Corporate Taxation

Corporate Taxation

Fifth Edition

Cheryl D. Block
Professor of Law
Washington University Law School

Ari Glogower
Associate Professor of Law
The Ohio State University Moritz College of Law

Joshua D. Blank
Professor of Law
University of California, Irvine School of Law

ASPEN
PUBLISHING

To contact Customer Service, e-mail customer.service@aspenpublishing.com, call 1-800-950-5259, or mail correspondence to:

> Aspen Publishing
> Attn: Order Department
> PO Box 990
> Frederick, MD 21705

Printed in the United States of America.

2 3 4 5 6 7 8 9 0

ISBN 978-1-4548-4810-3

Library of Congress Cataloging-in-Publication Data

Names: Block, Cheryl D., 1955- author. | Glogower, Ari, author. | Blank, Joshua D., author.
Title: Corporate taxation : examples and explanations / Cheryl D. Block, Professor of Law, Washington University Law School; Ari Glogower, Associate Professor of Law, The Ohio State University Moritz College of Law; Joshua D. Blank, Professor of Law, University of California, Irvine School of Law.
Description: Fifth edition. | Frederick, MD: Aspen Publishing, 2021. | Series: Examples & explanations series | Includes index.
Identifiers: LCCN 2021045266 | ISBN 9781454848103 (paperback) | ISBN 9781543831047 (ebook)
Subjects: LCSH: Corporations—Taxation—Law and legislation—United States.
Classification: LCC KF6465 .B557 2021 | DDC 343.7305/267—dc23/eng/20211006
LC record available at https://lccn.loc.gov/2021045266

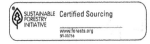

SUSTAINABLE FORESTRY INITIATIVE Certified Sourcing
www.forests.org
SFI-00756

About Aspen Publishing

Aspen Publishing is a leading provider of educational content and digital learning solutions to law schools in the U.S. and around the world. Aspen provides best-in-class solutions for legal education through authoritative textbooks, written by renowned authors, and breakthrough products such as Connected eBooks, Connected Quizzing, and PracticePerfect.

The Aspen Casebook Series (famously known among law faculty and students as the "red and black" casebooks) encompasses hundreds of highly regarded textbooks in more than eighty disciplines, from large enrollment courses, such as Torts and Contracts to emerging electives such as Sustainability and the Law of Policing. Study aids such as the *Examples & Explanations* and the *Emanuel Law Outlines* series, both highly popular collections, help law students master complex subject matter.

Major products, programs, and initiatives include:

- **Connected eBooks** are enhanced digital textbooks and study aids that come with a suite of online content and learning tools designed to maximize student success. Designed in collaboration with hundreds of faculty and students, the Connected eBook is a significant leap forward in the legal education learning tools available to students.

- **Connected Quizzing** is an easy-to-use formative assessment tool that tests law students' understanding and provides timely feedback to improve learning outcomes. Delivered through CasebookConnect.com, the learning platform already used by students to access their Aspen casebooks, Connected Quizzing is simple to implement and integrates seamlessly with law school course curricula.

- **PracticePerfect** is a visually engaging, interactive study aid to explain commonly encountered legal doctrines through easy-to-understand animated videos, illustrative examples, and numerous practice questions. Developed by a team of experts, PracticePerfect is the ideal study companion for today's law students.

- The **Aspen Learning Library** enables law schools to provide their students with access to the most popular study aids on the market across all of their courses. Available through an annual subscription, the online library consists of study aids in e-book, audio, and video formats with full text search, note-taking, and highlighting capabilities.

- Aspen's **Digital Bookshelf** is an institutional-level online education bookshelf, consolidating everything students and professors need to ensure success. This program ensures that every student has access to affordable course materials from day one.

- **Leading Edge** is a community centered on thinking differently about legal education and putting those thoughts into actionable strategies. At the core of the program is the Leading Edge Conference, an annual gathering of legal education thought leaders looking to pool ideas and identify promising directions of exploration.

To Chad, Hannah, and Aaron
And to the memory of Sugar, Pepi, and Elizabeth
— Cheryl

To Katy, Lilah, and Simon
—Ari

To my wife and children
—Josh

Summary of Contents

PART I. SOME PRELIMINARY MATTERS   I

PART II. CORPORATE FORMATION   65

PART III. CORPORATE MIDLIFE EVENTS   139

PART IV. CORPORATE LIQUIDATION AND RELATED ISSUES   273

Contents

Chapter 3   The Corporate Capital Structure   43

PART III. CORPORATE MIDLIFE EVENTS — 139

Chapter 5 — Nonliquidating Distributions — 141

Chapter 6   Redemption Distributions   181

Chapter 7 Stock Dividends   237

PART IV. CORPORATE LIQUIDATION AND
RELATED ISSUES   273

Chapter 8 General Liquidation Rules   275

SUBPART B. TAX-FREE REORGANIZATIONS   371

Chapter 11   Introduction to Basic Corporate Reorganization Principles   373

Chapter 14   Recapitalization and Other Corporate Restructuring   539

Contents

Preface

Corporate taxation has a reputation, among law students at least, as being one of the most difficult courses in the law school curriculum. This perception magnifies as Congress continues its seemingly endless amendment process, regularly revising the Internal Revenue Code and Subchapter C. Some of these revisions appear eminently sensible, and others do not. Few of them can be said to simplify, however.

With this book, we hope to assist in unraveling the mysteries of Subchapter C, dealing with corporate taxpayers and their shareholders. The Tax Cuts and Jobs Act of 2017 introduced some significant changes to Subchapter C, and followed a long series of legislative revisions in recent decades. At the time of this publication, Congress is considering further changes to the corporate tax rules, as the next stage in a continuous process of legislative reform.

This book describes the changes to Subchapter C in recent years resulting from the 2017 legislation and subsequent reforms, and how these changes can affect business structures. For example, the significant reduction in the corporate tax rate to 21% in 2017 can affect how a taxpayer might choose to organize a business entity, and new limitations on the deductibility of interest expenses can affect the choice of whether to fund the business with debt or equity.

Even as Congress has introduced changes with major consequences for structuring businesses, these changes have not significantly impacted the fundamentals of Subchapter C covered in this book. As long as Congress retains a separate corporate tax, Subchapter C will address basic questions in characterizing the tax consequences of corporate formations, distributions, liquidations, reorganizations, and divisions, which are the central concerns of this book.

In corporate tax, important changes also result from the government's application and evolving interpretation of Subchapter C. The Treasury Department continues to rethink and revise several of its long-standing positions, particularly in the area of tax-free reorganizations and divisions. In particular, Treasury Department rulings reflect the department's movement away from literal interpretation of several reorganization provisions in favor of a more flexible interpretation consistent with underlying tax policy objectives.

Two unique features of this book distinguish it from other books on corporate taxation. First, and most important, are the series of questions and answers (referred to as "Examples" and "Explanations") at the end of each chapter, with the exception of introductory Chapter 1. These problems should help to test your understanding and give you an opportunity to apply the textual material from each chapter. While we have attempted to make the problems as realistic as possible, they are unlike transactions in the real world in that the problems at the end of each chapter focus on the particular issues addressed in that chapter alone. Real-world corporate transactions may not be quite so "compartmentalized," but instead involve multiple issues in the same transaction. Once you have mastered the problems in these chapters, you should be in a position to advance to problems that combine multiple corporate tax issues. Although different professors look for different things in student responses to examination questions, the answers provided in the Explanations sections reflect the kind of answers we hope to see from our students.

The second unique feature of this book is that it includes numerous diagrams. In many cases, the most difficult aspects of corporate taxation involve understanding the underlying transaction itself. Once you can see the transaction, the tax consequences often fall right into place. We encourage you to get into a regular habit of diagramming corporate transactions. You can practice by diagramming the transactions described in the Examples and Explanations sections.

One last problem in studying corporate tax is simply deciding where to start. One possibility is to start with incorporation, or birth, of the corporation and end with liquidation, or death, of the corporation. This is sometimes referred to as the "cradle-to-grave" approach. Another possibility is to begin with distributions. Since corporations are first taxed on their profits and shareholders are taxed again on those profits when they are distributed as dividends, double taxation really is the heart of the corporate tax regime. Why not start at the heart with distributions? A strong case can be made for either technique. Texts and courses on corporate taxation take different approaches. This book adopts the cradle-to-grave approach, modified by considering corporate liquidations prior to the more complex materials on tax-free reorganizations. Nevertheless, each of the chapters that follows is designed to operate independently so that the book can be used as a study guide regardless of the approach used in your particular course of study.

Perhaps the best advice that we can offer students is to work always to see the big picture and not to get lost in the minutia that can sometimes be so overwhelming. In particular, we hope to assist students in developing skills that will enable them to identify the details that really matter in getting at the big picture. With the proper focus, corporate tax turns out not to be nearly as difficult as one first imagined. Better yet, corporate tax can be — dare we say it? — fun.

Cheryl D. Block
Ari Glogower
Joshua D. Blank
November 2021

Acknowledgments

We would like to thank our students and colleagues who have helped us think through the issues reflected here, including Professors Karen Brown, Sarah Lawsky, Robert Peroni, Adam Rosenzweig, Peter Wiedenbeck, and Chancellor Kent Syverud, and research assistants Pamela Burke, Stephen Cassarino, Tejpal Chawla, Daniel Fisher, Bernard Gallagher, Karen Howat, Jim Keller, Patricia Kuendig, and Kevin Schopp.

We are grateful to Elizabeth Dengler for her research assistance in preparing this revised Fifth Edition. We also thank the Washington University Law School, the Ohio State University Moritz College of Law, and the University of California, Irvine School of Law, which provided funding for research assistance and summer research grants.

Corporate Taxation

Some Preliminary Matters

PART I

Introduction

THE CORPORATE INCOME TAX — A DOUBLE TAX REGIME

Beginning immediately after passage of the Sixteenth Amendment in 1913[1] and continuing to the present, Congress has imposed a direct tax on both personal and corporate incomes.[2] Corporate profits are subject to a corporate level tax under §11 of the Internal Revenue Code[3] and a second tax on the same profits is imposed when the profits are distributed to the shareholders in the form of dividends.[4] Even if the shareholders sell their stock before receiving distributions, the price received for the stock presumably

---

1. The Sixteenth Amendment permits Congress to "lay and collect taxes on incomes, from whatever source derived, without apportionment among the several states." U.S. Const. Amend. XVI.

2. An earlier statute imposing an income tax upon both personal and corporate income was held unconstitutional. In 1909, Congress successfully levied a tax on corporations that was held to be constitutional as an indirect or *excise* tax not subject to the apportionment clause. Flint v. Stone Tracy Co., 220 U.S. 107, 171 (1911).

3. A small business corporation that makes a proper election under Subchapter S generally will not be subject to the corporate level tax imposed by §11. See I.R.C. §1363. See also Chapter 2 for further discussion of Subchapter S corporations. There also are three exceptions to the corporate tax listed in §11, for mutual savings banks conducting a life insurance business, insurance companies, and regulated investment companies and real estate investment trusts. I.R.C. §11(c). Each of these types of business entities is covered under different Subchapters of the Internal Revenue Code and is beyond the scope of this book.

4. I.R.C. §301. For further discussion of nonliquidating corporate distributions, see Chapter 5.

3

will include the stock's pro rata share of profits. As a result, the gain reported from sale of the stock should reflect the stockholder's share of undistributed profits. One way or the other, the shareholders will pay a tax. Since the corporation pays taxes on profits and is not entitled to any deduction for dividends paid to shareholders, the general effect of the corporate and shareholder taxes is double taxation of corporate income.

Prior to 2003, there was one important distinction between dividends and gains from the sale of stock. Dividends received by shareholders were considered ordinary income taxable at the individual income tax rates provided in I.R.C. §1, whereas gains from the sale of stock generally were, and continue to be, considered capital gains taxable under preferential capital gains rates provided in §1(h). Since 2003, however, qualified dividends from domestic corporations have also been eligible for the preferential capital gain rates.[5]

For tax years starting in 2018, an additional change also significantly altered the consequences of earning income through a corporation. Starting in 2018, Congress reduced the corporate tax rate to a flat 21% rate,[6] replacing the prior graduated rate schedule which resulted in a top average rate of 35%.[7] The reduction in the corporate tax rate and the preferential rate on qualified dividends both have significant implications which are discussed in the section that follows and throughout the remaining chapters of this book. These rate dynamics are almost certain to change again in the future. At the time of the publication of this edition, policymakers were considering proposals to increase the corporate tax rate once again, although future reforms are unlikely to restore the prior 35% top average rate.

The double tax imposed on corporations should be distinguished from the single layer of tax imposed on other forms of business organization. A partnership, for example, is not subject to income tax at the partnership entity level.[8] Instead, income, loss, deductions, and credits are "passed-through" and reported on each participant's individual tax return. If a partnership has income for the year, the partnership itself will have no tax liability, but each partner will report a share of the income on his or her individual tax return. In addition, certain corporations with a limited number

---

5. The Jobs and Growth Tax Relief Reconciliation Act of 2003, Pub. L. No. 108-27, 117 Stat. 752, §302 (codified at I.R.C. §1(h)(11)).

6. Pub. L. No. 115-97, 131 Stat. 2054, §13001 (2017) (codified at I.R.C. §11).

7. I.R.C. §11 (2017). Before the changes in the 2017 legislation, corporations were subject to marginal tax rates of 15%, 25%, 34%, and 35%, with additional surtaxes at particular income levels to yield an overall average rate of 35% on corporations earning taxable income of $18.33 million. Because of tax reduction opportunities, few corporations, in fact, bore this maximum 35% average rate. A 2016 Treasury study estimated that the actual effective average tax rate on corporations with more than $10 million in assets was 22% between 2007 and 2011. Dept. of Treas. Office of Tax Analysis, Average Effective Corporate Tax Rates (2016).

8. I.R.C. §701. Partnerships generally are governed by Subchapter K. I.R.C. §§701-761.

of shareholders may achieve similar pass-through status by making an election to be an S corporation under Subchapter S of the Internal Revenue Code.[9] Like a partnership, an S corporation is usually not itself a taxpaying entity, but instead generally passes items of income, loss, deduction, and credit through to its shareholders for reporting on their individual returns. In addition, changes to state business law in all 50 states and the District of Columbia have created authority for an increasing number of new types of business entities, such as limited liability companies (LLCs) and limited liability partnerships (LLPs). Under the check-the-box regulations, such entities with two or more members will automatically be treated as partnerships for tax purposes unless they elect to be treated as corporations.[10]

For the most part, this book focuses on corporations that have not made an election under Subchapter S and, thus, are subject to the rules of Subchapter C of the Internal Revenue Code.[11] Unless otherwise specified, references to the tax consequences of a corporation in this book refer to the tax consequences for a C corporation, or to rules that apply to all corporations generally. In contrast to pass-through entities—such as partnerships, S corporations, or LLCs—when C corporations earn a profit, the shareholders pay no immediate tax. Although the value of the stock may increase, a shareholder pays no tax until the corporation makes a distribution or the shareholder sells the shares. Similarly, the shareholder is not entitled to immediately deduct a share of the corporation's losses. The decreased value of the shares will be reflected in less gain, or perhaps a loss, on the ultimate sale of the shares.

At this point you may be wondering why two otherwise similar businesses, one operated as a partnership, S corporation, or LLC, and the other operated as a C corporation, should have different tax burdens. You would not be alone in having this thought. Over the years, policy makers and commentators have debated the wisdom of the separate corporate income tax.[12] Several proposals have recommended eliminating the corporate level tax altogether or otherwise fully "integrating" the corporate and individual

---

9. I.R.C. §1362 (election); §1361 (S corporation defined); §1363 (effect of election). Subchapter S corporations are considered briefly in Chapter 2.

10. For further discussion of these new types of business entities, see Chapter 2.

11. The modern statutory provisions on the corporate income tax can be found primarily in Subchapter C ("Corporate Distributions and Adjustments"), located within Subtitle A ("Income Taxes"), Chapter 1 ("Normal Taxes and Surtaxes") of Title 26 of the United States Code ("The Internal Revenue Code"). Corporations governed by the provisions of Subchapter C often are simply referred to as "C corporations."

12. For discussion of arguments in favor of the corporate tax, see Reuven S. Avi-Yonah, Corporations, Society, and the State: A Defense of the Corporate Tax, 90 Va. L. Rev. 1193 (2004); Steven A. Bank, A Capital Lock-In Theory of the Corporate Income Tax, 94 Geo. L.J. 889 (2006); Ari Glogower & David Kamin, The Progressivity Ratchet, 104 Minn. L. Rev. 1499 (2020); David M. Schizer, Between Scylla and Charybdis: Taxing Corporations or Shareholders (or Both), 116 Colum. L. Rev. 1849 (2016).

income taxes. Alternative proposals for partial integration have also been considered. Such proposals for partial integration would provide corporate deductions for dividends paid or shareholder credits on dividends received.[13] The preferential rate for qualified dividends introduced in 2003 and the 2017 reduction in the corporate tax rate to 21% might be viewed as compromises creating "partial integration" of a sort, although these changes also introduced other distortions to the tax system. Although Congress did not provide a shareholder deduction or credit for dividends received or entirely eliminate the corporate-layer of tax, it did reduce the burden of the double tax through these changes.

Despite its critics, the basic structure of the double corporate tax regime reflected in Subchapter C of the Internal Revenue Code has proved quite durable. The percentage of revenue generated by the corporate income tax, however, has declined in recent decades, as a result of tax rate changes, tax reduction opportunities, and opportunities to operate businesses through other tax entities. In 2020, for example, the federal government raised approximately 7.1% of its revenue from the corporate income tax, as opposed to approximately 48.9% from the individual income tax.[14] While the percentages are small, the volume of revenue raised by the corporate income tax is still substantial, and elimination of the corporate income tax would be politically quite difficult.[15] Corporate income taxation continues to be a subject of great interest and importance to taxpayers, policy makers, and academics alike.

COMPUTATION AND RATE STRUCTURE FOR THE TAX ON CORPORATE AND SHAREHOLDER INCOME

General Computation and Rates

The corporation is regarded as a separate person for federal income tax purposes and computes income in much the same way that individual taxpayers do.[16] The corporation will first determine its gross

---

13. For discussion of corporate integration options, see Michael J. Graetz & Alvin Warren, Jr., Integration of Corporate and Shareholder Taxes, 69 Nat'l Tax J. 677 (2016).

14. Joint Comm. on Tax'n, JCX-18-21, Overview of the Federal Tax System as in Effect for 2021, at 33 Tbl. A-3 (Comm. Print 2021).

15. In 2020, for example, the corporate income tax raised approximately $263 billion. Id. At 31 Tbl. A-1. For an interesting discussion of the political dynamics behind the persistence of the corporate tax, see Michael Doran, Managers, Shareholders, and the Corporate Tax, 95 Va. L. Rev. 517 (2009).

16. The Internal Revenue Code itself provides that "where not otherwise distinctly expressed or manifestly incompatible with the intent [of Title 26, t]he term 'person' shall be construed to mean and include . . . An association, company or corporation." I.R.C. §7701(a)(1).

income[17] and then subtract available deductions to determine taxable income. Of course, there are some differences in the types of income that corporations, as opposed to individuals, are likely to receive and also some differences in allowable deductions and credits.

Differences in the Tax Treatment for Corporate and Noncorporate Income: The Influence on Subchapter C

As of the time of this edition's publication, C corporations are taxed at a flat rate of 21%,[18] whereas an individual is taxed on ordinary income at rates nearing or exceeding 40%,[19] and on net capital gains and qualified dividends at a maximum rate of 23.8%.[20] Business income earned through a pass-through (such as a disregarded entity, a tax partnership, or an S corporation) may also qualify for the temporary 20% "qualified business income" deduction under §199A, which can further reduce the effective rate on business income that is not earned through a C corporation.[21]

As discussed in the section that follows and in subsequent chapters, these tax rate differentials substantially impact the ways in which taxpayers structure their corporate transactions and on the development of statutory and regulatory provisions under Subchapter C. Further, Congress may change some or all of these rates in the future, which would introduce new dynamics in the interaction between these tax regimes and new structuring considerations for taxpayers. At the same time, these rate dynamics do not alter the basic structure of Subchapter C which is the focus of this book.

For federal income tax purposes, gain and loss from the sale of a "capital asset" is treated differently from ordinary income and loss. Corporations are allowed losses from the sale or exchange of capital assets only to the extent

---

17. I.R.C. §61(a) makes no distinction between individuals and corporations in its definition of gross income.

18. I.R.C. §11(a).

19. Ordinary income is current subject to a top marginal rate of 37% under I.R.C. (a)-(d), (j), and may also be subject to the 3.8% net investment income tax in I.R.C. §1411 or the payroll and self-employment taxes in I.R.C. §3101(b) and I.R.C. §1401(b).

20. This 23.8% maximum rate accounts for both the 20% top rate on net capital gains and qualified dividends in I.R.C. §1(h) and the 3.8% net investment income tax in I.R.C. §1411. The preferential 20% maximum rate on net capital gains does not apply to gain from collectibles. I.R.C. §1(h)(4)-(5). Individual taxpayers investing in certain "qualified small business stock" may also defer tax on gain from the sale of such stock by purchasing other "qualified small business stock" within 60 days of the sale. I.R.C. §1045. Ultimately, even the sale of this replacement stock may be eligible for an exclusion under special provisions for the sale of "qualified small business stock" in I.R.C. §1202.

21. I.R.C. §199A. Because C corporations do not qualify for this deduction, a full discussion of §199A is beyond the scope of this book.

of gain from such sales or exchanges.[22] Thus, for any given taxable year, capital losses may be used only to offset capital gains. Individual taxpayers are subject to similar capital loss restrictions, but can deduct a maximum of $3,000 in capital losses even if capital losses exceed capital gains for the taxable year.[23] Capital gains and losses are further divided into short- or long-term gains or losses. A long-term capital gain or loss is a gain or loss from the sale or exchange of an asset held for more than one year.[24] The preferential net capital gains rates for individuals are applied to the excess of a taxpayer's net long-term capital gains over net short-term capital losses.[25]

For purposes of an introductory course in corporate taxation, one need not master all of the complexities of the capital gain and loss rules. It should be sufficient to recognize that capital loss restrictions and the rate differential for taxation of ordinary income versus capital gains raise especially significant issues for corporate taxpayers and their shareholders. For example, corporations may attempt to classify a *loss* as ordinary, rather than capital, in order to avoid the loss limitation rules. On the other hand, corporations may try to classify a *gain* as capital rather than ordinary so that they can use the gain to offset existing losses.

Another issue of concern to distributing corporations and their shareholders is the classification of corporate distributions to shareholders as a dividend or as something else, such as compensation to a shareholder who also happens to be an employee, or interest payments to a shareholder who also happens to have lent money or property to the corporation. From the corporation's perspective, it is generally preferable to avoid dividend classification since corporations *cannot* deduct dividends. On the other hand, corporations *can* in many cases deduct business interest expense under §163 and compensation to employees under §162, subject to the restrictions under both of these provisions.[26] Until 2003, shareholders in most cases generally were generally indifferent regarding the classification of distributions. Income from dividends, compensation, and

---

22. I.R.C. §1211(a). Unused corporate capital losses are subject to carryback and carryforward rules under §1212(a).

23. I.R.C. §1211(b). Unused individual capital losses may be carried forward under rules provided in §1212(b).

24. I.R.C. §1222(3), (4). The period of time during which the taxpayer has held a capital asset typically is referred to as the "holding period." One recurring issue in corporate taxation is whether the sale or exchange of stock or other assets begins a *new* holding period or whether, instead, an earlier holding period should be "tacked on." I.R.C. §1223 resolves many of these questions. Discussion of §1223 and specific holding period issues will be included in subsequent chapters as the issues arise.

25. "Net long-term capital gain" is defined as "the excess of long-term capital gains for the taxable year over the long-term capital losses for such year." I.R.C. §1222(7). "Net capital gain" is defined as the "excess of the net long-term capital gain for the taxable year over the net short-term capital loss for such year." I.R.C. §1222(11).

26. These issues regarding distributions to shareholders are discussed further in Chapter 5. The limitations of interest deductibility under §163(j) are discussed further in Chapter 3.

interest were all classified as ordinary income and therefore subject to the higher marginal rates of §1 regardless of the distribution's classification. Now that qualified dividends are taxed at the preferential rates for net capital gains, shareholders are more likely to prefer to receive payments classified as dividends rather than as ordinary compensation or interest.

A Brief History of Dividend Taxation

Under §1(h)(11)(A) net capital gain eligible for the preferential capital gains rates is defined as "net capital gain (determined without regard to this paragraph) *increased by qualified dividend income*."[27] This provision, introduced by Congress in 2003, has important implications which permeate much of the discussion that follows throughout this book. The changes to the tax treatment of dividends over time also help to explain many structural features of Subchapter C.

Historically, individual shareholders almost always preferred to receive capital gain rather than ordinary income in order to take advantage of the preferential tax rates provided in §1(h).[28] As noted earlier in this chapter, shareholders generally will be taxed on the return from their stock investment one way or the other. When corporations choose to distribute profits, the shareholders generally reflect their share of these profits upon receipt as taxable dividend income. If the corporation chooses instead to retain and invest its profits, resulting in increased share value, the shareholders generally will reflect their share of these profits upon subsequent sale of the stock as taxable gain on the appreciated value of the stock. Sale treatment offered two tax advantages. First of all, shareholders could in some cases benefit from deferring tax until they later sold the shares.[29] Second, individual shareholders benefited from the preferential rates applicable to a sale of stock, which is generally considered a capital asset.[30]

---

27. I.R.C. §1(h)(11)(A) (emphasis added). Under these rules, shareholders are not subject to the one-year holding period otherwise applicable to long-term capital gain, but instead subject to a different set of holding period rules provided in §1(h)(11)(B). These rules and other details regarding the operation of the "qualified dividend" provision are considered in Chapter 5.

28. Corporate shareholders, on the other hand, generally *preferred* to receive dividends eligible for the dividends-received deduction available to them under §243. The §243 deduction and its implications are discussed in more detail in Chapter 5.

29. For discussions of when taxpayers could benefit from earning income through a corporation and deferring tax until a sale, and when they could not achieve a tax benefit through this strategy, see Ari Glogower and David Kamin, Sheltering Income Through a Corporation, 164 Tax Notes Fed. 507 (July 22, 2019); Michael S. Knoll, The TCJA and the Questionable Incentive to Incorporate, 162 Tax Notes 977 (Mar. 4, 2019).

30. The capital asset definition is discussed later in this chapter.

I. Introduction

An individual shareholder's preference to "bailout" corporate profit at preferential capital gain rather than ordinary income rates previously applicable to dividends was so great that it kept legions of tax planners busy structuring transactions to achieve such results. In fact, much of Subchapter C and the regulations and case-law doctrines interpreting it are addressed to precisely these issues. As new and creative transactions emerged, Congress and the Treasury Department would respond with new or amended statutory or regulatory provisions designed to thwart such efforts. Taxpayers, in turn, would come up with new transactions taking advantage of "loopholes" in the revised statutory or regulatory provisions, thus stimulating another statutory or regulatory response. This dynamic has contributed substantially to the length and complexity of Subchapter C and regulations.

Section 1(h)(11) altered this dynamic and taxpayer incentives, both in terms of investment strategy and transaction structure. Whereas shareholders historically took extraordinary measures to avoid dividends and to bail out profit at capital gains rates, they may now welcome dividend income. In addition, prior to the statutory amendments, shareholders were often indifferent as to the distinction between dividend, compensation, or interest income. After the introduction of §1(h)(11), corporations may continue to prefer nondividend payments while their shareholders may now prefer dividend classification of corporate distributions. The 2017 reduction in the corporate tax rate to 21% and restrictions on the deductibility of interest under §163(j)[31] also mitigate this dynamic, however, and lessen the consequences for the corporation between classifying a distribution as a dividend or as certain nondividend payments.

Economists have long debated the impact of lower dividend rates on corporate and investor behavior. Under the "traditional view," reducing dividend tax rates should stimulate investment and lead to higher dividend payouts. In contrast, the "new view" predicts dividend tax rate cuts are not likely to result in significantly increased investment since most new equity financing comes from retained earnings rather than from selling new equity.[32] The 2003 dividend tax rate cut provided an interesting new laboratory for economists to test competing views. Some studies reported a substantial post-2003 increase in dividend payouts, but not a clear increase in investment activity.[33]

---

31. This limitation is discussed in greater detail in Chapter 3.

32. For an analysis of the competing views, see Daniel N. Shaviro, Decoding the U.S. Corporate Tax 73-88 (2009).

33. See Alan J. Auerbach and Kevin A. Hassett, Dividend Taxes and Firm Valuation: New Evidence, 92 Am. Econ. Rev. 119 (2006); Raj Chetty and Emmanuel Saez, Dividend Taxes and Corporate Behavior: Evidence from the 2003 Dividend Tax Cut, 120 Q.J. Econ. 791 (2005); Danny Yagan, Capital Tax Reform and the Real Economy: The Effects of the 2003 Dividend Tax Cut, 105 Am. Econ. R. 3531 (2015). As these and other studies indicate, many other factors must be taken in account in assessing the impact of rate cuts, including, for example, the relative age or "maturity" of the firm and the extent to which stock is owned by corporate managers.

I. Introduction

Commentators have long suggested that much of Subchapter C's complexity could be eliminated simply by providing for taxation of ordinary income and capital gains at the same rates. Many reformers had high hopes for the Tax Reform Act of 1986, which briefly eliminated the difference in rates. Even in 1986, however, it was clear that the equalization of rates would not last very long. Anticipating a possible future increase in ordinary income rates, Congress provided in 1986 that the rate on net capital gains would not exceed the top capital gain rate, which was then 28%.[34] Congress indeed increased ordinary income rates in 1990 and again in 1993, but the capital gains rate was protected from these increases as a result of the congressional preemptive strike included in the 1986 Act. The 2003 qualified dividend provision at least eliminated the disparate treatment of dividends and capital gains. Since the qualified dividend rule substantially reduced shareholder incentives to convert ordinary dividend income into capital gains, it could justify repeal or simplification of provisions described in this book enacted primarily to address government concerns about such behavior.

One common theme underlying much of the discussion that follows is the influence of the capital gains/ordinary income distinction on corporate transactions and on the development of Subchapter C. An in-depth discussion of the capital asset definition and the substantial volume of case law surrounding it is beyond the scope of this book on corporate tax. What follows in this introduction is a very brief discussion of the capital asset definition as applied in the corporate setting.[35] Specific transactions that raise capital gain versus ordinary income issues appear throughout the text and, particularly, in the examples at the end of chapters.

Overview of Capital Asset Definition

The term "capital asset" is rather expansively defined in I.R.C. §1221(a) as "property held by the taxpayer" *except* eight specifically listed items that are *not* considered capital assets.[36] Four of these exceptions are especially relevant for corporate businesses.[37] First, the §1221 definition excludes

---

34. Pub. L. No. 99-514, §101(a), 100 Stat. 2085.

35. For a useful detailed analysis of the capital asset definition, see Edward Yorio, Federal Income Tax Rulemaking: An Economic Approach, 51 Fordham L. Rev. 1 (1982).

36. Continuing the tradition of definitions in the negative, "ordinary income" is defined as "any gain from the sale or exchange of property which is neither a capital asset nor property described in section 1231(b)." I.R.C. §64.

37. In addition to the four exceptions discussed in the text, §1221 includes exceptions in §1221(a)(3) for copyrights, literary, musical, or artistic compositions; in §1221(a)(5) for publications of the United States government; in §1221(a)(6)-(7) for certain financial instruments; and in §1221(a)(8) for supplies used or consumed in the ordinary course of business.

I. Introduction

"stock in trade," inventory, or "property held by the taxpayer primarily for sale to customers in the ordinary course, of . . . [the taxpayer's] trade or business."[38] Thus, when a corporation sells goods or services to customers in the ordinary course of its business, the profit or loss will be treated as ordinary income or loss. In addition, when a corporation sells its inventory, any profit or loss will be treated as ordinary. Congress later added a second, and related, exception for "supplies of a type regularly used or consumed by the taxpayer in the ordinary course of a trade or business of the taxpayer."[39] This exception should reduce technical arguments as to whether or not a particular asset fits the definition of "stock in trade" or property "primarily for sale to customers" under §1221(a)(1) and clarifies that regular business assets, as opposed to investment assets, generally will not be classified as capital assets. Third, the capital asset definition excludes "accounts or notes receivable acquired in the ordinary course of trade or business for services rendered or from the sale of property described in paragraph (1)."[40] Fourth, the capital asset definition explicitly excludes depreciable trade or business property or real property used in a trade or business.[41] Thus, according to the terms of the capital asset definition itself, a corporate sale of depreciable equipment or real estate used for business purposes should result in ordinary income or loss. With regard to such sales of depreciable equipment or real estate, however, Congress has provided a special set of rules in §1231 under which gains or losses are treated as capital when gains from the sale of §1231 assets exceed losses from §1231 assets for the taxable year.[42] Thus, sales of depreciable property or real property used in a trade or business may be treated as capital gain or loss pursuant to §1231 even though these assets have otherwise been excluded from the definition of a "capital asset" under §1221(2). Such §1231 assets are sometimes referred to as "quasi-capital assets." Assets which are "substitutes for ordinary income," such as the right to earn ordinary income payments, will also be treated as ordinary, even if they do not fall within one of the categories listed in §1221.[43]

From the shareholder's perspective, stock generally is considered a capital asset.[44] Thus, when a shareholder sells his or her stock, the gain will be considered capital gain. The shareholder is entitled to this favorable treatment even though the stock reflects an indirect interest in the underlying

---

38. I.R.C. §1221(a)(1).
39. I.R.C. §1221(a)(8).
40. I.R.C. §1221(a)(4).
41. I.R.C. §1221(a)(2).
42. I.R.C. §1231(a).
43. See, e.g., Hort v. Comm'r, 313 U.S. 28 (1941); Lattera v. Comm'r, 437 F.3d 399 (3d. Cir. 2006).
44. However, if the shareholder is a dealer in securities, her gains from the sale of securities generally will not be considered gain from the sale of a capital asset. I.R.C. §1236.

assets of the corporation, which may or may not be capital assets. An individual shareholder's qualified dividend income is similarly eligible for capital gains rates.

The Corporate Alternative Minimum Tax

Under prior law, corporations were subject to the corporate alternative minimum tax (AMT), which was designed "to ensure that no taxpayer with substantial economic income [could] avoid significant tax liability by using exclusions, deductions, and credits because, however worthy their goals, they [became] counterproductive when taxpayers [were] allowed to use them to avoid virtually all tax liability."[45] The AMT prevented taxpayers with financial income from significantly reducing or eliminating their income for tax purposes by making various adjustments to taxable income.[46]

Congress repealed the AMT for corporations starting in the 2018 tax year,[47] although individuals are still subject to these rules. A detailed discussion of the mechanics of the AMT calculation is consequently beyond the scope of this book. The corporate AMT can still have some relevance for corporations in the years following its repeal, however, since a corporation may be able to offset taxable income in subsequent years with unused AMT credits.[48] It is also possible that a future Congress could restore the corporate AMT in connection with an increase in the corporate tax rate.

Penalty Taxes on Undistributed Corporate Income

Recall that the distinctive feature of corporate taxation generally is a *double* tax on corporate profits through imposition of both a *corporate* level tax on income and a *shareholder* level tax on distributions. Some corporations developed techniques to avoid the shareholder level tax by simply not making corporate distributions. Congress responded with penalty taxes on accumulated earnings and personal holding companies. Each of these provisions is designed to prod corporations into making distributions that will be subject to the shareholder level tax. Beginning in the 1980s, taxpayers generally had less incentive to earn income through a corporation and delay a distribution, since the combined effect of the corporate "double tax" significantly exceeded the top rates on income earned directly by an individual. The qualified dividend rules in 2003 further reduced the incentive to defer

---

45. S. Fin. Comm. Rep. No. 313, 99th Cong., 2d Sess. 518-519 (1986).
46. The AMT rules are in I.R.C. §55-58.
47. Pub. L. No. 115-97, 131 Stat. 2054, §12001 (2017) (codified at I.R.C. §55(a)).
48. I.R.C. §53.

corporate distributions. As a result, these rules have been less important during this period.

These rules may become more important, however, following the 2017 reduction in the corporate tax rate to 21%.[49] As described in greater detail in Chapter 2, if the corporate tax is substantially reduced, taxpayers may again be able to achieve a lower effective rate of tax by earning income through a corporation and deferring distributions.

a) The Accumulated Earnings Tax

The accumulated earnings penalty tax is imposed upon corporations "availed of for the purpose of avoiding the income tax with respect to its shareholders . . . by permitting earnings and profits to accumulate instead of being divided or distributed."[50] Such an inquiry obviously depends upon facts peculiar to the particular corporation. According to §533, a corporation that permits earnings and profits to "accumulate beyond the reasonable needs of the business" has acted with the prohibited tax avoidance motive. Not surprisingly, disputes between the taxpayer and the government in accumulated earnings penalty tax cases center upon identifying the "reasonable needs of the business." Special provisions in §537 and corresponding regulations address these issues.[51] Once it is factually determined that the corporation is subject to the accumulated earnings penalty tax, a tax is imposed equal to 20% of "accumulated taxable income."[52] For this purpose, "accumulated taxable income" is computed based upon taxable income, with adjustments as provided in §535. Perhaps most important among these adjustments is a credit for amounts that were retained for reasonable needs of the business.[53] Corporations may be subject to this penalty tax in addition to the regular corporate tax provided in §11.

b) The Personal Holding Company Tax

When the personal holding company rules were first adopted in 1934, individual income tax rates were much higher than corporate tax rates. Individual taxpayers found that they could reduce their tax liability on personal service income or income from personal assets by incorporating. The

---

49. For discussion of the renewed relevance of these rules in the context of a relatively low corporate tax rate, see David Kamin et al., The Games They Will Play: Tax Games, Roadblocks, and Glitches Under the 2017 Tax Legislation, 103 Minn. L. Rev. 1439, 1447-1454 (2019).
50. I.R.C. §532(a). Since personal holding companies are subject to a separate set of penalty provisions, such corporations are exempted from the accumulated earnings tax. I.R.C. §532(b)(1).
51. The details of these provisions are beyond the scope of these introductory materials.
52. I.R.C. §531.
53. I.R.C. §535(c).

problem was especially acute in the case of small, closely held businesses, whose shareholders could easily manipulate corporate affairs for nonbusiness purposes. In response, Congress adopted the personal holding company (PHC) rules to prevent this abuse by taxing certain shareholders on undistributed corporate earnings at the top marginal individual tax rate.

In some scenarios, today's individual and corporate tax rates could again present individual taxpayers an incentive to shelter their personal income at lower corporate rates. An incentive remains to retain corporate earnings so as to avoid, or defer, the shareholder level of the corporate double tax. As a practical matter, the accumulated earnings penalty is often difficult to impose since it requires a subjective finding of tax avoidance. The personal holding company rules offer an alternative and more objective set of rules for preventing the strategic use of corporations to reduce taxes.

Under the PHC provisions, a 20% penalty tax is imposed upon undistributed personal holding company income.[54] Since the PHC penalty tax is directed at small businesses whose shareholders can easily manipulate corporate affairs, the penalty only applies to corporations if "at any time during the last half of the taxable year more than 50 percent in value of its outstanding stock is owned, directly or indirectly, by or for not more than 5 individuals."[55] In addition, the penalty only applies if at least 60% of the corporation's adjusted ordinary gross income constitutes "personal holding company income."[56] Taxpayers can thereby avoid the effect of the PHC penalty tax by structuring around either of these requirements.

"Personal holding company income" is defined as the portion of adjusted ordinary gross income consisting of listed types of personal service or personal asset income, such as amounts under personal service contracts, dividends, rents, and the like.[57] The details and mechanics of the personal holding company penalty tax are beyond the scope of most introductory corporate taxation courses. As with the Accumulated Earnings Tax, corporations may be subject to the PHC penalty tax in addition to the regular corporate tax provided in §11. If a corporation meets the criteria for both penalty taxes, then only the PHC penalty tax applies.[58]

Affiliated Corporations

Each corporation subject to tax under Subtitle A of the Internal Revenue Code is required to file a corporate tax return.[59] Certain "affiliated groups

---

54. I.R.C. §541.
55. I.R.C. §542(a)(2).
56. I.R.C. §542(a)(1).
57. I.R.C. §§543(a)(7), 543(a)(1), 543(a)(2).
58. I.R.C. §532(b)(1).
59. I.R.C. §6012(a)(2).

of corporations," however, are extended the privilege of filing a "consolidated return" in lieu of separate returns.[60] Affiliated groups are chains of corporate entities connected through stock ownership with a common parent corporation.[61] A parent corporation is "affiliated" to its subsidiary if it possesses at least 80% of the total voting power *and* 80% of the total value of the stock of the subsidiary.[62] Congress granted affiliated corporations the privilege of filing consolidated returns, but left most of the details regarding consolidated filing to the Treasury Department.[63] Complex and extensive regulations now govern the computation of federal income tax for corporations filing consolidated returns. In fact, many modern corporate transactions are structured by tax lawyers and accountants to take advantage of special consolidated return provisions. While this book does not attempt a comprehensive analysis of the consolidated return regulations, some of the more significant issues related to consolidated return reporting are considered throughout the chapters that follow.

NONRECOGNITION IN THE SUBCHAPTER C WORLD

Under general federal income tax principles, realized gains and losses must be recognized for tax purposes unless the Code provides an explicit nonrecognition rule.[64] Familiar examples of such explicit nonrecognition rules in the noncorporate setting include the provisions allowing for like-kind exchanges and involuntary conversions.[65] The basic rationale for these rules is that a transaction that merely changes the form of a taxpayer's investment should not yet be considered a taxable event. The usual corollary to such nonrecognition rules is a substituted basis provision designed to assure that the gain or loss left unrecognized will be preserved for the future. Subchapter C contains numerous nonrecognition provisions as well. For example, if structured properly, the formation of a corporation will be a nonrecognition event.[66] In addition, certain corporate reorganizations are covered by nonrecognition rules.[67] Given the possibility of a tax-free reorganization, parties to a corporate acquisition are confronted with the choice between a tax-free acquisition with substituted basis rules or a taxable acquisition

---

60. I.R.C. §1501; see also §6012(e).
61. I.R.C. §1504(a)(1).
62. I.R.C. §1504(a)(2).
63. I.R.C. §1502 grants broad authority to the Treasury Secretary to prescribe regulations governing consolidated returns for affiliated corporations.
64. I.R.C. §§61(a)(3), 1001(c).
65. I.R.C. §§1031 (like-kind exchanges), 1033 (involuntary conversions).
66. I.R.C. §351. For a detailed discussion of this provision, see Chapter 4.
67. I.R.C. §§354, 361. For a detailed discussion of tax-free reorganizations, see Chapters 11-14.

with cost or fair market value basis rules. These issues will be considered in depth in subsequent chapters. For the moment, it is worth noting that non-recognition and substituted basis rules play an important part in Subchapter C and corporate tax planning. These principles serve as a thread that runs through much of the study of corporate taxation.

INCIDENCE OF THE CORPORATE TAX

Although the corporation itself pays the corporate-level tax, controversy continues in identifying the taxpayers who bear the ultimate burden of the corporate income tax. Economists describe the problem as determining the *incidence* of the corporate income tax. Since the corporation itself is a legal entity, it cannot bear the ultimate burden of taxation. To say that the incidence of the corporate tax falls upon the corporation, then, really is to say that the shareholder "owners" of the corporation bear the tax. Taxes paid by the corporation arguably reduce profits otherwise available for distribution to the shareholder owners. Focusing on the short run, it may well be that the corporation's shareholders bear the corporate tax burden. Over time, however, corporations may discover that they can shift the burden of the tax forward to consumers of the corporation's goods or services. By increasing the price of goods or services to cover tax costs, corporations can preserve profits for the shareholders and shift the corporate tax burden to consumers. Alternatively, corporations in the long run may shift the burden of taxation backwards to suppliers or to employees by reducing the amount paid for goods or services purchased. Savvy investors will move their investments to those corporations that successfully shift the tax burden. The extent to which such shifting occurs, and the direction of such shifting, is the subject of much debate and the incidence question remains unresolved. For example, one study by U.S. Treasury researchers estimated that approximately 82% of the corporate tax is borne by capital income, and approximately 18% by labor income.[68] Resolution of this debate fortunately is not essential for a thorough investigation of the laws governing Subchapter C.[69]

---

68. Julie Ann Cronin et al., Distributing the Corporate Income Tax: Revised U.S. Treasury Methodology, 66 Nat'l Tax J. 239 (2013).
69. For a discussion of the literature, see Daniel N. Shaviro, Decoding the U.S. Corporate Tax 57-71 (2009).

Choice of Form and Entity Classification

INTRODUCTION

Before jumping full speed into Subchapter C, students of corporate taxation should consider a few preliminary matters. Advisors of new businesses often assist the client in choosing an appropriate business form. Once the business form is chosen, the advisor next must assure that the business entity achieves the desired classification for tax purposes. Changes in state law have created a substantial number of new types of unincorporated business entities. In addition to the Subchapters C and S incorporated forms, business taxpayers also face a sometimes dizzying array of options for unincorporated entities.[1] "Check-the-box" rules make tax classification effectively elective for many business entities (with some important exceptions), thus making it reasonably simple to achieve the taxpayer's desired tax status.[2] These explicit tax classification rules have altered the balance for business taxpayers such that the choice of business form is often far less tax-driven than in the past.

---

1. In light of the number of different forms of business entities, several commentators have argued that state governments should adopt a unified business entity code. See, e.g., Thomas F. Blackwell, The Revolution Is Here: The Promise of a Unified Business Entity Code, 24 Iowa J. Corp. L. 333 (1999); Harry J. Haynsworth, The Unified Business Organization Code: The Next Generation, 29 Del. J. Corp. L. 83 (2004); John H. Matheson and Brent O. Olson, A Call for a Unified Business Organization Law, 65 Geo. Wash. L. Rev. 1 (1996).
2. A discussion of these "check-the-box" regulations follows later in this chapter.

This chapter first briefly addresses the nontax and tax issues surrounding the choice of a particular type of entity or organization for engaging in business activity. The second part of this chapter provides an overview of eligibility rules and certain tax issues unique to Subchapter S corporations. The third considers the entities to which Subchapter C applies and the proper classification of business entities for federal income tax purposes.

CHOICE OF BUSINESS FORM

The Options

At the outset, any business entity must consider the various options for structuring the business, both for tax and nontax purposes. A single individual who owns and operates a business may choose either to incorporate or to operate as a sole proprietor (a "disregarded entity") for tax purposes, simply reporting income and loss on a separate business schedule on an individual tax return.[3] Assuming more than one participant in the enterprise, the most common options for the nontax legal classification of a business are as a general or limited partnership, a limited liability company (LLC), a limited liability partnership (LLP), and a limited liability limited partnerships (LLLP).[4] The most common options for the tax classification of a business are as a tax partnership, a "disregarded entity," a Subchapter S corporation (referred to as an "S corporation"), and a Subchapter C corporation (referred to as a "C corporation"). As described later in this chapter, in some cases the legal classification of the entity will determine its tax classification, but in other cases it will not.

Ideally, the choice of business form should be animated largely by nontax considerations. Tax factors, however, often play a significant, if not determinative, role in choosing the form of doing business. Horizontal equity generally requires that similarly situated taxpayers be taxed alike. If one accepts that a business operated as a partnership is similarly situated to the same business operated as a corporation, the two entities should arguably be taxed in similar fashion. This is a significant "if." Some would argue that there are significant differences.[5] Proposals for integrating the corporate

---

3. All states and the District of Columbia also recognize single-member limited liability companies (LLCs). Certain single-owner organizations, including LLCs, "can choose to be recognized or disregarded as entities separate from their owners." Treas. Reg. §301.7701-1(a)(4). These entities are often colloquially referred to as "tax nothings." A limited liability company with only one member is considered a "disregarded entity." Id.
4. Most states impose more filing and registration requirements on these new types of entities than on the more traditional partnerships.
5. Some say that the corporation is a more efficient producer of surplus and that taxation of this surplus value justifies the double tax. Others rationalize the double tax on the grounds

and individual income taxes so as to reduce or eliminate the separate tax on corporate income arguably would go some of the way toward creating more horizontal equity between different forms of business organization. On the other hand, corporate integration could introduce new distortions or inequalities to the tax system. A complete discussion of these issues is beyond the scope of this book. What follows is a brief overview of the non-tax and tax issues that businesses will consider in choosing the appropriate form of doing business.

Nontax Factors

The key nontax factor that most businesses consider is limited liability. For high-risk businesses, limited liability often is essential in order to attract sufficient capital from investors. Sole proprietors and partners in a general partnership generally are personally liable for the torts, debts, and other obligations of the business and are entitled to actively participate in business management.[6] Whether under Subchapter C or Subchapter S, the corporate form offers the advantage of limited liability and centralized management. Shareholder investors cannot participate directly in management, but simply are entitled to elect a Board of Directors to manage corporate business affairs. The S corporation, often also referred to as a small business corporation, is typically a business entity formally incorporated pursuant to state law and, in this sense, is no different from any other corporation. An eligible corporation must *elect* under Subchapter S to be treated as an S corporation.[7] Although it offers the advantage of limited liability and centralized management, the availability of the S corporation option is limited to those entities that meet Subchapter S eligibility and filing requirements.[8]

The traditional option for investors seeking limited liability without incorporating has been the limited partnership. Several restrictions make the limited partnership unattractive to some businesses, however. First, a limited partnership offers limited liability only to the limited partners; the partnership must have at least one general partner who will be personally liable. The general partner, however, may be structured as an LLC to avoid liability. Second, limited partners may not actively engage in the management of business affairs.

---

that corporations have greater access to nationwide or even worldwide financing through stock markets or that corporations exercise greater economic and political power than other forms of business operation.

6. A business organized as a general or limited partnership may be able to avoid this problem by structuring the general partner as an LLC.

7. I.R.C. §1362.

8. These rules are discussed later in this chapter.

2. Choice of Form and Entity Classification

Every state and the District of Columbia have adopted statutes authorizing new and different business entities with some measure of limited liability, but without the restrictions imposed on limited partnerships. The limited liability company (LLC) generally is an unincorporated business organization all of whose members have limited liability, but whose members still are entitled to participate in the management of the business.[9] The limited liability partnership (LLP) is a general partnership that provides its partners with limited liability for some or all partnership obligations. The early LLP statutes provided protection only from vicarious liability for the malpractice or negligence of another partner sounding in tort. Later generation LLP statutes extended this protection to cover negligence and malpractice actions, whether sounding in tort, contract, or otherwise. Third generation LLP statutes finally provide full vicarious liability protection.[10] Another variation is the limited liability limited partnership (LLLP). This entity is a limited partnership providing traditional limited liability to the limited partners, but also providing limited liability to the *general* partners to the same extent permitted a partner in an LLP.[11]

A second nontax factor in choosing a business form is management. A corporation offers the centralized management of an elected Board of Directors. While it is possible to achieve comparable centralization of management in other business forms, the formal and simple structure of a corporate Board of Directors is appealing to many desiring centralized management for the business. On the other hand, the LLC offers greater flexibility with regard to management, effectively permitting management by either members or managers. In addition, even an otherwise manager-managed LLC can provide authority to nonmanagers to bind the LLC on particular matters through a specialized operating agreement. In choosing between a member-managed LLC and an LLP, one must keep in mind that partners generally have equal management rights. In contrast, the LLC offers the flexibility of majority rule through a specialized operating agreement. Along with this flexibility, however, comes the risk of a "squeeze out" for minority LLC members.[12]

---

9. The first LLC statute was adopted by Wyoming in 1977. Wyo. Stat. §§17-15-101 to 136 (1977 & Supp. 1995). Since that time, all 50 states and the District of Columbia have adopted LLC statutes. For a history of the development of LLC statutes, see generally Susan Pace Hamill, The Origins Behind the Limited Liability Company, 59 Ohio St. L.J. 1459 (1998); Larry E. Ribstein, The Emergence of the Limited Liability Company, 51 Bus. Law. 1 (1995).

10. LLPs generally do not provide protection against liability for activities in which the partner was personally involved or was directly responsible for the supervision of the individual personally involved. For a useful discussion of the evolution of these different generations of LLP statutes, see Robert R. Keatinge, Allan G. Donn, George W. Coleman, and Elizabeth G. Hester, Limited Liability Partnerships: The Next Step in the Evolution of the Unincorporated Business Organization, 51 Bus. Law. 147 (1995).

11. See, e.g., Colo. Rev. Stat. Ann., §§7-60-144, 7-62-109 (1995).

12. In this scenario, a minority member's economic interest or participation in the LLC is reduced or terminated by controlling members.

As a third nontax factor, businesses must consider access to capital markets. Corporate stock may be easier to market to investors and may provide greater ease of transferability. Fourth, the corporate form may offer advantages with respect to benefits available to employees such as qualified deferred compensation plans, profit-sharing and stock-option plans.

A fifth consideration in the choice of business form is the "ease of exit" or dissolution. Corporations generally have an indefinite life, while partnerships can be dissolved easily through the withdrawal of any partner. LLCs generally fit somewhere in the middle. Many state LLC statutes provide no statutory right to disassociate or withdraw.

As a sixth consideration, business participants choosing among different types of unincorporated business entities should carefully examine the state statute with regard to restrictions on distributions, rules with regard to profit-sharing ratios, and other financial matters.

A final factor is the cost of formation. A corporation, whether Subchapter C or S for tax purposes, requires Articles of Incorporation and By-Laws and registration with the jurisdiction of incorporation and often with other jurisdictions in which it does business. LLCs and LLPs also generally must register with the state. The legal costs of generating the necessary documents along with filing and registration fees makes the expense of incorporating a significant factor, particularly for many small businesses. Although a business would be well advised to have a partnership agreement, such an agreement is not required. Similarly, an LLC operating agreement is advisable for LLCs, but is not required in all states. Additionally, in most cases, partnerships need not register with the state or pay fees associated with such registration.

Tax Factors

a) Double Taxation

From a tax point of view, the double taxation provided for in Subchapter C presents a potential disadvantage.[13] This disadvantage to Subchapter C may not appear as serious if the corporation plans to reinvest profits as working capital and not pay out regular dividends. In addition, the preferential tax treatment of qualified dividends[14] and the lower corporate tax rate both reduce the burden of the corporate double tax. These factors may increase the relative attractiveness of the corporate business form.

---

13. For a contrary view, see John W. Lee, A Populist Political Perspective of the Business Tax Entities Universe: Hey the Stars Might Lie But the Numbers Never Do, 78 Tex. L. Rev. 885 (2000).
14. These new rules are discussed in further detail in Chapters 1 and 5.

By lowering the corporate tax rate, the 2017 tax legislation altered the traditional choice of entity calculus for some taxpayers. Under a reduced corporate tax, a taxpayer could experience an equivalent or even lower effective tax rate by earning income through a corporation rather than directly, even if the income is subject to both layers of the corporate double tax. For example, starting in 2018, corporate income that is earned and immediately distributed to an individual shareholder will be subject to an effective maximum rate of 39.8%,[15] which is slightly lower than the maximum possible rate on ordinary income earned by an individual (including both ordinary rates and surtaxes).[16]

Taxpayers may be able to benefit further by *not* receiving distributions from a corporation, and thereby reducing or avoiding the second individual layer of the corporate tax. Several issues should be considered, however, before choosing the corporate form of doing business for this reason. First, the Code imposes penalty taxes on certain undistributed corporate earnings.[17] Second, even though the double tax impact can be delayed through certain accumulations of capital, it generally cannot be avoided entirely.[18] Upon liquidation or upon sale of the stock, the shareholders must report gain or loss.

Pass-through entities, such as general or limited partnerships, Subchapter S corporations, LLCs, LLPs, and LLLPs offer the advantage of a single individual layer of federal income tax.[19] The tax treatment of pass-through entities with multiple owners *other than S corporations* is governed by Subchapter K.[20] The tax treatment of S corporations, on the other hand, is governed by special pass-through rules in Subchapter S.[21] The key feature of both Subchapters K and S is that the business entity *itself* pays no income tax.[22] In other words, both subchapters represent *single*, as opposed to double, tax

---

15. Under the rates in effect at the time of this edition's publication, income earned through a corporation will first be subject to a corporate tax rate of 21%. The after-tax corporate earnings will then be subject to the individual layer of tax at a maximum rate of 23.8% (as either qualified dividends or as capital gains if the taxpayer sells the corporate stock).

16. The top ordinary rates and surtaxes are described later in this chapter.

17. See the discussion of the accumulated earnings and personal holding company penalty taxes in Chapter 1.

18. One exception arises, however, when shareholders transfer stock ownership through inheritance or bequest. In such cases, the beneficiaries take the assets with a fair market value, frequently resulting in a "stepped-up" basis and thereby eliminating the shareholder level tax on the appreciated value of the stock. I.R.C. §1014. Thus, the corporate form may be attractive if a significant number of shareholders anticipate foregoing distributions and retaining their shares until death.

19. Although the single tax advantage is available to pass-through entities for *federal* tax purposes, some states *do* impose an entity level income and/or franchise tax.

20. I.R.C. §§701-777.

21. I.R.C. §§1361-1399.

22. I.R.C. §§701, 1363(a).

regimes. Although there are some differences, the basic pass-through principles of both subchapters are quite similar.[23]

Where there are profits, the advantage of a single layer of tax may be obvious. Furthermore, business income earned through a pass-through entity may also qualify for the 20% §199A deduction, which reduces the effective rate of tax on this income. In addition, if the partnership or other pass-through entity suffers an operating loss, each partner, S shareholder, or member will report his or her share of the loss on an individual tax return. Individual taxpayers often seek out such losses in order to reduce gains from other activities. An individual investor's ability to use such losses from a pass-through entity is severely restricted, however, through various provisions in the Code.[24] On the other hand, a shareholder in a Subchapter C corporation will never have the opportunity to report a corporate loss on her individual tax return.

Subchapter S corporations can offer the best of both worlds, but this entity choice also faces other limitations. On the one hand, the shareholder can have limited liability. At the same time, the business profits are subject to only one layer of tax. Availability of the Subchapter S election is limited, however. For example, the election is available only to corporations with 100 or fewer shareholders, which must be individuals or certain specified types of tax-exempt corporations or "electing small business trusts."[25] In addition, the S corporation can issue only one class of stock.[26] The LLC and LLP provisions in many states seem to solve many of these problems. A properly structured LLC or LLP provides the double advantages of limited liability and a single layer of taxation on business income, assuming that the LLC or LLP elects partnership classification for federal income tax purposes.[27] In addition, LLCs, in particular, allow members more flexibility to "custom fit" an operating agreement to their business needs. At the same time, state provisions for such businesses do not restrict the number of members that can participate.

---

23. A more detailed discussion of Subchapter S follows later in this chapter.

24. For example, a partner's losses are limited to the extent of the partner's basis in the partnership interest. I.R.C. §704(d). In addition, partners can only deduct losses to the extent that their partnership interest basis reflects amounts for which the partner is personally "at risk." I.R.C. §465. Finally, passive investors, such as limited partners, can only deduct losses from investments in passive activities to the extent that they have gain from passive activities. I.R.C. §469. A comprehensive discussion of these provisions is beyond the scope of this book.

25. I.R.C. §1361(b), (c)(2), (c).

26. These rules, and other S corporation restrictions are addressed later in this chapter.

27. The entity classification issues under "check-the-box" regulations are discussed later in this chapter.

b) Tax Rate Issues

In prior decades, taxpayers used the corporate entity itself as a tax shelter. Shortly after World War II, the individual income tax rate was significantly higher than the corporate tax rate. Individuals would place their assets in a corporation so that profits would be taxed at the significantly lower corporate rate. Even though there was a second shareholder-level tax on distributed earnings, this shareholder tax could be deferred for significant periods of time by accumulating earnings, or it could be eliminated entirely by leaving the stock upon death to beneficiaries who acquired the stock with a stepped-up basis under I.R.C. §1014.

In subsequent decades, the differential between the top corporate and individual income tax rates dwindled, but this rate dynamic remains sensitive to cycles of tax reform.

Prior to the 2017 tax changes, the top corporate tax rate of 35% was equivalent to the top rate on individual income, and few thought of a Subchapter C corporation as a tax shelter opportunity any longer. This dynamic has changed with the lower corporate rate, and in some cases earning income through a corporation may again be preferable.

One must look carefully at the anticipated earnings of the business, the anticipated tax bracket of primary shareholders, and the availability of the §199A pass-through deduction, among other factors, before making any decisions regarding business form based upon rate structure. The preferential tax rates available for qualified dividends offer an additional potential incentive toward choosing a corporate form of business. Another factor that should be considered is the extent to which any corporate income will be capital gain. Since individual taxpayers are eligible for significantly lower tax rates on their capital gain income under §1(h), capital gains earned by the corporation will not be taxed at a significantly higher rate than those earned by individual high-bracket taxpayers.

Some larger entities simply have no option other than to choose the corporate form. In some cases, state law may preclude doing business in noncorporate form. In addition, lenders are sometimes willing to charge significantly lower interest rates to corporations than to other business entities. In addition, the business may need the corporate advantages of limited liability and centralized management and may be ineligible for Subchapter S status. The centralized management permitted to an LLC under various "opt out" provisions under state law may prove too unwieldy. Another reason for choosing the corporate form may be that the business plans to make distributions only rarely. If the shareholders of such a corporation hold onto the stock until death, the stock basis is stepped up to fair market value under §1014, with the result that little or no shareholder level tax is paid. Many larger business entities wish to provide certain profit-sharing and stock-option plans that can be offered only through the corporate form. Finally, as described further below, "publicly traded partnerships" can be taxed as C corporations under §7704 regardless of their legal classification.

SUBCHAPTER S CORPORATIONS

Eligibility and Election

Absent a proper election, a business entity formally incorporated under state law will be governed by Subchapter C of the Code. Eligible corporations, however, may *elect* to be treated as an "S corporation."[28]

a) Eligible Corporations

i) Number and Types of Shareholders and S Corporation Ownership Interests

Common parlance often refers to Subchapter S business entities as "small business corporations." One important initial observation is that the term "small" in this context is *not* a reference to the volume of business. A multibillion-dollar corporation may still be an S corporation. Rather, "small," for purposes of Subchapter S, refers to the total *number of shareholders*. To be eligible for a Subchapter S election, the incorporated entity must be a domestic corporation with *no more than 100 shareholders*.[29] As a practical matter, however, a Subchapter S corporation actually may appear to have more than 100 shareholders, as a result of special counting rules under which certain family members together are counted as only one shareholder. The term "members of a family" for purposes of these counting rules is rather broadly defined to include not only husband and wife but also "common ancestors," along with their lineal descendants and spouses, as long as such ancestors are no more than six generations removed.[30]

Treasury Department interpretation of statutory eligibility requirements suggests another way to use the S corporation form yet, for all practical purposes, have more than 100 shareholders. In Rev. Rul. 94-43, the Treasury Department ruled that multiple S corporations may participate as partners in a joint venture *even* if the primary purpose of breaking into multiple entities is to bypass the 100-shareholder limit.[31] Imagine, for example, a group

---

28. Subchapter S spans I.R.C. §§1361-1379.

29. I.R.C. §1361(b)(1)(A). The number of permitted shareholders was originally limited to ten when Congress first enacted Subchapter S in 1958, but was increased over time to the current 100 shareholder limit. Even if they meet the other requirements, some domestic corporations, including certain financial institutions and banks, are ineligible for the Subchapter S election. See I.R.C. §1361(b)(2).

30. I.R.C. §1361(c). Even former spouses are included within this definition.

31. Rev. Rul. 94-43, 1994-2 C.B. 198, revoking Rev. Rul. 77-220, 1997-1 C.B. 263.

of 200 otherwise eligible individual investors whose interest in joining together in S corporation form is thwarted by the 100-shareholder limit. They can achieve something very close to their desired business structure by creating two separate S corporations, each with 100 shareholders, and then having the two corporate entities join together as partners in a partnership. In other cases, however, structuring to avoid the shareholder limitation may still be subject to challenge.[32]

In addition to the shareholder *number* restrictions, Subchapter S limits the *types* of permissible shareholders. For example, S corporations may not have any nonresident alien shareholders,[33] and subchapter S corporation shareholders generally must be *individuals*.[34] Over time, Congress has loosened this individual shareholder restriction through explicit statutory exceptions, which now permit some entities — certain family trusts and estates, voting trusts, and nonprofit entities — to be Subchapter S corporation shareholders.[35] Even under the loosened requirements, however, corporate and partnership entities cannot be small business corporation shareholders.[36]

Subchapter S also includes special rules with respect to interests that an S corporation may hold in other business entities. An S corporation may hold a partnership interest. Prior to 1996, however, S corporations could not hold an interest in a controlled subsidiary. Such subsidiaries now are not only permitted, but Subchapter S includes special provisions under which an S corporation can elect to treat a 100%-controlled subsidiary as a "qualified Subchapter S subsidiary," referred to in regulations as a "Qsub."[37] A Qsub will not be treated as a separate corporation for tax purposes.[38] This type of structure can be advantageous to a business wishing to isolate certain liabilities in a separate corporate entity without having to deal with complex intracorporate transaction or affiliated corporation tax rules.

ii) One Class of Stock Restriction

Another important Subchapter S eligibility requirement is that the corporation have only one class of stock.[39] Particularly with respect to managerial control, the "one class of stock" restriction leaves greater flexibility than might initially appear, however. For example, §1361(c)(4) explicitly states

---

32. See James S. Eustice, Joel D. Kuntz & John A. Bogdanski: Federal Income Taxation of S Corporations ¶3.04[10] (5th ed. 2015).
33. I.R.C. §1361(b)(1)(C).
34. I.R.C. §1361(b)(1)(B).
35. I.R.C. §1361(c)(1), (2), (3), (6).
36. Treas. Reg. §1361-1(f).
37. I.R.C. §1361(b)(3); Treas. Reg. §1361-2(a).
38. I.R.C. §1361(b)(3)(A).
39. I.R.C. §1361(b)(1)(D). For further general discussion on the corporate capital structure, see Chapter 3.

that the S corporation may be structured so that some common shareholders have greater voting rights than others. The restriction does prevent, however, an S corporation from having classes of stock with different economic entitlements. Regulations elaborate that stocks will be considered of the same class so long as they have "identical rights to distribution and liquidation proceeds."[40] The regulations go on to extend their blessing to S corporations with "voting and nonvoting common stock, a class of stock that may vote only on certain issues, irrevocable proxy agreements, or groups of shares that differ with respect to rights to elect members of the board of directors."[41]

The "one class of stock" restriction may raise thorny questions about when additional interests will be classified as additional classes of stock, thus violating the "one class" rule. Although a financial instrument on its surface may appear to represent debt, it risks reclassification as equity to the extent that it incorporates equity-like features.[42] This threat of debt reclassification is lessened to some extent, however, through "safe harbor" rules, which provide details describing "straight debt" instruments that will not be classified as another class of stock.[43]

b) Election and Termination

Although consent of *all* shareholders is required for an initial Subchapter S election,[44] only a majority vote is required to revoke it.[45] A corporation's Subchapter S status is also terminated by any event that causes the corporation to fail to meet the small business corporation definition. For example, if an S corporation issues a second class of stock or exceeds the 100-shareholder limit, it will cease to be an S corporation at the time of the disqualifying event.[46] Once a corporation's Subchapter S status is terminated, it generally will not be eligible to make another small business corporation election for five years.[47] The Treasury Secretary has explicit statutory authority, however, to grant an exception to this five-year restriction in the case of certain inadvertent terminations.[48]

An S corporation with remaining earnings and profits from a prior life as a C corporation faces another possible threat of termination.[49] Under a

---

40. Treas. Reg. §1.1361-1(l)(1).
41. *Id.*
42. A more detailed discussion of issues related to the debt-equity distinction follows in Chapter 3.
43. I.R.C. §1361(c)(5). For example, interest rates and payment dates cannot be contingent on profits, and the debt cannot be convertible into stock. *Id.*
44. I.R.C. §1362(a).
45. I.R.C. §1362(d)(1).
46. I.R.C. §1362(d)(2).
47. I.R.C. §1362(g).
48. I.R.C. §1362(f).
49. For further discussion of Subchapter C earnings and profits, see Chapter 4.

complex set of rules in §1362(d)(3), the Subchapter S election will terminate if the S corporation has such accumulated earnings and profits at the close of three consecutive years, and if more than 25% of the S corporation's gross receipts during those years consists of passive income, defined to mean income from royalties, rents, dividends, interest, and annuities.[50]

Tax Treatment of S Corporations and Their Shareholders

a) Background

The basic idea behind Subchapter S when it was first enacted in 1958 was to provide a vehicle through which small corporate businesses could avoid the double tax otherwise imposed on incorporated entities yet retain the advantage of corporate limited liability. Through Subchapter S, Congress gave birth to a new tax creature—a hybrid somewhere between a regular Subchapter C corporation and a pass-through partnership-type entity governed by Subchapter K. In its early iterations, Subchapter S incorporated more corporate-like tax features than it does today. Although formally incorporated under state law, an S corporation for tax purposes today really is much more akin to a partnership, LLC, or other pass-through type business entity. That said, however, one important distinction between S corporations and their pass-through cousins is what might be called the Subchapter C "default rule" in §1371(a), which provides that "[e]xcept as otherwise provided in this title, and except to the extent inconsistent with this subchapter, Subchapter C shall apply to an S Corporation and its shareholders."[51]

b) Basic Pass-Through Rules

By far the most important distinction between S and C corporations is that the S corporation generally is not a taxable entity.[52] Instead, the S corporation

---

50. I.R.C. §1362(d)(3)(B).

51. Thus, for example, formation of the corporation will be subject to the same nonrecognition rules applicable to C corporations (see Chapter 4) and ongoing and redemption distributions subject to subchapter C distribution rules (see Chapters 5 and 6). Although the applicable rules may be the same, the outcome may differ once the rules are read through the "Subchapter S lens," however. One possible disadvantage to the S corporation as opposed to partnership or LLC is that S corporations may trigger a taxable gain upon a distribution of appreciated property to shareholders under §311. See further discussion at the end of this chapter and in Chapter 5.

52. I.R.C. §1363(a) ("[e]xcept as otherwise provided in this subchapter, an S corporation shall not be subject to the taxes imposed by this chapter"). An S corporation may be subject to an entity-level tax if it has undistributed accumulated earnings and profits (if it was previously a C corporation) and if more than 25% if its gross receipts are passive investment income. I.R.C. §1375. See Chapter 5 for a discussion of earnings and profits in a C corporation.

is treated as a "pass-through" entity, meaning that its shareholders will report their pro rata share of income, loss, deductions, and the like on their individual tax returns.[53] Thus, the good news for S corporation investors is that business income is spared the corporate double tax.[54] The bad news is that, in contrast to C corporation shareholders who pay tax only on *distributed* dividends,[55] S corporation shareholders are responsible for tax on their pro rata share of income *even if they receive no distributions at all.*

Although the S corporation generally is not a taxable entity, it must compute income and loss at the entity level, file S corporation returns, and may be subject to audit. In general, the S corporation computes its taxable income in the same manner as an individual taxpayer.[56] Shareholders then are responsible for reporting their pro rata shares of S corporation income and loss on their individual income tax returns.[57]

One significant computational difference is that instead of aggregating all of its items of income, loss, deduction, or credit, the S corporation must separately state any such items "the separate treatment of which could affect the liability for tax of any shareholder."[58] For example, the S corporation must separately state capital gains and losses grouped by holding period.[59] Individual shareholders then will aggregate their pro rata share of these separately stated amounts with any such gains and losses they may have from other investments in their personal portfolios.

One factor to consider in choosing between Subchapter S and partnership or other pass-through forms of business is the strict Subchapter S requirement that each shareholder report his or her *pro rata share* of separately stated items and non-separately computed income or loss.[60] Despite the many parallels, one difference between the pass-through rules of Subchapter S and Subchapter K is that the latter offers greater flexibility to specially allocate certain items of income and loss through special provisions in the partnership agreement.[61]

---

53. I.R.C. §1366.

54. Subchapter S does include an exception, however, applicable to built-in gains for corporations that convert from C corporation to S corporation status. I.R.C. §1374. This exception to the otherwise "single tax" Subchapter S regime is not a concern for corporations that have always been S corporations.

55. See Chapter 5 for a detailed discussion of the shareholder-level tax on corporate distributions.

56. I.R.C. §1363(b).

57. I.R.C. §1366(a). The *character* of any item of income or loss is determined at the entity level. *Id. At* §1366(b).

58. I.R.C. §1366(a)(1)(A).

59. See Treas. Reg. §1.1366-1(a)(2), which lists such capital gains and losses along with other examples of items requiring separate statement.

60. I.R.C. §§1366(a), 1377(a).

61. Whereas §1366 requires pro rata allocations for S corporation shareholders, §702 provides that each partner shall take into account his *distributive share*, which may be determined by the partnership agreement. I.R.C. §704.

c) Distributions

Because S corporation shareholders are taxable on their pro rata share of the business income as the corporation earns it, they should not be taxed again when they receive distributions.[62] Subchapter S effectively achieves this result through a complex set of basis and distribution rules in §§1367 and 1368. Unlike the C corporation shareholder, the S corporation shareholder's basis is a fluid number constantly being adjusted upward to reflect previously taxed separately and non-separately stated income and downward to reflect loss and nontaxable distributions.[63]

At the corporate level, a distribution of appreciated property technically will trigger taxable gain to the entity as if the property had been sold at fair market value pursuant to the same rules applicable to C corporation.[64] Of course, since the S corporation is not a taxable entity, there will be no tax to the corporation. Rather, the individual S corporation shareholders will be responsible for tax on their individual pro rata shares of the gain.

d) Loss Limitations

Congress has long been concerned with potential tax avoidance opportunities open to pass-through business entity investors who might use their pass-through share of items of loss or deduction to offset otherwise taxable income from other sources. Its statutory response includes a complex array of loss limitation rules. One such rule specifically applicable to S corporation shareholders is that the aggregate loss and deductions for any taxable year cannot exceed the shareholder's adjusted basis in the S corporation stock and the shareholder's adjusted basis in any indebtedness of the S corporation to the shareholder.[65] S corporation shareholders also are subject to additional loss limitation rules more broadly applicable to investors in any type of pass-through entity.[66]

---

62. There may be some tax on distributions, however, to the extent that the S corporation has earnings and profits left over from a prior life as a C corporation. I.R.C. §1368(c).

63. I.R.C. §1367. Subchapter K provides similar ongoing adjustments to a partner or other pass-through entity investor's basis in I.R.C. §705.

64. I.R.C. §311. See Chapter 5.

65. I.R.C. §1366(d)(1). Unused losses generally can be carried forward indefinitely, however. Id. At §1366(d)(2). The Subchapter S rule here is more restrictive than the parallel Subchapter K rule, in which a partner's basis includes his or her share of partnership debt. Id. At §752. S corporation shareholders cannot include their share of the S corporation debt to third-party lenders in their stock basis.

66. See, e.g., I.R.C. §465 (at-risk rules) and §469 (passive loss rules).

CLASSIFICATION OF THE BUSINESS ENTITY

Initial Classification Issues

Federal tax law includes three primary categories of organizations recognized as entities separate from their owners: corporations (or other entities taxable as corporations), partnerships, and trusts.[67] Since each of these entities is governed by a distinct tax regime with its own special rules, proper classification of the organization is essential in determining the proper tax consequences of the organization's activities and transactions.[68] The "check-the-box" regulations, finalized in 1996, have added flexibility and reduced uncertainty in the business planning process. As before, however, the label attached to a particular enterprise for state law purposes will not be determinative for federal income tax purposes.[69]

The first step under the entity classification regulations is to be sure that a separate tax entity has actually been created. The mere co-ownership of property or sharing of expenses does not necessarily create a separate tax entity. A joint venture or other contractual arrangement creates a separate entity for tax purposes only if the participants "carry on a trade, business, financial operation, or venture and divide the profits therefrom."[70] Once it is established that the organization is a separate entity for tax purposes, the entity must further be classified as a corporation, partnership, or trust under rules provided in Treasury regulations §§301.7701-2, 3, and 4.

According to the regulations, a separate tax entity not properly classified as a trust, or otherwise subject to special treatment, is a "business entity."[71] Such a business entity with two or more members will be classified as a corporation or a partnership for tax purposes.[72] Before turning to the distinction between corporations and partnerships, then, it is necessary first to establish that the organization is not an ordinary trust.[73] Generally speaking, an ordinary trust does not involve "associates in a joint enterprise for the conduct of business for profit."[74] Instead, the usual trustee simply is responsible for protecting and conserving property for trust beneficiaries. The §7701 regulations distinguish such an ordinary trust from a business

---

67. Treas. Reg. §301.7701-1(b).
68. Corporations generally are subject to Subchapter C (§§301-384) or, upon proper election, to Subchapter S (bashabasha1361-1378) partnerships to Subchapter K (§§701-761), and trusts to Subchapter J (§§641-692).
69. Treas. Reg. §301.7701-1(a)(1).
70. Treas. Reg. §301.7701-1(a)(2).
71. Treas. Reg. §301.7701-2(a).
72. Id.
73. Treas. Reg. §301.7701-4.
74. Treas. Reg. §301.7701-4(a).

or commercial trust, providing that "[t]he fact that any organization is technically cast in the trust form, by conveying title to property to trustees for the benefit of persons designated as beneficiaries, will not change the real character of the organization if the organization is more properly classified as a *business* entity."[75] Once it is established that the organization in question is a *business* entity with two or more members, the entity must be further classified as either a corporation or a partnership.

Incorporated Entities

An entity properly incorporated under state law or properly organized under a state joint-stock company or joint-stock association statute generally will be treated as a corporation for federal income tax purposes.[76] In rare cases, however, a corporation otherwise properly incorporated under state law will be disregarded for federal income tax purposes. For example, the Supreme Court case of Commissioner v. Bollinger[77] involved a group of real-estate partnerships that created a corporation for the sole purpose of holding nominal title to property and borrowing necessary funds for the partnership real-estate business. The lender had suggested that the partnerships establish a corporation to hold nominal title to the collateral and borrow the necessary funds since the interest rate the lender could charge corporate borrowers under the state usury law was higher than the rate for noncorporate borrowers. The corporation had no other assets, liabilities, employees, or bank accounts. In *Bollinger*, the Court disregarded the corporation, finding that the corporate entity was acting as agent for the partnerships, which were the true owners of the property. Thus, the Court upheld the partnerships' reporting of income and loss on their partnership tax returns and the pass-through of such income and loss to the individual partners. This is not to suggest, however, that the *Bollinger* result will be common. As a general rule, once investors choose to incorporate, the corporation is viewed as a separate entity for tax purposes and the shareholders generally will be bound for tax purposes by their decision to incorporate, for better or for worse, until they liquidate the corporation. The *Bollinger* decision does leave open the possibility, however, that in certain limited circumstances, a properly incorporated entity could be disregarded for tax purposes.

---

75. Treas. Reg. §301.7701-4(b).
76. Treas. Reg. §301.7701-2(b)(1), (3). If eligible, of course, the corporation may elect to be treated as a Subchapter S corporation.
77. 485 U.S. 340 (1988).

Unincorporated Entities: Publicly Traded Partnerships and Per Se Corporations

In addition to formally incorporated businesses and joint-stock companies or associations, the Internal Revenue Code and regulations also automatically classify certain *unincorporated* entities as corporations for federal tax purposes. For example, §7704 automatically classifies certain publicly traded partnerships as corporations. For purposes of this provision, a publicly traded partnership is "any partnership if (1) interests in such partnership are traded on an established securities market, or (2) interests in such partnership are readily tradeable on a secondary market (or the substantial equivalent thereof)."[78] This Code provision was a response to the growth of "master limited partnerships" in the 1980s. Such investments were often available on established securities markets and gave investors, otherwise ineligible for pass-through tax treatment under Subchapter S, the advantages of limited liability and the opportunity to participate in huge business conglomerates without the disadvantage of the corporate double tax. Since these publicly traded partnerships so resemble corporations, §7704 *deems* them to be corporations for federal tax purposes. The §7701 regulations also automatically classify as corporations certain other business entities such as insurance companies,[79] certain state-chartered banks,[80] government-owned businesses,[81] and certain foreign entities.[82]

Associations Taxable as Corporations: Movement from the "Corporate Resemblance" Test to an Elective Regime

The Internal Revenue Code itself defines the term "corporation" to include "associations, joint-stock companies, and insurance companies."[83] Before adopting its "check-the-box" approach, the Treasury Department

---

78. I.R.C. §7704(b). As of the first day that it is classified as a publicly traded partnership, the partnership is deemed to have transferred all of its assets to a newly formed corporation in exchange for stock and to have distributed the stock to its partners in liquidation of their partnership interests. I.R.C. §7704(f).
79. Treas. Reg. §301.7701-2(b)(4).
80. Treas. Reg. §301.7701-2(b)(5).
81. Treas. Reg. §301.7701-2(b)(1), (6).
82. Treas. Reg. §301.7701-2(b)(8). This provision contains a list of particular business entities formed in specifically named foreign countries that will be treated as per se (or automatic) corporations. Other foreign business entities will be eligible to elect partnership or corporate status for U.S. Tax purposes. Issues related to foreign corporations and the general international implications of the entity classification regulations are beyond the scope of this book.
83. I.R.C. §7701(a)(3).

distinguished between "associations" taxable as corporations and unincorporated business entities *not* taxed as corporations under a six-part "corporate resemblance" test taken from the Supreme Court's 1935 decision in Morrissey v. Commissioner.[84] The old §7701 regulations identified six characteristics ordinarily found in a pure corporation, which, taken together, distinguished it from other organizations.[85] Based upon this old facts and circumstances analysis, if an organization more nearly resembled a corporation than a partnership or trust, the organization was classified as an association taxable as a corporation.

In proposing its "check-the-box" classification regulations, the Treasury Department noted that "[o]ne consequence of the increased flexibility under local law in forming a partnership or other unincorporated business organization is that taxpayers generally can achieve partnership tax classification for a nonpublicly traded organization that, in all meaningful respects, is virtually indistinguishable from a corporation."[86] The "check-the-box" regulations eliminate the corporate resemblance test, replacing the earlier formalistic rules "with a much simpler approach that generally is elective,"[87] and making explicit the previously de facto elective nature of the entity classification rules.

Elective "Check-the-Box" Classification Regulations

Under "check-the-box" regulations, a business entity that is not *automatically* classified as a corporation under §301.7701-2 is considered an "eligible entity."[88] An eligible entity with two or more members can elect classification as either an association taxable as a corporation or a partnership.[89] An eligible entity with a single member can elect classification as an association taxable as a corporation or to be disregarded as an entity separate from its owner.[90] The regulations provide a default partnership classification rule—if no election is filed for a domestic eligible entity with two or more members, the entity will be treated as a partnership. The default rule also provides that if no election is filed for a domestic single-owner entity, the entity "will be disregarded as an entity separate from its owner."[91]

---

84. 296 U.S. 344 (1935).
85. The six factors were (1) associates, (2) objective to carry on business for joint profit, (3) continuity of life, (4) centralization of management, (5) limited liability, and (6) free transferability of interests. Id. At 360.
86. Notice of Proposed Rulemaking, PS-43-95, Fed. Reg. (May 10, 1996).
87. T.D. 8697, 61 Fed. Reg. 66,584 (Dec. 18, 1996) (explanation of provisions).
88. Treas. Reg. §301.7701-3(a).
89. Id.
90. Id. See also Treas. Reg. §301.7701-2(a).
91. Treas. Reg. §301.7701-3(b)(1).

Since the default rules are explicit, the regulations clarify that "elections are necessary *only when* an eligible entity chooses to be classified initially as other than the default classification or when an eligible entity chooses to change its classification." In other words, an eligible entity that wishes *corporate* tax status must make a formal election; other entities need do nothing. The regulations define a partnership for tax purposes as "a business entity that is not a corporation . . . And that has at least two members."[92] Thus, for example, even though it is not a partnership under state law, a nonelecting LLC with two or more members is classified as a partnership for federal tax purposes.

Given that "check-the-box" rules permit an election to change entity classification, a business entity need not be stuck with its initial tax classification choice.[93] However, the regulations include special rules aimed at taxpayer attempts to use repeated changes in tax status for manipulative or abusive purposes. Thus, if an eligible entity elects to change its classification, it generally will not be permitted *again* to change its classification for a period of 60 months.[94] The regulations include details regarding tax consequences that flow from an elective change in classification.[95] For example, if a partnership elects to become an association, the regulations provide that the partnership is thereby deemed to contribute its assets and liabilities to the association in exchange for stock, followed by an immediate liquidation of the partnership in which stock is distributed to the partners.[96] If an eligible entity that previously elected to be classified as an association later elects to change its classification to partnership, the association will be deemed to have distributed all of its assets and liabilities to the shareholders in liquidation, followed by an immediate contribution of the assets and liabilities to the partnership.[97]

Summary and Implications

Current elective regulations simplify and liberalize entity classification rules. Given the availability of LLC and other alternate business forms, these

---

92. Treas. Reg. §301.7701-2(c)(1).
93. Treas. Reg. §301.7701-3(c)(1)(i).
94. Treas. Reg. §301.7701-3(c)(1)(iv). The Commissioner has authority, however, to waive this rule upon a greater than 50% change in ownership. *Id.*
95. Treas. Reg. §301.7701-3(g).
96. *Id. At* §301.7701-3(g)(1)(i). Tax consequences of the "deemed formation transaction" would be governed by §351, which is discussed in Chapter 4. Tax consequences of the "deemed partnership liquidation" would be governed by Subchapter K partnership rules.
97. Treas. Reg. §301.7701-3(g)(1)(ii). Tax consequence of the "deemed liquidation transaction" would be governed by §§331 and 336 or §§332 and 337, which are discussed in Chapters 8 and 9. The "deemed partnership contribution" would be governed by Subchapter K partnership rules.

"check-the-box" regulations effectively offer business owners the opportunity to easily achieve limited liability without incurring the double taxation of Subchapter C. Under the old "corporate resemblance" test, a limited partnership, LLC, LLP, or LLLP bore the risk that the Treasury Department might reclassify it as a corporation for tax purposes if the organization had more corporate than noncorporate characteristics. Under the "check-the-box" regulations, such eligible business entities simply can choose a tax classification by election.

The "check-the-box" rules were intended to simplify tax classification issues and reduce the extraordinary number of hours government and private accountants and lawyers were spending on them. Yet major simplification continues to appear elusive. A familiar cycle has emerged. Taxpayers design complex transactions to use new statutes or regulations to their tax advantage in ways that were unanticipated or were not desired by Congress or the Treasury Department. The government then responds to such "loopholes" with an amendment to the statute or regulations designed to attack the transaction. The government response often is complex and narrowly focused on the tax shelter of the moment, thus adding to the complexity of the Code and regulations. This dynamic has been especially acute in transactions involving foreign entities. Many taxpayers have taken advantage of complex interactions between check-the-box regulations and the tax rules applicable to foreign entities to eliminate or substantially reduce their U.S. Tax liability.[98]

The Internal Revenue Code includes specific definitions of the terms "corporation" and "partnership" in §7701. Given these definitions, some have questioned even the Treasury Department's authority to promulgate elective classification rules.[99] Several federal circuit courts have answered that question by upholding the validity of the check-the-box rules.[100]

As the Joint Committee on Taxation observed, the enhanced ability to choose partnership treatment, "places increased pressure on the rules governing the taxation of partnership income, making it more important to identify and, if possible, correct provisions in the partnership tax rules that give

---

98. The most frequently used statutory provisions have been the controlled foreign corporation (CFC) rules in I.R.C. §§951-965 (Subpart F). For a discussion of some of these transactions and the possible policy responses to them, see, e.g., Adam H. Rosenzweig, Harnessing the Costs of International Tax Arbitrage, 26 Va. Tax Rev. 555 (2007). These international rules, as well as tax reforms designed to prevent abuse, are beyond the scope of this book.
99. Staff of Joint Comm. on Tax'n, Review of Selected Entity Classification and Partnership Tax Issues, 105th Cong., 2d Sess. (Comm. Print 1997).
100. Littriello v. United States, 484 F.3d 372 (6th Cir. 2007), cert. denied, 128 S. Ct. 1290 (2008) (case of first impression). See also McNamee v. Dep't Treas., 488 F.3d 100 (2d Cir. 2007). Both of these cases involved single-member LLC individual owner's personal liability for federal payroll taxes. Regulations have since been adopted to provide that an otherwise disregarded entity nevertheless shall be treated as an entity for federal payroll tax purposes. Treas. Reg. basha301.7701-2(c)(iv).

anomalous results, create problems in application, or are anachronistic."[101] More significantly, the "check-the-box" regime undoubtedly will continue to stimulate policymakers to rethink the need for the different tax regimes in Subchapter C (corporations), Subchapter K (partnerships), and Subchapter S (small business corporations) and may place increased pressure on proposals for integrating the federal individual and corporate income taxes.

Examples

Basic Classification Questions

1. a. The Weasley twins, Fred and George, recently inherited as joint owners a substantial commercial rental property from a wealthy wizard uncle. They agree on a mutual arrangement to collect rents and arrange for necessary maintenance and repair. Do the Weasley twins have an "eligible entity" for which they could elect under check-the-box regulations to be treated as an association taxable as a corporation?
   b. What if the twins decided to add to the inherited property by purchasing several other commercial rental properties and hiring a rental management company to collect rents and take care of the repairs and maintenance?
   c. How will the Weasley real estate holdings in Example 1b be classified if they do nothing?

2. a. One hundred members from several recent Hogwarts graduating classes have decided to start a wizardry consulting business. Several members have spouses, sisters, brothers, and cousins who also would like to invest. The total number of investors, including relatives, comes to 120. Would they be eligible to make a Subchapter S election?
   b. Assuming that the investors initially made a valid election, would the Subchapter S status terminate if one shareholder dies so that the stock is owned by the deceased shareholder's estate?
   c. Again assuming a valid initial election, would Subchapter S status terminate if one shareholder sells her S corporation shares to a corporation?

Some Planning Questions

3. a. Harry, Hermione, and Ron have recently come into some money and are planning to start a retail sporting goods business, which will carry the widest selection anywhere of flying broomsticks for Quidditch. Ron's sister, Ginny, is also interested in the business. Since Quidditch players fly at high speeds and altitudes, the three friends are worried

---

101. Joint Comm. Entity Classification report, *supra*, note 94, at 1.

about potential liability for personal injuries to players using their products. What general advice would you offer regarding choice of business form?

b. Imagine that the others are reluctant to give Ginny much say with respect to management decisions. Would the S corporation option be unavailable if they decide to give Ginny nonvoting common stock? What if they wanted to give her nonvoting preferred stock?

c. How might your choice of form advice change if Harry, Hermione, and Ron told you that they expected to borrow significant funds from third-party lenders?

d. How might your choice of form advice change if Harry, Hermione, and Ron told you that they expected the business to hold various properties than might appreciate in value and that they might wish later to distribute to the investors?

Explanations

1. a. Mere co-ownership, rental, and maintenance of the property will not create a *business entity* for tax purposes. Absent evidence that they have created a trade, business, or venture, the Weasley twins simply will be treated as co-owners and will not be an eligible entity under check-the-box regulations. Treas. Reg. §301.7701-1(a)(2).

   b. These additional facts suggest that the twins now are more than mere co-owners and have created a business entity. The entity will be treated as a tax partnership, unless the election is made to be treated for tax purposes as a corporation. Treas. Reg. §301.7701-3(a).

   c. An election is necessary only "when an entity chooses to be classified initially as other than the default classification." Treas. Reg. §301.7701-3(a). Pursuant to "default classification" rules, a domestic eligible entity with two or more members will be treated as a partnership. Treas. Reg. §301.7701-3(b). Thus, if the Weasley's do nothing, they will automatically be classified for tax purposes as a partnership subject to pass-through rules.

2. a. To be eligible at all to elect under Subchapter S, the investors first will have to file articles of incorporation and follow any other procedures required to establish a valid corporation under state law. Once they have incorporated, they are no longer eligible to elect to be treated as a partnership governed by Subchapter K under check-the-box regulations. If all of the shareholders consent, however, they can elect to treat the business as a Subchapter S corporation pass-through type entity. Family members, as defined under §1361(c)(1), are treated as one shareholder. Thus, despite the 120 individual investors here, the group should still be within the 100-shareholder limit if the familial relationships meet the statutory requirements.

b. To be eligible to elect under Subchapter S, the corporation generally must have no more than 100 shareholders, who—with limited statutory exceptions—must be *individuals*. The estates of individual shareholders are permitted, however. I.R.C. §1361(c)(1)(A).

c. By definition in §1361(b)(1), a Subchapter S "small business corporation" cannot have corporations or partnerships as shareholders. Under §1362(d)(2), a previously valid Subchapter S election terminates when the corporation ceases to be a "small business corporation." A shareholder sale of S corporation stock to a corporation will terminate the Subchapter S election. If this occurs during a taxable year, the corporation will be treated as an S corporation only for the portion of the year prior to the termination ("S short year") and will be treated as a C corporation for the other portion of the year ("C short year"). I.R.C. §1362(e).

3. a. A general partnership would leave all investors exposed to potential personal liability. Even a limited partnership would require that there be a least one general partner with personal liability, unless the general partner is structured as an LLC. The primary remaining choices that offer limited liability include a corporation, with or without a Subchapter S election, or a limited liability company (LLC). The corporate form offers the advantage of centralized management, but this is not likely to be a significant concern here given the small number of investors involved. The disadvantages of the corporate form without a Subchapter S election, of course, is the double tax on distributed earnings, which is reduced now on account of the qualified dividends rules and the lower corporate tax rate. Assuming that they can steer clear of accumulated earnings tax penalties, shareholders can delay the shareholder-level tax as long as the corporation does not distribute its profits as dividends. Moreover, the shareholders can avoid the shareholder-level tax on corporate earnings altogether by leaving stock to their heirs, who will take the stock with a fair market value at death basis under §1014. Finally, a C corporation will also not qualify for the §199A qualified business income deduction. If the business income would qualify for this deduction, then an entity structured as a pass-through is likely to be favored.

A corporation with a Subchapter S election or an LLC both offer limited liability and pass-through tax treatment. They should have little trouble meeting the Subchapter S eligibility requirements: There are fewer than 100 individual investors, and they are unlikely to need more than one simple class of voting common stock. The S corporation form may be slightly more expensive than the LLC because of formal state law filing requirements and fees.

In choosing between the LLC and S corporation forms, you might also want to advise that the latter requires pro rata allocations of income, loss, deductions, and credits under §1366(a), whereas the parallel rules in §705 applicable to the LLC provide for allocations based on "distributive shares." This difference becomes significant in the event that the investors wish to specially allocate certain items or amounts to specific investors. The LLC form offers greater flexibility in this regard.

b. Under §1361(b)(1)(D), a corporation is ineligible for Subchapter S if it has more than one class of stock. For purposes of this rule, however, §1361(c)(4) disregards differences in common stock voting rights. Thus, they would still be eligible to elect under Subchapter S if Ginny receives nonvoting common stock or voting common stock with fewer votes or with rights to vote only on certain corporate matters. They would *not* be eligible for Subchapter S, on the other hand, if Ginny received *preferred* stock, which would be classified as a second class of stock.

c. The pass-through rules in Subchapters K and S are very similar, but there are some exceptions with respect to basis. Although individual investors in pass-through type entities generally report their share of business income and loss on their individual tax returns, special loss limitation rules generally limit the reporting of loss for any given year to the investor's basis. Under §752, LLC investors increase basis in their LLC investment by their share of business liabilities. In contrast, S corporation shareholders' bases under §1366(d) do not include their share of the business debts owed to third-party lenders. Thus, if the business expects to incur debt to third party lenders, the LLC form offers the potential for a greater pass-through of loss than the S corporation form.

d. As discussed later in Chapter 5 with respect to C corporations, a corporate distribution of appreciated property to its shareholders will trigger taxable gain under §311(b). Although the tax treatment of Subchapter S corporations generally is much more similar to tax partnerships than it is to C corporations, it is important to be mindful that Subchapter C rules generally still apply to the S corporation as provided in §1371(a). One circumstance in which the regular corporate tax rules make a difference is upon the distribution of appreciated property. There is no entity-level taxable gain when a tax partnership or disregarded entity distributes appreciated property. The S corporation, on the other hand, is subject to §311. This does not mean that the S corporation will pay a tax; it is, after all, a nontaxable entity. However, the distribution will trigger an entity-level gain and each shareholder will be responsible for reporting his or her pro rata share. In the end, structuring the entity as a tax partnership might be preferred in the event that the investors anticipate significant distributions of appreciated property.

The Corporate Capital Structure

INTRODUCTION[1]

Once a business chooses to operate in the corporate form, it must decide how to raise capital and otherwise structure the corporate organization. Corporations typically raise capital through issuing stock or through borrowing. The investor who purchases stock holds an equity interest while the lender holds a debt or creditor interest in the corporate enterprise. In either case, the investor or lender expects a return on funds placed or "invested" with the corporation. Shareholders may receive that return from dividends paid on the stock and from profit upon later sale of the stock. Lenders receive their return from interest payments.[2] The corporation is obligated to pay its lenders before it pays its shareholders. Thus, an equity interest is regarded as *subordinate* or *junior* to a debt interest in the corporation. Put another way, the debt interest is regarded as *preferred* or *senior* to the equity interest. An equity interest generally carries greater risk than a debt interest in *the same corporation*.[3]

---

1. This chapter provides only a brief overview of the corporate capital structure as necessary to understand the related tax issues. For a more detailed analysis, see Bayless Manning and James J. Hanks, Jr., Legal Capital (4th ed. 2013); Alan R. Palmiter, Corporations: Examples and Explanations, ch. 4 (9th ed. 2021).

2. A lender might also receive value by selling or exchanging the note at a gain. Such a gain generally would result from changes in interest rates and should not be regarded as gain from the investment in the corporation itself.

3. Generalizations are more difficult when comparing different corporations. A debt interest in a new, highly speculative corporation may be riskier than an equity interest in a well-established, economically healthy corporation.

Creditors generally are entitled only to a repayment of the principal and a fixed rate of interest. As a result, although creditors are preferred in the sense that they are entitled to payment before the common shareholders they are limited in that their rate of return generally is fixed. Unlike the creditor, the common shareholder's rate of return is unlimited, giving the shareholder the opportunity to participate in the economic growth of the corporation. A holder of stock or equity decides "to embark upon the corporate adventure, taking the risks of loss . . . so that he may enjoy the chances of profit."[4]

Many smaller corporations have only one class of equity outstanding. This simple voting common stock typically allows the shareholders to vote for members of the board of directors. It also gives the shareholders an unlimited interest in the earnings of the corporation after all creditors have been paid and an unlimited right to share in assets upon liquidation.[5] Other corporations may have more complex capital structures, including additional classes of common stock either with greater or lesser voting rights, or sometimes, no voting rights at all. Corporations may also issue preferred stock, which also may be either voting or nonvoting. Preferred stock generally provides for a fixed rate of return before the common shareholders are entitled to be paid. Thus, for example, 6% preferred stock may offer investors a fixed 6% rate of return on the stock's stated value before the common shareholders are paid. Unlike a creditor, the preferred shareholder is not entitled to a 6% return regardless of corporate performance.[6] Preferred shareholders are paid only after creditors have been paid, but before the common shareholders. Thus, in the corporate pecking order, preferred shareholders are senior or preferred to common shareholders, but subordinate or junior to creditors or note holders.

The design of any particular corporation's capital structure is driven by nontax and tax considerations. One important nontax factor is the anticipated investment strategy of potential investors. For example, decisions on relative amounts of preferred stock, common stock, debentures, and bonds will be made, in part, based upon the extent of risk that investors are prepared to bear. Management concerns also may determine the classes and amounts of common and nonvoting preferred issued. For example, a closely held corporation may wish to have both voting common and nonvoting

---

4. United States v. Title Guarantee & Trust Co., 133 F.2d 990, 993 (6th Cir. 1943).

5. This is not to suggest that the shareholders are entitled to dividends by operation of law. Dividends will be paid by the corporation only when they are declared by the board of directors. If the corporation should liquidate, however, the holders of common stock are entitled to all residual assets left after the creditors and other more senior equity holders have been paid.

6. Preferred stock that is cumulative has a priority right to accrued, but unpaid, dividends from prior years before common shareholders may receive a dividend. If the preferred stock is noncumulative, the corporation has no continuing obligation to later pay undeclared dividends from prior years. Preferred stock also may be either participating or nonparticipating. Participating preferred shareholders are entitled not only to their specified preferred rate of return, but also share with the common shareholders when additional dividends are declared.

preferred shares to distinguish those with only a financial stake from those with a management stake in the enterprise. Another factor is the extent to which investors will demand high-yield stocks that pay frequent dividends as opposed to shares offering their return through the appreciated value of the stock. The corporation may also be concerned with how the capital structure will be viewed by potential lenders. Tax factors influencing the capital structure include the extent to which the corporation wishes to pay and investors wish to receive dividend as opposed to interest payments. The rules on the tax treatment of qualified dividends also affect how corporations and investors weigh these considerations.[7]

DISTINGUISHING DEBT FROM EQUITY

Why Does It Matter?

Many corporate tax provisions cannot be properly applied until one first identifies the instrument at issue as debt or equity. The descriptions that follow provide a brief sampling of the kinds of issues that require a distinction between debt and equity instruments.

One issue of great concern to corporations is whether payments with respect to a particular instrument will qualify as deductible interest expense. Interest payments are generally deductible to the corporation[8] whereas distributions to shareholders with respect to stock are not deductible.

In 2017 Congress amended §163(j) to significantly limit the deductibility of interest expenses in certain cases.[9] Section 163(j), which applies to both corporate and noncorporate taxpayers, limits the deduction for any "business interest" to the sum of the taxpayer's "business interest income" and 30% of "adjusted taxable income."[10] For these purposes, business

---

7. See also discussion in Chapter 1.

8. I.R.C. §163. In addition to the limitation in I.R.C. §163(j) discussed in this section, there are a limited number of additional circumstances in which interest will not be deductible. See, e.g., I.R.C. §§247, 265(a)(2), 267A, 279.

9. Pub. L. No. 115-97, 131 Stat. 2054, §13301 (2017). Prior to this change, §163(j) provided for a much narrower "earnings stripping" limitation for a corporation with interest expenses above certain thresholds and in transactions with certain parties.

10. I.R.C. §163(j)(1). As part of the 2020 CARES Act Congress increased the 30% limitation to 50% for taxable years beginning in 2019 and 2020. I.R.C. §163(j)(10). The allowable deduction under §163(j)(1) also includes the amount of the taxpayers' "floor plan financing interest," which is defined in §163(j)(9). An anti-avoidance rule in the final regulations under §163(j) also includes in the definition of interest any expenses "economically equivalent to interest" if a principal purpose in structuring the payments is reduce the amount of interest that would otherwise be subject to the limitation. Treas. Reg. §1.163(j)-1(b)(22)(iv)(A).

interest is interest allocable to a trade or business,[11] business interest income is income includible in the taxpayer's gross income allocable to a trade or business,[12] and adjusted taxable income is income from a trade or business, net of interest income and expenses and certain other deductions.[13] These rules have the general effect of limiting the interest expense deduction for highly leveraged businesses. The taxpayer can carry forward disallowed business interest expenses to subsequent years.[14] Small businesses meeting the "gross receipts" test in §448(c) that are also not treated as "tax shelter" under §448(a)(3) are exempt from the limitation.[15]

The distinction between debt and equity will also have consequences for the investor receiving the corporate payments, who must distinguish interest receipts from dividend receipts. A corporation holding stock in another corporate enterprise is entitled to a dividends-received deduction on payments with respect to an equity interest,[16] but is not entitled to any deduction on interest receipts with respect to a debt instrument. In addition, holders of debt issued with "original issue discount"[17] (OID) will be required to include the interest reflected in this discount for each day during the taxable year that he or she held the debt instrument.[18] These OID rules generally will not apply to equity instruments.[19]

The debt-equity distinction also is critical in determining the tax consequences of incorporation. Upon formation of a corporation, contributors will be entitled to nonrecognition of gain upon receipt of *stock* in exchange for the property contributed.[20] If the investor receives a debenture or some other form of debt instead of stock in exchange for a contribution to a corporation, the transfer of property will not qualify for nonrecognition

---

11. I.R.C. §163(j)(5).

12. I.R.C. §163(j)(6). The legislative history suggests Congress's intent that, in case of a corporation, all interest income and expense will be treated as allocable to a trade or business. H.R. Rep. No. 115-466, at 386 n. 688 (2017).

13. I.R.C. §163(j)(8).

14. I.R.C. §163(j)(2).

15. I.R.C. §163(j)(3). Under this test, the average annual gross receipts of the entity for the preceding 3 years cannot exceed $25 million. A "tax shelter" is defined in §6662(d)(2)(C) as any entity or arrangement with a significant purpose of avoiding or evading Federal income tax. The statute also exempts certain trades or businesses listed in §163(j)(7).

16. I.R.C. §243. For further discussion of the §243 deduction, see Chapter 5.

17. "Original issue discount" is defined as the excess of the stated redemption price at maturity over the issue price. I.R.C. §1273(a)(1).

18. I.R.C. §1272(a)(1).

19. Rules similar to the OID rules may apply, however, to certain preferred stock redeemable at a price higher than the issue price. Here, the difference between the redemption and issue price resembles the discount element in an OID debt instrument. Under its authority under §305(c), the Treasury Department requires ratable inclusion of income of the redemption premium over the period of time during which the stock cannot be called for redemption. Treas. Reg. §1.305-5(b). For further discussion of §305(c), see Chapter 7.

20. I.R.C. §351. The nonrecognition rules for contributions in return for stock are discussed in more detail in Chapter 4.

treatment. In somewhat parallel fashion, the corporate reorganization rules provide non-recognition where the shareholders receive stock in a reorganization.[21] When shareholders receive notes or other evidence of indebtedness in the reorganization they may be treated as receiving taxable boot. Thus, distinguishing debt from equity will be important to shareholders participating in an otherwise tax-free reorganization.

Redemption provides another example of the significance of the distinction between equity and debt. Payments to a shareholder in redemption of stock will be governed by §302 whereas retirement of debt instruments will be governed by special rules in §1271.[22] Another example involves the loss of corporate value. When corporate stock loses its value, the shareholders may be entitled to a deduction for the loss of worthless stock under §165. On the other hand, when a debt becomes worthless, the lender may be entitled to a bad debt deduction under §166. The distinction also is important in determining eligibility for an election to be treated as a Subchapter S corporation. To be eligible for such an election, the corporation generally may have only one class of stock.[23] The corporation must be careful that any other financial instruments issued not be classified as equity or stock for purposes of these rules.

Why Should It Matter?

Corporate issuances of stock and debt are simply alternative methods of raising corporate capital. From a finance theory perspective, an argument can be made that changes in a firm's capital structure will not change the firm's overall value.[24] In other words, from an *economic*, as opposed to a tax, point of view, it should make little difference whether the corporation raises funds through debt or equity. Why, then, should there be any difference in the tax treatment of debt and equity? This question goes to the very heart of the corporate tax itself. One could eliminate much of the discrepancy between debt and equity by treating all corporate financial instruments as debt. Thus, corporations would be entitled to deduct all payments to investors and all holders of financial instruments would be required to report "interest" income as it accrued under rules similar to the original issue discount rules. The double tax on corporate earnings effectively would be eliminated. On the other hand, one could treat all financial instruments

---

21. For discussion of corporate reorganizations, see Chapters 11-14.
22. For a more thorough discussion of redemptions, see Chapter 6.
23. I.R.C. §1361(b)(1)(D).
24. See discussion of this theory in Richard A. Brealey, Stewart C. Myers, & Franklin Allen, Principles of Corporate Finance, chs. 17-19 (13th ed. 2020). This theoretical conclusion only holds, however, before taking into account the costs of the corporate tax, bankruptcy and certain other expenses.

as equity, thus disallowing any interest deductions on corporate financial instruments. Unless the interest deduction was eliminated for all business taxpayers, this would discriminate in favor of noncorporate businesses still eligible for the interest deduction. The bottom line is that a distinction between debt and equity is necessary so long as Congress remains committed to the corporate double tax.

The Relative Tax Advantages of Debt Versus Equity

Common wisdom has suggested that debt is encouraged by tax provisions favoring debt over equity. Perhaps the most frequently cited tax advantage to issuing debt vs. equity from the corporation's perspective is the potential deductibility of corporate interest payments on debt in contrast to the non-deductibility of corporate dividend payments on stock. Thus, in balancing corporate capital structure, corporations often include a substantial proportion of debt issue, which provides them with regular interest deductions. Before 2003, investors might have been somewhat indifferent between receiving returns to debt or equity investments. In either case, their receipt of interest or dividends was taxable at ordinary income rates. Investors with an equity interest also could be expected to be reasonably content with a corporation that chooses to accrue earnings rather than distribute them as dividends. After all, the accrued earnings will presumably be reflected in an increased value for the shares. Shareholders with an interest in a corporation that accrues, rather than distributes, its earnings thus benefit from deferral of the shareholder-level tax on corporate profits.[25] When the shareholders sell their stock, gain will be reported as capital gain. Moreover, the gain on the shares may never be taxed to the shareholders at all if they hold the shares until they die, leaving the stock to their heirs with a stepped-up basis under §1014.[26]

Prior to the 2003 qualified dividend provisions, an equity interest offered the dual advantages of deferring the shareholder-level tax on accrued corporate profit and converting what would have been ordinary dividend income into capital gain eligible for preferential tax rates. Thus, there was some tension between investors who preferred these equity interest advantages and the corporation, which might prefer to raise capital through debt. Currently, the qualified dividend rules can offer an additional advantage to

---

25. For a discussion of when a taxpayer would and would not benefit from deferring taxes by earning income through a corporation, see Ari Glogower & David Kamin, Sheltering Income Through a Corporation, 164 Tax Notes Fed. 507 (July 22, 2019); Michael S. Knoll, The TCJA and the Questionable Incentive to Incorporate, 162 Tax Notes 977 (Mar. 4, 2019).
26. The accumulated earnings tax, personal holding company rules, and related provisions in the Code were designed to prevent some of the perceived abuses from such accumulations. See Chapter 1.

equity investors, whereas the §163(j) limitation can reduce the corporation's preference for debt financing. Moreover, a *corporate shareholder* may also favor equity investments, since dividends paid to corporations are entitled to a dividends-received deduction under §243.[27] In the end, the potential tax advantages to debt from the paying corporation's perspective must be balanced against the preference that the individual and corporate shareholders may have for equity.

In addition to the limitation in §163(j), Congress has also responded to the perceived bias toward debt at the corporate level by disallowing corporate interest deductions in certain cases thought to be abusive or where interest deductions seemed particularly inappropriate. For example, in an effort to curb the growing numbers of tax-induced leveraged buy-outs, §279 disallows interest deductions on corporate indebtedness incurred to acquire certain stock of another corporation.

Absence of a Precise Standard

Although distinguishing debt from equity is important in determining the proper tax consequences of many corporate transactions, actually making the distinction often is no easy task. Variations in the types and terms of financial instruments are as boundless as the creativity of financial planners, tax lawyers, and accountants. Making the debt-equity distinction can be a frustrating exercise. There are no precise rules, but rather a number of factors to be applied in a facts and circumstances balancing act. As the court pointed out in one major case:

> neither any single criterion nor any series of criteria can provide a conclusive answer in the kaleidoscopic circumstances which individual cases present. . . . The various factors . . . Are only aids in answering the ultimate question whether the investment, analyzed in terms of its economic reality, constitutes risk capital entirely subject to the fortunes of the corporate venture or represents a strict debtor-creditor relationship. Since there is often an element of risk in a loan, just as there is an element of risk in an equity interest, the conflicting elements do not end at a clear line in all cases.[28]

Reclassification of a debt instrument as equity for tax purposes will result in disallowance of interest deductions to the corporation and taxation of dividends to the shareholders. Reclassification of an equity interest as a debt interest will result in disallowance of the §243 dividends-received deduction

---

27. See Chapter 5 for detailed discussion of the §243 dividends-received deduction.
28. Fin Hay Realty Co. v. United States, 398 F.2d 694, 696-697 (3d Cir. 1968) (citations omitted).

to any corporate shareholder and the allowance of interest deductions to the paying corporation.

Despite decades of effort, there are no precise rules distinguishing debt from equity. In 1969, Congress authorized the Treasury Department to "prescribe such regulations as may be necessary or appropriate to determine whether an interest in a corporation is to be treated . . . As stock or indebtedness (or as in part stock and in part indebtedness)."[29] An unusual Code provision, §385, offers merely suggestions to the Treasury Department as to factors it may include in regulations distinguishing debtor-creditor relationships from corporation-shareholder relationships.[30] These suggested factors are:

1. whether there is a written unconditional promise to pay on demand or on a specified date a sum certain in money in return for an adequate consideration in money or money's worth and to pay a fixed rate of interest;
2. whether there is subordination to or preference over any indebtedness of the corporation;
3. the ratio of debt to equity of the corporation;
4. whether there is convertibility into the stock of the corporation; and
5. the relationship between holdings of stock in the corporation and holdings of the interest in question.[31]

The Treasury Department first issued regulations under §385 in the early 1980s which were ultimately withdrawn in 1983.[32] More than three decades passed before Treasury issued final regulations in 2016,[33] which were subsequently modified in the following years.

The 2016 regulations did not add additional detail to the general factors listed in §385. Rather, the final regulations generally provide, somewhat vaguely, that in general the determination of "whether an interest in a corporation is treated for purposes of the Internal Revenue Code as stock or indebtedness . . . is determined based on common law, including the factors prescribed under such common law."[34] The final regulations instead focus

---

29. I.R.C. §385(a). The parenthetical language at the end of the sentence was actually added later. Pub. L. No. 101-239, §7208(a)(1) (1989).

30. Under §385(c), characterization of the instrument by the issuer is binding on the issuer and on all holders, but not binding on the Internal Revenue Service. Provision was made, however, for holders to treat an instrument inconsistently with the issuer's classification upon proper disclosure. I.R.C. §385(c)(2).

31. I.R.C. §385(b).

32. T.D. 7920, 48 Fed. Reg. 50,711 (Nov. 3, 1983).

33. T.D. 9790, 81 Fed. Reg. 72,858 (Oct. 21, 2016), promulgating final and temporary regulations in Treas. Reg. §1.381-1 et seq.

34. Treas. Reg. §1.385-1(b).

on certain transactions where the parties may take advantage of the distinction between debt and equity to generate deductible interest payments to a corporation. Under the "distribution regulations," a debt instrument distributed by a corporation to a related person will be treated as an equity interest in certain circumstances when the recipient has not made an additional investment in the corporation.[35]

It seems unlikely that Treasury will provide additional detailed guidance under §385 on the basic distinction between corporate debt and equity. Where does that leave things? No worse, and perhaps just a tiny bit better than before §385 was enacted. Before §385, courts were using a facts and circumstances analysis in deciding the difference between debt and equity and continue to do so. In the meantime, §385 provides at least a sense of the Congress regarding the types of factors that courts should examine in deciding cases.

Rather than thinking of debt and equity as two distinct categories, one should imagine a continuum with debt at one extreme and equity at the other. Financial instruments appear in many different forms, some with both debt and equity characteristics. These instruments are often referred to as hybrid securities. Taxpayers, tax advisors, the Treasury Department, and courts struggle with these hybrid securities to determine whether they are closer on the continuum to debt and therefore should be classified as debt or whether, instead, they are closer to equity and therefore should be classified as equity for tax purposes.[36]

Overview of Factors Used to Distinguish Debt from Equity

This overview of factors is designed to give you a flavor of the inquiry used to distinguish debt from equity. Keep in mind that the analysis adopts an overall facts and circumstances test and that no one of the following factors will determine the outcome.[37]

---

35. Treas. Reg. §1.385-3. A complete discussion of the distribution regulations is beyond the scope of this book. The 2016 regulations also included documentations requirements for certain debt transactions within an expanded group in Treas. Reg. §1.385-2, but these regulations were withdrawn in 2019. T.D. 9880, 84 Fed. Reg. 59,297 (Nov. 4, 2019).

36. Congress, the Treasury Department, and the courts have also considered the possibility of bifurcating financial instruments so that they may be treated as part debt and part equity. For further discussion of these bifurcation possibilities, see discussion in the sections that follow.

37. Federal circuit courts vary in the precise articulation and weights given to various factors used to distinguish debt from equity. The circuits also are split over classification of the debt-equity issue as a question of fact, law, or mixed fact and law, and over proper standards for appellate review. For a discussion and analysis of these splits, see Nathan R. Christensen, The Case for Reviewing Debt/Equity Determinations for Abuse of Discretion, 74 U. Chi. L. Rev. 1309 (2007).

a) Observing the Formalities of a Debt Instrument

The first factor listed in §385 may be useful in identifying those instruments that come closest to classic or straight debt. Where there is a "written unconditional promise to pay on demand or on a specified date a sum certain in money in return for an adequate consideration in money or money's worth, and to pay a fixed rate of interest," the instrument is likely to be regarded as debt.[38] Such a written obligation has the earmarks of a debt instrument. A key element here is the payment of reasonable interest. An instrument that fails to provide for the payment of interest will virtually never be classified as debt. In addition, to be sure that an instrument will be classified as debt, it is best to have a reasonably close fixed maturity date rather than a demand note or a maturity date long after the issuance of the note.[39]

To be respected as genuine debt, it is also important that certain formalities be observed. The note holder should act like a reasonable creditor, taking reasonable steps to enforce payment. In addition, it should be relatively clear that the corporation will have sufficient cash flow to meet its debt obligation. If the holder of the corporate note agrees to extensions of the maturity date or does not otherwise insist on payments in accordance with the terms of the note, the note may be suspect. Another related factor is the extent to which the note is backed by collateral. An instrument with adequate security is more likely to be respected as debt than one without. Even if the formalities normally associated with debt instruments are strictly observed, the debt may nevertheless be classified as equity if, after consideration of other relevant factors, the instrument more resembles equity than debt. A discussion of some of those factors follows.

b) The Debt-Equity Ratio or Thin Capitalization

When a corporation issues excessive liabilities relative to the capital contributions that it has received, the holders of corporate notes bear significant risk. Such a corporation is regarded as "thinly capitalized." Even though the instrument may bear all of the formalities normally associated with a debt instrument, the holders of this debt are depending largely on the profitability of the enterprise rather than underlying assets to assure payment. This type of risk is more typically associated with an equity investment. At some point, the debt-equity ratio is so large that the instrument should be regarded as an equity investment. For many years, the courts have

---

38. I.R.C. §385(b)(1).
39. At least one court classified shareholder advances to the corporation in the form of a demand note with no specified maturity date as debt, stressing that the note carried a fixed rate of interest and the corporation made regular interest payments. Indmar Prods. Co., Inc. v. Comm'r, 444 F.3d 771, 781 (6th Cir. 2006).

considered the debt-equity ratio as one of the many factors to be considered in distinguishing debt from equity. Congress also listed the debt-equity ratio as one of the five factors that the Treasury was to consider in promulgating regulations.[40] Although there is general agreement that the debt-equity ratio is significant, it is hard to quantify just how excessive the ratio needs to be before serious red flags should be waved. One commentator reports that a ratio of debt to equity that does not exceed 3:1 will generally withstand challenge.[41] Another set of issues involves the proper method for computing a debt-equity ratio. These include debates over whether to use aggregate debt figures as opposed to separate figures for debt to inside shareholder lenders and outside lenders, or separate figures for recourse and nonrecourse debt.

c) Subordination to Other Claims

Another important factor in distinguishing debt from equity is subordination to other claims. Creditor's claims generally take priority over equity holder's claims. Thus, if an instrument specifies that the holder's claims are subordinate to general creditor claims, the instrument is more likely to be classified as equity. A corporation may issue several different classes of debt, some of which are subordinated to other classes of debt. By itself, the subordination to some other creditor claims will not cause the subordinated debt to be reclassified as equity if the subordinated debt continues to be senior to preferred and common shares.

d) Contingency of Payment

In the case of straight or classic debt, the obligation to pay interest is unconditional. On the other hand, a corporation's obligation to pay interest to the holder of a financial instrument may be contingent upon a certain level of corporate profits or may be left to the discretion of the board of directors in some way. The risk associated with a debt instrument subject to such a contingency is more like the risk associated with an equity interest in the corporation. Such contingency is an important factor suggesting that the financial interest is an equity interest.

e) Right to Participate in Profits

One key element that distinguishes an equity holder from a debt holder is the right of the equity holder to participate in the corporation's economic

---

40. I.R.C. §385(b)(3).
41. Boris I. Bittker and James S. Eustice, Federal Income Taxation of Corporations and Shareholders ¶4.05[3] (7th ed. 2015).

growth. When the holder of an obligation is entitled to share in profits of the corporate enterprise above and beyond the interest specified in the note, this factor will weigh heavily in favor of an equity classification.[42]

In addition, when a note or debenture is convertible into stock, the note holder has the potential to ultimately share in the corporation's economic growth by exercising the conversion privilege. Thus, the conversion privilege is another factor weighing in favor of an equity classification.[43]

f) Voting and Other Rights of Control

Voting rights and managerial rights are equity characteristics. Lenders typically are not entitled to vote or otherwise participate in the management of the corporation. The presence of such rights can be a factor that causes a financial instrument to be classified as equity. Some debt instruments carry limited voting or other managerial rights designed to protect the lender. For example, the lender may be entitled to vote only on specific major corporate changes such as a merger or acquisition or only if quarterly earnings fall below a specified amount. Such limited voting rights should not cause the debt to be reclassified as equity.

g) Identity Between Shareholders and Creditors

When the shareholders of a corporation also lend money to the corporation, the notes taken in return should be regarded with special scrutiny. The notes are particularly prone to being reclassified as equity if the shareholders hold these notes in the same proportions that they own stock. Put another way, the debt classification is safer where the identity of debt and equity holders is different and where those who own both debt and equity hold different proportions of each.

h) Acquisition of Essential Assets

Some courts have considered the fact that a note was issued to shareholders in return for essential assets necessary for the corporation's business as an equity factor. The idea here is that corporations do not typically acquire their core assets through debt issued to shareholders. A shareholder who purports to sell such essential assets to a corporation in return for a note will be subject to special scrutiny. This is perhaps the most questionable of the many debt-equity factors discussed. The premise behind this factor appears to be flawed. There is no reason to believe that a corporation would

---

42. It also may be possible to bifurcate the instrument so that the fixed interest received is treated as interest and the additional profit treated as dividend.
43. See I.R.C. §385(b)(4).

not acquire its essential assets with debt. Many corporations borrow from outside lenders in order to acquire the core assets needed to start a business; a loan from a shareholder to acquire such assets should not be viewed differently.

i) Intent of the Parties

Some courts have explored the intent to establish a debtor-creditor relationship in deciding whether to reclassify a note as equity. Intent tests are difficult to apply. Best applied, an intent test should look to the reasonable expectation of the lender that the debt will be repaid, focusing on objective criteria.[44] Many of the criteria that a lender will look to in developing an expectation regarding repayment are the same factors discussed above. The factors begin to circle upon themselves and overlap.

Bifurcation of Hybrid Securities

Many financial instruments include both features of ordinary debt and ordinary equity. Previously, it was necessary to classify such hybrid securities entirely as either debt or equity. Under this "unitary" approach, one must examine all of the instrument's characteristics to determine whether the instrument is more "debt-like" or "equity-like." Amendments to §385 now authorize the Secretary to prescribe regulations to determine "whether an interest in a corporation is to be treated . . . As stock or indebtedness (*or as in part stock and in part indebtedness*)."[45] This bifurcation approach would eliminate the need to pick one characterization or the other in the case of complex hybrid securities. On the other hand, the bifurcation process itself may be complex and controversial as well.[46] The final regulations under §385 issued in 2016 did not include a general bifurcation rule, and merely stated that Treasury and the IRS would "continue to study the issue."[47]

---

44. One case that took this approach to intent was Gilbert v. Commissioner, 248 F.2d 399 (2d Cir. 1957), *appeal after remand*, 262 F.2d 512 (2d Cir.), *cert. denied*, 359 U.S. 1002 (1959).

45. I.R.C. §385(a) (emphasis added). The parenthetical language was added in 1989. Pub. L. No. 101-239, §7208(a)(1), 103 Stat. 2337.

46. An earlier Treasury Department proposal called for bifurcation with respect to certain debt obligations with both fixed and contingent obligations. The Treasury Department later withdrew its proposal to treat the noncontingent portion as debt and the contingent portion "in accordance with economic substance." In other words, the contingent portion would likely have been treated as equity. 59 Fed. Reg. 64,884 (Dec. 16, 1994). The Treasury Department's notice accompanying the withdrawal cited commentators who "argued that there is rarely a unique set of components into which a contingent payment debt instrument can be bifurcated. In addition, commentators questioned whether it is appropriate to bifurcate a contingent debt instrument because it is often unclear how the contingent components should be taxed." *Id. At* 64,885.

47. T.D. 9790, 81 Fed. Reg. 72,858, 72,859 (Oct. 21, 2016),

One example of a bifurcation rule already in place is a special rule applicable to certain high-yield discount obligations. Under §163(e)(5), such obligations are bifurcated for tax purposes into a "debt portion," for which an interest deduction will be permitted to the corporation and a "dividend portion" on which no deductions will be permitted to the corporation. If the recipient shareholder is a corporation, it will be entitled to a dividends-received deduction on the dividend portion.[48]

LOSSES FROM INVESTMENTS IN THE CORPORATE ENTERPRISE

General Losses

Losses suffered by shareholders or creditors generally will be deductible. The key question for investors, however, is whether the loss will be treated as capital or ordinary loss. For most taxpayers, ordinary loss is preferable for several reasons. First, it can be deducted against ordinary income. Second, in limited circumstances the taxpayer may be permitted to carryback the loss to earlier tax years under §172. A capital loss, on the other hand, is more limited. Individual taxpayers' capital losses first can be used to offset capital gains. Excess losses are deductible, but subject to a $3,000 cap for any single taxable year.[49] Individual losses beyond the $3,000 limit may be carried forward, but not backward.[50]

Losses from worthless securities are considered capital losses under §165(g). For purposes of this provision, a security includes not only shares of stock, but also options to acquire stock, and bonds, debentures, notes, certificates or other evidence of indebtedness issued by the corporation with interest coupons or in registered form.[51] Thus, for purposes of §165, if an instrument is classified as stock or equity, the loss when the stock becomes worthless will be a capital loss. Moreover, even if the instrument is classified as debt, if the debt carries interest coupons or is in registered form, the loss will also be capital loss.

On the other hand, if the taxpayer owns a debt instrument that is not registered and that has no interest coupons, a loss when debt becomes worthless will be subject to the rules of §166. A nonbusiness bad debt held by an individual taxpayer is deductible only as a short-term capital loss.

---

48. I.R.C. §163(e)(5)(B).
49. I.R.C. §1211(b).
50. I.R.C. §1212(b).
51. I.R.C. §165(g)(2).

Business bad debts, on the other hand, can be deducted as ordinary losses. To constitute a business bad debt, the loss must be proximately related to the taxpayer's business.[52] This has proven to be a very difficult test for many taxpayers to meet.[53]

Section 1244 Stock Losses

Before the enactment of §1244, investors who suffered a loss from sale or exchange of the stock in a small business were limited to a capital loss. This result seemed particularly inequitable to such investors given the alternative of Subchapter S or partnership provisions under which the investors would have been entitled to pass-throughs of ordinary losses from the business investment. Responding to this concern, Congress created a special class of stock in §1244.[54] When an individual or a partnership suffers certain losses on §1244 stock, the loss can be treated as an ordinary loss.[55] This ordinary loss treatment is only available to the individual or partnership to which the stock was issued. In addition, there is a $50,000 cap for individuals and a $100,000 cap for joint filers on the ordinary loss that can be taken. Any excess loss will be treated as a capital loss. Since the ordinary loss provisions are available only to the person who was issued the shares initially, a transferor who receives §1244 stock from the individual or partnership to which it was originally issued will not be entitled to the special loss treatment provided by §1244. Early versions of §1244 contained many technical requirements creating many traps for the unwary. Over the years, the restrictions and technical requirements have eased substantially, making the present version of §1244 much less complex. Although §1244 ordinary loss treatment originally was available only with respect to common stock, it is now available for losses on preferred stock as well.

To qualify as §1244 stock, the corporation must be a domestic United States corporation. In addition, the corporation must be a small business

---

52. Treas. Reg. §1.166-5(b).

53. See, e.g., Whipple v. Comm'r, 373 U.S. 193 (1963); United States v. Generes, 405 U.S. 93 (1972).

54. In connection with the so-called "bailout" legislation in 2008, Congress enacted a special provision permitting ordinary loss treatment upon the sale of "applicable preferred stock by any applicable financial institution." Emergency Economic Stabilization Act of 2008, tit. III, §301, Pub. L. No. 110-343, 122 Stat. 3765, 3802 (2008). This limited provision applied to the preferred Fannie Mae and Freddie Mac stock that was hit especially hard during the economic crisis. The status of these corporations was unique; they were previously government-owned and, even as private entities, they received numerous tax and regulatory advantages over other private entities.

55. Congress imposes certain limitations on the amount of ordinary loss in cases where the shareholder contributed loss property in the first instance to the corporation in return for the stock. In effect, losses that were built-in through the contribution of loss property are not permitted as §1244 ordinary losses. See I.R.C. §1244(d)(1).

corporation at the time the stock is issued. A corporation will qualify as a small business corporation if, at the time the stock is issued, the aggregate money and property received for stock, contributions to capital, or paid in surplus does not exceed $1 million.[56] In addition, the stock must have been issued in return for money or other property. Finally, during the five-year period prior to sustaining loss, the corporation must have received more than 50% of its receipts from sources other than royalties, rents, dividends, interest, annuities, and sale or exchanges of stock or securities.[57] Put more simply, more than 50% of the income during that five-year period should not be from passive sources. This requirement was designed to limit the ordinary loss provisions to those corporations that are substantially engaged in an active trade or business.

GAINS FROM INVESTMENT IN THE CORPORATE ENTERPRISE

Investors' gains received from the sale or exchange of stock or debt generally are treated as capital gain.[58] The lower capital gains rate is designed, in part, to encourage more corporate investment. Some policymakers have been interested in stimulating investment in smaller, new, higher-risk enterprises. Responding to this concern, Congress added several new provisions applicable to "qualified small business stock," as defined in §1202. "Qualified small business corporations" are distinguished from other C corporations based largely upon aggregate gross assets.[59] Also, the corporation must be engaged in an active trade or business during substantially all of the taxpayer's holding period for the stock.[60] The Taxpayer Relief Act of 1997 added a provision that permits individual investors to defer, or "roll over," gain from the sale of "qualified small business stock" by acquiring other qualified small business stock within 60 days.[61] Ultimately, individual shareholders are entitled to exclude up to 50% of "eligible gain" from a sale or exchange

---

56. For purposes of this provision, the amount taken into account for property is the adjusted basis of the property to the corporation less any liability relating to the property. I.R.C. §1244(c)(3).

57. I.R.C. §1244(c)(1)(C).

58. Among others, there are exceptions for certain recapture items and in the case of collapsible corporations.

59. The aggregate gross assets of a qualified small business cannot exceed $50 million. See I.R.C. §1202(d)(1)(A).

60. I.R.C. §1202(c)(2), (e).

61. Taxpayer Relief Act of 1997, Pub. L. No. 105-34, III Stat. 788, §313 (codified at I.R.C. §1045).

of such stock held for more than five years,[62] or up to 100% of any eligible gain with respect to stock acquired after September 27, 2010.[63] Through this special category of stock, Congress, in effect, provides reduced capital gains rates for investors in §1202 "small business stock" corporations.

CONCLUSION

The corporation makes two basic decisions regarding its capital structure. First, the corporation must decide on the types and classes of stock that will make up the equity structure of the enterprise. Second, the corporation must decide on the appropriate mix of debt and equity. Such decisions ideally should be made independent of tax considerations. The first category of decisions on the equity structure itself come closer to meeting this ideal. Most corporations decide on the equity structure of the enterprise based largely on nontax considerations. Different classes and kinds of stock are issued to reflect the different types of contributions made and the different levels of risk that investors are willing to undertake. On the other hand, decisions regarding the appropriate mix of debt and equity often are heavily influenced by tax considerations.

An in-depth discussion of all of the financial and other nontax considerations that factor into determining corporate capital structure is beyond the scope of this book. The above materials on capital structure are meant only to provide a brief introduction to the alternative capital structures and categories of financial instruments available and some of the tax issues involved.

Examples

1. Since his death, megastar Michael's extended family has been planning to keep his legacy alive through a corporation that would collect royalties, contract licensing arrangements, and develop theme parks and casinos. Based upon a careful market analysis, Michael's brothers, Gerry, Joe, and Tom expect significant profits in the long term. Each contributes to the copyrights and royalty rights to the corporation, with a total basis of $100,000 and a total fair market value of $3 million. They arrange a $1 million ten-year loan from MegaBank to the corporation at a market

---

62. I.R.C. §1202(a). The gain eligible for such preferential treatment is subject to limitations provided in §1202(b).
63. I.R.C. §1202(a)(4). Sept. 27, 2010 is the enactment date of the Creating Small Business Jobs Act of 2010 referenced in the statute. The amount of eligible gain excludible is also limited to $10 million or 10 times the adjusted basis of stock sold during the taxable year. I.R.C. §1202(b).

interest rate. In addition, each of the three brothers plans to lend the corporation $500,000 in cash in exchange for a 20-year promissory note. The note terms required regular interest payments at a rate set one-half point below the prime rate. Would the notes be classified as debt or equity for federal income tax purposes? What different federal income tax consequences would result from a classification as equity versus debt?

2. a. What if the corporation in Example 1 borrows $1.5 million under similar terms from Gerry alone and nothing from Joe and Tom? Would your answer be different if the promissory note was due in 5 rather than 20 years?

   b. What if, after five years, the corporation has made no interest payments as otherwise required by the promissory note terms, and Gerry has not made any efforts to collect the missing interest payments?

   c. What if, instead of promissory notes, the three shareholders received ten-year debentures, which provided that for the first five years interest was to be paid only in the event that the corporation had net profits? What if the debenture holders were subordinated to other creditors?

Explanations

1. Classification of the promissory notes issued to the shareholders as debt or equity will be determined based upon the facts and circumstances. No one factor will be determinative. In calling them promissory notes, the corporation has attached a debt-like label to these financial instruments. Although it may be suggestive of the parties' intent, the label attached to the financial instruments will not determine their classification. The first, and perhaps most important, factor to examine is the form of the notes. The closer the note terms come to observing typical debt obligation formalities, the more likely the notes are to be classified as debt. That these notes have a fixed maturity date, a fixed principal amount, bear interest at a stated rate, and require regular interest payments surely are factors that weigh in favor of debt classification. The real question here is whether the notes establish the type of relationship that one would expect to see between lender and borrower.

   One slight concern here might be that the note—at 20 years—is relatively long term. Equity investors typically make longer-term investments than lenders. Thus, an extremely long-term note appears more like equity than debt. On the other hand, 20-year debentures are not extraordinarily uncommon. This factor alone should not result in equity classification. Another concern might be that the interest rate is set below the prime rate. One would expect the lender in an arm's-length transaction to demand the full interest that the market will bear. Yet, lenders sometimes lend at below market rates. Since the rate here is just slightly below prime, this one factor alone is not likely to result in equity classification.

Another classification consideration is the debt-equity ratio. A significantly undercapitalized corporation that purports to "borrow" from its shareholders may raise suspicion that the purported "loans" are really disguised equity contributions. A related factor is the expected source of repayment on the debt. Courts have been more tolerant of higher debt-equity ratios when it has been clear that the corporation was likely to have sufficient funds for repayment.

Unfortunately, there are no clear rules about how debt-equity ratios should be computed and no magic numerical line that, when crossed, identifies a corporation with too high a ratio. One initial measurement question is whether to look just at the "inside" ratio — the amount of *shareholder* "debt" relative to capital — or an "outside" ratio, which compares *total* outstanding debt to capital.

In this Example, the corporation has total assets valued at $3 million and $2.5 million in total debts, leaving a *net* value of $500,000. Thus, the shareholder debt is $1.5 million relative to total net capital of $500,000, for an inside ratio of 3:1. A comparison of total outstanding debt of $2.5 million to the $500,000 net capital leaves an outside ratio of 5:1. Although they were withdrawn, initial debt-equity regulations suggested that an inside ratio of 3:1 and an outside ratio of 10:1 would not be considered excessive. Courts in several cases have been far more generous. The ratios in this Example are within a reasonably comfortable range, and the brothers' market analysis indicates that the corporation should have sufficient profits to repay the loans. Both these factors should weigh in favor of debt classification.

One factor weighing *against* debt classification is that each brother holds one-third of the total stock and one-third of the total shareholder debt. Such proportional contributions of the equity and purported loans raise suspicion that the debt is really equity in disguise. This factor is unlikely, I think, to outweigh the other factors weighing in favor of a debt classification. Although one can never be certain, the promissory notes in this Example are likely to be respected as genuine debt.

From the corporation's perspective, such debt classification is quite significant. Regular payments on genuine promissory notes are generally deductible as interest expense under §163, subject to §163(j) and the other possible limitations noted earlier in this chapter. In contrast, if the notes were classified as equity, corporate payments on the purported note would be viewed as nondeductible shareholder distributions.

The classification stakes are not quite as high, perhaps, from the shareholders' perspective. In either case, the shareholders are likely to have taxable income because interest payments are included in gross income pursuant to §61(a)(4) and dividends are similarly included under §61(a)(7). Nevertheless, there are significant differences. If the notes were classified as equity, the so-called "interest payments" to the shareholders would be treated as corporate distributions governed by §301. Unlike interest payments on debt instruments, which are *always* taxable, §301 distributions will not be fully taxable to the shareholders unless they are considered "dividends," a term of art defined in §316. Treatment of the distributions as dividends would depend on the extent to which they were paid out of earnings and profits.[64] If the distributions were considered dividends, they would be eligible for preferential capital gains rates as provided in §1(h)(11).[65] A second tax difference for the shareholders if the note is classified as debt is that if the corporation fails to make payments and the shareholders otherwise meet the statutory requirements, they may be entitled to §166 bad debt deductions.

2. a. The classification factor that has changed in the event that the corporation borrows $1.5 million from Gerry alone is proportionality. Under these changed facts, Gerry holds all of the purported debt and only one-third of the equity. Removing proportionality as a factor would make the debt classification case even stronger. Likewise, changing the promissory note from a 20-year to a 5-year note would strengthen the argument for debt classification because debt-type instruments generally tend to be shorter term than equity instruments.

   b. A new concern about possible reclassification of the promissory notes as equity arises if the corporation fails to make interest payments and Gerry fails to enforce the corporation's binding obligation to make those payments. Debt holders typically expect and insist upon timely payments of interest and principal in accordance with the lending instrument. On the other hand, an informed equity holder understands both the potential for profit and the risk of loss. A note holder who permits years to pass without payments begins to resemble an investor with more of an equity stake in the enterprise. This is not to say with certainty here that the notes would be reclassified as equity. This change in facts, however, would put a substantial weight on the scale in the equity direction.

   c. As discussed above, a shorter time period is one factor that would weigh in favor of debt classification. That these are 10-year debentures makes this a stronger case for debt than the 20-year notes in Example 1. Far greater weight, however, will be placed on the provision requiring interest payments over the first five years only in the event that the corporation has net profits. Lenders expect to be repaid

---

64. See Chapter 5 for a full discussion of nonliquidating corporate distributions.
65. See discussion in Chapter 1.

whether the borrower is profitable or not, and they typically demand security to ensure such repayment. When the brothers agree to forgo financial return for five years in the event that the corporation has no net profits, they are engaged much more in equity investor than true lender-type behavior. This factor would weigh extremely heavily toward equity classification. The brothers surely would emphasize that this restriction applied only for the first five years. As noted above, the debt versus equity determination is entirely based on a court's analysis of the facts and circumstances. If the brothers can provide an explanation for the five-year restriction that is consistent with viewing the debentures as genuine debt and additional evidence in favor of debt classification, they might counteract the heavy equity weight that undoubtedly would be placed on the profits feature of these debentures. A subordination clause similarly would weigh heavily in the direction of an equity classification.

Corporate
Formation

PART

II

Incorporation and Other Contributions to Capital

4

INTRODUCTION

The corporate enterprise typically receives funds in one of three ways. First, the corporation raises capital through equity contributions.[1] Second, the corporation may borrow funds. Third, the corporation receives operating funds through the sale of its goods or services and through returns on its investments. This chapter will consider primarily the first of these forms of fundraising—equity contributions from shareholders. At the time of formation, the initial shareholders of the corporation make equity contributions in return for stock. Keep in mind, however, that the principles considered in this chapter are not limited to the initial incorporation transaction. The provisions considered in this chapter cover subsequent capital contributions as well.[2]

In the typical incorporation transaction, the incorporating shareholders transfer cash, other property, or services to the corporation in return for stock.[3] Cash contributions in return for stock do not raise tax consequences

---

1. Although equity contributions usually come from shareholders, non-shareholders may occasionally make capital contributions as well.
2. Some of the peculiar issues raised by capital contributions made *after* the initial formation of the corporation are considered later in this chapter. In addition, §351 often will have a role to play in connection with various corporate reorganizations. The relationship between §351 and the reorganization provisions is discussed in detail in Chapters 11 and 12.
3. The transferring shareholders may be individuals or corporations. The newly formed corporation may be a new business or a continuation of an existing business previously operated in sole proprietorship, partnership, or other noncorporate form.

of great significance to the contributing shareholders. There is no unrealized gain or loss to be recognized by the shareholders in the case of a cash purchase at fair market value.[4] A shareholder who purchases stock for cash simply holds the stock with a cost basis. More significant tax issues arise when shareholders contribute appreciated or depreciated property in return for stock. When a shareholder contributes property in exchange for stock, two assets are created out of one—the original asset and the corporate stock now reflecting an indirect ownership of the same asset. The value of the contributed property, now held by the corporation, is also reflected in the newly issued stock held by the shareholder. Subchapter C addresses not only the questions of gain or loss to the respective parties, but also the appropriate basis of the contributed property in the corporation's hands and of the stock in the shareholder's hands. Absent special nonrecognition rules, gain or loss realized from the exchange would be recognized to the shareholder and to the corporation.[5] As we shall see, however, a properly structured shareholder contribution to capital will be treated as a nonrecognition event to the contributing shareholders under §351 and to the corporation under §1032. The shareholder nonrecognition provided by §351 will not necessarily be permanent, however. Corollary basis rules defer shareholder gains or losses not recognized at the time of the §351 exchange for potential taxation upon later sale or exchange of stock received in the exchange.

SHAREHOLDER NONRECOGNITION: §351 ELIGIBILITY REQUIREMENTS AND UNDERLYING POLICY

Overview

Shareholders in an incorporation transaction will not recognize any gain or loss on the exchange if they satisfy the three major requirements of §351(a). First, there must be a contribution of property. Second, the contribution must be solely in exchange for stock and, third, the contributors must control the corporation immediately after the exchange. This overview will

---

4. Different issues emerge if the shareholder purchases stock from the corporation at less than fair market value. If a shareholder is permitted to purchase stock at a discount, it will be important to know the underlying circumstances. For example, if the discount was offered in exchange for services rendered and was not offered as part of a qualified stock purchase or stock option plan, the discount will be taxable as compensation under the provisions of §§61 and 83.

5. I.R.C. §§61(a)(3), 1001(c). Treas. Reg. §1.1002-1(c) (listing §351 as an exception to the recognition requirement of §1001(c)). Some might argue that the corporation does not even realize a gain upon receipt of a contribution to capital. This argument is considered later in the section of this chapter on tax consequences to the corporation.

summarize each of these three elements and the tax policy considerations behind them. A more detailed discussion of each requirement follows in subsequent sections.

The first requirement for nonrecognition treatment is that the shareholders transfer *property*. Congress does not provide a comprehensive definition for purposes of applying these provisions, but merely identifies items that will *not* be considered property.[6] The Internal Revenue Service and the courts construe the term "property" broadly to include cash and real or intangible property.[7] Most important among the exceptions to the broad scope of the property definition is the contribution of services.[8] Individuals establishing a corporation often contribute past or future services in return for stock. Such service contributions are not considered contributions of property and will *not* qualify for nonrecognition treatment. The rationale for excluding service contributions is that payment for services, regardless of the form of payment, is compensation and should be taxed to the recipient shareholder as ordinary income. Horizontal equity — the principle that similarly situated taxpayers should face similar tax consequences — would be violated if those receiving cash compensation for services to the corporation were taxed, but those receiving stock compensation were not.

The second requirement to qualify for shareholder nonrecognition treatment is that property be contributed *solely in exchange for stock*.[9] By taking only stock in return for property, the shareholders continue their relationship with the contributed assets. This "continuity of interest" requirement is really the heart of §351.[10] The clearest example of this continuity of interest is the sole proprietor who incorporates an ongoing business by contributing all of the business assets to a newly formed corporation in return for 100% of the corporation's stock. Immediately before incorporating, the sole proprietor held a direct interest in the assets used in the business enterprise. Immediately after incorporation, the shareholder holds 100% of the stock of a new corporation and, thus, holds a continued, albeit now indirect, interest in the business assets. The assets contributed presumably are no different than they were before and business customers probably will not even notice a difference in operations.

---

6. I.R.C. §351(d).

7. The shareholder who contributes only cash does not have any realized gain or loss, but nevertheless has contributed property. Shares received for cash will count toward meeting the §351 control tests discussed below. See, e.g., Holstein v. Comm'r, 23 T.C. 923, 924 (1955).

8. I.R.C. §351(d)(1); Treas. Reg. §1.351-1(a)(1)(i).

9. I.R.C. §351(a). Certain types of preferred stock will not qualify for purposes of §351. This "nonqualified preferred stock" exception is considered later in this chapter.

10. Continuity of interest also is the heart of similar nonrecognition rules applicable to reorganization transactions. See Treas. Reg. §1.368-1(b). For complete coverage of reorganizations, see Chapters 11-14.

At first blush, the "solely in exchange for stock" language suggests that shareholders will not be eligible for nonrecognition treatment unless they receive *only* stock in return for contributed property. As is often the case with the Internal Revenue Code, the bark of the "solely in exchange for stock" language is louder than its bite. In fact, shareholders *may* receive something in addition to stock from the corporation in the incorporation exchange. Such additional property often is referred to as "boot."[11] Receipt of boot from the corporation will not completely disqualify the shareholder from nonrecognition treatment, but the shareholder receiving boot in an incorporation transaction will be taxed on realized gain to the extent of the boot.[12]

The third requirement for nonrecognition treatment is that the person or persons contributing property be in *control* of the corporation immediately after the exchange.[13] Control is arguably also an important element in considering "continuity of interest." It is not sufficient that contributors simply receive stock in the incorporation exchange. To qualify for tax-free treatment, they must receive *enough* stock to reflect a substantial continuity of their investment in the business assets. The control test provided in §368(c) includes two parts. To satisfy the control test, the contributing shareholder group must own (1) "stock possessing at least 80% of the *total combined voting power* of all classes of stock entitled to vote," and (2) "at least 80% of the *total number of shares* of all other classes of stock."[14] As a shorthand, this book will sometimes refer to both parts of the test together as the "80% control test" or simply the "control test."

Exceptions to Nonrecognition Rules

Even if an exchange meets the above three requirements under §351, nonrecognition treatment is not available in the case of a transfer of property to an investment company.[15] According to Treasury regulations, a transfer is made to an investment company when the transfer results in the diversification of the transferor's assets *and* the transferee company is "a regulated investment company, a real estate investment trust, or a corporation more than 80% of the value of whose assets . . . Are held for investment and are

---

11. To help with this concept, think of the shareholder as receiving stock and other property to boot.

12. I.R.C. §351(b)(1).

13. I.R.C. §§351(a), 368(c).

14. I.R.C. §368(c) (emphasis added). For purposes of meeting the total number of shares part of the control test, the Service takes the position that 80% of the total number of shares of *each class* of non-voting stock is required. Rev. Rul. 59-259, 1959-2 C.B. 115. This same control test is used for purposes of the tax-free reorganization provisions considered in Chapters 11-14.

15. I.R.C. §351(e)(1).

readily marketable stocks or securities, or interests in regulated investment companies or real estate investment trusts."[16] In such cases, Congress was concerned that, absent a special §351 exception, it would be too easy for a shareholder to diversify investments without recognition of taxable gain by contributing appreciated property in exchange for stock in a highly diversified investment corporation. Congress has expanded the definition of investment corporation, adding to the types of assets considered in applying the regulatory 80% test. A corporation will be considered an investment corporation if more than 80% of the value of its assets includes stock, securities, other equity interests in a corporation, debt, options, futures contracts, foreign currencies, and other specifically listed items.[17]

Another transaction not covered by §351 is a transfer of property by a debtor in a Title 11 bankruptcy case where the stock received in the exchange is used to satisfy indebtedness of the debtor.[18] Nevertheless, such a bankruptcy transaction can be structured to obtain nonrecognition under the reorganization provisions in §368(a)(1)(G).[19]

Why Permit Nonrecognition for Incorporation Transactions?

Now that we have briefly considered the three major requirements for nonrecognition treatment, let's take a step back to consider the policy behind §351. Why does Congress permit shareholders to defer recognition of gain or loss from transfers of property to a controlled corporation? For one thing, corporations need capital to function. To tax either the shareholder or the corporation on transactions through which corporations raise capital might serve as an impediment to incorporation or capital formation. Thus, the simplest explanation for the §351 nonrecognition rule is that Congress wished to encourage, or at least not to discourage, corporate formations. More generally, the legislative history reflects an interest in "facilitating business adjustments."[20]

A second justification often given for §351 is that the transaction reflects a mere change in form.[21] A contributing shareholder group that

---

16. Treas. Reg. §1.351-1(c)(1).
17. I.R.C. §351(e)(1).
18. I.R.C. §351(e)(2).
19. See Chapter 11.
20. The legislative history of one of the early predecessors to §351 suggests that nonrecognition was provided, in part, to "permit business to go forward with readjustments required by existing conditions." S. Rep. No. 275, 67th Cong., 1st Sess. 11-12 (1921); S. Rep. No. 398, 68th Cong., 1st Sess. 17-18 (1924).
21. "The underlying assumption [of §351] is that the new property is substantially a continuation of the old investment still unliquidated." Treas. Reg. §1.1002-1(c).

satisfies the "continuity of interest" requirement established through the "solely in exchange for stock" element, and also meets the 80% control test, arguably is merely changing the form of the business investment. The shareholders have a continued interest in their old assets now reflected in stock and they continue to exercise control over those assets through their controlling interest in the corporation.

Despite its mere change-in-form rationale, the scope of §351 is quite broad, extending nonrecognition to several transactions that arguably reflect more than a simple change in form. For example, §351 does not limit the number of transferors. Hundreds, thousands, or even millions of transferors may exchange property in return for stock. This often is the case in underwriting transactions where the public is considered to be part of the transferring control group. As another example, imagine a sole proprietor who, along with hundreds of similar investors, exchanges an interest in a small convenience store for stock in a large corporation operating a nationwide chain of convenience stores. A sole proprietor who transfers property in return for a minority interest in a large corporation effectively loses direct control over assets contributed. Nevertheless, this minority shareholder will receive nonrecognition treatment as part of the control group in a §351 transaction.

Given the breadth of transactions to which §351 nonrecognition applies, one challenge is to explain the policy behind limiting nonrecognition to transferors who receive an 80% controlling interest in the corporation.[22] And, even if the control requirement can be justified, why does Congress use 80% control rather than 50% or some other measure of control?[23] There is little legislative history explaining the rationale for requiring control. One limited explanation for the control test is that it prevents "corporations with readily marketable stock from using their stock to buy goods and supplies on a tax-free basis to their vendors."[24] Without the 80% control requirement, a vendor could accept a small percentage of another corporation's stock as payment for goods and services. The vendor could effectively sell property without recognizing any gain or loss. Perhaps the best explanation one can offer for the control requirement, however, is that it does appear to strengthen the continuity of interest element and the chance that the exchange represents a mere change in form.

---

22. It should be noted, for example, that parallel nonrecognition is provided in Subchapter K for transfers to a partnership in return for a partnership interest. These provisions do not require receipt of a controlling partnership interest. I.R.C. §721.

23. Since many significant corporate events such as acquisition or liquidation require a supermajority vote of the shareholders, 80% control is sometimes referred to as organic control whereas 50% control is referred to as managerial control.

24. Ronald Jensen, Of Form and Substance: Tax-Free Incorporations and Other Transactions Under Section 351, 11 Va. Tax Rev. 349, 398 (1991).

A Closer Look at the §351 Requirements

a) The Transfer Requirement

As its first requirement, §351 permits nonrecognition of gain or loss only "if property is transferred to a corporation." Two terms are important here. Notice that §351 refers to *transfers* of property. The transfer requirement generally will not be problematic. Most §351 contributions represent complete conveyances of property. Questions may arise, however, in the case of transfers falling short of complete conveyance. The courts have tended to interpret the transfer of property requirement broadly, holding, for example, that a contribution of a lease qualifies for nonrecognition treatment.[25] For purposes of §351, the term transfer does not carry the same meaning as "sale or exchange." For example, the Court of Claims held that contribution of a nonexclusive license to use certain patents qualified as a "§351 transfer" even though the license transfer would not have been considered a "sale or exchange" under §1001.[26]

b) The Property Requirement

i) Broad Notion of Property

To qualify for §351 nonrecognition, the transferors must contribute *property*. As noted earlier, the term property is rather broadly construed for purposes of §351.[27] Thus, property includes cash and other assets, including a transferor corporation's own stock[28] or a corporate or individual transferor's note. In addition, in the case of an existing corporation, the holder of a corporation's debt may exchange the debt obligation in return for stock.

---

25. R&J Furniture Co. v. Comm'r, 20 T.C. 857 (1953), *acq.* 1954-1 C.B. 6, *rev'd on other grounds*, 221 F.2d 795 (6th Cir. 1955); see also Rev. Rul. 55-540, 1955-2 C.B. 39, 43.

26. E.I. DuPont de Nemours & Co. v. United States, 471 F.2d 1211 (Ct. Cl. 1973).

27. Note that the definition of property in §317(a), which excludes stock in the corporation making the distribution, applies only to Part I of Subchapter C (Distributions by Corporations) and, thus, is not applicable to §351.

28. Rev. Rul. 74-503, 1974-2 C.B. 117. This 1974 ruling, subsequently revoked, involved a parent corporation's §351 contribution of its own stock in exchange for stock in a newly formed subsidiary. The ruling does not question the §351 nonrecognition exchange itself, but instead addresses the question of the subsidiary's basis in the parent corporation's stock and the parent corporation's basis in the subsidiary's stock received in the exchange. The controversial ruling relied on §362 to answer both basis questions, concluding that both the parent and subsidiary stock had a zero basis. In revoking the 1974 ruling, the Treasury Department announced that its reliance on §362 to determine the parent's stock basis was incorrect and that other conclusions in the ruling were under study. Rev. Rul. 2006-2, 2006-1 C.B. 261. These basis issues are discussed further later in this chapter. Although it has formally revoked its 1974 ruling, the Treasury Department is unlikely, we think, to alter its basic underlying premise that a corporation's own stock constitutes "property" for purposes of §351.

The debt will be considered property as long as it is evidenced by a security. Thus, a bond or debenture holder who exchanges the debt interest for equity (stock) will not recognize any gain or loss on the exchange attributable to the *principal* amount of the debt. Gain or loss will be recognized with regard to *interest* accrued while the transferor held the debt.[29] Debts of the transferee corporation that are *not* evidenced by a security are explicitly excluded from the definition of property under §351.[30] Since open-account indebtedness is not considered "property" for purposes of §351, a transferor of such indebtedness for stock will recognize gain or loss — generally loss in the form of a bad-debt deduction.

ii) Contribution of Services

The most significant exception to the breadth of the §351 transfer of property requirement is the exception for services. A transfer of either past or future *services* is not considered a transfer of property.[31] A transferor who contributes only services will not qualify for nonrecognition treatment and the entire value of stock received for such services will be taxable as ordinary compensation income. If the shareholder contributes both property *and* services, nonrecognition will apply only to the extent that stock was received in return for property. The amount eligible for nonrecognition and the amount subject to tax will be determined based upon the relative fair market value of the property and the services contributed. To illustrate, suppose that a shareholder contributed property worth $90,000 and services worth $10,000 in return for $100,000 worth of stock. In this case, $90,000 worth of stock has been received in return for property. Gain or loss on the property exchange will not be taxed. The remaining $10,000 worth of stock has been received for services, resulting in $10,000 of ordinary compensation income to the contributing shareholder.[32]

A combination of the service contribution restriction and the control test may generate further problems. Because services are not considered property for purposes of §351, a transferor who has contributed only services does not count as part of the control group. Consequently, if one shareholder contributes services in return for 21% of the stock and another

---

29. I.R.C. §351(d)(3) explicitly excludes from the definition of property, "interest on indebtedness of the transferee corporation which accrued on or after the beginning of the transferor's holding period for the debt." Similarly, if the bond was a market discount bond, the accrued market discount must be recognized upon an exchange of the bond for stock. I.R.C. §§1276(a), (c), (d)(1)(C).

30. I.R.C. §351(d)(2).

31. I.R.C. §351(d). The regulations clarify that stock "issued for services rendered or to be rendered to or for the benefit of the issuing corporation will not be treated as having been issued in return for property." Treas. Reg. §1.351-1(a)(1)(i).

32. For a similar example with similar results, see Treas. Reg. §1.351-1(a)(2), ex. 3.

contributes property in return for 79% of the stock, nonrecognition treatment is unavailable to *both* the service *and* the property contributor. The service contributing shareholder has taxable compensation income. Moreover, the property contributing shareholder fails the control test and is ineligible for nonrecognition treatment.[33] The lesson here is that in order to assure nonrecognition treatment for the property contributing shareholders, the "service only" shareholder should never receive more than 20% of the stock.

Another concern under §351(d) is determining whether certain "service-flavored" property is "property" or "service" for purposes of the §351 rules. The case of United States v. Frazell[34] provides a good illustration. The taxpayer in *Frazell* performed geological services for an oil and gas partnership in return for a contingent interest in the assets of the partnership. The court held that the taxpayer's contribution of this contingent partnership interest to a corporation in return for stock was not a contribution of "property" for purposes of §351.[35] Despite the taxpayer's loss in *Frazell*, the courts have been reasonably liberal in holding that various contributions of "service-flavored" property were eligible for nonrecognition treatment.[36]

Contributions of intellectual property would appear to be particularly vulnerable to attack under the §351(d) service restriction. As one court observed, "[t]he difficulty in determining whether payments to a creator of an invention or valuable commercial process are compensation for services or payments for the sale of a patent or other capital assets stems from the fact that an invention is merely the fruit of the inventor's labor, and that payment for the invention itself necessarily compensates the inventor for his services in creating the invention."[37] Despite this difficulty, the courts generally have held that stock issued in return for patents, copyrights, trademarks, and trade secrets is stock issued for property rather than for services.

---

33. If the service shareholder also contributed some property, then *all* of his shares could be counted toward meeting the control test unless the property contribution was of nominal value and made primarily for the purposes of qualifying the property contributor for nonrecognition treatment. See Treas. Reg. §1.351-1(a)(1)(ii). See also Treas. Reg. §1.351-1(a)(2), ex. 3.

34. 335 F.2d 487 (5th Cir. 1964), *cert. denied*, 380 U.S. 961 (1965).

35. There was some dispute in *Frazell* as to whether the taxpayer's partnership interest had vested prior to his making the corporate contribution. The court found that either the taxpayer had already received a vested partnership interest in return for services ineligible for nonrecognition under I.R.C. §721 or received stock in return for services ineligible for nonrecognition under I.R.C. §351. The §721 rules for contributions to a partnership parallel the §351 rules for contributions to a corporation. In either case, the court held that the taxpayer made a *service* contribution in return for compensation, as opposed to a *property* contribution in return for a partnership interest or for stock. 335 F.2d at 490.

36. See, e.g., United States v. Stafford, 727 F.2d 1043 (11th Cir. 1984) (letter of intent held to be "property" for purposes of §721); E.I. DuPont de Nemours & Co. v. United States, 471 F.2d 1211 (Ct. Cl. 1973) (nonexclusive license on patent held to be "property" for purposes of §351).

37. Ofria v. Comm'r, 77 T.C. 524, 535 (1981), *nonacq.* 1983-2 C.B. 1.

Moreover, even the Service agrees that where a "transferor agrees to perform services in connection with a transfer of property, tax-free treatment will be accorded if the services are *merely ancillary and subsidiary to* the property transfer."[38] Thus, receipt of stock in return for property and ancillary know-how will receive nonrecognition treatment under §351.[39]

iii) Ordinary Assets and Assignment of Income

When a business previously operated in sole proprietorship, partnership, or other noncorporate form later incorporates, a transferor may contribute the accounts receivable from prior business operations, which would be ordinary property in the hands of the transferor.[40] A transferor may also contribute other ordinary assets.[41] In exchange, the transferor receives corporate stock, which is generally a capital asset. The transferor could benefit in this way by assigning the receivables income to another taxpayer (the corporation) and by effectively converting ordinary property into a more favorably taxed capital asset. The courts and the IRS have held that §351's general nonrecognition principle generally trumps assignment of income concerns, absent evidence of improper tax avoidance.[42] Historically, the taxpayer also incurred a significant cost in this transaction: subjecting the contributed property to the corporate double tax. In an environment with a lower corporate tax rate, a taxpayer may achieve a greater benefit by contributing ordinary property or assigning ordinary income to a corporation.

c) The Solely in Exchange for Stock Requirement

To qualify for §351(a) nonrecognition, shareholders contributing property must receive *stock* in return. Anything other than stock will be considered "boot" and will be covered by special rules in §351(b). In addition, under special rules in §351(g), certain limited kinds of preferred stock will also be treated as boot.[43] Although determining whether or not the shareholders have received "stock" is not usually difficult, a few issues have emerged under the §351 exchange for stock requirement. Treasury Department regulations take the position that "for the purpose of §351, stock rights or

---

38. Rev. Rul. 64-56, 1964-1 C.B. 133, 134 (emphasis added).
39. For an excellent overall discussion of §351 "transfer of property" concerns in intellectual property cases, see J. Clifton Fleming, Jr., Domestic Section 351 Transfers of Intellectual Property: The Law as It Is vs. The Law as the Commissioner Would Prefer It to Be, 16 J. Corp. Tax 99 (1989).
40. I.R.C. §1221(a)(4).
41. I.R.C. §1221(a)(1)-(8)
42. See Hempt Bros., Inc. v. United States, 490 F.2d 1172 (3d Cir. 1974), *cert. denied*, 419 U.S. 826 (1974); Rev. Rul. 80-198, 1980-2 C.B. 113.
43. I.R.C. §351(g) is considered more fully below.

stock warrants are not included in the term 'stock.'"[44] On the other hand, the Tax Court has held that a contract right to receive additional shares of stock upon the corporation's achieving a specified net earnings goal was "stock" under §351.[45]

Although §351 once permitted nonrecognition where property was exchanged for "stock" or "securities," securities are now considered boot. In some limited circumstances, however, a long-term corporate security or debt may have so many equity characteristics that it will be reclassified as an equity interest for tax purposes.[46] Receipt of a debt instrument that has been reclassified as stock should be considered receipt of stock under §351 and the transferors receiving such an instrument should be eligible for nonrecognition.

d) Control Immediately After the Exchange Test

i) Who Can Be Considered a Member of the Control Group?

Under §351(a), the "person or persons" transferring property in return for stock must control the corporation immediately after the exchange. Members of the control group may include individuals, trusts, estates, partnerships, associations, companies, or corporations.[47] Several transferors may be involved, and because it is often impractical or impossible for all of them to simultaneously transfer property in return for stock, the regulations permit some flexibility. According to the regulations, a simultaneous exchange by all parties is not required, but the rights of the parties must have been previously defined and "the execution of the agreement [must] proceed with an expedition consistent with orderly procedure."[48] In other words, if the transactions

---

44. Treas. Reg. §1.351-1(a)(1). The Treasury Department has issued regulations defining the circumstances under which stock rights or warrants will be considered securities for purposes of the *reorganization* nonrecognition provisions. Treas. Reg. §1.354-1(e). This "warrant rule" is discussed in Chapters 11-13.

45. Hamrick v. Comm'r, 43 T.C. 21 (1964) acq. 1966-2 C.B. 5, *vacated and remanded* per parties' agreement, 17 A.F.T.R. 2d 357 (4th Cir. 1965). See also Carlberg v. United States, 281 F.2d 507 (8th Cir. 1960), where the court held that "stock" included "certificates of contingent interest" for purposes of §354. These certificates entitled the holders to reserved shares of stock to be released pending the settlement of substantial corporate liabilities. The Service takes the position that ordinary stock rights and warrants are distinguishable from the unusual contractual rights in *Hamrick* and *Carlberg*. Rev. Rul. 66-112, 1966-1 C.B. 68. For a critical view of the Service's position, see Boris I. Bittker & James S. Eustice, Federal Income Taxation of Corporations and Shareholders, ¶3.03[2] (7th ed. 2015).

46. See, e.g., Burr Oaks Corp. v. Comm'r, 43 T.C. 635 (1965), aff'd, 365 F.2d 24 (7th Cir. 1966), *cert. denied*, 385 U.S. 1007 (1967), where the court held that a promissory note issued by the corporation should be treated as preferred stock. As a result, the exchange was recast as a §351 contribution rather than a sale. A discussion of the distinction between §351 contributions and sales to the corporation follows later in this chapter. For a general discussion of the debt-equity distinction, see Chapter 3.

47. Treas. Reg. §1.351-1(a)(1).

48. Id.

can be viewed as part of an integrated plan of incorporation, contributing shareholders under the plan will be considered part of the "control group" even if all of the exchanges did not take place simultaneously.

Prior to regulatory changes, the Treasury Department took the position that the control test should be applied differently for two distinct types of underwriting agreements. In a *best efforts* underwriting contract the underwriter agrees to exercise his or her best efforts to sell a specified amount of stock to the public. The underwriter does not purchase stock directly and incurs no risk, other than loss of rights to stock and other commissions, upon failure to sell the specified number of shares. Since the underwriter serves merely as agent selling stock on behalf of the corporation, the underwriter in a best efforts contract is not part of the §351 transferor group and stock received by the underwriter is not be counted toward meeting the 80% control test. On the other hand, the purchasing public is considered part of the control group, and the shares acquired by the public in the public offering are counted toward the 80% control test.

In contrast, the underwriter in a firm commitment contract actually purchases stock from the corporation and undertakes to sell the shares to the general public. The underwriter in a firm commitment contract must retain the shares if efforts to sell them are unsuccessful. Since the firm commitment underwriter actually transfers its own property and assumes the risk of reselling the stock, the Treasury Department originally took the position that the underwriter, and not the public, should be counted as a member of the control group.[49] The Treasury Department now recognizes that the successful firm commitment underwriter's stock ownership is merely transitory. Thus, current regulations take the position that the same control measuring principles should apply whether the underwriting agreement is a best efforts contract or firm commitment contract in which the underwriter's stock ownership is transitory. In both cases, "if a person acquires stock of a corporation from an underwriter in exchange for cash . . ., the person who acquires stock from the underwriter is treated as transferring cash directly to the corporation in exchange for stock of the corporation and the underwriter is disregarded."[50] In other words, the purchasing public is considered part of the control group for both types of underwriting and the underwriter is not.

ii) Control "Immediately After the Exchange": Is Momentary Control Sufficient?

Another significant issue in interpreting the "immediately after the exchange" requirement is the length of time that the control group must

---

49. Rev. Rul. 78-294, 1978-2 C.B. 141 (Situation 2) (rendered obsolete by Treas. Reg. §1.351-1(a)(3)).
50. Treas. Reg. §1.351-1(a)(3)(i).

retain control. What if the transferor group has momentary control of the corporation, but then falls below the required 80% control as a result of stock transfers to others who were not part of the control group? Early case law suggested that where the transferor group had a binding agreement at the time of incorporation to transfer shares to members not in the control group, those shares would not be counted toward meeting the control test.[51]

The major case on point was American Bantam Car Co. v. Commissioner,[52] in which the incorporators entered into a best efforts contract with an underwriter. Immediately after transferring property to the corporation in return for common stock, the incorporators met the 80% control test. Some of the incorporators' stock was placed in an escrow account from which the underwriter was to receive common shares upon successfully marketing preferred shares to the general public. More than a year later, the underwriter had satisfied the best efforts contract requirements and received stock from the escrow account. Transfer of the stock from this account caused the incorporators' control to fall below the required 80%. The Court held that the incorporators had obtained the necessary 80% control immediately after the exchange and that the transaction was covered by the nonrecognition rules of §351.[53]

Despite its off-hand remark that the "statutory words 'immediately after the exchange' require control for no longer period; in fact, momentary control is sufficient,"[54] the Court recognized that in some cases apparent momentary control would not be sufficient. If the series of steps involved in the incorporation were part of an integrated plan, the "exchange" would not be viewed as complete until the necessary steps in the plan had been completed and the control test should be applied after completion of steps in the integrated plan. Applying a "mutual interdependence" test to the facts in *American Bantam*, the Court concluded that the underwriting arrangement was not a "sine qua non in the general plan, without which no other step would have been taken."[55] The underwriter's right to the escrowed shares was contingent and ownership of the shares remained with the incorporators until the underwriter satisfied the best efforts contract conditions.

Based upon cases such as *Intermountain Lumber* and *American Bantam*, it would seem that a post-incorporation sale of stock by the transferor group

---

51. See, e.g., Intermountain Lumber Co. v. Comm'r, 65 T.C. 1025 (1976).
52. 11 T.C. 397 (1948), *aff'd per curiam*, 177 F.2d 513 (3d Cir. 1949), *cert. denied*, 339 U.S. 920 (1950).
53. Interestingly enough, the taxpayer in *American Bantam* was the *corporation*, not the incorporators. In a §351 transaction, the corporation takes a substituted basis from the incorporating shareholders. To avoid this result and instead receive a cost basis, American Bantam took the position that the incorporators did *not* meet the 80% control test and that the transaction was not covered by §351.
54. 11 T.C. At 404.
55. Id. At 406.

pursuant to a binding contract could cause an incorporation exchange to fail §351 control requirements. All of this analysis has been called into question, however, as a result of the Treasury Department's significant change in position with regard to parallel nonrecognition rules applicable to reorganization transactions. Continuity of interest regulations applicable to *tax-free reorganizations* now provide that post-reorganization stock transfers, even if pursuant to a binding contract, will not cause a reorganization to violate continuity-of-interest principles as long as the transfers are made to unrelated parties.[56] Although these regulations do not technically apply to §351 transactions, they could have implications for the tax treatment of post-incorporation transfers of stock by members of the §351 control group.[57] In assessing this impact, it is important to understand the parallels between §351 and the similar nonrecognition rule in §354 for shareholders who exchange stock in one corporation for stock in another corporation as part of a reorganization transaction.[58]

The Treasury Department avoided a strict application of the post-incorporation control requirement under the facts in Revenue Ruling 2003-51,[59] involving two unrelated corporations wishing to consolidate certain business activities. The transferor in that ruling (W) first transferred the assets desired for purposes of a consolidation to a newly formed corporation (Newco) in exchange for all of Newco's stock. The other corporate party to the transaction (X) held the assets desired for consolidation in a wholly owned subsidiary (Y). After W's initial incorporation of Newco and pursuant to a prearranged binding commitment, W immediately joined X in a transaction in which W contributed all of its recently acquired Newco stock and X contributed needed cash to Y solely in exchange for Y stock. Immediately after the second transaction, W held 40% and X held 60% of the Y stock. The consolidation was complete: Y corporation continued to hold its own assets desired in the consolidation along with all of the stock in Newco, which in turn held the desired assets contributed by W.

Viewed independently, each of these transactions clearly qualified for nonrecognition under §351. The first transaction simply involved a sole transferor (W) contributing assets in exchange for 100% of the Newco stock. The second transaction involved contributions to an existing corporation by one historic shareholder (X) and one newcomer (W), solely

---

56. Treas. Reg. §1.368-1(e)(1)(i), (e)(8), ex. 1. These continuity-of-interest regulations are discussed in detail in Chapter 11.

57. Commentators still presume, however, that post-exchange stock transfers can cause a 351 transaction to fail the control requirement, when the contributor transfers enough of their stock to lose control pursuant to a prearranged agreement. See, e.g., Boris I. Bittker & James S. Eustice, Federal Income Taxation of Corporations and Shareholders, ¶3.09 (7th ed. 2015)

58. Although the shareholder nonrecognition rule is found in §354, the term "reorganization" is defined in §368. These provisions are discussed in detail in Chapters 11-14.

59. 2003-1 C.B. 938.

in exchange for stock, after which the contributors together held 100% of the Y stock.[60] Given W's binding commitment to the second exchange, however, one would be hard pressed not to consider the two steps as an integrated transaction after which W had only 40% control of Y and, thus, indirectly only 40% control of Newco. Since X made no transfers to Newco in the initial exchange, prior case law and rulings suggested that X would not be considered part of the control group. Thus, X's 60% would not count toward control. W alone would appear to fail the 80% control test.

Nevertheless, the Treasury Department concluded in Revenue Ruling 2003-51 that the §351 control requirement was met even though W had a binding commitment to transfer the Newco shares. Although the transaction seems to violate the literal requirements of §351, the ruling concluded that "treating a transfer of property that is followed by a nontaxable disposition of the stock received as a transfer described in §351 is not necessarily inconsistent with the purposes of §351."[61] After all, from an economic perspective the transferor in this case was simply rearranging its interest in the property through corporate consolidation and, thus, could claim a significant continuity of interest. The ruling emphasizes that W *could* simply have joined X in a single straightforward §351 transaction in which W contributed assets and X contributed cash to Y in exchange for Y stock. This is a rather remarkable concession from the Treasury Department, which typically holds taxpayers to the form of their transactions. Ordinarily, one does not expect a transaction that fails to meet statutory requirements for nonrecognition to nevertheless qualify because there is an alternate form of the transaction that *would* have qualified. Surprising as the ruling may seem, it does appear consistent with a trend in which the government has dramatically loosened its interpretation of the literal tax-free reorganization requirements, making it far easier for taxpayers to qualify for nonrecognition treatment.[62]

Disproportionate Contributions and Other Variations

Ordinarily, stock received by contributing shareholders is proportionate to the value of property contributed. Thus, if shareholders A and B each contribute 50% of the total value to Corporation X, one would expect each to

---

60. Keep in mind that the nonrecognition provisions of §351 are not limited to initial incorporations but also apply to contributions to capital of an existing corporation in exchange for stock. Issues regarding subsequent contributions to the capital of an existing corporation are considered later in this chapter.

61. 2003-1 C.B., at 940. Notice, however, that the ruling limits itself to a subsequent *nontaxable* disposition, leaving open the question of a subsequent *taxable* disposition of shares received in a §351 exchange.

62. These developments are discussed in Chapters 11 and 12.

get 50% of the value of X stock in return. Nevertheless, stock received need not necessarily "be substantially in proportion to . . . [the] interest in the property immediately prior to the transfer."[63] In the case of a disproportion-ate contribution, however, "the entire transaction will be given tax effect in accordance with its true nature."[64]

To illustrate, suppose that mother and daughter decide to incorporate a family business. They agree that each will receive 50% of the stock. The com-bined capital contributions will be $100,000. In a proportionate contribution, each would contribute $50,000 of the total $100,000 in return for 50% of the stock. Instead, mother contributes property worth $90,000 and daughter contributes property worth only $10,000. According to Treasury regulation §1.351-1(b)(1), the disproportionate nature of the contributions will not dis-qualify mother and daughter from §351 nonrecognition treatment. However, the transaction will be "given tax effect in accordance with its true nature." In deciding the "true nature" of the transaction, it will be necessary to examine the facts and circumstances to determine the reason that the "losing" party in the disproportionate exchange agreed to take less than her fair share. In the mother/daughter case, the most likely explanation is that mother was making a gift to daughter.[65] Mother will be viewed as first contributing 90% of the total contributions ($90,000) in return for 90% of the stock and then as making a gift of 40% of the shares ($40,000 worth of stock) to daughter. The daughter is viewed as first contributing 10% of the total contributions ($10,000) in return for 10% of the stock and then as receiving an additional 40% ($40,000 worth of stock) as a gift from mom. The daughter is deemed to receive a tax-free gift[66] and her basis for the gift shares will be governed by the gift-basis rules.[67] Mother may be required to pay a gift tax on this transfer.[68]

OPERATION OF SHAREHOLDER NONRECOGNITION RULES

Overview of Basis Rules: Deferral of Gain or Loss

If a contribution to the corporation meets the requirements of §351(a), gain or loss will not be recognized to the contributing shareholder. The

---

63. Treas. Reg. §1.351-1(b)(1).

64. Id.

65. See, e.g., Treas. Reg. §1.351-1(b)(2), ex. 1, 2. Other explanations for disproportionate contributions may be that one contributor is paying another for services rendered or to sat-isfy other obligations.

66. I.R.C. §102.

67. I.R.C. §1015.

68. I.R.C. §2501.

nonrecognitionwillnotnecessarilybepermanent,however.Congresspreserves unrecognized gain or loss through the basis rules in §358.[69] Section 358(a) provides that the shareholder's basis in property permitted to be received without recognition of gain or loss (the stock) shall be the same as that of the property exchanged (the property transferred to the corporation), subject to certain adjustments that will be considered below. This is a type of substituted basis labeled by Congress as "exchanged basis."[70] The nonrecognition and corollary deferral of gain or loss through substituted basis is reminiscent of similar rules applicable to like-kind exchanges.[71]

A simple example is perhaps the best way to illustrate the deferral provided by the combination of §§351 and 358. Suppose that shareholder A has been operating a business as sole proprietor and decides to incorporate, transferring real estate with a basis of $20,000 and a fair market value of $200,000 to a newly formed corporation in return for 100% of the corporation's common stock. The value of the stock received presumably is equal to the value of the corporation's only asset — $200,000. Under §351, the shareholder's $180,000 *realized* gain will not be recognized. A's basis in the common shares received will be an "exchanged basis" of $20,000 from the contributed real estate. If A later sells the stock for $200,000, A will then recognize the $180,000 gain previously deferred.[72] Thus, recognition of gain from the incorporation is deferred until ultimate disposition of the shares.[73]

---

69. The shareholder may permanently escape recognition only if he or she dies before disposing of the shares. In such event, the shareholder's heirs will inherit the stock with a fair market value basis at the time of death. I.R.C. §1014.

70. See I.R.C. §7701(a)(44), which defines "exchanged basis" as basis "determined in whole or in part by reference to other property held at any time by the person for whom the basis is to be determined."

71. I.R.C. §1031. These rules are not part of Subchapter C. They apply more broadly to exchanges of business or investment property.

72. In addition to determining the *amount* of gain, the shareholder will need to know the *character* of the gain. I.R.C. §1223(1) allows the shareholder to compute the stock's holding period by including the period of ownership of the transferred asset if (1) the stock received has the same basis in whole or in part as the property exchanged; and (2) the property exchanged was a capital asset. In the example in text, the shareholder received an exchanged basis under §358, thus satisfying the first condition. Assuming that the real estate transferred was a capital asset and assuming that A had held the real estate for more than one year, A's gain from sale of the stock will be long-term capital gain even if A has held the stock itself for less than one year. These holding period rules will be considered further in the Examples and Explanations section below.

73. Use of the term "deferred" does not mean that the gain or loss later recognized upon sale of the stock will be precisely the amount of gain or loss realized at the time of contribution. The value of the property contributed may increase or decrease. If so, the value of the stock presumably will also increase or decrease. Gain later recognized may be more or less than the $180,000 realized gain at the time of contribution. Note, though, that the same would be true if the shareholder had retained the property. Later sale of the property at a price lower than $200,000 would reduce the gain below $180,000. The important point here is that the "exchanged basis" preserves the gain or loss at the level it would have been if the shareholder had retained the contributed property and later sold it directly.

Effect of Boot

a) Taxation of "Boot Gain": §351(b)(1)

Under §351(a), the transfer to the corporation must be *solely in exchange for stock*. Any property other than qualified stock of the transferee corporation received by the shareholders in the §351 exchange is referred to as boot.[74] After setting out the "solely in exchange for stock" requirement in §351(a), Congress then loosens the requirement with the "boot exception" in §351(b). If §351(a) would apply but for the fact that some boot was received in the exchange, §351(b) provides that gain (if any) will be recognized, but not in excess of the boot received.[75] Returning to shareholder A in the example above, assume that instead of receiving $200,000 worth of stock in exchange for her real estate (basis $20,000), A received $170,000 worth of stock and $30,000 in cash boot. A's *realized gain* is still $180,000.[76] A's receipt of $30,000 boot will not jeopardize the nonrecognition transaction altogether, but she will be required to report gain to the extent of the money (boot) received. Of the $180,000 realized gain, A will recognize only a $30,000 "boot gain." The remaining $150,000 of realized gain remains unrecognized; it is not affected by the boot.[77]

After computing A's gain from the transaction, the next step is to determine A's basis in the $170,000 worth of stock. A begins with a §358(a) exchanged basis of $20,000 from the contributed real estate. She must then make adjustments, first decreasing basis by the amount of money received ($30,000)[78] and next increasing basis by the amount of gain recognized upon the exchange (also $30,000).[79] To better understand these adjustments, think of basis as a running account of the taxpayer's investment. To the extent of the $30,000 cash received, shareholder A has "cashed out" of her investment in the corporate enterprise. Since she took this cash out, shareholder A has already recovered this part of her investment and her basis

---

74. Boot may take the form of cash, other property, or "nonqualified preferred stock" as provided in I.R.C. §351(g). Under §357(a), however, the corporation's assumption of a transferring shareholder's liability is not considered boot. Incorporations involving assumption of liabilities are considered later in this chapter.

75. I.R.C. §351(b). The boot rules in §351(b) are quite similar to boot rules applicable to like-kind exchanges. See I.R.C. §1031(b).

76. Her realized gain is the amount realized (including stock and cash, totaling $200,000) less her basis of $20,000.

77. As a practical matter, the payment of cash boot upon formation of a new corporation is rare. Keep in mind that while §351 is most often associated with the initial formation of a corporation, it is not so limited. In fact, §351 applies to *any* transfer to a corporation controlled by the transferror that meets the §351 requirements. Cash boot may be more common in connection with such subsequent contributions. The more common form of boot in an initial incorporation is a corporate security.

78. I.R.C. §358(a)(1)(A)(ii).

79. I.R.C. §358(a)(1)(B)(ii).

must be reduced accordingly. On the other hand, this "cashing out" caused shareholder A to have $30,000 in taxable gain. This gain is an increased cost ("tax cost") in her corporate investment and should increase her basis. Even after these adjustments, shareholder A's basis remains at $20,000.

If shareholder A later sells her stock for $170,000, her gain from the sale will be $150,000.[80] Adding together the $30,000 boot gain from the initial transaction and the $150,000 gain collected upon later sale, we discover that her total gain from the two transactions is $180,000. This is precisely the unrealized appreciation lurking in the property when she transferred it to the corporation in the first place. The §351 exchange rules required her to report $30,000 of gain at the outset, but permitted her to defer the remaining $150,000 until ultimate sale of the stock.

You probably noticed that when the dust settled after shareholder A's §358 adjustments, basis had been reduced by $30,000 and then increased by $30,000, leaving her where she started with an exchanged basis in her common shares of $20,000. Why bother with these adjustments if they simply wash each other out? Although this particular example results in a wash, this will not be the outcome in all cases. A variation on the above hypothetical will help to illustrate. Suppose that shareholder A's basis in the contributed property had been $185,000 as opposed to $20,000. Again assume that the property is valued at $200,000 when she contributes it to the corporation in return for $170,000 worth of stock and $30,000 cash boot. Remember that §351(b) requires recognition of gain, if *any*, but not in excess of the boot. In this variation, A's *realized* gain from her contribution is only $15,000.[81] Thus, shareholder A will recognize "boot gain" of only $15,000 under §351(b). The receipt of $30,000 boot results in full recognition of her realized gain. Surely, shareholder A should not be taxed on more than her realized gain. As for basis, shareholder A must first decrease her exchanged basis of $185,000 by the $30,000 money received and then must increase by the $15,000 gain recognized, leaving a $170,000 basis in the stock. If she should later sell her shares for $170,000, she will have no further taxable gain. This is sensible, since she has already been fully taxed on her realized gain from the contributed property. The downward and upward adjustments required by §358 do not precisely wash each other out in this variation of the hypothetical.

If shareholder A received other property instead of cash boot, the analysis would be similar to that considered above. Assume, for example, that shareholder A transferred her real estate (basis $20,000) to the corporation in return for stock worth $170,000 and a piece of artwork worth $30,000.

---

80. From her $170,000 amount realized, subtract her §358 exchanged basis of $20,000.
81. A's amount realized is $200,000 ($170,000 worth of stock plus the $30,000 cash she received). From this amount, she subtracts her $185,000 basis.

The gain from this transaction is precisely the same as it was above. Of the $180,000 realized gain, a "boot gain" of $30,000 (the fair market value of the property received) will be recognized. Two basis questions now must be addressed, however. As for A's basis in the stock received, the answer remains the same—the exchanged basis of $20,000 is first decreased by the fair market value of the property ($30,000) and then increased by the gain recognized on the exchange (also $30,000).[82] The basis in the artwork is simply its fair market value of $30,000.[83] Shareholder A's fair market value basis in the boot makes sense. After all, she was taxed on the full value of the artwork. It is as if she received cash boot and then used the cash to purchase the asset. In effect, she has a "tax cost" basis in the boot property.

If shareholders transfer *multiple* properties in exchange for stock and boot, §351(b) gain must be computed on an asset-by-asset basis. A portion of the boot received must be allocated to each asset based upon the fair market value of the asset.[84] Boot gain will be recognized with respect to each gain asset transferred. Boot gain from each asset will be reflected as ordinary income, short-term capital gain, long-term capital gain, or recapture income, as appropriate. Thus, the asset-by-asset approach effectively preserves the character of gain for each individual asset.

b) Securities, Notes, or Other Evidence of Indebtedness as Boot

Prior to the Omnibus Budget Reconciliation Act of 1989, securities of the transferee corporation issued in a §351 exchange were not considered boot. Today, however, any securities transferred to a contributing shareholder in return for property in a §351 exchange are considered boot.[85] Ordinarily, when a shareholder receives boot, the gain, if any, is taxed to the extent of the fair market value of the boot. The gain must be reported entirely in the taxable year of the §351 exchange. When a shareholder receives boot in the form of notes or securities, however, timing issues arise. Given that payments on the boot notes or securities will occur over time, the shareholder may be entitled to take advantage of installment reporting under §453. Under the installment method, the shareholder would recognize boot gain as payments were received, thus deferring tax on the gain and spreading the recognition over the period of the installment obligation. There is no explicit statutory authority for treating notes or securities received in a §351 transaction under the installment method. However, Congress did provide special rules for installment reporting with respect to notes or securities

---

82. I.R.C. §358(a)(1)(A)(i), (a)(1)(B)(ii).
83. I.R.C. §358(a)(2).
84. Rev. Rul. 68-55, 1968-1 C.B. 140.
85. That is, §351(a) now only provides for nonrecognition upon the receipt of stock in the §351 exchange.

received as boot in other similar nonrecognition transactions such as like-kind exchanges and reorganizations.[86] In proposed regulations, the Service explicitly takes the position that transferors who receive corporate notes, securities, or other evidence of indebtedness as boot in a §351 transaction are entitled to installment reporting of boot gain.[87]

c) "Nonqualified Preferred Stock" Treated as Boot

Prior to the Taxpayer Relief Act of 1997, §351(a) nonrecognition extended to qualifying exchanges of property for *any* type of stock of the transferee corporation. Anything *other* than stock received by the transferors is considered boot. As noted in the preceding paragraphs, such boot includes corporate securities and other evidences of indebtedness. Over the years, the number of different types of stock, debt, and other financial instruments has exploded. In particular, tax and financial planners have created categories of preferred stock that closely resemble debt. By offering investors "debt-like" preferred stock or preferred stock with built-in redemption features, planners were able to structure incorporation transactions without any §351(b) boot gain in which the transferors received a preferred stock instrument much like a security or one that was reasonably certain to be quickly redeemed.

The Taxpayer Relief Act of 1997 added §351(g), which declares that §351(a) nonrecognition shall *not* apply to the transfer of property to a corporation in exchange for "nonqualified preferred stock." Instead, "nonqualified preferred stock" will be treated as boot under §351(b). For purposes of this provision, preferred stock is "stock which is limited and preferred as to dividends and does not participate in corporate growth to any significant extent."[88] Preferred stock is classified as *nonqualified* under any of four stated circumstances, the first three of which relate to redemption rights. Preferred stock is nonqualified (1) if the stockholder has a right to require that the issuing corporation or a related person redeem or purchase the shares within 20 years of issue,[89] (2) if redemption of the shares is mandatory

---

86. I.R.C. §453(f)(6).
87. Prop. Treas. Reg. §1.453-1(f)(3)(ii). Based on these proposed regulations, shareholders would be entitled to use §453 installment reporting for any taxable gain from "installment boot" in a §351 exchange, thus reporting taxable gain as payments are received. Despite this tax deferral, the regulations would permit an *immediate* increase to the shareholder's §358 stock basis for the full realized gain. However, the regulations would increase the *corporation's* §362(a) basis in the property received only as gain is reported by the shareholders under the installment method. This approach effectively treats the transaction as a simple §351 exchange with respect to stock received, and a separate installment sale with respect to boot received in the form of securities or notes. See also Prop. Treas. Reg. §1.453-1(f)(3)(iii), exs.
88. I.R.C. §351(g)(3).
89. I.R.C. §351(g)(2)(A)(i). Such shares often are referred to as "puttable."

within 20 years of issue,[90] or (3) if the issuing corporation or a related person has the right to redeem or purchase the shares within 20 years and "it is more likely than not that such right will be exercised."[91] The focus in these three cases is on shares that are reasonably likely to be redeemed and, thus, converted to cash in the hands of the holders. Congress is no longer willing to offer nonrecognition to those who transfer property to a corporation in exchange for such redeemable stock.[92] The last listed circumstance that will result in a nonqualified preferred stock classification is when the dividend rate for the preferred stock "varies, in whole or in part . . ., with reference to interest rates, commodity prices, or other similar indices."[93] Where dividends on stock are tied to such market factors, rather than to the earnings of the corporation itself, the preferred stock resembles debt. Since securities are now treated as boot under §351(b), Congress has decided to treat such debt-like preferred stock as boot as well.

To illustrate §351(g), imagine that shareholder A again transfers real estate with a basis of $20,000 and a fair market value of $200,000 to a newly formed corporation in exchange for 100% of the corporation's common stock, valued at $170,000, and 100% of the corporation's preferred stock, valued at $30,000. Shareholder A has a right to "put" the preferred shares within five years from the date of issue; in other words, shareholder A can *require* the corporation to redeem these preferred shares. Under §351(g), the redemption feature makes the preferred stock *nonqualified*. As a result, the preferred shares will be treated as boot. Shareholder A will recognize $30,000 "boot gain" just as if she had received cash or other boot.

Although nonqualified preferred stock is treated as boot for purposes of §351(b), the Conference Report clarifies that, until Treasury regulations require a different result, the nonqualified stock will still be treated as stock for purposes of the control test under §§351(a) and 368(c).[94] Imagine, for example, that two individual shareholders transfer appreciated property to a newly formed corporation in exchange for stock. Shareholder A receives all of the corporation's common stock and Shareholder B receives all the corporation's nonqualified preferred stock. Shareholder B surely will have "boot gain" under §351(b). Nevertheless, the preferred shares will be considered stock for purposes of determining control under §368(c). Since Shareholders A and B have "control" of the corporation immediately after

---

90. I.R.C. §351(g)(2)(A)(ii).
91. I.R.C. §351(g)(2)(A)(iii). Such shares often are referred to as "callable."
92. Despite incorporating one of the three redemption features, preferred stock will not be classified as nonqualified if the redemption right or obligation to purchase is subject to a contingency which makes the likelihood of redemption or purchase remote. I.R.C. §351(g)(2)(B). Other specific exceptions to the classification rules appear in I.R.C. §351(g)(2)(C).
93. I.R.C. §351(g)(2)(A)(iv).
94. H.R. Rep. No. 105-220, 105th Cong., 2d Sess. 561 (1997).

the exchange, Shareholder A will be entitled to §351(a) nonrecognition treatment.

d) No Recognition of Loss: §351(b)(2)

Although the payment of boot triggers recognition of gain, losses are not recognized. Section 351(b)(2) specifically disallows loss recognition when property other than stock (boot) is received in connection with a §351 exchange. The rationale here probably is that it otherwise would be too easy for shareholders to have it both ways, avoiding gain on §351(a) exchanges, but recognizing loss under §351(b) merely by including boot along with the transfer of stock from the corporation.

When shareholders receive boot in exchange for multiple assets in a §351 exchange, they may be tempted to argue that the "gain (if any)" language in §351(b) refers to *aggregate* gain from the assets contributed. If successful, the shareholders could use losses from the loss assets to offset gains from the gain assets contributed, resulting in a lower boot gain on the exchange. The asset-by-asset approach to multiple asset contributions prevents this end-run around §351(b)(2). Under this approach, no gain is recognized and no loss is permitted with respect to the boot allocated to the loss assets.[95]

TAX CONSEQUENCES TO THE CORPORATION

Nonrecognition Rule: §1032

With regard to the corporation, Congress provides a nonrecognition rule that somewhat parallels the §351 shareholder nonrecognition rules. Under §1032(a), "no gain or loss shall be recognized to a corporation on the receipt of money or other property in exchange for stock."[96]

One explanation for the nonrecognition provided in §1032 is potential hardship. Corporations need capital to begin operations. Taxing capital contributions would impose additional financial burdens on a corporation just as it was trying to get off the ground.[97] Put differently, §1032

---

95. See discussion earlier in this chapter and Example 6, *infra*.
96. See Treas. Reg. §1.1032-1(a), which provides that the "disposition by a corporation of shares of its own stock (including treasury stock) for money or other property does not give rise to taxable gain or deductible loss to the corporation regardless of the nature of the transaction or the facts and circumstances involved."
97. Note, however, that §1032 is not by its terms limited to contributions at the time of incorporation. In this respect, §1032 is similar to §351.

nonrecognition may be simply an encouragement to incorporate. Another explanation for §1032 may be that most contributions arguably do not involve genuine gain to the corporation. At least upon initial incorporation, the corporation's stock has not appreciated in the corporation's hands. The stock has no value until it is issued.

Although it is useful to think of §1032 as a parallel to §351, several differences between the two provisions should be pointed out. First, under §1032 *any* issuance of the corporation's own stock in return for money or other property is a nonrecognition event to the issuing corporation. Unlike §351, there is no requirement that a group receiving the shares meet an 80% control test. In addition, distributions of stock for services are covered by §1032. Treasury Regulation §1.1032-1(a) provides that a "transfer by a corporation of shares of its own stock . . . As compensation for services is considered, for purposes of section 1032(a), as a disposition by the corporation of such shares for money or other property." Finally, the basis rules that apply on the corporate side are similar, but not quite the same as the shareholder basis rules provided in §358.

The Corporate Basis Rules: §362

a) Basic Substituted Basis Rules: §362(a)

Operating together, the §351 shareholder nonrecognition rule and the §358 shareholder basis rule establish a deferral rather than permanent nonrecognition of the shareholder's gain or loss with respect to assets contributed to the corporation. The effect of the §1032 *corporate* nonrecognition rule in conjunction with the §362 basis rule is slightly different. First of all, arguably there is no corporate level gain from the shareholder contribution that should be deferred. Unlike the shareholder, the corporation has not disposed of appreciated or depreciated assets. Thus, §362 does not adopt an "exchanged" basis rule parallel to §358. Instead, the corporation's basis in property acquired in a §351 exchange is "the same as it would be in the hands of the transferor, increased in the amount of gain recognized to the transferor on such transfer."[98] In other words, the corporation takes the *contributing shareholder's* basis or "steps into the shoes of" the contributing shareholder. The Code refers to this variety of substituted basis as "transferred basis."[99] Suppose again that shareholder A contributes real estate with

---

98. I.R.C. §362(a).

99. I.R.C. §7701(a)(43) defines "transferred basis property" as property having a basis "determined in whole or in part by reference to the basis in the hands of the donor, grantor, or other transferor." Both "exchanged basis" and "transferred basis" are forms of "substituted basis." I.R.C. §7701(a)(42).

a basis of $20,000 and a fair market value of $200,000 to Corporation X in return for 100% of X's common stock. Corporation X will have no taxable gain from receipt of the property under §1032. Corporation X's basis in the property under §362 will be a "transferred basis" from the shareholder of $20,000. This transferred basis assures that the *shareholder* level gain or loss from the §351 contribution is preserved in the *corporation's* hands. If Corporation X sold the real estate contributed by A for $200,000, the corporation would be required to report a taxable gain of $180,000. This is precisely the amount of gain that the shareholder would have had if she sold the property herself.[100]

The only required adjustment to the corporation's basis in contributed property under §362(a) is an *increase* in the amount of the shareholder's gain recognized on the §351 exchange.[101] Since the corporation's §362 basis is designed to preserve the *shareholder* level gain or loss from the contributed property, this upward adjustment is necessary to reflect the portion of shareholder realized gain that has already been recognized. If shareholder A received $170,000 worth of stock and $30,000 boot from Corporation X in exchange for real estate with a basis of $20,000 and a fair market value of $200,000, shareholder A would report $30,000 in gain pursuant to §351(b)(1).[102] Corporation X's basis in the real estate now would be a transferred basis from shareholder A of $20,000, increased by the $30,000 gain recognized to shareholder A. Thus, the real estate would have a basis of $50,000 in the corporation's hands. If the corporation were to sell the real estate for $200,000, it would recognize a $150,000 gain—precisely the portion of $180,000 realized shareholder gain that was left unrecognized at the time of the §351 exchange.

Notice that both §§358 and 362 use a form of "substituted basis" and both provisions preserve the gain or loss left unrecognized to the shareholder under §351. Congress thus has preserved the shareholder level gain in two places. The shareholder will recognize the gain deferred upon later sale of the stock and the corporation will recognize the same gain upon later sale of the contributed property. Is this overkill? Will it result in double taxation of the same gain? The answer to the latter question is yes. Surely, there lurks the possibility that shareholder A's unrecognized gain from

---

100. If the asset in question was a capital asset, the gain would be capital gain. With regard to holding periods, the corporation will be entitled to include or "tack" the shareholder's holding period because the property in the corporation's hands has the same basis as it would have in the hands of the shareholder from whom the property was acquired. I.R.C. §1223(2).

101. Amendments to §362 added §362(d), which limits the amount of this increase in certain cases involving the assumption of liabilities by the corporation. A discussion of this new provision is included in the discussion of the effect of liabilities later in this chapter.

102. Shareholder A's tax treatment in this example is considered in detail in the section on boot earlier in this chapter.

appreciation in the contributed real estate will be taxed once at the shareholder level and again at the corporate level. The answer to the first question is more difficult and controversial. By its very nature, Subchapter C creates a double tax. Certainly, corporate income is taxed first to the corporation and again to the shareholders when it is distributed. The combination of §§358 and 362 extends this double tax to pre-contribution *appreciation* as well.[103]

b) Limitations on Built-In Losses: §362(e)

i) Background

As just described, the dual substituted basis rules in §§358 and 362 effectively preserve the shareholder's unrecognized gain from a §351 exchange for potential later taxation in both the shareholder's *and* the corporation's hands. Thus, even pre-incorporation appreciation in assets contributed to the corporation is potentially subject to double tax. Symmetrical application of the rules would result in a similar potential for duplication of pre-incorporation losses.

Imagine, for example, that shareholder A contributes real estate with a basis of $250,000 and a fair market value of $200,000 in exchange for $200,000 worth of X Corporation common stock. Because §351(a) nonrecognition applies to both gains and losses, shareholder A will not be permitted to recognize the $50,000 *realized loss* upon this exchange. Her $250,000 substituted basis in the X shares under §358 effectively preserves the $50,000 loss for recognition upon subsequent sale of the X stock. Under §362(a), X Corporation also would take a $250,000 basis in the contributed real estate. If the corporation later were to sell the real estate, it too would recognize the $50,000 loss.

Congressional concern for the potential doubling of so-called "built-in" losses has led to a number of different statutory loss restrictions enacted at different times and sometimes without adequate consideration of potential overlaps and complexities. Among these are the §362(e) corporate basis limitations enacted in 2004.[104]

---

103. In a case where a shareholder challenged the double taxation of pre-contribution appreciation, the court upheld the constitutionality of the provisions. In Perthur Holding Co. v. Comm'r, Judge Learned Hand commented that the double tax "may be unfair, but it is not unconstitutional. This was something the shareholder should have considered when he 'put on a corporate dress.'" 61 F.2d 785, 786 (2d Cir. 1932), cert. denied, 288 U.S. 616 (1933).

104. American Jobs Creation Act of 2004, Pub. L. No. 108-357, §836, 118 Stat. 1418, 1594-1596 (codified at I.R.C. §362(e)). Earlier statutory responses in §§358(h) and 362(d) to loss duplication issues in the context of liabilities assumed in a §351 transaction are considered later in this chapter. The §362(e) rules were adopted after the §336(d) loss limitation rules applicable to liquidating distributions. See Chapter 8 for a discussion of the §336 liquidating distribution rules and the potential overlaps between those provisions and §362(e).

ii) Importation of Losses: §362(e)(1)

The primary force driving the §362(e) loss limitation rules was congressional concern with certain Enron tax-avoidance transactions involving §351 transfers of loss properties by foreign entities not subject to U.S. Tax to a domestic corporation in exchange for the latter corporation's stock. The domestic corporation would then take advantage of the §362(a) substituted basis rule to recognize a loss on sale of the contributed loss property.[105] Rules in §362(e)(1)(A) were designed to prevent a U.S. corporation from importing and recognizing a loss in property contributed by a nontaxable foreign entity. Under these rules, if the aggregate adjusted basis exceeds the aggregate fair market value of contributed or "imported" properties, the transferee corporation's basis in each "imported" asset, notwithstanding §362(a) or (b) substituted basis rules, will be its fair market value immediately after the exchange.[106] Since the subject of this book is domestic corporate taxation, this chapter will not provide further detailed discussion of the §362(e)(1) limits on cross-boundary importation of losses from foreign entities. The §362(e) loss limitation rules, however, also included provisions more broadly applicable to domestic transactions, which are discussed in the sections that follow.[107]

iii) Limitations on Built-In Losses: §362(e)(2)

The §362(e)(2) built-in loss limitation rules operate as an exception to the §362(a) substituted basis rule otherwise applicable to §351 exchanges. Pursuant to §362(e)(2), and notwithstanding §362(a), the transferee corporation's aggregate adjusted bases in the assets received in a §351 exchange or as a contribution to capital "*shall not exceed the fair market value of such property immediately after such transaction.*"[108] Thus the "built-in loss" addressed by §362(e)(2) is the difference between the aggregate basis and fair market value of contributed properties as measured immediately after the §351 exchange; in other words, the loss in value that occurred during the transferor's term of ownership and before the asset became corporate property.

To start simply, consider a single shareholder, A, who contributes a single "loss property"—real estate with a $250,000 basis and a $200,000 fair

---

105. S. Rep. 192, at 124-125, 108th Cong., 1st Sess. (2003)

106. The operation of §362(e)(1) here is somewhat different from that of §362(e)(2), which applies the basis adjustment only to built-in loss assets.

107. To the extent that there is any overlap, §362(e)(2)(A) clarifies that the (e)(1) "importation" rules trump the (e)(2) "built-in loss" rules.

108. I.R.C. §362(e)(2)(A) (emphasis added). The regulations provide exceptions to this rule, such as in a case where the built-in-loss is subsequently eliminated without recognition. Treas. Reg. §1.362-4(c).

market value—in exchange for all of newly formed X Corporation's stock. Absent special rules, the combination of shareholder A's §358 basis in the stock ($250,000) and X Corporation's §362(a) basis in the real estate (also $250,000) would result in a potential duplication of the $50,000 realized, but unrecognized, loss. The idea behind the §362(e)(2) loss limitation rule is to preserve the loss only once. The statute achieves this result by limiting X Corporation's basis in the real estate to its $200,000 fair market value and leaving shareholder A's §358 stock basis unchanged.[109] Thus, the previously unrecognized loss is preserved in the shareholder's, but not the corporation's, hands.

An elective alternative to achieve the "single loss" result is provided in §362(e)(2)(C), which allows the transferring shareholder and transferee corporation to file a joint election, under which the corporation is not required to reduce its basis in the assets under §362(e)(2). Instead, the transferring shareholder's §358 basis will be limited to the fair market value of the transferred property.[110] Under this alternative, the single loss is preserved in the corporation's hands rather than through the shareholder's stock basis.

Application of the §362(e)(2) restrictions can be slightly trickier for transactions involving multiple assets and multiple transferors. The statutory language clearly states that the basis limitation rule applies in the aggregate. In the case of multiple assets, the corporation must reduce its basis in assets received in the §351 exchange by an amount equal to the difference between the *aggregate* bases and fair market values of the contributed properties immediately after the exchange. The corporation then is instructed under §362(e)(2)(B) to allocate this basis reduction among the properties received in proportion to "respective built-in losses immediately before the transaction." Despite some initial questions about whether the language in (e)(2)(A) also required aggregating the asset contributions of multiple *transferors*, Treasury regulations provide that the rules should be applied on a separate transferor-by-transferor basis.[111] This interpretation is also supported by a careful reading of the statutory text.

---

109. Regulations applicable to consolidated returns for affiliated corporations already include complex rules designed to prevent loss duplication. Consequently, Treasury regulations indicating that the §362(e)(2) loss limitation rules generally do not apply to intercompany transfers among members of a consolidated group. Treas. Reg. §§1.362-4(a)(2); 1.1502-80(h).

110. Once made, the election is irrevocable. I.R.C. §362(e)(2)(C)(ii). Notice 2005-70, 2005-2 C.B. 694.

111. Treas. Reg. §1.362-4(b) ("whether and the extent to which this section applies is determined separately for each Transferor"). See also Treas. Reg. §1.362-4(g)(3). The regulations also indicate that aggregate bases and fair market value should be compared for purposes of §362(e)(2) only after basis adjustment for any "boot gain." Id. At §1.362-4(h), ex. 6.

The practical impact of §362(e)(2)'s aggregate approach is that a built-in gain on one asset can be used to offset the built-in loss on another. For example, imagine that shareholder A in a §351 exchange transfers asset 1 with a basis of $90 and a fair market value of $60 and asset 2 with a $110 basis and a $120 fair market value. In other words, asset 1 has a $30 built-in loss and asset 2 a $10 built-in gain. Under §362(e)(2), the aggregate basis of $200 exceeds the aggregate fair market value of $180, thus requiring a $20 basis reduction, all of which will be allocated to asset 1, the loss asset. In the end, the corporation will own asset 1 with a $70 basis and asset 2 with a $110 basis. Even though asset 1 had an actual built-in loss of $30, the aggregate rules of §362(e)(2) require only a $20 basis reduction.[112]

NON-EQUITY TRANSACTIONS

The rules considered up to this point deal with contributions of property to a controlled corporation in exchange for stock in transactions qualifying under §351. Sometimes, however, taxpayers may wish to transfer property to the corporation in transactions not qualifying under §351. In such transactions, the corporation may transfer money or property to the taxpayer in exchange for the property it receives, or the corporation may issue a promissory note to the taxpayer in exchange for the property. Whether the taxpayer transfers property to the corporation in exchange for money or a promissory note or contributes property to the corporation in exchange for stock, the transferor's proceeds from the transaction will ultimately be taxable. In the case of a transfer in exchange for the corporation's promissory note, the transferor's return beyond consideration for the property sold takes the form of interest taxable as ordinary income.[113] In the case of an equity contribution in exchange for the corporation's stock, the transferors' return takes the form of dividends, previously taxable as ordinary income,

---

112. Treas. Reg. §1.362-4(h), ex. 1. This approach is different from the §336(d) built-in loss limitation rules applicable to certain liquidating distributions. These liquidation rules and their relationship to the §362(e) rules considered here are discussed later in Chapter 8. Additional problems involving multiple assets and multiple transferors are included in the Examples at the end of this chapter.

113. Payments of *principal* will be taxable to the extent of the gain upon the asset sold. This gain will be capital or ordinary depending upon the character of the asset sold. Assuming that the shareholder takes a promissory note in return for the sale, the sale will be treated as an installment sale unless the shareholder elects not to use the installment method. I.R.C. §453(d)(1).

but now eligible for preferential capital gains rates to the extent of qualified dividends.[114]

Given the valuable nonrecognition provided by §351, why might a taxpayer prefer to sell an asset to the corporation in a transaction not qualifying under this provision? Remember that §351 is a two-way street, providing nonrecognition for both gains *and losses*. A shareholder may wish to sell property to the corporation in order to recognize a loss. Unfortunately for certain taxpayers attempting to avoid §351 nonrecognition of loss by selling the property to the corporation in a taxable transaction, the related party rules of §267 may prohibit the shareholder from deducting any loss in such a transaction.[115] Thus, a *controlling* shareholder cannot recognize a loss upon a sale of property to the controlled corporation.

Another reason that a taxpayer might arrange a sale to the corporation rather than an equity contribution is to limit risk. A creditor's relationship with the corporation is less risky than an equity holder's relationship with the corporation. A corporate shareholder seeking to reduce risk by transferring property to the corporation in exchange for its promissory note should proceed with caution, however. Other creditors may turn to corporate law in order to achieve priority over creditors who are also major or controlling shareholders.

A shareholder also may attempt to transfer property to the corporation in a transaction not qualifying under §351 to provide the corporation with a cost basis in the property under §1012 rather than a transferred basis under §362. A corporation may find it particularly attractive to acquire depreciable property from the shareholder when the cost basis would result in significantly higher depreciation allowances than a transferred basis. A final reason the shareholder may arrange a sale to the corporation is to provide the corporation with a deduction for interest payments. A corporation can generally deduct interest payments on a promissory note,[116] but cannot deduct dividend payments to shareholders.

Given that §351 applies only to transfers in exchange for stock, transfers of property in exchange for long-term securities generally are taxable to the extent of the securities received as boot. There remains a risk, however, that a sale for a long-term note will be reconstrued as a contribution for *stock*. In some cases, the promissory note received had so many equity characteristics that the purported sale was deemed to be an exchange of property for *stock*

---

114. For a complete discussion of corporate distributions, including the qualified dividend rules, see Chapter 5. See also Chapter 1.

115. An individual owning, directly or indirectly, more than 50% of the value of the corporation's outstanding stock is considered "related" to the corporation for purposes of §267. See I.R.C. §267(b)(2).

116. I.R.C. §163(a). The corporation may be subject, however, to the §163(j) limitation on the deductibility of business interest. The rules for the treatment of corporate debt are discussed in Chapter 3.

and, thus, treated as a §351 nonrecognition exchange rather than a sale.[117] Thus, a formal sale in exchange for a debenture or note may be disregarded and viewed, in substance, as a disguised equity contribution in return for stock. Among the factors that courts have considered in distinguishing a sale from an equity contribution are (1) the capital and credit structure of the corporation, (2) the extent of risk borne by the noteholders, (3) the extent of control of the noteholders over business operations, (4) whether the "price" of the property was proportionate to its fair market value, and (5) whether payments on notes were subordinated to other creditors and dividends.[118]

ADDITIONAL CONTRIBUTIONS TO CAPITAL

Shareholder Level Issues

a) Nonrecognition

So far, this chapter has focused upon the initial formation of a corporation. Neither §351 or §1032, by its terms, is limited to contributions upon the initial formation of the corporation. Subsequent transfers to a corporation also will qualify for shareholder nonrecognition treatment if they meet all of the §351 requirements. Most importantly, the person or persons transferring property to the corporation in return for stock must be in control of the corporation immediately after the exchange. This requirement is easily met if all members of the original transferor group again transfer property to the corporation. On the other hand, if one or more members of the initial transferor group subsequently contribute additional appreciated property for additional shares of stock and, immediately after the transfer, the subsequent contributors hold less than 80% control, the exchange will not qualify for §351 nonrecognition unless the subsequent contributions are part of an "integrated plan" under which a group of persons meeting the control test contributes additional property to the corporation.[119] Suppose

---

117. See, e.g., Burr Oaks Corp. v. Comm'r, 43 T.C. 635 (1965), aff'd, 365 F.2d 24 (7th Cir. 1966), cert. denied, 385 U.S. 1007 (1967) (promissory notes received by the taxpayers in return for property treated as preferred stock for §351 purposes).
118. For more discussion of the distinction between debt and equity investments, see Chapter 3.
119. Given that the contribution does not qualify for §351 nonrecognition, the §358 basis rules also will not apply. Therefore, the contributing shareholder's basis in the stock received will be a cost basis. In this case, the cost would include both the actual cost of the property contributed (the shareholder's basis) plus "tax cost" incurred from the taxable contribution. In other words, the shareholder's basis in the new shares should be equal to the fair market value of the property contributed.

that, aware of this lurking problem, the subsequent contributors convinced enough other shareholders to make nominal contributions so that the group of contributing shareholders now had control immediately after the exchanges? Although the combined contributions might literally satisfy all of the requirements of §351, the Treasury Regulations provide that stock "issued for property which is of relatively small value in comparison to the value of the stock . . . Already owned . . . by the person who transferred such property, shall not be treated as having been issued in return for property if the primary purpose of the transfer is to qualify under this section the exchanges of property by other persons transferring property."[120] In other words, if the primary purpose of the nominal contributions of the other shareholders was to qualify the subsequent contributors or §351 nonrecognition treatment, the stock held by the nominal contributors will not be counted toward meeting the control test.[121] One question that comes to mind here is what constitutes property that is "of relatively small value in comparison to the value of stock already owned"? At what point are the contributions of the other shareholders substantial enough to be counted? The answer to this question is not entirely clear, but the Treasury Department has suggested in a Revenue Procedure that the transaction should be safe if the purchase represents 10% of the value already owned.[122]

Another question that may arise involves subsequent shareholder contributions for which the shareholder receives no additional shares of stock. Suppose, for example, that one of the original shareholders voluntarily contributes additional appreciated property to the corporation and gets nothing in return? The shareholder simply is making an additional contribution to capital. At least as to voluntary pro rata payments by shareholders, Treasury Regulations confirm this treatment, providing that such payments "are in the nature of assessments upon, and represent an additional price paid for, the shares of stock held by the individual shareholders."[123] In other words, if all shareholders contribute additional money or property in proportion to their stock interests, the contributions simply will be treated as additional price paid for the original shares. No taxable gain to the shareholders will result from contributions of appreciated property under such circumstances. The regulations do not speak as clearly to additional voluntary contributions that are not pro rata. It has generally been assumed that even voluntary non-pro rata contributions will not trigger taxable gain or

---

120. Treas. Reg. §1.351-1(a)(1)(ii) (emphasis added).
121. The validity of this regulation was tested and upheld in Kamborian v. Comm'r, 56 T.C. 847 (1971), aff'd, 469 F.2d 219 (1st Cir. 1972).
122. Rev. Proc. 77-37, 1977-2 C.B. 568 (stating requirements for purpose of receiving an advance letter ruling).
123. Treas. Reg. §1.118-1.

loss to the contributing shareholders.[124] Further support for this view is provided by the Supreme Court's opinion in Commissioner v. Fink.[125] In order to increase the attractiveness of the corporation to outside investors, the controlling shareholders in Fink voluntarily surrendered a non-pro rata portion of their shares, receiving no consideration in return. The Supreme Court disallowed the shareholders' ordinary loss deduction, holding that the stock surrender effectively was a contribution to capital or additional cost of stock.[126]

b) Basis

When a shareholder makes a subsequent contribution to the corporation that qualifies for §351 nonrecognition, basis in the new shares is determined under the "exchanged" basis rules of §358. If the contribution does not qualify for nonrecognition, the shareholder will receive a cost basis in the new shares. If no new shares are received for the subsequent contribution, the contribution to capital regulations discussed above simply view the contribution as an additional price paid for the stock.[127] Thus, in the simple case where a shareholder makes a cash contribution to capital, the shareholder's basis in his existing shares of stock is increased by the amount of money contributed. Upon a subsequent contribution of appreciated property, however, the question is whether the existing stock's basis should be increased by the basis of the property contributed or by the fair market value. If the difference between basis and fair market value does not result in taxable gain or loss, as assumed above, the original stock basis should be increased by the basis of the property contributed.[128] This approach applies an "exchanged basis" principle consistent with §358. An increase to the original stock basis, reflecting the fair market value of contributed property, should be permitted only in cases where the gain or loss was recognized to the shareholder upon the subsequent contribution.

Corporate Level Issues

Under §1032, a corporation issuing its own stock in return for money or other property has no taxable gain. Money or other property received by the corporation without issuing stock also will not be taxed according to

---

124. Boris I. Bittker and James S. Eustice, Federal Income Taxation of Corporations and Shareholders ¶3.13 (7th ed. 2015).

125. 483 U.S. 89 (1987).

126. Id. At 99-100. The basis in the surrendered shares was reallocated among the shares retained.

127. Treas. Reg. §1.118-1.

128. This approach is confirmed by dicta in Comm'r v. Fink, 483 U.S. 89, 94 (1987).

§118(a), which simply provides that "[i]n the case of a corporation, gross income does not include any contribution to the capital of the taxpayer." This general provision covers even non-shareholder contributions to capital. The §118 capital contribution exclusion does not apply, however, to "any contribution in aid of construction or any other contribution as a customer or potential customer."[129] Apparently, the focus of this "contribution in aid" exception is contributions to public utilities by transferors who stand to directly benefit from the contribution.[130] Contributions from such "direct beneficiaries" generally are not considered contributions to capital.[131] The §118 capital contribution exclusion also does not apply to "any contribution by any governmental entity or civic group (other than a contribution made by a shareholder as such)."[132]

The §362 "transferred basis" rules explicitly apply not only to §351 contributions, but also to property acquired "as paid-in surplus or as a contribution to capital."[133] Thus, the corporation's basis in property received as a contribution to capital generally is the same basis as in the hands of the transferor.[134] If the contribution to capital comes from a non-shareholder, however, the basis in property other than money will be zero.[135]

EFFECT OF LIABILITIES: §357 AND RELATED MATTERS

The General Rule: §357(a): Contributions with Liabilities

Sole proprietors, partners, and other noncorporate business entities may choose to incorporate after operating for a time in the noncorporate setting. As part of the incorporation transaction, it is quite common for the newly formed corporation to assume liabilities of the old business. In addition, contributions of property to the corporation may be subject to an outstanding mortgage or the corporation may assume the mortgage on the property.

For example, suppose that shareholder A purchased real estate for $20,000, paying $10,000 down and incurring a $10,000 mortgage for the remainder of the purchase price. After the property has appreciated to a fair market value of $200,000, but before making any payments on the mortgage, shareholder A transfers the property to the corporation in return

---

129. I.R.C. §118(b)(1).
130. H.R. Rep. No. 426, 99th Cong., 1st Sess. 644 (1985).
131. One exception is for certain qualifying contributions to water and sewerage disposal utilities. I.R.C. §118(c).
132. I.R.C. §118(b)(2).
133. I.R.C. §362(a)(2).
134. But see Treas. Reg. §1.1032-3, discussed at the end of this chapter.
135. I.R.C. §362(c).

for 100% of the common stock plus the corporation's assumption of the $10,000 mortgage. In this example, the net value of shareholder A's contribution to the corporation is $190,000. In return for her contribution shareholder A receives $190,000 worth of stock and is relieved of a $10,000 liability. Her *realized* gain is $180,000.[136] Under the basic §351 rules, shareholder A should be eligible for nonrecognition except that gain, if any, will be recognized to the extent of the boot. The tax issue here is whether or not relief from liability is considered boot, requiring shareholder A to report a $10,000 "boot gain."

Early in corporate tax history, the Supreme Court held in United States v. Hendler that the corporation's assumption of liabilities in a nonrecognition transaction was the equivalent of the receipt of boot by the shareholder.[137] As a result, many incorporators were required to report "boot gain" where liabilities were transferred to the corporation in an incorporation exchange. Shortly thereafter, Congress legislatively overruled *Hendler*. Today, the general rule of §357(a) provides that if another party assumes a liability of the transferor as part of the consideration in a §351 exchange, the assumption shall not be treated as boot and shall not prevent the exchange from being within §351.[138] Thus, the corporation's assumption of shareholder A's $10,000 mortgage in the above hypothetical is not considered boot.

The next question in a §351 exchange involving liabilities is the shareholder's basis in shares received upon the exchange. Recall that under §358(a), the shareholder's basis in stock received in the §351 transfer is an "exchanged basis" from the property contributed, reduced by the amount of money received and increased by the amount of gain recognized. Even though the assumption of liability is *not* considered money received under the general rule of §357(a), §358 provides that the assumption "shall, *for purposes of this section*, be treated as money received by the taxpayer on the exchange."[139] In other words, the corporation's assumption of the transferor's liability is *not* considered boot in applying the basic §351 nonrecognition rule, but it *is* considered boot for purposes of computing the shareholder's stock basis. This dichotomy can best be understood by focusing on the value received by the shareholder upon a contribution of liabilities in an

---

136. Amount realized ($200,000) less adjusted basis ($20,000). The amount realized from a disposition must include the fair market value of property received plus any liabilities assumed. Crane v. Comm'r, 331 U.S. 1 (1947); Comm'r v. Tufts, 461 U.S. 300 (1983). The taxpayer's original cost basis in this situation is $20,000, including the $10,000 down payment plus the $10,000 borrowed cost.

137. 303 U.S. 564 (1938).

138. I.R.C. §357(a). Originally, §357 was not limited to the *assumption* of liability, but also included a reference to another party acquiring property from the transferor *subject to* a liability. Congress amended §357 in 1999, eliminating references to transfers subject to liabilities. These changes will be discussed in detail later in this chapter.

139. I.R.C. §358(d)(1) (emphasis added).

incorporation transaction. The contributing shareholder gains from the corporate transaction to the extent that he or she is relieved of a liability. This gain is analogous to "discharge of indebtedness" income. In §357(a), Congress simply provides temporary relief from taxation on this gain. At the same time, the §358 basis rules attempt to preserve this "discharge of indebtedness type" gain for later taxation by treating the liability as money received for purposes of computing *basis*, reducing the shareholder's stock basis by the amount of the liability.

Shareholder A in our example received $190,000 worth of stock and $10,000 worth of relief from liability, totaling $200,000. Her total *realized* gain was $180,000. Since §358 now requires a decrease in basis for the liability assumed, shareholder A will reduce her exchanged basis of $20,000 from the real estate by the $10,000 liability, resulting in a stock basis of $10,000.[140] If she later sells her stock for $190,000, her taxable gain will be $180,000—precisely the amount of gain deferred in the §351 transaction. Failure to reduce her basis by the $10,000 liability would result in a taxable gain of only $170,000 on the later sale, thus permitting her to permanently escape taxation on her earlier "discharge of indebtedness type" income.

The Tax Avoidance Purpose Exception: §357(b)

An assumption of liability will be considered boot if the principal purpose of the taxpayer was to avoid federal income tax on the exchange or was not a bona fide business purpose. When might this be the case? Suppose that shareholder A from the earlier example had purchased the real estate for $20,000 cash many years ago. After the property had appreciated to $200,000, but before incorporating, A pledged the real estate as collateral for a $10,000 bank loan, using the borrowed funds to take a personal vacation. If A later transfers the property along with the liability to the corporation in return for $190,000 worth of stock, the assumption of liability arguably is for a tax avoidance purpose or, at least, is not for a bona fide business purpose. Shareholder A has effectively "cashed out" $10,000 from corporate solution, using the funds for personal reasons. In such a case, shareholder A would be required under §357(b) to treat the $10,000 as money (boot) received in the exchange and would be required to report a $10,000 "boot gain." Under §358, the exchanged basis of $20,000 from the real estate would be first reduced by the $10,000 liability and then increased by the $10,000 gain recognized, leaving shareholder A's stock basis at $20,000. If she were later to sell her shares for $190,000, the taxable gain would be only $170,000. Since she already would have been taxed on $10,000 of the

---

140. I.R.C. §358(a), (d)(1).

$180,000 realized gain at the time of the initial incorporation, this application of the §358 basis adjustments provides a sensible result.

A colorful case illustrates an especially egregious §357(b) tax avoidance transaction. The transaction was designed by Burton Kanter, a well-known Chicago tax and estate lawyer who "hobnobbed with the Pritzkers [of Hyatt Corporation fame] and Hollywood producers and who participated in countless extremely large and lucrative business ventures" yet reported negative adjusted gross income on all his tax returns from 1979 to 1989 and paid no federal income taxes.[141] A developer was interested in acquiring real estate interests owned by various Kanter family grantor trusts. The assets' liabilities exceeded their bases, and a straight sale would have triggered significant taxable gain.[142] In a series of transactions, Kanter caused the trusts to transfer their real estate interests to a Kanter-controlled inactive shell corporation in a §351 transaction. Almost immediately after the §351 exchange, the trusts sold the stock received in the exchange to another Kanter-controlled entity in return for installment notes. This entity, in turn, transferred the stock to the purchasing developer, who promptly liquidated the corporation, thus acquiring direct ownership of the real estate interests. The court had little trouble finding that the only purpose of this convoluted transaction structure was to sell real estate interests and to avoid federal income tax on the sale.[143] Thus, despite the general rule of §357(a), the assumption of liabilities in the initial §351 transaction triggered taxable boot gain under §357(b).

Liabilities in Excess of Basis: §357(c) General Rule

The second exception to the general rule of §357(a) is invoked simply when liabilities assumed exceed the shareholder's basis in the property transferred. Going back to the example above, suppose that shareholder A's contribution to the corporation was depreciable business machinery that she purchased for $20,000 and was worth $200,000 at the time of contribution. As in the original example, the purchase price was paid with $10,000 in cash and $10,000 was acquisition debt secured by the machinery. Now imagine

---

141. Estate of Kanter v. Comm'r, 337 F.3d 833, 838 (7th Cir. 2003); rev'd and remanded sub nom., Ballard v. Comm'r, 544 U.S. 40 (2005) (reversal based on procedural issues). In an opinion of over 400 pages, only a very small portion of which was devoted to the §357 liabilities issues, the Tax Court affirmed the §357(b) ruling against the taxpayer. Estate of Burton W. Kanter, T.C. Memo 2007-21 (Feb. 1, 2007). This opinion in turn was reversed and remanded on other grounds. Ballard v. Comm'r, 522 F.3d 1229 (11th Cir. 2008).

142. Under §1001, the full amount of liabilities assumed upon the sale of property must be included in amount realized regardless of the fair market value of the property. Treas. Reg. §1.1001-2(a)(1), (b). Comm'r v. Tufts, 461 U.S. 300 (1983).

143. 337 F.3d at 864.

that the shareholder took $15,000 in depreciation deductions with respect to the machinery before contributing the machinery to the corporation, thus reducing her basis in the building to $5,000.[144] Upon contribution, the corporation assumes the $10,000 liability. Although the assumption of liability *ordinarily* will not be considered boot under the general rule of §357(a), §357(c) requires treating the excess of liabilities assumed over the total adjusted basis of the property transferred as "gain from the sale or exchange of a capital asset or of property which is not a capital asset, as the case may be." Under this provision, shareholder A would report a taxable gain of $5,000 — the excess of the $10,000 liability assumed by the corporation over the $5,000 basis of the machinery at the time of contribution.[145] Under §358, shareholder A's basis in the stock would be an exchanged basis from the machinery ($5,000) decreased by the $10,000 liability assumed,[146] and increased by the $5,000 gain recognized.[147] After these adjustments, shareholder A's stock basis will be zero.[148]

To better understand the logic of §357(c), recall that the general rule in §357(a) gives shareholders the benefit of nonrecognition even though gain was technically realized from the corporation's assumption of liabilities. In most cases, the §358 basis rules will be sufficient to defer this "discharge of indebtedness type" income for taxation upon the later sale or disposition of the shares. If the shareholder's basis is reduced by the full amount of the liability, subsequent gain from sale or disposition of the stock will include an additional amount reflecting the previously realized, but unrecognized, gain. Problems arise, however, when the liability is *greater* than the shareholder's basis in the property. Returning to our hypothetical, recall that shareholder A had a *realized* gain of $195,000 on the §351 exchange.[149]

---

144. I.R.C. §1016(a)(2) requires a downward adjustment to basis for depreciation on the theory that the depreciation is an advance recovery of the taxpayer's capital or investment. The original $20,000 cost basis was thus reduced by the $15,000 in depreciation previously deducted.

145. Note that the property in this example is likely to be §1245 "recapture" property. I.R.C. §1245(a)(3). Under §1245(a), gain from the exchange would be ordinary income. Although §1245 generally applies notwithstanding other provisions, §1245(a), Congress provided an exception for certain tax-free exchanges, including §351. Under this exception, the §1245(a) gain shall not exceed the gain that would have been taken into account absent §1245. I.R.C. §1245(b)(3). In other words, shareholder A will report only the $5,000 taxable gain under §357(c). This gain will be treated as ordinary income under §1245(a).

146. I.R.C. §358(d)(1).

147. I.R.C. §358(a)(1)(B)(ii). Under §362(a), the corporation's basis in the property would be a substituted basis of $5,000 from the property transferred increased by the $5,000 gain recognized to shareholder A on the exchange, totaling $10,000.

148. Exchanged basis ($5,000) less liability ($10,000) plus gain recognized ($5,000).

149. Her $200,000 amount realized includes the fair market value of the stock ($190,000) plus the relief from liability ($10,000). Subtracting her basis of $5,000 leaves a gain of $195,000. Note that her realized gain in this example is $15,000 higher than in previous examples. In effect, this additional gain is a recapture of the $15,000 taken in prior depreciation deductions.

Absent the §357(c) exception, shareholder A in our example would be subject to the general rule in §357(a) and would report no gain upon transferring the building to the corporation along with the corresponding mortgage. Under §358, the stock basis would be the exchanged basis of $5,000 from the building reduced by the liability of $10,000, resulting in a basis of—5,000—a *negative* basis. At least in theory, shareholder A could be left with a negative basis in the shares.[150] Upon later sale of the stock for $190,000, the shareholder simply would report a $195,000 taxable gain.[151]

Despite this theoretical possibility, Congress, the Treasury Department, and most courts remain unwilling to embrace the notion of a negative basis.[152] Recognizing this "hang-up" over negative basis helps to explain the need for §357(c). Without negative basis, the §358 basis rules cannot preserve all of A's discharge of indebtedness type gain for later taxation. Since her basis in the building is only $5,000, but her relief from liability is $10,000, the best that can be achieved is a reduction in basis to zero, thus preserving only part of the realized, but unrecognized, gain from the corporation's assumption of liabilities. The legislative solution to this dilemma adopted by §357(c) is to force shareholder A to recognize $5,000 of the realized gain (the excess of liabilities over basis) at the time of her transfer to the corporation. Now we need not be concerned that her basis in the stock will be zero and that her gain on subsequent sale of the shares for $190,000 will be limited to $190,000. The other $5,000 in gain was already taxed at the time of the incorporation transfer, for a total taxable gain of the proper $195,000.

Comparison of §357(b) and (c)

When the liability assumed exceeds the basis of property transferred, §357(c) provides for recognition only of the excess at the time of the transfer. In contrast, if §357(b) applies, the entire assumption of liability is treated as boot. Thus, if shareholder A contributed property with a basis of $5,000 subject to a mortgage of $10,000, the §357(b) exception would result in a $10,000 gain whereas the §357(c) exception would result in only a $5,000 gain at the time of incorporation. In cases involving tax avoidance or lack

---

150. For a discussion of the theoretical possibilities, see George Cooper, Negative Basis, 75 Harv. L. Rev. 1352 (1962); J. Clifton Fleming, Jr., The Highly Unavoidable Section 357(c): A Case Study in Traps for the Unwary and Some Positive Thoughts About Negative Basis, 16 J. Corp. L. 1 (1990). See also Judge Kozinski's colorful discussion of negative basis in Peracchi v. Comm'r, 143 F.3d 487, 491 (9th Cir. 1998) ("But skeptics say that negative basis, like Bigfoot, doesn't exist.").

151. Amount realized ($190,000) less adjusted basis (−$5,000).

152. But see Easson v. Comm'r, 294 F.2d 653 (9th Cir. 1961); Parker v. Delaney, 186 F.2d 455 (1st Cir. 1950) (concurring opinion of Judge Magruder), cert. denied, 341 U.S. 926 (1951).

of bona fide business purpose, Congress imposes the harsher provision, requiring that the *entire* assumption of liability be considered boot. In other cases, Congress imposes tax only to the extent necessary to avoid the sticky negative basis problem and, at the same time, to assure that the entire realized gain at the time of the transfer is deferred through use of the substituted basis provisions in §358. In situations where both exceptions apply to the transaction, the harsher rule of §357(b) will prevail.[153]

Special Rules Applicable to Accounts Payable: §357(c)(3)

a) Regular Accounts Payable and Receivable

As described earlier in the chapter, when a business previously operated as a pass-through later incorporates, the newly formed corporation may collect the accounts receivable from prior business operations. Similarly, the new corporation may also assume the business accounts payable for goods and services purchased prior to incorporation. To treat accounts payable as liabilities for purposes of §357(c) would create hardships for some taxpayers. To illustrate, suppose that shareholder B decides to incorporate his business, transferring assets with a basis of $50,000 and a fair market value of $150,000 to a new solely owned corporation. Shareholder B also transfers $200,000 in accounts receivable and has the new corporation assume business accounts payable totaling $200,000.[154] Assume further that B's business was using the cash basis method of accounting. If the accounts payable were considered liabilities for purposes of §357(c), shareholder B would have a $150,000 gain—the excess of the $200,000 in liabilities over the $50,000 basis in the property contributed. If shareholder B had paid the accounts before incorporating, he could have taken a business expense deduction. As a cash basis taxpayer, however, he cannot take business deductions for payables that have not yet been paid, nor will transfer of the accounts payable to the corporation trigger a business deduction for shareholder B. Absent some statutory relief, the taxpayer in this case would have §357(c) gain resulting from the corporation's assumption of the accounts payable, but no offsetting deduction for the business expense.

Responding to this hardship, Congress added §357(c)(3)(A), which provides that liabilities that would give rise to a deduction will not be considered liabilities for purposes of §357(c)(1). Thus, in the above example, shareholder B would not take any business deductions for the $200,000 in accounts payable not yet paid, the payables would not be counted as

---

153. Treas. Reg. §1.357-2(a).
154. Assume that these payables included salaries due employees and other payables for which a business expense deduction would be available.

liabilities, and shareholder B would have no gain or loss from the incorporation transaction.[155] Assuming a business purpose for the transfer of accounts receivable, the corporation — and not shareholder B — will be taxed on the receivables as they are collected, and the corporation now will be entitled to deduct its payments on the accounts payable.[156]

Notice that the hardship to which Congress responded with §357(c)(3) generally is not a concern with accrual basis taxpayers. If shareholder B's business had used the accrual method of accounting, the accounts receivable already would have been taxed when they first accrued. Thus, as an accrual basis taxpayer, shareholder B would have a $200,000 basis in the accounts receivable. Adding this to the $50,000 basis from the other assets, his overall basis of $250,000 in the assets transferred would exceed the assumed liabilities of $200,000. As an accrual basis taxpayer, he may well have already deducted the accounts payable as well. In any event, he would no longer have to worry about §357(c) gain.

b) Exceptions to the Exception: §357(c)(3)(B)

i) Liabilities That Create or Increase Basis

To be clear that the §357(c)(3)(A) exception applies only to liabilities that would give rise to a deduction, Congress added an "exception to the exception" in §357(c)(3)(B), which provides that the (c)(3)(A) exception does not extend to any liabilities that result "in the creation of, or an increase in, the basis of any property." So, for example, payables incurred in connection with the purchase of, and reflected in the basis of, depreciable property will not be protected by the §357(c)(3) exception. If incurrence of a liability has created or increased basis, the hardship addressed in §357(c)(3) is not present. In such cases, the effective right to a deduction or basis offset for the business expense that gave rise to the liability is not lost, but is preserved in the corporation's hands through a substituted basis. Such liabilities are ineligible for the (c)(3)(A) exception. Thus, they will be treated as liabilities for computing any potential §357(c) gain, and the transferring shareholders will be required under §358(d)(1) to reduce their stock basis by the liabilities.

ii) Contingent Liabilities

One circumstance seems to have slipped through the cracks between §357(c)(3)(A) and (B), however. Even an accrual basis taxpayer may have

---

155. The assumption of such accounts payable will not cause a reduction in the contributing shareholder's basis under §358 either. I.R.C. §358(d)(2).
156. See Rev. Rul. 80-198, 1980-2 C.B. 113. See earlier discussion in this chapter on assignment of income.

contingent liabilities that do not necessarily "give rise to a deduction" under §357(c)(3)(A), nor have they yet created a basis under §357(c)(3)(B). The Treasury Department addressed just such a case involving a transfer of contingent environmental liabilities for potential soil and ground water remediation as part of a §351 exchange.[157] The Service concluded that although §357(c)(3)(A) explicitly addressed liabilities that gave rise to deductions, the same principles applied to contingent liabilities that "had neither given rise to deductions ... nor resulted in the creation of or increase in basis in any property."[158] The corporate transferor had not yet taken any deduction with respect to the contingent liabilities, nor had the liabilities resulted in the creation of basis. The Service determined that such liabilities should not be counted in determining whether liabilities exceed basis pursuant to §357(c) and that such contingent liabilities should not reduce the shareholder's basis under §358(d).

Aggressive tax planners quickly took advantage of Rev. Rul. 95-74 on contingent liabilities to develop and market a popular tax shelter transaction. The contingent liability tax shelter story offers yet another illustration of the now familiar dynamic of creative taxpayer transaction, followed by narrowly focused government response to close the loophole, followed by yet more creative transactions. The basic idea was to use the §351 contribution of cash along with substantial contingent liabilities to create a high-basis, low-value stock, which the corporation could sell at a substantial tax loss. In one of the most familiar contingent liability cases, the Black & Decker corporation (B&D) transferred $561 million in cash plus $560 million in contingent employee health claims for all of the stock of a newly formed subsidiary in a §351 exchange.[159] Given the $560 million in assumed liabilities, the *net value* of B&D's contribution and, hence, the value of the subsidiary stock was only $1 million. Shortly thereafter, B&D sold the subsidiary stock for $1 million, claiming a $560 million loss, which it then used to offset significant capital gains from other transactions.

The key to this tax shelter's success was classification of the contingent liabilities as eligible for the §357(c)(3) exception. Relying on Rev. Rul. 95-74, B&D claimed that the assumed contingent liabilities were of the type that eventually would give rise to deductions and, as such, should not be counted as liabilities for §357(c) purposes. More significant for purposes of the tax shelter, B&D made the corollary claim under §358(d)(2) that it was not required to reduce its $561 million basis in the subsidiary stock by the amount of contingent liabilities.[160]

---

157. Rev. Rul. 95-74, 1995-2 C.B. 36.
158. Id. At 37.
159. B&D had borrowed the $561 million in cash on a short-term basis from a third-party lender. Shortly after transferring it to the subsidiary, B&D "borrowed" the same cash back from its own subsidiary in order to pay off the short-term loan.
160. The lower court denied the government's motion for summary judgment based upon a statutory analysis of §§357(c)(3) and 358(d). Black & Decker Corp. v. United States, 340

4. Incorporation and Other Contributions to Capital

To combat the B&D-style transaction, Congress added a new provision in §358(h) governing liability transfers to a corporation when the transferring shareholder is not required to reduce basis in the stock received under §358(d)(1).[161] In an effective statutory override of §358(d)(1) for such cases, §358(h) mandates a reduction in the transferor's stock basis by the amount of the liability, but not below fair market value.[162] If this provision had applied at the time, B&D's basis in the subsidiary stock would have been limited to $1 million, thus depriving B&D of its tax advantage.

Congress included an exception to the §358(h)(1) basis limitations, however, in §358(h)(2) for transactions in which the trade or business or substantially all of the assets with which the liability is associated are simultaneously transferred to the corporation assuming the liability. Congress also explicitly gave the Treasury secretary unusual authority to create regulatory exceptions. On their face, the §358(h)(2) exceptions suggest that taxpayers still can transfer contingent liabilities without being required to reduce the stock basis under §358(d)(1) as long as they simultaneously transfer the underlying assets giving rise to the liability.

The Internal Revenue Service, however, continues to take an aggressive position against contingent liability tax shelters, even those that technically fit within the statutory language.[163] In a 2006 case, Coltec Industries transferred a third-party note and contingent asbestos liability claims along with the assets that gave rise to the asbestos claims in exchange for subsidiary stock. Although both the lower and appellate courts ruled in the taxpayer's favor based upon statutory interpretation, the Federal Circuit on appeal denied the taxpayer's loss, agreeing with the government that the transaction had no economic substance.[164] The Treasury Department also used its

---

F. Supp. 2d 621 (D. Md. 2004). The Fourth Circuit affirmed the lower courts statutory interpretation in favor of the taxpayer, but remanded for trial on the government's alternative argument that the tax shelter transaction had no economic substance. Black & Decker Corp. v. United States, 436 F.3d 431 (4th Cir. 2006). The case eventually settled without a trial on the economic substance question.

161. Community Renewal Tax Relief Act of 2000, Pub. L. No. 106-554, tit. VIII, §836(a), 118 Stat. 1418, 1594-95 (codified at I.R.C. §358(h)).

162. I.R.C. §358(h)(1). For purposes of this provision, liability is defined to include "any fixed or contingent obligation to make payment, without regard to whether the obligation is otherwise taken into account for purposes of this title." I.R.C. §358(h)(3).

163. See, e.g., Notice 2001-17, 2001-1 C.B. 730, in which the Service warned that it planned to attack these shelters using a number of different arguments and designated the transaction as a "listed transaction" (subject to reportable transaction disclosure and penalty rules). The many tools at the IRS's disposal now include §358(h), as well as §§269, 357(b), and 362(e), along with common law-type business purpose, tax avoidance, and economic substance doctrines. The economic substance doctrine is codified at §7701(o).

164. Coltec Indus. Inc. v. United States, 454 F.3d 1340 (Fed. Cir. 2006), *cert. denied*, 549 U.S. 1206 (2007). The tax years at issue in *Coltec* technically were not governed by the §358(h) rules, but it appears likely that the case would have been decided in the same way even under §358(h).

statutory authority effectively to eliminate the (h)(2) exception for corporations that transfer substantially all of the assets with which the liability is associated, reasoning that "making the exception of section 358(h)(2)(B) unavailable is necessary to prevent abuse."[165]

Avoiding the §357(c) "Trap"

A contributing shareholder faced with the possibility of a §357(c) gain may wish to avoid tax upon the excess of liabilities over basis in one of two basic ways: (1) decrease the liabilities assumed by the corporation, or (2) increase the basis of assets transferred. The most direct and obvious way to achieve either of these results, however, requires the commitment of additional resources. Surely, the contributing shareholder may pay off some or all of the liabilities prior to transferring assets to the corporation. In the alternative, the contributing shareholder may invest additional resources in the corporation, thus increasing the basis of property transferred. For example, the shareholder might simply increase the basis of the assets transferred to the corporation by contributing additional cash to cover the difference between the liabilities assumed and the basis in the property contributed.[166] Shareholders unwilling or unable to invest additional resources of their own might first borrow the necessary cash from a third-party lender and then transfer the cash to the corporation along with the other property subject to liabilities.[167] This option not only avoids §357(c) by increasing the basis in the assets transferred, but also may produce interest deductions on the borrowing.

Another approach recently attempted by several taxpayers is for the contributing shareholder to issue a promissory note to the corporation covering the difference between liabilities assumed and basis of the transferred assets. This option is not very different from borrowing cash and then contributing the cash to the corporation. The shareholder simply is borrowing from the corporation itself rather than a third-party lender. As long as the shareholder's promissory note is a bona fide debt to the corporation, the source of the borrowing arguably should not alter the outcome. In each case, the shareholder is making a contribution with borrowed funds. The economic effect of the transactions is the same. The problem with this approach is that the statute itself does not support it. Based upon the traditional tax wisdom that the maker does not have a basis in his own note, the Internal Revenue

---

165. See T.D. 9397, 73 Fed. Reg. 26321 (May 9, 2008), promulgating finalized regulations in Treas. Reg. §1.358-5.

166. For purposes of §357(c), cash contributed is treated as having a basis equal to the cash amount.

167. See, e.g., Edwards v. Comm'r, 19 T.C. 275 (1952), acq. 1953-1 C.B. 4.

Service has taken the position that contribution of the shareholder's own note does not increase the basis of the assets transferred and, thus, is ineffective in avoiding §357(c) gain.[168]

Until the late 1990s, most courts addressing the issue had agreed with the Service.[169] Two controversial opinions then reached a different result, however. In a case before the Second Circuit, Lessinger v. Commissioner, the taxpayer incorporated a business previously operated as a sole proprietorship. The liabilities transferred exceeded the basis of the property transferred by approximately $250,000, resulting in a potential §357(c) gain. In fact, the liabilities transferred exceeded even the fair market value of the assets transferred. In other words, the business had a negative net worth at the time of incorporation.[170]

In addition to the other assets and liabilities transferred, Mr. Lessinger undertook an obligation to the corporation for the $250,000 difference between liabilities and basis.[171] Mr. Lessinger argued that his obligation was additional "property" transferred to the corporation in return for stock and that this additional property had a basis equal to the $250,000 face value of the note. The effect of including this additional basis in the overall basis of the assets transferred was to eliminate the §357(c) gain, since the liabilities assumed no longer exceeded the basis of the assets transferred.

The obvious problem with this logic is that a taxpayer ordinarily has no basis in his *own* obligation to pay. Even if the obligation is considered "property" for purposes of §351, transfer of the obligation does not alter the §357(c) computation if the obligation has a zero basis. The Second Circuit in *Lessinger* conceded that the note had a zero basis in Mr. Lessinger's hands. On the other hand, the court found that the note in the *corporation's* hands had a basis equal to its face amount.[172] Moreover, the Second Circuit concluded that, at least in the situation presented, §357(c)'s reference to liability in excess of basis is a reference to the *transferee corporation's* basis in the obligation.[173] The combined effect of these two unusual holdings was that Mr. Lessinger's obligation was found to be effective in increasing the basis

---

168. See, e.g., Rev. Rul. 68-629, 1968-2 C.B. 154.
169. See, e.g., Alderman v. Comm'r, 55 T.C. 662 (1971).
170. Lessinger v. Comm'r, 872 F.2d 519 (2d Cir. 1989).
171. The original obligation was not in the form of a promissory note and both the shareholder's and the corporation's record keeping were somewhat sloppy. The shareholder later executed a promissory note for the debt. Despite the initial informalities and the failure to pay interest on the note, the court concluded that the obligation was a real debt. Id. At 524.
172. The court stated that "the corporation should have a basis in its obligation from Lessinger, because it incurred a cost in the transaction involving the transfer of the obligation by taking on the liabilities of the proprietorship that exceeded its assets, and because it would have to recognize income upon Lessinger's payment of the debt if it had no basis in the obligation." 872 F.2d at 525.
173. Id. At 526.

of the assets transferred for purposes of §357(c), thus eliminating any gain from the excess of liabilities over the basis of the transferred property.

It is easy to understand the court's sympathy for Mr. Lessinger. In an economic sense, he did not realize any gain from incorporating a sole proprietorship with a negative net worth. Moreover, Mr. Lessinger could have avoided §357(c) gain by borrowing cash from a third party and then contributing the cash. The only difference between the cash and the note transactions is that in the latter case, the taxpayer is borrowing from the corporation rather than a third party.[174] Finally, the court did not see this as a case of deliberate tax evasion. In fact, Mr. Lessinger incorporated his business only when his lender refused to provide additional working capital to him as a sole proprietor because state usury laws allowed the lender to charge higher interest rates to corporations. The court noted that if the government had prevailed in the case, it would be "the factor's demand for higher interest [that] led Lessinger into a §351 'trap.'"[175]

While most commentators seem to agree that the result in Lessinger is sensible from a policy point of view, they have been critical of the opinion.[176] Providing the corporation with a face value basis in the transferring shareholder's note is inconsistent with §362's requirement that the corporation's basis in a §351 transaction be the same as that of the transferring shareholder.[177] Moreover, §357(c)'s reference to the excess of liabilities over the "adjusted basis of the property transferred" is virtually always interpreted to mean the adjusted basis in the transferring shareholder's (not in the corporation's) hands.[178]

Despite its loss in the Second Circuit, the government continued to litigate vigorously, presumably hoping to create a split among the circuits and take the issue to the Supreme Court. Much to everyone's surprise, these

---

174. The court explicitly noted the similarity of the two transactions and expressed its fear that a contrary ruling would create a "trap for the unwary." Id. At 528.

175. Id. At 523, n.1.

176. See, e.g., Fleming, supra note 151; Michael Megaard and Susan Megaard, Can Shareholder's Note Avoid Gain on Transfer of Excess Liabilities?, 71 J. Tax'n 244 (1989); Louis S. Nunes, Comment, Taking Section 357(c) Out of the Scheme of Things: Has the Second Circuit Stranded This Section of the Internal Revenue Code?, 65 Tul. L. Rev. 663 (1991). Contra Kenneth Brewer, The Zero Basis Hoax, 63 Tax Notes 457 (1994).

177. To get around §362, the court simply says in a footnote that §362 "cannot be applied to the corporation's valuation of its receivable from the taxpayer" because the purpose of §362 was to prevent the corporation from getting a new, stepped-up basis for depreciation purposes. 872 F.2d at 525, n.4.

178. Treas. Reg. §1.357-2(a). The court responds by noting that in most cases, the corporation takes its basis from the shareholder under §362. Here, however, the court concludes that §362 does not apply to the note. "Consideration of 'adjusted basis' in section 357(c) . . . normally does not require determining whether the section refers to the 'adjusted basis' in the hands of the transferor-shareholder or the transferee-corporation, because the basis does not change." 872 F.2d at 526.

efforts backfired when the Ninth Circuit issued its decision in Peracchi v. Commissioner.[179]

In response to a demand for additional capital to meet state minimum premium-to-asset ratios for his closely held corporation, Mr. Peracchi contributed real estate encumbered by liabilities in excess of his basis in the property. In an attempt to avoid the §357(c) trap, Peracchi also contributed his own unsecured personal promissory note to the corporation, arguing, as Mr. Lessinger had, that the note had a basis equal to its face amount.

The Ninth Circuit shared the *Lessinger* court's concern that the §357(c) trap could have been avoided through transactions that were economically equivalent to the contribution of a promissory note. For example, the court noted that "Peracchi could have borrowed $1 million from a bank and contributed cash to [the corporation] along with the properties. Because cash has a basis equal to face value, Peracchi would not have faced any section 357(c) gain."[180] On the other hand, the Ninth Circuit was unwilling to adopt the Second Circuit's twisted and unconventional interpretation of the statutory language in §§357(c) and 362. Instead, the court rejected the traditional tax wisdom regarding a taxpayer's basis in his or her own note, finding that Mr. Peracchi *did* have a basis in his personal promissory note contributed to the corporation. To reach this conclusion, the court reasoned that the corporation's creditors could enforce Peracchi's note in the event of the corporation's bankruptcy. Since the corporation was "an operating business which is subject to a non-trivial risk of bankruptcy or receivership,"[181] the court found that Peracchi had increased his exposure to risk and was entitled to "a step-up in basis to the extent he will be subjected to economic loss if the underlying investment turns unprofitable."[182] The court was careful, however, to limit its holding to cases where the note was worth approximately its face amount.[183]

Although the *Peracchi* opinion's reasoning is superficially more appealing than that of *Lessinger*, criticism of the opinion has been similarly severe.[184] Most significant, its finding that the taxpayer had a basis in his own note is

179. 143 F.3d 487 (9th Cir. 1998).
180. Id. At 493.
181. Id. At 493, n.14.
182. Id. At 493.
183. Since the taxpayer's net worth far exceeded the face value of the note, the court was prepared to conclude, in this case, that Peracchi's note was worth its face value. Id. At 493-494, n.15.
184. The opinion itself includes an unusually vigorous dissent. Id. At 497 ("Peracchi says a lot about economic realities. I see nothing real about that maneuver. I see, rather, a bit of sortilege that would have made Merlin envious. The taxpayer has created something—basis—out of nothing.") See also Richard M. Lipton and Joseph E. Bender, *Peracchi and Making Something Out of Nothing, or Does Debt Have a Zero Basis to Its Maker and Further Ruminations on the Substance and Form of Transactions*, 77 Taxes 13, 20 (1999) ("One of the interesting aspects of the Ninth Circuit's decision in *Peracchi* is its total disregard for authorities . . .").

contrary to well-established precedent. While the court was careful to limit its holding to the facts of the case before it, this holding could have serious implications far beyond the §357 context.

In a case decided after *Lessinger* and *Peracchi*, the taxpayers incorporated a business previously operated as a joint venture.[185] Liabilities of the transferred assets exceeded their basis, thus threatening the shareholders with §357(c) gain. Like Mr. Lessinger, they would not otherwise have incorporated, but did so only upon the insistence of secured creditors. Unlike Lessinger and Peracchi, however, the shareholders did not transfer a personal promissory note to the corporation to cover the excess liabilities. Instead, they remained liable by executing personal guarantees of the debt. The Seggermans argued that their personal guarantees were essentially equivalent to the promissory notes held to successfully avoid §357(c) gain in *Lessinger* and *Peracchi*. The court disagreed, finding that the personal guarantees differed from promissory notes in that the guarantees reflected a mere promise to pay in the future and did not constitute economic outlays.[186] In the alternative, the shareholders cited *Lessinger* and *Peracchi* as evidence of an "emerging equitable interpretation" and urged the court to use its equitable power to save them from §357(c) gain. While it recognized the harsh tax consequences for the Seggerman family, the court rejected this suggestion, stating that "it is the province of the legislative branch, rather than the judiciary, to safeguard the taxpayer from undue hardship . . . ,"[187]

Most agree that some solution to the §357(c) hardship is necessary, however. If shareholders can borrow cash from third parties to get around §357(c), they arguably should be able to borrow from the corporation as well. One proposed narrow solution would be to treat the shareholder in the Lessinger-type situation as having purchase-money debt owed to the corporation. Ordinarily, a buyer who borrows from the seller is deemed to first borrow cash from the seller and then to transfer the cash in exchange for the property. In this way, the buyer with purchase money debt has the same basis in the property that a buyer with a third-party mortgage would have. If the shareholder who transfers a personal note to the corporation is deemed first to have borrowed the cash and then to transfer the cash as part of the §351 exchange, the §357(c) trap is avoided without distorting the language of the statute.[188] A broader solution would be to repeal §357(c) altogether and simply have taxpayers reduce their basis in the stock by the full amount of liabilities *even* if this results in a negative basis.[189] In the meantime, the §357(d) definition of "assumption of liability" added to the Code

---

185. Seggerman Farms, Inc. v. Comm'r, 308 F.3d 803 (7th Cir. 2002).

186. Id. At 807.

187. Id. At 808.

188. J. Clifton Fleming, Jr., A Second Look at the Zero Basis Hoax, 64 Tax Notes 811 (1994).

189. See Fleming, *supra* note 151.

in 1999 provides some, albeit imperfect, relief.[190] The primary motivation for these changes was not the §357(c) hardship concern, however. Congress was instead focused on a particular abusive transaction involving the transfer of multiple assets secured by the same liability. These provisions and their potential impact are considered in a subsequent section in this chapter on multiple asset transfers.

What Constitutes Assumption of Liability?

a) Different Types of Liability

To better understand the meaning of §357(d) liabilities and when they are assumed for purposes of §357, one should first be familiar with two different terms often used to refer to liability that is secured by a lien on property. When property is merely subject to a *nonrecourse* mortgage, this generally means that the property transferred is subject to forfeiture, but the borrower is not otherwise personally liable for payment of the debt. On the other hand, when property is subject to a *recourse* mortgage, the property itself is subject to forfeiture *and* the borrower is also personally liable for nonpayment. In other words, the borrower's other assets may be required to satisfy the debt obligation.

Prior to 1999, §357 and related provisions generally referred to circumstances in which "another party assumes a liability of the transferor or acquires property from the transferor subject to a liability." As interpreted, this meant that the same tax treatment applied regardless of whether the mortgage attached to the property transferred was recourse or nonrecourse and regardless of any particular understanding between the parties as to who would actually pay the debt. Amendments to §357 deleted the references to property acquired subject to a liability.[191] Today, §357(a)(2) reads more simply, covering only the case where, "as part of the consideration, another party to the exchange *assumes a liability of the taxpayer.* . . ." At the same time, however, the §357 amendments added §357(d), which defines the extent to which liabilities shall be treated as having been assumed. As a result of this provision, "assumption of liability" has become a statutory term of art. Rest assured that any apparent simplification in §357(a) is outweighed by the potential complexities added by new §357(d).[192]

---

190. The 1999 amendments were not applicable to the facts in *Seggerman Farms* since the transactions at issue predated 1999.

191. Miscellaneous Trade and Technical Corrections Act of 1999, Pub. L. No. 106-36, 113 Stat. 127, §3001 (codified, as amended, at I.R.C. §357).

192. For a discussion of some of these complexities, see Karen C. Burke, Contributions, Distributions, and Assumption of Liabilities: Confronting Economic Reality, 56 Tax Law. 383 (2003); John A. Bogdanski, Section 357(d) — Old Can, New Worms, 27 J. Corp. Tax'n 17, 23 (2000).

When Congress added §357(d) in 1999, it simultaneously added a new subparagraph to the §362 rules regarding the corporation's basis in property received in a §351 exchange.[193] The immediate impetus for both of these revisions was a very particular series of abusive transactions brought to the attention of Congress. The focus was upon very specific §351 exchanges through which foreign corporations transferred multiple properties securing the same liability to a domestic subsidiary. The U.S. subsidiary was able to take advantage of the prior §362 basis rules to overstate basis in the cross-collateralized properties received in the exchange. This overstated basis, in some cases well in excess of the transferred asset's fair market value, was then used to dramatically increase the U.S. corporation's depreciation deductions. For the moment, you should not concern yourself with the details of these complicated transactions.[194] On the other hand, a general awareness of this legislative history might be useful as you attempt to understand the impact of the revised approach to assumptions of liability reflected in §357(d). Despite the narrow concern driving the revisions, Congress drafted rules that apply quite broadly. Unfortunately, Congress left in its wake a set of rules that adds uncertainty and complexity for taxpayers who are not necessarily engaged in abusive transactions. The good news is that most of the complexity involves transactions in which multiple assets secure the same liability. The impact of the 1999 revisions is less dramatic in the case of more straightforward exchanges involving multiple assets.

b) Assumption of *Recourse* Liabilities

Under prior rules, any property transferred subject to a lien was automatically and mechanically treated as a liability that could trigger §357(c) gain.[195] Although this approach had the virtue of simplicity, it sometimes created hardships for taxpayers like the Lessingers and the Seggermans. The §357(d) rules now provide that recourse liabilities are considered assumed "if the transferee has agreed to, and is expected to, satisfy . . . [the] liability . . . whether or not the transferor has been relieved of such liability."[196] In other words, a *recourse* liability is only assumed for purpose of §357 if transfer of the liability meets

---

193. I.R.C. §362(d).

194. A brief discussion of these multiple-asset transactions is included in sections that follow in this chapter.

195. Prior to the addition of specific rules in §357(d)(1)(A) defining assumption of recourse liabilities for purposes of §357, computation of gain under §357(c) upon transferring liabilities in a §351 exchange was inconsistent with the analogous §1001 computation of gain from a sale or exchange. For the latter, regulations provided that amount realized would include liabilities transferred only if "another person agrees to pay the liability." Treas. Reg. §1.1001-2(a)(4)(ii). The changes enacted in §357(d)(1)(A) go a long way toward eliminating the inconsistency. Even now, however, computations under the two provisions are not precisely parallel since §357(d) includes an "expectation of the parties" test absent from the §1001 regulations.

196. I.R.C. §357(d)(1)(A).

two requirements. First, recourse liabilities are not considered assumed unless the corporation formally agrees to be responsible for the debt. Second, it must be expected that the corporation will, in fact, do so. Whether the transfer meets these requirements will be determined under a facts-and-circumstances analysis. Under prior law, the transfer of property subject to a recourse liability in excess of basis automatically triggered §357(c) gain. Under the revised rules, the presumption is that recourse liabilities are *not* assumed and, thus, will *not* trigger §357(c) gain. The presumption is overcome only upon the corporation's realistic agreement to satisfy the debt. In effect, §357(d)(1)(A) now establishes a "non-assumption" default rule.

The §357(d)(1)(A) "assumption of recourse liability" definition offers some relief to shareholders who previously faced §357(c) hardships. At least with respect to *recourse* liabilities, shareholders can now avoid triggering §357(c) gain by being careful *not* to have the corporation formally assume or contractually agree to satisfy the liability.[197] Absent the corporation's agreement, there simply is no liability assumption at all and the §357(c) problem disappears entirely. Shareholder transferors must be careful in using this technique, however. To be safe, the shareholder and corporation may want to execute formal documents making it clear that the sharehold-ers, and *not* the corporation, have agreed to be responsible for the debt. Even so, the IRS may use the facts-and-circumstances analysis to challenge the bona fide nature of the agreement. The IRS may be especially suspicious that the shareholders and the corporation, who are related parties, have "cooked the books" to make it appear that the shareholders continue to be responsible when they really expect the corporation to satisfy the debt. As a practical matter, the lender is likely to first attempt collection through forfeiture proceedings against the property itself rather than by pursuing individual shareholders. If shareholders want to ensure success in avoiding §357(c) gain through this device, they should probably execute an agree-ment to indemnify the corporation in the event that the property is forfeited. Concerns about the extent to which the IRS will use the §357(d) facts-and-circumstances analysis to challenge such agreements between the corpora-tion and its shareholders and the factors that it will consider in connection with such analysis simply add to the uncertainty and complexity generated by the §357(d) rules.[198] If the shareholders originally avoided §357(c) gain

---

197. This technique will not work for nonrecourse debt since it will be treated as assumed sim-ply because the transferred asset continues to be subject to the liability. I.R.C. §357(d)(1)(B). This provision and its impact are discussed in the section that follows in this chapter.
198. Other complex issues generated by the assumption "term of art" in §357(d) include identifying *whose* expectations are relevant and what constitutes a corporate or shareholder "agreement" to satisfy the liability. See Bogdanski, *supra* note 186. In an unusual move, in 2003 the Treasury Department announced that it was "*considering publishing a notice of proposed rulemaking* proposing rules regarding the amount of liability a transferee of property is treated as assuming . . . And certain tax consequences that result from the transferee's assumption of such a liability." Announcement 2003-37, 2003-1 C.B. 1025.

by persuading the IRS that the shareholders would continue to be responsible and that the corporation did *not* assume the liability, another question emerges. What happens if the corporation ultimately *does* end up satisfying the recourse liability? It seems unlikely that the government would impose a retroactive §357(c) gain. More likely, the subsequent corporate payment of the debt would be viewed as a taxable constructive dividend under §301 or simply as discharge of indebtedness income.[199]

c) Assumption of *Nonrecourse* Liabilities

As noted in the preceding section, the §357(d)(1)(A) "assumption" definition, added in 1999, can significantly change the tax treatment of recourse liabilities transferred to the corporation in a §351 exchange. By contrast, the parallel §357(d)(1)(B) definition of *nonrecourse* liability changes very little in most cases. Nonrecourse liabilities transferred to a corporation were, and continue to be, treated as assumed to the full extent of the liability. The §357(d)(1)(B) rule simply provides that "a nonrecourse liability shall be treated as having been assumed by the transferee of any asset subject to such liability." Shareholders who transfer nonrecourse mortgages in excess of liabilities will find themselves essentially where they were before 1999. They may still have to resort to the *Lessinger/Peracchi* promissory note technique and hope that the courts will continue to be sympathetic.

In some respects, taxpayers may even be *worse* off in the nonrecourse setting than they were before. To understand how this might be so, one must look at the *corporate-level* tax consequences of a shareholder §357(c) gain. When Congress added the §357(d) assumption definitions in 1999, it simultaneously amended the §362 basis rules applicable to the corporation in a §351 exchange. Under prior law, when shareholders recognized a §357(c) gain, the corporation received a reciprocal increase in the transferred asset's basis for the full amount of gain recognized to the shareholders.[200] In other words, the shareholder's §357(c) gain and the corporation's step-up in basis were always symmetrical. Under the revised §362 rules, such symmetry will not always result from "liability in excess of basis" exchanges.

To illustrate, imagine a §351 incorporation transaction in which shareholder A transfers zero basis property to X Corporation.[201] Assume that the property has a fair market value of $80,000 and is subject to a $100,000 nonrecourse mortgage. Shareholder A will have a $100,000 §357(c) gain

---

199. The §301 dividend rules are discussed in Chapter 5.
200. I.R.C. §362(a).
201. This zero basis is likely to be the result of previous depreciation deductions subtracted from basis under §1016.

on this exchange.[202] Previously, the §362 rules imposed no limit on the corporation's corollary basis increase. Thus, X Corporation would have been entitled to increase its substituted basis of zero by the full $100,000 of shareholder A's §357(c) gain, leaving X with a $100,000 basis in the property. Under §362(d), added in 1999 along with the §357(d) "assumption of liability" definitions, X's basis following this exchange now cannot exceed the transferred property's fair market value. Current law will thus restrict X Corporation's basis in the transferred asset to $80,000.[203]

Notice the lack of symmetry in this example: X Corporation has only an $80,000 basis even though shareholder A reported a $100,000 taxable gain on the exchange. One might disagree about whether this asymmetry makes policy sense and whether it is appropriate to give the corporation a basis in the transferred property that exceeds the property's fair market value. On the other hand, there should be no disagreement that the §362(d) restriction alters the tax consequences of this transaction. Previously, even though the shareholders were stuck with §357(c) gain, they might at least have taken some comfort from the corporation's reciprocal basis increase. While shareholders transferring *recourse* liabilities in excess of basis in a §351 exchange may be better off as a result of the revised assumption of liability rules, shareholders transferring *nonrecourse* liabilities may actually be worse off. It is unclear whether Congress really intended this result or whether it is simply the unintended byproduct of rules designed to combat certain narrow abusive transactions.

Fortunately, when shareholders contribute only *one* asset that is subject to only *one* liability, the application of the §357(d) "assumption of liability" definition is rather straightforward. Tax life gets complicated rather quickly, however, when the §351 exchange involves multiple assets secured by the same liability. These issues are addressed briefly in the following section.

Multiple Assets Securing the Same Liability

a) Basic Multiple Asset Transfer

Under a special exception in §357(d)(2), the amount of nonrecourse liabilities assumed will be reduced in certain cases where the transferor owned *multiple* assets subject to the liability transferred. Related provisions in §362(d) may restrict the increase to the corporation's basis in the property

---

202. This amount reflects the excess of the $100,000 liability assumed by the corporation over the shareholder's zero basis in the property transferred.
203. The revised basis rule provides that "[i]n no event shall the basis of any property be increased . . . Above the fair market value of such property . . . by reason of any gain recognized to the transferor as a result of the assumption of a liability." I.R.C. §362(d)(1).

received that would otherwise result from the transferring shareholder's §357(c) gain. For the well-advised taxpayer, the §357(d)(2) exception to the nonrecourse debt assumption definition may offer some flexibility in transactions involving multiple assets secured by the same liability. On the other hand, this provision may create a trap for the ill-advised taxpayer.

To illustrate, imagine that shareholder A owns Asset 1 (zero basis and $300 fair market value) and Asset 2 (zero basis and $200 fair market value). Both assets are secured by the same $500 nonrecourse liability. Upon incorporation, A transfers Asset 1 to X Corporation subject to the $500 nonrecourse mortgage in exchange for 100% of X's stock, but retains Asset 2. Prior law provided no guidance as to how the nonrecourse liability should be allocated under such circumstances. Under current law, absent a special agreement between the shareholder and the corporation, the "default" rule in §357(d)(1)(B) presumes that X Corporation is assuming the entire liability. Thus, shareholder A would report a $500 §357(c) gain. This tax treatment may not accurately reflect the economics of the transaction, however. As a practical matter, if X defaults on the mortgage, the lender will be entitled to foreclose on Asset 1, effectively collecting only $300 in satisfaction of the $500 debt. Since the mortgage is nonrecourse, X has little incentive to satisfy any more than $300. Although shareholder A has been relieved of only a $300 portion of the debt from an economic perspective, §357(c) treats her as having discharged the entire $500 liability. Even so, the corporation will not be entitled to the full $500 increase to its basis under §362(a); its basis will be limited to the $300 value of the property received pursuant to §362(d)(1).

The well-advised taxpayer in shareholder A's situation will execute a formal agreement with X providing that she agrees to, and is expected to, satisfy a $200 portion of the nonrecourse liability.[204] If she does so, §357(d)(2)(A) will reduce the nonrecourse liability viewed as "assumed" by the $200 portion for which shareholder A formally retains responsibility.[205] Armed with such an agreement, shareholder A would limit her §357(c) gain to only $300. This tax treatment is more consonant with the economics of the

---

204. Notice that this agreement between shareholder A and Corporation X simply provides for a pro rata allocation of the nonrecourse debt to each asset based upon its relative fair market value. The agreement need not necessarily provide for such pro rata allocation, however. The §357(d)(2) definition flexibly permits reduction of the nonrecourse debt by "the amount of such liability which an owner of other assets not transferred" to the corporation has agreed to and is expected to satisfy subject to a fair market value limitation provided in §357(d)(2)(B).

205. Under this exception to the "default" presumption that the entire debt is assumed, the nonrecourse liability is reduced by "the lesser of— (A) the amount of such liability which an owner of other assets not transferred to the transferee and also subject to such liability has agreed with the transferee to, and is expected to, satisfy, or (B) the fair market value of such other assets . . . ." I.R.C. §357(d)(2). Notice that the "lesser of" clause effectively places a $200 cap on the amount of reduction that shareholder A could take.

transaction in any event. Most shareholders would be foolish not to execute such an agreement. Thus, §357(c) and its relatives now potentially create yet another trap for the ill-advised. Again, these results may be the unintended byproduct of legislation designed to address particular abusive transactions. In its haste to respond to these abusive transactions, Congress did not carefully consider the impact of the §357(d) rules on basic multiple asset transactions. In fact, the Treasury Department itself has indicated its concern with this and other "anomalies" created by §357(d)(2) and announced that it is considering regulations providing that "in certain cases where the transferor and the transferee have no agreement regarding the satisfaction of a nonrecourse liability, the transferee will not be treated as assuming the entire amount of the nonrecourse liability."[206]

b) Abusive Multiple Asset Transactions

Perhaps the best way to make at least some sense of §§357(d) and 362(d) is to look at the transaction it was designed to attack. Imagine that X Corporation has three separate assets, each with a basis of zero and a fair market value of $50. All three assets are subject to the same $100 nonrecourse liability. In other words, the properties are cross-collateralized. X decides to incorporate subsidiaries A, B, and C, transferring one of the three assets to each subsidiary. Each of the assets remains subject to the entire $100 liability. If §357(c) imposes a tax on the excess of the full $100 liability over basis for *each* of the three assets, X Corporation will be required to report a $100 §357(c) gain for each transfer, totaling $300. Instead, §357(d)(2) provides that the nonrecourse liability treated as assumed will be reduced by the lesser of "the amount of such liability which an owner of other assets not transferred to the transferee and also subject to the liability has agreed with the transferee to, and is expected to, satisfy" or the fair market value of the other property. In effect, the amount of liability viewed as assumed by each subsidiary in the above example must be reduced by the portion of nonrecourse liability attributable to assets *not* transferred. Thus, the liabilities considered assumed by each A, B, and C will be $33.33, resulting in an overall §357(c) gain of only $100. If anything, the *old* result appeared harsh and the new result seems preferable from the taxpayer's point of view. Where was the abuse? Recall that the transferee corporation's basis in the assets under §362 is a transferred basis, *increased in the amount of the gain recognized by the transferor.* Under the old rules, if subsidiaries A, B, and C were each entitled to increase basis in the assets received by the §357(c) gain, each of them would have a $100 basis in the asset received from X. In fact, the real concern driving the

---

206. Announcement 2003-37, 2003-1 C.B. 1025. See also Liabilities Assumed in Certain Transactions, 68 Fed. Reg. 23931 (May 6, 2003).

amendments was the use of §357(c) to create artificial basis under §362. The abuse becomes especially clear if A, B, and C are domestic corporations entitled to the step-up in basis under §362, while X is a foreign corporation not subject to U.S. Tax on the §357(c) gain. Not surprisingly, Congress also added a new §362(d) as a corollary to §357(d), denying the full step-up in basis.[207]

The Corporation's Transfer of Its Own Stock — Special Issues Under §351

A corporate transferor may transfer its own stock to a newly formed or existing subsidiary in return for subsidiary stock under §351.[208] As noted earlier, the transferor corporation's stock is considered property for purposes of §351. Nonrecognition treatment is available under §351 as long as the transferor corporation has control immediately after the exchange. In measuring such control immediately after the exchange, the Code specifically provides that "the fact that any corporate transferor distributes part or all of the stock in the corporation which it receives in the exchange to its shareholders shall not be taken into account."[209] Thus, the transferor corporation may distribute the subsidiary stock to its shareholders, maintaining only brief direct control. This subsequent distribution of subsidiary stock to the parent corporation's shareholders may be eligible for nonrecognition as a tax-free corporate division.[210]

Related issues upon a parent corporation's creation of a subsidiary are the subsidiary corporation's basis in the parent stock and the parent's basis in the subsidiary's stock. Under §362, the subsidiary's basis will be the

---

207. I.R.C. §362(d), added by Pub. L. No. 106-36, §3001(e) (codified, as amended, at I.R.C. §362). This provision includes two limitations on the corporation's increase in basis to reflect gains recognized by the shareholders on the exchange. First, §362(d)(1) provides that "in no event shall the basis of any property be increased . . . Above the fair market value of such property . . . by reason of any gain recognized to the transferor as a result of the assumption of a liability." Second, §362(d)(2) directly addresses the concern with multiple assets securing the same liability. If a transferor with multiple assets securing a liability does not transfer all of those assets to the corporation, and if nobody was subject to tax on the §357(c) gain with respect to the transferred assets, the corporation's increase in basis under §362 "shall be determined as if the liability assumed by the transferee equaled such transferee's ratable portion of such liability determined on the basis of the relative fair market value . . . of all the assets subject to such liability." I.R.C. §362(d)(2)(B).

208. If a corporate parent contributes 80% control of its own stock to its subsidiary in a §351 exchange, the subsidiary effectively becomes the parent and the parent becomes the subsidiary. This role reversal, referred to in the trade as a "corporate inversion," raises a number of complex tax issues, which will be considered briefly in subsequent chapters.

209. I.R.C. §351(c).

210. For a detailed discussion of §351(c), divisive reorganizations, and other tax-free corporate divisions, see Chapter 14.

same as it would be in the hands of the transferor corporation, increased in the amount of any gain recognized by the transferor. One might expect the parent corporation's basis in its subsidiary's stock to be governed by the §358 basis rules for stock received by a contributing shareholder in a §351 exchange. When the transferor is a corporation exchanging its own stock or securities, however, the §358 rules do not apply.[211] For many years, the Treasury Department took the position that both the parent's and subsidiary's stock basis should be determined under §362. Because a corporation has a zero basis in its newly issued stock or reissued treasury stock, it reasoned that the subsidiary should take a §362(a) substituted basis of zero upon receipt of the parent's stock in a §351 exchange. The same zero substituted basis also would apply to the parent upon a second application of §362(a).[212]

The use of §362 in determining the transferor's basis in a §351 exchange at best is a strained statutory construction. In addition, commentators have criticized the "zero basis" rule arguing that "[t]he concern with the zero basis result is that the parent that contributes its stock to a subsidiary appears improperly to have been denied its statutory right to issue its stock without recognition, because the subsidiary may recognize gain when it later disposes of the zero basis parent stock."[213] In 2006, the Treasury Department revoked its earlier "zero basis" ruling and made the unusual concession that it was incorrect in using §362 to determine the parent corporation's basis in the subsidiary stock, adding that all other conclusions in the 1974 ruling were "under study."[214] The 2006 ruling did not suggest, however, what the parent corporation's basis *should* be, leaving at least the possibility that the Treasury Department might later use different reasoning to reach the same zero basis conclusion.

In the meantime, §1032 regulations offer limited relief to subsidiaries confronted with this "zero basis" problem upon acquiring money or property in exchange for parent corporation stock. For example, imagine that a parent corporation (P) issues additional shares of its stock to its subsidiary (S) in order to enable the subsidiary to acquire a truck from a third party. In accordance with the plan, S immediately exchanges the recently issued P stock for the truck. Without special relief, S would recognize gain to the extent that the fair market value of the truck received exceeded S's zero basis in the P stock. Under limited conditions, the regulations treat the transaction as if, immediately before the exchange of P stock for the

---

211. I.R.C. §358(e).
212. Rev. Rul. 74-503, 1974-2 C.B. 117 (citing Treas. Reg. §1.1032-1(d)), *revoked by* Rev. Rul. 2006-2, 2006-1 C.B. 261.
213. Jasper L. Cummings, Jr., The Silent Policies of Conservation and Cloning of Tax Basis and the Corporate Applications, 48 Tax L. Rev. 113, 133 (1992).
214. Rev. Rul. 2006-2, 2006-1 C.B. 261.

truck, S *purchased* P's stock from P for fair market value with cash contributed to S by P.[215] The effect of this deemed purchase is to provide S with a fair market value basis, as opposed to a zero basis, in the P shares. Assuming an immediate arm's-length exchange of the P stock for the truck, there should be no taxable gain to S upon the exchange. In addition to a plan to acquire money or other property, eligibility for such special treatment requires that (1) S *immediately* transfer the P stock in exchange for money or property from someone other than P; (2) S acquire the P stock in a transaction in which, but for the special rule, S would have a §362 basis in the P stock; (3) the party receiving the P stock not get a substituted basis (i.e., the transaction must be taxable to the third party); and (4) the P stock not be exchanged for other P stock.[216]

Examples

The following questions apply the materials just discussed and add some nuances and details not specifically considered.

An Easy Question

1. Viola and Sebastian agree to form Sail Away, Inc., a small family boat rental business. Viola contributes 20 sailboats purchased for $70,000 but worth $170,000 at the time of incorporation. Sally previously ran a boat dealership business and held the sailboats as inventory. Sebastian contributes a small piece of waterfront property and a dock purchased many years ago for $30,000, with a fair market value of $150,000, plus cash of $20,000. In return for the contributions, each receives 50% of the 200 authorized common shares of Sail Away stock. Tax consequences to Viola? To Sebastian? To Sail Away, Inc.?

Variations on a Theme from Question 1

2. a. What result if Viola's sailboats were originally purchased for $180,000?
   b. What result if Viola received 75% of the stock and Sebastian 25%?
   c. What result if Sebastian's contribution consisted of services worth $70,000 and property worth $100,000 (basis still $30,000)? What if he contributed only services valued at $170,000?

---

215. Treas. Reg. §1.1032-3(b), (e)(1), ex. 1. The regulations also provide some relief in the context of certain tax-free triangular reorganizations in which the first step in a multistep acquisition is a transfer by the purchasing corporation of its own stock to a new subsidiary in a §351 exchange. Treas. Reg. §1.1032-2. Tax-free reorganizations are discussed later in Chapters 11-14.
216. Treas. Reg. §1.1032-3(c).

d. What result if Viola made her contribution in exchange for $160,000 worth of stock plus a Sail Away security valued at $10,000? How would your answer change if Viola's basis in the property contributed had been $180,000?

e. What if Sebastian in Example 1 later makes an additional contribution of $20,000 cash and receives no additional shares? Would your answer be different if he contributes property worth $20,000 (basis $5,000)? What if he receives some additional shares for the subsequent contribution?

Transfer of Control

2. Antonio incorporated his shipping business by contributing all of his ships and their cargo to a newly formed corporation in return for 100% of the stock. At the time of incorporation, Antonio committed himself to transferring 25% of the stock to his good friend Bassanio in exchange for cash in order to help him with some financial problems. What tax consequence to Antonio and the newly formed corporation?

The Publicly Held Setting

3. Sir Falstaff has decided to incorporate a publishing business and needs to raise capital through sales of stock to the public. He arranges for Falstaff's, Inc., to have two classes of stock: Class A common and Class B 6% nonvoting preferred. The articles of incorporation authorized 1,000 shares of Class A common and 5,000 shares of Class B preferred. The preferred shares are to be sold to the public for cash. Falstaff incorporates by transferring a printing press and other assets to the corporation in return for 75% of the common stock. His friend Nym contributes additional capital in return for 25% of the Class A common shares. Together, they approach an underwriter who agrees to sell 4,500 Class B preferred shares to the public. If successful, the underwriter is to receive the remaining 500 Class B preferred shares. What tax consequences to Falstaff, Nym, the corporation, the underwriter, and the public if the underwriter is successful?

Return of Boot

4. Oberon and Puck agree to establish Oberon Spirits, Inc., (OSI) to manufacture and sell fine wines and spirits. At the time of incorporation, two classes of stock are authorized: (1) voting common stock and (2) 6% nonvoting preferred stock with a redemption feature mandating redemption of the shares at a specified premium ten years from the date of issue. Oberon contributes land for a winery with a basis of $75,000 and a fair market value of $500,000. Puck contributes a wine cellar already filled

with fine wines he has collected over the years. Puck's basis for the wines and the cellar was $20,000, and its fair market value at the time of contribution was $500,000. In return for his contribution, Oberon receives 100 shares of common stock. Puck, on the other hand, receives only 50 shares of common stock valued at $250,000 and OSI securities bearing 8% interest and payable over ten years, also valued at $250,000.

a. What tax consequence to Oberon, Puck and the corporation?

b. What if, instead of the OSI securities, Puck received OSI 6% non-voting preferred stock valued at $250,000?

c. What if Puck received only OSI 6% nonvoting preferred stock valued at $500,000 in exchange for his contribution?

d. What if, in Example 5a, Puck's basis for the wine cellar and wines had been $450,000?

Problems with Boot, Liabilities, and Other Twists

6. a. Prospero and his daughter Miranda decide to establish a corporation to sell island real estate. Prospero has been collecting real estate over the years. He has one parcel with a basis of $30,000 and a fair market of $100,000, and another parcel has a basis of $170,000 and a fair market value of $100,000. Prospero has held parcel one for six months and parcel two for five years. Prospero contributes the two parcels in return for 80% of the stock (worth $190,000) plus $10,000 cash boot. Miranda contributes only one parcel with a basis of $70,000, a fair market value of $90,000, to the corporation in return for 20% of the stock (worth $50,000). The corporation takes Miranda's property subject to a mortgage of $40,000. What tax consequence to Prospero, Miranda, and the corporation?

b. What result if Miranda's parcel was subject to a mortgage in the amount of $80,000?

c. How might your answer to 6b change if Miranda had taken out the $80,000 mortgage against her property just one week prior to contributing the property as part of the incorporation exchange, using the $80,000 to pay off her personal debts?

7. Assume that Prospero in Example 6a had been operating a real-estate business as a sole proprietor prior to incorporation. At the time of incorporation, he had already contracted for the sale of the land parcel with a basis of $30,000 and a fair market value of $100,000, but had not yet received payment. He contributes the sale contract to a new corporation in exchange for all of the corporation's stock. In addition, the corporation assumes $150,000 in accounts payable previously incurred by the proprietorship for salaries and other business expenses. What tax consequence to Prospero and the corporation?

Explanations

1. Viola has contributed property to the corporation, solely in exchange for stock, and immediately after the exchange, she and Sebastian together control 100% of the stock of the corporation. Thus, Viola will qualify for nonrecognition under §351. Presumably, the value of her 50% stock interest is equal to 50% of the value of the corporation's assets — $170,000. Her $100,000 realized gain ($170,000 amount realized less $70,000 basis in the sailboats) will not be recognized. Viola's basis in her 100 shares of Sail Away stock will be an exchanged basis of $70,000 under §358. Should she later sell the stock for $170,000, she will recognize a $100,000 gain at that time. Note that her stock is a capital asset, the sale of which will result in capital gain or loss. The sailboats Viola contributed were inventory, and therefore not capital assets or §1231 assets. I.R.C. §§1221(a)(1), 1231(b)(1)(A). As a result, she will not be able to tack the period during which she owned the boats onto the stock holding period under §1223(1). If Viola sells the stock within the first year, her gain will be short-term capital gain. If she waits more than one year before selling the shares, her gain will be long-term capital gain from the sale of stock.

    Sebastian also has met the requirements of §351. Sebastian's 50% stock interest presumably is also worth $170,000. He effectively purchased $20,000 worth of stock for cash and received the remaining $150,000 worth of stock in exchange for property. His $120,000 realized gain from transfer of the waterfront property ($150,000 amount realized less $30,000 basis in the property) will not be recognized. Sebastian's basis in the stock will include his exchanged basis of $30,000 from the property plus the $20,000 cash contributed for a total of $50,000. Should he later sell the stock for $170,000, he will recognize a capital gain of $120,000. A stock sale within the first year, however, will raise an interesting holding period question in determining whether that gain is long or short term. The §1223(1) tacking rules apply only if the stock received in the exchange takes a substituted basis *and* if the property transferred to the corporation was a capital asset or §1231 asset at the time of contribution. Even assuming that the real estate is a capital asset, recall that Sebastian also contributed $20,000 in cash, which clearly is not. Under the Treasury Department's interpretation, Sebastian will have a *split holding period* for each share based on the relative fair market values of the real estate and the cash.[217] Thus, Sebastian will tack on the holding period from the real estate to the holding period for the stock with respect to 150/170 of each share. His holding period for

---

217. Rev. Rul. 85-164, 1985-2 C.B. 117.

20/170 of each share begins at the time of the §351 exchange. Things are much simpler if Sebastian waits for more than one year to sell the stock, in which case all of his gain will be long-term capital gain.

Sail Away, Inc., will have no gain from the receipt of the sailboats, the waterfront property, or the cash under §1032. Its basis in the boats under §362 will be a transferred basis from Viola of $70,000. Since these are not capital assets, any gain from the sale of these boats would result in ordinary income unless the gain qualified for capital gain-like treatment under §1231. As for the waterfront property, it will have a transferred basis from Sebastian of $30,000. If the property is considered a capital asset in Sail Away's hands, any gain from sale of the property will be capital gain. Moreover, Sail Away will be entitled to tack on the period during which Sebastian owned the land so that the gain will be long-term capital gain even if the property is sold within the first year. I.R.C. §1223(2).

2. a. If Viola's sailboats originally had been purchased for $180,000, but were worth only $170,000 at the time of contribution, she would have realized a loss of $10,000 upon the exchange. Notice that §351 nonrecognition is not elective and applies to both gains and losses. Thus, Viola will not be able to recognize the loss. Her basis in the stock will be an exchanged basis of $180,000 from the sailboats contributed. Should she later sell her shares for $170,000, she will recognize the $10,000 loss at that time. If Viola wanted to recognize her loss immediately, she should have sold the boats to a third party and contributed cash to the corporation. Prior to 2004, Sail Away's basis in the boats under §362 would have been $180,000. Under §362(e), however, some adjustments to the corporation's basis will be necessary. The statutory language, which refers in (e)(2)(A)(i) to a transferor, suggests that the rules should be applied on a transferor-by-transferor basis. This reading is confirmed by Treas. Reg. §1.362-4(b), (g)(3). Since the value of Sebastian's contribution exceeded its basis, the §362(e) adjustment analysis is necessary here only with respect to Viola's contribution of loss property. Although the statute refers to aggregates, the answer here is simple because Viola contributed just the sailboats. The sailboats' $180,000 basis exceeded their $170,000 fair market value immediately after the exchange. Thus, §362(e)(2)(A) limits Sail Away's basis in the sailboats to their $170,000 fair market value.

   b. If Viola received 75% of the stock and Sebastian only 25% in return for equal contributions from each of $170,000, it would be important to know why Viola received a disproportionately greater share of stock than she would otherwise be entitled to. The disproportionate exchange still qualifies for §351 nonrecognition, but regulations make clear that "the entire transaction will be given tax effect in accordance with its true nature." Treas. Reg. §1.351-1(b)(1). For example, if Sebastian agreed to allow her the extra shares simply as a gift out of "detached and disinterested generosity,"[218] the transaction will be viewed in two steps. It will be assumed that the stock first was received in proportion to the relative contributions from each and then that Sebastian made a gift to Viola. Thus, Sebastian will be viewed as first receiving 50% of the stock with a basis of $50,000 ($30,000 exchanged basis from the property plus $20,000 cash). He next will be viewed as transferring half of his stock (25% of the total shares) to Viola as a gift. The receipt of the gift will be tax-free to Viola under §102. Her basis in the gift shares will be $25,000 under §1015.[219] Thus, Viola's basis for her full 75% will now be $95,000 (her $70,000 exchanged basis from the property contributed plus $25,000 §1015 basis in the gift shares). Sebastian may be required to pay a gift tax on the transfer of the shares to Viola under §2501. After the gift, Sebastian's basis in his remaining stock will be $25,000.

If Sebastian agreed to allow Viola to take the extra 25% because Viola had worked for several years in Sebastian's real-estate firm without any salary and was due $85,000 in back pay, the transaction still would first be viewed as if each received 50% of the stock worth $170,000. Sebastian would then be viewed as transferring half ($85,000 worth) to Viola as compensation. Viola will report the $85,000 as taxable compensation income. Her basis in the 75% will include her exchanged basis of $70,000 plus a tax cost basis of $85,000 for a total of $155,000. Sebastian, on the other hand, will be left with a basis of $25,000 in his remaining shares and will be entitled to a business expense deduction for salary paid to Viola, assuming that his business was on a cash basis and he had not previously deducted the expense.

c. If Sebastian contributed services worth $70,000 and property worth $100,000 in exchange for $170,000 worth of stock, he effectively is receiving $70,000 worth of stock as compensation for services and $100,000 worth of stock in exchange for property. He should report $70,000 as ordinary compensation income. The $70,000 realized gain from the property contribution ($100,000 amount realized less $30,000 basis in the property) will not be recognized. Sebastian's basis in the stock will include an exchanged basis of $30,000

---

218. See Comm'r v. Duberstein, 363 U.S. 278, 285 (1960); Comm'r v. LoBue, 351 U.S. 243, 246 (1956).
219. Since she received half of Sebastian's shares, she will take half of his basis.

from the property *plus* a "tax cost" basis of $70,000 from the stock received for services totaling $100,000. Note that even though part of Sebastian's contribution was in the form of services, his full 50% can be counted for purposes of the control tests since he also contributed property. Treas. Reg. §1.351-1(a)(1)(ii), (a)(2), ex. 3. Thus, Viola and Sebastian together will still satisfy the §368(c) control tests. Viola is entitled to §351 nonrecognition as above. Sail Away would be entitled to a $70,000 §162 ordinary and necessary business expense deduction for compensation paid.

If Sebastian made his entire contribution in the form of services worth $170,000, he would be required to report $170,000 in ordinary compensation income and would hold the stock with a $170,000 basis. Moreover, since he contributed no property, his 50% share would not be counted toward meeting the control test. By itself, Viola's 50% interest does not meet the control test, making her ineligible for §351 nonrecognition. Viola now must report her $100,000 gain ($170,000 amount realized less $70,000 basis in the sailboats) from the exchange of property for stock. Her basis in the stock now will be a $170,000 "cost" or fair market value basis. Sail Away would be entitled to a $170,000 §162 ordinary and necessary business expense deduction for compensation paid.

d. The $10,000 in Sail Away securities will be treated as boot to Viola. Of her $100,000 realized gain from the §351 exchange ($170,000 amount realized from stock and securities received less $70,000 basis in the sailboats), she will recognize gain only to the extent of the $10,000 boot. I.R.C. §351(b)(1). Assuming that the sailboats were not capital assets, her gain will be ordinary income. To compute her basis in the stock, Viola will start with a §358 exchanged basis of $70,000, decreased by the $10,000 fair market value of the boot securities and increased by the $10,000 gain. I.R.C. §358(a)(1)(A)(i), (B)(ii). Thus, her basis in the shares will remain at $70,000. Her basis in the Sail Away securities will be the $10,000 fair market value. I.R.C. §358(a)(2). Sail Away's basis in the sailboats under §362(a) would be $80,000 ($70,000 transferred basis increased by the $10,000 gain recognized by Viola).

If Viola's basis in the contributed property had been $180,000, she would have a realized loss of $10,000. Under §351(b)(2), however, she will not be entitled to recognize this loss. Under §358, her $180,000 exchanged basis in the stock would be decreased by the $10,000 fair market value of the boot securities received, leaving her with a basis of $170,000. If she later sells hers shares for $160,000, she will recognize the $10,000 loss at that time. Although §362(a) generally provides for a substituted basis, §362(e) will limit Sail Away's basis here to the $170,000 fair market value of the sailboats.[220]

e. If Sebastian later makes an additional cash contribution without receiving any additional shares of stock, he simply has made a cash contribution to capital and will be entitled to increase the basis in his stock to reflect the additional $20,000 payment. Treas. Reg. §1.118-1. Thus, his total basis for the shares now will be $70,000.

Sebastian's contribution of property worth $20,000 (basis $5,000) for no additional shares should also be viewed as an additional contribution to capital. Section §351 is not invoked here since this was not an exchange of property for stock. Sail Away would not report any gain upon receipt of the cash pursuant to §118.

One issue here is whether or not Sebastian must recognize a gain of $15,000 from disposition of this appreciated property. Unless the transfer of property is being used in payment of an assessment, at least one commentator assumes that the realized gain will not be taxed. Boris I. Bittker and James S. Eustice, Federal Income Taxation of Corporations and Shareholders ¶3.13 (7th ed. 2015). Assuming that Sebastian is not taxed on the transfer, he should increase his basis in the stock by the $5,000 basis (rather than the fair market value) of the property contributed. Sail Away's basis in the property under §362(a)(2) would then be $5,000.

If Sebastian received additional shares in return for his subsequent contribution of property, the transaction would be tested under §351. Sebastian now has contributed property solely in exchange for stock. Unless Sebastian alone meets the 80% control tests immediately after this transfer, he will not be eligible for nonrecognition. He should try to convince Viola to make more than a nominal contribution at the same time.

3. Given Antonio's binding commitment, the transaction might be viewed as an "integrated transaction," which is not complete until after Antonio transfers the 25% interest to Bassanio. As such, Antonio would be viewed as controlling only 75% of the stock and so would not have the requisite 80% control immediately after the exchange. Since his friend Bassanio contributed no property to the corporation, his 25% would not be counted toward meeting the control test. Antonio would be required to recognize any gain or loss from his contribution. On the other hand, Antonio might persuade the IRS to permit him §351 nonrecognition

---

220. Although the result would not change in this case of an unrecognized loss, Treasury regulations require that §362(e)(2) computations be done *after* increasing the corporation's basis in the amount of the shareholder's boot gain as required in §362(a). Treas. Reg. §1.362-4(h), ex. 6.

despite his binding commitment to sell 25% of his stock. Revised regulations defining the continuity of interest in the reorganization context disregard "mere dispositions" of stock received in a potential reorganization to unrelated parties. Treas. Reg. 1.368-1(e)(1)(i). Example 1 of the regulation approves tax-free treatment for the shareholders under §354 despite a binding commitment to sell. Treas. Reg. §1.368-1(e)(7), ex. 1. Given the parallels between §§351 and 354, the same nonrecognition approach arguably should apply to Antonio. In addition, Antonio might point to Revenue Ruling 2003-51 involving an "integrated" post-incorporation transfer of stock by the §351 transferor to a third party that did not participate directly in the §351 exchange. Despite the integrated transaction, the Treasury Department approved the transferor's §351 nonrecognition treatment. While it might suggest the government's changing position with regard to continuity of interest, Antonio should keep in mind that this ruling is not directly on point. The subsequent transfer under the facts at issue in the ruling was itself part of a tax-free reorganization. In Antonio's case, in contrast, the subsequent transfer was a taxable cash transaction.

4. To qualify for nonrecognition treatment, the person or persons contributing property must have control immediately after the exchange. To meet this requirement, the group must have 80% of the total combined voting power. Falstaff and Nym together meet this requirement since only the common shares have voting rights. The question here involves the second part of the control test. Under §368(c) the transferor group must also have 80% of the total number of shares of all other classes of stock. Thus, to qualify for §351 nonrecognition, the transferor group must show that it controls more than 80% (4,000) of the total 5,000 nonvoting preferred shares immediately after the exchange. To meet the tests of control *immediately after the exchange*, Treasury regulations indicate that the contributions of property in exchange for stock test need not be simultaneous, but the rights of the parties must be previously defined and the execution of the agreement must proceed with an expedition consistent with orderly procedure. Treas. Reg. §1.351-1(a)(1). Since the underwriter in a best efforts underwriting is acting merely as agent on behalf of the corporation, the underwriter is not considered part of the control group. On the other hand, the shares sold to the public will be counted toward meeting the control tests as long as the underwriting plan has proceeded expeditiously. The public is viewed as transferring cash directly to the corporation in return for stock and, therefore, is included in the control group along with Falstaff and Nym. See Treas. Reg. §1.351-1(a)(3). The group now has 100% of the voting stock and 90% (4,500 out of 5,000) of the total number of all other classes of stock. Consequently, Falstaff and Nym are eligible for §351 nonrecognition

upon their transfers of property in exchange for stock. The corporation is eligible for nonrecognition upon the receipt of property and cash under §1032. Its basis in contributed property is determined under §362. The underwriter must report ordinary compensation income upon receipt of the 500 Class B preferred shares. The public simply has contributed cash in exchange for stock. The public's basis in the shares will be equal to the cash contributed.

5. a. Oberon's realized gain of $425,000 ($500,000 amount realized less $75,000 basis in winery) will not be recognized. His stock will take a §358 exchanged basis of $75,000 from the winery property contributed. Of Puck's $480,000 realized gain ($500,000 amount realized less $20,000 basis in wines and cellar), he will recognize gain under §351(b)(1) to the extent of the $250,000 boot received in the form of OSI securities.[221] Puck's common stock basis under §358 will be his $20,000 exchanged basis decreased by the $250,000 boot and then increased by the $250,000 gain recognized, leaving him still with a basis of $20,000 in the stock. His basis in the OSI securities will be fair market value ($250,000) pursuant to §358(a)(2). OSI will report no gain or loss upon receipt of the land, wine cellar, and wines under §1032. Its basis in the land will be a transferred basis of $75,000 under §362. Its basis in the wine cellar and wines under §362 will be $270,000 (a transferred basis of $20,000 increased by the $250,000 gain recognized by Puck).

   b. Since the 6% OSI nonvoting preferred stock received by Puck is subject to a mandatory redemption clause within less than 20 years from the date of issue, the stock will be classified as "nonqualified preferred stock" under §351(g)(2)(A)(ii). As a result, the preferred stock will be treated as boot pursuant to §351(g)(1). Again, of his $480,000 realized gain, Puck will recognize "boot gain" to the extent of the $250,000 boot received in the form of OSI nonqualified preferred stock. Puck's common stock basis under §358 will be the same as it was in the answer to Example 5a. His basis in the preferred stock will be fair market value ($250,000) pursuant to §358(a)(2). OSI's basis in the wine cellar and wines would still be $270,000, as above.

   c. If Puck received only OSI 6% nonvoting preferred stock in exchange for his contribution, Puck will not be eligible for §351(a) nonrecognition, since he will have received only boot in exchange for his contribution. In this case, Puck received $500,000 worth of boot. Under §351(b), Puck must report gain, if any, to the extent of the boot received. Thus, Puck will report his entire $480,000 realized

---

221. Under proposed regulations, Puck would be entitled to report boot gain from the ten-year debt instrument under the installment method. Prop. Treas. Reg. §1.453-1(f)(3).

gain. Since Puck's preferred shares are considered "other property," the basis of these shares will be fair market value ($500,000) under §358(a)(2). This fair market value basis makes sense since Puck has now been fully taxed with respect to the appreciated value of the wine cellar contributed to the corporation.

One remaining concern is whether Oberon remains eligible for §351(a) nonrecognition. Recall that §§351(a) and 368(c) require the transferors to have both 80% of the total combined voting power and 80% of the total number of shares of all other classes of stock immediately after the exchange. If Puck's nonvoting preferred shares cannot be counted for purposes of the control test, Oberon's eligibility for nonrecognition is threatened. The legislative history behind §351(g) notes Congress's view that the preferred stock will be considered stock for purposes of §§351(a) and 368(c). Conference Report for the Taxpayer Relief Act of 1997, H.R. Rep. 105-220 at 561 (1997). Thus, the control test should be viewed as met and Oberon should remain eligible for §351(a) nonrecognition on the winery contribution in exchange for common stock. OSI will have a $500,000 basis in the wine cellar and wines and a $75,000 basis in the land for the winery.

d. If Puck's basis in the wines and cellar had been $450,000, his realized gain upon the contribution would have been only $50,000 ($500,000 amount realized less $450,000 basis in contributed property). Although he received $250,000 boot, he can be taxed only to the extent of his $50,000 gain. Puck's stock basis under §358 will be his $450,000 exchanged basis decreased by the $250,000 boot and increased in the amount of the $50,000 gain, leaving him with a basis of $250,000 in the OSI stock. Notice that his basis in the boot now is equal to its fair market value of $250,000. Since he has already been taxed upon the full realized gain, there should be no further taxable gain upon a sale of the boot for $250,000. OSI's basis in the wine cellar and wines under §362 will be $500,000 (a transferred basis of $450,000 increased by the $50,000 gain recognized by Puck).

6. a. The tax consequences to Prospero are a bit tricky in this problem. Note that Prospero has made an overall contribution of property worth $200,000 and that the overall basis in the property contributed was $200,000. Taking these two contributions together, it would appear that there is no realized gain or loss. Although Prospero has received $10,000 in boot, he will argue that there is no taxable gain from the boot since no gain was realized. Remember, however, that §351(b)(2) specifies that no loss shall be allowed in §351 transactions even where boot is paid by the corporation. To accept Prospero's argument here would be to allow his $70,000 loss from the second parcel to

offset the $70,000 gain from the first parcel, thus allowing him a loss. Rev. Rul. 68-55 addresses this problem by requiring an asset-by-asset approach in such cases. An allocation must be made based upon the fair market value of each asset. Since the two parcels were of equal value, each represents 50% of the total property contributed. Thus, 50% of the boot ($5,000) will be deemed to have been received for the first parcel and 50% (the remaining $5,000) for the second parcel. The realized gain on the first parcel was $70,000. Of this gain, $5,000 will be recognized as boot gain. As for parcel two, no loss will be recognized despite the receipt of $5,000 boot attributable to it pursuant to §351(b)(2).

The appropriate character of Prospero's boot gain raises some interesting questions. Notice that parcel one was a capital asset held for only six months, while parcel two was a capital asset held for five years. Example 1, included in Treas. Reg. §1.357-2(b), seems to suggest that since half of the assets contributed, by reference to fair market value, were short term and the other half were long term, half of the boot gain should be short-term capital gain and the other half should be long-term capital gain. This result would not make sense as applied to Prospero. Only parcel one had any realized gain at all. In Prospero's case, the most sensible result would be to attribute the boot gain entirely to parcel one, resulting in $5,000 of short-term capital gain.

Prospero's stock basis will be an overall exchanged basis of $200,000 from the two properties contributed decreased by the $10,000 cash boot and increased by the $5,000 taxable gain, leaving him with a $195,000 stock basis. Should he later sell the shares for $190,000, he will recognize a $5,000 loss. This later loss will offset the $5,000 gain recognized at the time of incorporation. In the end, his overall net gain or loss from both transfers is zero.

Miranda's contribution of property with a basis of $70,000, fair market value of $90,000, and subject to a mortgage of $40,000 results in a realized gain of $20,000 ($90,000 amount realized less $70,000 basis).[222] Under the general rule of §357(a), the corporation's taking property subject to a liability is not considered boot. Consequently, Miranda will not be required to recognize gain upon the transfer. This result assumes that there was no tax avoidance motive triggering the inclusion of liability as boot under §357(b). Notice also that Miranda has no §357(c) gain since the $40,000 liability transferred

---

222. Given the $40,000 mortgage, the net value of Miranda's contribution of property is only $50,000. Her amount realized on the exchange includes $50,000 worth of stock received and $40,000 from the liability, for a total of $90,000.

does not exceed the $70,000 basis in the contributed property. Even though the liability is not considered boot under §357, her §358 exchanged basis of $70,000 in the stock must be decreased by the $40,000 liability under §358(d), leaving her with a basis of $30,000 in the stock. If she later sells her stock for $50,000, she will report the $20,000 realized gain left unrecognized upon the §351 exchange.

Under §1032, the corporation would not recognize any gain upon receipt of the properties from Prospero and Miranda. Under §362, the corporation would take a $70,000 transferred basis in the parcel contributed by Miranda. As for the properties contributed by Prospero, the corporation would begin with a transferred basis of $30,000 in parcel one and $170,000 in parcel two. Pursuant to §362, the corporation is entitled to increase its basis in assets contributed by the $5,000 in boot gain recognized by Prospero. Since parcel one had a realized gain, while parcel two had a realized (but unrecognized) loss, the most sensible approach would be for the corporation to add $5,000 to its basis in parcel one, leaving the corporation with a total basis of $35,000 for parcel one and $170,000 for parcel two.[223]

This problem also raises some interesting issues under §362(e)(2). When there are multiple transferors, Treasury regulations provide that the §362(e)(2) analysis should be applied separately for each transferor. Treas. Reg. §1.362-4(b). There are no §362(e)(2) issues with respect to Miranda's contribution of a single "gain property." There may be some issues regarding Prospero's contributions, though. One of his contributed parcels had a $70,000 built-in gain and the other a $70,000 built-in loss. Before taking Prospero's $5,000 boot gain into account, the corporation's $200,000 aggregate basis in the assets received under §362(a) does not exceed the $200,000 fair market value immediately after the exchange. For purposes of measuring §362(e)(2) net built-in loss, however, the regulations would require the corporation first to increase its basis under §362(a) or (b) for any gain recognized by the transferor. Treas. Reg. §1.362-4(h), ex. 6. After adding Prospero's $5,000 boot gain, the corporation's $205,000 aggregate basis now does exceed the $200,000 aggregate fair market value. As applied here, the regulation requires a $5,000 reduction in the corporation's basis, all of which would be allocated to the loss asset. The basis of Prospero's second parcel in the corporation's hands thus would be reduced to $165,000.

---

223. The regulations, however, suggest that the §362 basis increase should be apportioned based upon the relative fair market values of the contributed assets. See Treas. Reg. §1.357-2(b), ex. 1, 2. This result does not make sense, as applied to the situation in Example 6, where one of the assets is a gain asset and the other asset is a loss asset.

b. If Miranda contributed the same property to the corporation subject to an $80,000 mortgage, the results would be different. Now the mortgage of $80,000 exceeds her $70,000 basis in the contributed property by $10,000. Under §357(c), this $10,000 excess of liabilities over basis must be recognized as gain from the sale of the contributed property. Her basis in the stock under §358 will be an exchanged basis of $70,000 reduced by the $80,000 liabilities assumed and increased by the $10,000 gain recognized. Thus, her basis in the shares will be zero. Under §362, the corporation's basis would be $80,000 (a transferred basis of $70,000 increased by the $10,000 gain recognized by Miranda).

c. When Miranda took out a mortgage just before incorporating and then used the mortgage proceeds for personal reasons unrelated to the business, she distinctly raised the likelihood that the Service will assert, pursuant to §357(b), that her principal purpose with respect to the corporation's assumption of her liability was to avoid federal income tax or that her principal purpose was not a bona fide business purpose. Recall that in question 6b. Miranda recognized only $10,000 in boot gain (the excess of the $80,000 of liabilities over her $70,000 basis in the contributed property). In contrast, if the exchange is governed by §357(b), the *entire* $80,000 of liability assumed will be treated as money received by Miranda on the exchange. As a result, she would recognize her *entire* realized gain of $20,000. Under §358, Miranda would begin with a $70,000 exchanged basis, reduced by the $80,000 of liabilities assumed and increased by the $20,000 gain recognized, resulting in a $10,000 basis in her stock. This result makes sense. Since she contributed property with a $10,000 net value to the corporation ($90,000 fair market value less $80,000 mortgage liability), she presumably received stock worth $10,000 on the §351 exchange. Since she has already recognized her entire realized gain with respect to the contributed property, she has no further gain to be deferred through substituted basis rules. Under §362, the corporation would take a $70,000 transferred basis increased by the $20,000 gain recognized to Miranda, resulting in a total basis of $90,000.

7. If Prospero contributed parcels of land which he had already contracted to sell, the first question that arises is whether this might be an impermissible assignment of income to the corporation. Assignment of income issues under §351 are decided on a case-by-case basis. Since the real estate was contributed for use in the real estate business, and since there does not appear to be a tax-avoidance motive, §351 nonrecognition should trump the assignment of income doctrine in this case. The corporation will report income upon the receipt of payments from the land sale contract and will take deductions upon payment of the accounts payable for salary and other business expenses.

Another problem is that if the accounts payable of $150,000 are considered liabilities for purposes of §357(c), the overall liabilities exceed the $30,000 basis of property contributed, resulting in a potential $120,000 taxable gain under §357(c)(1). Since the accounts payable would give rise to a deduction to Prospero if he had paid them, §357(c)(3) does not consider them liabilities for purposes of §357(c)(1). As before, Prospero's stock basis under §358 would be $195,000. Pursuant to §358(d)(2), he is not required to reduce his basis by the accounts payable since they are excluded under §357(c)(3).

PART III

Corporate
Midlife Events

CHAPTER 5

Nonliquidating Distributions

INTRODUCTION

A useful place to begin studying the tax consequences of corporate distributions is the relationship of shareholders to the corporations in which they hold shares. A shareholder is essentially an owner of the corporate enterprise whose ownership interest typically provides three significant rights: (1) the right to exercise control through voting,[1] (2) entitlement to a share of the corporation's earnings when distributions are declared, and (3) entitlement to a share of the corporation's net assets upon liquidation.[2] One obvious way that shareholders receive payment for their share of previously undistributed earnings and assets is through sale of the stock itself. Short of terminating their stock ownership, however, shareholders often receive their share of earnings and/or assets through different types of corporate distributions.

This chapter considers nonliquidating corporate distributions (also referred to as "operating distributions") made to shareholders during the corporation's lifetime. The most common example is a simple pro rata cash distribution in which the amount of each shareholder's distribution is determined according to his or her proportionate interest in the corporation.

---

1. Not all shares carry the right to vote, however. Certain classes of stock may be designated nonvoting. Nonvoting preferred stock is a common example.
2. This three-part ownership analysis is nicely spelled out in Himmel v. Comm'r, 338 F.2d 815, 817 (2d Cir. 1964).

141

Immediately after the distribution, the shareholders continue to hold the same proportionate interests that they held immediately before the distribution. In other words, the distribution has not altered the basic relationship among shareholders or between the shareholders and the corporation. One may be tempted to think of this distribution as a "dividend." For tax purposes, however, "dividend" is a term of art with a precise statutory meaning.

Before embarking upon a detailed discussion of typical nonliquidating or operating distributions, it will be useful to note other types of corporate distributions through which shareholders may receive their shares of earnings and/or assets. In a redemption, the corporation distributes cash or other property to its shareholders in return for its own stock, thus reducing the number of outstanding shares.[3] In a liquidating distribution, the corporation distributes its remaining assets after payment of liabilities to its creditors at or about the time of its termination as a going concern.[4] Other distributions may be made in connection with a formal corporate restructuring such as a reorganization.[5] This chapter will cover only nonliquidating distributions other than redemptions.[6] Keep in mind that the distribution rules considered in this chapter generally preserve the double tax on corporate income. Income is taxed once when it is earned by the corporation and again when it is distributed to the shareholders.

TAX CONSEQUENCES TO THE SHAREHOLDERS

Overview of §301 Distributions with Respect to Stock

The starting point for determining tax consequences to shareholders receiving corporate distributions is §301, which addresses distributions of property by a corporation to a shareholder *with respect to* the corporation's stock.[7] For purposes of §301, property includes money, securities, and any other property *except* stock in the corporation making the distribution (or rights

---

3. A redemption is a unique type of nonliquidating distribution that is considered fully in Chapter 6. For the moment, however, note that a pro rata redemption does not alter the basic relationship among shareholders. As a result, such redemptions are treated for tax purposes according to the nonliquidating or operating distribution rules. See I.R.C. §302(d).

4. Liquidating distributions are governed by I.R.C. §§331, 332, 336, and 337. For complete coverage of liquidations, see Chapters 8 and 9.

5. The term "reorganization" is defined for tax purposes in I.R.C. §368. For complete coverage of reorganizations, see Chapters 11-14.

6. As a form of shorthand, the remainder of this chapter will refer to these distributions as "nonliquidating" or "operating distributions."

7. I.R.C. §301(a) (emphasis added).

to acquire such stock).[8] The §301 rules apply only to distributions made "with respect to" the distributing corporation's stock. Corporations may make distributions for other reasons, however. For example, a shareholder also may be an employee of or a lender to the corporation. In such cases, the distribution may not be made "with respect to" stock, but instead with respect to an employment or lender relationship. What appears to be a §301 distribution actually may be payment of salary or repayment of a debt.[9] When the shareholder wears more than one hat, a facts and circumstances analysis will be necessary to distinguish distributions made with respect to stock, and thus subject to §301, from payments covered by other provisions of the Code.

Section 301(c) breaks nonliquidating corporate distributions into three distinct parts. First, the portion of the distribution that is a dividend is includible in the shareholder's gross income under §301(c)(1). Until 2003, distributions classified as dividends were taxed as ordinary income. Under §1(h)(11), "qualified dividends" are now eligible for preferential capital gains rates.[10] Second, the portion of the distribution that is not a dividend shall be applied against and reduce the shareholder's adjusted basis in the stock pursuant to §301(c)(2). Finally, any remaining portion of the distribution shall be treated as gain from the sale or exchange of property under §301(c)(3).

A Closer Look at the §301 Trilogy

By including the dividend portion of the corporate distribution in gross income, §301(c)(1) repeats what we already know from the general definition of gross income in §61(a)(7), which specifically lists dividends as items to be included in gross income. Neither of these provisions provides a definition of "dividend," however. A "dividend" is defined in §316 as any distribution of property made by a corporation to its shareholders out of earnings and profits accumulated after 1913 (accumulated e&p) or out of earnings and profits of the taxable year (current e&p).[11] Without getting

---

8. I.R.C. §317(a). A corporation distributing its own stock is making a "stock dividend." Stock dividends are covered by §305 and are considered in Chapter 7.

9. The reverse situation also presents concerns. A payment that appears to be salary, repayment of a debt, or other nondividend payment in fact may be a disguised or constructive dividend. Constructive dividends will be considered later in this chapter.

10. The operation and implications of this provision are discussed in Chapter 1 and also are considered later in this chapter.

11. Current e&p is computed "as of the close of the taxable year without diminution by reason of any distributions made during the taxable year." I.R.C. §316(a)(2). Thus, the status of current e&p on the precise date of the distribution generally is not relevant. In contrast, accumulated e&p on the date of the distribution will be relevant. These details are explored further in Example 3 of the Examples and Explanations section below.

into details for the moment, it should at least be clear that an operating distribution may be entirely a dividend, partially a dividend (to the extent that it is paid to shareholders out of earnings and profits), or not a dividend at all (if the corporation has no earnings and profits).[12]

The last two parts of the §301(c) trilogy deal with the excess portion of the distribution determined *not* to be a dividend after application of the §316 dividend test. The portion of the distribution that is *not* a dividend is applied against and reduces the shareholder's adjusted basis in the stock under §301(c)(2). This second part of the distribution rule trilogy provides for a tax-free recovery of the taxpayer's investment (basis) in the stock. Finally, since basis cannot be reduced below zero,[13] and since the shareholder should not receive *more* than his or her investment back tax free, §301(c)(3) requires the shareholder to treat any remaining portion of the distribution as gain from the sale or exchange of property. Since stock generally is held as a capital asset, the gain or loss from this deemed sale or exchange generally will be capital gain or loss.

Why Limit Dividends to Amounts Paid Out of Earnings and Profits?

A closer look at the "dividend" definition in §316 will help to understand the e&p limitation. Imagine that shareholder A contributes $100 to form a new solely owned corporation.[14] Before the corporation has earned any profit, the corporation distributes $100.[15] Shareholder A arguably has no economic gain from this receipt and should report no taxable gain since the distribution was simply a return of the original investment. This is precisely the result achieved by §§301 and 316. Since the corporation has no earnings and profits, the distribution will not be treated as a dividend. Instead, under §301(c)(2), the portion of the distribution that is not a dividend (in this case, the full $100) is a tax-free recovery of capital and will be applied against shareholder A's stock basis. Applying the $100 distribution against

---

12. Several details concerning the §316 dividend rules are not addressed here in the text. The Examples and Explanation section below explores additional details, including a discussion of the differences in computing current as opposed to accumulated e&p.

13. Negative basis certainly is a theoretical possibility. See, e.g., George Cooper, Negative Basis, 75 Harv. L. Rev. 1352 (1962). Nevertheless, Congress and the Treasury Department have never opted to use it. The concept of negative basis was addressed in connection with the discussion of §357(c) in Chapter 4.

14. Assume for purposes of discussion that the contribution was tax free under §351 and that the shareholder's stock basis under §358 was also $100.

15. You may be wondering how the corporation could distribute the $100 and still survive. Assume that the corporation had excess cash on hand, either from borrowing or from gross receipts before paying expenses. In other words, the corporation had available cash, but no economic profit.

the $100 original stock basis now will reduce shareholder A's stock basis to zero. Additional distributions to the shareholder before the corporation has earned a profit will be treated under §301(c)(3) as gain from a fictional sale or exchange of the shareholder's stock.[16]

Imagine now that shareholder A's corporation earns a $100 profit in its first year of operations. The corporation's distribution of $100 to the shareholder at the end of the first year theoretically might be construed either as a distribution of the $100 profit or as a distribution of the underlying $100 capital contributed by the shareholder. The statutory provisions in §§301 and 316 effectively adopt a "profits first" ordering rule under which earnings and profits are deemed to be distributed before capital. Since the corporation has current e&p, the $100 distribution to shareholder A in this example is a taxable dividend under §301(c)(1) and the shareholder's $100 stock basis is not reduced.

The underlying rationale of §316 appears to be that when a corporation makes distributions that are not out of e&p or profit, the corporation is dipping into its capital. In a tax regime that taxes only net income, shareholders must be entitled, at some point, to receive a tax-free return of their original investment. When the corporation makes a distribution before it has a profit, the shareholders arguably are recovering the capital they have invested in the corporation and which is reflected in the shareholder's stock basis. Since the shareholder has recovered this investment from the corporation without tax, basis in the stock should be reduced by the amount of the distribution. Failure to reduce basis would permit a potential double tax-free recovery of capital.

Although the recovery of capital notion often is cited as the rationale for the dividend definition, it is not an entirely satisfactory explanation of §316. The use of both accumulated and current e&p sometimes produces results inconsistent with a logical application of recovery of capital principles. To illustrate, imagine that shareholder A contributes $100 to form a corporation. In the first year of operations, the corporation incurs a deficit. In year 2, the corporation has some current earnings, but not enough to make up the prior year's deficit. The corporation thus has an accumulated deficit or a negative accumulated e&p account. From shareholder A's perspective, the corporation has not yet been profitable overall. Nevertheless, a distribution will result in dividend income to shareholder A to the extent of current e&p. A corporation with an accumulated deficit, but current earnings, might avoid this "nimble dividend" result for its shareholders simply by deferring distributions until a subsequent year in which there is no current e&p. Thus, not only can the §316 two-part dividend definition sometimes

---

16. Since the stock basis has already been reduced to zero, no further basis remains to be recovered tax free under §301(c)(2).

produce results inconsistent with recovery of capital principles, but the rules also can be manipulated by careful timing of distributions.

Application of the two-part e&p definition can yield results inconsistent with a recovery of capital rationale in other ways as well. Suppose that shareholder A above sold his stock to shareholder B at the end of year 1 (a deficit year) and before any distributions were made. Concerned about buying into a deficit corporation, shareholder B agreed to pay only $90 for the shares. Assume further that the corporation remains in a deficit position for year 2. Shareholder B will have no dividend income upon a corporate distribution of $100 in year 2, since the corporation has no e&p. Instead, the $100 distribution will be treated first as a tax-free recovery of shareholder B's $90 basis in the shares under §301(c)(2) and then as a $10 gain from the sale or exchange of stock under §301(c)(3). Notice that the corporate investment *has* been profitable as to shareholder B, who received a distribution in excess of the price paid for the shares. To the extent of the excess $10 received over the $90 paid for the stock, application of the dividend definition arguably results in windfall basis recovery treatment to shareholder B.

Given the weaknesses of recovery of capital theory as a satisfactory explanation for the §316 two-part dividend definition, one must look elsewhere for answers. The corporate tax history books may shed some light. Until 1936, the dividend definition referred only to accumulated e&p. At that time, corporations were subject to an undistributed profits tax. Corporations were entitled to deduct dividends paid in computing undistributed earnings subject to the old tax, but distributions out of *current* earnings made by a corporation with an *accumulated deficit* were not considered dividends. Hence, they were not deductible for purposes of the undistributed earnings tax. As relief for these corporations, Congress added what is now §316(a)(2) including distributions out of *current* e&p as dividends. The undistributed profits tax was repealed long ago, but the two-part dividend definition remains.

The Tax Stakes: Timing and Character of Shareholder Income

a) A Matter of Timing

What is really at stake for the shareholder applying the §301 distribution rules is the timing and character of income reporting. Sooner or later, the shareholder will be required to pay tax on his or her share of corporate profit.[17] Profits retained by the corporation presumably increase the value

---

17. One notable exception is the shareholder who holds onto stock until death and passes the stock on to heirs with a stepped-up basis under I.R.C. §1014.

of the corporation's stock. This increased value should be reflected in a higher gain to the shareholder upon ultimate sale of the stock. If instead, the corporation passes profit on to its shareholders through distributions, the shareholders will report immediate income to the extent that the distributions are dividends under §316. In effect, the corporation's dividend payments accelerate the shareholder's liability for tax upon his or her share of corporate profit. This is consistent with realization principles. A shareholder who receives a distribution has realized a gain to the extent of the distribution. Distributed profits have left the corporation and are no longer reflected in an increased value in the shares themselves. If no shareholder tax on the dividend is collected at this point, there may never be an opportunity to collect a shareholder level tax upon this profit.

Timing also is at stake when the corporation makes a distribution that is not out of e&p. Typically, the owner of a non-wasting asset must wait for final disposition of the asset to recover his or her capital through a basis offset to the amount realized from the sale under §1001, or would only be entitled to a partial basis recovery upon a disposition of a portion of the asset.[18] Owners of stock arguably should be subject to the same rules. After all, if the corporation has truly dipped into capital so as to reduce its overall net worth, this will ultimately be reflected in a lower price paid for the shares. Just like any other owner of a non-wasting asset, the shareholder simply would report a lower gain, or perhaps even report a loss, upon sale of the asset. Nevertheless, the §301 rules offer shareholders a uniquely accelerated recovery of capital. Unlike owners of other non-wasting assets, shareholders may receive a tax-free recovery of capital under §301(c)(2) without disposing of the shares. In the meantime, they have in hand the value represented by the corporate distribution. Proposals have been made to repeal the §316 e&p limitation altogether so that shareholders would be taxed on distributions regardless of their corporate source.[19] Overall gain or loss from the stock ownership would be computed upon final disposition of the shares. Since no such proposals have been adopted, shareholders retain the privilege of an advanced recovery of stock basis upon receipt of certain corporate distributions without disposing of the underlying stock.

---

18. See, e.g., the rules for proportional basis recovery upon the disposition of a portion of a larger property in Treas. Reg. §1.61-6(a).

19. Among the first of these proposals was from Professor William Andrews in an article entitled Out of Its Earnings and Profits: Some Reflections on the Taxation of Dividends, 69 Harv. L. Rev. 1403 (1956). See also Staff of the Senate Comm. on Finance, The Reform and Simplification of the Income Taxation of Corporations, 98th Cong., 1st Sess. 77 (1983); S. Rep. No. 99-47, 99th Cong., 1st Sess. (1985).

b) The Character Issue

i) Ordinary Income Versus Capital Gain?

The increased value from a corporation's retained profits presumably will be reflected in the gain reported by the shareholders upon sale or exchange of the stock. Gain from a shareholder's sale or exchange of stock held for investment typically is capital gain, historically eligible for lower preferential tax rates.[20] Until 2003, however, profits distributed to shareholders as dividends were taxed to the shareholders at higher ordinary income rates. Thus, in addition to accelerating the timing of a shareholder level tax, corporate dividend distributions often changed the *character* of the shareholder level tax from capital gain to ordinary income.[21] Put differently, under prior law the Code's approach to timing and character issues offered two advantages to individual shareholders who received their share of corporate profit in the form of capital gains as opposed to dividends. Investors often benefited both from deferred recognition of gain and lower rates.

ii) "Qualified Dividend" Rules

The §1(h)(11) qualified dividend rules have significantly changed the stakes for corporations and their shareholders with regard to dividend distributions. Although dividends still result in immediate taxable income to recipient shareholders, most dividends to individual shareholders will no longer be subject to ordinary income tax rates but instead will be taxed at the same preferential rates as "net capital gains."

Taxpayers historically have been eligible for preferential tax rates on gains from the sale of capital assets. "Net capital gain" eligible for capital gains rates is computed under a series of "netting rules" and holding period requirements provided in §1222.[22] The preferential rates applicable to "net capital gain" is generally limited to the net amount of "long-term capital gains," which are defined as gains "from the sale or exchange of a capital asset held for more than 1 year."[23] The netting rules in §1222 calculate net capital gain as long-term capital gains, offset by any long-term capital losses and then by any net short-term capital losses.[24]

Although stock itself generally is considered a capital asset, dividends are not. When Congress added the "qualified dividend income" rule, it did not

---

20. For a brief discussion of capital gains preferences, see Chapter 1.

21. The Code imposes some penalties on excessive retention of earnings in order to prevent corporations from deliberately using a retained earnings technique to reduce ordinary dividend income to their shareholders. These issues are considered briefly in Chapter 1.

22. "Net capital gain" is defined as "the excess of the net long-term capital gain for the taxable year over the net short-term capital loss for such year." I.R.C. §1222(11).

23. I.R.C. §1222(3).

24. I.R.C. §1223(7), (11).

alter the "capital asset" definition provided in §1221 or change any of the capital asset holding period rules in §1223. Instead, Congress provided that *only* for purposes of the rate provisions in §1(h), "'net capital gain' means net capital gain (determined without regard to this paragraph) increased by *qualified dividend income*."[25] The term "qualified dividend income" itself is a term of art, defined as "dividends received during the taxable year from (I) domestic corporations, and (II) qualified foreign corporations."[26] Despite the apparent simplicity of this definition, provisions in §1(h)(11)(B)-(D) include many provisos and exceptions.[27]

The decision to add "qualified dividend income" to the top of "net capital gains" *only* for purposes of the §1 *rate* provisions rather than to include such dividend income in the §1221 asset definition itself has interesting implications. First, the effect of this creative approach is that dividend income is not included in the netting process used to compute net capital gain. Thus, although dividends benefit from capital gains rates, they cannot be offset by any net capital losses. Second, dividends are not subject to the one-year holding period otherwise used to compute long-term capital gain. Instead, §1(h) includes its own unique, and much shorter, holding period. To be classified as "qualified dividend income," the dividend must be paid with respect to stock that meets a complex 60-day holding period under which the shareholder must have held the stock for at least 60 days during a 121-day period beginning 60 days before the stock becomes "ex-dividend."[28] The holding-period rules and many of the other exceptions to the "qualified dividend income" definition are addressed to perceived abuses of investors who engage in arbitrage, quick trades, hedging transactions, short sales, and the like.

Although it does not technically operate as an *exception* to the "qualified dividend income" definition, another special rule was included in §1(h)(11) to prevent potential manipulation of the reduced tax rates on dividend income. Absent a special rule, an investor might buy stock, the cost basis of which reflects an anticipated dividend, expecting to treat the dividend as "qualified dividend income" taxable at preferential capital gains rates. Given the high basis in the shares, the investor might shortly thereafter expect to sell the stock at a loss, using the loss as a short-term capital loss to reduce income that would otherwise be taxed at higher ordinary income rates.

---

25. I.R.C. §1(h)(11)(A) (emphasis added).
26. I.R.C. §1(h)(11)(B).
27. Dividends from "qualified foreign corporations" are subject to a number of special restrictions contained in §1(h)(11)(C). The definition also includes exceptions for dividends paid by tax-exempt corporations, I.R.C. §1(h)(11)(B)(ii)(I), by mutual funds, I.R.C. §1(h)(11)(B)(ii)(II), and by regulated investment companies (RICs) and real estate investment trusts (REITs), I.R.C. §1(h)(11)(D)(iii). Issues with respect to these special exceptions are not considered further in this book.
28. I.R.C. §1(h)(11)(B)(iii).

To prevent such manipulation, §1(h)(11)(D)(ii) classifies certain large dividends on stock owned by the shareholder for relatively short periods of time as "extraordinary dividends." Such dividends remain eligible for the qualified dividend rates, but any subsequent loss from the sale or exchange of the stock will be treated as long-term capital loss to the extent of prior extraordinary dividends.[29]

To be sure, the exceptions and special rules included in §1(h)(11) add significant complexity to what otherwise might have been a rather straightforward provision. As a practical matter, however, most dividends paid to most individual shareholders of U.S. domestic corporations should qualify for the qualified dividend preferential rates. Further discussion of the mechanics of §1(h)(11) is beyond the scope of most introductory courses on corporate taxation.

In-Kind Distributions

Not all distributions to shareholders are made in the form of cash or its equivalent. On occasion, particularly in the case of small, closely held corporations, distributions are made in-kind. For example, a corporation might distribute an asset in its investment portfolio or an asset no longer needed for ongoing operations. From the shareholder's perspective, such distributions are governed by the same rules in §§301 and 316 discussed above.

There will be some practical differences in application of the rules, however. First, determining the amount of the distribution will be slightly more difficult than it is in the case of cash distributions. Section 301(b)(1) provides that the amount of the distribution is the amount of money received plus the fair market value of other property received.[30] Thus, determining the amount of an in-kind distribution will require valuation of the property distributed. Once the amount of an in-kind distribution has been determined, the tax consequences will depend upon the outcome of the §301(c) trilogy. In other words, the shareholder will have dividend income to the extent of e&p, tax-free recovery of capital on excess amounts to the extent of stock basis, and sale or exchange gain on the remainder of the distribution.

---

29. I.R.C. §1(h)(11)(D)(ii). For a definition of "extraordinary dividend," §1(h)(11) cross-references §1059, an "extraordinary dividend" rule previously only applicable to corporate shareholders. In general, a dividend is classified as an "extraordinary dividend" if it equals or exceeds 10% of the shareholder's adjusted basis in the stock. I.R.C. §1059(c). A brief discussion of the "extraordinary dividend" rules as applied to corporate shareholders follows later in this chapter.
30. When the shareholder assumes or takes property subject to liabilities, the amount of the distribution is reduced by the amount of the liability. I.R.C. §301(b)(2). This point is considered below in a separate section on distributions involving liabilities.

The recipient shareholder of an in-kind distribution does have one additional concern that the cash recipient does not—determining basis in the property received. Section 301(d) simply provides that the basis of such property shall be its fair market value. This fair market value basis makes sense because the shareholder has taken the value of the distribution into account for tax purposes. Since the receipt is taxable, the shareholder receives a "tax cost" basis as if she had first received cash and then purchased the property.

DEFINITIONS OF EARNINGS AND PROFITS

General Concepts

Given the importance of earnings and profits in identifying dividends for purposes of §316, it is surprising that the Internal Revenue Code provides no definition.[31] Even the Treasury Department regulations are of limited assistance. Because the Code has not provided a definition, the rules regarding computation of e&p have been developed in an ad hoc fashion through scattered legislation, cases, regulations, rulings, and common sense accounting.

The concept of earnings and profits is distinct from that of taxable income.[32] Nevertheless, taxable income is a useful place to start in computing e&p. A corporation generally must use the same method of accounting for e&p purposes that it employs for computing taxable income.[33] In order to arrive at e&p from taxable income, corporate accountants must make various upward and downward adjustments to taxable income. The Internal Revenue Code fails to provide a comprehensive list of such adjustments, but Congress at least provides a hint as to the purpose of the adjustments in its title to §312(n): "Adjustments to Earnings and Profits to More Accurately Reflect Economic Gain and Loss." In computing *taxable* income, Congress permits certain exemptions and deductions purely for economic or social policy reasons and not because the exemptions or deductions are necessary to accurately represent the corporation's economic profits. The earnings and profits account theoretically provides a truer picture of the corporation's *economic* income or profit than taxable income can.

---

31. Despite its lack of a statutory definition, the Code does list certain necessary adjustments to earnings and profits "to more accurately reflect economic gain and loss." I.R.C. §312(n). Some of these adjustments are considered later in this section.
32. Accountants and others familiar with financial accounting should be aware that e&p for purposes of §316 also is distinct from the concept of "retained earnings" for purposes of the corporate balance sheet.
33. Treas. Reg. §1.312-6(a).

Upward Adjustments

Two basic categories of upward adjustments must be made to taxable income to compute e&p. The first category involves certain items that were excluded from taxable income, but must be added back for e&p purposes. One major upward adjustment in this first category is contained not in the Code itself, but in Treas. Reg. §1.312-6, which provides that e&p includes tax-exempt income. Even though certain corporate income may be exempt from federal income tax, it must be added back to taxable income in computing e&p. A common example is interest on certain bonds and other obligations excluded from gross income under §103. In addition, a corporate shareholder must add back to taxable income the amount subtracted under the §243 dividends-received deduction. The rationale for these upward adjustments is that income exempt from tax at the corporate level nevertheless represents part of the corporation's profit or economic income. Distributions of such profits to the shareholders should be taxable to the same extent as other distributions of profit. Failure to include this income in e&p would provide a *double* benefit; income would be exempt at both the corporate and the shareholder level.

The second category of upward adjustments involves differences in timing for e&p purposes. Although Treas. Reg. §1.312-6(a) generally requires the taxpayer to use the same method of accounting for taxable income and e&p purposes, certain timing-related e&p adjustments operate as exceptions. A good example of an upward adjustment in this category is found in §312(n)(5), which requires that e&p be computed as if the installment method had not been used even though the corporation uses the installment sale method in determining taxable income. Although §453 installment reporting permits deferral for taxable income purposes, the full gain from an installment sale is realized at the time of sale. To arrive at e&p from taxable income, the corporate taxpayer here must add back any gain from the sale that has been deferred through use of the installment method.

Another example of a timing related upward adjustment to taxable income involves depreciation. Although the corporation may use an accelerated method of depreciation for income tax purposes, §312(k) requires the corporation to compute depreciation on a straight-line method for e&p purposes. Thus, to arrive at e&p from taxable income, the corporate taxpayer must add back the excess of accelerated over straight-line depreciation.

Downward Adjustments

In addition to upward adjustments, corporate taxpayers will also make some downward adjustments to taxable income to determine e&p. The corporation will be entitled to deduct certain items for e&p purposes that are not otherwise deductible for tax purposes. As with the upward adjustments, these downward adjustments to taxable income assure that e&p is a more accurate reflection of economic gain or loss. The adjustments reflect expenses that deplete economic resources but are otherwise nondeductible for tax purposes. The most common example is federal income tax.[34] Although not deductible for taxable income purposes, federal income tax is deductible in computing e&p. The timing of the downward adjustment for federal income tax paid has been settled through rulings and case law. A cash basis taxpayer, for example, reduces earnings and profits for the year in which the tax is actually paid.[35] An accrual basis taxpayer, on the other hand, can deduct federal income tax liability from e&p in the year that the liability accrues.[36] Although the corporation cannot deduct dividends paid in computing its taxable income, dividends paid will reduce e&p as provided in §312.[37]

Additional Timing Issues

The Internal Revenue Code contains several provisions that allow temporary nonrecognition or deferral of income. The e&p related issues presented by such nonrecognition items are different from those raised by the exempt income adjustment discussed above. The exempt income items discussed above are permanently excluded from the tax base. If they are to be included in e&p, they must be included when they are received. Nonrecognition/deferral items, on the other hand, will be included in the taxpayer's taxable income for some later year. Such deferral items generally enter into e&p in the year they are recognized, not in the year they are realized.[38] We studied one example of nonrecognition/deferral rules earlier in §351. Additional examples can be found in the like-kind exchange rules of §1031, involuntary conversion rules of §1033 and the relief from discharge of indebtedness income in §108.

In the case of affiliated corporations, a member of a corporate consolidated group will compute its e&p in the same manner as if it had filed a separate return. The consolidated return regulations provide a few exceptions, however. For example, under the consolidated return regulations, if one

---

34. Certain tax penalties paid also will reduce e&p. See Rev. Rul. 57-332, 1957-2 C.B. 231.
35. Helvering v. Alworth Trust, 136 F.2d 812 (8th Cir.), *cert. denied*, 320 U.S. 784 (1943); Rev. Rul. 70-609, 1970-2 C.B. 78.
36. James Armour, Inc. v. Comm'r, 43 T.C. 295, 310 (1964).
37. The §312 adjustments to earnings and profits following a corporate distribution will be considered later in this chapter.
38. See I.R.C. §312(f)(1); Bangor and Aroostook R.R. v. Comm'r, 193 F.2d 827 (1st Cir. 1951), *cert. denied*, 343 U.S. 934 (1952).

member of a consolidated group sells property to another, the gain or loss from the intercompany transaction is deferred.[39] The intercompany gain or loss is not included in taxable income in the year of sale, but instead will be included later "to produce the same effect on consolidated taxable income (and consolidated tax liability) as if [the corporations] were divisions of a single corporation, and the intercompany transaction were a transaction between divisions."[40] So, for example, gain or loss from the property sale would be included in taxable income when the property is disposed of *outside* of the consolidated group. In computing e&p, the selling member of the group will not take the deferred gain or loss into account until it is included in the taxable income of the group.[41] This special rule for deferred intercompany transactions is consistent with the treatment of other deferral transactions, such as like-kind exchanges, in which the item is not included in e&p until the income is included in taxable income. Under consolidated return regulations, the e&p of the lower-tier members of a consolidated group is annually transferred or "tiered up" to the common parent so that the common parent reflects the e&p for the entire group.[42]

SPECIAL RULES FOR CORPORATE SHAREHOLDERS

The Dividends-Received Deduction: §243

Corporations often wear two hats. In addition to paying a corporate level tax, a corporation may own shares in another corporation and thus be subject to a shareholder level tax as well. When a corporation wearing its shareholder hat receives a distribution from another corporation, it will be subject to the same §301 rules discussed above. Unlike an individual shareholder, however, a corporate shareholder receiving a distribution from a domestic (U.S.) corporation will be entitled to a special dividends-received deduction under I.R.C. §243.

Under the current rules in §243, Corporations that are members of an affiliated group and receive "qualifying dividends" are eligible for a 100% deduction of dividends received.[43] Small business investment companies are also entitled to a 100% deduction.[44] Under the default rules in §243(a),

---

39. Treas. Reg. §1.1502-13(c)(1). See particularly Treas. Reg. §1.1502-13(c)(7), ex. 1. A realized gain or loss to the selling corporation that is deferred under the consolidated return regulations is called an "intercompany item."
40. Treas. Reg. §1.1502-13(c)(1).
41. Treas. Reg. §1.1502-33(a).
42. Treas. Reg. §1.1502-33(b).
43. I.R.C. §243(a)(3), (b).
44. I.R.C. §243(a)(2),

other corporations are entitled to only a 50% deduction.[45] The dividends-received deduction increases to 65%, however, for corporate shareholders owning 20% or more of the stock of the distributing corporation.[46]

The rationale for this special deduction is reasonably straight-forward. Without the deduction, corporate profits would be taxed first to the corporation that earned them, again to the corporate shareholder receiving the distribution, and yet again to the individual shareholder upon receipt of a distribution from the second corporation. Although Congress provided for a double tax on corporations, it did not intend a triple, or potentially even more extensive, multi-tiered tax in the case of longer corporate ownership chains.

Special Rules for Corporations Filing a Consolidated Return

Corporations that are affiliated, as defined in §1504, are entitled to file a consolidated return. Although the same basic §301 rules will apply to a distribution from one member to another member of a consolidated group, there are some differences. In most cases, an intercompany distribution is not included in the gross income of the member receiving the distribution.[47] This exclusion effectively achieves the same result as taking a 100% dividends-received deduction. Notice, however, that it also permits the distributee to exclude the excess distribution that would otherwise have been taxable as capital gain under §301(c)(3). In keeping with the "single entity" theory underlying the consolidated return regulations, both the dividend income under §301(c)(1) and the capital gain under §301(c)(3) are deferred through a corresponding negative adjustment to the distributee corporation's basis in stock in the distributing corporation.[48]

Congressional Response to Dividends-Received Deduction Abuses

Although the dividends-received deduction is designed to eliminate multiple layers of taxation beyond the existing double tax, it also has been subject

---

45. I.R.C. §243(a)(1),

46. I.R.C. §243(c). In the 2017 tax legislation Congress lowered the dividends-received deduction amounts to their current levels in connection with the reduction of the corporate tax rate. Pub. L. No. 115-97, 131 Stat. 2054 §13002 (2017). Before this change corporate shareholders owning between 20% or more (but less than 80%) of the stock of the distributing corporation were entitled to an 80% deduction, and corporate shareholders owning less than 20% were entitled to a 70% deduction.

47. Treas. Reg. §1.1502-13(f)(2)(ii).

48. *Id.*; Treas. Reg. §1.1502-32. See particularly Treas. Reg. §1.1502-13(f)(7), ex. 1.

to abuse by corporations seeking to classify otherwise taxable receipts as deductible dividends. Congress on several occasions has reconsidered the deduction, adding several anti-abuse provisions.[49] For example, Congress has imposed holding period requirements to prevent corporations from purchasing stock immediately before and selling immediately after a distribution simply to take advantage of the §243 deduction.[50]

Another restriction disallows the §243 deduction when the distributing corporation is a tax-exempt organization. Section 243 is designed to eliminate multiple layers of tax *beyond* the basic double tax of Subchapter C. It is not designed to eliminate the corporate level tax altogether. Assuming that the tax-exempt distributing corporation paid no tax on the income when it was received, a §243 deduction to the recipient corporate shareholder would eliminate the corporate level tax altogether. Consequently, §246(a) denies the dividends-received deduction in the case of distributions from tax-exempt corporations.

Corporations also arguably abused the §243 deduction in certain leveraged stock investments. For example, corporations would purchase stock for their investment portfolios with borrowed funds. Absent statutory restrictions, dividends from such leveraged stock would be entitled to a dividends-received deduction, effectively excluding all, or a portion, of the dividend from taxable income. In addition, the corporation would be entitled to deduct interest expense incurred in connection with the debt-financed purchase. The combination of §243 and interest deductions provided a net tax loss from the transaction that could be used to shelter other corporate income. Congress responded with limitations on the §243 deduction in the case of debt-financed portfolio stock. Section 246A restricts the §243 deduction in the case of dividends on debt-financed portfolio stock through a formula that reduces the dividends-received deduction to the extent of the "average indebtedness percentage."[51] Well-advised taxpayers have discovered that they can bypass the §246A restrictions, however. Stock will be subject to §246A only if it has been acquired through "portfolio indebtedness," defined to mean "any indebtedness directly attributable to investment in the portfolio stock."[52] When a corporation deposits borrowed funds into general accounts along with funds from other sources, the fungibility of money makes it difficult to determine which funds were actually used for the portfolio stock. At least one court has interpreted the "directly attributable"

---

49. This book will not provide in-depth coverage of anti-avoidance provisions in this area. What follows in the text is a brief discussion of some of the anti-abuse rules.

50. See I.R.C. §246(c).

51. I.R.C. §246A(a)(2). Another investment-related abuse of the dividends-received deduction has been the use of hedging transactions. Congress responded to hedging designed to reduce the risk of loss by disallowing the §243 deduction in certain hedging transactions. I.R.C. §246(c)(1)(B).

52. I.R.C. §246A(d)(3).

language very narrowly, making it virtually impossible for the IRS to make a successful §246A case. In conclusion, the court conceded "that §246A's current statutory and regulatory regime makes it virtually impossible for the Service to trace debt proceeds and thus assess tax deficiencies under §246A against companies . . . who engage in numerous investment transactions. However, any decision to loosen the 'direct' connection required between debt-proceeds and the purchase of dividend-paying stocks must be made by Congress or the Service, not the courts. . . ."[53]

Another transaction designed by corporations to take advantage of the §243 deduction is known as "dividend stripping." To illustrate, assume that Corporation X hears that Corporation Y is about to distribute a substantial dividend. It purchases Y shares for $200 and shortly thereafter receives a $50 dividend. As a corporate shareholder, X is entitled to a dividends-received deduction with respect to the $50 distribution. Given a 50% dividends-received deduction under §243(a)(1), only $25 of the $50 distribution is subject to tax and the remaining $25 effectively is excluded. After the dividend distribution, the value of the Y shares drops to $150. Corporation X now sells the shares for $150 and, absent statutory restrictions, would take a $50 capital loss. Congress responded to this type of transaction with the "extraordinary dividend" rules in §1059. In the case of an "extraordinary dividend"[54] issued on stock held for less than two years,[55] the corporate shareholder must reduce basis in the stock by the nontaxed portion of the dividend.[56] In the example above, Corporation X's $200 cost basis is reduced by $25 to $175. Thus, X's capital loss will be limited to $25.[57]

---

53. OBH, Inc. v. United States, 397 F. Supp. 2d 1148, 1164 (D. Neb. 2005).

54. Extraordinary dividends are those where the amount of the dividend equals or exceeds specified percentages of the taxpayer's adjusted basis in the stock. I.R.C. §1059(c). In other words, §1059 applies only to the receipt of certain large dividends relative to the corporate shareholder's investment in the distributing corporation's stock. Even if the distribution is not an "extraordinary dividend" subject to §1059, an alternative "dividend stripping" rule is designed to prevent §243 abuses by limiting the corporation's §243 dividends-received deduction with respect to dividends received on stock held for less than 45 days during a specified 90-day period. I.R.C. §246(c).

55. Certain exceptions will apply. See, e.g., §1059(d)(6), (e)(3).

56. I.R.C. §1059(b). An extraordinary dividend under §1059 may even trigger an immediate gain to the extent that the nontaxed portion of the dividend exceeds the corporate shareholder's basis in the stock. I.R.C. §1059(a)(2).

57. In the "dividend stripping" illustration, a *corporate* shareholder hoped to take advantage of the §243 dividends-received deduction to reduce or eliminate dividend income and then report an "artificial loss" on the subsequent sale of the stock. Absent special rules, the reduced tax rates applicable to "qualified dividend income" now offer *individual* shareholders similar opportunities. In place of the §243 deduction, the individual shareholder might use §1(h)(11) to reduce tax on dividend income, and subsequently try to report a similar "artificial loss" upon sale of the stock. Although the mechanics are somewhat different, the §1059 "extraordinary dividend" concept, previously applicable only to corporate shareholders, has now been extended to noncorporate shareholders as well. See the discussion earlier in this chapter.

Dividends-Received Deduction in a "Bootstrap Acquisition"

Another creative use of the §243 dividends-received deduction is to reduce a corporate shareholder's potential gain from the sale of stock. One of the landmark cases in this area is Waterman Steamship Corporation v. Commissioner.[58] The parent corporation, Waterman Steamship, received a $3.5 million cash offer for all of its stock in two subsidiary corporations. Since the parent's basis in the subsidiary shares was only $700,000, such a sale of stock would have resulted in a $2.8 million taxable capital gain. Waterman Steamship counterproposed a sale at the reduced price of $700,000 to be completed after its subsidiaries had declared and paid dividends amounting to $2.8 million. This might appear to be quite a deal to the buyer. How often does the counteroffer from the seller come in at a substantially lower price? The rub was that the dividend was paid in the form of a short-term (30-day) promissory note. This note was paid with funds borrowed by the purchasing corporation from its major stockholder shortly after the purchaser acquired control of Waterman Steamship's subsidiaries. The end result here is that the selling corporation has received $3.5 million cash ($2.8 million in distributions from its subsidiaries and $700,000 from the buyer) in connection with the sale of its subsidiaries. This type of transaction sometimes is called a "bootstrap acquisition" since a substantial portion of the funds for the acquisition appear to come from the seller itself rather than from the buyer. The seller thus uses its own funds to "bootstrap" the sale.

Waterman Steamship argued that the $2.8 million was a cash dividend received when it was both legal and equitable owner of the subsidiaries' stock. It argued that the cash dividend should not be taxed pursuant to the consolidated return regulations, which effectively exclude inter-corporate dividends in provisions paralleling §243. The government, on the other hand, argued that the so-called dividend in substance was part of the sales price paid for the stock. The Tax Court agreed with the taxpayer, but the Fifth Circuit reversed, holding that the subsidiaries acted as "a mere conduit for passing the payment through to the seller. We agree with the Commissioner. The so-called dividend and sale were one transfer. The note was but one transitory step in a total, pre-arranged plan to sell the stock."[59] The selling corporation in Waterman Steamship wound up with a busted bootstrap acquisition.

---

58. 430 F.2d 1185 (5th Cir. 1970), cert. denied, 401 U.S. 939 (1971), nonacq., 1975-2 C.B. 3.
59. Id. At 1192.

5. Nonliquidating Distributions

Other corporate sellers have avoided the pitfalls displayed in this case and arranged successful sales of stock with pre-sale distributions of cash or other unwanted assets.[60] For example, in TSN Liquidating Corporation v. United States,[61] the selling corporation (TSN) arranged for an in-kind distribution of approximately $1.8 million of assets from its target subsidiary immediately prior to selling the subsidiary stock to the purchasing corporation for approximately $800,000. Immediately after the sale transaction, the purchaser contributed substantial capital to the target subsidiary, the effect of which was to reinfuse the value of the target's assets previously distributed to TSN. TSN, of course, claimed the distribution as a dividend eligible for a §243 deduction. Relying on *Waterman Steamship*, the government countered that the alleged dividend should be treated as part of the purchase price upon sale of the subsidiary stock. The Fifth Circuit disagreed and held for the taxpayer. The court noted that the distribution in *Waterman Steamship* "was clearly a sham, designed solely to achieve a tax free distribution of assets ultimately funded by the purchaser."[62] In contrast to the *Waterman Steamship* "sham" distribution, TSN's subsidiary distributed assets that were unwanted by the buyer and ultimately were retained by TSN. The court also noted that there was no suggestion that TSN had a tax avoidance motive, adding that "[t]he fact that the dividend may have had incidental tax benefit to the taxpayer, without more, does not necessitate the disallowance of dividend treatment."[63]

The *TSN* and *Litton Industries* cases illustrate that it still is possible to successfully structure a bootstrap acquisition through a pre-sale dividend distribution of assets by a target subsidiary, deductible by the selling parent under §243. Taxpayers should tread carefully, however, in planning such transactions. First, it is important that there be some business reason for the distribution, usually that the distributed assets are unwanted by the buyer. The parent ideally should avoid an immediate sale or exchange of the assets received in the pre-sale distribution. Finally, the taxpayer must take into account the basis reduction in its subsidiary stock, and potential taxable gain that can result if the distribution is treated as an "extraordinary dividend" under §1059.[64]

---

60. See, e.g., Litton Industries, Inc. v. Comm'r, 89 T.C. 1086 (1987), *acq. in result in part*, 1988-2 C.B. 1.

61. 624 F.2d 1328 (5th Cir. 1980).

62. *Id.* At 1335.

63. *Id.* At 1336.

64. The selling parent corporation must also take into account that in determining the extent of the dividend, special rules for computing e&p are imposed on distributions to 20% shareholders by I.R.C. §301(e).

TAX CONSEQUENCES TO THE DISTRIBUTING CORPORATION

In-Kind Distributions: §311

a) In General

A corporation does not realize or recognize any gain or loss upon a simple cash distribution to its shareholders. In contrast, in-kind distributions can have significant tax consequences. Do not be misled by §311(a), which provides a general nonrecognition rule for the distributing corporation upon distributions of property with respect to stock. This so-called general rule is virtually swallowed by the exception provided in §311(b). When a corporation distributes *appreciated* property, §311(b) requires that the distributing corporation recognize gain "as if such property were sold to the distributee at its fair market value." In other words, the distributing corporation must treat the appreciated property as if it had been sold to the shareholders, triggering taxable gain.[65] Given the gain recognition required by §311(b), what remains of the §311(a) "general rule" simply is a loss disallowance rule. In the end, Congress does *not* provide a two-way street for in-kind operating distributions. Corporations must recognize gain upon distribution of appreciated property, but cannot recognize loss upon distribution of loss property.[66]

The explanation for the statutory inversion of the "general rule" and its "exception" in §311 is historical. At one time in corporate tax history, corporate level nonrecognition of *both* gain and loss upon in-kind distributions was the general rule. This old nonrecognition rule often is attributed to the famous 1935 decision of the United States Supreme Court in General Utilities & Operating Company v. Helvering.[67] The General Utilities company owned stock in the Islands Edison Company originally purchased for $2,000, but worth approximately $1 million. Rather than sell the stock directly, General Utilities distributed the stock to its shareholders, who then sold the shares. The issue for the court was whether the distribution of this

---

65. If the in-kind distribution is from one member to another member of a consolidated group, a distribution of appreciated property still triggers a gain under §311(b). However, under the consolidated return regulations, the §311(b) gain will be deferred as if property had been transferred within divisions of a single corporation. In general, the deferred gain will be taxed when the distributed property leaves the consolidated group. Treas. Reg. §1.1502-13(f)(7), ex. 1.

66. This should be contrasted with liquidating distributions. Unlike §311, §336 provides that "gain *or loss* shall be recognized to a liquidating corporation on the distribution of property in complete liquidation." I.R.C. §336(a) (emphasis added). Liquidating distributions are considered in Chapter 8.

67. 296 U.S. 200 (1935).

highly appreciated stock required General Utilities to report a taxable gain on the difference between the fair market value of the stock and its $2,000 basis. The Supreme Court held that there was no taxable gain.[68] The government's concern with this transaction should not be hard to discern. The distributing corporation disposed of its highly appreciated Islands Edison stock, transferring $1 million in value to its shareholders. Although the $1 million value was reported as dividend income to the shareholders, the corporation reported no gain or loss. The corporation effectively escaped the corporate level portion of the double tax on corporate income. If the corporation had sold the Islands Edison stock directly to the buyer and distributed the cash proceeds from the sale to its shareholders, two levels of tax would have been collected.

Surprisingly, Congress first indicated its approval of the *General Utilities* decision by initially codifying the nonrecognition rule in §311(a).[69] In piece-meal fashion over the years, however, Congress has chipped away at, and finally repealed, the *General Utilities* nonrecognition rule as applied to distributions of appreciated property. Rather than repeal §311(a) entirely, Congress left it in place and added §311(b). The gain recognition rule now in §311(b) reflects the congressional judgment that corporations should not be able to escape corporate level taxation on appreciation in corporate assets distributed to shareholders.

Imagine that Corporations X and Y each hold an asset with a basis of $110 and a fair market value of $150. Corporation X arranges to sell the asset for $150 and later distributes $150 cash to its sole shareholder. In contrast, Corporation Y distributes the asset directly to its sole shareholder, who later sells the asset for $150. These two economically similar transactions now will result in similar tax consequences. Corporation X will recognize a $40 taxable gain on the sale under §§61(a)(3) and 1001 and the shareholder will report income from the cash distribution under the §301 rules. Similarly, Corporation Y will recognize a $40 gain upon the distribution under §311(b) and the shareholder will report gain from the in-kind distribution under the §301 rules. In each case, the character of the corporation's gain as capital or ordinary will depend upon the character of the asset.

Switching to loss property, suppose that Corporation X sold an asset with a basis of $110 and a fair market value of $100 and later distributed the $100 cash proceeds to its sole shareholder, while Corporation Y simply distributed the loss asset directly to the shareholder. Corporation X is

---

68. In quite cursory fashion, the Court simply said that the corporation derived no taxable gain from the distribution of appreciated stock: "This was no sale; assets were not used to discharge indebtedness." *Id.* At 206.
69. Congress initially provided a parallel nonrecognition rule for liquidating distributions as well. These rules and the relevant *General Utilities* history in the liquidation context are considered in Chapter 8.

entitled to recognize the $10 loss upon sale of the asset, but Corporation Y will *not* be entitled to deduct the $10 loss. Since this is not a distribution of appreciated property, the §311(a) nonrecognition rule will apply. In this case, the two similar economic transactions do *not* have similar tax results.

b) Why the Lack of Symmetry in §311?

Why does Congress require recognition of gain upon distributions of appreciated property but prohibit recognition of loss upon distributions of depreciated property? Congress has historically been concerned with the possibilities for manipulation of loss recognition.[70] This is particularly true where the parties to the transaction are related.[71] If both gains and losses were recognized upon corporate distributions, corporations might be motivated to leave gains unrealized by holding onto appreciated assets, but realize losses by distributing loss assets. One might respond with the observation that a corporation wishing to avoid gains but realize losses can achieve this result by holding onto appreciated property and selling depreciated property in the marketplace. Cash received from the sale could then be distributed to the shareholders. A sale of loss property in the marketplace can be distinguished from a distribution of loss property to the shareholders, however, since the marketplace sale actually causes the property to leave the corporate family. Recognition of the loss in this case comes at a price; the corporation *and* its shareholders must relinquish control over the property. If losses were recognized upon in-kind distributions, corporations would be able to receive the tax benefit of the loss while keeping the property in the corporate family's hands.[72]

Adjustments to E&P: §312

Remember that shareholders report taxable dividends only to the extent of the corporation's e&p. Once a distribution is made out of earnings and profits, the e&p distributed is no longer available for future dividend

---

70. In fact, even in connection with liquidating distributions, upon which loss recognition is generally allowed, §336(d) imposes limitations on loss recognition in certain cases. These limitations are discussed further in Chapter 8.

71. See, e.g., I.R.C. §267(a), which disallows losses from sales or exchanges between related parties. Related parties, for purposes of §267, include an individual and a corporation in which the individual owns more than 50% in value of the outstanding stock. I.R.C. §267(b)(2).

72. The real concern for manipulation evolves from the relationship of corporation and shareholder. Congress fears that the corporation will take a loss, but still retain control of the property indirectly through its shareholders. This is more likely to be a problem with respect to controlling shareholders. Some would argue that the §267 restriction on losses between related parties is a sufficient response to the loss manipulation possibility and that the §311 restriction is overly broad.

distributions. Accordingly, §312(a) requires the distributing corporation to decrease its earnings and profits after making a distribution with respect to its stock. Although a corporation might find itself with a negative e&p account from operating business losses, §312(a) effectively prohibits the corporation from *creating* a deficit in e&p through distributions since e&p can only be reduced after a corporate distribution "to the extent thereof."

Following a cash distribution, the distributing corporation simply decreases e&p by the amount of money distributed.[73] Adjustments following in-kind distributions of property can be slightly more involved. To illustrate, suppose again that Corporation Y distributes an asset with a basis of $110 and a fair market value of $150. As a result of this in-kind distribution of appreciated property, §312(b)(1) first requires the distributing corporation to *increase* e&p by the excess of fair market value over basis of the property distributed. In other words, e&p is increased to the extent of the $40 corporate gain just recognized under §311(b).[74] As described earlier in this chapter, a corporation also adjusts e&p downward for federal income taxes, when the tax liability is either paid or accrued, depending on the corporation's accounting method.[75] As a result, Corporation Y would also adjust its e&p downward by the amount of any additional income tax liability to the corporation resulting from gain recognized on the distribution.[76]

Corporation Y next must *decrease* e&p to reflect the distribution. Under the "general rule" for e&p adjustments following corporate distributions, the corporation would decrease e&p by the *adjusted basis* of the property distributed.[77] In the case of *appreciated* property, however, the Code instructs the corporation to substitute the words "fair market value" for "adjusted basis."[78] In other words, Corporation Y in the above example would now decrease e&p by the full $150 fair market value of the distributed asset. While the statutory language is cumbersome, the result is sensible. If Corporation Y had never been taxed upon the $40 gain from appreciation in the distributed asset and had never reflected that gain in e&p, it might make sense to limit the downward adjustment to e&p from the distribution to the $110 basis in the asset. In fact, the "general" e&p adjustment rule in §312(a)(3) actually is a relic left over from the days when the *General Utilities* nonrecognition rule prevailed, and even distributions of appreciated property did not result in

---

73. I.R.C. §312(a)(1).
74. In fact, since the §311 gain is included in the corporation's taxable income and since the e&p computation will begin with taxable income, the language of §312(b)(1) may be unnecessary. The gain certainly should not be counted in e&p twice.
75. Bittker & Eustice, Federal Income Taxation of Corporations & Shareholders, Chapter 8.05; Rev. Rul. 70-609, 1970-2 CB 78.
76. See Bittker & Eustice, Federal Income Taxation of Corporations & Shareholders, Chapter 8.22[1].
77. I.R.C. §312(a)(3).
78. I.R.C. §312(b)(2).

taxable gain to the distributing corporation. Just as the §311(b) exception virtually swallows the §311(a) "general rule" regarding recognition of gain or loss upon in-kind distributions of property, the §312(b) exception similarly virtually swallows the §312(a)(3) "general rule" regarding corporate adjustments to e&p after in-kind distributions.

The §312(a)(3) "general rule" decreasing e&p by the adjusted basis of the property distributed will apply to distributions of loss property. Suppose again that Corporation Y distributes property with a basis of $110 and a fair market value of $100. When loss property is distributed, §312(a)(3) simply requires that e&p be reduced by the adjusted basis of the property. Although §311(a) disallows the loss for tax purposes, the corporation is still entitled to reduce e&p by the $110 adjusted basis of the property distributed, thus reducing the e&p amounts available for future distributions. This is a sensible result since the corporation's "cost" or investment in the distributed property was $110 and this amount has left the corporation and is no longer available for future distribution.

No Deductions for Dividends Paid

As opposed to many other corporate payments, dividends are not deductible to the distributing corporation. On the other hand, interest expense incurred by a corporation generally is deductible under §163.[79] In addition, reasonable salary payments to employees (including shareholder employees) are deductible trade or business expenses under §162. Distinguishing between nondeductible dividend payments and other deductible corporate expenses has historically been a thorny problem with significant tax implications for both shareholders and corporations. First, corporations may raise capital through issues of equity or debt instruments and the distinction between the two types of instruments can be blurry. Among the major considerations taken into account in deciding between debt and equity as a method of raising capital is the interest deduction that is generally available to the corporation (but subject to limitations) upon corporate interest payments to debt holders.[80] Before 2003, shareholder concern with the distinction was low, given that both dividends and interest were taxable at the same ordinary income rates in any event.[81]

---

79. The corporation may be subject, however, to the §163(j) limitation on the deductibility of business interest. The rules for the treatment of corporate debt are discussed in Chapter 3.
80. See Chapter 3 for discussion of corporate capital structure and the factors used to distinguish debt from equity.
81. On the other hand, individual shareholders might prefer dividend classification of a corporate distribution if the distributing corporation had zero or low e&p. In such a case, all or some of the distribution would be a tax-free recovery of capital under §301(c)(2).

Shareholders often wear multiple hats, adding to the difficulty in distinguishing debt from equity. For example, a taxpayer may be both a shareholder and a seller. It can sometimes be difficult to tell whether the assets were *contributed* to capital in exchange for a dividend-paying equity interest or *sold* to the corporation in exchange for an interest-bearing note.[82] If a shareholder is also an employee, it can be difficult to determine whether a particular payment constitutes deductible compensation or a nondeductible dividend.

In the past, the government position generally was to argue that corporate payments, particularly those to individual shareholders, were dividends taxable as ordinary income to the shareholder and nondeductible to the corporation. As long as tax rates applicable to "qualified dividend" income remain much lower than the rates applicable to compensation and interest income, the government may not be as vigorous in its "dividend" assertions in these cases.[83]

DISTRIBUTIONS INVOLVING LIABILITIES

Shareholder Tax Consequences

If the shareholder either assumes a liability, or takes property subject to a liability, in connection with an in-kind distribution, §301(b)(2) provides that the amount of the distribution will be reduced (but not below zero) by the amount of such liability. After all, when a shareholder takes on a liability in connection with an in-kind distribution, the value of the property to the shareholder is reduced to the extent that she must incur debt in order to retain the property. Imagine, for example, that the corporation distributes property with a fair market value of $150 that is subject to a $100 mortgage to shareholder A. The *amount* of shareholder A's distribution under §301(b)(2) is $50—the *net* value of the distribution after taking the liability into account.[84]

Even though the fair market value of the property distributed is reduced by liabilities to determine the *amount* of the distribution, the shareholder still is entitled to a fair market value *basis* in the property under §301(d). Thus,

---

82. See the discussion in Chapter 4.

83. See Chapter 1 for an additional discussion of the dynamics resulting from the "qualified dividend income" rules.

84. The extent to which this $50 distribution is taxable as a dividend depends on the outcome of the same §§301 and 316 shareholder distribution analysis considered earlier in this chapter.

shareholder A's basis in the distributed property is $150. This full fair market value basis simply extends to the shareholder the same right to include borrowing in basis that is provided to all taxpayers;[85] the shareholder is given the benefit of a presumption of repayment of the debt and is entitled to include borrowing in advance as a "cost."

Interesting issues arise when the shareholder takes on a debt with respect to the distributed property that *exceeds* the fair market value of the property. For example, imagine that shareholder A took the distributed property worth $150 subject to a $200 mortgage. The *amount* of the distribution now would be zero, since §301(b)(2) prohibits a reduction below zero. Under §301(d), shareholder A's basis in the distributed property would be limited to its $150 fair market value. As a result, the shareholder cannot include the full amount of the $200 liability in the distributed property's basis. What is *really* happening when a shareholder receives an in-kind property distribution where a recourse liability assumed exceeds the value of the property? In this example, shareholder A must pay $50 more for the property than its worth. At least in the case of operating distributions, such a situation might be construed as a shareholder contribution of $50 to the corporation's capital. The shareholder arguably should receive an increase in his or her stock basis reflecting the excess of the liability over fair market value.[86]

Distributing Corporation Tax Consequences

When a corporation makes an in-kind distribution in connection with which the shareholders either assume a liability or take property subject to a liability, additional corporate level considerations arise. According to general tax principles, the amount realized to the seller must include the amount of liabilities when a buyer either assumes or purchases property subject to liabilities.[87] Since §311(b) requires the corporation to treat the distribution as a sale to the shareholder, the "amount realized" to the corporation upon the distribution includes liabilities taken on by the shareholders. Corporate level gain upon an in-kind distribution ordinarily is measured by

---

85. In its landmark opinion in Crane v. Comm'r, 331 U.S. 1, 11 (1947), the Supreme Court concluded that the taxpayer's basis in property included her mortgage. The Court reached this result in *Crane* even though the liability involved was a *nonrecourse* mortgage. The Court noted the longstanding practice of the Treasury Department allowing taxpayers to use the full value of property (undiminished by liabilities) for purposes of depreciation and continued acceptance of this practice by Congress. It is now well settled that basis includes borrowing. Comm'r v. Tufts, 461 U.S. 300 (1983).
86. Treas. Reg. §1.118-1. For an in-depth discussion of contributions to capital, see Chapter 3.
87. This rule serves as a corollary to the rule that borrowing is included in basis. If borrowing was included in the seller's basis in the property, the buyer's assumption of the liability must be included in amount realized upon resale. Comm'r v. Tufts, 461 U.S. 300 (1983); Crane v. Comm'r, 331 U.S. 1 (1947); Treas. Reg. §1.1001-2(a).

the fair market value of the property distributed over its adjusted basis.[88] Suppose, for example, that Corporation X distributes property with a basis of $80 and a fair market value of $150 to shareholder A, subject to a $100 mortgage on the property. Corporation X will report a taxable gain of $70 under §311(b). In this case, the $150 amount realized includes both the $100 liability taken on by the shareholder and the additional $50 value in the appreciated property.

While the term "fair market value" *ordinarily* refers to the price that a willing seller and an unrelated buyer would agree to in the marketplace, the Code requires that the fair market value of the property "be treated as *not less than* the amount of [the] liability" when liabilities are involved in an in-kind distribution.[89] Thus, when the liabilities *exceed* fair market value, corporate level gain under §311 will be measured by the excess of *liabilities* over adjusted basis. To illustrate, imagine that the mortgage in the above example was $200 instead of $100. Even though the fair market value of the property was only $150, the amount realized to the corporation upon its distribution of the property to its shareholder now would be $200, resulting in a $120 taxable gain.[90] This twist on the general rule is simply a codification in the corporate distribution context of the holding in Commissioner v. Tufts.[91] In *Tufts*, the Supreme Court held that when a buyer assumes or takes property subject to a liability, the amount realized from the sale must include the full amount of the liability *even* if the liability *exceeds* the fair market value of the property.[92]

For distributions involving liabilities, §312(c) requires that "proper adjustment" be made to e&p for liabilities to which distributed property is subject or which are assumed by shareholders. This language is not very helpful. What

---

88. I.R.C. §311(b). This gain formula is no different from the formula used upon sales of property generally. See I.R.C. §1001.

89. I.R.C. §336(b). Section 336 generally covers the tax consequences to corporations upon *liquidating* distributions, which are considered in Chapters 8 and 9. With respect to nonliquidating distributions, §311(b)(2) entitled "Treatment of Liabilities," provides that "[r]ules similar to the rules of section 336(b) shall apply for purposes of this subsection." Notice that §336(b) applies to both recourse and nonrecourse debt. Cf. Treas. Reg. §1.1001-2(c), ex. 8.

90. Notice that this gain reflects $70 appreciation in the property's value and an additional $50 from excess liability over the value of the property.

91. 461 U.S. 300 (1983).

92. Since the acceptance of excess recourse liabilities might be viewed as a shareholder contribution to capital, one might argue that the corporation should receive this excess as a tax-free contribution to capital under §§118 or 1032. For a detailed discussion of these sections, see Chapter 3. Under this view, the corporation's gain, contrary to *Tufts*, should be limited to fair market value over basis. This view would require repeal of §336(b). The argument against this view is that *Tufts* requires full inclusion of liabilities in amount realized because the liabilities were included in the corporation's basis when the funds were borrowed. This basis from borrowing may have resulted in depreciation or other deductions. *Crane* and *Tufts* require symmetry in the inclusion of borrowing in both basis and amount realized. Thus, full inclusion of the recourse liability as provided in §336(b) may be warranted. Resolution of this debate is beyond the scope of this book.

is the proper adjustment? Relief from a liability generates income or profit. In the old world under *General Utilities*, "proper adjustment" required an increase in e&p to the extent of the liability.[93] "Proper adjustment" for liabilities under §312(c) in the world after repeal of *General Utilities* is more confusing. A more detailed analysis of the necessary adjustment is provided in the Examples and Explanations section below.[94]

CONSTRUCTIVE DIVIDENDS

In addition to actual dividends, corporations sometimes engage in activity which is *deemed* to result in dividend treatment. One common example is the closely held company in which the shareholders also are involved in day-to-day management activities for which they receive salary. If the corporation pays salaries in excess of what is reasonable, the excess may be viewed as a constructive dividend to the employee-shareholder to the extent that the corporation has sufficient e&p to cover the excess payment. Of course, if an excess payment is treated as constructive dividend to the shareholder, it also will be a nondeductible dividend payment for the corporation. In other words, the corporation's §162 salary deduction for the excess salary payment would be disallowed. Even if a salary payment is not deemed to be a constructive dividend, the IRS still may challenge corporate salary deductions simply on the grounds that the payments are unreasonable.[95] In a 2004 case, the Tax Court denied approximately $12.9 million of a corporation's approximately $20 million deduction for salary paid in 1998 to a CEO who was also the founder and sole voting shareholder of the closely held corporation, on the grounds that the excess payment was unreasonable and that it was a disguised dividend.[96] In a somewhat blistering finding of clear error, the Seventh Circuit reversed the Tax Court's decision that the payments were excessive.[97] The appellate court's observation that "[a]ll businesses are different, all CEOs are different, and all compensation packages for CEOs are different" signals that the IRS may continue to face serious burden of

---

93. In convoluted fashion, the regulations talk about "reducing the reduction." Treas. Reg. §1.312-3. The effect of reducing the reduction is an increase.

94. See Example 7.

95. Treas. Reg. §1.162-7(b)(3) (defining "reasonable" as?only such amount as would ordinarily be paid for like services by like enterprises under like circumstances?).

96. Menard, Inc. v. Comm'r, 88 T.C.M. 229 (2004), reconsideration denied, 89 T.C.M. 656 (2005), rev'd, 560 F. 3d 620 (7th Cir. 2009).

97. Menard, Inc. v. Comm'r, 560 F.3d 620, (7th Cir. 2009) (applying the Seventh Circuit presumption that salary is reasonable if investors are obtaining a higher return than they have reason to expect); Id. At 627 (referring to the Tax Court's numerical adjustments as "arbitrary and dizzying"); Id. At 626 (complaining of the Tax Court's comparison of CEO's base salary to other corporations in the industry without comparing total compensation packages).

proof obstacles in attempts to disallow an arguably excessive salary deduction claimed by a closely held corporation.[98] Current law also reduces the incentive for corporations to pay compensation rather than dividends to an employee-shareholder, since the latter are now taxed at a lower rate to the recipient as a qualified dividend.

Another common constructive dividend is free service or property provided by the corporation to a shareholder-employee or officer — free personal use of the corporation's private jet, for example. From the shareholder's perspective, both dividends and salary are fully taxable. There is one important distinction, however. Salary payments are taxable without regard to the corporation's e&p account. On the other hand, a constructive dividend is taxable as a dividend under §301 only to the extent of the corporation's e&p.[99] From the corporation's perspective, the distinction is even more significant. Salary payments are deductible business expenses whereas dividend distributions are not deductible.

Examples

Some Beginning Questions

1. Curly is the sole shareholder of Beautiful Pups, Inc., (BPI) a dog-grooming business. Curly's basis in the shares is $5,000. BPI employs Moe to run the day-to-day operations. At the end of the year in question, BPI has current e&p of $100,000 and accumulated e&p of $300,000. BPI distributes cash of $100,000 to Curly. Tax consequences to Curly? Tax consequences to BPI? What issues are raised if, instead of hiring incompetent Moe as the manager, Curly manages the business himself?

2. a. What if BPI in the above problem had no current e&p?
   b. What if BPI had $100,000 in current e&p, but no accumulated e&p?
   c. What if BPI had $100,000 in current e&p, but an accumulated deficit?
   d. What if BPI had $25,000 in current e&p and $25,000 in accumulated e&p?
   e. What if BPI had no e&p at all?

3. a. Curly, Moe, and Larry each were the sole owners of Stooges Plumbing during one-third of the first taxable year of Stooges operations.

---

98. Id. At 623. In the case of publicly held corporations, §162(m) already prohibits deductions for excessive employee remuneration, defined as remuneration in excess of $1 million with respect to CEOs and certain other highly compensated employees.
99. Historically, of course, the other significant distinction was that dividends were taxed as ordinary income. Under the qualified dividend rules, most domestic corporate dividends are now taxed at net capital gains rates.

Curly owned all the shares for the first period from January 1 through March 31, during which time the company had $100,000 in current e&p. Moe owned the shares from April 1 through June 30, during which time the company had $200,000 in current e&p. Larry owned the shares for the final period, during which time the corporation suffered a $150,000 loss. Each received a $100,000 distribution from the corporation during his term of ownership. How should Curly, Moe, and Larry treat these distributions for tax purposes?

b. What if the above distributions took place in the second year of operations, the year 2 current earnings were the same as year 1 above, and, in addition to the current e&p, Stooges had $25,000 in its accumulated e&p account?

Computing Earnings and Profits

4. Stooges Plumbing is a cash basis corporation.[100] Its income and expenses for the taxable year were as follows:

Gross receipts from plumbing services	$200,000
Ordinary and necessary expenses for salaries and supplies	50,000
Income from tax-exempt bonds	10,000
Accelerated depreciation on equipment: a ten-year asset with an original basis of $5,000	750
Realized but unrecognized gain from like-kind exchange under §1031	1,000
Federal income tax liability for the prior taxable year paid in the current taxable year	5,000

Compute Stooges' e&p for the taxable year.

Adding Complexities at the Corporate Level

5. a. On December 31, Minstrel Singers, Inc., distributes to its shareholders an old Boesendorfer grand piano with a fair market value of $125,000 and a basis to the corporation immediately before the distribution of $75,000. Assume that the corporation had sufficient e&p to cover the distribution. What tax consequence to Minstrel Singers, Inc.? To the shareholders?

---

100. Under §448(a) C corporations generally cannot use the cash method of accounting. Assume, however, that Stooges is excepted from this restriction by §448(b)(3), which allows C corporations with average annual gross receipts of less than $25 million in the prior three years to use the cash method.

b. What if Minstrel Singers had no e&p for the year in which the distribution was made?

6. In Example 5, what if the basis of the property to the corporation immediately before the distribution had been $60,000 and the fair market value of the property had been $50,000?

7. a. What if the property described in Example 5 was subject to a mortgage of $100,000 and the shareholders took the property subject to the mortgage?
   b. What if the mortgage amount in Example 7a was $130,000?

The Corporate Shareholder

8. a. MicroMac, Inc., is a large computer corporation that owns 80% of MiniMac, Inc., a subsidiary corporation. The remaining 20% of MicroMac's stock is owned by individual minority shareholders. The two corporations do not file a consolidated return. MiniMac has been extremely profitable and declares a pro rata distribution from e&p of $50,000. Of this total amount, $40,000 is distributed to MicroMac as the parent company and $10,000 is distributed to the minority shareholders. What are the tax consequences of the distribution to both MicroMac and to the minority shareholders? Would the results be different if the subsidiary corporation was tax exempt?
   b. How would your answer to Example 8a change if MicroMac and MiniMac *did* file a consolidated return as affiliated corporations under §1504?

9. On January 1, MicroMac, Inc., purchased shares of IBM stock for $100,000. On January 15 of the same year, IBM paid a $2000 dividend on these shares. MicroMac sold its IBM shares on January 30 of the same year. What are the tax consequences to MicroMac upon receipt of the dividend?

A Sneaky Question

The precise issue raised by the following question was not discussed in the text above. Test your skills by intuiting an answer based on concepts that were discussed:

10. Corporation Y is a publishing company and Corporation Z manufactures paper. Both corporations are wholly owned by shareholder A. Last year, Corporation Y spent $500,000 for paper purchased from Corporation Z. If Y had paid the prices normally charged to Z's other customers, the bill would have been $750,000. What are the tax consequences, if any, of these events to shareholder A and Corporations Y and Z?

Explanations

1. Curly will have a fully taxable dividend of $100,000 under §§301(c)(1) and 61(a)(7) since the corporation has sufficient e&p to cover the distribution. His $5,000 basis in the BPI stock will remain unchanged. After the distribution, BPI's e&p account must be reduced by the amount of money distributed pursuant to §312(a)(1). The question here is whether the distribution comes out of current or accumulated e&p since there is enough of either to cover the distribution. The flush language of §316(a) provides that "except as otherwise provided, . . . every distribution is made out of earnings and profits to the extent thereof, *and from the most recently accumulated earnings and profits*." See also Treas. Reg. §1.316-2(a) (emphasis added). Under these rules, current e&p must be exhausted before dipping into accumulated earnings. BPI's current e&p will be reduced to zero or "wiped out." I.R.C. §312(a)(1). The accumulated e&p account remains at $300,000. There will be no deduction to BPI for the dividend paid.

   The issue raised if Curly manages the business himself is whether the distribution was "made by a corporation . . . *with respect to its stock*." I.R.C. §301(a) (emphasis added). Where the same person wears both an employee and shareholder hat, the §301 rules may not apply at all if the distribution is viewed as made to an employee. Whether the distribution is made to Curly as employee or shareholder will be determined under the facts and circumstances. If the payment to Curly is viewed as compensation for his services, Curly will have §61(a)(1) salary or compensation income. If viewed as a payment with respect to stock, Curly will have §61(a)(7) dividend income. Before the §1(h)(11) "qualified dividend income" rules, Curly may well have been indifferent regarding classification of the distribution as compensation or dividend. Either way, the distribution would have been taxed at ordinary income rates. On the other hand, as a sole shareholder of a closely held corporation who probably bears the incidence of both the corporate and the shareholder level tax, Curly might have had some preference for compensation classification since the ordinary and necessary business expense deduction to the corporation would result in lower corporate income subject to tax. If classified as a dividend pursuant to the rules in §§301 and 316, the distribution should be "qualified dividend income" to Curly eligible for preferential capital gain rates under §1(h)(11). If viewed as a payment to an employee, BPI can take a §162(a)(1) deduction for an ordinary and necessary salary expense. In contrast, a dividend payment to a shareholder is nondeductible.

2. a. Even if BPI had no current e&p, Curly would still be required to report $100,000 in §301 dividend income, since there is sufficient

accumulated e&p to cover the distribution. I.R.C. §316 clearly refers to accumulated *or* current e&p. BPI's accumulated e&p account would be reduced to $200,000. I.R.C. §312(a)(1).

b. If BPI had only current e&p of $100,000, but no accumulated e&p, Curly would still have a fully taxable dividend. Section 316 includes dividends paid out of current *or* accumulated e&p. This distribution would wipe out BPI's e&p.

c. If BPI had an accumulated deficit, but nevertheless had $100,000 of current earnings, the dividend to Curly would still be taxable, again because §316 uses the word "or" rather than "and." This "nimble dividend" result arguably is inconsistent with recovery of capital principles. Since Curly is the original shareholder and the corporation has not yet been profitable, the distribution of funds arguably should be treated as a recovery of capital.

d. If BPI had only $25,000 in current and $25,000 in accumulated e&p, Curly's taxable dividend would be limited to the extent of the $50,000 combined e&p. He would receive $5,000 as a tax-free recovery of his basis under §301(c)(2) and reduce the basis in his shares from $5,000 to zero. The remaining $45,000 would be treated as gain from the sale or exchange of stock under §301(c)(3). If Curly has held the stock for the proper holding period under §1222, the gain will be treated as long-term capital gain. Regarding the corporation's e&p adjustment following the distribution, recall that the distribution can only reduce e&p *to the extent thereof.* I.R.C. §312(a). Consequently, both BPI's current and accumulated e&p accounts are reduced to zero, but not below.

e. If the corporation had no e&p at all, Curly would receive $5,000 as a tax-free recovery of capital under §301(c)(2) and reduce his basis in the shares to zero. The remaining $95,000 would be §301(c)(3) gain. If Curly held the stock for the proper holding period under §1222, the gain would be long-term capital gain.

3. a. Since this is the first year of Stooges operations, it has no accumulated e&p. The *net* current e&p at the end of year 1 was $150,000. I.R.C. §316(a) provides that *current* e&p is to be "computed as of the close of the taxable year without diminution by reason of any distributions made during the taxable year and without regard to the amount of the earnings and profits at the time the distribution was made." Thus, the particular status of the *current* e&p account at the time of each distribution is irrelevant. Current e&p of $150,000 was not sufficient to cover the $300,000 total distributions, however. Under these circumstances, the dividend portion of each distribution is determined by using a ratio, the numerator of which is total current e&p and the denominator of which is total distributions. See Treas. Reg.

§1.316-2(b). In our case, this ratio would be $150,000/$300,000 or 50%. Thus, Curly, Moe, and Larry will each be taxed upon a dividend of $50,000, one-half of the $100,000 each received. The remaining half of each distribution will be tax-free recovery of capital to the extent of their bases in the stock under §301(c)(2) with any excess treated as gain from the sale of stock under §301(c)(3). The corporation's e&p account is reduced to zero or "wiped out," leaving nothing to carry into the second year as accumulated e&p.

b. If, in addition to this year's e&p, Stooges also had $25,000 in accumulated e&p, you would first look to and "wipe out" the current e&p account as described above so that each still would have a $50,000 dividend from current e&p. In addition, according to Treas. Reg. §1.316-2(b), istributions not out of *current* e&p shall be considered taxable dividends to the extent of accumulated e&p "available on the date of the distribution." Under this rule, Curly, as the first shareholder receiving a distribution during the taxable year, would have an additional $25,000 in taxable dividend (for a total of $75,000), thus wiping out the accumulated e&p account. Moe and Larry would be left with only the $50,000 dividend computed above. This problem illustrates that, in contrast to current e&p, the status of accumulated e&p account on the date of the distribution is relevant. See also Treas. Reg. §1.316-2(c) (example). See also Rev. Rul. 74-164, 1974-1 C.B. 74.

4. The first step in computing e&p for Stooges Plumbing is to determine taxable income. To compute taxable income, deductible expenses must be subtracted from gross receipts received for plumbing services:

Gross receipts	$200,000
Less ordinary expenses	$50,000
	$150,000
Less accelerated depreciation	$750
	$149,250 taxable income

To arrive at e&p from taxable income, Stooges must make two upward adjustments. First, the $10,000 in exempt income must be added back. Treas. Reg. §1.312-6. In addition, Stooges must add back the excess of accelerated over straight-line depreciation. I.R.C. §312(k). If Stooges used straight-line depreciation for its ten-year asset with a $5,000 basis, yearly depreciation would be $500 per year. Thus the excess of accelerated ($750) over straight-line ($500) is $250. Stooges' total upward adjustments amount to $10,250:

Exempt income	$10,000
Excess depreciation	$250
	$10,250 upward adjustment amount

5. Nonliquidating Distributions

Stooges also must adjust taxable income downward for its $5,000 federal income tax liability. Since Stooges is a cash basis taxpayer, federal income tax paid in the taxable year reduces e&p for the taxable year even though the tax was due for the prior taxable year. To summarize, Stooges' e&p for the taxable year is computed as follows:

Taxable income	$149,250
plus upward adjustments	$10,250
	$159,500
less downward adjustment	$5,000
	$154,500

The realized, but unrecognized, gain from the like-kind exchange will not be taken into account for taxable income *or* e&p purposes. This gain will enter into taxable income and e&p when it is recognized. I.R.C. §312(f)(1).

5. A. Upon distribution of the piano, Minstrel must report a taxable gain as if the piano had been sold to the shareholders at its fair market value. I.R.C. §311(b). Thus, Minstrel will report a gain of $50,000 ($125,000 fair market value less $75,000 basis). Minstrel's e&p first will be increased by the $50,000 gain and then decreased by the $125,000 fair market value of the distributed piano. I.R.C. §312(a), (b). The amount of the distribution to the shareholders in this case is $125,000, the fair market value of the property distributed. I.R.C. §301(b). There was sufficient e&p to cover the distribution. Thus, the entire $125,000 will be treated as dividend to the shareholders. The shareholders will have a basis of $125,000 (fair market value) in the piano. I.R.C. §301(d).

b. If there was otherwise no e&p on December 31, the issue is whether the distribution *itself* creates any e&p that will result in dividend treatment to shareholders. The answer is yes. Under §312(b) e&p is increased by the excess of fair market value over adjusted basis. Thus, the $50,000 gain recognized to Minstrel under §311(b) will also increase its e&p. As a result, the shareholders will report $50,000 of the distribution as taxable dividend. The remaining $75,000 will be recovery of capital to the extent of basis in the shares with any excess treated as gain from the sale of stock.

The $50,000 gain recognized to Minstrel upon the distribution will also increase the corporation's tax liability for the year. As a result, this additional tax liability would also reduce the corporation's e&p when it is accrued or paid, depending upon the corporation's accounting method. Reducing the corporation's e&p by this amount in the year of the distribution would also reduce the amount of the distribution that is taxable to the shareholders as a dividend.

After an in-kind distribution, §312(a)(3) requires that e&p be decreased by the adjusted basis of property distributed. In the case of appreciated property, however, §312(b) provides that "(a)(3) shall be applied by substituting 'fair market value' for 'adjusted basis.'" Although the fair market value here is $125,000, the §312(a) adjustment cannot reduce e&p below zero. In our problem, e&p will be decreased from $50,000 to zero.

Unfortunately, the mechanics of §312 here can be rather confusing. One distribution causes three significant tax events. First, the distribution results in corporate gain. This gain increases e&p. Second, the distribution results in a taxable dividend to the shareholders to the extent of e&p. Finally, the distribution reduces e&p. Since all of these tax events are taking place simultaneously through one economic event, one may be confused as to the order in which to consider the tax consequences. Sections 312(a) and (b) provide an inelegantly drafted, but common sense, answer requiring the corporation to first increase e&p by the gain recognized and then decrease e&p by fair market value of the property distributed. Tax consequences to the shareholders must be determined after the increase to e&p, but before the decrease reflecting the distribution.

After working through the problem, you probably noticed that we first increased e&p from zero to $50,000 and then immediately decreased e&p back to zero again. If these two numbers simply wash each other out, you may be asking: why bother? The reason is that unless we went through this exercise, the shareholders would have wound up with no dividend. By temporarily increasing e&p, the corporation generated at least some e&p to cover the distribution, thus making the distribution at least partially taxable to the shareholders.

One final issue here is the basis of the piano now in the shareholders' hands. Section 301(d) simply provides that the basis is fair market value, here $125,000. Since the corporation paid tax on the corporate level gain and the shareholders paid tax on the distribution to the extent provided in §301(c), this result now seems appropriate.

6. Although the corporation has realized a $10,000 loss, the loss will not be recognized. This question illustrates the limited remaining function of the general rule of §311(a), which provides that no gain or loss shall be recognized on corporate distributions. Given the §311(b) exception for appreciated property, the "general rule" in §311(a) now effectively operates as a disallowance of loss rule. After the distribution, the corporation's e&p will be reduced under §312(a)(3) by the $60,000 adjusted basis of the property distributed. E&p cannot be reduced below zero by the distribution. If the corporation had no e&p before the distribution was made, e&p would remain at zero.

5. Nonliquidating Distributions

The shareholders in this case received a distribution of $50,000 — the fair market value of the property. I.R.C. §301(b)(1). If the corporation has sufficient e&p, this will be a dividend to the shareholders. If the corporation had no e&p, the distribution would be treated as a tax-free recovery of capital to the extent of basis and thereafter as gain from the sale of stock. The shareholders' basis in the property is its fair market value of $50,000. I.R.C. §301(d).

7. a. Adding the assumption of a mortgage to Example 5 will not change the tax results to the corporation. The corporation must still report a gain of $50,000 ($125,000 amount realized less $75,000 basis) upon distribution of the piano. The corporation is treated as if it sold the property to the shareholders at fair market value. The amount realized of $125,000 incorporates the $100,000 mortgage just as it would in an ordinary sale.

From the shareholders' perspective, the distribution must be reduced by the amount of the liabilities under §301(b)(2). Thus, the shareholders have received a $25,000 distribution ($125,000 less $100,000). The distribution will be treated as a dividend to the extent of e&p. Despite receiving only a $25,000 distribution, the shareholders will take the piano with a full fair market value basis of $125,000 under §301(d). This too reflects the *Crane* notion that borrowed amounts are included in basis. Including the liability in basis presumes that the taxpayer will pay the liability.

One sticky issue remains — what adjustment to e&p should be made following the distribution? E&p will first be increased by the amount of the gain ($50,000) under §312(b)(1), and may be reduced by the corporation's additional tax liability resulting from the additional taxable gain recognized on the distribution. Thereafter, e&p must be reduced by the fair market value of the property ($125,000) under §312(a) as modified by §312(b)(2). In addition, however, §312(c) requires "proper adjustment" for liabilities. The role of §312(c) after repeal of *General Utilities* is not entirely clear. On the one hand, given repeal of *General Utilities*, the corporation now must include the liability in amount realized on the distribution under §311. The resulting gain is included in taxable income and e&p. As a result, one might argue that no further adjustment is "proper." On the other hand, a closer look at what has been distributed out of corporate solution shows that the corporation has distributed property worth $125,000 subject to a mortgage of $100,000, or a *net* distribution of only $25,000. (Remember that this is the amount of the distribution to the shareholders figured above.) After taking the gain of $50,000 into account, then, perhaps the corporation should be limited to an e&p reduction of $25,000. Perhaps, then, "proper adjustment" for liabilities *does* require something further. Using the convoluted language of Treas. Reg. §1.312-3, we might reduce the $125,000 reduction by the $100,000 mortgage, leaving a decrease to e&p of $25,000. The latter approach seems to be the right answer here because it more accurately reflects the economic substance of the distribution.

b. Notice that the $130,000 liability exceeds the $125,000 fair market value of the property distributed. For purposes of computing Minstrel's §311(b) gain, §311(b)(2) instructs that "rules similar to the rules of section 336(b) shall apply." Under §336(b), otherwise applicable to liquidating distributions, the fair market value of the property distributed "shall be treated as not less than the amount of [the] liability." Thus, Minstrel's taxable gain upon the distribution would be $55,000 (amount realized $130,000 less $75,000 basis).

For the shareholders, the amount of the distribution is the fair market value of $125,000 reduced by the liability. I.R.C. §301(b)(1), (2). In this case, decreasing fair market value by the full amount of the liability would result in a *negative* distribution, an admittedly odd notion. The §301(b) amount of the distribution to shareholders in this case would surely be zero. There are no explicit rules in the statute or regulations addressing how the shareholders should treat the excess $5,000 liability. They might take the position that the $5,000 excess liability is a contribution to capital, which should increase their basis in the Minstrel stock.

8. a. Both MicroMac, Inc., and its minority shareholders have received a §301(c)(1) dividend. The minority shareholders will report their $10,000 share as ordinary dividend income. As a corporate shareholder, MicroMac can take a dividends-received deduction under §243. If the affiliated group has made the proper election and if the dividend is otherwise a "qualifying dividend" under §243(b), MicroMac will receive a 100% dividends-received deduction. I.R.C. §243(a)(3). The effect of this 100% deduction is to exclude the dividend from MicroMac's income.

If the subsidiary paying the dividend was a tax-exempt entity, the parent MicroMac, would not be entitled to a dividends-received deduction. I.R.C. §246(a)(1). The dividends-received deduction is designed to eliminate multiple layers of tax *beyond* the double tax. If the distributing corporation is exempt from tax and the corporate shareholder can take a dividends-received deduction, the government would collect a full tax only at the shareholder level.

b. The only change would be that MicroMac, the distributee member of the consolidated group, would simply exclude the amount of the dividend, rather than first include the dividend and then take a

§243 deduction. The effect of this treatment is the same as the §243 deduction — no tax upon the dividend distribution. In addition, under the consolidated return regulations, MicroMac would be required to reduce its basis in its MiniMac shares by the amount of the excluded dividend. Treas. Reg. §1.1502-13(f)(2).

9. MicroMac is not eligible for the §243 deduction since it did not own the IBM shares for the required holding period. I.R.C. §246(c). Thus, the dividend would be taxable to MicroMac to the extent of IBM's e&p. This holding period requirement prevents corporations from taking the §243 deduction on stock purchased recently in anticipation of a quick dividend payment otherwise eligible for a dividends-received deduction. Since §246(c) disallows the §243 deduction, no portion of the dividend is left untaxed for purposes of §1059(b). Thus, no further restrictions will apply.

10. Corporation Z has made a bargain sale to Corporation Y. Ordinarily, such a bargain would have no immediate tax consequence. Given the relationship of the two corporations, however, some interesting tax consequences emerge. Here, Corporation Z has given up $250,000 in value that has been transferred to Corporation Y. The reason for the special arrangement here was the common ownership of the two corporations. The sale might be viewed as a *constructive dividend* of $250,000 from Corporation Z to shareholder A followed by a contribution by A of the same $250,000 to Corporation Y. Under this approach, A would have dividend income to the extent that Corporation Z has e&p to cover the distribution and would receive an increase to basis in the Y shares reflecting the $250,000 contribution.[101]

---

101. See, e.g., Rev. Rul. 69-630, 1969-2 C.B. 112. Of course, not all payments between commonly controlled corporations will be treated as constructive dividends. This problem is designed simply to point out that possibility and to give some sense of the scope of constructive dividend principles.

6

Redemption Distributions

INTRODUCTION

A redemption distribution is a special type of nonliquidating distribution with one major distinguishing feature: The corporation in a redemption distributes cash or other property *in return for its own stock*.[1] At a minimum, a corporation's purchase of its own shares alters the capital structure by reducing the total shares outstanding. Moreover, unless the redemption is pro rata as to all shareholders, the redemption will alter the relative ownership interests of shareholders. In contrast, the nonliquidating distributions discussed in Chapter 5 generally did not alter the capital structure of the corporation or the relationships among shareholders or between shareholders and the corporation.

In some cases, a redemption simply reduces the number of outstanding shares and otherwise leaves the relative shareholder interests unchanged. For example, imagine a corporation with two unrelated shareholders, each of whom holds 1,000 shares of stock representing 50% of the total 2,000 outstanding shares. If the corporation pays cash to redeem 200 shares from each shareholder, the total number of shares outstanding is reduced from 2,000 to 1,600. Each shareholder now owns 800 shares. Despite this reduction in the *number* of shares, each shareholder still holds a 50% interest in

---

1. I.R.C. §317(b) provides that "stock shall be treated as redeemed by a corporation if the corporation acquires its stock from a shareholder in exchange for property, whether or not the stock so acquired is cancelled, retired or held as treasury stock."

the corporation. The corporation has less cash in its coffers and each of the shareholders has more cash in his or her pocket. How is this different from an operating distribution by which the corporation might distribute the same cash to the shareholders? The obvious answer is that in the redemption case, the corporation purchased back its own stock. From an economic perspective, however, the transactions are not very different. In either case, the shareholders have taken cash out of the corporation without changing their relative interests in the corporation. If the transaction had been structured as an operating distribution when the corporation had sufficient earnings and profits, the shareholders would have treated the distribution as a taxable dividend. When redemptions take on the quality of an operating distribution, they too will be handled under the §301 distribution rules considered in Chapter 5.

Varying the example above, imagine that the corporation decided to redeem completely the 1,000 shares from one of its shareholders, reducing the total number of outstanding shares from 2,000 to 1,000. The redeemed shareholder no longer holds any shares and the remaining shareholder's interest has increased from 50% to 100%.[2] Unlike the pro rata redemption described above, this redemption rather dramatically alters the shareholders' relative interests. The redeemed shareholder effectively has sold her entire interest back to the corporation, thus reducing her interest in the corporation from 50% to zero. From the redeemed shareholder's perspective, this redemption takes on the quality of a sale.[3]

Taken together, these examples should begin to illustrate the challenge for drafters of the Internal Revenue Code with regard to redemptions. The key problem is distinguishing those redemptions that should be handled under the §301 distribution rules and those that should be treated simply as sales of stock by the shareholders to the corporation. Individual shareholders generally will prefer sale or exchange treatment.[4] First of all, such treatment allows a basis offset that would not be available if the redemption was treated as a §301 distribution.[5] Second, if the stock has lost value, the shareholder will be entitled to use the loss for tax purposes at the time of the

---

2. Potential tax consequences to the remaining shareholders upon this increase in their proportionate interests in the corporation are considered in a separate section later in this chapter.

3. The redemption distribution will be treated as a sale under the §302(b)(3) "complete termination of interest" provision, which is discussed in detail later in this chapter.

4. Corporate shareholders, on the other hand, may prefer dividend treatment to take advantage of the §243 dividends-received deduction. For discussion of the dividends-received deduction available to corporate shareholders, see Chapter 5. Special issues related to redemptions from corporate shareholders are considered later in this chapter.

5. Assuming that there is sufficient e&p to cover the distribution, a §301 distribution will result in taxable income without any basis offset. If there is not sufficient e&p, the shareholder may receive a tax-free recovery of basis under the §301(c) rules. For complete discussion of the §301 distribution rules, see Chapter 5.

redemption.[6] Finally, since stock generally is a capital asset, sale treatment at a gain will result in capital gains eligible for preferential capital gains rates. Prior to 2003, the individual shareholder's preference for sale or exchange treatment of a redemption distribution was driven largely by the lower capital gains rates applicable to such redemption exchanges.[7] Today, however, the advantage of lower rates is available even for dividend-like redemptions, thus reducing the relative attractiveness of sale or exchange classification to individual shareholders. Even so, sale or exchange treatment of a redemption distribution still offers the advantage of a basis offset that would not generally be available under the §301 dividend rules. In addition, since qualified dividends are included in net capital gain *only* for purposes of the tax rate provisions in §1, shareholders will not be able to use any loss from the redemption distribution to offset other income in the event that the distribution is treated as a dividend under the §302 rules.

This chapter focuses primarily upon the rules designed to distinguish "sale redemptions" from "distribution redemptions." Note that these rules concern the proper tax treatment of the shareholders. From the corporation's perspective, a redemption distribution is not significantly different from other nonliquidating distributions. The final sections of this chapter consider tax consequences to the corporation.

TAX CONSEQUENCES TO REDEEMED SHAREHOLDERS

Overview

Prior to 1954, redemption distributions simply were treated as sales *unless* they were "essentially equivalent to the distribution of a taxable dividend."[8] This early statutory language was simple, but not especially helpful. After all, the very point of the redemption distribution rules was to distinguish those redemptions that should be treated as sales from those that should be treated as dividends. In this early period, decisions as to when distributions were essentially equivalent to a dividend and, therefore, taxable as a dividend, were left to the courts. Each such case required a facts and circumstances analysis and shareholders were left with tremendous uncertainty as

---

6. In assessing the value of this advantage, one must consider that the shareholder's ability to deduct the loss may be limited since the loss is likely to be capital loss.

7. On the other hand, the shareholder might have been indifferent in cases where the redeemed shares were held for less than one year, resulting in short-term capital gain on the redemption exchange. In addition, shareholders likely preferred dividend classification when the corporation had zero or low e&p.

8. Internal Revenue Code of 1939, §115(g).

to the outcome. In 1954, Congress enacted §302, under which individual shareholders could be certain of sale or exchange rather than dividend treatment upon receipt of redemption distributions meeting the precise tests provided within its §302(b) "safe harbor" provisions.[9] For the most part, the provisions enacted in 1954 are those still found in §302(b) today.

A brief look at the structure of §302 is a good place to start. First, §302(a) provides that if one of the four paragraphs of subsection (b) applies, a corporate redemption of stock will be treated as "a distribution in part or full payment in exchange for the stock"—a sale. If the redemption does not fit within one of the paragraphs of subsection (b), the redemption will be treated as a distribution of property to which the distribution rules of §301 apply.[10] Thus, §302 is designed to distinguish sale or exchange redemptions from distribution redemptions to be treated under the nonliquidating distribution rules considered in Chapter 5. *Unless* the exchange fits within one of the descriptions in §302(b), the redemption will be treated under the §301 distribution rules.[11]

The §302(b) Tests for Sale or Exchange Treatment

a) Complete Termination of Interest: §302(b)(3)

The simplest of the §302(b) rules provides sale or exchange treatment for redemptions "in complete redemption of all of the stock owned by the shareholder." A classic illustration of §302(b)(3) is a redemption distribution to one of two 50% shareholders in exchange for all of the redeemed shareholder's stock. Treating the redemption as full payment in exchange for the stock in accordance with §302(a) makes sense if the shareholder's interest in the corporation is terminated by a complete redemption. Sale or exchange gain would result from the shareholder's sale of the stock to an independent third party. The tax consequences should be no different simply because the buyer happened to be the corporation itself.

A few twists should be noted here. First, in determining whether or not a particular shareholder's interest has been completely terminated, constructive ownership rules shall apply.[12] Under these constructive ownership or attribution rules, the redeemed shareholder is deemed to own shares owned by certain related parties for purposes of testing the redemption

---

9. The benefit to individual shareholders from the §302(b) "safe harbors" is lower now that qualified dividends are also taxed preferential rates.

10. I.R.C. §302(d).

11. Note that §302(a) is entitled "General Rule." Given that only those redemptions that meet the requirements of subsection (b) are covered, this title can be a bit misleading.

12. The §318 constructive stock ownership rules will apply for purposes of all of the §302(b) tests. I.R.C. §302(c)(1). These rules are considered in detail later in this chapter.

distribution under §302(b). For example, if the two shareholders in the above example were husband and wife, the redemption of all of the shares from one of them would not qualify under §302(b)(3), since the redeemed shareholder would be considered to own the spouse's shares even after the redemption and thus, the redeemed shareholder's interest will not have been completely terminated.[13]

Second, a complete redemption need not take place at one instant. A series of redemption distributions may be considered part of a complete termination of interest if the "individual redemptions constitute, in substance, the component parts of a single sale or exchange of the entire stock interest" and if the "redemptions are pursuant to a firm and fixed plan to eliminate the stockholder from the corporation."[14] Deciding whether a series of redemptions is part of an integrated plan to completely terminate the shareholder requires a facts and circumstances analysis.[15]

b) Substantially Disproportionate Distribution: §302(b)(2)

Even if the shareholder's interest is not completely terminated, sale or exchange treatment may be available if his or her interest in the corporation is substantially reduced. In the §302(b)(2) "substantially disproportionate distribution" safe harbor, Congress provides precise mathematical tests to measure the extent of the shareholder's reduction in interest. This mathematical rule is designed to provide some certainty to shareholders concerning the percentage of stock that must be redeemed so as to qualify as a substantially disproportionate distribution. Congress determined by fiat that when there has been greater than a 20% reduction in the shareholder's voting interest *and* where the resulting interest is not a controlling interest, the shareholder has relinquished sufficient interest in the corporation to qualify for sale treatment. Thus, §302(b)(2) imposes the following two-part test:

i) The 50% Threshold Test

As a threshold, §302(b)(2) shall not apply "unless immediately after the redemption the shareholder owns less than 50% of the total combined voting power of all classes of stock entitled to vote."[16] If the redeemed

---

13. I.R.C. §318(a)(1)(A)(i).
14. Bleily & Collishaw, Inc. v. Comm'r, 72 T.C. 751, 756 (1979), aff'd, 647 F.2d 169 (9th Cir. 1981).
15. The Court in *Bleily & Collishaw* stated: "Generally, a gentleman's agreement lacking written embodiment, communication, and contractual obligations will not suffice to show a fixed and firm plan. . . . On the other hand, a plan need not be in writing, absolutely binding, or communicated to others to be fixed and firm although these factors all tend to indicate that such is the case." *Id.*
16. I.R.C. §302(b)(2)(B).

shareholder holds 50% or more of the combined voting power immediately after the redemption, the shareholder retains majority control of the corporation. A proportionate reduction that still leaves the shareholder with a controlling voting interest immediately after the redemption is not substantial enough to qualify for §302(b)(2) sale or exchange treatment.

ii) The 80% Disproportionate Distribution Tests

The second part of the mathematical test involves a before and after analysis of stock ownership. The percentage of voting stock owned by the shareholder immediately *after* the redemption must be less than 80% of the percentage of voting stock owned by the shareholder immediately *before* the redemption.[17] This test in effect requires at least a 20% reduction in the shareholder's voting interest in the corporation. The idea is that if less than 20% of the shareholder's voting interest is "sold" back to the corporation through the redemption, the shareholder's interest in the corporation relative to the other shareholders has not changed substantially. In such cases, Congress has determined that the transaction looks more like a distribution and should not qualify for sale treatment under §302(b)(2).

To illustrate, suppose that Corporation X has two unrelated shareholders, A and B, each of whom owns 50 of the 100 common voting shares outstanding and the corporation redeems 25 shares from A for cash. Immediately *before* the redemption, shareholder A owned 50% of the stock and immediately *after* the redemption, owns 25 of the remaining 75 shares or 33⅓%. Shareholder A meets the 50% threshold test since her interest is less than 50% of the voting stock immediately after the redemption. Also, the 33⅓% owned immediately after the redemption is less than 80% of the 50% owned immediately before the redemption, so the redemption will qualify under §302(b)(2).[18]

In addition to the 80% test applied to *voting* stock, §302(b)(2) requires another application of the 80% test to the common stock of the corporation,

---

17. I.R.C. §302(b)(2)(C). The language of the statute refers to the "ratio which the voting stock of the corporation owned by the shareholder immediately after the redemption bears to all of the voting stock of the corporation at such time," I.R.C. §302(b)(2)(C)(i), and the "ratio which the voting stock of the corporation owned by the shareholder immediately before the redemption bears to all of the voting stock of the corporation at such time," I.R.C. §302(b)(2)(C)(ii). For simplicity, these ratios simply will be referred to as the percentages of stock owned by the shareholder immediately after and immediately before the redemption respectively.

18. One way to figure the results under the 80% test is to create the ratio that the percentage ownership after the redemption bears to the percentage ownership before the redemption. In our example, this ratio would be 33⅓/50 or 66⅔%. Since this ratio is less than 80%, the redemption meets the 80% test. Another is first to compute 80% of the pre-redemption ratio. Since 80% of 50% is 40%, anything *less than* a 40% interest immediately after the redemption would be sufficient to qualify shareholder A for sale treatment under the §302(b)(2).

whether voting or nonvoting. Thus, if the corporation has outstanding any nonvoting common stock in addition to voting stock, the 80% test must be met for the total voting and nonvoting common shares as well as for the voting shares alone.[19]

c) Redemptions Not Equivalent to Dividends: §302(b)(1)

i) History

Section 302(b)(1) simply provides for sale treatment "if the redemption is not essentially equivalent to a dividend." Unlike the other provisions in §302(b), the "not essentially equivalent to a dividend" rule has a long history and interpretation of the statutory language in §302(b)(1) has been developed substantially through case law. This language carried over from the simple, but not especially helpful, provision in the 1939 Internal Revenue Code. The House version of the 1954 Code would have eliminated the "essentially equivalent to a dividend" language,[20] but the Senate insisted on retaining the old language, noting that the House version "appeared unnecessarily restrictive, particularly in the case of redemptions of preferred stock that might be called by the corporation without the shareholder having any control over when the redemption may take place."[21]

Given this history, modern §302(b)(1) has been quite narrowly construed and is the §302(b) sale or exchange provision of last resort for most individual shareholders. The landmark case interpreting §302(b)(1) is United States v. Davis,[22] which involved a closely held corporation owned by the taxpayer, his wife, and his children. Responding to the corporation's need for additional capital, the taxpayer contributed cash in return for some nonvoting preferred stock. The corporation was to "repay" the cash by later redeeming the shares. Since the taxpayer's basis in the nonvoting preferred shares was equal to the cash contributed, he expected little or no taxable gain from the later redemption. Unfortunately for Mr. Davis, the redemption did not qualify as a complete termination of his interest under §302(b)(3) since only his preferred shares were redeemed. Similarly, the redemption did not qualify for the §302(b)(2) substantially disproportionate distribution safe harbor. In the end, the taxpayer's argument for sale treatment hinged upon the §302(b)(1) "essentially equivalent to a dividend" test. Since his wife and children owned all of the other shares of the corporation, the taxpayer

---

19. If a corporation has only one class of voting common stock outstanding, the result of the application of the two 80% tests in §302(b)(2)(C) is the same. Rev. Rul. 87-88, 1987-2 C.B. 81.

20. H.R. Rep. No. 1337, 83d Cong., 2d Sess. 35 (1954).

21. S. Rep. No. 1622, 83d Cong., 2d Sess. 44 (1954).

22. 397 U.S. 301 (1970). The Supreme Court in *Davis* provides a rather detailed and useful description of the history behind §302(b)(1).

was deemed to be a 100% owner of the corporation both before and after the redemption through operation of the constructive ownership rules.[23] Developing what is commonly known as the "meaningful reduction" test, the Court ruled that to be eligible for sale or exchange treatment under §302(b)(1), "a redemption must result in a meaningful reduction of the shareholder's proportionate interest in the corporation."[24] Since Mr. Davis was deemed to be a 100% owner both before and after the redemption, he had experienced no reduction in interest at all. The redemption distribution in exchange for his nonvoting preferred stock was treated as a dividend.

If a shareholder's reduction in interest is to be meaningful, there at least must be some reduction. The import of the Davis decision is that redemption of a sole shareholder (or a "constructive" sole shareholder such as Mr. Davis) is always equivalent to a dividend and can never get sale treatment. The hardship in Davis should be reasonably evident. If the taxpayer had lent the necessary capital to the corporation and later been repaid, he would have had no taxable gain from the corporation's repayment of principal. By providing the needed capital to the corporation in the form of a contribution in exchange for stock, the taxpayer in Davis found himself with a taxable dividend upon redemption of the stock.[25] The dissenters in Davis argued vigorously for a bona fide business purpose exception, particularly in the case of closely held corporations. Despite this call for a bona fide business exception, the Davis meaningful reduction test continues to rule the day. A redemption from a sole shareholder, actual or constructive, will never qualify for sale treatment under §302.

ii) The Aftermath of Davis

Although the Davis case gave birth to the meaningful reduction test, the Court in that particular case found no reduction at all. Thus, the Court left open the question of how much reduction would qualify as "meaningful" in cases where a corporate redemption causes at least some reduction in the shareholder's interest. The Davis meaningful reduction test requires a facts and circumstances analysis and each case must be examined on its own merits. Nevertheless, cases and rulings interpreting the meaningful reduction test appear to fall into two categories.

The first includes redemptions from majority shareholders. When the shareholder held a majority interest immediately before the redemption and continues to hold a dominant voting interest immediately after the

---

23. I.R.C. §318(a)(1).

24. United States v. Davis, 397 U.S. 301, 313 (1970).

25. Note, however, that the taxpayer in the Davis case was entitled to add the basis in the redeemed preferred stock to his basis in the common shares he continued to hold, thus reducing future gain from the sale of the common shares. Id. At 307, n.9.

redemption, virtually *no* reduction in interest will be considered meaningful. Rev. Rul. 75-502 provides a good illustration of the Treasury Department's position. In that ruling the shareholder's interest in the corporation was reduced from 57% to 50%. The remaining 50% was owned by a single unrelated shareholder. Although the shareholder (an estate) continued to hold 50% after the redemption, its voting control was eliminated since the other 50% shareholder now held effective veto power, or at least the power to create a stalemate. The Treasury Department ruled that the redemption qualified for sale or exchange treatment under §302(b)(1). The Ruling added that if the reduction had been less than 7% "the redemption would not qualify under section 302(b)(1) because the estate would continue to have dominant voting rights in X by virtue of its ownership of more than 50% of the X stock."[26] The logic here resembles the 50% threshold test under §302(b)(2). The reduction in interest is not thought to be substantial enough to justify sale or exchange treatment if the shareholder still exercises majority voting control even after the redemption. Despite this similarity, the Treasury Department's interpretation of §302(b)(1) allows more flexibility than the rigid 50% threshold test of §302(b)(2). The redemption involved in Rev. Rul. 75-502 would not have met the threshold test of §302(b)(2), which requires that the shareholder's interest immediately after the redemption be *less than* 50%. Under the facts and circumstances of that ruling, the reduction was considered meaningful since only two shareholders remained after the redemption. By implication, the Ruling suggests that had the remaining 50% of the stock been held by many shareholders, as opposed to one, the 50% interest owned by the taxpayer after the redemption would have left effective dominant voting rights with the redeemed shareholder. The reduction in that instance would not have been considered meaningful.

Although a shareholder who retains dominant voting rights after a redemption will have difficulty using §302(b)(1), there is one set of circumstances in which a case for meaningful reduction might succeed. For example, in Wright v. United States,[27] the court held that a reduction from 85% to 61.7% was meaningful since the shareholder lost the two-thirds voting control required by state law for various corporate actions. The shareholder in *Wright* retained *managerial* control, but nevertheless lost what might be referred to as *organic* control.[28] The Treasury Department, however, refused to consider the loss of organic control as a meaningful reduction in

---

26. Rev. Rul. 75-502, 1975-2 C.B. 111.
27. 482 F.2d 600 (8th Cir. 1973).
28. Since most states and articles of incorporation provide supermajority voting rules only in the case of major organic changes such as merger or acquisition, we will refer to loss of such a supermajority interest as a loss of organic control.

a case where no action requiring a two-thirds vote was contemplated at the time of the redemption.[29]

The second category of §302(b)(1) cases involves redemptions from minority shareholders, who will have a much easier time arguing that a meaningful reduction has taken place. In contrast to the uphill battle facing the majority shareholder in qualifying for §302(b)(1) sale treatment, it appears that even very small reductions in interest will qualify the minority shareholder. For example, in Rev. Rul. 76-385[30] a reduction from a 0.0001118% interest to a 0.0001081% interest in Z Corporation was considered meaningful. The ruling points out that the redemption "involves a minority shareholder whose relative stock interest in Z is minimal and who exercises no control over the affairs of Z."[31] This was precisely the kind of case the Senate was worried about when it added back the "not essentially equivalent to a dividend" provision. Recall that the Senate Finance Committee voted to leave this language in the statute to protect "redemptions of preferred stock which might be called by the corporation without the shareholder having any control over when the redemption may take place."[32] Even though a minuscule reduction may be sufficient for many minority shareholders, there remain circumstances in which a minority shareholder may be denied §301(b)(1) treatment. For example, Rev. Rul. 85-106 suggests that a minority shareholder who owns both voting and nonvoting stock and has only nonvoting stock redeemed will face strong opposition from the Service, which continues to see loss of voting power as a key factor.[33] Even though the redeemed trust in this ruling experienced a reduction in its *economic* interests, the absence of any reduction in *voting* power was a significant factor in the ruling's conclusion that there was no 301(b)(1) meaningful reduction. In addition, the Treasury Department continues to insist on at least *some* reduction in the shareholder's proportionate interest. For example, in Rev. Rul. 81-289, the proportionate interest of the minority shareholders remained at exactly 0.2% before and after the redemption distribution. The minority shareholder in this ruling was not entitled to sale treatment under §302(b)(1) since he or she experienced no reduction in rights to vote, to participate in earnings distributions, or to net assets upon liquidation.[34]

---

29. Rev. Rul. 78-401, 1978-2 C.B. 127.
30. 1976-2 C.B. 92. Although it did not rule directly on the "meaningful reduction" issue, the Third Circuit has favorably cited the Treasury Department's 1976 ruling. Conopco, Inc. v. United States, 572 F.3d 162, 165, n.4 (3d Cir. 2009).
31. Id.
32. S. Rep. No. 1622, 83d Cong., 2d Sess. 44 (1954).
33. See, e.g., Rev. Rul. 85-106, 1985-2 C.B. 116. Although a minority shareholder, the redeemed trust in this ruling had the potential to participate in a control group by acting in concert with two other shareholders.
34. Rev. Rul. 81-289, 1981-2 C.B. 82.

d) Partial Liquidations: §302(b)(4)

The last sale or exchange redemption in §302(b)(4) has a rather different focus from the first three. The first three of the §302(b) tests focus on the extent of the *shareholder's* proportionate reduction in interest in the corporation relative to other shareholders. In contrast, the (b)(4) partial liquidation provision views the redemption from the *corporation's* perspective, looking to the extent of corporate contraction. In fact, even a pro rata redemption distribution might qualify for sale or exchange treatment under §302(b)(4).[35] In addition, unlike the other §302(b) provisions, §302(b)(4) is limited to *noncorporate* shareholders. Section 302(b)(4) permits sale or exchange treatment to a noncorporate shareholder if the distribution is "in partial liquidation of the distributing corporation."

Unfortunately, the general definition of "partial liquidation" in §302(e)(1) is quite vague. This provision sets out two requirements for classification as a partial liquidation. First, the distribution must be "not essentially equivalent to a dividend (*determined at the corporate level rather than at the shareholder level*)."[36] Second, the distribution must be "pursuant to a plan and occur within the taxable year in which the plan is adopted or within the succeeding taxable year."[37] Although some issues may arise regarding what constitutes a "plan" and the date on which the plan was adopted, this second requirement is reasonably straightforward.

The first requirement is more problematic. One might immediately notice parallels with the language in §302(b)(1). Recall that, as interpreted by the Supreme Court in the *Davis* case, a (b)(1) "not essentially equivalent to a dividend" distribution required a "meaningful reduction" in the *shareholder's* interest. Although it uses the same initial language, §302(e) asks us to make the "not essentially equivalent to a dividend" determination at the *corporate* level. Taking this instruction to heart, it should be clear that the *Davis* shareholder level meaningful reduction test will not apply to partial liquidation distributions. The meaning of "not essentially equivalent to a dividend" determined at the corporate level lies in old case law and regulations promulgated under the predecessor to §302(b)(4).[38] Under these cases and regulations, a distribution was not essentially equivalent to a dividend from the corporate perspective when the distribution reflected a "genuine

---

35. See I.R.C. §302(e)(4).
36. I.R.C. §302(e)(1)(A) (emphasis added).
37. I.R.C. §302(e)(1)(B).
38. Much of the language in §302(b)(4) originated in old §346. Thus, the regulations under this now repealed provision may be instructive. See Treas. Reg. §1.346-1. Oddly enough, even though the old partial liquidation provision in the statute itself has been repealed, the regulations remain in place.

contraction of the corporate business."[39] Even in its earlier incarnations, the "corporate contraction" doctrine was highly fact specific and the outcome of any particular case was difficult to predict.

Responding to this uncertainty, Congress provides a partial liquidation "safe harbor within a safe harbor" in §302(e)(2). Taxpayers meeting the more specific requirements in §302(e)(2) will be assured that the distribution is a partial liquidation for purposes of §302(b)(4).[40] Here again, the definition has two requirements. First, the distribution must be "attributable to the distributing corporation's ceasing to conduct, or consists of the assets of, a qualified trade or business."[41] Second, the distributing corporation must be "actively engaged in the conduct of a qualified trade or business immediately after the distribution."[42] A qualified trade or business is one that was "(A) actively conducted throughout the 5-year period ending on the date of redemption, and (B) was not acquired by the corporation within such period in a transaction in which gain or loss was recognized in whole or in part."[43] In this safe-harbor definition, we see more clearly the concept of corporate contraction. The safe harbor here envisions a corporation that was engaged in two or more businesses and is distributing the assets of, or ceasing to conduct, one of its businesses.[44]

A LOOK AT ATTRIBUTION RULES: §318

Overview

In determining the percentage ownership of stock before and after a redemption for purposes of applying the §302(b) rules discussed above,[45] the shareholder must include not only shares *actually* owned but also shares

---

39. Treas. Reg. §1.346-1(a)(2). An example in the regulations taken from an earlier case is "the distribution of unused insurance proceeds recovered as a result of a fire which destroyed part of the business causing a cessation of a part of its activities." Id.
40. The "safe harbor" definition in §302(e)(2) is not exclusive. It states that "distributions which meet the requirement of paragraph (1)(A) [the general definition] shall include (but *shall not be limited to*) a distribution meeting the requirements of . . . This paragraph." I.R.C. §302(e)(2) (emphasis added).
41. I.R.C. §302(e)(2)(A).
42. I.R.C. §302(e)(2)(B).
43. I.R.C. §302(e)(3).
44. One should note the similarities between a partial liquidation as defined in §302(e)(2) and a corporate split-off pursuant to §355. Split-offs and the similarities to partial liquidations are considered further in Chapter 13.
45. Since §302(b)(4) focuses on the extent of corporate contraction rather than on the shareholder's proportionate interest, the attribution rules will have little or no bearing in the case of a partial liquidation.

constructively owned. The rationale for these constructive ownership or attribution rules is that shareholders are presumed to exercise control over shares held by certain related parties. For example, suppose that taxpayer W's shares are completely redeemed by a closely held corporation in which she and her husband own all of the stock. Even though the wife no longer owns any shares *directly,* she is considered to own her husband's shares *indirectly.* The constructive ownership rules *presume* that she still exercises control over the corporate enterprise to the extent of her husband's interest.

The constructive stock ownership rules in §318 come into play only when another provision of the Code expressly makes them applicable.[46] The §302 stock redemption rules are among the Code provisions expressly referring to §318.[47] Pursuant to §302(c), the attribution rules apply only for purposes of testing the *redeemed* shareholder's proportionate interest in the corporation immediately before and immediately after the redemption distribution and then applying the various §302(b) tests for sale or exchange treatment.

One interesting issue to arise over the years is whether the presumption of control that underlies the family attribution rules in §318(a)(1) can be rebutted by evidence of family hostility. A series of colorful cases involving family discord has raised this issue with mixed results. Most courts have taken the view that evidence of discord cannot be used to avoid family attribution. These courts view the §318 rules as irrebuttable.[48] As most colorfully put by the court in *David Metzger Trust,* "The pattern, intensity, and predicted duration of a family fight are difficult enough for the solomonic justice of our domestic relations courts. It is hardly the basis for a soundly administered tax policy. The fixity of the attribution rules then in this sense is not their weakness but their strength."[49] Evidence of family discord may nevertheless be relevant in one limited context. In connection with the "not essentially equivalent to a dividend" safe harbor in §302(b)(1) at least one court has indicated that family discord may be taken into account in determining whether or not a reduction in interest is meaningful under the *Davis* test.[50]

---

46. I.R.C. §318(a).

47. I.R.C. §302(c)(1) states that "section 318(a) shall apply in determining the ownership of stock."

48. David Metzger Trust v. Comm'r, 693 F.2d 459 (5th Cir. 1982), *cert. denied,* 463 U.S. 1207 (1983); Cerone v. Comm'r, 87 T.C. 1 (1986). *Contra* Robin Haft Trust v. Comm'r, 510 F.2d 43 (1st Cir. 1975).

49. David Metzger Trust v. Comm'r, 693 F.2d at 467.

50. Cerone v. Comm'r, 87 T.C. At 22. Note, however, that the attribution rules must first be applied in determining whether or not there has been any reduction in interest and to determine the extent of the reduction. Evidence of family discord then might be considered as a factor in assessing whether or not the reduction was meaningful.

Categories of Attribution

The §318 attribution rules include four categories of relationships that will cause the shares of one shareholder to be constructively owned by another. First, §318(a)(1) provides for attribution among certain family members. Second, §318(a)(2) provides for attribution from entities such as partnerships or corporations to the individual partners or shareholders and, third, §318(a)(3) provides for attribution to entities such as partnerships or corporations from the individual partners or shareholders. Finally, §318(a)(4) provides that persons who have an option to purchase stock shall be considered as owning the shares over which they hold the option.

a) Family Attribution: §318(a)(1)

An individual will be considered to own stock that is owned directly or indirectly by his or her spouse, children, grandchildren, or parents under §318(a)(1). Notice that the relationships specified here are, for the most part, lineal. This provision does *not* call for attribution between siblings, for example.[51]

b) Attribution *from* Entities: §318(a)(2)

Section 318(a)(2) provides attribution rules for stock owned by a partnership, estate, trust, or corporation. Stock owned directly or indirectly by a partnership or estate shall be considered as owned *proportionately* by its partners or beneficiaries.[52] For example, suppose that partners A and B each hold a one-half interest in Partnership X. Partnership X owns 100 shares in Corporation Y. Each partner will be considered to constructively own one-half of the partnership's stock for purposes of §302.

---

51. In contrast, different constructive ownership rules applicable for purposes of other provisions of the Code *do* provide attribution for siblings. I.R.C. §267(b)(1). Note too that §318(a) limits the lineal attribution to children, grandchildren, and parents, whereas §267 applies attribution to all lineal descendants. I.R.C. §267(c)(4).

52. I.R.C. §318(a)(2)(A). According to the regulations, beneficiary "includes any person entitled to receive property of a decedent pursuant to a will or pursuant to laws of descent and distribution. A person shall no longer be considered a beneficiary of an estate when all property to which he is entitled has been received by him, when he no longer has a claim against the estate arising out of having been a beneficiary, and when there is only a remote possibility that it will be necessary for the estate to seek the return of property or to seek payment from him by contribution or otherwise to satisfy claims against the estate or expenses of administration." Treas. Reg. §1.318-3(a).

6. Redemption Distributions

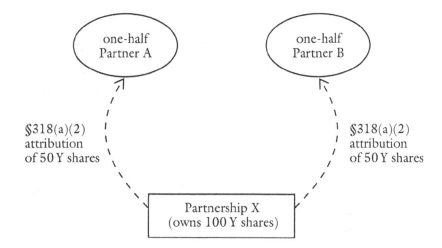

Similarly, beneficiaries of a trust will be considered to own stock of the trust in proportion to their actuarial interests in the trust.[53] Finally, any person[54] who directly or indirectly owns 50% or more in value of the stock in a corporation will be considered to own stock owned by the corporation in proportion to the value of stock owned.[55] For example, imagine that shareholders A and B each own a 50% interest in Corporation X and Corporation X holds 100 Y shares. Each shareholder is deemed to own 50% of the stock owned by Corporation X.

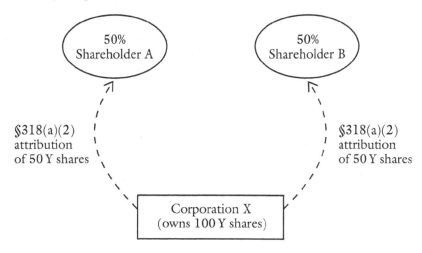

---

53. I.R.C. §318(a)(2)(B)(i). In addition, stock owned by any portion of a trust of which a person is considered a "grantor" will be considered owned by the grantor. I.R.C. §318(a)(2)(B)(ii).

54. It should be noted that the statute uses the term "person" as opposed to "individual" for purposes of the entity attribution rules in §318(a)(2) and (a)(3). "Person" is a broad term that includes corporations and other entities. See I.R.C. §7701(a)(1).

55. I.R.C. §318(a)(2)(C).

Notice the difference between the partnership/estate attribution rule and the corporation attribution rule. The former applies regardless of the extent of the partner or beneficiary's interest in the entity. Thus, even a 10% partner would be considered to own 10% of the partnership's stock. A 10% shareholder in a corporation, on the other hand, would not be viewed as constructively owning any stock owned by the corporation. The difference here simply reflects differences in the entities themselves. A shareholder has little control over affairs of the corporation unless he or she holds a controlling interest permitting election of his or her chosen representatives to the Board of Directors. On the other hand, partners generally have control proportionate to their interest in the partnership. Under §318(a)(2) from the entity attribution, only stock proportionate to the person's interest in the entity will be attributed from the entity to the individual.

c) Attribution *to* Entities: §318(a)(3)

Section 318(a)(3) provides attribution rules for stock owned by persons *to* entities in which they hold an interest. Stock owned directly or indirectly by a partner in a partnership or a beneficiary of an estate is considered owned by the partnership or estate respectively. Stock owned by a beneficiary of a trust is considered owned by the trust unless the beneficial interest is a remote contingent interest.[56] Finally, if any person owns 50% or more of the stock in a corporation, the corporation will be considered to own that person's stock. Note that unlike the §318(a)(2) from the entity rules, the rules for attribution *to* the entity are not proportional rules. In other words, when the §318(a)(3) constructive ownership rules apply, *all* of the stock owned by the related person is attributed to the entity. When a person is in control of a corporation, the corporation is considered to own *all* of that person's stock. Imagine, for example, that shareholders A and B each own 50% of the stock in Corporation X. Each of the shareholders also owns 50 shares of stock in Corporation Z. All of these Z shares will be attributed to Corporation X under §318(a)(3).

---

56. A beneficial interest is considered remote if "under the maximum exercise of discretion by the trustee in favor of such beneficiary, the value of such interest, computed actuarially, is 5 percent or less of the value of the trust property." I.R.C. §318(a)(3)(B)(i).

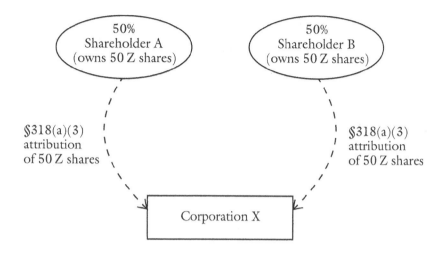

d) Options Treated as Stock: §318(a)(4)

Under §318(a)(4), a person with an option to acquire stock is considered to actually own the shares over which she holds the option for purposes of testing a redemption distribution under §302(b). A warrant or convertible security will be considered an option under this rule if it provides the holder a right to obtain stock at his or her election and if there are no contingencies with respect to the election.[57]

Multiple Attribution

Each of the attribution rules discussed above provides that stock owned directly or *indirectly* by one person shall be considered owned by another. A person may own stock *indirectly* via attribution from another. Lest there be any doubt, the operating rules in §318(a)(5) provide, with two exceptions, that stock *constructively* owned shall be considered *actually* owned for purposes of applying the attribution rules. For example, suppose that A is a partner in Partnership X. A's mother owns 50 shares in Corporation Z. Under §318(a)(1), A is considered to own her mother's shares. In a second application of attribution rules under §318(a)(3)(A), the partnership is considered to own the stock just attributed to A. Thus, the partnership constructively owns shares actually owned by the mother of one of its partners.

---

57. Rev. Rul. 68-601, 1968-2 C.B. 124. See also Rev. Rul. 89-64, 1989-1 C.B. 91.

Although the general operating rule of §318(a)(5) allows unlimited multiple attribution, two exceptions to the general rule provide for a cut-off of attribution in certain cases. The first exception applies to family attribution. Stock constructively owned by an individual under the family attribution rules shall not be considered as owned by her for purposes of *again* applying the family attribution rules in order to make another the constructive owner of such stock.[58] This family attribution cut-off prevents multiple applications of the attribution rules to pass constructive ownership to family members not included in the §318(a)(1) provision directly. For example, recall that §318(a)(1) does not provide for direct attribution between siblings. Without the family attribution cut-off, one sibling's stock might have been attributed to another in a two-step process. First, one child's stock is attributed to a parent under §318(a)(1). Next, absent the cut-off rule, the stock would be attributed from the parent to the other child in a second application of §318(a)(1). Since §318(a)(5)(B) prevents a double application of family attribution, one sibling will not be considered to own stock of another.[59]

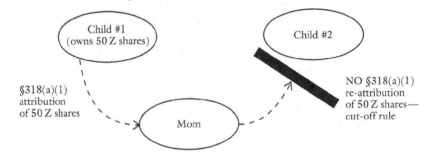

---

58. I.R.C. §318(a)(5)(B).
59. The §318(a)(5)(B) rule is sometimes referred to as the "(1)/(1) cut-off."

6. Redemption Distributions

A second exception to the general multiple attribution operating rule applies to entities. Under §318(a)(5)(C), "stock constructively owned by a partnership, estate, trust, or corporation by reason of the application of paragraph (3) shall not be considered as owned by it for purposes of applying paragraph (2) in order to make another the constructive owner of such stock."[60] This attribution cut-off is similar to the family attribution cut-off above. As an example, suppose that Partnership X has two equal and unrelated partners, A and B. Partner A owns stock in Z corporation. The Z stock is constructively owned by the partnership under §318(a)(3). Absent the special cut-off, partner B now might be considered to own one-half of these shares under §318(a)(2).[61] The attribution of shares from one partner to another partner is prevented through the attribution cut-off found in §318(a)(5)(C) much in the same way that the attribution between siblings is prevented by §318(a)(5)(B).

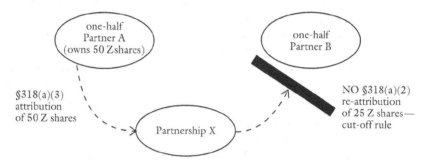

This seems a sensible result. There is no reason to assume that one partner has control over a corporation in which an unrelated partner happens to hold stock.

As you can imagine, multiple application of the attribution rules and operation of the attribution cut-offs can be quite complex. In each case above, we considered only one example of operation of the attribution cut-offs. Keep in mind that many other applications are possible. Moreover, where multiple attribution is not cut off by one of the operating rules, applications of the rules can be seemingly endless. Since application of the constructive ownership rules tends to be somewhat mechanical, more involved problems can best be considered in the Examples and Explanations section below.[62]

---

60. The §318(a)(5)(C) rule is sometimes referred to as the "(3)/(2) cut-off."
61. Keep in mind that §318(a)(2) provides for proportionate attribution and partner B holds a one-half partnership interest.
62. See Examples 5 and 6 at the end of this chapter.

Waiver of Family Attribution Rules: §302(c)(2)

a) Waiver by Individual Shareholders

In the family business setting, application of constructive ownership rules made it virtually impossible for a redeemed shareholder to receive sale treatment on the redemption. Even if his or her shares were completely redeemed, constructive ownership from other family members prevented the redemption from qualifying as a complete termination of interest under §302(b)(3). Responding to these concerns, Congress allows the redeemed shareholder to waive only family attribution under §318(a)(1) and only in the case of §302(b)(3) complete terminations of interest.[63] Using the family attribution waiver, it is now possible for one family member to retire from the family business by having the corporation purchase all of his or her shares in a redemption that qualifies as a complete termination of interest under §302(b)(3). If the proper waiver is filed, shares held by the remaining family members will not be attributed to the redeemed shareholder.

To qualify for the waiver, three important conditions must be met. First, immediately after the redemption, the redeemed shareholder must have "no interest in the corporation (including an interest as officer, director, or employee), other than an interest as a creditor."[64] Remember that the attribution rules are based on the assumption that related parties retain control and influence over the corporation even though they may not own any shares directly. The redeemed shareholder's agreement to forgo any interest in the corporation undercuts this assumption of control. Second, the redeemed shareholder cannot acquire any such interest in the corporation within ten years of the redemption distribution.[65] Third, the redeemed shareholder must file an agreement to notify the Secretary of any reacquisition within the ten-year period. Should such reacquisition occur, the statute of limitations will be extended for one year from the date of notification to the Secretary.[66] In such cases, the taxes for the year of redemption will be recomputed to treat the redemption as a §301 distribution rather than as a sale.

---

63. I.R.C. §302(c)(2)(A).

64. I.R.C. §302(c)(2)(A)(i).

65. I.R.C. §302(c)(2)(A)(ii). The statute provides an exception for stock acquired by bequest or inheritance.

66. I.R.C. §302(c)(2)(A)(iii). Another concern in applying the family attribution waiver provisions was that family businesses would engage in pre-redemption stock shuffling so as to permit a later redemption of one family member to receive sale treatment. Congress responded to this concern by creating an exception to the waiver rules in cases where the distributee received any of the redeemed stock within ten years prior to redemption from a related party. This "look-back" exception will apply only if one of the principal purposes of the acquisition was tax avoidance. I.R.C. §302(c)(2)(B).

6. Redemption Distributions

The requirement that the redeemed shareholder forgo any interest in the corporation other than an interest as a creditor is really the heart of the waiver provision. Congress is willing to ignore the presumption of continued control through other family members' shares only if the retiring family member no longer has any interest in the corporate enterprise other than as a creditor. The precise boundaries of the "no interest" condition have been somewhat difficult to define, however.

The statutory language permitting the retiring shareholder to continue as a creditor gives corporations flexibility to completely redeem a family member with a promissory note providing for payment on an installment basis. This will be a convenient tool where corporate funds are limited or otherwise needed for operations or expansion or where the retiring shareholder wishes to arrange for a steady stream of income through installment payments. The Treasury Department was concerned, however, that corporations might create special creditor relationships with retiring family members that really disguised a greater continuing interest in the corporate enterprise than one would expect for the ordinary creditor. Responding to this concern, the regulations provide that

> a person will be considered a creditor only if the rights of such person with respect to the corporation are not greater or broader in scope than necessary for the enforcement of his claim. Such claim must not in any sense be proprietary and must not be subordinate to the claims of general creditors. An obligation in the form of a debt may thus constitute a proprietary interest. For example, if under the terms of the instrument the corporation may discharge the principal amount of its obligation to a person by payments, the amount or certainty of which are dependent upon the earnings of the corporation, such a person is not a creditor of the corporation. Furthermore, if under the terms of the instrument the rate of purported interest is dependent upon earnings, the holder of such instrument may not, in some cases, be a creditor.[67]

Several courts have held arrangements to create only a creditor interest even under circumstances where the retiring shareholders maintained an interest in the corporation with some arguably proprietary characteristics. For example, in Dunn v. Commissioner,[68] an installment agreement with the retiring shareholders provided for postponement of any installment payment that would cause the corporation to fall below the net working capital requirement or to violate the 50% net profit retention clause under the corporation's franchise agreement with General Motors. The government argued that the postponement provision in the redemption agreement subordinated the shareholder's claim and that the payments were

---

67. Treas. Reg. §1.302-4(d).
68. 615 F.2d 578 (2d Cir. 1980).

dependent upon the corporation's earnings. Ruling for the shareholders, the Second Circuit noted that only the timing of the payments, as opposed to the amounts, were in any way dependent upon the corporation's earnings. While conceding that an ordinary trade creditor would have greater right to insist on payment than the retiring shareholders, the court observed that this "is just the difference between any trade creditor selling on current account and a long-term creditor, secured or unsecured."[69] The court found that general creditors would have no greater rights than the retiring shareholders if the corporation were to liquidate. The rulings in Dunn and several other cases suggest that the courts will be somewhat lenient and allow the corporation some leeway in structuring installment agreements with retiring shareholders to take unusual circumstances into account.[70] Even the Service has agreed that an arm's-length leasehold interest retained by the redeemed shareholder is not prohibited under the waiver rules as long as the rental payments to the redeemed shareholder are not subordinated to general creditor claims or dependent upon the corporation's earnings.[71]

Another issue in interpreting the "no interest" condition is whether the retiring family member can continue in some advisory or independent consultant capacity as long as he has no formal interest as an officer, director, or employee. The Tax Court took the rather liberal position that the test for purposes of §302(c)(2)(A)(i) was whether the taxpayer had "a financial stake in the corporation or continued to control after the redemption."[72] Merely providing services to the corporation, even for compensation, was not considered by the Tax Court to be an interest in the corporation for purposes of applying the waiver rule. The Ninth Circuit, at least, disagrees. In Lynch v. Commissioner, the Ninth Circuit Court of Appeals rejected the Tax Court approach, stating that "[a]n individualized determination of whether a taxpayer has retained a financial stake or continued to control the corporation after the redemption is inconsistent with Congress' desire to bring a measure of certainty to the tax consequences of a corporate redemption. We hold that a taxpayer who provides post-redemption services, either as an employee or an independent contractor, holds a prohibited interest in the corporation because he is not a creditor."[73]

---

69. Id. At 583.
70. See, e.g., Estate of Leonard v. Comm'r, 61 T.C. 554 (1974), nonacq. 1978-2 C.B. 3.
71. Rev. Rul. 77-467, 1977-2 C.B. 92. See also Hurst v. Comm'r, 124 T.C. 16, 18-20 (2005) (lease of headquarters from former shareholder at fixed rent and not conditioned on corporate financial performance was not a prohibited interest despite former shareholder's persuading the corporation to surrender an option to buy the property).
72. Lynch v. Comm'r, 83 T.C. 597, 606-607 (1984), rev'd, 801 F.2d 1176 (9th Cir. 1986). Similar language was used in Cerone v. Comm'r, 87 T.C. 1, 31 (1986); Seda v. Comm'r, 82 T.C. 484, 488 (1984); Lewis v. Comm'r, 47 T.C. 129, 135 (1966).
73. 801 F.2d 1176, 1179 (9th Cir. 1986).

6. Redemption Distributions

One Tax Court opinion displays remarkable leniency in interpreting the §302(c)(2) "prohibited interest" interest restriction. In Hurst v. Commissioner,[74] the Tax Court held that an actual post-redemption *employment* relationship did not constitute a prohibited interest when the employee was the wife of the redeemed shareholder, who had not herself owned any stock in the corporation. In addition to the wife's employment, the redeemed shareholder and his wife in *Hurst* personally owned the corporation's headquarters, which they continued to lease to the corporation after the redemption. Moreover, the retired shareholder received promissory notes in exchange for his redeemed shares, which were secured by the redeemed stock and were subordinate to the corporation's obligation to its bank. The court noted that such security arrangements were common in such sales agreements, that the notes were not subordinate to *general* creditors, and that neither the amount nor certainty of payments on the note was dependent on the corporation's earnings.[75] The Commissioner argued that, taken together, all of these continuing relationships with the corporation violated the §302(c)(2) "prohibited interest" test even though each of the relationships alone might have passed muster.[76] The court seems to reject this "holistic approach" and concludes in any event that the various legal claims, "[e]ven looked at all together . . . were in no way contingent upon the financial performance of the company except in the obvious sense that all creditors have in their debtors' solvency."[77]

b) Waiver by an Entity

As originally drafted, the waiver rules permitted only the waiver of family attribution under §318(a)(1) by *individual* distributees. In 1982, Congress added a narrow provision permitting *entities* to waive family attribution under limited circumstances.[78] If a person with an interest in an entity owns stock indirectly by family attribution under §318(a)(1), the stock will again be attributed to the entity under §318(a)(3). As a result, an otherwise complete redemption of the entity's interest will fail the §302(b)(3) complete termination of interest test. Under §302(c)(2)(C), the *entity* may waive the *family* attribution to its beneficiary. Notice, however, that the waiver is limited to §318(a)(1) family attribution. If the person owned any shares *directly,*

---

74. 124 T.C. 16 (2005).

75. *Id. At* 16-18. In fact, the shareholder's retirement arrangements involved a complex mix of promissory notes from the corporation and its new owners, all of which were secured by the corporation's stock and subject to cross-default clauses.

76. *Id. At* 16.

77. *Id. At* 28.

78. I.R.C. §302(c)(2)(C).

these would be attributed to the entity under §318(a)(3). No waiver is available to the entity under §318(a)(3).

To illustrate, suppose that A is the beneficiary of X's estate. X's estate owns 50 Corporation Z shares. The remaining 50 Z shares are owned by A's mother.[79] Z Corporation redeems all of the shares owned directly by Estate X. Absent a waiver, multiple application of the attribution rules[80] will result in the Estate's constructively owning A's mother's shares.

Under these circumstances, the estate may waive the attribution from A's mother to A if the conditions of §302(c)(2)(C) are met. These conditions require that the entity and each related person meet the (c)(2)(A) waiver requirements.[81] In our example, both Estate X and beneficiary A must have no interest other than as a creditor and agree not to acquire such an interest within ten years. In addition, each related party must agree to be jointly and severally liable for any deficiency resulting from acquisition of an interest within the ten-year period.[82] If the estate and its beneficiary meet the conditions and file an appropriate waiver, the estate will qualify for sale or exchange treatment under §302(b)(3). If A owned 50% of the Z stock directly rather than by attribution from her mother, A's Z shares would be attributed to the estate and the estate would be ineligible for sale or

---

79. Notice that A herself owns no Z shares.
80. This would be an (a)(1)-(a)(3) combination. Notice that this multiple attribution is similar to the multiple attribution rule in the partnership example discussed previously in this chapter. The partnership in that example also could use the entity waiver rule discussed here to avoid family attribution from Partner A's mom.
81. I.R.C. §302(c)(2)(C)(i)(I).
82. I.R.C. §302(c)(2)(C)(i)(II).

exchange treatment under any of the safe harbors since the estate constructively would be a 100% owner both before and after the redemption.

The Mystery of Disappearing Basis

Assuming sufficient earnings and profits, application of the §318 attribution rules in connection with a §302 redemption distribution may result in dividend treatment without any basis offset. In the ordinary dividend situation, the absence of a basis offset is not especially troubling. After all, the shareholder receiving a dividend distribution still owns the stock and will recover the basis by subtracting it from the amount realized upon ultimate sale of the stock. On the other hand, the shareholder in the redemption setting actually relinquishes shares. Unfortunately, §302 itself offers no guidance on how to properly account for the shareholder's basis in the shares relinquished. Surely, there should be some mechanism through which the shareholder can ultimately recover the basis in these shares without tax. It would be unfair to allow the basis in the redeemed stock to quietly disappear. The "mystery of disappearing" basis is the search for a mechanism to preserve the shareholder's basis in the redeemed shares after a dividend redemption.

Two variations of the mystery emerge from redemptions treated as dividends under §302. First, the shareholder may retain some stock after a redemption treated as a dividend under the §302(b)(1), (b)(2), or (b)(4) "safe harbors." The mystery in such cases is resolved rather simply by adding the basis from the redeemed shares to the basis in the shares retained after the redemption.[83] The plot thickens, however, in the case of a complete termination of interest redemption after which the redeemed shareholder no longer holds any stock. In such a case, sale treatment was prevented due to application of the constructive ownership rules. What happens to the redeemed shareholder's basis in the shares no longer owned? For example, consider the simple closely held family corporation in which stock is owned entirely by the husband and wife. Even if the husband's shares are completely redeemed upon his retirement, the redemption distribution will not meet any of the §302(b) sale or exchange tests unless the husband files a proper waiver of family attribution. He is deemed to own 100% of the corporation both immediately before and immediately after the redemption. As a result, the husband will have dividend income to the extent of the corporation's earnings and profits and will receive no offset for his basis in the redeemed shares.

---

83. Treas. Reg. §1.302-2(c), ex. 1.

The best clue to an answer to the "mystery of disappearing basis" after a §302(b)(3) complete termination of interest redemption is found in a regulatory example. In Treasury Regulation §1.302-2(c), example (2), husband and wife (H and W) each owned one-half of Corporation X. H had originally purchased all of the stock for $100,000 and had later given one-half to W. All of H's stock is later redeemed in a transaction determined to be a dividend as opposed to a sale redemption. Without further elaboration, the example states that "immediately after the transaction, W holds the remaining stock of Corporation X with a basis of $100,000."

The regulatory example resolves the mystery by permitting the husband's basis in the shares redeemed to be transferred to the wife. When she later sells the remaining shares, she will get the basis offset. Keeping in mind that the mystery should arise only in cases where attribution rules prevent sale treatment, it appears that basis in the redeemed shares should be transferred to those remaining shareholders from whom the attribution occurred. These mysteries are explored further in the Examples and Explanations section below.

SPECIAL ISSUES FOR CORPORATE SHAREHOLDERS

Prior to the 2003 "qualified dividend income" rules,[84] individual shareholders thought of the §302(b) provisions as "safe harbors" since they preferred the preferential capital gains rates and basis offset available in a §302 sale or exchange redemption to §301 ordinary dividend income. Individual shareholders often insisted that the corporation carefully structure a redemption transaction to fit within one of the §302(b) provisions. The "qualified dividend income" provisions have altered the equation, reducing the extent to which individual shareholders think of the §302(b) provisions as "safe harbors." Although individual shareholders still can take advantage of the basis offset and the ability to recognize loss on the redemption exchange, the reduction in dividend tax rates makes the distinction between dividend and exchange redemptions less significant for individual shareholders than it was before.

Corporate shareholders, on the other hand, have different interests with respect to redemption transactions; they are unlikely to think of the §302(b) provisions as "safe harbors" at all. Instead, corporate shareholders tend to prefer §301 dividend treatment so that they can take advantage of the §243 dividends-received deduction available only to corporate shareholders.

---

84. See Chapters 1 and 5.

6. Redemption Distributions

Rather than adopt special §302 redemption rules applicable to corporate shareholders, Congress responded to perceived dividends-received deduction abuses with narrowly targeted special provisions in the §1059 extraordinary dividend rules. Under §1059(e), certain redemption distributions to corporate shareholders are treated as §1059(a) "extraordinary dividends."[85] If the redemption distribution is classified as an "extraordinary dividend" under §1059(e), the corporate shareholder receiving the redemption distribution will be required to reduce its basis in its remaining shares by the nontaxed portion of the dividend—in other words, to the extent that it was able to escape tax on the distribution through the §243 dividends-received deduction. This presumably will result in a larger gain upon subsequent sale of the stock. In addition, to the extent that the nontaxed portion of the distribution exceeds the shareholder's basis in the remaining shares, §1059(a)(2) now triggers an immediate recognition of capital gain.

Details of the §1059 rules are beyond the scope of most basic courses in corporate taxation. For the moment, the lesson to be highlighted from this episode is that individual shareholders and corporate shareholders may have different interests with regard to classification of redemption distributions. Historically, the Treasury Department has been rather rigid in its application of the §302(b) tests, making them harder to satisfy. This government strategy was designed to prevent individual shareholders from too easily achieving sale or exchange treatment on redemption distributions, thus escaping §301 dividend treatment. The government's rigid application of the §302(b) rules, however, has played into the hands of corporate shareholders, who actually prefer §301 treatment.

REDEMPTIONS OF STOCK TO PAY DEATH TAXES: §303

After the death of one of its shareholders, a closely held corporation often redeems shares from the decedent's estate. Absent special rules, the estate might be required to report the distribution as a dividend under the §301 distribution rules after applying the §302 redemption analysis incorporating constructive ownership from other family members. Responding to the hardship faced by some family businesses forced to liquidate in order to pay estate and other death taxes, Congress enacted §303, which provides sale or exchange treatment upon the redemption of shares included in determining the gross estate of a decedent.[86]

Pursuant to §303(a), a redemption distribution will be treated as a sale or exchange to the extent that it does not exceed the sum of death taxes and

---

85. See the discussion of §1059 in Chapter 5.
86. I.R.C. §303(a).

the funeral and administrative expenses allowed as deductions. Special limitations in §303(b) require that the distribution be made within specified periods measured from the date of death of the decedent.[87] More important, as a threshold, §303(b)(2) limits the application of the special sale or exchange rule of §303(a) to cases where the value of the corporation's stock included in the gross estate exceeds 35% of the excess of the value of the gross estate over funeral, administrative, taxes, and other expenses.[88] The idea here is to limit this antihardship provision to those estates for which stock in the corporation represents a substantial proportion of the estate's assets.[89]

REDEMPTIONS RELATED TO INTER-SHAREHOLDER TRANSFERS AND BOOTSTRAP ACQUISITIONS

Inter-Shareholder Transfers

a) In General

Redemption distributions sometimes are used as part of a plan to transfer control of a corporation. Imagine, for example, that shareholder A wishes to retire from a corporation equally owned by unrelated shareholders A, B, and C. If shareholders B and C simply "bought out" shareholder A's interest using their own funds, shareholder A would report gain or loss upon the sale. As an alternative, the corporation might redeem shareholder A's stock using corporate funds. Such a redemption would eliminate shareholder A's one-third interest and simultaneously increase shareholder B and C's interests from one-third to one-half each. Since the shareholders are unrelated, no shares would be attributed under §318, and shareholder A would treat the redemption as a §302(b)(3) complete termination of interest sale or exchange. Notice that the tax consequences to shareholder A are no different than they were in the case of a direct sale — sale or exchange gain upon disposition of the shares. Thus, A may well be indifferent as to the structure of

---

87. I.R.C. §303(b)(1). This period will vary depending upon circumstances, but is generally tied to the period for assessment, redetermination of deficiency, or payment of estate tax by installment.

88. I.R.C. §303(b)(2)(A)(i), (ii) (referring to the value of the gross estate over the sum allowable as deduction under §§2053 and 2054). Section 303(b)(2)(B) provides special rules for purposes of computing stock ownership in meeting the 35% requirement.

89. On the other hand, notice that §303 sale or exchange treatment is available even if the family does not use redemption proceeds to pay death taxes. To some, this provision might appear to be a windfall to the estate, which already benefits from the stepped-up basis in assets provided in §1014.

the transaction. On the other hand, B and C are likely to prefer the redemption approach since it effectively allows them to acquire A's interest without using their own funds.

What about the remaining shareholders whose interest in the corporation is increased by reason of a redemption of another? If A, B, and C structure the above transaction as a redemption, will B and C's increase in their relative interests in the corporation be taxable? To answer this question, a closer look at what has really happened is necessary. The corporation in the above example presumably redeemed shareholder A's stock at fair market value. Although shareholder B and C's *percentage* of shares has increased, the *net worth* of the shares they own remains unchanged. For example, assume that the corporation's overall net worth was $3 million, so that each of the three shareholders' interests immediately before the redemption was worth $1 million. After the $1 million redemption distribution to shareholder A, shareholders B and C each hold a 50% interest in the corporation with an overall net worth of $2 million. Thus, the value of shareholder B and C's interests remains $1 million apiece. As a general rule, the increase in the remaining shareholders' proportionate interests resulting from the redemption of another shareholder is not taxable.[90] Interestingly enough, in Holsey v. Commissioner,[91] the court reached this result even though the redemption was at *less* than fair market value. Imagine that shareholder A in the above hypothetical received only $750,000 in redemption of his one-third interest in the corporation. In other words, the redemption price was 25% below the fair market value of his interest. In such a case, shareholders B and C receive not only an increase in their *percentage* interests from one-third to one-half, but also an increase in the *value* of their shares from $1 million to $1,125,000.[92] Under similar circumstances, the Third Circuit in *Holsey* conceded that "the taxpayer was benefited indirectly by the distribution. The value of his own stock was increased, since the redemption was for less than book value, and he became sole stockholder. But these benefits operated only to increase the value of the taxpayer's stock holdings; they could not give rise to taxable income within the meaning of the Sixteenth Amendment until the corporation makes a distribution to the taxpayer or his stock is sold."[93] In other words, the court found no *realized* gain to the continuing shareholder.

One key exception to the general rule that the continuing shareholder's interest increase resulting from redemption of another shareholder is not

90. See, e.g., Holsey v. Comm'r, 258 F.2d 865 (3d Cir. 1958).
91. *Id.*
92. Before the redemption, shareholders B and C each owned one-third of a corporation worth $3 million. After the redemption, they each own one-half of a corporation worth $2.25 million.
93. 258 F.2d at 868.

taxable is the "primary and unconditional obligation" exception. According to the Treasury Department and the courts, when the continuing shareholder is subject to an "unconditional obligation to purchase the retiring shareholder's stock, the satisfaction by the corporation of his obligation results in a constructive distribution to him."[94] Imagine, for example, that shareholders B and C had a binding "buy-sell" agreement obligating them to purchase shareholder A's shares. If, instead, the corporation redeems shareholder A's stock, the corporation has relieved shareholder B and C's obligation.[95] Since the redemption distribution satisfied shareholder B and C's "primary and unconditional obligation," they will be required to report their increase in proportionate interest as a constructive dividend.[96]

b) Redemptions Incident to Divorce

Unique tax issues arise in the divorce setting when a redemption of shares from one spouse effectively transfers control of the corporation to the other spouse. A common scenario is a corporation owned entirely by husband and wife. Upon divorce, the parties may choose to have the corporation completely redeem the shares of one spouse, leaving the other spouse as sole owner of the corporation. Under the general redemption principles just considered, the redeemed spouse would report sale or exchange gain under §302(b)(3).[97] The nonredeemed spouse would not have any taxable income from the resulting increased interest in the corporation unless the redemption distribution satisfied a "primary and unconditional obligation" to purchase the redeemed spouse's shares.

---

94. Rev. Rul. 69-608, 1969-2 C.B. 42. This ruling is especially useful since it provides numerous illustrations of corporate buy-sell agreements, indicating those that do, and those that do not, create an unconditional obligation to purchase. See also Wall v. United States, 164 F.2d 462 (4th Cir. 1947); Sullivan v. United States, 363 F.2d 724 (8th Cir. 1966), cert. denied, 387 U.S. 905 (1967).

95. Notice that the courts and the Service view the satisfaction of the obligation by the corporation as a constructive dividend to the continuing shareholder. This suggests that the earnings and profits of the corporation are relevant. If the corporation had no e&p, there would be no dividend, but rather recovery of capital and sale or exchange gain under §301(c). On the other hand, if the transaction is viewed as a pure cancellation of indebtedness, the extent of the corporation's earnings and profits would not be relevant.

96. Another risk for the shareholders whose interests are increased as a result of another shareholder's redemption is that their proportionate interest increase will be treated as a "deemed" stock dividend taxable under §305(c). Discussion of the §305(c) constructive stock dividend rules appears in Chapter 7. In the meantime, note simply that the risk to the remaining shareholders of a taxable "deemed" stock dividend is low as long as their increase in proportionate interest results from an "isolated redemption," as opposed to a series of periodic redemptions.

97. Since the spouses are no longer married, the ex-spouse's shares are not constructively owned under the §318 attribution rules.

6. Redemption Distributions

The unique twist in the divorce setting, however, is the §1041 non-recognition rule for property transfers "incident" to divorce.[98] Ordinarily, §1041 permits nonrecognition to both the transferring and the transferee spouse or former spouse on direct transfers of property incident to divorce. In addition, the Treasury Department has concluded that certain property transfers to third parties *on behalf* of a spouse also should be eligible for §1041 nonrecognition.[99] Past applications of this rule to stock redemptions required by a divorce or separation instrument led to odd and sometimes inconsistent results.

For example, in a controversial case involving a corporation wholly owned by husband and wife, the Ninth Circuit held that the wife's transfer of her shares to the corporation in complete redemption pursuant to a divorce decree was a transfer "on behalf of" the husband covered by the temporary regulation.[100] As a result, the wife was entitled to §1041 nonrecognition rather than §302 sale or exchange treatment upon receipt of cash from the corporation in exchange for her redeemed stock. She paid no tax upon receipt of funds from the redemption. Given this §1041 treatment to the wife, the transaction *should* have been viewed under the regulations as a direct transfer of the stock from the wife to her husband, followed by a transfer of the stock by the husband to the "third party" corporation in complete redemption. In other words, the wife's transfer of shares to the corporation "on behalf of" her husband should have shifted tax liability for the sale or exchange gain on redemption to the husband.

Odd results emerged, however, because the tax consequences to the husband were decided in a separate case in which the Tax Court decided that it was not bound by the Ninth Circuit's holding. The Tax Court believed that the legal issue in the husband's case did not turn on §1041, but rather on whether there was a constructive dividend to the husband. The court held that there was no constructive dividend to the nonredeemed husband whose proportionate interest in the corporation increased as a result of the wife's redemption since he did not have a "primary and unconditional obligation" to purchase the wife's shares.[101] In the end, neither husband nor wife paid tax on the approximately $450,000 paid out by the corporation in the redemption distribution.

---

98. I.R.C. §1041(a)(2). The nonrecognition provided in §1041 applies more broadly to transfers of property between spouses generally and to transfers between former spouses that are incident to divorce. Since the redemption issue tends to arise in the divorce context, this discussion is limited to transfers incident to divorce.

99. Treas. Reg. §1.1041-1T(c).

100. Arnes v. United States, 981 F.2d 456 (9th Cir. 1992). See also Craven v. United States, 215 F.3d 1201 (11th Cir. 2000).

101. Arnes v. Comm'r, 102 T.C. 522 (1994).

This end result arguably is inconsistent with the policies underlying both §1041 and §302. Nonrecognition is provided under §1041 for property transfers between spouses and between ex-spouses incident to divorce because married taxpayers are thought to represent a single economic unit. Although §1041 provides nonrecognition at the time of transfer, the transferee spouse takes the property with a substituted basis from the transferring spouse.[102] This substituted basis is designed to preserve gain or loss unrecognized at the time of transfer for recognition upon later disposition of the property. In other words, gain or loss will be recognized when the property leaves the marital unit.

In the case of the Arnes divorce, the wife's shares were not transferred to the husband, but were completely redeemed for cash. In contrast to the ordinary §1041 transaction, Mr. Arnes took no property with a substituted basis. Unless one of the spouses is subject to tax at the time of the redemption, gain or loss with respect to the redeemed shares will never be recognized for tax purposes, resulting in a "whipsaw" to the government.[103] This result is inconsistent with §302, which requires shareholder level recognition of taxable income when funds or property are withdrawn from the corporation in a redemption distribution.[104]

The Treasury Department responded to the "whipsaw" problem with regulations addressed specifically to stock redemptions incident to divorce or separation.[105] The regulations provide that stock redemptions in the divorce setting will not be governed by the "transfers on behalf of a spouse" language from the temporary regulations. Instead, the regulations distinguish between two different types of stock redemptions: (1) a redemption that is treated under applicable tax law as a constructive dividend to the nonredeemed spouse whose proportionate interest in the corporation is increased as a by-product of the redemption of shares from the other spouse and (2) a redemption that is not treated as a constructive dividend to the nonredeemed spouse. In distinguishing between these two types of redemption, recall that a redemption of stock from one shareholder is treated as a constructive dividend to another only if the redemption satisfies a "primary and unconditional obligation" of the nonredeemed shareholder to buy the redeemed shares.

Under the regulations, the form of the redemption is respected in cases where the redemption distribution does not result in a constructive dividend to the other spouse — i.e., a redemption in which the nonredeemed spouse

---

102. I.R.C. §1041(b).
103. In a case appealable to the Sixth Circuit, the Tax Court declined to follow and announced its disagreement with the Ninth Circuit's decision in the *Arnes* case. *Blatt v. Comm'r*, 102 T.C. 77 (1994).
104. Recall that the focus of §302 simply is to distinguish redemption distributions treated as sales or exchanges from those treated under the §301 distribution rules.
105. Treas. Reg. §1.1041-2.

had no primary and unconditional obligation to purchase the redeemed shares. In other words, the redemption distribution to the redeemed shareholder in exchange for stock will be taxed either as a dividend or as a sale or exchange under §302 and will not be eligible for tax-free treatment under §1041.[106] On the other hand, if the redemption distribution *does* relieve the nonredeemed spouse of a primary and unconditional obligation to purchase the redeemed shares, the transaction is viewed as if the spouse who is "retiring" from the corporation first transferred his or her shares to the other spouse and the shares were then redeemed from the latter. In other words, the transaction is *deemed* to be a §302 redemption to the nonredeemed spouse. The redemption proceeds actually paid to the redeemed spouse are then *deemed* to have been received from the other spouse tax-free pursuant to §1041.[107] In the end, the regulations ensure that one, and only one, of the spouses is taxed on the redemption distribution; the other gets the benefit of §1041 nonrecognition.[108]

Other Bootstrap Acquisitions

The inter-shareholder "buy out" situations just discussed involved the departure of one shareholder from the corporation and the acquisition of his or her interest by the remaining shareholders. Instead of using their own funds, the remaining shareholders use *corporate* assets to fund the acquisition. Such an acquisition may be called a "bootstrap acquisition." Even outside purchasers can structure a corporate acquisition so that all or a part of the funds for the acquisition come from the target corporation's assets. The landmark case in this area is Zenz v. Quinlivan.[109]

In *Zenz*, the buyer intended to acquire complete control over a target corporation owned by a single shareholder. Instead of a direct purchase of all of the shares, the buyer first purchased a small amount of stock from the selling shareholder. Shortly thereafter, the corporation redeemed all the selling shareholder's remaining shares. The selling shareholder presumably was indifferent as to whether she sold *all* of her stock to the buyer directly or sold only part of the stock and had the rest redeemed. Assuming that the redemption qualified as a §302(b)(3) complete termination of her interest,

---

106. Treas. Reg. §1.1041-2(a)(1), (b)(1).
107. Treas. Reg. §1.1041-2(a)(2), (b)(2).
108. The regulations provide special rules under which the parties can reverse the tax consequences that would otherwise result from application of the regulations if they so provide in the divorce or separation instrument or a valid written agreement. Treas. Reg. §1.1041-2(c). In the end, the Treasury Department is content as long as it is assured that one or the other spouse will be taxed upon the redemption proceeds.
109. 213 F.2d 914 (6th Cir. 1954).

she would treat all of her gain as capital gain from the sale of stock in either case.

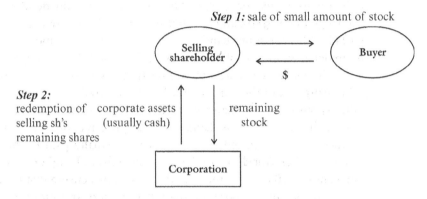

Step 1: sale of small amount of stock

From the buyer's viewpoint, the transaction was arranged in this fashion for at least two reasons. First, the buyer was concerned about the corporation's high earnings and profits accounts, which would later prove to be a source of taxable dividends should he receive distributions from the corporation. By buying only a small amount of stock and having the corporation use its earnings and profits to redeem the rest from the sole shareholder, the e&p account was reduced pursuant to §312.[110] Second, the buyer would otherwise have to come up with substantial funds to purchase *all* of the stock. By buying a small amount and having the corporation redeem the rest, the buyer got 100% control of the corporation without having to use substantial funds of his own. This type of acquisition is also known as a "bootstrap acquisition," since the buyer is bootstrapping on the acquired corporation's funds to take over the corporation.

Concerned that this structure was a deliberate device to evade tax, the Service argued in *Zenz* that the shareholder should not be entitled to §302(b)(3) complete termination of interest treatment and instead should report the redemption distribution as a dividend. Conceding that the transaction was arranged to minimize taxes for both parties, the court nevertheless held that the redeemed shareholder was entitled to sale treatment. She literally satisfied the requirements of §302(b)(3) and she *intended* a complete liquidation of her holdings in the corporation.[111]

Notice that the redemption in the *Zenz* case took place *after* the sale of stock. This too was part of the overall plan. If the redemption had *preceded* the acquisition, it would have been a partial redemption from a sole

---

110. I.R.C. §312(n)(7). See further discussion later in this chapter.
111. Under the 2003 "qualified dividend income" rules, the government is unlikely to be as troubled by this type of transaction. The distribution would likely be eligible for capital gains rates in any event. Even under the qualified dividend rules, however, sale or exchange treatment would still offer a basis offset and recognition of a loss in the event that the shareholder's basis exceeded the distribution amount.

shareholder and, thus, arguably taxable as a dividend to the shareholder. By having the acquisition precede the redemption, this problem was avoided and the redeemed shareholder qualified for §302(b)(3) sale or exchange treatment. Since *Zenz*, several courts have held, and the Service has conceded, that a "*Zenz*-like" bootstrap acquisition still will qualify as a §302(b)(3) sale or exchange redemption treatment to the selling/redeemed shareholder even if the redemption precedes the purchase of shares, as long as the two steps clearly are part of an overall integrated plan.[112]

The Service has also approved the *Zenz* bootstrap technique for acquisition transactions that do not completely terminate the selling shareholder's interest. In Rev. Rul. 75-447, for example, shareholders A and B, each with 50 shares, wanted to bring a new equal shareholder, C, into the business.[113] The corporation first issued 25 new shares to C and then caused the corporation to redeem 25 shares each from A and B. The Service announced that it was proper to rely on *Zenz* in determining whether the redemption distributions to A and B satisfied the §302(b)(2) "substantially disproportionate distribution" test. As long as the issuance of new shares and the redemption are "clearly part of an integrated plan to reduce a shareholder's interest, effect will be given only to the overall result for purposes of section 302(b)(2) and the sequence in which the events occur will be disregarded."[114] A and B met the §302(b)(2) mathematical tests and were entitled to sale or exchange treatment, since each were viewed as having a 50% interest immediately before and a 33⅓% interest immediately after the overall redemption transaction.

Not surprisingly, taxpayers were delighted with the *Zenz* bootstrap acquisition approach and it became an important component of acquisition planning. Notice that a bootstrap acquisition may include a redemption as part of the plan when the selling shareholder is an *individual* taxpayer. The goal of the individual taxpayer is to get §302(b) sale or exchange gain treatment for the amount received for stock, while simultaneously lowering the purchase price to the buyer. A bootstrap acquisition generally will not include a redemption where the selling shareholder is a *corporate* taxpayer. The interest of the *corporate* seller is to classify any pre-sale distribution as a *dividend* in order to take advantage of the §243 dividends-received deduction or the consolidated return provisions.[115]

---

112. United States v. Carey, 289 F.2d 531 (8th Cir. 1961); Rev. Rul. 77-226, 1977-2 C.B. 90.
113. Rev. Rul. 75-447, 1975-2 C.B. 113.
114. *Id.* At 114.
115. Bootstrap acquisitions involving a corporate shareholder seeking to take advantage of the §243 dividends-received deduction are considered in Chapter 5.

REDEMPTIONS BY RELATED CORPORATIONS: §304

Overview

The §302 redemption distribution rules covered in this chapter apply not only to *actual* redemptions, but also to certain sales of stock that are *deemed* to be redemptions for policy reasons. Section 304 provides a complex set of rules by which sales of stock involving related corporations will be treated as redemptions. Perhaps the best way to begin to approach §304 is through an example. Suppose that shareholder A owned 100% of the stock of both Corporations X and Y. In other words, X and Y Corporations are commonly controlled, sometimes referred to as brother-sister corporations. Assume that shareholder A sells some of his X shares to Corporation Y for cash. Absent §304, shareholder A would simply report gain or loss from the sale of stock under §§61(a)(3) and 1001, presumably as a capital gain. This transaction appears to be a straightforward sale of stock by shareholder A to Corporation Y. Why might it be necessary to complicate the universe by recharacterizing the transaction as something other than a simple stock sale? The concern here is that the shareholder controls the corporation from which he is receiving the sales proceeds (Y Corporation). In effect, he is taking property out of Corporation Y in exchange for stock in a related corporation over which he also has control (X Corporation). Viewed in this fashion, the transaction looks very much like a redemption and §304 requires that it be tested under the redemption rules.

Notice that §304 simply recharacterizes certain sales as redemptions. It says nothing directly about the tax consequences of such redemptions. Once a particular sale is recharacterized as a redemption for purposes of §304, tax consequences of the redemption to the shareholders will be governed by the §302 provisions considered at length earlier in this chapter. If the deemed redemption is treated as a sale or exchange under §302(b), any gain will be treated as capital gain. If the deemed redemption fails the §302(b) sale or exchange tests, the property received will be treated under the §301 distribution rules. The §304 rules were largely designed as anti-abuse provisions to prevent shareholders from bailing out corporate profits at capital gains rates rather than ordinary income rates, and from offsetting the amount of the distribution by their stock basis for distributions that resemble dividend distributions.[116] This abuse concern applied primarily to *individual* shareholders, who generally preferred sale or exchange redemption treatment. *Corporate* shareholders, on the other hand, may *prefer* a §304 redemption that

---

116. The result for the corporate shareholder may be more difficult to achieve given that under §1059(e), a §304 redemption to which §301 applies may be treated as an extraordinary dividend.

will be considered a §301 distribution. Here again, the "qualified dividend income" rules have altered the stakes. Even if the deemed redemption is now classified as a dividend, most individual shareholders will be eligible for the lower tax rates available under §1(h)(11). Thus, individual shareholders may well be indifferent regarding the redemption classification. At the same time, corporate shareholders will continue to *prefer* a §304 deemed dividend redemption.

Deemed redemptions covered by §304 fall into two categories. The first involves acquisitions by related corporations other than subsidiaries, sometimes referred to as commonly controlled or brother-sister corporations.[117] The second involves acquisitions by subsidiaries.[118] Before getting into the details of each of these transactions, however, it will be useful to consider the special definition of control used for purposes of §304.

Measuring Control for Purposes of §304

Determining whether §304(a)(1) or (a)(2) applies to a particular sale or exchange of stock will first require an assessment of whether one or more persons is in *control* of each of two corporations (§304(a)(1)) or whether one corporation *controls* another (§304(a)(2)). The term "control" has a unique definition for purposes of §304, meaning "the ownership of stock possessing at least 50 percent of the total combined voting power of all classes of stock entitled to vote, or at least 50 percent of the total value of shares of all classes of stock."[119] In applying this 50% test, §304 explicitly provides that the constructive ownership rules of §318 shall apply, with some variations. These variations tend to broaden application of the constructive ownership rules and increase the likelihood that a particular transaction will be governed by §304.

First, if a person or persons controls one corporation, which in turn controls another corporation, the shareholders of the first corporation will also be in control of the second.[120] Second, for purposes of §304, the §318(a)(2)(C) and (a)(3)(C) attribution rules shall be applied by substituting 5% for 50%.[121] Ordinarily, §318 constructive ownership to and from the corporation only kicks in where the shareholder is a majority shareholder; that is, where the shareholder owns 50% or more of the value in

---

117. I.R.C. §304(a)(1).
118. I.R.C. §304(a)(2).
119. I.R.C. §304(c)(1) (emphasis added). Notice that §304 uses a 50%, as opposed to 80%, control test. Compare I.R.C. §368(c).
120. Without this variation, the shareholders of the first corporation would only receive *proportionate* attribution from the corporation under §318(a)(2)(C).
121. I.R.C. §304(c)(3).

stock in a corporation. Under §318(a)(2)(C), a person who owns, directly or indirectly, more than 50% of the stock of a corporation shall be considered as owning stock owned by the corporation *in that proportion which the value of the stock owned bears to the value of all of the stock in the corporation.* So, a 50% shareholder of Corporation X will be deemed to own 50% of the stock that Corporation X owns.[122] For the purpose of measuring control under §304, however, a shareholder who has more than 5% of the stock of a corporation will be deemed to own the stock owned by the corporation. The attribution here still will be in proportion to the value of the stock owned by the shareholder. Thus, if shareholder A owns 5% of Corporation X, shareholder A will be deemed to own 5% of the stock that Corporation X owns.

Under §318(a)(3)(C), if a shareholder owns, directly or indirectly, more than 50% of the value of stock in a corporation, that corporation will be deemed to own the stock owned, directly or indirectly, by that shareholder. Thus, if shareholder A owns 50% of Corporation X and also owns 10% of Corporation Y, Corporation X will be deemed to own *all* of the shareholder's Corporation Y stock. Notice here that, unlike the §318(a)(2) rules, attribution under (a)(3) is not proportionate. Once the shareholder has 50% control, *all* stock owned by the shareholder is attributed to the controlled corporation. The §304 variation to the constructive ownership rules reduces the 50% threshold to 5%, but also provides that in any case where §318 would not apply but for this variation, the attribution rules shall be applied proportionately.[123] Assume, for example, that shareholder A owns 5% of the stock in Corporation X and also owns 50% in Corporation Z. Ordinarily, under the constructive ownership rules of §318, no shares would be attributed from shareholder A to Corporation X. Under the §304 variation, however, Corporation X will be deemed to own 5% of the Z shares that shareholder A owns.

Commonly Controlled or Brother-Sister Corporations: §304(a)(1)

Imagine that unrelated shareholders A and B each own 50% of the stock (50 out of 100 outstanding shares) of both Corporations X and Y and that Shareholder A sells 10 of her X shares to Corporation Y for cash.

---

122. Note that under the first variation described above, if Corporation X is in control of Corporation Y, the 50% shareholder here will be deemed to control both Corporations X and Y. I.R.C. §304(c)(1).
123. I.R.C. §304(c)(3)(B)(ii)(II).

Brother-Sister Corporations: §304

commonly controlled corporations

Under §304(a)(1), if "one or more persons are in control of each of two corporations, and in return for property, one of the corporations acquires stock in the other corporation from the person (or persons) so in control, then . . . such property shall be treated as a distribution in redemption of the stock of the corporation acquiring such stock." Slow and careful parsing of the words will help. First of all, A in our example is in control of each of the two corporations, X and Y, since she owns 50% of each corporation. Next, one of the corporations (Y Corporation) has acquired stock in the other corporation (X Corporation) from a person or persons in control of each of the corporations (shareholder A) in return for property (cash).

According to §304(a)(1), the property transferred by Y Corporation to shareholder A (cash) shall be treated as a distribution in redemption of Y Corporation.[124] Thus, the next step is to test the deemed redemption to determine whether it will get sale or exchange as opposed to dividend treatment. For the most part, this will involve application of the same §302 rules considered earlier in this chapter. A few special considerations should be noted in the §304 context, however. For example, notice that the deemed redemption under §304(a)(1) is of the *acquiring* corporation's stock, in this

---

124. For purposes of the §302 before and after analysis in testing the redemption, the §318(a)(2)(C) and §318(a)(3)(C) attribution rules are applied "without regard to the 50 percent limitation contained therein." I.R.C. §304(b)(1). Recall that for purposes of *measuring control*, the 50% threshold was reduced to 5%. Keep in mind that the provisions in §304(c) go only to the definition of control. These rules determine whether or not §304 will govern a particular transaction in the first instance. In contrast, the §304 elimination of the 50% threshold altogether is only for the purposes of testing the redemption under §302.

case, Y Corporation. Since the funds are transferred from Y Corporation to shareholder A, this treatment initially makes some sense. There is a major logistics problem, however. We are told to test this case under §302 as a Corporation Y redemption. Ordinarily, this would require a before and after analysis of shareholder A's interest in Y *Corporation*. Here, however, there has been no change at all in the ownership of Y stock. Thus, for purposes of testing the redemption under §302(b), the statute looks to stock of the issuing corporation, here Corporation X.[125]

If the shareholder is entitled to sale or exchange treatment under §302(b), she will simply report the distribution as her amount realized from the sale, offsetting this by her basis in the 10 X shares transferred to Corporation Y. If the deemed redemption fails the §302(b) tests and is treated as a §301 distribution, the statute expressly provides that the stock transferred by the shareholder and received by the acquiring corporation (10 X shares) should be treated as transferred in a §351(a) transaction followed by a redemption by the acquiring corporation of the shares it was treated as issuing in the hypothetical §351 exchange.[126] In the above example, shareholder A owned 50% (50 out of 100 shares) of Corporation X immediately before the deemed redemption. Immediately after the deemed redemption, she owns 45% (45 out of 100 shares).[127] Shareholder A does not qualify for complete termination of interest treatment under §302(b)(3), nor will she qualify for the §302(b)(2) safe harbor.[128] Unless she can qualify the distribution for sale or exchange treatment under §302(b)(1) "not essentially equivalent to a dividend" test, shareholder A must report the amount received from Corporation Y as a §301 distribution, treated as a dividend to the extent of earnings and profits.[129] In the end, §304(a)(1) creates a number of fictional events to work its magic. In effect, the transaction is treated as if shareholder A first transferred 10 X shares in exchange for fictional shares of the acquiring corporation (Corporation Y). These

---

125. I.R.C. §304(b)(1).

126. I.R.C. §304(a)(1) (last sentence).

127. Shareholder A retains 40 X shares. In addition, since she is a 50% owner of Y Corporation, 5 of the 10 she just transferred to Y will be "reattributed" to her under §318(a)(2)(C). For an example involving similar "reattribution," see Treas. Reg. §1.304-2(c), ex. 1.

128. Although she meets the less than 50% test, she fails the 80% test, since her interest immediately after the redemption (45%) is more than 80% of her interest immediately before the redemption (50% × 0.8=40%).

129. The §301 distribution rules are considered fully in Chapter 4. To calculate the amount which is a dividend, §304 first looks to the acquiring corporation to the extent of its earnings and profits, and then to the issuing corporation to the extent of its earnings and profits. I.R.C. §304(b)(2). In other words, the earnings and profits of both corporations effectively are pooled when necessary. Given the relationship between the entities, it makes sense to look also to the other corporation's earnings and profits in the case where those of the acquiring corporation are insufficient to cover the dividend.

fictional Y shares are immediately redeemed, but the redemption is tested with reference to shareholder A's ownership of stock in the issuing corporation (Corporation X). If the deemed redemption is treated as a §301 distribution, shareholder A is viewed as making a §351 contribution to the acquiring corporation. Thus, the shareholder should increase her basis in shares of the acquiring corporation (Corporation Y) by her basis in the 10 shares she transferred in Corporation X.[130] If the shareholder owns no remaining shares in the acquiring corporation directly, she may increase her basis in remaining shares of the issuer (Corporation X).[131] Here again, we see a variation of the mystery of disappearing basis.[132]

The acquiring corporation in the above example now owns 10 shares of stock in Corporation X. Ordinarily, a stock purchaser would simply take a cost basis in the purchased shares under §1012. Again, to the extent that the deemed redemption distribution is treated as a §301 distribution to the "selling" shareholder, §304(a)(1) treats the acquired shares as a §351 contribution.[133] As such, the purchasing corporation will take the shareholder's basis — a substituted basis — in the acquired stock.[134] In the above example, Corporation Y would hold the 10 X shares transferred by shareholder A with the same basis that shareholder A had.

Acquisitions by Subsidiaries: §304(a)(2)

A slightly different set of rules applies under §304 when the corporations involved are parent and subsidiary, as opposed to brother-sister corporations. For example, suppose now that shareholders A and B each own 50% of the stock of Corporation X. Corporation X, in turn, owns 100% of Corporation Y. In other words, Corporation X is a parent and Corporation Y is its wholly owned subsidiary.

---

130. Treas. Reg. §1.304-2(a), (c), ex. 1.
131. Treas. Reg. §1.304-2(a).
132. If the shareholder holds no direct shares in either the acquiring or the issuing corporation, the Service's view is that the seller's basis in the shares sold really does disappear. Rev. Rul. 70-496, 1970-2 C.B. 74. See also Treas. Reg. §1.304-2(c), ex. 2. This is unfair to the shareholder. Some way should surely be found at an appropriate time to permit the shareholder or related parties the recovery of basis to which they are entitled. See Coyle v. United States, 415 F.2d 488, 493 (4th Cir. 1968) (discussion to the effect that basis will not disappear).
133. I.R.C. §304(a)(1) (last sentence).
134. I.R.C. §362(a)(2).

Parent-Subsidiary Corporations: §304

Assume again that shareholder A sells 10 of her X shares to Corporation Y for cash. Absent special statutory provisions, shareholder A would simply report gain or loss from the sale of stock. Again, however, §304 requires that the property she receives from Corporation Y be treated as a deemed redemption. The operation of the rules in this parent-subsidiary case is a bit different, however. Section 304(a)(2) provides redemption treatment "if in return for property, one corporation acquires from a shareholder of another corporation stock in such other corporation, and the issuing corporation controls the acquiring corporation." In our example, the issuing corporation (X) owns 100%, and thus controls, the acquiring corporation (Y). In return for property (cash), Y Corporation acquired stock in the issuing or parent corporation from shareholder A. Under §304(a)(2), the cash received by shareholder A "shall be treated as a distribution in redemption of the stock of the issuing [parent] corporation." One might envision this transaction as if X Corporation (the parent) first transferred cash to its subsidiary, Y Corporation, which in turn used the cash to acquire the X stock on behalf of its parent.

Notice some technical differences between the deemed redemption provided under (a)(2) as opposed to (a)(1). In the parent-subsidiary case covered by (a)(2), the deemed redemption is a redemption by X Corporation—the issuing corporation. Since shareholder A has parted with some of her X Corporation shares, the before and after analysis of her interest in X required by §302 can be performed without the logistics dilemma produced in the brother-sister case covered by (a)(1).[135] If the

---

135. I.R.C. §304(b)(1) states that in the case of any acquisition of stock to which subsection (a) of this section applies, determinations as to whether the acquisition is by reason of §302(b), to be treated as distribution in part or in full payment in exchange for stock shall be made by reference to stock of the issuing corporation.

deemed redemption meets one of the §302(b) sale or exchange tests, the shareholder simply will report the amount received from Corporation Y as an amount realized, offset by her basis in the X shares transferred. On the other hand, if the deemed redemption fails the §302(b) tests, the transaction will be governed by the §301 distribution rules. Unlike the brother-sister context, however, this transaction in the parent-subsidiary context is not envisioned as a contribution to capital. As a consequence, shareholder A will not increase her basis in Corporation Y stock by the basis in the X shares transferred. Instead, the regulations provide that basis in the remaining parent corporation stock is determined by including the basis in the shares sold to the subsidiary.[136] In other words, shareholder A will have the same basis in the 40 X shares retained that she previously had in the full 50 X shares. The acquiring subsidiary's basis in the parent corporation stock will be a §1012 cost basis.[137]

Overlaps Between §304(a)(1) and (a)(2)

Determining whether a particular transaction falls within §304(a)(1) or (a)(2) can become tricky. Bizarre results occur after application of the constructive ownership rules. For example, any parent-subsidiary relationship can be seen as a brother-sister relationship. Take, for example, our earlier parent-subsidiary case in which A and B each own 50% of the stock in Corporation X and Corporation X, in turn, owns 100% of Corporation Y. Under the constructive ownership rules as modified in §304(c), since A and B control Corporation X, they shall be treated as in control of the subsidiary, Corporation Y.[138] Thus, A and B are persons in control of each of two corporations and §304(a)(1) also would appear to apply. Section §304(a)(1) explicitly prevents this overlap, however, stating that it will apply "unless paragraph (2) applies." Thus, the §304(a)(2) parent-subsidiary rule trumps the commonly controlled corporation rule in §304(a)(1).

One can also argue that every brother-sister relationship also is a parent-subsidiary relationship after application of the constructive ownership rules. If A and B each own 50% of both Corporations X and Y, Corporation X is considered as owning all of the stock that A and B own in Corporation Y.[139] In other words, Corporation X is deemed to be the parent of Corporation Y.[140] If the statute is taken literally, §304(a)(1) is superfluous, since every 50%

---

136. Treas. Reg. §1.304-3(a).
137. Rev. Rul. 80-189, 1980-2 C.B. 106.
138. I.R.C. §304(c)(1) (last sentence).
139. I.R.C. §318(a)(3)(C).
140. One could also do this attribution in reverse. In reverse, Corporation Y is deemed to own all of A and B's stock in Corporation X. In other words, Corporation Y is the deemed parent of Corporation X.

control relationship could be recharacterized as a parent-subsidiary relationship. Here, however, the regulations suggest that the direct brother-sister relationship will prevail over the constructive parent-subsidiary relationship.[141]

TAX CONSEQUENCES TO THE CORPORATION

From the corporation's perspective, the distribution of cash or property to the shareholder in a redemption distribution is a "distribution with respect to stock" for purposes of §311. Thus, the corporate tax consequences will be governed by the nonliquidating distribution rules considered in Chapter 5. When the corporation uses appreciated property in a redemption distribution, gain will be recognized.[142] Losses from the distribution of depreciated property will not be recognized.[143]

With regard to earnings and profits adjustments, redemptions that are treated as dividend distributions will be treated exactly as any other dividend distribution would be.[144] Different earnings and profits rules apply, however, with respect to redemptions treated as sales. Some reduction to earnings and profits is appropriate, since the corporation is, after all, distributing earnings to repurchase its shares. On the other hand, in order for the distribution to be classified as a sale or exchange for purposes of §302(a), the selling shareholder generally must have experienced a substantial reduction in proportionate interest. To some extent, then, the corporation is dipping into its capital to restore a portion of the selling shareholder's investment. A reduction in earnings and profits to the full extent of the redemption distribution would reduce the amount of dividend income on subsequent distributions to the remaining shareholders. Thus, the amount distributed in redemption would never be treated as a dividend with respect to the redeemed shares or the remaining shares. The statutory solution in §312(n)(7) is to limit the earnings and profits reduction to an amount "not in excess of the ratable share of earnings and profits . . . Attributable to the stock so redeemed." This provision imposes a ceiling, or cap, on the e&p reduction following a redemption distribution that is treated as a sale or exchange to the redeemed shareholder. Thus, for example, if the corporation completely redeems a 50% shareholder, the redemption distribution could not generate an e&p reduction greater than the 50% of earnings and profits attributable to the shares redeemed.

---

141. See Treas. Reg. §1.304-2(c), ex. 1.
142. I.R.C. §311(b).
143. I.R.C. §311(a).
144. I.R.C. §312(a), (b). For a detailed discussion of these e&p adjustment rules, see Chapter 5.

6. Redemption Distributions

As a final observation regarding tax consequences to the distributing corporation, note that §162(k) denies deductions for amounts paid or incurred in connection with the corporation's redemption of its own stock.[145] A number of cases have raised interesting questions and a split in the federal circuit courts over the intersection of §162(k)(1), the §302 redemption rules, and special rules in §404(k)(1), which permit corporations with employee stock option plans (ESOPs) to deduct "applicable dividends" paid in cash with respect to applicable employer securities. Corporations with ESOPs generally make contributions of their own stock over time on behalf of their employees to an ESOP trust, which then allocates the stock to employee-participants' accounts. Upon retirement, employees may be entitled to take the stock in their accounts or, instead, to elect to take an equivalent value in cash. When employees select the cash option, the corporation typically redeems its stock from the trust, which then distributes cash to the employee. A redemption that does not fit within any of the §302(b) "safe harbors" will be treated as a dividend to the redeemed shareholder, the ESOP trust. From the corporation's perspective, the general corporate tax rule providing that corporations cannot deduct dividend distributions comes into conflict with §404(k)(1), which allows deductions for applicable dividends in the ESOP setting. In any event, even if the cash payments to the shareholder are viewed as meeting the "applicable dividend" requirements, the corporation still faces restrictions in §162(k)(1), which disallow deductions "for any amount paid or incurred by a corporation in connection with the reacquisition of its stock." One circuit court has held that the cash payments to the employees are distinct from the redemption distribution and are not in connection with the corporation's reacquisition of stock, thus permitting the §404(k) deduction.[146] Two others, however, have rejected this approach and disallowed corporate deductions for cash payments in redemption of stock held by the corporation's ESOP trust.[147]

Example

1. Springfield, Inc. (Springfield) is a media company that produces animated sitcoms. Springfield has five shareholders: Marge, Homer, Ned, Moe, and Marge's grandmother. Marge and Homer are married, and Ned and Moe are unrelated to the other shareholders. Each of the shareholders owns

---

145. I.R.C. §162(k)(1). The Code states an exception, however, for interest allowable as a deduction under §163. I.R.C. §162(k)(2).

146. Boise Cascade Corp. v. United States, 329 F.3d 751 (9th Cir. 2003).

147. Conopco, Inc. v. United States, 572 F.3d 162 (3d Cir. 2009); General Mills, Inc. v. United States, 554 F.3d 727 (8th Cir. 2009). Treasury Department regulations promulgated in 2006 specify that "[a]mounts paid or incurred in connection with reacquisition of stock include amounts paid by a corporation to reacquire its stock from an ESOP that are used in a manner described in section 404(k)(2)(A)." Treas. Reg. §1.162(k)-1(a).

20% of the 1,000 shares of Springfield's outstanding common voting stock. The overall net value of the corporation is $5 million. The corporation decided to redeem Marge completely and distributed $1 million cash to her in return for all of her stock. The corporation's current earnings and profits for the year of the redemption is $2.5 million. It has no accumulated e&p. Marge's basis in her shares was $300,000. What tax consequence to Marge? To Springfield? To the remaining shareholders?

Variations on Example I

2. a. What if Springfield distributed property worth $1 million (with a basis to Springfield of $250,000) instead of cash to redeem Marge's stock?
   b. What if Springfield redeemed only ten shares of Moe's stock and no stock from Marge? Moe's basis in the redeemed shares was $20,000.
   c. Would the results in Example 1 change if all five shareholders had agreed to a "buy out" arrangement pursuant to which each agreed to first offer sale of the shares to the other shareholders before selling to a third party?
   d. Would your answers to any of the above change if, in addition to their interests in Springfield, Marge and Moe were partners in an unrelated partnership?

Meaningful Reductions?

3. SlimFaster, Inc., is a corporation engaged in the business of selling weight loss products and consulting with individuals seeking weight loss advice. Mr. Jim Slim, founder of the corporation, and his two daughters each own 250 of the 750 shares of common voting stock. In addition, the corporation recently issued 750 shares of nonvoting preferred stock. Mr. Slim holds all of the preferred shares. What are the tax consequences to Slim and the corporation if the corporation redeems all of Slim's preferred stock for cash? What if the corporation redeems all of Slim's common *and* preferred stock?

4. a. Assume the same facts as in Example 3, except that Slim owns only 250 shares of preferred stock with the remaining 500 held by the public. What are the tax consequences now if all of Slim's preferred shares are redeemed?
   b. One member of the public originally bought 100 shares of SlimFaster nonvoting preferred stock. The corporation redeems 10 shares from this shareholder. What result?

Fun and Games with Attribution

5. Mr. Smith owns 50 of the 100 outstanding common shares of Corporation X. X, a parent corporation, owns 100% of Corporation Y. Corporation Y

owns 40 of the 100 outstanding shares in Corporation Z. Mr. Smith owns 60 shares of Corporation Z stock. What tax consequence if Z redeems the 60 Z shares owned by Mr. Smith?

6. a. Would your answer to Example 5 change if Mr. Smith did not own any X shares directly, but his wife owned 50 X shares?
   b. Would your answer to Example 5 change if Mr. Smith did not own any X shares directly, but his mother-in-law owned 50 X shares?
   c. What tax consequences in Example 5 if Z redeems the 40 Z shares owned by Corporation Y?

Related Corporations

7. a. Three unrelated shareholders, Rex, Alexia, and Lee, each owned 600 of the 1,800 outstanding common shares of Oedipus Yarn and Needles, Inc. And 600 of the 1,800 outstanding common shares of Queens Eyeglasses, Inc. Oedipus had a substantial e&p surplus, while Queens Eyeglasses had no current earnings and a deficit in its accumulated e&p account. Queens had cash reserves, while Oedipus held inventory and other assets of value. On the same day, Rex and Lee each sold 300 shares of their Oedipus stock to Queens in return for cash. How should Rex and Lee treat the sale for tax purposes?
   b. Would your answer in Example 7a differ if Oedipus held all of the shares in Queens Eyeglasses and the individual shareholders owned no direct shares in Queens?
   c. How would your answer to Example 7a differ if Rex and Alexia were husband and wife?
   d. How would your answer to Example 7b differ if Rex and Alexia were husband and wife?
   e. How would your answer to Example 7a differ if Rex and Lee sold 450 of their Oedipus shares to Queens?

Explanations

1. Although at first blush, the redemption appears to qualify for sale treatment to Marge as a §302(b)(3) complete termination of interest, this will not be the case. Marge is deemed to own her husband Homer's shares under §318(a)(1) and, thus, has not been completely terminated. Marge directly owned 200/1,000 or 20% and indirectly owned an additional 200/1,000 or 20% by attribution from her husband immediately before the redemption. Thus, immediately before the redemption, Marge held 400/1,000 or 40%. Marge is not deemed to own her grandmother's shares. Immediately after the redemption, Marge no longer held any shares directly, but continued to constructively own her husband's shares. Unless Marge files an appropriate waiver of family attribution under

§302(c)(2), immediately after the redemption, she will be deemed to constructively own 200/800 or 25%. Even without a waiver, however, since the percentage owned immediately after the redemption is less than 50%, Marge satisfies the threshold test of §302(b)(2)(B). In addition, Marge meets the 80% test since his post-redemption ratio of 25% is less than 80% of his pre-redemption ratio of 40%.

Since Marge qualifies under the §302(b)(2) safe harbor, §302(a) provides that the redemption will be treated as a sale. The amount realized upon the sale is the $1 million received from the corporation. From this, she will subtract her $300,000 basis in the shares, resulting in a taxable gain of $700,000. This gain will be capital gain, assuming that the stock was a capital asset in Marge's hands. Since the corporation distributed cash, there is no gain or loss to worry about from the corporation's perspective. The corporation will be required to reduce its earnings and profits to reflect the distribution. Pursuant to the §312(n)(7) limitations to §312(a), the corporation's e&p reduction shall not exceed the redeemed stock's ratable share of e&p. Thus, the reduction will be limited to 20% of $2.5 million, or $500,000. The remaining e&p after the redemption is $2 million.

Since the remaining shareholders had no primary and unconditional obligation to buy out his shares, there should be no tax consequence to the remaining shareholders from the redemption of Marge's shares.

2. a. If the corporation used property instead of cash to redeem Marge's stock, the tax consequences to Marge would be the same. She has still received property worth $1 million in a "sale" redemption under §302(a). Her gain will still be $700,000. Since the transaction was taxable to Marge, she should be entitled to a basis equal to the property's fair market value at the time of the redemption distribution, in this case, $1 million ("tax cost basis"). If the corporation uses property with a fair market value of $1 million and a basis of $250,000 to redeem Marge's shares, the corporation will have a $750,000 taxable gain under §311(b). This reflects appreciation in the value of the property that was not previously taxed at the corporate level. The character of the gain will depend upon the asset distributed. The corporation's e&p would first be increased by the $750,000 gain to $3.25 million. I.R.C. §312(b). Depending on its accounting method, the corporation's e&p may then be reduced by the federal income tax liability to the corporation resulting from the corporation's $750,000 gain on the distribution. E&P would then be reduced by $650,000. Note that while §312(a), (b) would otherwise permit an e&p reduction in the amount of the $1 million value of the property, the reduction here is limited by §312(n)(7) to the redeemed stock's ratable

shares of e&p (20% of $3.25 million).[148] There would still be no tax consequence to the remaining shareholders.

b. If the corporation redeemed ten shares from Moe, he would clearly not qualify for sale treatment as a complete termination of interest. It appears that he also would not qualify under the §302(b)(2) substantially disproportionate distribution test. Immediately before the redemption, Moe owned 200/1,000 or 20%. Immediately after the redemption, he owns 190/990 or 19%. In order to qualify under the 80% test, Moe's post-redemption ratio must be less than 16% (80% of his pre-redemption ratio of 20%). Although he meets the 50% threshold test because he owns less than 50% immediately after the redemption, he fails the 80% test.

To determine whether Moe might receive sale treatment under the §302(b)(1) "not essentially equivalent to a dividend" test, a facts and circumstances analysis will be necessary. The Senate legislative history indicated that §302(b)(1) was intended primarily for the protection of preferred minority shareholders who had no control over redemptions. Moe, however, is a minority voting common shareholder. He might argue that prior to the redemption, he shared voting control equally with four others and that immediately after the redemption, his interest is slightly lower than the remaining shareholders, thus eliminating his shared control. If successful with this argument, Moe will be eligible for sale treatment. He would subtract his basis of $20,000 from the amount received from the corporation to figure his gain or loss.

If Moe is unsuccessful in his argument that §302(b)(1) applies, the corporate distribution will be treated as a §301 dividend since the corporation has sufficient e&p. Assuming that it qualified under §1(h)(11), this dividend amount will be added to net capital gain and taxed at capital gains rates. He will not get any basis offset. His $20,000 basis in the redeemed shares should not be lost. He should be entitled to add the $20,000 back into the basis of the Springfield shares he continues to hold. The corporation simply will reduce its e&p by the cash distribution. Notice that the §312(n)(7) limitation only applies to sale or exchange redemptions.

c. From Marge's perspective, there would be no change. She would still have a $700,000 taxable gain. Moreover, there should be no effect on the remaining shareholders. The agreement here was only that the

---

148. The amount of the e&p reduction under §312(n)(7) would be slightly lower if the corporation also reduced its e&p upon the distribution by the accrued tax liability resulting from the distribution of appreciated property (and the corporation's e&p at the time was consequently less than $3.25 million).

shareholders would first offer to the other shareholders. There was no binding obligation to purchase. If the remaining shareholders had previously entered into a binding contract to "buy out" Marge's shares and if, instead, the corporation redeemed the shares in satisfaction of that obligation, the remaining shareholders would be viewed as receiving a constructive dividend.

d. No, the answers would not change if Marge and Moe were partners in an unrelated partnership. In such a case, each of the partners' 200 shares would be attributed to the partnership under §318(a)(3)(A). Absent a special rule, the shares might then be reattributed to the partners under §318(a)(2)(A). The attribution cut-off rule in §318(a)(5)(C) prevents this result. One partner will not be deemed to own the shares of an unrelated partner.

3. This question is close to the facts in the *Davis* case. Mr. Slim owns one-third of the common voting stock directly and owns the remaining two-thirds indirectly through attribution from his daughters. After application of the constructive ownership rules, he is the sole shareholder. He surely does not qualify for the complete termination of interest safe harbor since only his preferred shares were redeemed. Moreover, he will not qualify for §302(b)(2) since there has been no reduction in his interest. He also fails the "not essentially equivalent to a dividend" test since there has been no reduction in his interest, meaningful or otherwise. As the *Davis* case indicated, a sole shareholder can never qualify for the §302(b)(1) "not essentially equivalent to a dividend" safe harbor. Since Slim will fail all of the §302(b) tests, the redemption will be treated as a dividend, probably eligible for preferential capital gains rates under §1(h)(11), to the extent of the corporation's e&p. Since he continues to own common stock, his basis for the preferred shares redeemed will be added to the basis of his common stock. The corporation simply will reduce its e&p by the cash distributed pursuant to §312(a).

If the corporation redeemed both Slim's common and preferred stock, Slim would own no shares directly immediately after the redemption. Nevertheless, Slim would still own 100% of the remaining stock by attribution from his daughters and would therefore not qualify under any of the §302(b) sale or exchange tests. The redemption distribution would be taxed as a dividend to the extent of e&p. Slim can avoid this dividend result by filing a waiver of family attribution and by agreeing to have no further interest in the corporation other than an interest as a creditor under §302(c)(2). Now Slim would qualify for sale or exchange treatment as a complete termination of interest under §302(b)(3). He would simply subtract his basis in the shares redeemed from the distribution received from the corporation to measure his gain or loss.

If Slim does not file a waiver and the distribution is treated as a dividend, Slim must address a potential mystery of disappearing basis problem. Unlike the situation above, Slim no longer holds any shares of his own to which he can add the basis of the redeemed stock. The mystery should be resolved here by giving Slim's basis to his two daughters in proportion to their relative stock holdings. Again, the corporation simply will reduce e&p by the cash distributed.

4. a. If Slim held only 250 of the preferred shares all of which were redeemed, he still would not qualify for §302(b)(3) complete termination of interest treatment since he still would own one-third of the common stock directly and two-thirds indirectly, unless he files a family attribution waiver. In addition, he cannot qualify for the §302(b)(2) safe harbor because he does not meet the 50% threshold test. Directly and through attribution, he owns 100% of the common voting stock. The only possibility here is §302(b)(1). There was no reduction in Slim's voting stock interest. Since two-thirds of the preferred stock was owned by the public, there was some reduction in his preferred stock interest. Was this reduction meaningful under the *Davis* test? Probably not. Since Slim continues to have voting control, he would most likely fail the *Davis* meaningful reduction test.

   b. If one member of the public purchased 100 shares of SlimFaster stock and 10 shares are redeemed, there is no complete termination of interest, since the shareholder still holds 90 shares. The §302(b)(2) substantially disproportionate interest test is not applicable here since the minority shareholder owned no voting stock in the first place. This case represents precisely the situation that the Senate Finance Committee was concerned with in keeping the "essentially equivalent to a dividend" language in the statute. A minority shareholder of nonvoting preferred stock has little or no control over corporate redemptions. Consequently, the §302(b)(1) safe harbor is liberally applied in such cases. Even minor reductions in the shareholder's interest have been considered meaningful. See, e.g., Rev. Rul. 76-385, 1976-2 C.B. 92. The minority shareholder should be entitled to sale treatment of the redemption distribution under §302(b)(1) and §302(a). The corporation will reduce its e&p, subject to the limitations in §312(n)(7).

5. If Z Corporation redeems the 60 Z shares owned by Mr. Smith, at first blush it would appear that he qualifies for sale or exchange treatment under the complete termination of interest safe harbor. This will not be the case, however. Mr. Smith will be deemed to own 20 Z shares by attribution in two steps. First, since X Corporation owns 100% of Y Corporation, X will be deemed to own 100% of the shares that Y owns under §318(a)(2)(C). Thus, X constructively owns Y's 40 Z shares. And,

since Mr. Smith owns 50% of X Corporation, he will be deemed to own 50% of the 40 Z shares that X owns through attribution from Y. This multiple application of the attribution rules involves a (2)/(2) combination, which is not cut off by any of the operating rules in §318(a)(5).

After determining the proper attribution, Mr. Smith must compare the pre-redemption ratio to the post-redemption ratio. Immediately before the redemption, Mr. Smith owned 60% of the Z shares directly and 20% indirectly for a total of 80%. Immediately after the redemption, he owns no shares directly, but 50% of the remaining 40 shares through attribution. The reduction from 80% to 50% will not qualify for the §302(b)(2) substantially disproportionate distribution safe harbor. Note that the 50% threshold test requires that the shareholder hold *less than* 50% of the voting stock immediately after the redemption. Since Mr. Smith holds exactly 50%, this test is not met. The next question, then, is whether a reduction from 80% to 50% is a meaningful reduction under §302(b)(1). Since Mr. Smith shares control with a "friendly" party, the Service in this case will likely conclude that the reduction is not meaningful. If so, the redemption distribution will be treated as a dividend to the extent of earnings and profits. What about Smith's basis in his 60 Z shares? The mystery of disappearing basis appears again. Mr. Smith's basis in the redeemed shares might be added to Y Corporation's basis in the remaining 40 Z shares. On the other hand, Smith might argue that the change from a position of absolute power to one of equally shared power should be considered meaningful. If he wins, the redemption distribution will be entitled to sale treatment and Smith will get his basis offset through the §1001 computation on the exchange.

6. a. No. The answer would be the same. Mr. Smith would still be deemed to constructively own one-half of Y's 40 Z shares, now through a three-step application of the attribution rules. As above, the 40 Z shares would be constructively owned by X under §318(a)(2)(C). Mr. Smith's wife would be considered to own one-half of these shares (20 Z) through a second application of this attribution rule. Finally, Mr. Smith will be deemed to own the 20 Z shares just attributed to his wife through the family attribution provisions of §318(a)(1). This (2)/(2)/(1) punch is also not prohibited by any of the cut-off rules in §318(a)(5).

   b. Yes. The first two attribution steps in this variation of the facts would not change, however. X Corporation would be deemed to own the 40 Z shares under §318(a)(2) and X's mother-in-law would be deemed to own one-half of the 40 Z shares through a second application of §318(a)(2). There is no direct attribution between in-laws, however. The mother-in-law's stock could only be attributed to Mr. Smith by going through his wife. This double application of the family attribution rules of §318(a)(1) is cut off by the operating rule in §318(a)(5)(B). Thus, the redemption of Mr. Smith's stock will completely terminate his interest under §302(b)(3) and he will be entitled to report the redemption distribution as a sale.

c. If Z Corporation redeemed the 40 Z shares owned by Y Corporation, again it would first appear to be a complete termination of interest. However, Y Corporation will be deemed to own Mr. Smith's Z stock. Since Mr. Smith owns 50% of X, X Corporation will be deemed to own Mr. Smith's 60 Z shares under §318(a)(3)(C). Since X owns 100% of Y, Y will be deemed to own X's shares under a second application of §318(a)(3)(C). Note that the attribution rules here are not proportionate. Thus, *all* of Mr. Smith's shares will be attributed to Y Corporation. As a result, Y will be considered a 100% owner of the Z shares both immediately before and immediately after the redemption and will fail all of the §302(b) tests. Y Corporation will report the redemption distribution as a dividend to the extent of Z's e&p. Y Corporation will take a §243 dividends-received deduction. Since this is a non-pro rata redemption, it will be treated as an "extraordinary dividend" to Y Corporation subject to the special rules of §1059(a)(1) and (2). Y Corporation's basis in the Z stock will first be reduced by the nontaxed portion of the dividend under §1059(a)(1). To the extent that the nontaxed portion of the dividend exceeds Y Corporation's basis in the Z shares, gain will be recognized under §1059(a)(2).

7. a. Since the shareholders are unrelated and each owns only one-third of the corporation's stock, no single shareholder controls either corporation, as control is defined in §304(c). One's initial instinct might be to say that §304 does not cover this case at all. If so, the sales would simply be treated as sales under §§61(a)(3) and 1001. Nevertheless, §304(a)(1) refers to "one or more persons . . . in control of each of two corporations." The issue here is whether to aggregate at least the shares owned by the two transferring shareholders for purposes of §304. The regulations provide that §304 will apply in such a case "provided the sales by each of such persons are related to each other." Treas. Reg. §1.304-2(b). Whether the sales are related will depend upon the facts and circumstances. In our case, the sales took place on the same day. In addition, the corporation is closely held. One suspects that the two shareholders consulted with each other, and probably with the third shareholder, regarding these sales. Assuming that the sales are related, both sales will be governed by §304(a)(1). In return for property (cash) one corporation (Queens) acquired stock of the other corporation (Oedipus) from the persons in control. The sales are deemed under §304(a)(1) to be a distribution in

redemption of Queens stock. This redemption must now be tested under the §302 redemption rules. Even though §304(a)(1) tells us that this is a redemption of Queens stock, the statute tells us to test the redemption by reference to stock of the issuing corporation, in this case, Oedipus. I.R.C. §304(b)(1). Immediately before the redemption, each of the transferring shareholders had 600/1,800 or one-third of the Oedipus stock outstanding. Immediately after the redemption, each of the transferring shareholders had 500/1,800.[149] Remember here that this is a *deemed* redemption. The shares were not really redeemed, but are now owned by Queens. Nevertheless, for purposes of §304, we treat these shares as if they were, in fact, redeemed. The shareholders here have gone from a 33⅓% ownership to a 28% ownership. Nothing in the facts suggests a corporate contraction. Thus, the (b)(4) partial liquidation exception will not apply. Since the shareholders still own stock, this is not a (b)(3) complete termination of interest redemption. They will not qualify, however, for the (b)(2) safe-harbor. Although they each have less than 50% of the stock immediately after the exchange, the 28% interest immediately after the exchange is not less than 80% of the 33⅓% interest immediately before the exchange. Thus, the cash received by Rex and Lee is treated as a distribution from Queens to which §301 applies. Even though Queens itself has no e&p, the distribution will still be classified as a §316 dividend since §304(b)(2) effectively directs the shareholders to look to Oedipus's e&p in the event that Queen's e&p is insufficient to cover the distribution. Rex and Lee will increase the basis in their Queens shares by the basis in the 300 Oedipus shares transferred. Queens will take a substituted basis from Rex and Lee in the 600 Oedipus shares it now owns.

b. No. If Oedipus was the parent and Queens was a subsidiary, the transaction technically would be covered by §304(a)(2) instead of (a)(1). The only difference here is that (a)(2) itself tells us that this is a deemed redemption of the issuing corporation's stock (Oedipus). The §302 analysis would be the same.

c. Although the end result would not change, the analysis differs for Rex if he is married to Alexia. Under the attribution rules, Rex is deemed to own the shares that Alexia owns. Thus, before the deemed redemption, he held a 2/3 interest in Queens. After the redemption, he has a 61% interest in the corporation, since he holds 300 shares directly, and 600 shares by attribution from his wife, and 200 shares

---

149. Rex and Lee each continued to own 300 Oedipus shares directly. In addition, 200 (1/3) of the 600 Oedipus shares now owned by Queens are "reattributed" to each of them under §318(a)(2)(C), as modified by §304.

by "reattribution" from Queens. There should be no difference in the tax consequences to Lee.

d. This deemed redemption would now be governed by §304(a)(2). The tax differences would be minor. Rex would still fail the safe-harbor tests and, thus, would be required to treat the distribution as a dividend to the extent of Queen's e&p. The differences would arise regarding basis issues. Rex would add the basis in the transferred shares to the remaining shares in *Oedipus,* rather than Queens. In addition, Queens would get a cost basis in the shares received.

e. If Rex and Lee sold 450 shares, as opposed to 300, they would have a 25% interest in Oedipus immediately after the redemption.[150] In other words, this is a sufficient reduction in their interest in the corporation to qualify as a §302(b)(2) sale redemption. The shareholders, then, will recover their basis in the Oedipus shares sold through the basis offset in the §1001 formula. Queens would hold the shares with a cost basis.

---

150. The ratio would be 450/1,800 (150 shares owned directly and 300 shares "reattributed" under §318(a)(2)(C), as modified by §304).

Stock Dividends

INTRODUCTION

From time to time during its lifetime, the corporation will make distributions of its own stock to its shareholders. The reasons for such stock distributions are varied. Often, the distribution reflects a corporate surplus that was retained as working capital rather than distributed to the shareholders. The stock dividend is tangible evidence to the shareholders of that surplus, even though the shareholders have withdrawn no assets from the corporation.

This was precisely the type of distribution involved in the landmark Supreme Court decision in Eisner v. Macomber.[1] In that case, Standard Oil of California issued a 50% stock dividend on its outstanding capital stock. The taxpayer, as owner of 2,200 shares, received a certificate for an additional 1,100 shares. At the time, Congress explicitly had provided for taxation of stock dividends.[2] The Supreme Court declared the taxation of stock dividends unconstitutional on the grounds that a stock dividend was not income under the Sixteenth Amendment.

The *Macomber* opinion provides a useful discussion of the "essential nature of a stock dividend" and, more broadly, the concepts of income and realization. First, the Court described the "essential nature of a stock dividend" as a distribution that "takes nothing from the property of the

---

1. 252 U.S. 189 (1920).
2. Revenue Act of 1916, §2(a), c. 463, 39 Stat. 756.

corporation and adds nothing to the interests of the shareholders. Its property is not diminished, and their interests are not increased. . . . The proportional interest of each shareholder remains the same. The only change is in the evidence which represents that interest, the new shares and the original shares together representing the same proportional interest that the original shares represented before the issue of the new ones."[3] The Court went on to describe a stock dividend as showing "that the company's accumulated profits have been capitalized, instead of distributed to the stockholders or retained as surplus available for the distribution. . . . Far from being a realization of profits of the stockholder, it tends rather to postpone such realization, in that the fund represented by the new stock has been transferred from surplus to capital, and no longer is available for actual distribution."[4]

The Supreme Court in *Macomber* correctly concluded that there is no realization of gain from the distribution of a pro rata stock dividend that does not alter the shareholder's proportionate interests in the corporation. The shareholder simply has additional pieces of paper reflecting the same interest that he had before. The key here is realization. As the corporation's surplus was building, the value of each shareholder's interest in the corporation was increasing. Economists would surely view this increase in value as income. Nevertheless, there is no *realization* of that income until the shareholder sells or disposes of the stock. Modern scholars take the view that the *Macomber* case developed an overly narrow definition of income and was wrongly decided as a constitutional matter. Most scholars today would agree that Congress could constitutionally tax stock dividends if it chose to do so. Yet, the principle of realization is so well-entrenched as a matter of tax policy that Congress has chosen not to tax most pro rata stock dividends.

The *Macomber* Court's description of the "essential nature of a stock dividend" does not apply to all stock dividends. Unless all shareholders participate in proportion to their interests in the corporation, a stock dividend will alter the proportionate interests of shareholders. Some shareholders may increase their interest in the corporate enterprise at the expense of other shareholders. Thus, the holding in Eisner v. Macomber was limited to "true stock dividends" that did not alter the shareholders' proportionate interests in the corporation. If the interest received by the shareholder was sufficiently different from the underlying stock upon which the stock dividend was issued, the stock dividend was taxable.[5] The lower courts had difficulty distinguishing stock dividends that were tax-free under the *Macomber* analysis from those that were taxable. Congress attempted to provide greater certainty by codifying rules on stock dividends in §§305 and 306. The

---

3. 252 U.S. 189, 202-203 (citing Gibbons v. Mahon, 136 U.S. 549, 559-560 (1890)).
4. 252 U.S. 189, 211 (1920).
5. See, e.g., Koshland v. Helvering, 298 U.S. 441 (1936) (common stock dividend on preferred stock).

remainder of this chapter is devoted to these statutory rules and their current interpretation.

TAX CONSEQUENCES TO THE SHAREHOLDERS

The Basic §305(a) Nonrecognition Rule

When a corporation distributes its own stock or rights to acquire such stock, the corporation is not making a distribution of "property" that would be covered by the §301 distribution rules.[6] Instead, stock dividends are governed by special provisions found in §305.

Under the §305(a) general rule applicable to stock dividends, distributions of the corporation's own stock or options to acquire such stock are not taxable to the shareholders.[7] Five exceptions to the general rule are enumerated in §305(b). In addition, Congress in §305(c) provided reasonably broad authority to the Treasury Department to promulgate regulations under which certain stock and option distributions and other transactions not covered by the five enumerated exceptions nevertheless may be treated as taxable distributions.

The nonrecognition rule reflected in §305(a) simply codifies the general nonrecognition principle established by the Supreme Court in Eisner v. Macomber. Recall that the thrust of the Court's ruling in that case was to protect stock dividends that did not alter the shareholders' proportionate interest in the corporation. In keeping with that spirit, §305 ordinarily protects from taxation pro rata distributions issued with respect to common stock. Non-pro rata distributions are likely to be covered by one of the exceptions to the general rule provided in §305(b).

Notice also that nonrecognition is limited under §305(a) to distributions of the corporation's stock made "with respect to its stock." Thus, only distributions to shareholders qua shareholders will be covered by §305. The stock dividend provisions of §305 will not apply to stock distributions when the facts and circumstances suggest that the distribution was intended as compensation for services or as satisfaction of corporate debt, for example.[8]

---

6. For purposes of the §301 rules, property includes "money, securities, and any other property; *except that such term does not include stock in the corporation making the distribution (or rights to acquire such stock).*" I.R.C. §317(a) (emphasis added). For a discussion of the rules applicable to nonliquidating distributions, see Chapter 5.

7. For purposes of §305, the term "stock" includes "rights to acquire such stock." I.R.C. §305(d)(1).

8. Section 301 contains a similar limitation. See discussion in Chapter 5.

Basis Rules: §307

There are no immediate tax consequences to the shareholder upon the receipt of a tax-free stock dividend under §305(a). However, the shareholder must compute basis for the dividend shares received. When new shares are received in a distribution to which the general rule of §305(a) applies, §307 requires an allocation of the old basis. More specifically, it provides that the "basis of such new stock and of the stock with respect to which it is distributed (referred to in this section as 'old stock'), respectively, shall . . . be determined by allocating between the old stock and the new stock the adjusted basis of the old stock." In other words, the shareholder will take the basis in the old stock with respect to which the new stock was issued and spread that basis over all of the shares, old and new, owned immediately after the stock distribution. The regulations specify that the allocation will be "in proportion to the fair market values of each on the date of distribution."[9] To determine the basis in dividend shares under this allocation rule, the shareholder will multiply the basis in the old stock by a fraction, the numerator of which is the fair market value of the new shares on the date of distribution and the denominator of which is the fair market value of all of the shares owned (old and new) on the date of the distribution.[10] Suppose, for example, that shareholder S owns 100 shares of stock in Corporation X ("old shares") with a basis of $1,500. Corporation X declares a 50% stock dividend pursuant to which S receives 50 new shares. Immediately after the distribution, the fair market value of the old shares is $10,000 and the fair market value of the new shares is $5,000. To determine her basis in the new shares, S will multiply her basis in the old shares of $1,500×5,000/15,000 or 1/3. One-third of her old basis is allocable to the new shares. Thus, the shareholder's basis in her 50 new shares will be $500. Her basis remaining in the old shares will be $1,000. Notice that the shareholder's overall basis in her stock ownership remains at $1,500 — the amount she originally invested. Although the basis in each individual share is reduced, the overall basis remains the same.

The Shareholder's Holding Period

Since stock generally is considered a capital asset, it will be important for shareholders to know the holding period for shares received by way of a stock dividend. A special holding period rule for stock with a basis

---

9. Treas. Reg. §1.307-1(a).
10. The calculation of fair market value should be made immediately after the stock distribution. Treas. Reg. §1.307-1(b) (example).

determined under §307 permits tacking of the period during which the underlying shares were held.[11] Returning to the example above, if shareholder S had owned her shares for three years, she would be entitled to add or "tack" that three year period to the holding period for the new shares. Remember that this stock dividend was tax-free under §305(a) and was subject to the §307 basis allocation rules. Like the stock dividend in Eisner v. Macomber, such stock dividends represent little other than a balance sheet adjustment whereby the shareholders receive additional shares of stock, but experience no change in their relative proportionate interest. In substance, shareholder S owns nothing different from what she had before. Under these circumstances, tacking of the holding period makes sense.

The §305(b) Exceptions

a) In General

Congress enumerates five specific types of stock dividends in §305(b) for which the general nonrecognition rule of §305(a) will not apply. The five §305(b) exceptions appear to be connected by a theme—the exceptions generally cover distributions that alter or may alter the proportionate interests of shareholders. The exceptions reflect a congressional effort to codify the "shift in proportional interest" test developed in Eisner v. Macomber and its progeny. When the stock dividend changes proportionate interests of the shareholders, the distribution is more than a mere paper transaction.

If one of the five §305(b) exceptions applies, the stock dividend will be treated as a §301 distribution. Remember that under the §301 rules, distributions will be treated as dividends to the extent of earnings and profits. Thus, to the extent that there are sufficient earnings and profits to cover the distribution, a §305(b) stock dividend will be taxable. The shareholder will report the fair market value of the stock distributed as dividend income and the shares will receive a fair market value basis under §301(d), rather than the §307 allocated basis that applies to stock received tax-free under §305(a).[12]

---

11. More specifically, the Code provides that "[i]n determining the period for which the taxpayer has held stock or rights to acquire stock received on a distribution, if the basis of such stock or rights is determined under section 307 . . . There shall (under regulations prescribed by the Secretary) be included the period for which he held the stock in the distributing corporation before the receipt of such stock or rights upon such distribution." I.R.C. §1223(4). The regulations clarify that the holding period for the dividend shares is the period for which the taxpayer held "the stock in respect of which the dividend was issued." Treas. Reg. §1.1223-1(e).

12. Such income is likely to qualify for preferential capital gains rates under the §1(h)(11) "qualified dividend income rules." These rules and the §301 distribution rules more generally are considered fully in Chapter 5.

b) Election to Take Other Property: §305(b)(1)

If any of the shareholders can elect to have a distribution payable either in stock or property other than stock, the stock dividend will be taxable to all shareholders receiving stock pursuant to §305(b)(1). Surely, any shareholder who elects to receive property *other than stock* should be taxable according to the §301 distribution rules. More important, §305(b)(1) also requires even those who receive stock to report the distribution under the §301 rules. If some shareholders receive stock and other shareholders receive cash or other property, the stock dividend recipients increase their proportionate interest in the corporation at the expense of the other shareholders. Even if only one shareholder had an election to take cash or other property, all shareholders will be tainted by this election and the entire stock distribution will be taxable.

Notice that the §305(b)(1) exception sweeps rather broadly to deal not only with distributions that actually are disproportionate, but even those that are *potentially* disproportionate. The §305(b)(1) exception will apply even if all shareholders with an election to take property other than stock choose to take stock after all.[13] It is conceivable that a perfectly pro rata stock distribution will fail to get §305(a) nonrecognition simply because some shareholder had an unexercised election to take other property. The logic behind the §305(b)(1) exception is that where one or more shareholders choose to take property, usually cash, and other shareholders take stock, a shift in proportionate interest occurs. Those who receive stock have received something different from what they had before. Theoretically, even the mere option to take something other than stock suggests that what has happened, in substance, is that those shareholders with elective rights first received cash and then simply chose to reinvest that cash in the corporation.

An election to take stock or property may not be obvious from the stock dividend declaration itself, but may be found in the corporate charter or, more generally, in the circumstances surrounding the distribution.[14] For example, if the corporation has two classes of stock, one of which pays cash dividends and the other stock dividends, the arrangement can be considered one through which the shareholders may elect to receive property or stock. The shareholders who receive stock dividends will be covered by the §305(b)(1) exception and, thus, will be taxable under §301 along with the other shareholders who received cash.[15]

---

13. The regulations state that the exception will apply regardless of "[w]hether the distribution is actually made in whole or in part in stock or in stock rights." Treas. Reg. §1.305-2(a)(1).

14. Treas. Reg. §1.305-2(a)(4).

15. There are some overlaps between §305(b)(1) and (b)(2) as a result of which this arrangement may also be covered by the latter. In any event, the tax consequences will be the same under either provision: the stock dividend will be taxable. The §305(b)(2) exception is discussed in the section that follows.

Shareholders who participate in an automatic dividend reinvestment plan generally will be taxable on the shares received through the plan under §305(b)(1).[16] Such plans permit shareholders to elect to have their cash dividends automatically reinvested in shares of the corporation, often at a slight discount below the fair market value of the shares and for a service charge paid for administration of the plan. In effect, participating shareholders under such a plan have an election to take dividends in the form of cash or stock. From an economic perspective, those who receive stock may be viewed as if they had first received cash and then chosen to reinvest that cash in the corporate enterprise.

c) Disproportionate Distributions: §305(b)(2)

Under the disproportionate distribution exception, a stock distribution will be taxable if it results in the receipt of property by some shareholders and an increase in the proportionate interest of others in assets or earnings and profits.[17] Under this provision the property received is often cash, but may be any other type of property. This requirement that some shareholders receive property sometimes is referred to as the "companion distribution" requirement. As a first illustration of a taxable stock dividend under §305(b)(2), suppose that a corporation has Class A and Class B common stock outstanding. It declares a dividend payable to the Class A shareholders in additional Class A shares and payable to the Class B shareholders in cash. The distribution to the Class A shareholders is a taxable stock dividend under §305(b)(2).[18] In the alternative, consider the example discussed in the §305(b)(1) analysis above of a corporation with two classes of stock, one of which pays cash distributions and the other pays stock distributions. This too is a §305(b)(2) taxable stock dividend. In both cases, those receiving the stock distribution will increase their proportionate interests in the corporation at the expense of those receiving cash. For purposes of §302(b)(2), the distributions need not be simultaneous, however. The §305(b)(2) exception applies to a distribution "or a series of distributions" that results in the receipt of property by some and an increase in proportionate interests of others.

Notice the breadth of §305(b)(2). First, if a series of distributions results in an increase in the proportionate interest of some shareholders and the receipt of cash or property by others, the stock distribution will be

---

16. Rev. Rul. 76-53, 1976-1 C.B. 87. Here again, there may be some overlaps with §305(b)(2). See, e.g., Rev. Rul. 78-375, 1978-2 C.B. 130, 132 (covering a dividend reinvestment plan under both §§305(b)(1) and (b)(2)).

17. Notice that §305(b)(2) does not require an increase in voting rights but only an increase in rights to assets or earnings and profits.

18. Treas. Reg. §1.305-3(e), ex. 1.

taxable "whether or not the stock distributions and the cash distributions are steps in an overall plan or are independent and unrelated."[19] Since no plan is required and since the Code and regulations provide no other definition of a "series of distributions," it is difficult to know when such a series exists. The regulations simply indicate that "[w]here the receipt of cash or property occurs more than 36 months following a distribution or series of distributions of stock, or where a distribution or series of distributions of stock is made more than 36 months following the receipt of cash or property, such distribution or distributions will be presumed not to result in the receipt of cash or property by some shareholders and an increase in the proportionate interest of other shareholders, unless the receipt of cash or property and the distribution or series of distributions of stock are made pursuant to a plan."[20] Given this lax interpretation of the "companion distribution" requirement, it seems silly to bother with it at all.[21] The requirement adds needless complexity. In addition, in the case of an insolvent corporation, the lack of a companion distribution of cash or other property may even result in a disproportionate stock dividend not being subject to the §301 distribution rules.

Second, the companion distribution need not come from the corporation itself. The regulations continue that "there is no requirement that the shareholders receiving cash or property acquire the cash or property by way of a corporate distribution with respect to their shares, so long as they receive such cash or property in their capacity as shareholders."[22] Although the cash or other property need not come from the corporation itself, it must be paid to the shareholders in their capacity as shareholders and must be a distribution governed by §301 or other similar dividend-like provision mentioned in the regulations.[23] By way of illustration, the regulation describes a transaction in which some shareholders receive a stock distribution and other shareholders sell their shares in a prearranged plan to a related corporation for cash. In such a case, the stock dividend will be taxable under §305(b)(2).

d) Distributions of Common and Preferred: §305(b)(3)

If a distribution or series of distributions results in some common shareholders receiving common stock and others receiving preferred stock, the entire stock distribution will be taxable under §305(b)(3). The logic here

---

19. Treas. Reg. §1.305-3(b)(2).

20. Treas. Reg. §1.305-3(b)(4).

21. For an excellent critique, see James Holden, Unraveling the Mysteries of Section 305, 36 N.Y.U. Inst. Fed. Tax'n 781 (1978).

22. Treas. Reg. §1.305-3(b)(3).

23. The distribution must be one to which §§301, 356(a)(2), 871(a)(1)(A), 881(a)(1), 852(b), or 857(b) applies. Treas. Reg. §1.305-3(b)(3).

presumably is that common shareholders' rights with respect to voting, earnings, and assets upon liquidation are significantly different from the rights of other shareholders. If a stock distribution results in some common shareholders receiving additional common shares and others receiving only preferred stock, a shift in proportionate interest has occurred. Notice, however, that the exception in §305(b)(3) applies only to distributions with respect to common stock. Distributions on preferred stock generally will be taxable under the exception provided in §305(b)(4).

e) Distributions on Preferred Stock: §305(b)(4)

A stock distribution issued with respect to preferred stock will be taxable under §304(b)(4), with one statutory exception for distributions to certain convertible preferred shareholders.[24] Unlike the other §305(b) exceptions, §305(b)(4) will apply even to a pro rata distribution. For example, if the corporation issues a pro rata stock distribution of additional preferred shares to all holders of preferred stock, this will be a taxable stock distribution unless it fits within the convertible preferred exception.

The logic behind the §305(b)(4) exception has a slightly different quality from that behind all of the other §305(b) exceptions, which are based on variations to the "shift in proportionate interest" theme. In each of the other cases, Congress identified situations that either shifted, or potentially shifted, the shareholders' proportionate interests and, thus, should not be covered by the Eisner v. Macomber reasoning. In contrast, the §305 legislative history notes that preferred stock generally pays specified cash dividends. Congress viewed stock dividends paid with respect to preferred stock as substitutes for cash dividends, concluding that such stock dividends should be taxed.[25]

f) Distributions of Convertible Preferred: §305(b)(5)

When shareholders receive a stock dividend in the form of preferred shares that are convertible into common stock, some shareholders may convert and others may not. If so, those shareholders who choose to convert increase their proportionate interest in the common stock relative to other shareholders. The final exception in §305(b)(5) provides that a distribution of convertible preferred will be taxable "unless it is established to the satisfaction of the Secretary that such distribution will not have the result described in paragraph (2)." In other words, a distribution of convertible preferred

---

24. The exception covers only distributions to convertible preferred shareholders in order to increase the conversion ratio solely to take into account a stock dividend or stock split with respect to the stock into which the stock may be converted. I.R.C. §305(b)(4).
25. See S. Rep. No. 522, 91st Cong., 1st Sess. 55 (1969).

will be taxable unless the shareholders can show that the distribution will not result in an increase in proportionate interest for some shareholders and the receipt of property by others. If *all* of the shareholders convert the shares or *all* of the shareholders choose not to convert, then the effect of the distribution is pro rata and the distribution is much like those covered by the general nonrecognition rule in §305(a). On the other hand, if some shareholders are likely to convert and others likely not to convert, the effect of the distribution is much like the taxable stock dividends provided for in §305(b)(2). The §305 regulations conclude that the distribution is likely to result in a disproportionate distribution when conversion rights must be exercised within a relatively short period of time and when factors such as dividend rates, redemption provisions, marketability and conversion price suggest that some shareholders will convert and some will not.[26] On the other hand, if conversion rights are available over a period of years and the dividend rates are consistent with market conditions, the regulations conclude that "there is no basis for predicting at what time and the extent to which the stock will be converted and it is unlikely that a disproportionate distribution will result."[27]

Deemed Stock Distributions: §305(c)

Recognizing that certain transactions may have the effect of a stock dividend even though no shares are actually distributed, Congress directed the Secretary to promulgate regulations under which certain transactions will be treated as distributions of stock for purposes of §305. Section 305(c) lists five categories of transactions that will be deemed constructive stock dividends to "any shareholder whose proportionate interest in the earnings and profits or assets of the corporation is increased" as a result of the particular transaction. The deemed stock distribution will be taxable under §301 if it has the result described in one of the five exceptions provided in §305(b).[28] In any constructive stock dividend case, one must first determine whether the transaction is a deemed distribution transaction that increases the proportionate interest of some shareholders and second, whether it would be taxable under one of the §305(b) exceptions.

The five categories of deemed transactions specified in §305(c) include:

1. a change in conversion ratio,
2. a change in redemption price,
3. a difference between redemption price and issue price,

---

26. Treas. Reg. §1.305-6(a)(2).
27. Id.
28. Treas. Reg. §1.305-7(a)(2).

4. a redemption treated as a distribution to which §301 applies, or
5. any transaction (including a recapitalization) having a similar effect on the interest of any shareholder.[29]

Looking first at conversion ratios, if the corporation has one class of stock that is convertible into another, a change in the conversion ratio can result in an increase in the proportionate interest of some shareholders. Even though no stock is actually issued, the effect of such a change is similar to a non-pro rata stock dividend.[30] For example, imagine a corporation that has two classes of stock outstanding. Class B shares initially are convertible into Class A at a ratio of one to one; that is, each Class B share can be converted into one Class A share. Imagine further that the corporation pays cash dividends to the Class A shareholders and increases the conversion ratio of the Class B shareholders so that each Class B share now can be converted into 1.5 Class A shares. Even though no stock was actually issued, this increase in the conversion ratio reflects an increase in the Class B shareholders' proportionate interest at the expense of the Class A shareholders.[31] The constructive stock dividend will be treated as a disproportionate stock distribution under §305(b)(2).[32] The Class B shareholders are deemed under §305(c) to have received a stock dividend in the amount of the fair market value of the additional one-half share per Class B share previously owned.[33]

The second category of transactions that may result in a deemed distribution is a change in the redemption price. Suppose, for example, that the corporation increases the price at which it will redeem preferred shares. Such a change increases the preferred shareholders' claim on corporate assets and may be viewed as a deemed stock distribution to the preferred shareholders.

Under the third category, §305(c) deemed distributions may result when stock terms provide for redemption at a price higher than the issue price—a redemption premium. Suppose, for example, that a corporation issues preferred stock for $100 per share that pays no dividends and is

---

29. I.R.C. §305(c).
30. Notice that a change in conversion ratio that accompanies an *actual* stock dividend distribution may be covered by §302(b)(2). See Treas. Reg. §1.305-3(d)(1)(i), (d)(1)(ii), exs. b, c, d.
31. Technically speaking, the increase in proportionate interest does not occur until the Class B shareholders actually convert their shares.
32. The companion distribution requirement of §305(b)(2) is met, since the Class A shareholders received cash dividends.
33. For a similar example, see Treas. Reg. §1.305-3(e), ex. 6. On the other hand, a change in conversion ratio sometimes may be necessary in order to prevent the dilution of the convertible shareholders' interest. The regulations provide that a change in conversion ratio "made pursuant to a bona fide, reasonable adjustment formula" to prevent dilution of the convertible shareholders' interest will not be considered a deemed distribution of stock. Treas. Reg. §1.305-7(b)(1).

subject to mandatory redemption in ten years for $200. The concern here is that the redemption premium is really a series of preferred-on-preferred stock dividends in disguise. Based upon a similar example, Treasury regulations conclude that "[u]nder sections 305(c) and 305(b)(4), the entire redemption premium . . . is deemed to be a distribution of preferred stock on preferred stock which is taxable as a distribution of property under section 301."[34]

This type of deemed preferred on preferred distribution also raises questions about the proper amount and timing of constructive income. Concern for the proper treatment of redemption premiums led Congress in 1990 to add provisions to §305(c), explicitly directing the Treasury Secretary to prescribe regulations for treating redemption premiums under the same principles applicable to original issue discount (OID) rules under §1272.[35] The logic behind the OID rules is that when a debt instrument is issued for a price below a higher fixed amount to be paid upon maturity, the difference is really a substitute for interest, which ordinarily would accrue daily and be reported as ordinary income. Rather than accrue ratably in equal daily amounts, the OID rules use economic interest accrual principles. These principles now are applicable as well to redemption premiums on stock that is mandatorily redeemable by the issuer, or on stock with respect to which the holder has an option to demand redemption by the issuer, often referred to as a "put."[36] The rules also apply to redemption premiums on stock that may be called for redemption by the issuer, often referred to as "callable" stock.[37] The bite of these rules as applied to redemption premiums may not be quite as harsh as the bark, however. First, redemption premiums benefit from the same de minimis exception applicable for OID purposes.[38] Second, §305(c) constructive distributions will apply with respect to premiums on stock callable by the issuer only "if, based on all the facts and circumstances as of the issue date, redemption pursuant to that right is more likely than not to occur."[39] The regulations further provide "safe harbor" rules under which the redemption will not be treated as more likely than not to occur

---

34. Treas. Reg. §1.305-3(e), ex. 15.

35. I.R.C. §305(c)(1)-(3) (added by the Omnibus Reconciliation Act of 1990, Pub. L. No. 101-508, §11322, 104 Stat. 1388).

36. Treas. Reg. §1.305-5(b)(2). The constructive distribution rules include an exception, however, for mandatory redemption obligations or "put rights" that are triggered by contingencies outside the parties' control. Id.

37. Treas. Reg. §1.305-5(b)(3).

38. See Treas. Reg. §1.305-5(b)(1), which cross-references to I.R.C. §1273(a)(3) (treating original issue discount as zero if it would be less than of 1 percent of stated redemption price at maturity multiplied by number of years to maturity).

39. Treas. Reg. §1.305-5(b)(3)(i). Even if the redemption is more likely than not to occur, it will not be covered by these constructive distribution rules if the premium is "solely in the nature of a penalty for premature redemption." Id.

if the issuer and holder are not related, there are no plans, arrangements, or agreements that would compel the issuer to redeem, and the exercise of the redemption right would not reduce the yield of the stock, as determining using OID principles.[40]

Another potential deemed stock dividend may result from a non-pro rata stock redemption. Recall that a redemption of stock from one shareholder causes an increase in the other shareholders' interests.[41] Under §305(c), Congress directed the Treasury Department to promulgate regulations addressing when a redemption treated as a §301 distribution to the redeemed shareholder should be treated as a deemed or constructive stock dividend to the remaining shareholders. The regulations include examples indicating that an isolated redemption from one shareholder resulting in an increase to other shareholders' proportionate interests will not be a constructive stock dividend to the shareholders whose interests are increased.[42] On the other hand, a redemption plan under which a portion of some shareholders' stock is periodically redeemed while the proportionate interests of other shareholders' increases will be a constructive dividend to the shareholders whose interests are increased.[43]

TAX CONSEQUENCES TO THE CORPORATION

Generally speaking, the issuance of a pro rata stock dividend has little or no tax consequence to the issuing corporation. For accounting purposes, the stock dividend merely is reflected on the corporation's balance sheet by appropriate changes to the equity and surplus accounts. Since no assets have left the corporation, §312(d) sensibly provides that there will be no reduction to the corporation's earnings and profits if the distribution was not taxable to the shareholders by reason of §305(a).[44] On the other hand, to the extent that all or a portion of a stock dividend is taxable to the shareholders by reason of one of the §305(b) exceptions, the regulations call for a reduction in earnings and profits by the fair market value of the taxable portion of the stock distribution.[45]

---

40. Treas. Reg. §1.305-5(b)(3)(ii).
41. For a complete discussion of redemption distributions, see Chapter 6.
42. Treas. Reg. §1.305-3(e), ex. 10.
43. Id., ex. 8 (describing method for computing the amount of distribution).
44. I.R.C. §312(d)(1)(B).
45. Treas. Reg. §1.312-1(d).

THE PREFERRED STOCK BAILOUT: §306 STOCK

Background and History

Despite the many different varieties of preferred stock, certain shared characteristics tend to predominate. For example, preferred stock generally is senior stock in that it has a right to its share (usually specified as a percentage much like an interest rate) of dividends before dividends are paid to common shareholders. On the other hand, preferred shareholders often have no voting rights at all, or perhaps junior voting rights, in relation to the common shareholders. In addition, since dividends available to preferred shareholders are usually fixed, preferred shareholders generally have a lesser right to share in the unlimited growth of the corporation.[46] Shareholders who own both common and nonvoting preferred stock often can sell off preferred shares without compromising their voting rights and their share in unlimited growth. Combined with the tax-free nature of stock dividends under §305 discussed above, this opportunity gave rise to what was referred to as the "preferred stock bailout."

The first step in such a bailout was for the corporation to issue a pro rata stock dividend of preferred shares—usually nonvoting—with respect to the outstanding common stock. Since none of the §305(b) exceptions applies to a pro rata distribution of preferred with respect to common, the distribution was a nontaxable stock dividend under §305(a). The second step was either for the corporation to redeem the preferred shares or for the shareholders to sell the preferred shares, usually in a prearranged plan. Upon sale or redemption of the stock, the shareholders reported any gain as capital gain. The preferred stock bailout was then complete. Instead of distributing its profits as a dividend, the corporation distributed its profits in a tax-free distribution of its own stock. The shareholders realized gain upon later sale of the stock, but at capital gains rates. Under pre-2003 law, this technique permitted shareholders to bail out corporate earnings that would otherwise have been taxed as ordinary income at capital gains rates and to delay imposition of the tax until ultimate disposition of the new shares.

The corporate bailout was easier to see in the case of a preferred stock dividend followed by a redemption of the dividend stock. The corporation

---

46. According to regulations, "'preferred stock' generally refers to stock which, in relation to all other classes of stock outstanding enjoys certain limited rights and privileges (generally associated with specific dividend and liquidation priorities) but does not participate in corporate growth to any significant extent." Compare the definition of preferred stock for purposes of identifying §351 nonqualified preferred stock. §351(g)(3) ("stock which is limited and preferred as to dividends and does not participate in corporate growth to any significant extent"). See Chapter 4 for a discussion of §351 nonqualified preferred stock.

used its own funds to repurchase stock previously issued as a tax-free stock dividend. Funds for the bailout were paid by the corporation directly to its shareholders. If the redemption was treated as a sale or exchange redemption under §302, the shareholder reported capital gain from a sale or exchange of stock as opposed to ordinary income from a dividend.[47] When the shareholder sold the preferred stock received from the stock dividend to an outside third party, the corporate bailout may have been more difficult to see. The funds for purchase of the shares came not from the corporation, but from some outside source. The case of Chamberlin v. Commissioner provides a good example of a successful preferred stock bailout through shareholder disposition of dividend shares to a third party.[48] The corporation in Chamberlin found itself with a substantial earned surplus. The primary shareholders objected to the distribution of such a surplus as a dividend taxable at ordinary income rates. Instead, the corporation and its primary shareholders contacted two insurance companies regarding investing in the corporation's preferred stock. The insurance companies carefully investigated the corporation and agreed to purchase the preferred shares. The corporation arranged a pro rata preferred stock dividend to the common shareholders. Shortly thereafter, and in accordance with a plan worked out in advance, the shareholders sold their preferred shares to the insurance companies. One important feature of the preferred shares was a mandatory redemption clause under which the shares would be redeemed by the corporation over a seven-year period. As the court put it, the "dominant and decisive issue" was whether the stock dividend, which "by reason of its redemption feature, enabled the corporation to ultimately distribute its earnings to its stockholders on a taxable basis materially lower than would have been the case by declaring and paying the usual cash dividend, was a bona fide one, one in substance as well as in form."[49] Although the shareholders received cash from the third party insurance companies as part of a stock sale, the corporation's cash was ultimately used to satisfy its mandatory redemption obligation to the insurance companies. The Commissioner argued that this transaction was a taxable dividend to the shareholders. Rejecting this claim, the court concluded that both the stock dividend and the sale to the insurance companies were bona fide. In a useful and candid passage the court noted that

> [i]n deciding this case it must be kept in mind that it does not involve a ruling that the profit derived from the sale of the stock dividend is or is not taxable income. Such profit is conceded to be taxable. The issue is whether it is taxable as income from a cash dividend or as income resulting from a long-term

---

47. For a more detailed discussion of the redemption provisions of §302, see Chapter 6.
48. 207 F.2d 462 (6th Cir. 1953), *cert. denied*, 347 U.S. 918 (1954).
49. *Id. At* 470.

capital gain. Accordingly, it is not the usual case of total tax avoidance. Congress has adopted the policy of taxing long-term capital gains differently from ordinary income. . . . [I]t has specifically excluded certain transactions with respect to stock dividends from the classification of a capital gain. The present transaction is not within the exclusion. If the profit from a transaction like the one here involved is to be taxed at the same rate as ordinary income, it should be done by appropriate legislation, not court decision.[50]

Congress responded rather quickly to the court's invitation to adopt appropriate legislation to combat the preferred stock bailout. In considering its legislative options, Congress was cognizant that an initial preferred stock dividend distribution itself did not necessarily result in a bailout of corporate earnings at capital gains rather than ordinary income rates. Since the bailout resulted not from the initial tax-free receipt of the stock dividend, but from the later disposition of the dividend shares, Congress responded by creating a special provision in §306, entitled "Dispositions of Certain Stock." Preferred stock dividends remain eligible for nonrecognition under §305(a). Once received, however, the stock may be designated as "§306 stock." When the shareholder disposes of this §306 stock, either through sale or redemption, the normal sale or redemption rules do not apply. Instead, the tax consequences of the transaction are governed by rules provided in §306. Although initial classification of distributed shares as §306 stock has no immediate tax consequence, the operative rules of §306(a) may trigger negative tax consequences upon subsequent disposition. Since the shares came burdened with such potentially negative tax consequences, many in the tax world came to refer to §306 stock as "tainted stock." As the section that follows illustrates, however, the negative tax consequence or "taint" is no longer as significant as it was prior to 2003.

Tainted Stock in the "Qualified Dividend Income" World

While Congress has not eliminated the distinction between capital gains and ordinary income in general, it has largely eliminated the distinction as it applies to individual shareholder gain from stock investments and dividend distributions. Since §1(h)(11) now provides preferential capital gains rates for most dividends paid to individual shareholders in any event,[51] such shareholders no longer have the same incentives to use preferred stock as a device to bail out corporate earnings at capital gains rather than ordinary income rates. Moreover, in assessing the impact of the qualified dividend

---

50. Id. At 472.
51. Chapters 1 and 5 discuss the qualified dividend rules at length. In addition, analysis of the impact of the rules on other relevant corporate transactions appears throughout the book.

rules upon §306, one should keep in mind that the §306 anti-bailout provisions were focused on individual shareholders. In contrast to individuals, *corporate* shareholders generally are delighted to find a sale or redemption treated as a dividend, which might be eligible for the §243 dividends-received deduction.[52]

In fact, the qualified dividend rules changed policy considerations underlying interpretation and application of §306. Some have even argued that the §306 rules should now be repealed, suspended, or significantly modified. If the government concern driving §306 is manipulation and tax avoidance, the importance of the §306 rules appears to diminish as applied to most individual shareholders and, in some cases, may be overly favorable to corporate shareholders. In some cases, individual shareholders may now even prefer "§306 dividends" to regular "§301 dividends" since the holding period required for a "qualified dividend" is shorter than the one-year period otherwise required for long-term capital gains.

Repeal of §306 may be premature, however. Even in a "qualified dividend" world, without §306 the preferred stock bailout still would offer the basis offset advantage upon sale or exchange of the stock that would not be available if the disposition was treated as a dividend.[53] In addition, absent §306, a shareholder might still use a preferred stock bailout to recognize a loss upon disposition of the §306 stock that would not have been available if the amount realized had been treated as a dividend.[54] Perhaps these continuing bailout opportunities explain why Congress has not yet moved to repeal or modify §306. In the meantime, the §306 provisions remain part of Subchapter C and its provisions may alter the tax consequences of certain dispositions or redemptions of stock.

Working Through the §306 Stock Rules

a) The Definition of §306 Stock

To unravel the mysteries of §306, one must start by identifying the stock that will be covered by its web. By its terms, §306 stock is "[s]tock (other than common stock issued with respect to common stock) which was distributed to the shareholder selling or otherwise disposing of such stock if, by reason of section 305(a), any part of such distribution was not includible

---

52. Corporate shareholder use of §306 stock to *create* dividends eligible for a §243 deduction may be subject to limitations under §1059 and similar provisions. These provisions might be simplified if they no longer need to take §306 stock into account.
53. The section that follows in this chapter provides an illustration of this continued bailout potential.
54. For an illustration, see Example 5e at the end of this chapter.

in the gross income of the shareholder."[55] Notice first that §306 only applies to stock initially received tax-free under §305(a). The bailout concern was that shareholders could receive a *nontaxable* stock dividend that they could later convert to capital gain income through disposition of the shares without significantly altering their relationship with the corporation. Consistent with this observation, §306 does not apply to common stock issued to common shareholders. Preferred shares were thought to be the perfect vehicles for corporate bailouts since shareholders can dispose of these shares without losing any of their proprietary interest reflected in the underlying common stock. If a corporation instead issues a common stock dividend to shareholders who later dispose of the dividend shares, the disposition causes a reduction in the shareholders' voting rights and rights to unlimited growth in the corporation. Thus, it makes some sense that Congress carved out common stock distributions from §306 coverage.

Since the adoption of §306, several rulings and cases have focused on the question of what constitutes "common stock" for purposes of §306. A corporation might create a class of stock that smells a lot like preferred, but label it common stock. Labels will not be determinative for purposes of §306.[56] In several rulings, the Service has indicated that in deciding whether particular stock is common stock for purposes of the §306(c)(1) definition, one must look to the underlying congressional purpose behind eliminating the preferred stock bailout.[57]

In addition to the definition provided in §306(c)(1), Congress included two other categories in the §306 stock definition. The second category classifies as §306 stock any stock other than common stock received tax-free in a reorganization, "but only to the extent that either the effect of the transaction was substantially the same as the receipt of a stock dividend, or the stock was received in exchange for §306 stock."[58] Under this definition, if the shareholder receives new preferred shares in a tax-free reorganization to replace previously owned preferred shares, the replacement preferred shares should not be classified as §306 stock. On the other hand, if the shareholder receives preferred shares designed to provide him with an additional preferred interest, these additional shares will be classified as §306 stock. In addition, if the shareholder previously had §306 stock and, as part of a tax-free reorganization, receives preferred shares to replace the §306 stock, the replacement shares will be considered §306 stock as well.

---

55. I.R.C. §306(c)(1)(A). Options to acquire stock and certain stock acquired through the exercise of options will also be considered §306 stock. I.R.C. §306(d).
56. See, e.g., Rev. Rul. 79-163, 1979-1 C.B. 131, where stock classified as common by the corporation was not considered common for §306 purposes because it did not have an unrestricted right in the corporation's equity growth.
57. Rev. Rul. 81-91, 1981-1 C.B. 123.
58. I.R.C. §306(c)(1)(B)(ii).

7. Stock Dividends

The third category of preferred stock is stock that has a substituted basis. Congress defines §306 stock to include "stock the basis of which (in the hands of the shareholder selling or otherwise disposing of such stock) is determined by reference to the basis (in the hands of such shareholder or any other person) of section 306 stock."[59] Here again, Congress was concerned with preserving the "taint" upon certain exchanges or transfers of §306 stock. For example, assume that a parent received §306 stock, as defined in the first definition above, from a stock dividend. Thereafter, the parent transferred the stock to a child by way of a gift. Since property received by gift generally takes a substituted basis, the gifted shares in the child's hands would retain the §306 stock classification. Congress often uses substituted basis rules when property is exchanged without immediate recognition of gain or loss. The substituted basis assures that the previously unrecognized gain or loss is preserved in some fashion. When a parent makes a gift of stock to a child, for example, the parent's gain or loss effectively is preserved in the child's hands through use of a substituted basis under §1015. If, in contrast, the child inherits the stock from a parent with a fair market value basis determined under §1014, then the "taint" will not be preserved.[60] The third category included in the §306 stock definitions assured that not only the gain or loss, but also the §306 "taint," remained with the shares when they were transferred.

As an exception to the three categories of §306 stock described above, §306 stock "does not include any stock no part of the distribution of which would have been a dividend at the time of the distribution if money had been distributed in lieu of the stock."[61] This exception goes to the heart of §306. It focuses on bailout *potential* by identifying the extent to which the stock distribution *would have been* taxable as a dividend if cash had been used instead of stock. Bailout potential existed if the corporation had sufficient earnings and profits to cover the distribution if it had been a cash distribution instead of a stock distribution. If a corporation issued preferred stock to common shareholders in a year for which there were no current or accumulated earnings and profits, no part of the distribution would have been a dividend if cash had been distributed under the §301 distribution rules. Thus, under the §306(c)(2) exception, the stock distributed is not §306 stock. This exception was consistent with the purpose of §306 to prevent bailouts of corporate profits at capital gains as opposed to ordinary income rates. Prior to 2003, if no part of the distribution would have been a dividend, there would have been no ordinary income from the distribution in any event.

---

59. I.R.C. §306(c)(1)(C).
60. Treas. Reg. §1.306-3(e).
61. I.R.C. §306(c)(2).

b) Disposition of §306 Stock

Shareholders may dispose of §306 stock either through a redemption or a sale or exchange other than a redemption. The §306 operating rules cover each of these types of dispositions separately.

i) Dispositions by Redemption

A redemption distribution ordinarily is treated as a sale or exchange to the redeemed shareholder only if it meets one of the §302(b) tests.[62] On the other hand, the amount realized to the shareholder upon redemption of §306 stock automatically is "treated as a distribution of property to which section 301 applies."[63] The effect of this provision is to bypass the redemption provisions of §302. Prior to 2003, this treatment had two disadvantages for redemptions that otherwise would have qualified for sale or exchange treatment under §302(a). First, the shareholder was not entitled to a basis offset and second, the redemption proceeds were treated as ordinary income to the extent that the corporation had sufficient earnings and profits to cover the distribution under the §301 rules. Under the qualified dividend income rules, only the first advantage remains.

One odd feature of the §306(a)(2) disposition by redemption provision is that the corporation's earnings and profits at the time of the initial tainted stock distribution appear to be irrelevant. The §306(a)(2) rules simply direct the shareholder to §301. Thus, the relevant earnings and profits used to determine tax consequences to the shareholder are those in the year of the disposition or redemption, not the year when the §306 stock was distributed. This seems inconsistent with §306's focus upon bailout potential and the extent to which the initial stock dividend would have been taxable as a dividend if it had been paid in cash. Perhaps testing the redemption disposition of §306 stock by e&p at the time of redemption can be explained by the fact that the bailout, if any, is achieved through a distribution of funds directly from the corporation. In a sense, the redemption is viewed as an actual bailout of corporate funds, as opposed merely to bailout potential. Another unique feature of the §306(a)(2) redemption bailout is that since the redemption simply is treated as a §301 distribution, a corporate shareholder will be entitled to a §243 dividends-received deduction. As a result, corporate shareholders often find the §306 stock label attractive.[64]

---

62. The redemption provisions of §302 are considered in Chapter 6.
63. I.R.C. §306(a)(2).
64. This attractiveness will be reduced, eliminated, or perhaps even become a disincentive to the extent that the redemption is treated as a §1059 "extraordinary dividend" under §1059. See Chapters 5 and 6 for further discussion of §1059.

ii) Dispositions Other than by Redemption

Sales or other dispositions of §306 tainted stock *other than by redemption* are governed by §306(a)(1). In contrast to §306(a)(2), the provisions in §306(a)(1) are rather complex and awkwardly worded. Before diving into the mechanics, it might be useful to provide an overview of what §306(a)(1) achieves in the end. First, a portion of the amount realized from disposition of the tainted stock will be treated as dividend income. This portion essentially reflects the amount that would have been a dividend if the corporation had distributed cash instead of stock. Second, to the extent permissible, the shareholder will be entitled to recover basis in the shares tax-free. Finally, any excess gain will be treated as gain from the sale of stock.[65] Notice that these three steps parallel the distribution rules in §301(c)(1), (2), and (3). This is precisely the idea—Congress is attempting here to provide for dividend-like treatment.

Suppose that Corporation X has two shareholders (A and B) who equally own all of the common stock. In a year when the corporation has ample earnings and profits, it distributes a §305(a) nontaxable stock dividend of $600,000 worth of nonvoting preferred stock ($300,000 to each shareholder). Shareholder A later sells the preferred shares for $300,000 to an unrelated third party. Assume that shareholder A's basis in the stock, determined after a §307 allocation, was $225,000. If shareholder A's stock was not §306 stock and she simply sold it to a third party for cash, her taxable gain under §1001 simply would be her amount realized of $300,000 less her basis of $225,000 for a capital gain of $75,000.

This example illustrates the extent to which "bailout" potential, while admittedly reduced, remains even in the "qualified dividend income" world. If shareholder A retains her common stock and sells only the nonvoting preferred stock, she receives $300,000 cash from her investment in X Corporation without sacrificing her voting rights or rights to her share in the unlimited growth potential in the corporation, which are still reflected in the underlying common stock. The transaction resembles a dividend, through which the shareholder receives cash out of her stock investment without relinquishing control or other significant shareholder interests. If the sale is treated as a straightforward §1001 sale or exchange, shareholder A reports only a $75,000 capital gain. Prior to 2003, when most dividends were taxed at ordinary income rates, this preferred stock bailout tempted shareholders with both the opportunity to reduce the taxable *amount* from $300,000 to $75,000 and to change the *character* of the gain from ordinary income to capital gain. The §306 rules were designed to prevent both of these moves. Under the "qualified dividend income" rules, the second move is unnecessary since most dividends are likely to be eligible for capital gains

---

65. I.R.C. §§306(a)(1)(A) and (B).

rates in any event. Even in this world, however, shareholder A would be able to reduce the taxable *amount* from her sale of preferred shares unless the §306 rules apply.

iii) §306(a)(1) Stock Disposition Mechanics

Working through the mechanics of §306(a)(1) can be confusing. The only solution is slow and patient analysis of the statute. The §306(a)(1) rules begin by treating the amount realized from a disposition of §306 stock (other than by redemption) as ordinary income.[66] Notice that the language of §306(a)(1)(A) itself provides that the amount realized "shall be treated as ordinary income" and does not explicitly classify the sale proceeds as *dividend* income. Prior to 2003, this language simply provided for taxation at ordinary income rates subject to the exceptions provided in §306(a)(2). When Congress added the "qualified dividend income" rules, however, it also amended §306 to provide that "[f]or purposes of section 1(h)(11) ... Any amount treated as ordinary income under this paragraph shall be treated as a dividend received from the corporation."[67] Thus, although *labeled* "ordinary income" under §306(a)(1)(A), the amount realized from a sale or disposition of §306 stock is treated as a *dividend* eligible for preferential capital gains rates as long as the distribution otherwise meets the §1(h)(11)(B) "qualified dividend" definition.

Although its initial language speaks broadly, §306(a)(1) does not necessarily treat the *entire* amount realized as "ordinary income"/dividend under the post-2003 rules. The statute goes on to provide that there shall *not* be "ordinary"/dividend income to the extent that amount realized exceeds the §306 stock's "ratable share of the amount which would have been a dividend at the time of the distribution if (in lieu of section 306 stock) the corporation had distributed money in an amount equal to the fair market value of the stock at the time of distribution."[68] This language asks a hypothetical question—if the corporation had distributed cash instead of stock, what would be the shareholder's ratable share of the amount that would have been a dividend? Unlike the disposition by redemption provision in §306(a)(2), this exercise requires the shareholder to look back to the year in which the §306 stock was initially distributed. Since there were ample earnings and profits in the year of the stock distribution in the example above, *all* of the distribution would have been a dividend if the corporation had distributed money in lieu of stock. In this case, the limitation in §306(a)(1)(A) does

---

66. I.R.C. §306(a)(1)(A).
67. I.R.C. §306(a)(1)(D).
68. I.R.C. §306(a)(1)(A)(ii).

not apply and the entire amount realized is treated as dividend income.[69] Thus, shareholder A must report the full $300,000 proceeds from the sale as dividend income with no basis offset. Although shareholder A may benefit from the lower tax rates now available under §1(h)(11), the stakes are still high. Without §306, her gain would be only $75,000.

The absence of a tax-free recovery of basis is common in the context of §301 dividend distributions. If a corporation has sufficient earnings and profits, the shareholder must report the entire distribution as a taxable dividend without any basis offset.[70] In the dividend scenario, however, the shareholder continues to own the shares, whereas the shareholder in the §306(a)(1) stock sale has sold her shares to an unrelated third party. Absent §306, the shareholder would be entitled to a full basis recovery. Shareholder A might argue that since she has a $225,000 investment in the stock that she was not entitled to recover tax-free, she should be entitled to a loss. She will be denied the loss because §306(a)(1)(C) explicitly provides that "no loss shall be recognized." She will not lose her basis, however. Although §306 disallows losses, shareholders are permitted to add any unrecovered basis from the §306 shares to the basis of the common shares with respect to which the §306 shares were issued.[71]

Returning to the illustration above, imagine instead that X Corporation made its $600,000 stock dividend distribution in a year when the corporation had only $100,000 in earnings and profits. This change in facts would alter the §306(a)(1) analysis and the tax consequences to shareholder A, who owns 50% of the outstanding X Corporation stock. If the corporation had only $100,000 of earnings and profits in the year the stock dividend was distributed, shareholder A's ratable share of the amount that would have been a dividend if she had received cash would be $50,000 (50% of $100,000). Although §306(a)(1) starts by suggesting that the entire $300,000 received for the preferred shares will be treated as "ordinary" / dividend income, it provides an exception to the extent that the amount realized ($300,000) exceeds the $50,000 ratable share. In other words, only $50,000 is treated as dividend income.

The next step under §306(a)(1) is to determine how the remaining $250,000 of her amount realized should be treated. Under §306(a)(1)(B), the excess of amount realized ($300,000) over the amount treated as "ordinary"/dividend income ($50,000) plus the adjusted basis of the stock ($225,000) will be treated as gain from the sale of the stock. Thus,

---

69. The provisions in §306(a)(1)(B) also are not applicable since there is no excess of the amount realized ($300,000) over the "ordinary income"/dividend amount plus Shareholder A's adjusted basis in the preferred shares.

70. See Chapter 5 for discussion of nonliquidating distributions.

71. Treas. Reg. §1.306-1(b)(2), ex. 2, 3. Notice the parallels to the "mystery of disappearing basis" issues considered in the redemption setting. See Chapter 6 for a discussion of basis issues in connection with dividend-type redemptions.

under §306(a)(1)(B), shareholder A will report the excess $25,000 as capital gain from the sale of stock. Notice that the *amount* of shareholder A's gain under §306(a)(1) remains the same $75,000 she would have reported under §1001 if the stock had not been tainted §306 stock. Prior to 2003, the critical difference had to do with the *character* of shareholder A's gain. A non-§306 stock sale would have resulted in a $75,000 capital gain in this variation to the hypothetical, whereas the "tainted" stock sale resulted in $50,000 of ordinary income and $25,000 of capital gain. Put differently, §306 breaks the amount realized into three pieces. In shareholder A's case, the $300,000 amount realized is broken into $50,000 ordinary income, (taxed at ordinary income rates prior to 2003), $225,000 tax-free recovery of capital, and $25,000 capital gain from the sale of stock. For the most part, the §306(a) operating rules parallel the provisions in §301(c). When a corporation makes a distribution to a shareholder, the dividend as defined in §316 based upon earnings and profits, is taxable income under §301(c)(1). Thereafter the shareholder is entitled to a tax-free recovery of basis under §301(c)(2). Finally, any excess is treated as gain from the sale of stock under §301(c)(3).

Despite the parallels to §301(c), there are some differences. For example, §306 refers to the shareholder's "ratable share" of earnings and profits whereas §301 does not. Oddly enough, shareholders may now actually find themselves *better off* under §306 than under §301 since the latter does not limit dividend income to the shareholder's ratable share of earnings and profits. For example, assuming that the distribution met the §1(h)(11) "qualified dividend income" definition, a $300,000 §301 distribution to shareholder A when the corporation's earnings and profits were only $100,000 would result in a $100,000 dividend under §301(c)(1), eligible for capital gains rates. Under §301(c)(2), the remaining $200,000 of the distribution would be treated as tax-free recovery of capital. Since she had a $225,000 basis in the preferred shares, she would be left with a $25,000 basis not yet recovered tax-free. In contrast, although the dividend is still eligible for preferential rates, only $50,000 of the $300,000 distribution is treated as a dividend under §306, and shareholder A receives a tax-free recovery of her entire $225,000 basis. In cases where the shareholder receives an amount in excess of the tax-free basis recovery, another possible advantage to a "§306 dividend" over a "§301 dividend" relates to required holding periods. Since §301(c)(3) treats such excess as "gain from the sale or exchange of property," the shareholder would be subject to the one-year holding period otherwise required for long-term capital gain eligible for preferential capital gains rates. In contrast, the "§306 dividend" classification appears to permit the shareholder to take advantage of the shorter 60-day holding period provided in the "qualified dividend" definition in §1(h)(11).

Exceptions to the §306 Rules: §306(b)

The §306(b) exceptions to the §306(a) "tainted" stock rules are connected by a common theme. Remember that Congress designed §306 to combat the preferred stock bailout. If the shareholders retain their interest in the underlying common stock with respect to which the preferred stock dividend was issued, they retain voting rights and rights to share in unlimited growth of the corporation. By disposing of the §306 shares and retaining the underlying common shares, the shareholders essentially have taken earnings from the corporation without sacrificing any of the proprietary interest reflected in the underlying common shares. The first two exceptions in §306(b) cover circumstances where the shareholder's interest in the corporation is completely terminated. In such cases, the shareholder has parted with not only the tainted stock, but also the underlying common with respect to which the "tainted" stock was issued. This is not the bailout scenario that Congress was concerned with. In the most extreme case, if the corporation redeems §306 stock as part of a complete liquidation of the corporation, *all* of the shareholders' interests are terminated. Thus, §306(a) will not apply to complete liquidations.[72] Short of complete liquidation, §306(a) also will not apply to complete termination of interest redemptions under §302(b)(3) or partial liquidation redemptions under §302(b)(4).[73] In addition, §306(a) will not apply if the disposition other than by redemption completely terminates the shareholder's interest and is not a disposition to a related party under the §318 attribution rules.[74]

As a third exception, §306(a) will not apply to the disposition of §306 stock to the extent that gain or loss is not recognized under any other income tax provisions in the Internal Revenue Code.[75] In other words, §306 will not trump other nonrecognition provisions. This exception is not as generous at it might seem at first glance. Keep in mind that most nonrecognition provisions in the Code come paired with substituted basis rules designed to preserve gain or loss left unrecognized. Since the §306 stock definition includes stock the basis of which is determined in reference to the basis of §306 stock (substituted basis), the stock will retain its taint even after a nonrecognition exchange. Although §306(a) does not apply on the disposition of the §306 shares in the nonrecognition exchange, the §306(a) rules will apply upon ultimate disposition of the shares in a taxable exchange. For example, the owner of §306 stock who transfers the shares by gift will not recognize any gain upon the disposition. The recipient of

---

72. I.R.C. §306(b)(2). For a full discussion of complete liquidations, see Chapters 8 and 9.
73. I.R.C. §306(b)(1)(B).
74. For a more detailed discussion of the §318 attribution rules, see Chapter 6.
75. I.R.C. §306(b)(3).

the gift, however, takes the shares with a substituted basis under §1015 and the stock retains its "taint" in the new owner's hands. In addition, a shareholder may exchange §306 shares for new shares as part of a tax-free reorganization. Although the disposition of the shares was tax-free, the shares received in exchange for the §306 shares are considered §306 stock under §306(c)(1)(B). Thus, §306(a) will apply to a later disposition of the shares received tax-free as part of the reorganization.[76]

The final exception to the §306(a) rules is for "transactions not in avoidance." Since the §306 rules were designed to combat certain deliberate and tax motivated bailouts, Congress left the taxpayer with an opportunity under §306(b)(4) to argue that the transaction was not motivated by tax avoidance. The §306(b)(4) exception contains two categories of transactions. First, the taxpayer can avoid §306(a) by establishing to the satisfaction of the Secretary that the distribution *and* the disposition or redemption were "not in pursuance of a plan having as one of its principal purposes the avoidance of federal income tax."[77] Second, where there is a prior or simultaneous disposition of the underlying stock with respect to which the tainted stock was issued, the taxpayer can avoid §306(a) by establishing to the satisfaction of the Secretary that the disposition of the tainted stock "was not in pursuance of a plan having as one of its principal purposes the avoidance of federal income tax."[78]

The standard in each case is the same: pursuance of a plan having tax avoidance as *one* of its principal purposes. This may prove a very difficult standard for the taxpayer to address. Most taxpayers choosing one route or another for a particular transaction consider tax consequences to some extent. Although there have not been many litigated cases to date, cases that have been decided suggest that the taxpayer will have an uphill battle in making a case for this exception. Even if there is an otherwise legitimate business reason for the transaction, at least one court has held that the transaction fails §306(b)(4) if *one* of the principal reasons for structuring the particular transaction was tax avoidance, apparently read "tax reduction."[79]

The rationale for the second category of nonavoidance exceptions is similar to the rationale for the complete liquidation and complete termination of interest exceptions discussed above. If the shareholder either already

---

76. Tax-free reorganizations are discussed in Chapters 11-14.

77. I.R.C. §306(b)(4)(A).

78. I.R.C. §306(b)(4)(B). With regard to the first nonavoidance exception category, the taxpayer must establish that *both* the initial stock distribution *and* the later disposition of the tainted stock meet the nonavoidance standard. With regard to the second category, involving prior or simultaneous sale of the underlying stock, the taxpayer must meet the standard only once with respect to the disposition.

79. Fireoved v. United States, 462 F.2d 1281 (3d Cir. 1972). Given the reduced bailout incentives in the "qualified dividend income" world, one might expect the Treasury Department to litigate §306 cases less frequently and, in any case, to be more lenient in its acceptance of taxpayer arguments under §306(b)(4).

has disposed of the underlying stock or is disposing of the underlying stock along with the §306 shares, the bailout abuse arguably is no longer present. After all, Congress was concerned that shareholders could get profits out of the corporation without sacrificing much proprietary interest in the corporation. In the case of Fireoved v. United States,[80] the shareholder had previously sold some, but not all, of the underlying common stock with respect to which the §306 stock had been issued. Rejecting his claim for a §306(b)(4) exception, the court observed:

> [I]t is reasonable to assume that Congress realized the general lack of a tax avoidance purpose when a person sells *all* of his control in a corporation and then either simultaneously or subsequently disposes of his section 306 stock. However, when *only a portion* of the underlying common stock is sold, and the taxpayer retains essentially all the control he had previously, it would be unrealistic to conclude that Congress meant to give that taxpayer the advantage of section 306(b)(4)(B) when he ultimately sells his section 306 stock.[81]

Under the particular circumstances in the *Fireoved* case, although the shareholder had sold some of his shares to another shareholder, he retained effective veto power, and hence, control over the corporation. A taxpayer with anything less than a prior or simultaneous sale of *all* of the underlying common will have a difficult time making a case under §306(b)(4). The case may be strengthened, however, if the prior or simultaneous sale of the underlying common results in a loss of effective control.

Charitable Bailout

In an early ruling, the Treasury Department ruled that although §306(a)(1) generally applies to dispositions other than redemptions, a disposition by gift is not a taxable event to the donor.[82] Thus, §306(a)(1) will not apply to dispositions by gift. Instead, the donee will receive a substituted basis under §1015 and, under the definition of §306 stock in §306(c)(1)(C), the donee will own §306 stock. In other words, the recipient of the gift takes the stock not only with the donor's basis, but also with the donor's §306 "taint." If the taxpayer donates §306 stock to a tax-exempt charitable organization, the taxpayer has no taxable gain from making the gift. The charity presumably has the stock with a substituted basis classified as §306 stock. The donor will never pay tax on the appreciation reflected in the shares received in the form of a stock dividend and later transferred to

---

80. *Id.*
81. *Id. At* 1289 (emphasis added).
82. Rev. Rul. 57-328, 1957-2 C.B. 229.

charity. Although the charity holds §306 stock, as a tax-exempt organization, it is unlikely to report any income from disposition of the shares. And, to add icing to the cake, the taxpayer donating the stock is entitled to a charitable contribution deduction under §170.

In a modest effort to combat this particular bailout transaction, Congress limits the amount of the taxpayer's charitable deduction. Ordinarily, a taxpayer can deduct the full fair market value of property contributed to charity.[83] Under a limitation in §170(e), however, the amount is reduced by "the amount of gain which would not have been long-term capital gain if the property contributed had been sold by the taxpayer at its fair market value." Recall that §1(h)(11) simply adds "qualified dividend income" to "net capital gain" but does not otherwise alter the general definition and holding periods for capital assets.[84] Since §170(e) refers to "long-term capital gain," the "qualified dividend" rules do not appear to change the outcome under §170(e). This is not necessarily an insensible result. Absent §170(e), shareholders presumably would receive a full fair market value deduction upon contribution of appreciated stock. A charitable contribution deduction for the value of contributed property that was never taxed to the donor puts that stock donor at a relative tax advantage to those who donate cash. If so, the full fair market value deduction may be overly generous in the first place. On the other hand, this concern arguably extends far beyond the §306 setting and perhaps suggests that taxpayers generally should not be allowed full fair market value deductions upon contributions of previously unrealized and untaxed gain.

Examples

Basic §305 Problems

1. Tara Corporation was an industrial farm owned and operated by the O'Hara family. Mr. And Mrs. O'Hara owned 75% of the common stock with a basis of $600,000 and their daughter, Scarlet, owned the remaining 25%, with a basis of $200,000. Tara declares and distributes a stock dividend of newly authorized nonvoting preferred shares valued immediately after the distribution at $1 million. Mr. And Mrs. O'Hara receive $750,000 worth and Scarlet receives $250,000 worth of the preferred shares. Immediately after the preferred stock distribution, the total value of the common shares outstanding is also $1 million. Assume that the corporation has sufficient e&p to cover any distribution falling under the §301 rules. What are the tax consequences of the stock distribution to the O'Hara family and the Tara Corporation?

---

83. Treas. Reg. §1.170A-1(c).
84. See Chapters 1 and 5.

Variations on a Theme from Example 1

2. a. If Scarlet was able to convince the corporation to make her share of the stock dividend payable in cash in lieu of stock, what tax consequences to Scarlet? To her parents?

   b. What if the corporation issues a stock dividend of convertible preferred shares? Assume that each preferred share can be converted into one common share.

   c. If the corporation had two classes of voting common stock, one owned entirely by Mr. And Mrs. O'Hara (Class A) and the other owned by Scarlet (Class B) and the corporation declares a preferred stock dividend on the Class A shares and a cash dividend on the Class B shares, what result?

   d. What if the corporation issues a stock dividend to the Class B shareholders and nothing to the Class A shareholders? Is it relevant that one year later the Class A shareholders have deeded to them a portion of the farm property with a small cabin in which they plan to retire?

   e. What result if several years after the preferred stock dividend described in Example 1, the corporation decides to distribute additional common shares with respect to the preferred shares?

Deemed Distributions

3. a. Miss Pitty Pat's Dress Shop started out as a small family business, but is now a large corporate chain with retail stores throughout the country. It has two classes of shares outstanding. Class A is regular voting common stock, while Class B is subject to mandatory, regular redemptions over a ten-year period. After the ten-year period, all of the Class B shareholders will have been completely redeemed. What tax consequences result from the regular, planned redemptions of the Class B shareholders? To the Class A shareholders?

   b. Now imagine that Miss Pitty Pat's simply had two classes of stock, one owned by the founding family and the other owned by the public, and as part of a plan to take the corporation private again and vest control in the family, the corporation was able to redeem all of the shares owned by the public through a one time tender offer. What tax consequences?

4. What if, in Example 2b above, Tara Corporation changed the conversion privileges of the preferred stock so that each share of preferred could now be converted into two shares of common stock?

§306 Stock Problems

5. a. Returning to Tara from Example 1, remember that Mr. And Mrs. O'Hara owned 75% of the common stock with a basis of $600,000

and their daughter, Scarlet, owned the remaining 25%, with a basis of $200,000. Tara declared and distributed in year 1 a stock dividend of newly authorized nonvoting preferred shares valued at $1 million. Mr. And Mrs. O'Hara received $750,000 worth and Scarlet received $250,000 worth of the preferred shares. Immediately after the preferred stock distribution, the total value of the common shares outstanding was also $1 million. Assume now that the current earnings and profits for year 1 were $1 million and that there were no accumulated earnings and profits. In year 2, Tara redeems the preferred shares held by Scarlet for $1.2 million in cash. Assume further that this is the only distribution for year 2, that the corporation's current earnings and profits for year 2 are $500,000, and that there are no accumulated earnings and profits for year 2. What tax consequences to Scarlet when her preferred shares are redeemed?

b. What are the tax consequences to Scarlet if instead of having her preferred shares redeemed for $1.2 million, she sells her shares to Rhett Butler in year 2 for $1.2 million?

c. Would your answers to Examples 5a or 5b change if Tara had no earnings and profits for year 1?

d. Would your answer to Example 5a change if the total earnings and profits for year 1 had been only $400,000?

e. Would your answer to Example 5a change if Tara redeemed Scarlet's shares in year 2 for $75,000?

f. Would your answer to Example 5e change if the corporation simultaneously redeemed all of Scarlet's stock (the preferred and the common) in year 2? What if the corporation simultaneously redeemed one-half of Scarlet's common stock along with the preferred?

6. a. Pitty Pat's Dress Shops, Inc. And Ashley Enterprises entered into merger negotiations and arranged for a tax-free reorganization. Melonie had 200 common and 100 preferred shares in Ashley Enterprises. As part of the reorganization, she traded her Ashley shares for 200 Pitty Pat's shares (of equal value to her original common shares) and 200 preferred shares (double the value of her original Ashley preferred shares). What are the tax consequences to Melonie upon receipt of these shares?

b. If Melonie gives her new preferred shares in Pitty Pat's to her daughter April on her birthday, any tax consequences to Melonie or April upon the initial transfer? What if April later sells the shares to an unrelated third party?

c. Would your answer to Example 6b change if April received the preferred shares in Pitty Pat's as an inheritance from Melonie, with a fair market value basis determined under §1014?

Explanations

1. The distribution of preferred shares to the Tara shareholders is a pro rata distribution of preferred stock with respect to common stock. As such, it will be a tax-free stock dividend under §305(a). Note, however, that the shares will be considered tainted §306 stock. This will be considered further in Example 5. The basis of the preferred shares received as part of the stock distribution is determined under §307 by allocating the basis in the common shares according to a ratio based upon the fair market value of the classes of stock immediately after the distribution. Since the preferred shares had a value of $1 million immediately after the distribution and the total fair market value of all of the shares immediately after the distribution was $2 million, the ratio will be 50%. Thus, Mr. And Mrs. O'Hara will now have a basis of $300,000 in their new preferred shares (50% of $600,000) and $300,000 in the common shares, and Scarlet will have a basis of $100,000 in her new preferred shares (50% of $200,000) and $100,000 in the common shares. There are no tax consequences to Tara. The corporation will not reduce its earnings and profits.

2. a. If Scarlet convinces the corporation to pay her distribution in cash, she will of course be taxable on the cash distribution under the §301 rules. In addition, the fact that she receives cash will also make the stock distribution to her parents taxable under the §301 distribution rules under either §305(b)(1) or (2). Her parents' basis in the new shares will be the $750,000 fair market value under §301(d). Tara will reduce its e&p by the full $1 million value of the distribution.

   b. If the corporation issues a dividend of convertible preferred shares, this distribution will be taxable under §305(b)(5) unless the shareholders can establish to the satisfaction of the Secretary that the distribution will not result in the increase in the proportionate interests of some shareholders and the receipt of property by others. In other words, if the shareholders can establish either that all of the shareholders will convert or that none of the shareholders will convert, either event would leave the shareholders in the same relative positions vis-à-vis the corporation that they had held before. In either of these two cases, the distribution would not be taxable. If the shareholders cannot establish either of these two cases, they will be taxable on the stock distribution in accordance with §301 distribution rules. They will take a fair market value basis in the shares under §301(d). Tara will reduce its e&p to the extent that the stock distribution was taxable to the shareholders.

   c. When there are two classes of stock, one of which receives cash and the other of which receives stock, the shareholders effectively have been able to elect (in deciding which class of stock to acquire) to receive either cash or stock. As such, the stock distribution would be taxable under §305(b)(1). In addition, under §305(b)(2), the distribution has the effect of the receipt of property by some shareholders (cash) and an increase in the proportionate interest of others. Whether you view it as under §305(b)(1) or (b)(2), the result is the same—a taxable dividend to all, a fair market value basis in the stock for those who receive stock, and a reduction to Tara's e&p.

d. If the corporation issues a stock dividend to one class of shareholders and nothing to the other class, the shareholders receiving stock have increased their proportionate interest in the corporation at the expense of the other shareholders. As a policy matter, one would think that this increase in proportionate interest alone would be enough to justify taxation of the stock dividend. Under §305(b)(2), however, a companion distribution is required. In other words, one group of shareholders must receive stock and another group of shareholders must receive other property. The fact that the class A shareholders received some property from the corporation a year later is relevant. The regulations provide a 36-month window of time during which the companion distribution requirement can be met. Treas. Reg. §1.305-3(b)(4). Thus, one group of shareholders in this problem has received stock and another group has received property. The stock distribution will fall under §305(b)(2) and is taxable under the §301 distribution rules. Tara will reduce its e&p by the amount of the distribution.

e. If the corporation issues common shares with respect to its preferred shares, this will be a taxable stock dividend under §305(b)(4). All stock distributions on preferred stock are taxable.

3. a. Tax consequences to the redeemed Class B shareholders will be governed by the §302 redemption rules. See Chapter 6. With regard to the Class A shareholders, the regular and ongoing redemption of the Class B shareholders caused the Class A shareholders' proportionate interests in the corporation to increase. Even though the Class A shareholders have received no formal stock distribution, this will be regarded as a deemed stock dividend under §305(c). The Class A shareholders whose interests are increased will be taxable pursuant to the §301 distribution rules. See Treas. Reg. §1.305-7 and Treas. Reg. §1.305-3(e), ex. 8.

b. Where an isolated redemption from one group of shareholders causes the interests of another group of shareholders to increase their proportionate interest, this isolated redemption does not give rise to a deemed distribution under §305(c). There will be no tax consequences to the family. Treas. Reg. §1.305-3(e), ex. 10.

4. If Tara alters the conversion ratio so that every share of preferred stock can now be converted into two shares of common, this dilutes the interest of the common shareholders and increases the interests of the preferred shareholders. Although there has been no formal stock distribution, the preferred shareholders will be taxed upon a deemed stock distribution under §305(c). Treas. Reg. §1.305-7(a)(2).

5. a. Since the preferred shares issued by Tara were other than common shares received tax-free §305(a), they are considered §306 stock. There was no tax consequence upon the initial receipt of the preferred stock dividend (review answer to Example 1). When Scarlet has her shares redeemed for $1.2 million in cash, she has a distribution governed by §306(a)(2). Under §306(a)(2), her $1.2 million amount realized is treated as a §301 distribution. Since the redemption took place in year 2, the §301 analysis be will applied for year 2. Since the corporation had only $500,000 in earnings and profits for year 2, Scarlet will have dividend income of $500,000. Assuming that the distribution meets the §1(h)(11) "qualified dividend income" definition, Scarlet will add $500,000 to her net capital gain for year 2. An additional $100,000 will be a tax-free recovery of her basis in the shares under §301(c)(2). (See answer to Example 1 for an analysis of the §307 basis allocation, arriving at a $100,000 basis for her preferred shares.) The remaining $600,000 will be gain from sale of a capital asset under §301(c)(3).

   b. If Scarlet sold her preferred shares to Rhett Butler for $1.2 million, the tax consequences would be slightly different. This is a disposition other than by redemption covered by §306(a)(1). We start with §306(a)(1)(A), which provides that the amount realized ($1.2 million) shall be treated as "ordinary" income. For purposes of §306, any amounts viewed as ordinary income will be considered dividend distributions. I.R.C. §306(a)(1)(D). Consequently, assuming that the dividends meet the requirements of §1(h)(11), they should be eligible for preferential capital gains rates. However, the provision continues that it shall not apply to the extent that the amount realized ($1.2 million) exceeds the stock's ratable shares of the amount which would have been a dividend at the time of the stock distribution if money had been distributed in lieu of stock. In this problem, the corporation had sufficient earnings and profits to cover the full stock distribution in year 1. Thus, Scarlet's ratable share of the amount that would have been a dividend is $250,000, the full fair market value of the preferred shares that she received. So, of the $1.2 million total amount realized, the dividend result shall not apply to the extent of $950,000. This leaves Scarlet with $250,000 dividend income under §306(a)(1)(A). In the end, notice that she has dividend income to the extent of her §306 stock's ratable share of the amount that would have been a dividend. Prior to 2003, $250,000 of the $1.2 million distribution would have been taxed at ordinary income rates. Under current law, the $250,000 will be added to Scarlet's net capital gain for year 2 if the distribution meets the requirements of §1(h)(11).

Next, we turn to §306(a)(1)(B). Any excess of amount realized ($1.2 million) over the sum of (i) the amount treated under (A) as ordinary income ($250,000) and (ii) the adjusted basis of the stock ($100,000) is treated as gain from the sale of stock. So, we subtract $350,000 from the $1.2 million to arrive at $850,000, which will be treated as capital gain. Notice what we've done here. The $250,000 was already accounted for as dividend income. This was her ratable share of e&p for the year of the §306 stock distribution. Section 306(a)(1)(B) then takes her $100,000 basis into account, giving her a tax-free recovery of basis. Scarlet's total taxable income from the sale to Rhett is $1.1 million ($250,000 dividend income and $850,000 capital gain). Compare this result with the tax consequences if §306 were not in the Code. Under §1001, she would simply report her amount realized ($1.2 million) less basis ($100,000) for a capital gain of $1.1 million. The total taxable income from the transaction is the same. Prior to 2003, the only difference was the character of the income. In the "qualified dividend income" world, the $250,000 dividend income and the $850,000 capital gain are likely to be taxed at the same rates. When the dust settles after all of the §306(a)(1) computations, her overall $1.1 million gain is likely to be taxed in the same way that it would have been under §1001. This is one illustration that might be used in a call for repeal or modification of §306.

c. The answers to Examples 5a and 5b would be quite different if Tara had no earnings and profits in year 1. Under such circumstances, the preferred stock distributed would not have been §306 stock in the first place under §306(c)(1)(C) since no part of the distribution would have been a dividend if the corporation had distributed money instead of stock. Thus, if there had been no earnings and profits in year 1, a redemption of Scarlet's shares simply would be dealt with under the §302 redemption provisions. A sale to Rhett Butler would be governed by the sale or exchange rules in §1001.

d. The answer to Example 5a would not change. Under §306(a)(2), Scarlet treats the redemption in year 2 as a §301 distribution. The relevant e&p is the e&p for year 2.

e. The answer to Examples 5a would be very different if Scarlet's shares were redeemed in year 2 for $75,000 instead of $1.2 million. Instead of a $1.1 million realized gain from the redemption of her preferred shares, Scarlet would now have a $25,000 realized loss ($75,000 amount realized less $100,000 basis in the preferred shares). Under

§306(a)(2), Scarlet is treated as receiving the $75,000 as a §301 distribution. Since Tara had sufficient e&p in year 2 to cover this distribution, the entire $75,000 would be treated as a dividend, which Scarlet would add to her net capital gain for year 2, assuming the $75,000 was classified as "qualified dividend income" under §1(h)(11). Notice that, unlike Example 5b, Scarlet here would be worse off under §306 than she would have been under §1001. She would report a $75,000 taxable gain even though she arguably realized a $25,000 *loss*. Her loss would not disappear, however. Her $100,000 basis in the preferred shares redeemed would be added to her $100,000 basis in the underlying common shares, leaving her with the same $200,000 basis in the common shares that she started with. The $100,000 "loss" would be available to her through a basis offset upon subsequent sale of the common stock.

f. Unlike the answer in 5e, Scarlet may be able to get sale or exchange treatment, thus permitting her to recognize her $25,000 loss. Under §306(b)(1)(B), the §306(a) rules do not apply where the redemption of §306 stock is part of a §302(b)(3) complete termination of the shareholder's interest. Although her interest appears to be completely terminated, she is still deemed to own her parents' stock under the §318 attribution rules. However, Scarlet would qualify for §302(b)(3) treatment and the redemption of the tainted shares would not be governed by §306(a) if she filed the appropriate waiver of attribution under §302(c)(2).

If the corporation simultaneously redeems only one-half of Scarlet's common stock, her only hope of avoiding §306(a) would be to argue under §306(b)(4) that the redemption "was not in pursuance of a plan" having tax avoidance as one of its principal purposes. The Service will not automatically consider Scarlet eligible for the §306(b)(4) exception unless she has parted with *all* of her underlying common stock in the corporation. To make a claim under §306(b)(4), Scarlet would have to show that she parted with a *substantial* interest in the corporation and must also negate the inference of a tax avoidance plan. The §306(b)(4) exceptions do not explicitly cross-reference the §318 attribution rules. The extent to which the Service will consider attribution from Scarlet's parents as a factor in assessing her claim for §306(b) relief is unclear.

6. a. When a shareholder receives shares in a tax-free reorganization, they will be considered tainted shares "to the extent that . . . The effect of the transaction was substantially the same as the receipt of a stock dividend." I.R.C. §306(c)(1)(B)(i). Here, since Melonie received twice the value in preferred shares that she held previously, the *excess* preferred shares that she received will be regarded as §306 stock. There

will be no immediate tax consequence other than designating the shares as "tainted."

b. When Melonie transfers the §306 shares by gift to her daughter, April, there is no immediate tax consequence to either Melonie or April. However, April will hold §306 stock since the stock in her hands has a basis that is determined by reference to the basis of §306 stock under §306(c)(1)(C). Assuming that the stock appreciated in value during Melonie's term of ownership, April takes the stock under §1015 with her mother's basis in the preferred tainted shares. Thus, the basis of these shares in April's hands is determined by reference to the basis of tainted stock. If April later sells the shares, her sale will be governed not by §1001, but by §306(a)(1).

c. In contrast to the gift scenario in 6b, the §306 "taint" does not carry over to a recipient who receives the shares as an inheritance with a fair market value basis determined under §1014. Treas. Reg. §1.306-3(e). If April later sells the shares, her sale will be governed by §1001, with no additional consequences under §306.

PART IV

Corporate Liquidation and Related Issues

IV

8

General Liquidation Rules

INTRODUCTION

The closing events of a corporate life involve liquidation of the corporate enterprise. Although these events have significant tax consequences, the Code and regulations fail to provide a precise definition of liquidation. Some guidance is offered by regulations providing that "[a] status of liquidation exists when the corporation ceases to be a going concern and its activities are merely for the purpose of winding up its affairs, paying its debts, and distributing any remaining balance to its shareholders."[1] Thus, it is useful to think of liquidation as a *process* through which the corporation winds up its affairs and distributes remaining assets to its shareholders rather than a single event.

A corporation may liquidate in one of two ways. After paying off creditors, it may distribute the assets remaining directly to the shareholders in-kind. Alternatively, the corporation may sell off its assets for cash or notes, first paying off creditors and then distributing the remaining cash or notes to its shareholders. In either case, since the liquidation distribution effectively terminates the shareholder's interest in the corporation, distributions in liquidation, whether in-kind or cash, are treated as taxable events as if the shareholders sold their stock back to the corporation in return for corporate assets in-kind or for cash.[2]

---

1. Treas. Reg. §1.332-2(c). The regulation also specifies that "legal dissolution of the corporation is not required." *Id.*
2. I.R.C. §331.

From the corporation's perspective, an in-kind liquidating distribution also will be a taxable event.[3] If the government is to collect a corporate level tax on appreciated assets or permit a loss on depreciated assets, this generally is the last opportunity to do so. If the corporation chooses instead to sell its assets and distribute cash in liquidation, it will report taxable gain or loss on the sale of assets.[4] Thus, the tax consequences of the two liquidating techniques are parallel for shareholders and the liquidating corporation — liquidation generally is a taxable event to both the shareholders and the liquidating corporation.[5]

You might have noticed that the birth and death of the corporation do not receive parallel treatment. Under §§351 and 1032, formation of the corporation generally is a nonrecognition event to both the shareholders and the corporation. The stated rationale for such nonrecognition treatment is that formation of the corporate enterprise represents merely a change in form.[6] Dissolution of the corporation arguably represents a mere change in form as well. Yet under §§331 and 336, dissolution *is* a taxable event to both the shareholders and the corporation. The justification for this difference in treatment is that assets distributed to shareholders on liquidation represent value that has not yet been subject to shareholder level taxation. Nonrecognition treatment to shareholders would permit a "bailing out" of this value without the double tax envisioned by Subchapter C. In addition, liquidation distributions often are cash distributions. Since cash is not an asset to which a substituted basis can attach, there is no opportunity to preserve gain for later taxation. If the shareholders are to be taxed on the previously untaxed amounts, the liquidation distribution is the last moment to do so. Similarly, previously unrealized gain or loss on the corporation's assets would never be subject to the corporate level tax unless liquidation was treated as a taxable event to the dissolving corporation.

In summary, one important reason for treating complete liquidation as a taxable event is commitment to the scheme of double taxation developed in Subchapter C. If liquidation of the corporate enterprise is not treated as a taxable event, the opportunity for imposing this double tax on previously untaxed items is lost. Prior to 2003, *distributed* earnings were first taxed to the corporation as ordinary income and, assuming sufficient earnings and profits, taxed again as ordinary income to the shareholders.[7] In other words,

---

3. I.R.C. §336.

4. I.R.C. §§1001, 61(a)(3).

5. Different rules will apply to the liquidation of a subsidiary. The parent-subsidiary context is considered in Chapter 9.

6. For a discussion of §351 and its policy underpinnings, see Chapter 4.

7. Although the top marginal tax rates on ordinary income at each level have differed over time, the current top marginal rate for corporate income is 21% and for shareholder's ordinary income is 40.8% (including the net investment income tax). For further discussion see Chapter 2.

corporate profits were taxed as ordinary income to the corporation and also included in the corporation's earnings and profits accounts available again for a second tax as ordinary income upon dividend distributions to shareholders.[8] In contrast, the shareholder-level tax on *undistributed* earnings, presumably still reflected in the stock's value, was imposed upon the shareholders only at capital gains rates upon subsequent sale or disposition of the stock or upon liquidation. Thus, a corporation with retained earnings offered shareholders both a *deferral* of the shareholder-level tax on their share of corporate earnings and a change in the *character* of the gain from ordinary income to capital gain which may be taxed at preferential rates.[9] Pursuant to §1(h)(11), this character difference is eliminated for "qualified dividends." Under these rules, eligible shareholders will report both dividend distributions and gains upon subsequent sale, disposition, or liquidation at capital gains rates.

TAX CONSEQUENCES TO INDIVIDUAL SHAREHOLDERS: §331

Overview

Amounts received by the shareholders in complete liquidation are treated under §331 as "full payment in exchange for the stock."[10] The gain or loss on this exchange is computed in the same manner that the taxpayer would compute gain from any other sale or exchange.[11] Thus, the amount realized by the shareholder will be the fair market value of property plus the cash received from the corporation upon liquidation. From this, the shareholder will subtract his basis in the shares.

Since stock for most shareholders is a capital asset, the resulting gain or loss generally will be capital gain or loss.[12] The amount realized on liquidation will be allocated to blocks of shares purchased at different times. So, for example, if the shareholder purchased two-thirds of his shares several years ago and one-third of his shares within the last two months, he will allocate

---

8. Nonliquidating distributions are considered in Chapter 5.

9. These basic consequences of earning income through the corporate form are discussed in Chapter 2.

10. A parent corporation that receives a liquidating distribution from a subsidiary will not be governed by §331. Instead, treatment of receipts by parent corporations in complete liquidation of a subsidiary are governed by §332. See Chapter 9.

11. Treas. Reg. §1.331-1(b). The regulation explicitly refers to §§1001 and 1002, which govern sales or exchanges in general.

12. Shares in the hands of a dealer in stock will not be capital assets with the exception of shares held for the dealer's own investment. I.R.C. §1236.

two-thirds of the amount realized to the first block and the remaining one-third to the more recently purchased block of shares. Long-term capital gain treatment will only be available for the first block of shares.[13] Moreover, the shareholder may have a gain on one block of shares and a loss on another.

If the shareholder receives an in-kind distribution and reports gain or loss under §331, the basis of the property received will be the fair market value of the property at the time of distribution under §334(a). This is a sensible result. Since the receipt of the property was a taxable event, the shareholder essentially is credited with a cost basis.

Dividends Distinguished

In contrast to liquidating distributions, shareholders must treat nonliquidating distributions under §301 as dividends to the extent that they are paid out of earnings and profits.[14] Several significant differences should be noticed here. First, earnings and profits are not relevant in determining the shareholder's taxable gain or loss on liquidation. They effectively go to "earnings and profits heaven" and are no longer available to trigger a shareholder-level tax upon distribution as dividend income. Second, upon liquidation, the shareholder is entitled to a basis offset that is not available in the §301 dividend setting unless the corporation has insufficient earnings and profits to cover the distribution.[15] In addition, prior to 2003, dividend income was treated as ordinary income, whereas liquidation gain generally was capital gain. Given the lower tax rates on capital gains and the opportunity for a basis offset, shareholders generally preferred sale or exchange treatment to dividend treatment.[16] Since 2003, most shareholders have been eligible to report both liquidating distributions and "qualified dividend" distributions at capital gains rates, diminishing the shareholder preference for §331 sales or exchanges over §301 dividends. In cases where the corporation has significant earnings and profits, however, this shareholder preference may not be completely eliminated since the sale or exchange treatment available under §331 still allows shareholders to subtract their basis in the stock from the amount received upon the liquidating distribution.

---

13. Treas. Reg. §1.331-1(e).

14. See Chapter 5. Section §331(b) states explicitly that the §301 distribution rules do not apply to complete liquidations.

15. The §301(c) dividend rules are considered in great detail in Chapter 5.

16. One exception is the corporate shareholder, which will generally prefer dividend treatment to take advantage of the §243 dividends-received deduction.

Liquidation in Installments

a) Series of Liquidation Payments

Since liquidation is a process of winding up the affairs of a corporation that may take place over a period of months or even years, §346(a) provides that a distribution "shall be treated as in complete liquidation of a corporation if the distribution is one of a series of distributions in redemption of all of the stock of the corporation pursuant to a plan." In other words, each distribution is considered part of a complete liquidation as long as the series of distributions is part of an integrated, overall plan of complete liquidation. A few special §331 issues arise, however, in determining the proper shareholder tax treatment of a series of distributions in complete liquidation.

First, as a factual matter, it may be difficult to determine when a series of payments amounts to a series of distributions in complete liquidation. More specifically, the difficulty is in distinguishing a series of distributions in complete liquidation from a series of dividend payments. Whether or not the series of distributions in fact is one in complete liquidation will be decided by a facts and circumstances test. If the corporation wishes §331 complete liquidation treatment for its shareholders, the careful tax advisor, at a minimum, will insist that the corporation adopt a formal plan of complete liquidation and make liquidating distributions in accordance with that plan.

A second issue stems from the resemblance between a series of payments in complete liquidation and an installment sale of the shares. Under §453, an installment sale is defined as a "disposition of property where at least 1 payment is to be received after the close of the taxable year in which the disposition occurs."[17] Particularly since §331 and its regulations explicitly treat the complete liquidation as a sale or exchange under §1001, a series of complete liquidation payments where at least one payment is received in any year after the disposition of the stock would appear to be an installment sale. It seems that in principle the shareholders should use the installment method, reporting gain under §453(c) as each payment is received.[18]

---

17. I.R.C. §453(b)(1).
18. On the other hand, if the stock was traded on an established securities market, the installment provisions would not apply at all pursuant to §453(k)(2), which requires all payments received upon the disposition of publicly traded stock to be treated as received in the year of disposition of the stock. In other words, §453(k)(2) denies the preferential installment sale reporting privilege on the sale of publicly traded stock. Thus, regulations disallow installment reporting for shareholders who receive installment obligations in liquidation of a corporation whose stock is traded on an established securities market. Treas. Reg. §1.453-11(a)(2).

Despite an apparent inconsistency with installment method reporting, the Service in Rev. Rul. 85-48 adopted the old basis recovery first approach in the complete liquidation setting.[19] Under this method, each payment that the shareholder receives in liquidation is tax-free until basis has been recovered. This ruling is not only inconsistent with §453, but also is contrary to the modern trend toward denial of deferral advantages in the case of certain publicly traded stock,[20] and toward generally substituting regular reporting requirements in lieu of deferral provisions.[21]

Although the Service has not technically revoked Rev. Rul. 85-48, its preamble to the proposed version of Treas. Reg. §1.453-11 acknowledged the inconsistencies of a "basis first" recovery method with installment reporting.[22] Notice that §453(h)(1), which authorizes installment method reporting for shareholders who receive a distribution of a promissory note "acquired in respect of a sale or exchange by the corporation," does not technically apply to a mere series of distributions in liquidation.

b) Contingent Payments over Time

Ordinarily, the fair market value of property distributed upon complete liquidation will not be difficult to determine. In some cases, however, the shareholders receive contingent payment assets that cannot be valued. For example, rights to royalties or mineral rights provide for a series of payments over time, the overall value of which may be difficult to discern. In such cases, the liquidation will be treated as an "open transaction." Open transaction treatment permits the shareholder to treat payments first as tax-free recovery of basis and thereafter as capital gain from the sale of stock.[23] It should be noted that this will be a "rare and unusual" circumstance. Although appraisals may be difficult and complex, the Service ordinarily will require valuation and a closing of the liquidation transaction. Moreover, most of the case law on the "open transaction" doctrine was decided before the addition of §453(j)(2), which directed the Treasury

---

19. 1985-1 C.B. 126. Oddly enough, this is essentially the "open transaction" approach adopted by the Court in Burnet v. Logan, 283 U.S. 404 (1931), and since rejected by the Treasury Department under most circumstances. See, e.g., Treas. Reg. §15A.453-1(c).

20. See, e.g., I.R.C. §453(k)(2).

21. See, e.g., rules requiring current inclusion in income of original issue discount on debt instruments. I.R.C. §1272.

22. 62 Fed. Reg. 3244, 3245 (Jan. 22, 1997) ("Generally, a shareholder that receives liquidating distributions in more than one taxable year may recover the basis in the shareholder's stock completely before recognizing any gain. This general rule is inconsistent with installment method reporting, which requires that basis be ratably recovered as payments are received.").

23. The landmark case on the "open transaction" doctrine is Burnet v. Logan, 283 U.S. 404 (1931). The doctrine was explicitly applied to the corporate liquidation context in Comm'r v. Carter, 170 F.2d 911 (2d Cir. 1948).

Secretary to promulgate regulations "providing for ratable basis recovery in transactions where the gross profit or the total contract price (or both) cannot be readily ascertained." In contingent payment cases where there is no maximum selling price and no fixed period over which payments will be made, the Treasury now requires that basis be recovered in equal increments over 15 years.[24] Again, however, it is not clear that the Service will apply the installment sale provisions to contingent payments received on complete liquidation.

c) Corporate Sale of Assets Followed by Distribution of Notes to Shareholders

Instead of distributing assets in-kind to the shareholders, the corporation may sell its assets in return for third party promissory notes and thereafter distribute these notes to the shareholders.[25] Ordinarily, the shareholders under §331 are required to include the fair market value of any property received, including promissory notes. Section 453(h), however, provides special rules permitting the shareholders to report gain under the installment method when they receive such third-party notes upon liquidation. Under §453(h), shareholders may treat the receipt of *payments* under the obligation, rather than the obligation itself, as the consideration received in exchange for stock under §331. This provision effectively extends to the shareholders the same installment reporting privilege that would have been available to the corporation if it had retained the notes.[26] To qualify for this treatment under §453(h), the installment obligation must have been acquired by the corporation from a sale during the 12-month period beginning upon adoption of a plan of complete liquidation and the liquidation, in fact, must be completed during the same 12-month period. In order to prevent abuse of this transfer of the installment reporting privilege, Congress includes some restrictions on the use of §453(h). For example, if the installment note was received in exchange for the corporation's sale of regular inventory, stock in trade, or property that the corporation otherwise held primarily for sale to customers, §453(h)(1)(B) would disallow shareholder use of the installment method unless the sale was part of the corporation's sale of substantially all of the property

---

24. Treas. Reg. §15a.453-1(c)(4).

25. The distribution of an installment note by the corporation will be considered a disposition of the note, triggering recognition of gain to the corporation on the difference between the fair market value of the obligation and the basis of the obligation. I.R.C. §453B(a). This rule will not apply to distributions in liquidation of a subsidiary. I.R.C. §453B(d). For further discussion, see Chapter 9.

26. Note, however, that regulations under §453(h) disallow the installment reporting privilege in the case of installment obligation distributions in liquidation of a corporation whose stock is traded on an established securities market. Treas. Reg. §1.453-11(a)(2).

attributable to a trade or business — essentially a bulk or lump-sum liquidation sale. This rule is designed to ensure that the installment privilege is passed on to shareholders only for liquidation-type sales and not for ordinary sales more consistent with day-to-day business operations. Another exception disallows shareholder use of the installment method in the case of certain sales where the obligor on the note and the shareholder are related.[27]

Distributions Involving Liabilities

If the shareholders assume a corporate liability or take property in liquidation subject to a liability, the liability will reduce the shareholder's amount realized in the initial liquidation exchange under §331. In the case of a contingent or uncertain liability that was not taken into account in the initial liquidation exchange, a shareholder who later pays the debt will be entitled to a deduction. Based upon the Supreme Court's decision in Arrowsmith v. Commissioner,[28] this deduction generally will be treated as a capital loss. In *Arrowsmith*, the corporation was completely liquidated and the shareholders reported capital gain on the liquidation exchange. In a subsequent year, the shareholders were held to have transferee liability for certain of the defunct corporation's debts. The shareholders reported payments on the debts as ordinary business losses. The Supreme Court, however, required the shareholders to take the losses as capital losses, noting that the shareholders "were required to pay the judgment because of liability imposed on them as transferees of liquidation distribution assets. And it is plain that their liability as transferees was not based on any ordinary business transaction of theirs apart from the liquidation proceedings."[29] The Court examined all of the liquidation transaction events occurring over several years to determine the proper character of the loss.[30]

---

27. I.R.C. §453(h)(1)(C).
28. 344 U.S. 6 (1952), *rehearing denied*, 344 U.S. 900 (1952).
29. Id. At 8.
30. The *Arrowsmith* decision is quite brief and subject to varying interpretations. Its implications extend far beyond the complete liquidation context, raising issues about the nature of our annual accounting system and the character of gains and losses from related events occurring in different tax years. These broader implications are beyond the scope of this book. For a useful discussion of the issues, see Deborah H. Schenk, *Arrowsmith* and Its Progeny: Tax Characterization by Reference to Past Events, 33 Rutgers L. Rev. 317 (1981).

TAX CONSEQUENCES TO THE LIQUIDATING CORPORATION: §336

Overview

Although there are some differences, the tax treatment to the corporation of liquidating distributions parallels the treatment of nonliquidating distributions under §311 considered earlier in Chapter 5. The general rule of §336 is that "gain or loss shall be recognized to a liquidating corporation on the distribution of property in complete liquidation as if such property were sold to the distributee at its fair market value." Just as the shareholders are viewed in §331 as selling their stock back to the corporation in return for corporate assets, the liquidating corporation is viewed as selling its assets to the shareholders. Thus, gain or loss will be recognized to the distributing corporation on in-kind distributions. In other words, a liquidating distribution generally is both a realization and recognition event to the distributing corporation.[31]

The Old World of General Utilities

The recognition rules presently found in modern-day §336 were not always so. Under the old *General Utilities* rule, as applied in the liquidation context, corporations did not recognize gain or loss upon in-kind liquidating distributions.[32] Moreover, in order to achieve parity between in-kind liquidation distributions and sales of assets followed by cash distributions in liquidation, old rules even permitted the corporation to avoid recognition of gain on the sale of assets in pursuance of a plan of complete liquidation. In 1986, Congress placed the final nail in the coffin of the old *General Utilities* rule. Prior to 1986, a corporate liquidation could be designed to avoid corporate level tax upon the distribution of appreciated property. The shareholders would report gain upon the receipt of corporate assets in liquidation under §331 and would receive a fair market value (stepped-up) basis in the distributed property under §334(a). Thus, subsequent sale of the assets by the shareholders to a third party resulted in no further gain to the shareholders

---

31. Section 337 provides an exception to these rules in the case of distributions to a parent corporation in complete liquidation of a subsidiary. See Chapter 9.
32. For a discussion of the old *General Utilities* rule, see Chapter 5. The present §336 rules providing for general recognition of gain or loss to the corporation upon liquidation were added by the Tax Reform Act of 1986.

on the appreciation that accrued up to the time of liquidation. The double corporate tax on asset appreciation was thus avoided. One danger in this technique from the taxpayer's perspective was that the Service might successfully argue that the substance of the transaction was a taxable sale of assets by the corporation followed by a distribution of cash to the shareholders in liquidation. This danger was especially great in cases where the shareholders technically sold the property recently received in liquidation, even though the corporation had done the groundwork of contracting with the buyer or negotiating the terms of the sale.[33] On the other hand, if the corporation was careful not to contract with a buyer or negotiate the details of a shareholder sale before the liquidation, the corporation might successfully avoid double taxation.[34]

Future generations of law students and tax lawyers may be able to forget the old *General Utilities* world. For the moment, however, the tax system continues to suffer the growing pains resulting from the demise of the *General Utilities* rule. Many important cases, regulations, and rulings were written in the old world. To understand current provisions in proper context, one must be aware of the history behind them. Moreover, as we will see in subsequent chapters, some small pieces of the old world survive. Taxpayers have been creatively designing transactions to take advantage of the few remaining vestiges of the old world.

At least with respect to appreciated assets, *General Utilities* repeal generally was not popular with corporate taxpayers since it mandated a §336 corporate level tax upon liquidation in addition to the §331 shareholder level tax. With respect to loss properties, however, Congress feared that corporate taxpayers might use *General Utilities* repeal to their advantage, potentially recognizing a second corporate level loss. This concern led to special §336 loss limitations rules, discussed later in this chapter.

Distributions Involving Liabilities

For purposes of computing gain or loss, the corporation is viewed as having sold the distributed property to the shareholders at fair market value. When the shareholders assume a liability or property is distributed subject to a liability, however, §336(b) provides that the amount realized on the sale "shall be treated as not less than the amount of such liability." This provision

---

33. The Commissioner successfully raised this argument in the landmark case of Comm'r v. Court Holding Co., 324 U.S. 331 (1945).
34. Through careful planning, the taxpayers in United States v. Cumberland Public Service Co., 338 U.S. 451 (1950), achieved what the taxpayers in *Court Holding* had been unable to — liquidation without corporate level tax on corporate asset appreciation.

simply codifies in the liquidation context the notion that amount realized on the sale or exchange of property subject to liabilities must include the full liability, even if the liability exceeds fair market value.[35]

Treatment of Losses

a) General Loss Recognition

Despite parallels between the §311 nonliquidating distribution and §336 liquidating distribution rules, one key difference between the two sets of rules involves the treatment of losses. Remember that §311 does not permit recognition of losses to the distributing corporation upon nonliquidating distributions. In contrast, if the same property is distributed in a liquidating distribution, the general rule is that the liquidating corporation will be permitted to recognize loss. The policy explanation for this difference is a bit of a mystery. One possible explanation is that an operating corporation is more likely to deliberately undervalue property for purposes of recognizing loss than a liquidating corporation. Another explanation is that operating distributions offer greater opportunities for manipulation or "cherry picking." A corporation may distribute loss property so as to recognize losses while retaining gain property and not recognizing gain on unrealized appreciation. On the other hand, when the corporation is liquidating, it is selling or distributing *all* of its assets and the cherry picking problem presumably is not present.

b) Loss Limitations

i) Introduction

Although Congress established a general loss recognition rule in §336, its concern with potential abuses led to some restrictions. Before diving into §336(d) loss limitation details and mechanics, it may be helpful to quickly review some basics. Recall that when shareholders contribute appreciated property in a §351 exchange, the shareholder's unrecognized gain is preserved for later taxation both through the shareholder's §358 substituted basis in the stock *and* through the corporation's §362 substituted basis in the property. In other words, pre-incorporation appreciation potentially is subject to corporate double tax. Absent special loss limitations, the same substituted basis rules would result in potential double recognition of pre-incorporation — or "built-in" — loss. The double loss concerns motivating the 2004 enactment

---

35. Comm'r v. Tufts, 461 U.S. 300 (1983). These issues were discussed earlier in the chapter on nonliquidating distributions. Remember that §311(b)(2) provides that "[r]ules similar to the rules of section 336(b) shall apply" for purposes of §311. See discussion in Chapter 5.

of §362(e) actually are quite similar to those behind the §336 loss limitation rules.[36] As the discussion in sections that follow and the Explanations at the end of this chapter will show, the §336(d) loss limitation rules have played a somewhat more limited role since the adoption of §362(e).[37] The sections that follow will explore two basic types of loss limitations in §336(d) and their potential overlap with §362(e).[38]

ii) Related Person Rule: §336(d)(1)

First, the "related party" rules in §336(d)(1) disallow certain losses on distributions to related persons. Before going any further with §336(d)(1), you should first determine whether any of the shareholders receiving the in-kind loss property distribution is a "related person." For a definition of "related person," §336 cross-references to §267. An individual shareholder is related under the latter provision if she directly or indirectly owns more than 50% in value of the outstanding stock of the corporation; in other words, if she is a controlling shareholder.[39] A corporate shareholder is related if it is a member of the same controlled group.[40]

Next, you must look carefully at the distribution in question. If the distribution to the related person is either non-pro rata or is a distribution of "disqualified property," §336(d)(1) will disallow the recognition of *any* loss.[41] Disqualified property, for purposes of §336(d)(1), is any property received in a §351 contribution or contribution to capital during the five years prior to the liquidating distribution.[42] In other words, §336(d)(1) disallows the loss where the corporation distributes back out to related shareholders property that was recently contributed in a nontaxable §351 transaction.

---

36. See Chapter 4 for a full discussion of §351 exchanges, the corollary substituted basis rules, and the loss restrictions in §362(e).

37. Given the enactment of §362(e), arguable flaws in the §336(d) rules themselves, and inconsistencies in application of the two provisions, some have even suggested the repeal of §336(d)(1)-(2). See, e.g., Douglas A. Kahn, Jeffrey H. Kahn, Prevention of Double Deductions of a Single Loss: Solutions in Search of a Problem, 26 Va. L. Rev. 1, 5, 23 (2006).

38. A third loss limitation in §336(d)(3) involving liquidation of a subsidiary is considered in Chapter 9.

39. I.R.C. §267(b)(2). Constructive ownership rules found in §267(c) will be used to determine stock indirectly owned.

40. I.R.C. §267(b)(3), (f). Section 267(f) adopts the controlled group definition from §1563(a) with the exception that a 50% control test is substituted for the 80% control test wherever it appears in §1563(a). Controlled groups include parent-subsidiary chains, brother-sister corporations commonly owned by five or fewer persons, and combinations of the two, as provided in §1563.

41. For purposes of this rule, "non-pro rata" refers to a non-pro rata distribution of the loss asset itself, as opposed to a distribution that is non-pro rata in the aggregate. See Boris I. Bittker and James S. Eustice, Federal Income Taxation of Corporations and Shareholders ¶10.21[3][a] (7th ed. 2015).

42. I.R.C. §336(d)(1)(B).

As a general matter, the §336(d)(1) provisions express a basic concern with non-arm's-length transactions between related parties. With respect to loss transactions in particular, related party transactions raise suspicion that the parties may have manipulated or undervalued properties in order to increase apparent losses to the parties' mutual tax advantage. In fact, this is the basic idea behind the §267 general loss disallowance rules. Instead of adding the somewhat oddly crafted §336(d)(1) rules, this manipulation concern might have been better served in this instance simply by extending the application of §267 to liquidating distributions. As they stand, however, the §336(d)(1) loss limitation rules appear to respond to two different perceived abuses, one of which reflects this more general concern for manipulation. Although its terms are not explicitly so limited, the other seems to reflect concern with built-in losses and, as such, overlaps somewhat with §336(d)(2).

The non-pro rata distribution rule addresses a transaction in which the liquidating corporation makes disproportionate distributions of loss property to related shareholders. In addition to undervaluing loss assets to maximize loss recognition, the corporation might choose to make a disproportionate distribution of loss property to related shareholders to generate a double loss while leaving the unrelated shareholders without a comparable distribution. This abuse would not only hurt the federal fisc, but also deprive the unrelated shareholders of a fair share of the distribution.

The disqualified property definition in §336(d)(1) apparently addresses a second potential abuse involving a major shareholder who makes a contribution of loss property, sometimes referred to as "built-in loss property," followed by a distribution of the contributed loss property in complete liquidation within five years. Imagine, for example, a shareholder who in year 1 contributed property with a basis of $50,000 and a fair market value of $10,000 in exchange for 100% of a new corporation's stock. The shareholder's $40,000 realized loss would not be recognized in this §351 exchange. Pursuant to §358, the shareholder would hold the stock with a $50,000 basis. Without §362(e), the corporation also would hold the property with a $50,000 substituted basis. If the property was still worth $10,000 in year 4 when it was distributed in complete liquidation, the shareholder would recognize a $40,000 loss under §331. Absent loss limitation rules, the corporation also would recognize a $40,000 loss under §336. Pursuant to §336(d)(1), however, the corporation's loss from this liquidating distribution of "disqualified property" to a related shareholder will be disallowed.

The addition of §362(e) both complicates the picture and emphasizes a certain incoherence with these overlapping provisions. If §362(e)(2) had applied upon the initial §351 exchange, the corporation's basis—which under §362(a) would have been $50,000—instead would have been limited to the property's $10,000 fair market value. In other words, §362(e)(2) addresses the built-in loss problem up front. If the corporation were to distribute the property in complete liquidation in year 4 when its value was still $10,000, there simply would be no realized loss and, thus, nothing for §336(d)(1) to disallow.

What, then, is the continued function of §336(d)(1)? For one, although the disqualified property rule appears to be focused upon built-in losses, notice that that §336(d)(1) disallows the *entire* loss when disqualified property is distributed to a related party. Suppose, for example, that the disqualified property's value had been only $8,000 when it was distributed in complete liquidation to a related party. The §362(e)(2) limitation of the corporation's basis already has effectively disallowed the $40,000 built-in loss. The additional $2,000 loss now would be disallowed under §336(d)(1). Notice also that the definition of "disqualified property" in §336(d)(1)(B) simply refers to property that was contributed to the corporation in a §351 transaction. Thus, §336(d)(1) will apply to a distribution of disqualified property to a related party even if there was no built-in loss, making it arguably overinclusive. Suppose, for example, that the shareholder contributed the $50,000 basis property in a §351 exchange when its fair market value was $70,000. The corporation's §362(a) substituted basis would be $50,000. No §362(e)(2) restrictions would apply since this was a contribution of appreciated property. If the property declined in value to $10,000 and was distributed to a related party in complete liquidation in year 4, §336(d)(1) still would disallow the corporation's loss.

iii) Anti-Stuffing Rules: §336(d)(2)

The second basic liquidation loss limitation rule also responds to the potential for double losses on contributed property. Because this provision is more explicitly and narrowly focused on congressional concern that the shareholders deliberately would "stuff" the corporation initially with loss property in a §351 transaction, it is sometimes referred to as the "anti-stuffing" rule. Absent the §336(d) loss limitations, "unstuffing," or liquidating, the corporation would result in both a loss to the corporation and a loss to the shareholder. As it turns out, this concern over double loss recognition drives the related party rules in §336(d)(1), the anti-stuffing rules in §336(d)(2), and the §362(e)(2) rules enacted in 2004. Congress perhaps was more troubled with the related party case, however, since related parties may more easily join together to cooperate for tax advantage. As you will see in the discussion below, the §336(d)(1) related party rules impose a more severe penalty than either the §362(e) corporate basis or the §336(d)(2) anti-stuffing rules. When it adopted §362(e) in 2004, Congress was probably not focused on the provision's overlaps and potential inconsistencies with §336(d)(2).[43] The mechanism used to combat potential double loss is similar in both provisions. Both essentially address the built-in loss or "loss stuffing" problem by limiting the corporation's basis to the fair market value of the contributed property at the time of contribution. In many cases, §336(d)(2) effectively will become moot once §362(e) has worked its magic. These overlaps are considered below after an initial discussion of §336(d)(2).

Two elements are necessary to trigger the §336(d)(2) limitation to apply. First, the property in question must have been acquired by the liquidating corporation in a §351 transaction or as a contribution to capital.[44] Second, the acquisition must have been "part of a plan the principal purpose of which was to recognize loss by the liquidating corporation with respect to such property in connection with the liquidation."[45] Determining whether the §351 acquisition was part of a plan with such a purpose will not be easy. Here, however, Congress created a *presumption* that any §351 or capital contribution within two years before adoption of a plan of complete liquidation was part of a plan the principal purpose of which was to recognize loss.[46] The statute provides that the presumption will be rebuttable "as provided in regulations," but the Treasury Department has yet to issue such regulations. In the meantime, the legislative history suggests some clues to transactions that may successfully rebut the presumption. The Conference Report issued in connection with the enactment of §336(d) stated that

> [t]he conferees intend that the Treasury Department will issue regulations generally providing that the presumed prohibited purpose for contributions of property two years in advance of the adoption of a plan of liquidation will be disregarded *unless* there is no clear and substantial relationship between the contributed property and the conduct of the corporation's current or future business enterprises.[47]

---

43. For example, in its explanation of proposed §362(e) regulations, the Treasury Department did not address any issues regarding potential interactions, but stated its belief "that, generally, sections 336(d) and 362(e)(2) are fully compatible where the parties do not make an election to apply section 362(e)(2)(C)." Limitations on Transfers of Built-In Losses, 71 Fed. Reg. 62,067, 62,070 (Oct. 23, 2006).

44. I.R.C. §336(d)(2)(B)(i)(I). In addition, if the originally contributed property was exchanged by the distributing corporation for other property that takes a substituted basis from the contributed property—a §1031 like-kind exchange, for example—distribution of the property received in that exchange will be covered by the §336(d)(2) anti-stuffing rule. I.R.C. §336(d)(2)(B)(i) (flush language). In other words, the corporation cannot avoid the anti-stuffing rules by exchanging the §351 property for alternate substituted basis property and then distributing the new property at a loss.

45. I.R.C. §336(d)(2)(B)(i)(II). Notice that this subjective intent-based rule differs from the objective test in §336(d)(1).

46. I.R.C. §336(d)(2)(B)(ii).

47. H.R. Rep. 841, 99th Cong. 2d Sess. At II-201 (1986).

For now, it appears that if the contributed assets were an integral part of the trade or business of the corporation or substantially related to the business, rebuttal of the two-year presumption should be relatively easy.

Unlike the "related person" limitation in §336(d)(1), the "anti-stuffing" rule does not necessarily disallow the *entire* loss upon a distribution of loss property. Rather than disallow loss outright, §336(d)(2) achieves its magic by adjusting the basis of the distributed property. The liquidating corporation must reduce the basis of the distributed property by the excess of the adjusted basis over the fair market value of the contributed property *immediately after its acquisition by the corporation*.[48] Using numbers from the example above, imagine that several unrelated shareholders contributed property with a basis of $50,000 and a fair market value of $10,000. The corporation is required under §336(d)(2) to reduce its §362 basis of $50,000 by the excess of basis over fair market value at the time of the §351 contribution — $40,000. Thus, the corporation's basis for purposes of determining gain or loss under §336(a) would be $10,000.[49] Since the fair market value of the property is $10,000, there would be no loss to the corporation upon liquidation. Section 336(d)(2) thus operates rather elegantly to disallow only the loss built-in at the time of contribution. If the contributed property had declined further in value to $8,000, the corporation's basis would still be $10,000. Of the overall decline in value of $42,000 the $40,000 built-in loss is disallowed and the remaining $2,000 loss is permitted. Recall that if the same distribution had been made to a related shareholder covered by §336(d)(1), the entire $42,000 loss would have been disallowed.

The loss limitation rules in §336(d)(1) and (d)(2) can overlap so that the same transaction is covered by the language of both sections. The General Explanation of the Tax Reform Act of 1986 explains that if a particular transaction could fit within either (d)(1) or (d)(2), the harsher provisions of (d)(1) will prevail.[50]

Although the related party rule is more severe than the anti-stuffing rule in most respects, one aspect of the §336(d)(2) provisions sweeps more broadly than its sister limitation in §336(d)(1). Notice that the "anti-stuffing" loss limitation in §336(d)(2) applies not only to distributions, but also to sales or exchanges of the previously contributed property covered by the rule.[51] Thus, if instead of distributing the loss property to its

---

48. I.R.C. §336(d)(2)(A) (emphasis added).

49. Under §362(e)(2) the corporation presumably *already* would have been required to reduce its basis in the property to $10,000, thus making §336(d)(2) superfluous here. See further discussion below.

50. Staff of the Joint Comm. on Tax'n, Gen. Explanation of the Tax Reform Act of 1986, at 342 n.86 (1987).

51. Some commentators suggest that §336(d)(2) is less severe than §336(d)(1) in order to compensate for the broader scope of the former. See, e.g., Boris I. Bittker and James S. Eustice, Federal Income Taxation of Corporations and Shareholders ¶10.21[3][b] (7th ed. 2015).

shareholders, the corporation *sold* the previously contributed property to a third party and distributed cash to the shareholders in liquidation, the built-in loss would still be disallowed under §336(d)(2).

As noted earlier, §336(d)(2) now may well be moot for many—perhaps even most—liquidation distributions of loss property that were contributed in a §351 exchange given the addition of §362(e) "up-front" corporate basis limitations for built-in loss property received in the initial §351 exchange. Suppose, for example, that several unrelated U.S. shareholders make a §351 contribution to a domestic corporation of a single jointly owned asset with a basis of $100,000 and a fair market value of $25,000—i.e., an asset with a $75,000 built-in loss. The shareholders' §358 substituted stock basis will be $100,000. Under §362(e)(2), however, the corporation's basis in the contributed property up front will be limited to $25,000, thus eliminating the potential for a duplication of the shareholders' $75,000 loss in the corporation's hands. Thus, §362(e) has *already* effectively reduced the corporation's basis by the $75,000 built-in loss at the time of the contribution, the same adjustment that later would be required by §336(d)(2) upon a liquidating distribution of the property. Whether achieved via §362(e)(2) or §336(d)(2), the result will be the same: The corporation will not be entitled to any loss if it distributes the property in complete liquidation when the property value still is $25,000.[52] Either way, if the property is distributed in liquidation when its value is *less than* $25,000, the corporation will be disallowed only the $75,000 built-in loss, but will be entitled to recognize any excess post-contribution loss.

One significant difference in the operation of §§362(e)(2) and 336(d)(2) that can lead to odd and inconsistent outcomes is that the former uses aggregate figures whereas the latter works on an individual asset basis. Imagine, for example, that the shareholders in the above example had contributed two assets, one with a basis of $100,000 and a fair market value of $25,000 and the other with a basis of $25,000 and a fair market value of $100,000. Since the aggregate $125,000 basis does not exceed the aggregate $125,000 fair market value, no §362(e)(2) restrictions would apply. In other words, the built-in $75,000 gain on one asset can be used to offset the built-in $75,000 loss on the other. The corporation's §362(a) basis in

---

52. Odd results may arise, however, if the shareholders and the corporation made an election under §362(e)(2)(C) to restrict the *shareholders'* §358 basis in the *stock* to the fair market value of the contributed property in lieu of limiting the corporation's basis under §362(e). If §336(d)(2) applies to the corporation's basis in the property upon liquidation, the result could be a disallowance of the loss to *both* the shareholders and the corporation, a potentially harsh result to the unwary. The Treasury Department invited public comments on this concern when it issued its proposed §362(e) regulations described earlier in this chapter. Limitations on Transfers of Built-In Losses, 71 Fed. Reg. 62,067, 62,070 (Oct. 23, 2006). Final regulations under §362(e) issued in 2013 did not address this issue and stated that "no comments were received" on this issue. Limitations on Duplication of Net Built-In Losses, 78 Fed. Reg. 54,156, 54,160 (Sept. 3, 2013).

the loss property would be $100,000. If the corporation were to distribute the assets in complete liquidation within two years, however, §336(d)(2) would presume a plan to recognize the built-in loss by the liquidating corporation on the first asset. In effect, Congress has imposed harsher built-in loss limitation rules in the context of certain liquidating distributions. It is not clear why this should be so.

Examples

A Basic Liquidation

1. a. ABC Corporation was initially formed with cash contributions from five unrelated shareholders, each of whom contributed $10,000 in exchange for 20% of ABC's voting common stock. The shareholders have made no further contributions. Assume that none of the shareholders are dealers in stock, so that their stock investment is a capital asset. After several years of operations, the corporation adopts a plan of complete liquidation and distributes assets with a basis to the corporation of $50,000 and a fair market value of $125,000. Thus, each shareholder receives $25,000 of the corporation's assets upon liquidation. At the time of liquidation, the corporation had $125,000 in its current earnings and profits account and no accumulated earnings and profits. What are the tax consequences to the corporation and its shareholders upon liquidation?

   b. How would your answer change if the fair market value of the assets distributed in liquidation was $30,000 instead of $125,000?

   c. What if the corporation sold these assets to a third party for $30,000 and distributed the cash to the shareholders upon liquidation?

   d. Assume that one 20% shareholder had purchased 50 of her 100 shares for $1,000 in one year and the remaining 50 for $10,000 15 years later. What are the tax consequences to the shareholder upon receipt of assets worth $15,000 on liquidation?

Adding Liabilities

2. How would your answers to Examples 1a and 1b change if the shareholders took the property in liquidation subject to a $100,000 mortgage?

Series of Distribution Problems

3. a. Confronted with competition from other children's book publishers and having lost its primary author, Cat in the Hat Books, Inc., has decided to liquidate. It adopts a plan of liquidation pursuant to which it will make three distributions over a two-year period. Mr. Weiss, the primary shareholder, holds 100 shares. His basis in the shares is $20,000. In the year the liquidation plan is adopted, he receives

distributions totaling $12,500. In the next year, he receives another $12,500. What are the tax consequences to shareholder Weiss upon receipt of these distributions in complete liquidation?

b. How would your answer change if there was no formal plan of liquidation?

4. Lorax, Inc., is a mining company with coal operations in West Virginia. Upon liquidation, it distributes $20,000 cash and a 30-year right to receive royalties on the Berkley seam of coal to shareholder Tim. Tim's basis in his Lorax shares is $15,000. What are the tax consequences to the Lorax corporation and to Tim?

Sale of Asset/Distribution of Note Problems

5. Yak Enterprises is a corporation that runs travel tours to Nepal. On January 1 it adopted a plan of complete liquidation. Its assets had a basis of $250,000. In February of the same year it sold its assets to an interested buyer for $1 million, payable in five equal installments of $200,000 over five years plus 8% interest reflected in a promissory note received from the buyer. In March, the corporation distributed the note to its shareholders in complete liquidation before the corporation had received any payments on the note. What are the tax consequences to Yak and its shareholders? For purposes of this Example, assume that the note had a $1 million fair market value at the time of receipt by the corporation and distribution to the shareholders.

Loss Limitation Problems

6. a. Horton Enterprises is owned by two unrelated shareholders. Daisy holds 60% and Yertle holds 40% of the outstanding common stock. The company engages in the business of real estate development. The corporation purchased real estate in New York for a purchase price of $10 million. Given the decline in real estate values, the property was worth only $7 million when the corporation distributed the real estate to its shareholders as tenants-in-common in complete liquidation. What are the tax consequences to Horton?

b. How would your answer to Example 6a change if the shareholders together had purchased the same real estate in 1 year for $10 million, contributed it to the corporation in a §351 transaction in year 5 when the fair market value was $7 million, and got the real estate back upon complete liquidation in year 12 when the property was still worth $7 million?

7. Grinch Greeting Cards, Inc., is owned by ten unrelated shareholders, each of whom owns 10% of the outstanding common stock. In a year 1 § 351 contribution, Lulu contributed a plant ($800,000 basis; $500,000 fair

market value) previously used in her sole proprietorship printing business, along with other assets with an aggregate basis of $200,000 and a fair market value of $500,000. The other shareholders in year 1 each contributed cash in exchange for stock. In year 2, Grinch distributed all of its assets pursuant to a plan of complete liquidation. As part of the liquidation plan, Grinch distributed to Lulu the printing plant, which had since declined in value to $450,000. How much loss, if any, will Grinch be entitled to recognize upon the liquidating distribution?

Explanations

1. a. ABC Corporation will be treated under §336(a) as if it sold its assets to the shareholders for fair market value. Thus, the corporation will report a gain of $75,000 upon the liquidating distribution ($125,000 fair market value of the distributed assets less $50,000 basis). The character of the gain will be determined by the character of the assets distributed. The corporation's stock will now be canceled and the corporation is effectively dissolved. Its earnings and profits account, along with its other tax characteristics, go to "tax heaven" along with the corporation.

   Under §331, the liquidation distribution will be treated as full payment in exchange for stock. Each shareholder will report a $15,000 capital gain ($25,000 amount realized less $10,000 stock basis). The earnings and profits account of the corporation is irrelevant in determining shareholder gain or loss under §331. Under §334(a), each shareholder's basis in assets received in the taxable §331 exchange will be the $125,000 fair market value of the assets received upon liquidation.

   b. Again, under §336(a), ABC Corporation will be treated as if it sold the assets to the shareholders for fair market value. In this case, since the fair market value of the assets is only $30,000 and the corporation's basis is still $50,000, the corporation will report a loss of $20,000. Unlike the §311 operating distribution rules, §336(a) does permit recognition of loss on liquidating distributions. The character of the loss will again depend upon the character of the asset distributed. Since none of the shareholders are related persons and none of the distributed property was acquired by the corporation from the shareholders in a §351 contribution, the §336(d) loss limitations are not applicable.

   Since each shareholder owns 20% of the stock, each presumably received $6,000 out of the total $30,000 in distributed assets. Given their bases of $10,000, each will report a $4,000 capital loss. The shareholders each will take a $6,000 fair market value basis in the assets received.

    c. If the corporation sold its assets to a third party for $30,000, it would also realize and recognize a $20,000 loss on the sale. Subsequent distribution of the cash would be taxable to the shareholders under §331 as in the answers to Examples 1a and 1b. Notice that the tax result is the same whether the corporation distributes the assets directly (as in 1b) or sells the assets and then distributes the cash.

    d. Since the shareholder has two blocks of shares, the amount realized on the liquidating distribution must be allocated between the two blocks, each of which represents 50% of her stock holdings. She will allocate one-half of the distribution—$7,500—to each block. She will report a $6,500 long-term capital gain from the first block of shares and a $2,500 long-term capital loss from the second block of shares. See Treas. Reg. §1.331-1(e). Note that if she had aggregated the shares, she would have had an overall gain of $4,000. The allocation approach more accurately traces gain and losses for specific blocks of shares. The shareholder will have a fair market value basis in the assets received upon liquidation under §334(a).

2. If the shareholders upon liquidation of the ABC Corporation took the $125,000 property subject to a $100,000 mortgage, the transaction still will be treated under §336(a) to ABC as if the property had been sold at fair market value to the shareholders. Thus, the corporation still will have a $75,000 gain. The answer to Example 1a does not change. In effect, the amount realized by ABC includes the $100,000 mortgage amount as well as the distributed property's value in excess of the mortgage.

    From the shareholders' perspective, however, addition of the liability does change the answer. The amount realized by the shareholders upon liquidation is net of the liability. Thus, the aggregate liability must be subtracted from the amount realized on the exchange. The net amount received by the shareholders is only $25,000 ($125,000 value less the $100,000 mortgage). Assuming that each shareholder upon liquidation received 20% of the assets subject to 20% of the liabilities, each would have received a $5,000 liquidating distribution. After subtracting their $10,000 basis, each shareholder would have a $5,000 capital loss. Under §334(a), each shareholder's basis will be the $25,000 fair market value in the property received (20% of $125,000). You might think of this $25,000 as including the mortgage amount in the same way the taxpayers generally are entitled to include borrowing in basis.

    If the fair market value of the assets upon liquidation is only $30,000, as in Example 1b, but the property is still subject to a $100,000 mortgage, the tax consequences to ABC will change. Although ABC is still treated under §336(a) as if it sold the property to the shareholders, under §336(b), fair market value shall be treated as not less than the liability. Thus, the amount realized on the exchange is $100,000—the amount of the liability. From this, the corporation will subtract its basis of $50,000, resulting in a $50,000 gain. Note that without the liability, this distribution resulted in a $20,000 loss to ABC. (See answer to Example 1b.) When shareholders take property subject to a corporate liability, the corporation benefits to the extent that it is relieved of the liability. Where the liability exceeds the fair market value, the amount realized must include the liability.

From the shareholders' perspective, the amount realized on liquidation should be net of liabilities. In this example, the fair market value of the liquidating distribution was $30,000 and the shareholders took the property subject to a $100,000 mortgage. There is actually a net negative value to this distribution from the shareholders' perspective. Corporations rarely make such distributions to their shareholders. One would expect shareholders to be unhappy to acquire liabilities that exceed the value of the assets. More often than not, the corporation probably avoids these problems by "dumping" the assets. Limited liability will protect the shareholders from the clutches of creditors. The presence of §336(b) suggests that Congress anticipated such transactions to occur from time to time. However, §336(b) only answers the corporate level questions. Section 331 itself says nothing about liabilities taken on by the shareholders at liquidation.

The most plausible outcome in this scenario is to treat this scenario from the shareholder's perspective under §165 rather than under §331.[53] In this case the shareholders would recognize an immediate capital loss in the amount of the mortgage plus their basis in the shares less the $30,000 fair market value of the property received. Their basis in the property received would then be the fair market value of $30,000.

3. a. The distribution will be treated as an exchange of shareholder Weiss's stock under §331. Although the shareholder is not receiving a formal promissory note, this series of distribution effectively is an installment sale. Under the §453 installment method, the shareholder would have a gross profit ratio of $5,000/$25,000 or 20% (gross profit from $25,000 payments less $20,000 basis over the total $25,000 contract price). Thus, 20% of each $12,500 distribution ($2,500) would have been taxable each year. Under the authority of Rev. Rul. 85-48, however, the shareholder may be permitted to recover his basis before reporting any gain. Since his receipts of $12,500 in the first year are less than his $20,000 basis, he would have no gain for year 1. The

---

53. See Boris I. Bittker and James S. Eustice, Federal Income Taxation of Corporations and Shareholders ¶10.22[3] (7th ed. 2015); see also Rev. Rul. 2003-125, 2003-2 C.B. 1243 (allowing a worthless security deduction under §165 upon the deemed liquidation of an entity, where the entity's liabilities exceeded the value of its assets).

$12,500 would be applied against his stock basis, however, leaving the shareholder with a $7,500 basis in the shares. When he receives the $12,500 distribution in year 2, he would report a $5,000 capital gain. This deferral of gain is inconsistent with the installment method, which technically should apply here. Since this was not an installment note from a corporate sale of assets in liquidation, §453(h)(1) is not technically applicable.

b. It is not necessary that there be a formal plan of liquidation in order for the provisions of §§331 and 336 to apply. Clear indication of an intent to liquidate should suffice. On the other hand, when liquidation involves a series of distributions, there is a risk that early distributions will be viewed as dividends. Whether a particular distribution is a dividend or part of a series of liquidating distributions is determined based on all of the facts and circumstances. To be safe, the corporation ordinarily will want to adopt a plan of liquidation. If the Service regarded the first payment in this series as a dividend and only considered the final payment as a liquidating distribution, the shareholder would report dividend income on the first $12,500 distribution (assuming sufficient earnings and profits to cover the distribution). The second distribution would be treated as a §331 exchange, resulting in a $7,500 capital loss ($20,000 basis less $12,500 distribution). Notice that although the overall net amount subject to tax is the same $5,000 that was taxed in Example 3a ($12,500 year 1 income offset by the $7,500 year 2 loss), the tax consequences are different in several ways. First, if the first-year distribution is treated as part of a series of distributions in liquidation, as it was in Example 3a, the shareholders will have no taxable income from the distribution in year 1. On the other hand, assuming sufficient earnings and profits, the $12,500 distribution in year 1 will be fully taxed if it is considered a dividend that is not part of the liquidation. Second, under a dividend approach to the first-year distribution, the $12,500 reported in year 1 as §301 dividend income and the $7,500 loss in year 2 is a capital loss. Although the net gain is $5,000, capital loss netting rules may prevent the shareholder from using the loss in year 2.

4. Tim's receipt of the cash and royalty rights should be treated as a distribution in a §331 liquidation exchange. The Service will expect Tim to make every effort to value the royalty rights, to include that amount in amount realized, and to "close" the transaction. Under a "closed transaction" approach, Tim would report capital gain on the difference between the value of the assets received (cash plus royalty rights) less his $15,000 basis in the shares. The royalty rights would then receive a basis equal to the fair market value assigned to them for purposes of §331. As Tim

received future royalty payments, he should be permitted to amortize this basis.

If the royalty rights truly cannot be valued, Tim may be entitled to treat this as an "open liquidation transaction." Since the cash of $20,000 exceeds his $15,000 basis by $5,000, he should report $5,000 in long-term capital gain upon liquidation. Thereafter, each royalty payment will be considered continuing payment in exchange for stock and, therefore, treated as capital gain. This open transaction treatment is inconsistent with installment sale provisions that otherwise require ratable basis recovery over a 15-year period. Treas. Reg. §15a.453-1(c)(1). The Service does not appear to be applying the installment sale provisions to distributions in complete liquidation, however.

5. When the corporation sells its assets to a third party in return for a promissory note, it is entitled to installment reporting. The corporation would report gain as payments were received. Since Yak received no payments, it would not report any gain upon receipt of the note. Its basis in the note would be its $250,000 basis in the underlying assets sold. I.R.C. §453B(b). Upon distributing the note in liquidation, Yak would report a $750,000 gain ($1 million value of the note less $250,000 basis). I.R.C. §453B(a). Assuming that the corporation also has not yet received any interest on the notes, it will not have any interest income.

Ordinarily, the shareholders would be required to report the full fair market value of the note as part of the amount realized on the §331 exchange. Under §453(h), however, the shareholders will be entitled to treat each payment as payment in the §331 exchange. Thus, each $200,000 payment will be treated under the installment method. The shareholders will use their stock basis to determine a gross profit ratio and report a portion of each payment as gain accordingly. I.R.C. §453. The shareholders will report this as capital gain or loss. Any interest on the note received by the shareholders will be treated as ordinary income.

6. a. Horton Enterprises should be permitted to recognize a $3 million loss upon distribution of the real estate in complete liquidation ($7 million value of real estate less $10 million basis). Daisy is a "related person" for purposes of §336(d)(1), since she owns 60% of the stock. I.R.C. §267(b)(2). However, the §336(d)(1) loss limitation rules apply only to non-pro rata distributions or distributions of disqualified property. Since the real estate in this problem was not contributed, but rather purchased by the corporation, it is not disqualified property. Since the distribution was made to Daisy and Yertle as tenants-in-common, it should be regarded as pro rata and the (d)(1) loss limitation would not apply. The §336(d)(2) "anti-stuffing" limitation would also not apply since the property was not acquired by the corporation in a §351 transaction or as a contribution to capital.

b. This is a good example of a situation in which the §362(e)(2) rule effectively trumps and sweeps more broadly than the §336(d)(1) related party rule. The §336(d)(1) loss limitations apply only to non-pro rata or disqualified property distributions. Since this property was acquired by the corporation in a §351 contribution more than five years before the date of distribution, it is not disqualified property. Assuming that the distribution was pro rata, §336(d)(1) would not have disallowed the $3 million loss. Similarly, the transaction would likely not be subject to the §336(d)(2) "anti-stuffing" limitation since the property was contributed to the corporation more than two years prior to the liquidating distribution (assuming that the property acquisition did not otherwise have a principal purpose of recognizing loss by the liquidating corporation).

The problem for the corporation in this Example would have occurred upon the §351 contribution in year 5. Assuming that this was the only property contributed, the "aggregate" basis of $10 million exceeded the "aggregate" $7 million adjusted basis. Thus, Horton Enterprise's basis in the property already would have been limited to the $7 million fair market value at the time of contribution. In the end, the loss is disallowed by virtue of §362(e)(2) even though §336(d)(1) otherwise would not have disallowed the loss upon liquidation.

7. Although the printing plant contributed by Lulu had a $300,000 built-in loss, Grinch still would have taken an $800,000 substituted basis in the plant following the §351 exchange pursuant to §362(a). Notice that the § 362(e)(2) corporate basis limitation rules would not have applied since the *aggregate* adjusted basis of Lulu's contributions did not exceed the *aggregate* fair market value at the time of her § 351 exchange. Grinch would realize a loss of $350,000 upon distributing the printing plant in complete liquidation. ($800,000 basis less $450,000 fair market value.) No § 336(d)(1) issues arise in this case since Lulu is not a related party. Since the distribution was within two years of the § 351 contribution, however, it will be presumed under § 336(d)(2)(B)(ii) to be "part of a plan the principal purpose of which was to recognize loss by the liquidating corporation." Although regulations have not been finalized, legislative history suggests that the presumed prohibited purpose may be rebutted where the property at issue is integrally related to the corporation's business operations and there are no other facts indicating a corporate purpose to duplicate the built-in loss. Assuming successful rebuttal of the presumed prohibited purpose, Grinch should be entitled to recognize the entire $350,000 loss upon distribution of the plant. Even if Grinch cannot successfully rebut the purpose presumption, the § 336(d)(2) loss limitation rules will not disallow the entire loss.

Instead, § 336(d)(2)(A) would reduce the corporation's adjusted basis in the property ($800,000) by the excess of its adjusted basis immediately after the acquisition by the corporation over the fair market value at that time ($800,000 less $500,000). In other words, for purposes of determining loss on the liquidating distribution, Grinch's basis must first be reduced by the amount of the $300,000 built-in loss, leaving Grinch with a $500,000 basis in the plant. Thus, Grinch still would recognize a $50,000 loss upon a liquidating distribution when the plant's value was $450,000.

Liquidation
of Subsidiaries

INTRODUCTION

Unlike general liquidations, which typically are taxable events to both the liquidating corporation and to the shareholders,[1] liquidations of subsidiary corporations generally are not taxable to either the liquidating subsidiary or to its shareholder parent corporation. One rationale for the different treatment of subsidiary liquidations is that Congress wished to encourage the simplification of complex corporate structures by permitting the elimination of subsidiary corporations without immediate tax consequence. A parent and its subsidiaries are part of the same "corporate family" of affiliated corporations and are eligible to file consolidated tax returns.[2] Since a distribution in liquidation does not cause assets to leave this larger corporate family, Congress decided not to impose an immediate tax upon liquidation of a subsidiary, but instead to defer taxation of gain or recognition of loss. Put another way, the liquidation of a subsidiary effectively is a merger of the subsidiary into the parent corporation. The nonrecognition treatment provided these transactions is similar to the nonrecognition otherwise provided to tax-free reorganizations.[3]

---

1. See Chapter 8.
2. I.R.C. §1501. Notice that affiliated corporations may *elect*, but are not *required*, to file consolidated returns. The basic §332 liquidation rules apply whether or not such an election is made.
3. For a detailed discussion of tax-free reorganizations, see Chapters 11-14.

The different tax treatment afforded to subsidiary liquidations can also be understood by thinking back to the basic double tax imposed by Subchapter C. The corporate tax regime is designed to impose a double tax on corporate earnings, but not multiple layers of taxation beyond the two tiers. Without special rules, the liquidation of a subsidiary would result in a triple, or even longer chain of multiple taxes. The liquidating subsidiary would be taxed upon making the distribution under §336. The parent would be taxed upon receiving the distribution under §331. Finally, the parent corporation's shareholders would report a third gain or loss under §331 when the parent corporation eventually liquidated and distributed the assets received from the subsidiary, or they would be taxed under §301 if the parent later distributed the assets in an operating distribution.[4]

The special subsidiary liquidation rules considered in this chapter avoid this potential triple or greater multiple tax. The rules are designed to collect *one* shareholder level tax and *one* corporate level tax in connection with the subsidiary liquidation. Since a shareholder level tax will be reported eventually by the parent corporation's shareholders, Congress chose to eliminate the shareholder level tax that would otherwise be imposed on the parent corporation under §331 at the time of liquidation of a subsidiary. As described in more detail below, §332 operates as an exception to the general recognition rule in §331, providing nonrecognition of the shareholder level tax to the parent upon receipt of a liquidating distribution from a subsidiary. In addition, §337 operates as an exception to the general recognition rule in §336, providing nonrecognition of the corporate level tax to the liquidating subsidiary. This corporate level gain or loss in the subsidiary's assets will be preserved, however, through use of substituted basis rules. The distributed assets will retain in the parent corporation's hands the same basis they had while in the subsidiary's hands. Let's turn now to some of the details.

TAX CONSEQUENCES TO THE PARENT CORPORATION: §332

Nonrecognition Rules

Section 332(a) provides that "[n]o gain or loss shall be recognized on the receipt by a corporation of property distributed in complete liquidation of another corporation." Despite the broad language used here, this

---

4. If the parent corporation shareholders sell their stock in the meantime, the sales price for the stock presumably will reflect the value of these assets as well.

nonrecognition rule will not apply to just *any* corporate shareholder that receives assets upon liquidation, but is limited by §332(b)(1) to corporations owning stock that meets the requirements of §1504(a)(2) — a direct reference to the provision that defines affiliated corporations eligible to file consolidated returns. To meet the requirements of §1504(a)(2), a corporation must own at least 80% of the total voting power *and* at least 80% of the total value of another corporation's stock.[5] Although the Code itself does not use the term "parent," a corporation meeting this two-part 80% ownership test is commonly referred to as a parent corporation. The corporation in which the parent holds this 80% interest is commonly referred to as a subsidiary.

In order to be eligible for §332(a) nonrecognition, the distribution must be in complete cancellation or redemption of all of the liquidating corporation's stock. In addition, the liquidating corporation must either transfer all of its property within the taxable year or make a series of distributions in accordance with a plan of liquidation under which all of the property is distributed within three years.[6] To be eligible for §332 nonrecognition, the parent corporation must meet the two-part 80% control test on the date of adoption of a plan of liquidation and at all times until receipt of the property in liquidation. Although §332 is a mandatory provision, the 80% control test effectively makes it elective. If the parent corporation disposes of enough stock to cause its ownership to fall below the required 80%, it will fail the control test and the liquidation will not be covered by §332.[7] Moreover, the regulations explicitly provide that §332 "applies only to those cases in which the recipient corporation receives at least *partial payment* for the stock which it owns in the liquidating corporation."[8] In other words, §332 does not apply at all to liquidation of an insolvent subsidiary. Upon complete liquidation of such a subsidiary, the parent corporation would instead be entitled to a §165(g) loss deduction with respect to worthless securities.[9]

If the subsidiary is indebted to the parent at the time of liquidation, payments in satisfaction of indebtedness will be taxable to the parent despite the nonrecognition rules of §332. Such payments are made to the parent in its capacity as a creditor rather than as a shareholder. As an example, the regulations provide that "if the parent corporation purchased its subsidiary's bonds at a discount and upon liquidation of the subsidiary the parent

---

5. Whether or not consolidated returns are filed, the corporation is eligible for §332 nonrecognition as long as it meets the §1504(a)(2) 80% ownership tests.

6. I.R.C. §332(b)(2), (3).

7. See, e.g., Comm'r v. Day & Zimmerman, Inc., 151 F.2d 517 (3d Cir. 1945) (holding that as long as the sale itself was bona fide, a preliquidation sale of shares successfully permitted the parent corporation to "flunk" §332 even though the sale had no other business purpose).

8. Treas. Reg. §1.332-2(b) (emphasis added).

9. Id.

corporation receives payment for the face amount of such bonds, gain shall be recognized to the parent corporation."[10]

Assuming that the corporate parent meets the control test and that the distributions in liquidation otherwise meet the requirements of §332, the parent corporation will recognize no gain or loss upon receipt of property in liquidation from the subsidiary. Property for purposes of §332 includes in-kind property as well as cash. Under §334(b) the basis of distributed property now in the parent corporation's hands "shall be the same as it would be in the hands of the transferor."[11] To use a simple example, assume that the subsidiary distributes property in liquidation with a basis of $25,000 and a fair market value of $100,000. The liquidating subsidiary is entitled to non-recognition of its $75,000 realized gain under §337.[12] In addition, the parent corporation will receive this $100,000 property without any immediate gain under §332(a). The parent corporation's basis in the property under §334(b) will be the same $25,000 basis that the subsidiary had. Thus, if the parent later were to sell the property for $100,000, it would report a $75,000 gain. The §334(b) basis rules effectively transfer responsibility for reporting the liquidating subsidiary's gain or loss on the liquidation distribution from the subsidiary to the parent. Special rules also provide that the parent corporation will "inherit" many of the subsidiary's tax characteristics, including earnings and profits accounts and net operating losses.[13] The parent's inheritance of such characteristics is subject to numerous complex limitations,[14] which are beyond the scope of most introductory courses in corporate taxation.

There is one exception to the transferred basis rule of §334(b)(1). If gain or loss is recognized by the subsidiary on the distribution of property in liquidation, the basis of the distributed property in the parent's hands will be fair market value. There are a few situations in which the subsidiary may be required to recognize gain or loss despite the general nonrecognition rule for the subsidiary provided in §337.[15] The fair market value basis in such cases is sensible. Since the subsidiary has already reported gain or loss, there is no need to preserve gain or loss through a transferred basis.

---

10. Treas. Reg. §1.332-7.

11. This is referred to as transferred basis. See I.R.C. §7701(a)(43).

12. Detailed discussion of §337 appears later in this chapter.

13. I.R.C. §381(a), (c). If the parent owns less than 100% of the subsidiary's stock, regulations provide that the inherited earnings and profits "shall be computed by taking into account the amount of earnings and profits properly applicable to the distributions to minority shareholders. . . ." Treas. Reg. §1.381(c)(2)-1(c)(2). This suggests that the parent will inherit only a proportionate share of earnings and profits.

14. I.R.C. §381(c).

15. For example, if the parent corporation is a tax-exempt organization, the subsidiary may not be eligible for §337 nonrecognition. The §337 provisions are considered in greater detail later in this chapter.

Observations About "Outside" and "Inside" Basis

A parent corporation owns stock in its subsidiary for which it has a basis. This stock represents the parent's indirect ownership interest in the underlying subsidiary's assets. The subsidiary's assets themselves also have a basis. A parent corporation's basis in its subsidiary's *stock* sometimes is referred to as its "outside" basis, while the subsidiary's basis in the *assets* themselves sometimes is called the "inside" basis. When a parent corporation sells or disposes of its subsidiary's stock, gain or loss in its investment in the subsidiary stock is measured by subtracting the outside stock basis from the amount realized on the stock disposition. When the subsidiary sells or disposes of its assets, gain or loss is measured by subtracting the inside asset basis from the amount realized on the asset disposition.

Notice the effect of the subsidiary liquidation rules. After liquidation, the subsidiary stock disappears and the parent is left owning the old subsidiary's assets directly. The parent corporation's "outside" basis in the subsidiary stock simply disappears and the unrealized gain or loss from the parent corporation's stock in the subsidiary will never be taxed. Instead, the parent takes a transferred basis in the old subsidiary's assets. By thus retaining the "inside" basis, Congress has chosen to preserve the unrealized gain or loss in the subsidiary's assets rather than the gain or loss in the stock. In some cases, the parent's "outside" basis in the stock and the subsidiary's "inside" basis in its assets will be the same. In such cases, the preservation of the subsidiary's asset basis rather than the parent's stock basis makes little difference. In either event, the basis figure is the same. Since Congress was concerned with collecting only one corporate level tax, it will be sufficient to collect that tax upon sale or distribution of the assets received in liquidation. Sometimes, however, the parent's "outside" basis in its subsidiary stock will not be equal to the subsidiary's basis in its assets.[16] This situation can create troubling distortions. For example, in the above hypothetical, assume that the parent corporation had a basis of $120,000 in the subsidiary stock. Since the fair market value of the assets received on liquidation is only $100,000, the parent corporation has suffered a $20,000 loss. However, the loss will not be recognized and the parent will take the assets with a $25,000 basis. In this case, the parent arguably is disallowed a loss that it should be entitled to recognize at some point. On the other hand, if the parent corporation's basis in its stock had been only $10,000, there would be a potential $90,000 gain in the stock. By giving the parent a

---

16. This situation occurs, for example, if the parent purchased the subsidiary's stock from a third party or acquired the subsidiary stock in a tax-free reorganization or other nonrecognition transaction.

$25,000 basis in the assets, only a $75,000 gain is preserved. In such a case, the government would come up short.

TAX CONSEQUENCES TO MINORITY SHAREHOLDERS: §331

If the parent corporation owns 100% of the subsidiary's stock, there obviously will be no other shareholders to worry about. Since §332 applies to corporations with as little as 80% of the subsidiary's stock, however, one needs to consider minority shareholders holding the remainder of the subsidiary's stock. These minority shareholders may be individuals or corporations. Since §332 does not apply to minority shareholders, such shareholders are left to the recognition rules of §331 applicable to general liquidations.[17] Minority shareholders generally will recognize gain or loss under §331 and take a fair market value basis in the assets received under §334(a).[18]

TAX CONSEQUENCES TO THE LIQUIDATING SUBSIDIARY: §337

Distributions to the Parent Corporation

The in-kind distribution of assets to the parent corporation in liquidation of a subsidiary generally is not a taxable event to the liquidating subsidiary. More specifically, §337(a) provides that "[n]o gain or loss shall be recognized to the liquidating corporation on the distribution to the 80-percent distributee of any property in a complete liquidation to which §332 applies." As noted earlier, the rationale behind this nonrecognition is that the parent corporation eventually will recognize gain or loss on its distribution or sale of the assets, since it takes a transferred basis from the subsidiary. Congress means to collect only one corporate level tax and, thus, provides nonrecognition to the liquidating subsidiary.[19] Albeit deferred, responsibility for reporting

---

17. See discussion in Chapter 8.

18. There can be overlaps between the §332 liquidation rules and the tax-free reorganization rules. Thus, minority shareholders may also be entitled to nonrecognition if the overall liquidation transaction fits within one of the reorganization definitions in §368. Reorganizations are covered in Chapters 11-14.

19. As further confirmation of this rationale behind §337, notice the exception provided in §337(b)(2) for distributions to tax-exempt distributees. If the parent corporation is tax-exempt, the subsidiary will not receive nonrecognition treatment unless the property

gain or loss from appreciation or depreciation in the subsidiary's assets is transferred upon liquidation to the parent. As an exception to the general rule for the satisfaction of debt with appreciated property, §337(b)(1) also provides that any transfer of property to the parent in satisfaction of indebtedness shall be treated as a distribution in the §332 liquidation. In other words, the subsidiary will not recognize gain or loss. Pursuant to §334(b), the parent must take a transferred basis in these, as well as any other, assets.

Notice here that if the subsidiary sells off its assets for cash, it will be subject to taxation on the cash sale, even if the cash is shortly thereafter distributed to the parent corporation in complete liquidation.[20] This may initially appear inconsistent with the observation in Chapter 8 on general liquidations that in-kind distributions and asset sales in liquidation followed by cash distributions should achieve similar tax results. The problem in the parent-subsidiary liquidation context is that §337 provides for nonrecognition, in part, because the subsidiary gain or loss is preserved by giving the parent a transferred basis in the subsidiary's assets. If the parent corporation receives only cash, there is no asset to which the Code can attach a transferred basis. If corporate level gain is to be taxed, the tax must be collected at the time of the cash sale by the subsidiary. One way around this problem is for the subsidiary to sell its assets for an installment note instead of cash. The installment note is an asset that can take a transferred basis. In addition, although §453B(a) generally requires recognition of gain or loss upon disposition of an installment note, the liquidating subsidiary here is protected from recognition by §453B(d), which provides an exception for distributions to which §337 applies.

Distributions to Minority Shareholders

Distributions to minority shareholders are not covered by §337, but instead are governed by the general liquidation rules in §336.[21] Recall that under §336, gain or loss shall be recognized *except to the extent provided in* §337. Since §337 limits its nonrecognition rule to distributions "to the 80% distributee," or parent, the liquidating subsidiary will recognize *gain* on any in-kind assets distributed to minority shareholders. However, no loss will be permitted to the liquidating subsidiary on such in-kind distributions. Losses are prohibited by §336(d)(3), which provides that "[i]n the case of any

---

distributed will be used by the parent in an unrelated business and, thus, subject to tax in the parent's hands.

20. This is in sharp contrast to the pre-1986 provisions. Old §337 (prior to *General Utilities* repeal) permitted certain sales of assets in connection with liquidation of the corporation to be tax-free. This provision was repealed along with *General Utilities*.

21. Treas. Reg. §1.332-5.

liquidation to which section 332 applies, no loss shall be recognized to the liquidating corporation on any distribution in such liquidation." Notice the double standard. Gains on distributions to minority shareholders must be recognized, but losses cannot be recognized.

To understand the loss limitation on distributions to minority shareholders, it will be helpful to take a step back for a moment to look at the big picture. Remember the general rule now codified in §336 that in-kind distributions in complete liquidation are taxable to the liquidating corporation. As discussed in Chapter 8, this provision overruled or repealed the old *General Utilities* nonrecognition rule. Subsidiaries still can get nonrecognition treatment on distributions in complete liquidation under §337. Thus, §337 stands as one of the remaining exceptions to the repeal of *General Utilities*. Under the circumstances, Congress and the Treasury Department were, and continue to be, sensitive to potential abuses. The concern reflected in §336(d)(3) is that a liquidating subsidiary might deliberately arrange its affairs so as to distribute *gain* assets to the parent, thus taking advantage of the nonrecognition provided in §337, and at the same time distribute *loss* assets to the minority shareholder, thus taking advantage of the general recognition rules of §336.

Additional Anti-Abuse Provisions

Given that §337 remains as an exception to repeal of the old *General Utilities* nonrecognition rules, taxpayers have been rather creative in designing gain transactions to fit within §337, thereby avoiding taxation of gains, and designing loss transactions to fall outside of §337, thereby recognizing loss. Many such transactions have taken advantage of special provisions in the consolidated return regulations. As taxpayers have come up with such transactions, Congress and the Treasury Department have promulgated statutory provisions and regulations to combat them.

For example, one consolidated return regulation allows several affiliated corporations to combine their shares for purposes of meeting the 80% control tests necessary to be eligible for §§332 and 337 nonrecognition.[22] This consolidated return provision led creative taxpayers to design a transaction known as the "mirror transaction." Assume that a purchasing corporation is interested in acquiring some, but not all, assets of a target corporation. Since the assets are highly appreciated, a direct sale of the wanted assets would result in a substantial taxable gain to the target. In a "mirror transaction," the wanted and unwanted assets would be isolated in different members of the target's consolidated group. For example, the target might hold the wanted assets in subsidiary

---

22. Treas. Reg. §1.1502-34.

9. Liquidation of Subsidiaries

T1 (asset basis $500, fair market value $2,000) and the unwanted assets in subsidiary T2 (asset basis $500, fair market value $2,000). The purchasing corporation would then create two subsidiaries, P1 and P2, to "mirror" the target's two subsidiaries. P would create these subsidiaries by contributing cash to P1 equal to the value of T1's assets ($2,000) and cash to P2 equal to the value of T2's assets ($2,000). P's basis in the stock of each of its new subsidiaries, P1 and P2, is $2,000.[23] P now causes P1 to purchase one-half of T's stock for $2,000 and P2 to purchase the other half of T's stock, also for $2,000.

T now liquidates, distributing the T1 assets in complete liquidation to P1 and the T2 assets in complete liquidation to P2. By themselves, P1 and P2 only own 50% of T's stock. Thus, the liquidation would not be treated as a liquidation of a subsidiary under §§332 and 337. Under the consolidated return regulations, however, P1 and P2, as members of a consolidated group, will aggregate their shares in determining whether or not §332 applies.[24] Together, P1 and P2 own all of T's stock. As a result, the liquidation will be tax-free to P1 and P2 under §332 and tax-free to T under §337. No gain is recognized on the appreciation of T's assets. Since T1 has the wanted assets, P1 presumably will retain the T1 stock or cause T1 to liquidate so that P1 can hold the assets directly. In the meantime, P can sell off its P2 stock, thus getting rid of the unwanted assets. Since the fair market value of the P2 stock is equal to $2,000 and P's basis in its P2 stock is also $2,000, no gain will result from this sale of stock. When the dust settles, P and T have accomplished the transfer of appreciated assets without tax recognition of any gain.

To eliminate this particular end-run around repeal of the *General Utilities* rule, §337(c) now provides that the term "80% distributee" includes only the corporation meeting the stock ownership requirements of §332(b) and that the determination of an 80% distributee "shall be made without regard to any consolidated return regulation." As a result of §337(c), T in the above example would not receive nonrecognition treatment under §337. Pursuant to §336, T now will report gain upon distribution of the T1 and T2 stock in complete liquidation.

In addition to this specific provision in §337(c), Congress in §337(d) gave the Treasury Secretary specific authority to prescribe regulations to ensure that the purposes of the Tax Reform Act of 1986 — most important, the repeal of the old *General Utilities* rule as applied to liquidations — not be circumvented. Shortly after Congress eliminated advantages of the "mirror transaction" with §337(c), creative taxpayers came up with yet a different transaction using another consolidated return regulation. The so-called "son of mirror" transaction took advantage of investment adjustment basis rules contained in the consolidated return regulations.[25] The Treasury Department

---

23. I.R.C. §1012.
24. Treas. Reg. §1.1502-34.
25. Treas. Reg. §1.1502-32.

has used its §337(d) authority to promulgate regulations disallowing losses in "son of mirror" as well as other potentially abusive transactions.[26]

Given their complexity, the consolidated return regulations in general and the loss disallowance regulations in particular are beyond the scope of most introductory corporate tax courses. On the other hand, dealing with the consolidated return regulations and their implications increasingly has become part of the corporate tax lawyer's work. The references to the consolidated return regulations and related issues in this chapter are not meant to be comprehensive, but rather simply to introduce the student of corporate taxation to some of the issues presented.

Examples

A Basic Subsidiary Liquidation

1. a. Queen of the Night, Inc. (QNI), a mattress and bed discounter, has only one class of voting common stock outstanding. Papageno, Inc. (PI) owns 80% of the QNI stock with a basis of $200,000. The remaining 20% is owned by Papagena. Papagena has a basis of $5,000 in her shares. The QNI shareholders adopt a plan of liquidation on January 1 and QNI distributes all of its assets in liquidation on December 31. The QNI assets distributed to PI on liquidation were as follows:

	basis	fair market value
real estate	$150,000	$750,000
building	$30,000	$25,000
mattresses	$20,000	$25,000

In addition, QNI distributes the following assets to Papagena:

	basis	fair market value
cash	—	$50,000
portfolio stock	$100,000	$150,000

What are the tax consequences of the liquidation to PI? To Papagena? To QNI?

b. If the basis in the portfolio stock that was distributed to Papagena had been $200,000 instead of $100,000, how would the tax consequences to QNI and Papagena be different?

c. What if PI's basis in its QNI stock had been $150,000 instead of $200,000?

d. What if PI's basis in its QNI stock had been $900,000 instead of $200,000?

---

26. Treas. Reg. §1.1502-36.

Effective Electivity of §332

2. a. Figaro, Inc., is a wholly owned subsidiary of Bridal Shops, Inc. Figaro's primary asset is real estate with a basis of $800,000. The real estate has declined in value to $300,000. After Figaro adopts a plan of liquidation, but before distribution of the property in liquidation, Bridal Shops sells 21% of its Figaro stock to unrelated Buyer Bob. Figaro shortly thereafter liquidates, distributing the property, still valued at $300,000, to Bridal Shops and cash to Buyer Bob in complete liquidation. Assume that the liquidation distribution was pro rata overall, meaning that Bridal shops receives 79% of the value and Buyer Bob receives 21% of the value upon liquidation. What are the tax consequences to Figaro, Bridal Shops, and Buyer Bob?

   b. Assume that instead of Bridal Shops selling shares to Buyer Bob, Figaro decides to sell its real estate to Buyer Bob for $300,000 cash. Shortly thereafter, Figaro distributes the cash to Bridal Shops in complete liquidation. What tax consequences to Figaro? To Buyer Bob? To Bridal Shops?

   c. How would your answers to Example 2a change if Figaro's real estate had a basis and fair market value of $300,000 and Bridal Shops had a $400,000 basis in its remaining interest in Figaro?

Installment Notes

3. Tutti Corporation is a wholly owned subsidiary engaged in the business of selling and renting musical instruments. It owns a piece of real estate with a basis of $250,000 and a fair market value of $1 million. In addition, it maintains an inventory of musical instruments, also with a basis of $250,000 and valued at $1 million. Tutti sold the real estate to Buyer Bob for a five-year installment note calling for payments of $200,000 at the end of each year (plus interest). Before receiving any payments on the note, Tutti liquidates, distributing the note and the instruments to its parent in complete liquidation. What tax consequences to Tutti and its parent?

Debt to Parent Corporation

4. JFC is an American company that imports paper fans from Japan. JFC owns all of the outstanding stock of Butterfly Corporation. Several years ago, when Butterfly was short of cash, it borrowed $500,000 from JFC. Upon liquidation, Butterfly distributes assets with an overall basis of $200,000 and a fair market value of $600,000. Of this amount, $500,000 is payment for the principal amount of the loan from JFC, $20,000 is payment for interest on the loan, and the remainder is payment for the stock in liquidation. What are the tax consequences to JFC and Butterfly?

Explanations

1. a. The parent corporation, PI, received assets with an overall fair market value of $800,000 upon liquidation. Absent §332, PI would report a gain of $600,000 under §331 (amount realized of $800,000 less $200,000 stock basis). However, since PI owns stock meeting the two-part control test of §1504(a)(2) and since QNI is completely liquidating and transferring all of its property within the taxable year, PI will be eligible for nonrecognition under §332(a). Thus, PI will report no gain or loss upon receipt of the property from QNI.

   The basis of the assets now in PI's hands will be the same as it was in QNI's hands under §334(b)(1). Thus, the real estate's basis will continue to be $150,000, the building's basis will be $30,000 and the basis in the mattresses will be $20,000. PI's $200,000 basis in the QNI stock will disappear.

   QNI, the subsidiary, has distributed three assets to its parent, PI, in a complete liquidation to which §332 applies. There is a potential gain of $600,000 in the real estate, a potential loss of $5,000 in the building, and a potential gain of $5,000 in the mattresses. Under §337(a), none of this gain or loss will be recognized to QNI. Since PI took the assets with a substituted basis under §334(b)(1), QNI's assets effectively retain their historic basis. QNI's unrecognized gain in the real estate and mattresses and its loss in the building are thus preserved and presumably will be recognized to PI when it sells or disposes of the assets.

   The minority shareholder, Papagena, has received cash and property with a total value of $200,000. From this, she will subtract her $5,000 basis, resulting in a $195,000 taxable gain under §331. This will be capital gain from the sale of her stock. Her basis in the portfolio stock received will be its fair market value of $150,000 under §334(a). Since §332 only applies to distributions to the 80% distributee, QNI will be taxed on a $50,000 gain upon distribution of its portfolio stock to Papagena under §336.

   b. Even if the basis of QNI's portfolio stock had been $200,000, Papagena's gain under §331 would still be $195,000. She still received cash and property worth $200,000 and can subtract her $5,000 basis. Her basis in the stock received will still be the fair market value of $150,000. The change in basis does affect the tax consequences to QNI, however. QNI now has a realized loss of $50,000 on the distribution of the portfolio stock, but it will not be entitled to recognize this loss under §336(d)(3).

   c. This variation presents a discrepancy between the parent's (PI's) outside basis in its subsidiary's (QNI's) stock and the subsidiary's inside basis in the assets. In the first version of the hypothetical, PI's outside basis in the stock was $200,000 and QNI's overall inside basis in the assets attributable to PI was also $200,000. Thus, the potential gain of $600,000 with regard to PI's stock was the same as the overall gain reflected in QNI's assets. With a combination of §§332, 334(b), and 337, Congress has chosen to preserve only one level of corporate tax. When, as in the first variation of this hypothetical, the parent's gain in the stock and the subsidiary's gain in the assets is the same, it doesn't much matter which of the gains is preserved (except, perhaps, for character issues). In variation 2c, however, PI's unrealized gain in the stock was $650,000. The potential gain reflected in QNI's assets, however, still is only $600,000. Nevertheless, the tax consequences of this variation are exactly the same as in problem 1a. PI still will receive the assets on liquidation without recognizing any gain under §332. QNI still will get nonrecognition treatment on the distributions of assets under §337. Moreover, PI's basis in the assets will be the same as it was in QNI's hands. Thus, only $600,000 of potential future gain is preserved through use of a transferred basis. PI's basis in the QNI stock disappears and along with it the opportunity for the government to collect the extra $50,000 unrealized parent gain in the subsidiary stock. This example illustrates that when the "outside" gain from the parent's stock investment exceeds the "inside" gain or loss reflected in the subsidiary's assets, the subsidiary liquidation rules may result in a "windfall" to the corporate family.

d. If PI's basis in its QNI stock was $900,000, PI would realize a $100,000 *loss* (an "outside" loss) upon receipt of QNI's $800,000 worth of assets, which it will not be entitled to recognize pursuant to §332(a). At the same time, there is an "inside" *gain* reflected in QNI's assets. Nevertheless, the §334(b)(1) still applies a substituted basis rule, leaving PI with a potential gain upon subsequent disposition of the assets. PI's loss goes to "loss heaven" without being recognized. In this case, the liquidation rules result in lost tax benefits to the corporate family. This is a situation in which PI may wish to deliberately "flunk" the §332 tests. See Example 2's discussion of "effective electivity."

2. a. The issue here is whether the transfer of 21% of the stock successfully takes the transaction outside the scope of §332. Under §332, the distributee corporation must meet the 80% control tests at the time of adoption of a plan of liquidation and at all times until the property is distributed in complete liquidation. In effect, §332 is an elective provision. Put differently, the rigid rules of §332 also can operate as a trap for the unwary. Since the parent, Bridal Shops, in this case

does not meet the 80% control test throughout the relevant period of time, the liquidation is not covered by §332. Upon receipt of the real estate, Bridal Shops will report gain or loss under §331 (amount realized of $300,000 less Bridal Shop's basis in its remaining 79% of the Figaro stock). The real estate now in Bridal Shop's hands will take a fair market value basis of $300,000. Figaro has realized a $500,000 loss in real estate that it would like to recognize upon the liquidating distribution. Since §337 nonrecognition only applies to complete liquidations under §332 and Bridal Shops failed the §332 80% distributee test, Figaro's liquidating distribution will be governed by §336, which generally provides for recognition of gain or loss to the distributing corporation upon complete liquidation. I.R.C. §336(a). Under this provision, it would appear that Figaro could recognize its $500,000 loss.

Figaro may face problems under the §336(d)(1) loss limitation rules, however. Notice that although the distribution was pro rata overall, it was not pro rata with respect to the loss asset itself. Bridal Shops received a 100% interest in the loss property even though it had only a 79% interest in Figaro. Since Bridal Shops owned more than 50% of the stock, it was a "related party" for purposes of §336(d)(1). The loss would be disallowed unless Figaro distributed the loss property to the shareholders as tenants-in-common. If the primary motivation behind the transaction structure was Figaro's recognition of loss, Figaro would have been better off selling the loss property and distributing the proceeds to Bridal Shop as in Example 2b.

Buyer Bob recently purchased stock for cash and took a cost basis in his shares. He will subtract this cost basis from the cash amount received on liquidation and report the resulting gain or loss under §331.

b. If Figaro sells the loss property to Buyer Bob, it will be entitled to recognize the $500,000 loss. By its terms, §337 nonrecognition applies only on distributions in liquidation. On the other hand, the Treasury Department has §337(d) authority to prescribe regulations as necessary or appropriate to carry out the purposes of the Tax Reform Act of 1986 — the critical purpose in this context is repeal of the *General Utilities* doctrine. Under this authority, the Treasury Department could extend the scope of regulations beyond simply dealing with actual liquidation distributions. The regulations to date do not prohibit the type of loss taken by Figaro in this problem. Although the sale of the loss property may well have been designed to avoid nonrecognition, the loss in this case is economic, as opposed to artificial. In addition, the culprit that leads to recognition of loss here is the Code's different treatment of sales as opposed to contributions and distributions. Similar problems arise in other areas as well. Shareholders with loss property will sell loss property and contribute cash to the corporation under §351 in order to be able to recognize the loss. Similarly, Corporations will sell property rather than distribute it under §311 in order to recognize the loss.

Bridal Shops will receive $300,000 cash without recognition of any gain under §332. Its basis in the Figaro stock disappears. Buyer Bob simply owns the real estate with a $300,000 cost basis under §1012.

c. Bridal Shops has now realized a $100,000 loss on its investment in Figaro stock, which it would not be able to recognize under §332. The preliquidation sale of 21% to Buyer Bob should successfully cause Bridal Shops to "flunk" §332. As a result, Bridal Shops should now be able to recognize the loss under §331. Although §336 now technically requires Figaro to recognize gain or loss, there is no gain or loss to recognize since the basis equals the fair market value of the distributed property. Bridal Shops will take the property with a $300,000 fair market value under §334(a). The tax consequences to Bob would remain the same.

3. Ordinarily, a corporation must recognize gain upon disposition of an installment note to the extent of the difference between the fair market value of the note and the basis of the obligation under §453B(a). In the case of liquidation distributions, however, §453B(d) provides an exception for distributions to which §337(a) applies. Since Tutti is distributing the notes in a §332/§337 liquidation, it will report no gain upon distribution of the installment note. Nor will it report any gain upon the distribution of the instruments under the terms of §337 itself.

The parent will take a $250,000 transferred basis in the note and a $250,000 basis in the instruments from Tutti under §334(b). Any installment gain that would have been reported by Tutti effectively will now be reported by the parent as payments are received. The special relief provided in §453(h) for shareholders who receive installment notes in a liquidation distribution is unnecessary here since receipt of the note is eligible for nonrecognition in any event. Notice that the §453(h) relief is limited to liquidations to which §331 applies. (See Chapter 8 for further discussion of this provision.)

4. The repayment of principal on the loan will not be taxable to JFC under the tax principles applicable to borrowing generally. The payment of interest will be taxable. Repayments of the principal and interest are considered to be paid to the parent in its capacity as a creditor, not as a shareholder. Such payments are therefore outside the scope of §332. Any

excess payments above the principal and interest on the loan will be tax-free under §332.[27]

Butterfly has repaid the full amount of the loan and there is no cancellation of indebtedness income to worry about. In any event, §337(b)(1) provides that distributions in satisfaction of indebtedness will be considered part of the §337 distribution. Therefore, the subsidiary Butterfly will report no gain or loss.

---

27. Note that if the subsidiary's debt to its parent had exceeded the fair market value of its assets—i.e., if the subsidiary had been insolvent—§332 would not have applied at all. Instead, the parent would look to §165(g) regarding losses on worthless securities. Treas. Reg. §1.332-2(b) (applying §332 only to cases where the "recipient corporation receives at least partial payment for the stock").

PART V

Corporate
Acquisitions and
Divisions and
Other Corporate
Restructuring

Taxable Acquisitions

CHAPTER 10

Taxable Mergers and Acquisitions

INTRODUCTION

Corporate Acquisitions in General

Corporations sometimes purchase stock in other corporations to hold for investment, or purchase assets from other corporations to hold for investment or to use for business operations. The tax lawyer or tax professional generally would not refer to these day-to-day corporate purchases of stock or assets as corporate acquisitions. In common tax parlance, "corporate acquisition" generally refers to an acquisition of *control* by one corporation over another.[1] One corporation may acquire control over another through two different transaction types. First, a simple *asset* acquisition from the target corporation itself offers the purchaser direct control over the selling corporation's assets. Second, a *stock* acquisition from the target corporation's shareholders provides the purchaser with indirect control over the selling corporation's assets through its ownership of the target corporation's stock.

In a stock purchase, the purchasing corporation (P) acquires a controlling interest in the target corporation's (T) stock from the target's shareholders, thus becoming a parent to its newly acquired subsidiary (T). The parent may continue to operate T as a separate entity or may cause T to

---

1. For purposes of this chapter, "control" refers to the 80% control requirement under I.R.C. §1504 ("Affiliated Group Defined").

distribute its assets in a complete liquidation. In the case of a stock purchase followed immediately by a liquidation of T, the purchasing corporation acquires control over T's assets upon the liquidation distribution. If the purchase of the target's stock and the subsequent liquidation of the target are viewed as an integrated transaction under the step transaction doctrine, the stock purchase transaction looks much like a direct asset acquisition. When the dust settles, T has disappeared, P has direct control over the T assets, and the T shareholders hold the consideration paid by P.

Over the years, the courts and Congress have developed rules to determine when certain stock acquisitions should be treated as asset acquisitions for tax purposes. The current provisions in §338 provide an election to qualified purchasing corporations to treat certain stock acquisitions as asset acquisitions. In the end, the acquiring corporation can choose among three basic techniques for a taxable acquisition of control: (1) an asset acquisition, (2) a stock acquisition without a §338 election, and (3) a stock acquisition treated as an asset acquisition pursuant to a §338 election.

For any corporate acquisition transaction to proceed substantially beyond the initial discussion stages, the parties to the transaction must make several basic decisions regarding the structure of the transaction. This chapter begins with a brief discussion on the choice of acquisition structure and corporate acquisitions tax planning. Following this introduction, the chapter considers the particular structure and tax consequences of taxable asset acquisitions, taxable stock acquisitions with a §338 election, and taxable stock acquisitions without a §338 election.

Choice of Acquisition Structure

a) Taxable Acquisition Versus Tax-Free Reorganization

The parties to a corporate acquisition must first decide whether the transaction is to proceed as a taxable acquisition or a tax-free reorganization.[2] The label "taxable acquisition" is used simply to indicate that the selling corporation is taxable upon the sale of its assets or that the selling shareholders are taxable upon the sale of their stock. Any particular transaction will be classified as a tax-free reorganization only if it fits within one of the precise meanings of the term "reorganization" as defined in §368(a).[3] By definition, a corporate acquisition transaction that fails to fit within such a statutory nonrecognition provision is a taxable acquisition.

Under the statutory nonrecognition provisions applicable to corporate organizations and reorganizations, classification of an acquisitive transaction as tax-free depends largely upon the consideration used by the purchasing corporation in the exchange. Generally speaking, where the consideration paid by the purchasing corporation provides the target corporation or its shareholders with a substantial continuing proprietary interest in the reorganized corporate entity, the transaction is likely to meet one of the "reorganization" definitions.

Two relatively easy cases appear at the extremes. Imagine first a purchasing corporation acquiring target assets or stock entirely for cash and/or notes. Surely, such consideration provides no continuing proprietary interest in the corporate enterprise to the target corporation or its shareholders. The simple corporate acquisition of assets or stock for cash and/or notes is the classic "taxable acquisition"—the target corporation is taxable upon the sale of its assets or the target shareholders are taxable upon the sale of their stock under §§61(a)(3) and 1001. At the other extreme, imagine that the purchasing corporation (P) acquires all of the target's assets in exchange for P voting stock or acquires all of the target's stock from the T shareholders in exchange for P voting stock. In either case, the P voting stock provides the target corporation or its shareholders with a continuing proprietary interest in the reorganized corporation. Both transactions will fit one of the "reorganization" definitions of §368(a).[4]

---

2. This chapter focuses upon *taxable* acquisitions of control. The brief material presented here on tax-free reorganizations is designed simply to illustrate the key distinctions between taxable and tax-free acquisitions. Most of the discussion of tax-free reorganizations appears in subsequent chapters. Chapter 11 provides an introduction to basic tax-free reorganization principles, and Chapter 12 includes a detailed analysis of acquisitive tax-free reorganizations in particular.
3. In addition, a transfer of property to a controlled corporation in return for stock will be a tax-free transaction under §351. See discussion in Chapter 4.
4. The asset acquisition will fit within §368(a)(1)(C) (Type C reorganization). The stock acquisition will fit within §368(a)(1)(B) (Type B reorganization). For a full discussion of both types of tax-free acquisitions, see Chapter 12.

The first, and most important, difference in tax consequence between taxable acquisitions and tax-free acquisitive reorganizations is that the seller typically recognizes gain or loss in a taxable acquisition, but is eligible for nonrecognition treatment in the case of a tax-free reorganization.[5] In a tax-free asset acquisition, the target corporation is entitled to nonrecognition upon the exchange of its assets for eligible consideration, usually purchasing corporation stock.[6] In a tax-free stock acquisition, the target shareholders will not recognize gain or loss upon the transfer of T shares for eligible consideration from the purchasing corporation, also usually P stock.[7]

The second key distinction in tax consequence between taxable acquisitions and tax-free reorganizations involves an important set of corollary basis rules. The purchasing corporation in a taxable asset acquisition is entitled to a §1012 cost basis in assets purchased from the target. Consequently, the term often used to describe a taxable asset acquisition is a "cost basis acquisition." In contrast, the purchasing corporation in a tax-free asset acquisition is not entitled to a "cost basis," but instead takes the target corporation's assets with the same basis that the target corporation had.[8] The effect of this basis rule is a deferral of gain or loss recognition with respect to the target's assets until the purchasing corporation later sells, exchanges, or otherwise disposes of the target's assets in a taxable transaction. The term often used to describe this type of tax-free acquisitive reorganization is a "transferred" or carryover basis acquisition.[9]

In a taxable stock acquisition, the purchasing corporation is entitled to a §1012 cost basis only in the T shares purchased.[10] In contrast, the purchaser in a tax-free stock reorganization is not entitled to a cost basis in the acquired stock, but instead takes the stock with the same basis that it had

---

5. This is not to say that the target or its shareholders will *never* recognize gain or loss in a tax-free acquisitive reorganization. Shareholders will be taxable immediately, for example, on boot received as part of the transaction as well as payments received for accrued interest. These particular instances are considered in detail in Chapter 12. On the flip side, this is not to say that the selling shareholder *always* recognizes gain or loss in a taxable acquisition. If the selling shareholder is a corporation, it might escape tax on the stock sale under §338(h)(10). See discussion later in this chapter.

6. I.R.C. §361. The tax-free asset acquisition may take the form of a direct transfer of assets by the target to the purchaser or, instead, a state-law merger of the target into the purchaser.

7. I.R.C. §354.

8. I.R.C. §362.

9. The Treasury Department itself, along with many practitioners, continues to use the term "carryover basis." The technically correct term provided in the Code is "transferred basis." Property with a transferred basis is defined as property the basis of which is "determined in whole or in part by reference to the basis in the hands of the donor, grantor, or other transferor." I.R.C. §7701(a)(43). For purposes of this chapter, the terms "transferred basis" and "carryover basis" are used interchangeably.

10. The purchasing corporation will not also get a "cost basis" in T's assets unless it makes a proper election pursuant to §338. These issues are considered in subsequent sections of this chapter.

in the shareholder's hands. In addition, the target corporation's assets will retain the same "historic" basis that they had before the acquisition, again deferring recognition of gain or loss with respect to target's assets.

Given the dramatic difference in tax consequence, proper classification of a corporate acquisition transaction as either a taxable acquisition or a tax-free acquisitive reorganization is critically important to the parties to the transaction and to the government. Unless otherwise indicated, however, the remainder of this chapter is devoted to taxable acquisitions. The definitional boundaries distinguishing taxable acquisitions from tax-free reorganizations are considered in subsequent chapters on tax-free reorganizations.

b) Stock Versus Assets

The second basic decision required of the parties to a corporate acquisition is whether the purchaser will acquire stock or assets. Both tax and nontax factors will influence this decision. With regard to nontax factors, the purchaser's choice between stock or assets may be limited because the corporation is unwilling to negotiate a transfer of assets, the shareholders are unwilling to negotiate a transfer of stock, or some other outside restrictions prevent the sale or transfer of the assets or the stock. In addition, the choice of a stock or asset acquisition may be heavily influenced by the purchasing corporation's desire to minimize its exposure to any outstanding target corporation liabilities to creditors. Finally, an asset acquisition makes it easier for the purchasing corporation to isolate and avoid acquiring any "unwanted assets."

Both buyer and seller also will have several tax factors to consider in deciding between a taxable stock or asset sale. The taxable sale of assets results in an immediate taxable gain to the selling corporation and a cost basis in the assets to the purchasing corporation. The purchasing corporation's desire to acquire assets will depend upon the extent to which the assets are depreciable or otherwise would benefit from a cost basis, which usually is higher than the target corporation's historic basis. The selling corporation's willingness to sell assets will depend on the extent of the gain or loss reflected in the assets and the possibility of using any offsetting losses to reduce gains. The selling corporation also must consider the tax consequences to its shareholders. After a simple sale of all of its assets for cash, the target company presumably will distribute the cash to its shareholders in a liquidation distribution taxable to the shareholders. Thus, an asset acquisition often involves a rather immediate double tax — the corporation recognizes gain or loss on the sale of its assets for cash or notes and the shareholders recognize gain or loss on receipt of the cash or note proceeds upon the liquidation of their stock holdings. In contrast, a stock sale by the shareholders generally results in the immediate recognition of only the shareholder level tax — the shareholders recognize gain or loss upon the sale of their stock while the target corporation's assets remain with the target and retain their historic bases. Since the stock sale results in only one immediate tax, such sales often are favored over asset sales. These tax considerations will be considered further throughout this chapter.

c) To Elect or Not to Elect Under §338

Finally, in the case of a qualifying stock acquisition, the parties must decide whether or not the purchasing corporation will make a §338 election. Such an election essentially will provide the purchaser with a "cost basis" in the target's assets, but will also require the target to recognize gain or loss as if it had sold all of its assets. These significant tax consequences to both buyer and seller are considered in detail in subsequent sections of the chapter.

TAXABLE ASSET ACQUISITIONS

The Transaction

In a typical taxable asset acquisition, the selling or target corporation (T) transfers all or substantially all of its assets to the purchasing corporation (P) or a P subsidiary (S)[11] in exchange for cash and/or notes.[12] As part of the taxable acquisition, the purchasing corporation often will assume some or all of the selling corporation's liabilities. Generally, the target corporation will liquidate shortly after the exchange, distributing cash, notes and other consideration received to the T shareholders in exchange for their T shares. Sometimes, however, T may be kept alive for various reasons. For example, elderly shareholders may wish to keep the corporation alive in order to assure a stepped-up basis in the stock upon their death.[13]

---

11. A taxable asset acquisition need not necessarily involve a purchasing corporation. Instead, the purchaser might be a partnership, sole proprietor, or other entity. For purposes of this chapter, however, discussion of taxable asset transfers assumes a corporate purchaser, except where §336(e) elections are discussed later in this chapter.

12. P also may use other consideration, including P stock. Even where some P stock is used, the transaction will continue to be classified as a taxable acquisition unless the type and amount of P stock otherwise cause the transaction to fit within one of the tax-free reorganization definitions or the §351 contribution to a controlled corporation provision.

13. I.R.C. §1014. The shareholders also might wish to keep the corporation alive as a personal holding company, regulated investment company, or Subchapter S corporation.

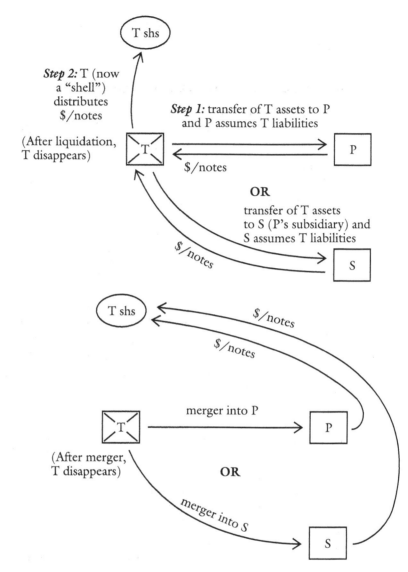

Another form of taxable asset acquisition is a state-law merger of the target into P or a P subsidiary[14] for cash, notes, or other consideration that would not qualify for tax-free reorganization treatment, sometimes referred to as a "cash merger." In this type of transaction, the consideration is transferred directly by P (or S) to the T shareholders and there is no need for T to formally liquidate. For tax purposes, however, the Service treats this transaction as a taxable asset transfer by T followed by T's complete liquidation.[15] For purposes of this chapter, reference to a "taxable asset acquisition" includes either the direct sale of assets or the taxable "cash merger."

---

14. Merger of the target into a P subsidiary is called a "forward triangular merger." Discussion of such forward mergers in the tax-free reorganization context appears in Chapter 12.
15. See Rev. Rul. 69-6, 1969-1 C.B. 104; Treas. Reg. §1.368-1(b).

327

Tax Consequences to the Selling Corporation and Its Shareholders

a) Tax Consequences to the Target Corporation

In a taxable asset acquisition, the selling target corporation (T) will recognize a taxable gain or loss immediately upon the sale of assets under §§61(a)(3) and 1001.[16] The amount and character of gain or loss on the sale of assets must be determined on an individual, asset-by-asset basis.[17] In the event of a sale of a going business for a lump-sum price, it will be necessary to allocate a portion of the purchase price to each asset sold. Since some of the assets sold will result in capital gain or loss while others will result in ordinary income,[18] the particular method used for allocating the purchase price will be important to the seller. Congress requires the "residual allocation method" for purposes of measuring the seller's gain or loss on the assets sold.[19]

Consistent with the rules for sales generally, T must include in its amount realized from the sale any liabilities assumed by the purchaser, and the amount of liability to which any property transferred was subject.[20] In addition, if the purchasing corporation assumes liabilities for accrued but as yet unpaid operating expenses of a cash basis target corporation, the liabilities assumed should be included in T's amount realized from the sale. If

---

16. To the extent that T receives notes from the purchaser in exchange for its assets, T may be entitled to report gain under the installment method provided in §453. However, use of the installment method is not permitted with respect to the sale of certain assets such as inventory. I.R.C. §453(b)(2)(B).

17. The landmark case requiring this fragmented, individual asset approach to a sale of business assets is Williams v. McGowan, 152 F.2d 570 (2d Cir. 1945).

18. In addition to ordinary income reported on ordinary income assets sold, the selling corporation may be required to report ordinary income on recapture items such as certain previously deducted depreciation, I.R.C. §§1239, 1245, 1250, and previously deducted tax benefit items. See I.R.C. §111. In addition, T will be required to report ordinary income with respect to any imputed interest on P notes bearing less than a market rate of interest, §483, or original issue discount (OID) with regard to P notes received in the exchange, §§1271-1275. A detailed discussion of recapture items, imputed interest, and OID rules is beyond the scope of this book.

19. The same method also will be used by the purchaser for purposes of allocating basis to the assets purchased. See discussion in subsequent section of this chapter entitled "Tax Consequences to the Purchasing Corporation." Regulations under §1060 explicitly cross-reference to and adopt the allocation rules in Treas. Reg. §1.338-6 and -7. Treas. Reg. §1.1060-1(c)(2). A discussion of the §§338 and 1060 residual allocation provisions follows in the section of this chapter entitled "Allocation of the Purchase Price."

20. The amount realized by T on any particular asset transferred subject to a mortgage will include the mortgage amount. Lest there be any doubt, the regulations explicitly state that, for purposes of determining the amount of the seller's gain or loss, "the fair market value of any property subject to a nonrecourse indebtedness will be treated as being not less than the amount of such indebtedness." Treas. Reg. §1.338-6(a)(2). On the other hand, the fair market value used for purposes of allocation of the purchase price is *gross* fair market value.

T has included the assumption of operating expense liabilities as proceeds from the sale, it follows that T should be entitled to deduct these assumed operating expenses.[21]

After a sale of all or substantially all of the target's assets, the target corporation is simply a "shell" holding the consideration received from the purchasing corporation along with any unsold assets. In most cases, a liquidation of the target quickly will follow the sale. Unless the target is making a liquidating distribution to a corporate parent,[22] the subsequent liquidation distribution will be a taxable event to the distributing target. In a simple sale of substantially all of the target's assets for cash, T will already have paid gain or loss upon the initial sale of assets. As a practical matter, there should be little remaining gain or loss to be reported by target upon subsequent liquidation distributions, since the distribution of cash to the shareholders will not trigger further gain. Keep in mind, however, that the target corporation still will be required to report gain or loss upon the liquidating distribution of any "unwanted assets" not sold to the purchaser as part of the asset acquisition.

b) Tax Consequences to the Target Shareholders

When the target corporation distributes cash and other assets to its shareholders in liquidation following T's taxable asset sale, the shareholders generally will report gain or loss upon the liquidating distribution pursuant to §331.[23] Consequently, a taxable asset acquisition usually results in a rather immediate double tax — the selling target is taxed upon receipt of consideration for the assets sold and the target shareholders subsequently are taxed when the target distributes this consideration to its shareholders.[24] If T sells assets in exchange for P installment notes and subsequently distributes the P notes in complete liquidation, the note distribution will trigger T's recognition of any gain previously deferred through installment reporting.[25]

---

21. See, e.g., Commercial Security Bank v. Comm'r, 77 T.C. 145 (1981); James M. Pierce Corp. v. Comm'r, 326 F.2d 67, 71-72 (8th Cir. 1964).
22. Subsidiary liquidations generally are not taxable to the distributing subsidiary pursuant to §337. See generally Chapter 9.
23. See Chapter 8. However, liquidation of a controlled subsidiary generally is treated as a nonrecognition event under tax rules more akin to the tax-free reorganization rules. See Chapter 9. If the target corporation is not liquidating, the distribution to the shareholders will be taxable pursuant to the §301 dividend rules. See Chapter 5.
24. The shareholder level reporting may be deferred to some extent if the target remains alive. In most cases, the liquidation of the target follows rather quickly upon the sale, and any period of deferral is likely to be brief.
25. T would have reported gain from the initial sale of assets only upon actual receipt of installment payments pursuant to §453. A subsequent distribution of the P notes to T's shareholders upon liquidation would be considered a "disposition of an installment obligation," triggering recognition of any gain previously deferred through use of the installment method. I.R.C. §453B.

Despite the general recognition provisions in §331, however, the T *sharehold-ers* who receive P notes upon T's liquidation may be eligible to report payments on the notes under the installment method as if they had sold their T stock on an installment basis directly to P.[26]

Tax Consequences to the Purchasing Corporation

The purchasing corporation in a taxable asset acquisition is entitled to a §1012 cost basis in assets purchased from the target.[27] Since the target corporation is fully reporting gain or loss on the asset transfer and since the purchasing corporation is paying full consideration for each asset, there is no reason to deny the purchaser the same cost basis generally available under §1012 for any purchase of assets. The overall price paid by the purchaser must be allocated among all the assets purchased in order to determine the cost basis of each particular asset in the purchaser's hands. Some of the acquired assets may be depreciable or amortizable and others may not, and some of the assets may be intended for resale and others not. Thus, the particular method used for allocating the purchase price also will be important to the purchaser.[28] Pursuant to §1060, the purchaser must use the same residual allocation method to compute basis in the purchased assets that was used by the seller to allocate purchase price in computing gain or loss on the asset sale.

Allocation of the Purchase Price

a) Tax Stakes for Buyer and Seller

Historically, buyer and seller in a taxable asset acquisition have had somewhat adverse interests regarding the allocation of purchase price to particular assets. Where appreciated capital assets are involved, the seller generally prefers as much as possible allocated to capital gain as opposed to ordinary income assets.[29] On the other hand, the buyer generally prefers as much as possible allocated to assets that are depreciable or amortizable or intended

---

26. See I.R.C. §453(h), (k). For a more detailed discussion of shareholder installment reporting under §453(h), see Chapter 8.

27. Assuming an arm's-length purchase, this cost basis should be equal to the fair market value of the assets.

28. Transaction costs are not taken into account for purposes of this allocation. Treas. Reg. §1.338-6(a)(2)(ii). Under §195 a taxpayer may elect to deduct a portion of "start-up expenditures" as defined in §195(c), with the balance amortizable over a 180-month period. These expenditures may include investigatory costs in determining whether to acquire a business and which business to acquire. See Rev. Rul. 99-23, 1999-1 C.B. 998.

29. In the case of loss assets, this preference would be reversed.

for resale, many of which are not considered capital assets. For example, sellers historically preferred allocation to goodwill or going concern value over covenants not to compete since sale of goodwill or going concern value generated capital gain while sale of covenants generated ordinary income. Buyers typically preferred allocation to covenants not to compete, since payments for such covenants were amortizable while payments for goodwill and going concern value were not. Because of these adverse interests, the Service generally respected an arm's-length agreement between buyer and seller containing a purchase price allocation.[30]

Although sellers generally still prefer allocations to capital assets and buyers generally still prefer allocations to depreciable or amortizable assets, tax changes over time have altered the tax landscape and the dynamics of the allocation of purchase price. First, purchased goodwill and certain other intangibles may be amortized pursuant to §197. Under this provision, specified purchased intangibles that are held in connection with the conduct of a trade or business or investment activity are amortizable over a 15-year period.[31] Most important from the buyer's point of view, the intangibles covered by §197 include goodwill, going concern value *and* covenants not to compete, along with several other intangibles. This change eliminates the buyer's incentive to allocate as much of the purchase price as possible to covenants not to compete as opposed to goodwill.

b) Special Allocation Rules: §1060[32]

i) Scope of the Special Allocation Rules

In addition to the §197 rules on amortization of purchased intangibles, the Code in §1060 also includes "special allocation rules for certain asset acquisitions." The §1060 special allocation rules apply only to "applicable asset acquisitions," defined to include transfers "of assets which constitute a trade or business" and "with respect to which the transferee's [buyer's] basis in such assets is determined wholly by reference to the consideration paid for such assets."[33] In other words, the rules are limited to taxable asset acquisitions of a *group* of assets that together constitute a trade or business.[34]

---

30. Comm'r v. Danielson, 378 F.2d 771 (3d Cir.), *cert. denied*, 389 U.S. 858 (1967).

31. See I.R.C. §197(a)-(d). Some limitations apply, however. For example, §197 amortization is not permitted "if the intangible is created in connection with a transaction (or series of related transactions) involving the acquisition of assets constituting a trade or business or substantial portion thereof." §197(c)(2). In addition, §197(f) disallows recognition of loss in the case of certain dispositions of §197 intangibles.

32. This section provides only an overview of the §1060 allocation rules.

33. I.R.C. §1060(c). Regulations clarify that the acquisition will be governed by §1060 if the "assets transferred constitute a trade or business in the hands of either the seller or the purchaser." Treas. Reg. §1.1060-1(b)(1).

34. The regulations here first cross-reference to the "active trade or business" requirement of §355(b), but continue to provide that even if the group of assets does not constitute a "trade

The classic example of a transaction covered by the §1060 allocation rules is a direct acquisition of all or substantially all of the target's assets for cash or notes.[35]

ii) The Residual Method

Under the residual allocation method prescribed by §1060, the "consideration received for the assets" is allocated to seven different classes of assets.[36] The overall purchase price for the group of assets is allocated to each class in sequence, with the "residual," or leftover, amount allocated to Class VII assets. Class I assets generally include cash and general deposit accounts.[37] The total amount to be allocated is first reduced by the amount of such Class I assets transferred, effectively allocating the purchase price to these assets on a dollar-for-dollar basis. Once the Class I assets are subtracted, the remainder is allocated first to Class II assets (actively traded personal property, including publicly traded stock, certificates of deposit, and foreign currency), then to Class III assets (accounts receivable, most debt instruments, and assets that the taxpayer marks to market at least annually), then to Class IV assets (inventory or property held primarily for sale to customers), then to Class V assets (all assets other than those in Classes I-IV and VI-VII), then to Class VI assets (all §197 intangible assets except goodwill and going concern value), and finally to Class VII assets (intangibles in the nature of goodwill and going concern value) in proportion to the fair market value of the assets on the purchase date.[38] An allocation to any particular asset cannot exceed the asset's fair market value.[39] This important restriction effectively assures that any surplus value paid for the assets will be allocated to Class VII assets such as goodwill.

---

or business" under §355, it will constitute a trade or business for purposes of §1060 "if its character is such that goodwill or going concern value could under any circumstances attach to such group." Treas. Reg. §1.1060-1(b)(2)(i). For discussion of the §355 "trade or business" requirement, see Chapter 13.

35. The discussion of §1060 here is limited to corporate transfers. Notice, however, that the special allocation rules are not limited to corporate asset sales.

36. Section 1060 and its accompanying regulations adopt the same allocation method used to allocate basis to various assets under §338(b)(5). The rationale for borrowing from §338 for the taxable asset acquisitions allocation rules was to provide roughly parallel treatment for taxable asset acquisitions and taxable stock acquisitions *treated as* asset acquisitions upon a proper §338 election. A detailed discussion of §338 transactions follows later in this chapter.

37. Treas. Reg. §1.338-6(b)(1). Class I assets are essentially cash and cash equivalents.

38. Notice that the common thread for Class I assets is extreme liquidity. Continuing this thread, Class II assets are highly liquid, but not *as* liquid as Class I assets, which, in turn, are not quite *as* liquid as those in Class III, which include "fast pay" assets such as accounts receivable.

39. Treas. Reg. §1.338-6(c)(1). See Treas. Reg. §1.338-6(a)(2) for the definition of "fair market value" for purposes of §§338 and 1060 allocations.

Early residual allocation method regulations were undoubtedly designed to ensure that any premium paid for the target's assets would be attributed to goodwill or going concern value. Since goodwill and going concern value were not then amortizable, the practical effect was to limit the buyer's ability to amortize. Put slightly differently, the residual method was designed to prevent the undervaluation of goodwill in the allocation process. The buyer's disadvantage from the residual method was often the seller's advantage. By allocating the premium paid to goodwill or going concern value, the method increased the portion of any gain eligible for capital gains treatment. As §197 provides 15-year amortization to intangibles, including goodwill and going concern value, the Treasury Department has retained the "residual method," but includes all of the amortizable §197 intangibles (as opposed to just goodwill and going concern value) in the residual Classes VI and VII.[40]

TAXABLE STOCK ACQUISITIONS

The Transaction

In a typical stock sale, the selling shareholders transfer some or all of their target corporation (T) stock to the purchasing corporation (P) or a P subsidiary (S) in exchange for cash and/or notes.[41] Assuming the purchase of a controlling interest, the purchasing corporation now becomes a parent to its newly acquired subsidiary. P may simply retain T as a distinct subsidiary. In this case, T remains intact as a corporate entity and remains liable to its creditors; P need not formally assume T's liabilities. As an alternative, the purchasing corporation may completely liquidate T, generally referred to as an "upstream merger." Upon such merger, P will become responsible for T's liabilities.

---

40. The separation of §197 intangibles into two separate classes probably reflects the notion that §197 intangibles such as customer lists, workplace in force, and patents (now included in Class VI) are slightly more "tangible" than goodwill and going concern value (now included in Class VII).

41. As in the case of taxable asset acquisitions, the consideration also may include other assets, and even P stock. The transaction will be classified as a taxable acquisition as long as it does not meet one of the reorganization definitions in I.R.C. §368(a). Although an individual or a noncorporate entity may also acquire a controlling interest in a target corporation, the focus of this chapter is upon corporate purchasers.

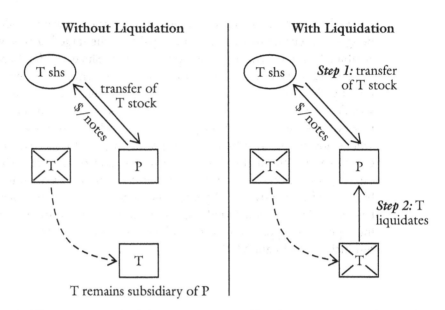

Tax Consequences to the Selling Corporation and Its Shareholders

The selling target shareholders will report gain or loss from sale of their T shares to P pursuant to §§61(a)(3) and 1001. If the T shareholders receive P notes in exchange for their T shares, they will be entitled to report gain under the installment method in §453.[42] The target corporation itself bears no immediate tax consequence. T simply remains intact, albeit now as a P subsidiary. Each T asset simply retains the same basis that it had prior to the stock acquisition. If T liquidates, it will recognize no gain or loss on the liquidating distribution pursuant to §337.[43]

A complex set of statutory and regulatory provisions addresses the extent to which the target corporation may continue to use any pre-existing net operating losses (NOLs) after the stock acquisition. In cases where the acquisition results in an "ownership change,"[44] the carryforward of unused NOLs is subject to limitations provided in §382.[45] If the target is liquidated or merged

---

42. I.R.C. §453(a), (b).
43. See Chapter 9.
44. There is an "ownership change," as defined in §382(g), if the percentage of target stock held by one or more 5% shareholders has increased by more than 50% over the lowest percentage of stock owned by such shareholders during the three-year testing period defined in §382(i).
45. In certain tax avoidance cases, the carryforward of NOLs may be denied entirely under special provisions in §269. The §382 rules are considered further in Chapter 12.

into P after the acquisition, P can continue to use T's unused NOLs, subject to restrictions provided in §381 and in the consolidated return regulations.[46] The details of these rules are beyond the scope of most basic courses in corporate taxation. In general, the idea behind the rules is to allow P to use the NOLs to offset T's future income, but not to offset P's future income.

Tax Consequences to the Purchasing Corporation

In a taxable stock acquisition, the purchasing corporation P is entitled to a §1012 cost basis in the T shares purchased. Since the T shareholders fully reported gain or loss on the sale of stock and P paid full consideration for the shares, there is no reason to deny such a cost basis in the stock. Absent an election under §338,[47] however, T (now a subsidiary of P) retains its assets with no change in asset basis. If T subsequently distributes its assets to P in a liquidating distribution, P will not recognize gain or loss pursuant to §332, and P will receive the assets with the same basis that T had in the assets.[48] Thus, even after liquidation, the T assets will retain their historic basis. In the end, notice that the tax consequences to both T and P are the same whether or not T liquidates. In either case, there is no immediate corporate level recognition of the gain or loss on T's assets, but instead a deferral of gain or loss until the purchasing corporation sells, distributes or otherwise disposes of the assets. In some cases, this deferral of the corporate level tax with respect to T's assets makes a stock acquisition more attractive than an asset acquisition.

STOCK ACQUISITIONS TREATED AS ASSET ACQUISITIONS: §338

Section 338: Roots and Background

When a purchasing corporation acquires a controlling stock interest in a target followed immediately by receipt of the target's assets in a liquidating distribution, the transaction begins to resemble an asset acquisition. The direct asset acquisition transfers assets from T to P in one step, whereas P's acquisition of T stock followed by T's liquidation transfers assets in two steps.

---

46. See Treas. Reg. §1.1502-21(c).
47. Detailed discussion of the §338 election appears later in this chapter.
48. I.R.C. §334(b). See Chapter 9 for a detailed discussion of subsidiary liquidations.

Direct Asset Acquisition | **Two-Step Asset Acquisition**

Consistent with the notion that economically equivalent transactions generally should receive equivalent tax treatment, Congress has attempted to achieve some parity between certain stock acquisitions and asset acquisition. The remainder of this chapter addresses those efforts, which culminated in the adoption of §338.

The starting point in any historical discussion of §338 is Kimbell-Diamond Milling Co. v. Comm'r.[49] The corporate taxpayer in Kimbell-Diamond sustained a fire casualty that destroyed its mill. In its search to replace the mill property, Kimbell-Diamond found Whaley, a target corporation with a comparable mill. Kimbell-Diamond purchased 100% of Whaley's stock and shortly thereafter liquidated the target, thus acquiring direct ownership of the mill. The issue before the court in Kimbell-Diamond was the proper basis in the mill for purposes of depreciation. Kimbell-Diamond argued that it had legitimately liquidated the target, Whaley, and that the mill should have the same basis in its hands that it had in the target Whaley's hands under the predecessor to §334(b). The Commissioner argued that since Kimbell-Diamond intended an asset acquisition of the mill, the purchase of stock and the subsequent liquidation should be integrated and viewed as a purchase of assets under the step transaction doctrine. The Court agreed that the transaction should be viewed as an asset acquisition, leaving Kimbell-Diamond with a cost basis in the mill instead of a substituted basis from the target, Whaley.[50]

---

49. 14 T.C. 74 (1950), aff'd per curiam, 187 F.2d 718 (5th Cir.), cert. denied, 342 U.S. 827 (1951).
50. The roles of the taxpayer and the Commissioner in Kimbell-Diamond are somewhat unusual. In acquisitions such as these, the purchaser's cost basis tends to be higher than a substituted basis in the target's assets. One would expect the purchaser to argue for cost basis. In Kimbell-Diamond, however, the purchaser's cost basis was lower than the target company's basis in the mill.

The government's success in *Kimbell-Diamond* was a Pyrrhic victory, however. Taxpayers quickly discovered that they could receive a cost basis in assets of an acquired subsidiary simply by establishing an *intent* to acquire assets. This intent-based standard led to great uncertainty. In 1954, Congress enacted old §334(b)(2), which codified the basic approach of *Kimbell-Diamond*, while attempting to eliminate the uncertainty of an intent-based test. Under old §334(b)(2), a purchaser of stock was entitled to a cost basis in the target company's assets if the purchaser acquired at least 80% of another corporation's stock during a 12-month period and the distribution of target assets was pursuant to a plan of liquidation adopted not more than two years after the stock purchase. Old §334(b)(2) was not elective and thus led to many traps for the unwary. In addition, the target corporation had to be liquidated in order to achieve a stepped-up basis for the purchasing corporation. In 1982, Congress replaced old §334(b)(2) with §338.[51] Since 1982, Congress has tinkered with details and ironed out kinks, but the *Kimbell-Diamond* case and the old §334(b)(2) roots of modern §338 remain unmistakable.

Qualifying Stock Purchases (QSPs)

Unlike the early statutory response to *Kimbell-Diamond* in old §334(b)(2), modern §338 is explicitly elective. The election is available only to corporations that have made a "qualified stock purchase," (QSP) defined as a transaction (or series of transactions) in which the purchasing corporation acquires stock in another corporation that meets the two-part 80% control test of §1504(a)(2) during a 12-month acquisition period.[52] In other words, §338 only applies to stock purchases of *control* sufficient to meet the 80% ownership test required for consolidated return reporting. Although such control need not be acquired in one transaction alone, it must be acquired during one 12-month period. The purchasing corporation must make a timely §338 election and, once made, the election is irrevocable.[53]

Note that §338 only applies to qualified stock *purchases*. The definition of "purchase" provided in §338(h)(3) excludes certain stock acquisitions. For example, target stock in which the purchasing corporation takes a

---

51. Tax Equity and Fiscal Responsibility Act of 1982, §224(a), Pub. L. No. 97-248.

52. I.R.C. §338(d)(3). The "acquisition period" is the "12-month period beginning with the date of the first acquisition by purchase of stock included in a qualified stock purchase." I.R.C. §338(h)(1).

53. To be timely, the election must be "not later than the 15th day of the 9th month beginning after the month in which the acquisition date occurs." I.R.C. §338(g)(1). The "acquisition date" is the "first day on which there is a qualified stock purchase," in general, the day on which the purchasing corporation's stock acquisitions during the 12-month period first meet the 80% tests. I.R.C. §338(h)(2).

transferred or substituted basis from the transferor or a §1014 basis from a decedent is not acquired by purchase. In addition, any stock acquired by P in a §351 or other tax-free reorganization is not acquired by purchase.[54] Finally, any stock acquired from a person the ownership of whose stock would be attributed to P under the §318 attribution rules is not acquired by purchase. A moment's reflection on these exclusions from the §338 "purchase" definition reveals an important underlying theme. The idea is that §338 should apply only to *taxable* acquisitions. In the ordinary taxable stock acquisition, the selling shareholders report gain or loss on the sale of stock and the purchasing shareholder takes the stock with a cost basis. Congress was willing to permit an elective cost basis[55] in the target's assets upon a transfer of control that was taxable to the selling shareholders.[56] For the most part, exclusions from the "purchase" definition provided in §338(h)(3) weed out stock transfers that were not taxable to the seller or transferor. Thus, for example, the §338 elective step-up is not available for acquisitions of control through a tax-free reorganization.

In addition to the shareholder level tax reported on the stock sale, §338 also ensures corporate level recognition to the target on the appreciation or depreciation in the value of its assets, using a "deemed sale" of the target's assets as a trigger for recognizing gain or loss. In the end, the tax consequences of a stock acquisition under §338 parallel the tax consequences of a direct asset acquisition. In each case, the target corporation recognizes a gain or loss on either the actual or the "deemed sale" of its assets and the target shareholders recognize capital gain or loss on either the sale of target stock to the purchasing corporation or the receipt of distributions in liquidation of the target. In addition, the purchasing corporation in either case effectively receives the target's assets with a cost basis. For purposes of this discussion, we use the term "cost basis"—at least in the §338 context—rather loosely. You may be surprised to discover that the term "cost basis" does not appear anywhere in the technical statutory language of §338. Although the statute and regulations tweak the language to address various particular circumstances, the conceptual force behind the §338 rules essentially is providing the purchaser a cost basis—often a stepped-up basis—in acquired assets. Keeping this basic concept in mind should help to clarify your understanding as you work through the technical statutory language.

---

54. To be acquired by "purchase" for purposes of §338, the stock must not have been acquired in an exchange to which §§351, 354, 355 or 356 applies. I.R.C. §338(h)(3)(A)(ii).
55. By its terms, §338 does not refer to the target's asset basis following a §338 election as either a "cost" or "stepped-up" basis, but instead as a "grossed-up" basis. This term and the mechanics of §338 are discussed later in this chapter.
56. Note the exception upon a §338(h)(10) election, discussed later in this chapter. Although the (h)(10) election permits the selling shareholder to avoid recognition of gain, the shareholder in that case is a corporation, whose shareholders, in turn, will presumably report taxable gain or loss in the future.

Deemed Sale and Repurchase of Assets by Target

If the purchasing corporation makes a §338 election following a QSP, the target corporation will be deemed to have engaged in two significant transactions. First, under §338(a)(1), the target is treated as if it "sold all of its assets at the close of the acquisition date at fair market value in a single transaction."[57] This sale triggers recognition of gain or loss to the target and is often described as the deemed sale by "old target" (old T). Second, under §338(a)(2) the target is treated "as a new corporation which purchased all of the assets referred to in paragraph (1)" on the following day. This deemed repurchase of the target corporation's assets is the transaction that effectively provides the purchaser with a "cost basis" in the target's assets and is often described as the deemed repurchase by "new target" (new T).

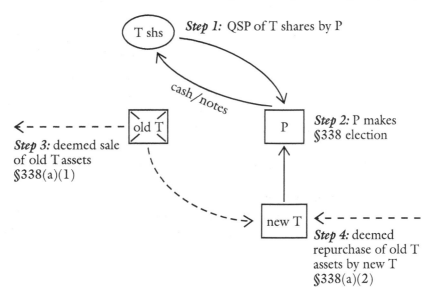

At first glance, the fictional two-step sale and repurchase provided by §338(a) seems unnecessarily complex. If Congress meant to permit a cost basis to the purchasing corporation in the target corporation's assets, why not just say so? First, step 1 of the two-step process extracts a heavy price for the "cost basis" ultimately permitted to the purchasing corporation in the target corporation's assets. Congress is unwilling to provide the cost — usually stepped-up — basis to the purchasing corporation unless the target corporation pays tax on the previously unrealized gain or loss in the target

---

57. Recall that under §338(h)(2), the acquisition date is the first date on which the purchasing corporation has acquired enough target stock to meet the 80% qualified stock purchase control tests.

assets. The §338(a)(1) deemed sale of target assets requires recognition of that gain or loss to the old target.

Second, notice that the deemed repurchase in step 2 takes place on the day *after* the acquisition date, and the target is treated as a new corporation. The new target created by the fiction in §338(a)(2) has lost most of its tax attributes. With few exceptions, "new target is treated as a new corporation that is unrelated to old target."[58] Thus, new target no longer has any earnings and profits, net operating losses or other relevant tax attributes.[59] By creating this new target for the deemed repurchase in step two, Congress meant to eliminate trafficking in tax attributes that might otherwise occur. For example, purchasing corporations might otherwise shop around for target corporations with net operating losses to acquire primarily for tax reasons.

Another consequence of having the deemed sale by the old target on one day and the deemed repurchase on the following day, is isolation of the old target's gain or loss from the §338(a)(1) deemed sale. Special rules included in §338 provide that "the target corporation shall not be treated as a member of an affiliated group with respect to the sale described in subsection (a)(1)."[60] This provision is also designed to prohibit trafficking—in this case, trafficking in the tax characteristics of the old target's deemed sale itself. Notice that §338(h)(9) restricts the target's membership in both the selling *and* purchasing affiliated groups with respect to the deemed sale. Thus, the restriction generally prevents the target from using gains or losses of other members of the selling consolidated group to offset gains or losses resulting from the §338(a)(1) deemed asset sale.[61] In addition, the old target is not considered a member of the purchasing corporation's affiliated group with respect to old T's deemed asset sale.[62] Consequently, the purchasing corporation will not be entitled to use the old target's gain or loss from the deemed sale to offset gain or loss on the purchasing group's consolidated return.

---

58. Treas. Reg. §1.338-1(b)(1).

59. The exceptions provided for in the regulations include various employee benefit, pension, annuity, profit sharing, stock bonus, or options plans. Treas. Reg. §1.338-1(b)(2). Thus, new target will continue to be liable for such obligations to its employees. In addition, new target will continue to be liable for old target's federal income tax liabilities. Treas. Reg. §1.338-1(b)(3)(i), (ii).

60. I.R.C. §338(h)(9).

61. Also in §338(h)(9), however, Congress authorized the Treasury Department to formulate exceptions. If old T is the common parent of an affiliated group, the deemed sale gain can be reported on a final consolidated return for old T. Treas. Reg. §1.338-10(a)(1). On the other hand, if the target is otherwise a member of a selling group, the old target is treated as "disaffiliated" from the group immediately before the deemed sale of its assets and will file a separate "deemed sale return," including only items resulting from the deemed sale and limited carryover items. Treas. Reg. §1.338-10(a)(2)(i).

62. Treas. Reg. §1.338-10(a)(5).

Mechanics of the §338(a)(1) Deemed Sale

The statutory language in §338(a)(1) merely provides that "the target shall be treated as having sold all of its assets at the close of the acquisition date at fair market value in a single transaction."

Instead of adopting a traditional "arm's-length buyer and seller" definition of fair market value, the Treasury Regulations use a grossed-up aggregate deemed sales price (ADSP) as the price at which target is deemed to have sold all of its assets for purposes of §338(a)(1).[63] Under the regulations, the ADSP is based on the amount realized by the target shareholders on the sale of stock to the purchasing corporation.[64]

In addition, ADSP includes any old target liability "that is properly taken into account in the amount realized under general principles of tax law that would apply if old target had sold its assets to an unrelated person for consideration that included the discharge of its liabilities."[65] This inclusion of liabilities in the §338(a)(1) deemed sales price is consistent with the general tax principle that the amount realized on any sale includes liabilities assumed by the buyer or liabilities to which the assets sold were subject. For purposes of computing ADSP, the target's liabilities also include any tax liability from the deemed asset sale itself, including recapture items arising from the deemed sale.[66] Since gain or loss from the deemed asset sale is determined on an asset-by-asset basis, old target must allocate the overall ADSP price among its assets. The allocation method used for this purpose generally will be the same allocation method used for determining the basis of each asset in the purchaser's hands.[67] Character of the old target's gain or loss as capital or ordinary will depend upon the character of each asset sold.

Notice that the statutory language in §338(a)(1) refers to a deemed sale by old T of *all* of its assets at fair market value. In other words, the target

---

63. Treas. Reg. §1.338-4(a), (b).

64. The regulations actually refer to the "grossed-up amount realized on the sale to the purchasing corporation of the purchasing corporation's recently purchased target stock." Treas. Reg. §1.338-4(b)(i). This amount realized is "determined as if . . . The installment method were not available. . . ." Id. At (c)(1)(i). The amount realized is then "grossed-up" by "divid[ing] by the percentage of target stock (by value, determined on the acquisition date) attributable to that recently purchased target stock. Id. At (c)(ii). Finally, old T is entitled to subtract from amount realized those selling costs that would ordinarily be permitted in a sale of stock to an unrelated third party. Id. At (c)(iii).

65. Treas. Reg. §1.338-4(d)(1).

66. Id. The regulations acknowledge that the deemed sale itself can increase or decrease ADSP by creating or reducing a tax liability. Thus, the determination of ADSP "may require trial and error computations." Treas. Reg. §1.338-4(e).

67. This is the residual method proscribed by the Treasury Department pursuant to authority granted in §338(b)(5). Treas. Reg. §1.338-6. See also discussion in this chapter on "Mechanics of the §338(a)(2) Deemed Repurchase." The residual method also is used for direct taxable asset acquisitions pursuant to §1060. See earlier discussion in this chapter on taxable asset acquisitions.

corporation is deemed to sell all of its assets, and gain or loss amounts should be the same whether the purchasing corporation made a QSP of 80% or 100%, or some percentage between the two. When the purchasing corporation makes a QSP of less than 100%, the regulation's approach alone will not achieve this result. Imagine, for example, a target corporation with assets worth $1 million and a basis of $250,000. P acquires 90% of the target's stock in a QSP for $900,000. If this $900,000 is used as the ADSP for purposes of computing old T's §338(a)(1) deemed asset sale gain, the §338 election will not have triggered full taxation on all the appreciation in old T's assets. The regulations address this problem by defining ADSP to include a *grossed-up amount realized* from the QSP.[68] To get *grossed-up* ADSP, the regulations divide the amount realized from the actual sale ($900,000) by the percentage of recently purchased, or QSP, stock (90%), thus arriving at a $1 million sales price for the deemed §338(a)(1) sale.

Mechanics of the §338(a)(2) Deemed Repurchase

Although the basic idea behind the deemed repurchase of assets by the new target is to provide a cost basis to the purchasing corporation in the target's assets, the mechanics of the repurchase can be a bit puzzling for the novice. Instead of using the term "cost basis," §338(b)(1) provides that the purchase price for purposes of the deemed repurchase is the sum of "(A) the grossed-up basis of the purchasing corporation's recently purchased stock, and (B) the basis of the purchasing corporation's nonrecently purchased stock."[69] There are two reasons for the complexity here. First, the purchasing corporation need only purchase the required 80% interest during the 12-month acquisition period. The purchasing corporation itself already may own additional target stock that it acquired before this acquisition period. The Code refers to this stock as "nonrecently purchased" stock. More colloquially, it is sometimes referred to as "old and cold" stock. The purchasing corporation generally is not entitled to a cost basis with respect to old and cold stock that was not part of the QSP. Thus, absent an additional special election, the cost basis is permitted only for the qualifying shares.[70]

---

68. Treas. Reg. §1.338-4(b), (c)(1).
69. The §338 regulations use the term "adjusted grossed-up basis" (AGUB) to refer to "the amount for which new target is deemed to have purchased all of its assets in the deemed purchase under section 338(a)(2)." Treas. Reg. §1.338-5(a). Under the regulations, AGUB "is the sum of (i) The grossed-up basis in the purchasing corporation's recently purchased target stock; (ii) The purchasing corporation's basis in nonrecently purchased target stock; and (iii) The liabilities of the new target." Id. At (b)(i)-(iii).
70. Ordinarily, the historical basis for the old and cold shares is simply added to the "grossed-up" basis of the recently purchased shares according to §338(b)(1)(B). If the purchasing corporation would like to receive a cost basis with respect to this old stock as well, it is

A second reason for the complexity is that the purchasing corporation will not necessarily own all of the target company's stock after the qualified acquisition. Up to 20% of the target stock still may be owned by minority shareholders. Nevertheless, since the old target recognized full gain or loss on the deemed asset sale, Congress wanted to provide a full step-up in basis for the target assets. This is achieved through use of a "grossed-up" basis. To figure the "grossed-up" basis, §338(b)(4) instructs the purchasing corporation to multiply the cost basis for stock purchased during the 12-month acquisition period by a fraction the numerator of which is 100% minus the old and cold (nonrecently purchased) stock and the denominator of which is the percentage of qualifying or recently purchased stock.[71] If there are no minority shareholders, this fraction always will be equal to one. Obviously, multiplying the cost basis of the stock by one will leave the cost basis unchanged. Thus, in the simple case with no minority shareholders and no complicating liabilities, the purchase price for the deemed repurchase by the new target simply will be the cost of the qualifying or recently purchased stock plus the purchasing corporation's basis in any old and cold or nonrecently purchased shares of target stock.

Assume, for example, that the purchasing corporation (P) acquired 10% of the target corporation (T) many years ago for $1,000. This 10% of the T stock in P's hands is nonrecently purchased or old and cold stock. In a qualified stock purchase, P acquires the remaining 90% for $900,000. As of the acquisition date, T owns assets with a basis of $250,000 and a fair market value of $1 million. Whether or not P makes a §338 election, the T shareholders will report gain or loss on the sale of their T shares. If P does not make a §338 election, T will simply be a new subsidiary of P, retaining its historical asset basis of $250,000. Even if P liquidates T, neither P nor T will recognize gain or loss under §§332 and 337, and the target assets still will have a $250,000 transferred basis in P's hands under §334(b).

If P makes a §338 election, old T will be deemed to sell all of its assets on the acquisition date. Old T will report a gain of $750,000 on this deemed sale.[72] On the following day, new T will be deemed to repurchase the same assets. The purchase price will be the grossed-up basis in P's recently purchased stock plus the basis of the nonrecently purchased stock. To determine grossed-up basis here, P will multiply the basis of the 90%

---

possible to do so by making a second election under §338(b)(3). The price extracted for this secondary election is recognition of gain on a deemed sale of the old and cold, or nonrecently purchased, target corporation stock.

71. "Recently purchased stock" is the T stock acquired by P during the 12-month acquisition period and held by P on the acquisition date (i.e., the 80% or more QSP). I.R.C. §338(b)(6)(A). "Nonrecently purchased stock" includes any T stock held by P on the acquisition date that is not recently purchased stock (i.e., P's "old and cold" T stock). I.R.C. §338(b)(6)(B).

72. The amount realized is the $1 million grossed-up ADSP ($900,000/0.9). See Treas. Reg. §1.338-4(b), (c)(1). From this, old T subtracts its $250,000 basis in the assets.

recently purchased stock ($900,000) by a fraction of 90%/90% or 1.[73] In other words, the grossed-up basis is simply the $900,000 cost basis of the recently purchased shares. This will always be the case where no minority shareholders are involved. To this grossed-up basis, P can add the $1,000 basis from the old and cold shares.[74] Thus, new T's basis in the assets after the deemed repurchase will be $901,000. This overall basis then must be allocated among new T's assets.[75] Notice that the asset basis is not fully stepped-up to the $1 million fair market value. This is because P is not eligible for the step-up in basis with respect to the 10% nonrecently purchased stock.[76]

Changing the facts slightly, assume that P purchases 90% in a QSP, but that the remaining 10% is owned by minority shareholders. If P makes a §338 election, old T still is deemed to sell all of its assets as of the acquisition date. Thus, old T will still report a $750,000 gain. Since P has no nonrecently purchased stock, the purchase price on the deemed repurchase by new T under §338(b)(1) is just the grossed-up basis of the 90% recently purchased stock. P now will multiply its $900,000 cost basis in the recently purchased shares by a fraction of 100%/90%.[77] Note that the grossed-up basis then is $1 million, the fair market value of T's assets as of the acquisition date. Since T reported full gain on the deemed sale of its assets, and since all of P's shares were recently acquired as part of a QSP, §338 here permits a full step-up in the basis of T's assets.[78]

Qualified Stock Purchase Without a §338 Election Followed by Liquidation or Reorganization of Target

One lingering question after the adoption of old §334(b)(2) and its §338 successor was whether a purchaser that failed to meet the formal statutory requirements for a stepped-up basis in assets under old §334(b)(2) or failed to make a §338 election following a QSP still could receive a stepped-up basis in the target's assets by arguing an intent to acquire assets under the Kimbell-Diamond step-transaction doctrine. The legislative history behind §338 attempted to resolve the lingering question, declaring that §338 was

---

73. Under §338(b)(4), the numerator of the fraction is 100% less the 10% old and cold stock, and the denominator is the 90% recently purchased stock.

74. I.R.C. §338(b)(1)(B).

75. I.R.C. §338(b)(5); Treas. Reg. §1.338-6, 7.

76. P may be able to get the additional step-up in basis with respect to these shares by making a secondary election under §338(b)(3) and recognizing gain on the appreciation in those old shares.

77. Under §338(b)(4), the numerator is 100% less the nonrecently purchased shares. In this case, there are no such shares. The denominator is the recently purchased stock, here 90%.

78. This chapter often uses the term "stepped-up basis" in lieu of "cost basis." I use this term since, in most cases, target assets have appreciated and the buyer's interest in a §338 election is stepped-up basis to fair market value. Keep in mind, however, that if the target's cost basis exceeds fair market value, a §338 election can result in a "stepped-down basis."

"intended to replace any nonstatutory treatment of a stock purchase as an asset purchase under the Kimbell-Diamond doctrine."[79] Despite this declaration, the *Kimbell-Diamond* doctrine has refused to disappear quietly.

In the case of Yoc Heating Corp. v. Commissioner,[80] the purchasing corporation (P) wanted to acquire T assets with a cost basis. Unable to negotiate a purchase of the target corporation's assets, P subsequently acquired 85% of the target corporation's stock for cash and notes.[81] Shortly after the stock acquisition, P formed a new subsidiary (X) and offered the T shareholders, including P itself, one share of X stock in exchange for every three shares of T stock. Not surprisingly, P accepted this offer to exchange its recently acquired 85% interest in T for additional X shares. The T minority shareholders were "bought out" for cash.

The government in *Yoc Heating* argued that the stock exchange was covered by the tax-free reorganization rules under which X received a substituted basis in T assets under §362(b). The purchaser, on the other hand, argued under the step-transaction doctrine that its various steps were integral parts of a plan to acquire a controlling interest in the target's assets. The Tax Court agreed to view the various steps as part of an integrated transaction. Before the overall integrated transaction, 85% of the target was owned by unrelated shareholders. After the integrated transaction, the purchaser held an 85% controlling interest. Since the historic shareholders no longer held a substantial interest in the corporate enterprise, the Tax Court found that the transaction failed to meet the continuity of proprietary interest test necessary to classify the acquisition as a tax-free reorganization.[82] Since it was not a tax-free liquidation of a subsidiary or a tax-free reorganization, the Tax Court held that the transaction was "by way of purchase with an accompanying step up in basis."[83] In the end, the taxpayer in *Yoc Heating* received a stepped-up basis in the appreciated target assets following an acquisition of the target's stock *without* satisfying the statutory requirements of old §334(b)(2).

The *Yoc Heating* integrated transaction rule seemed to support a stepped-up basis in target assets after a qualified stock acquisition even in some cases where the purchaser did *not* make a §338 election. The Treasury Department

---

79. H.R. Conf. Rep. No. 760, 97th Cong., 2d Sess. 467, 536 (1982). This approach was confirmed by Rev. Rul. 90-95, 1990-2 C.B. 67, 68 ("Section 338 of the Code replaced the *Kimbell-Diamond* doctrine and governs whether a corporation's acquisition of stock is treated as an asset purchase.") and later by regulations now found at Treas. Reg. §1.338-3(d). See T.D. 8940, 66 Fed. Reg. 9925, 9926 (Feb. 13, 2001) ("These rules . . . effectuate Congressional intent, in replacing former section 334(b)(2) with section 338, that the deemed sale results provided by section 338 not be available through transactions within the purchasing group after the acquisition.").

80. 61 T.C. 168, 178 (1973).

81. Under the current provisions in §338, this stock acquisition would be considered a QSP.

82. The Treasury Department has substantially changed its position regarding "historic" continuity of interest. For further discussion, see Chapter 11.

83. 61 T.C. 168, 178.

reacted by adding a provision to the §338 regulations, commonly known as the "anti-*Yoc Heating*" regulations.[84] The "anti-*Yoc Heating*" regulations apply only if target assets are transferred to the purchasing corporation (or an affiliate) following a qualified stock purchase for which a §338 election was *not* made.[85] Recall that the only element lacking for tax-free reorganization treatment in *Yoc Heating* was continuity of interest because the historic shareholders of T did not hold a substantial interest in X after the transaction. The §338 regulations solved the dilemma by effectively deeming the recent purchaser to be an historic shareholder.[86] As a result, the merger following the QSP can be treated as a tax-free reorganization, resulting in a substituted basis for the target assets pursuant to §362(b). Given the apparent demise of the historic shareholder continuity of interest requirements, the "anti-*Yoc Heating*" regulations are probably best understood as turning off the step-transaction doctrine and treating a first step QSP in a multistep acquisition as an independent event when the overall integrated transaction would otherwise be classified as a taxable acquisition.[87]

Notice the unusual and creative regulatory response provided by the Treasury Department in the "anti-*Yoc Heating*" regulations. The regulation effectively "bifurcates" the transaction, treating the transaction as a tax-free reorganization as to the purchaser and target, but a taxable acquisition as to minority shareholders. The regulation provides that tax-free reorganization treatment will not be available to minority shareholders unless the transaction would otherwise qualify as a reorganization.[88] Thus, the minority shareholders "bought out" for cash in the *Yoc Heating* transaction would not be eligible to treat the exchange of their old T shares as received in tax-free reorganization pursuant to §354. The Treasury Department defends this treatment as "the simplest and most effective means" of achieving the intent of §338.[89] It believed that extension of this regulatory reorganization treatment to minority shareholders was inappropriate as applied to an integrated transaction in which the "owner of the majority stake in the target receives solely cash. Thus, extension of reorganization treatment to the minority shareholders in this case would inappropriately alter general reorganization principles, and would not be grounded in the policies of section 338."[90]

---

84. Treas. Reg. §1.338-3(d). This Treasury Department position had previously been reflected in Rev. Rul. 90-95, 1990-2 C.B. 67. See note 79.

85. Treas. Reg. §1.338-3(d)(1). Compare Treas. Reg. §1.338-3(c), addressing the effect of post-acquisition events on eligibility to make a §338 election.

86. Treas. Reg. §1.338-3(d)(2). See also id. At (d)(5)(ii).

87. But see Treas. Reg. §1.338(h)(10)-1(c)(2), which *retains* the step-transaction approach when the integrated transaction would be classified as a tax-free reorganization. See Chapter 11 for a full discussion of the revised continuity of interest regulations and the potential overlaps between §338 and the tax-free reorganization provisions.

88. Treas. Reg. §1.338-3(d)(1). For further detailed discussion of acquisitive reorganization rules and their potential overlaps with §338, see Chapter 12.

89. T.D. 8626, 60 Fed. Reg. 54,942, 54,943 (Oct. 27, 1995) (preamble to "anti-*Yoc Heating*" regulations).

90. Id.

Deciding Whether to Make the §338 Election

Prior to the 1986 repeal of the *General Utilities* rule, §338 elections were rather attractive because the §338 deemed sale by old T did not result in taxable gain or loss.[91] As a result, the purchasing corporation could acquire a stepped-up basis in the target's assets without the target ever having recognized gain on its unrealized appreciation. Since 1986, however, the deemed sale by old T will trigger recognition of the target's gain or loss. Thus, the step-up in basis provided by a §338 election often comes at a heavy price. In our example above, old T was required to report a taxable gain of $750,000. Even though responsibility for this gain technically belongs to T, as a practical matter, the price to P of the overall acquisition often will increase substantially if the purchaser plans to make a §338 election. Given the large "toll charge" in the form of a taxable gain to T, a §338 election will be unwise for many taxpayers. On the other hand, if T's assets are depreciable or include unimproved property that P plans to sell reasonably quickly, a step-up in the basis of T's appreciated assets may be attractive to P. To decide whether such an election is sensible, the taxable gain from the deemed sale by the target must be weighed against the value to the purchasing corporation of the basis step-up. For example, it may be that the discounted present value of additional depreciation allowances provided by the higher basis will exceed the taxable gain to the target under §338(a)(1).[92]

SPECIAL PROBLEMS UNDER §338: AFFILIATED CORPORATIONS AND CONSISTENCY RULES

Target as Part of a Selling Affiliated Group

Special tax issues emerge when the target corporation is part of an affiliated group of corporations, and the target recognizes gain as a result of a §338 election. Imagine, for example, that T's sole asset is all of the stock of corporation T-1. In other words, T is a parent holding company of a wholly owned subsidiary. If P acquires all of T's stock and makes a §338 election with respect to its qualified stock purchase, T will be deemed to have sold its T-1 stock under §338(a)(1) and to repurchase the same T-1 stock under §338(a)(2). The deemed repurchase under §338(a)(2) is also a QSP. (See diagram on the next page.)

---

91. Prior to 1986, the deemed sale of assets by the target was considered to be a tax-free sale in connection with liquidation under *old* §337. For discussion of these rules prior to repeal of *General Utilities*, see Chapter 8.
92. For an effort to describe the assessments involved mathematically, see Mark Kotlarsky, Stepping-Up Basis: Purchase of Stock or Purchase of Assets, 39 Tax Notes 1011 (1988).

Absent special rules, if T makes a §338 election with respect to its deemed acquisition of T-1 stock, T-1 now will be deemed to have sold all of its assets under §338(a)(1). Thus, T would be taxed on the sale of its T stock and T-1 would be taxed on the deemed sale of its assets.

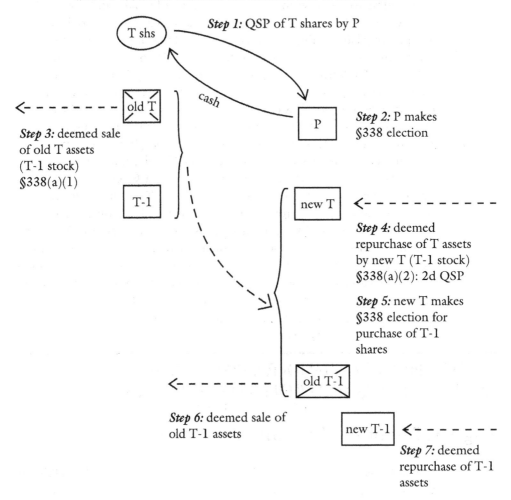

The potential for cascading taxes multiplies as the corporate chain of tiered subsidiaries lengthens. For example, assume that T-1's only asset, in turn, is all of the stock of second-tier subsidiary, T-2. T is taxed on its sale of T-1 stock to P. Again, assuming a §338 election by P and an actual or deemed §338 election by T and T-1, T-1 is taxed on its deemed sale of T-2 stock, and T-2 is taxed on the deemed sale of its assets. Under certain conditions, the §338 regulations provide relief from this multiple tax potential.[93]

---

93. Treas. Reg. §1.338-4(h)(1), (2). The regulation only applies to the deemed sale of a target affiliate where a §338 election was made for the target and the target affiliate. Treas. Reg. §1.338-4(h)(2), (8), exs. 1, 2. The relief provided for in this regulation is not available when a §338(h)(10) election has been made for the target affiliate. A discussion of §338(h)(10) appears in the next section.

If eligible for this regulatory relief, the target (T) will not recognize gain or loss from the deemed sale of the target affiliate's (T-1) stock, but T-1 still will be required to recognize gain or loss on the deemed sale of its assets. This regulatory provision is known as the "anticascading rule."

The Special §338(h)(10) Election

A related concern for a target and its affiliates arises when the target is a wholly owned subsidiary of a corporate seller, CS. Assume, for example, that purchaser P makes a cash purchase of all of T's stock from CS. CS will be taxed upon the sale of the T stock. CS's shareholders also will report gain or loss under §301 or §331 when the cash received from P is distributed to them in the form of a dividend or liquidating distribution.[94] In addition, if P makes a §338 election, T will report gain or loss from the deemed sale of its assets under §338(a)(1).

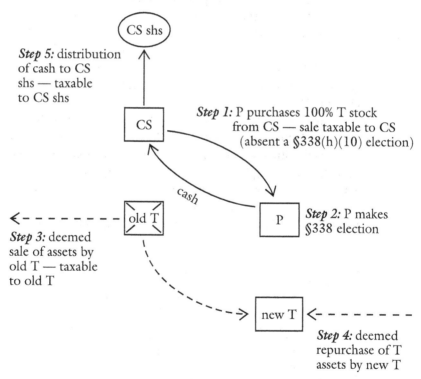

Step 5: distribution of cash to CS shs — taxable to CS shs

Step 1: P purchases 100% T stock from CS — sale taxable to CS (absent a §338(h)(10) election)

Step 2: P makes §338 election

Step 3: deemed sale of assets by old T — taxable to old T

Step 4: deemed repurchase of T assets by new T

The target group's concern is the multiple taxes imposed upon old T, CS and the CS shareholders. If T simply had distributed its assets to CS in complete liquidation, CS and T would have been entitled to nonrecognition under §§332 and 337.[95] CS then could have sold the T assets directly to P in

94. See Chapters 5 and 8.
95. See Chapter 9.

a taxable asset sale. As an alternative, T could have sold its assets directly to P in a taxable asset sale followed by a liquidating distribution to its parent, CS. Again, CS would have been entitled to nonrecognition under §332. In either case, these alternative transactions would provide a cost basis in assets to the purchaser while imposing only one layer of corporate tax on the selling target and its parent.

In some circumstances, however, P may demand, or require, a stock rather than an asset acquisition. To give P a cost basis in the T assets only when both the selling target *and* its parent recognize gain would be inconsistent with the general notion that economically equivalent transactions should result in reasonably equivalent tax consequences.[96] In response to this concern with the potential for more than two layers of tax, §338(h)(10) permits a special election,[97] as a result of which CS will recognize no gain or loss on the sale of its T stock.[98] Under the §338(h)(10) regulations, old T is treated as if it sold all of its assets to an unrelated person in a single transaction at the close of the acquisition date and subsequently transferred all of its assets to members of the selling consolidated group or selling affiliate.[99] This special (h)(10) election is available only if the purchasing corporation makes a QSP of target stock from a member of a selling consolidated group.[100] In addition, the election is available only if the target recognizes gain or loss from a §338(a)(1) deemed sale of assets resulting from a §338 election.[101]

While the attractiveness of §338 elections generally has diminished since the 1986 repeal of the *General Utilities* rule, a general §338(a) election combined with a secondary §338(h)(10) election can provide numerous advantages, making it one remaining stock acquisition transaction for which a §338 election often is sensible. The (h)(10) election will be especially attractive when the parent corporation's "outside gain" with respect to its investment in the target subsidiary *stock* is large relative to the "inside gain"

---

96. In addition, while Subchapter C imposes a double tax on corporate earnings, Congress has generally provided relief designed to prevent more than two layers of tax in the case of tiered corporations. See, e.g., the dividends-received deduction in §243.

97. Unlike the initial §338 election made by the purchasing corporation alone, the §338(h)(10) election is made jointly by P and the selling consolidated group or the selling affiliate. Treas. Reg. §1.338(h)(10)-1(c)(3). The timing of the (h)(10) election coincides with the timing required for the §338 election itself under §338(g).

98. I.R.C. §338(h)(10)(A).

99. Treas. Reg. §1.338(h)(10)-1(d)(3), (4). "In most cases, the [latter] transfer will be treated as a distribution in complete liquidation. . . ." Id. At (4)(i).

100. The statute itself provides for an (h)(10) election only when the target corporation was a member of a consolidated group filing a consolidated return. Pursuant to regulatory authority granted in §338(h)(10)(B), however, the Treasury Department extended eligibility for the (h)(10) election to cases in which the target merely is a member of an affiliated group of corporations, whether or not they file a consolidated return. Treas. Reg. §1.338(h)(10)-1(c)(1).

101. I.R.C. §338(h)(10)(A)(ii).

with respect to the target's *assets*. Another attraction of the §338(h)(10) election is that it allows the target corporation to be treated as a member of the selling consolidated group for purposes of the deemed sale.[102] Recall that the target generally is not considered to be a member of a consolidated group with respect to the §338(a)(1) deemed asset sale.[103] Absent a special §338(h)(10) election, the deemed sale would be reported on a single day special "deemed sale return." Thus, gain or loss from the target's deemed asset sale ordinarily cannot be consolidated or offset against other gains or losses within the target's affiliated group. The §338(h)(10) election will be especially attractive where the target has losses elsewhere in the selling group that can be used to offset gain from the deemed §338(a)(1) sale of assets.

Additional Potential Triple Tax Issues: §336(e)

With §338(h)(10), Congress offers relief from the triple-tax threat that would otherwise arise when a parent corporation transfers its subsidiary stock in a QSP to a buyer who makes a §338 election: a tax to the parent upon the stock sale, a tax to the target upon the deemed asset sale, and yet another tax to the parent shareholders upon the parent's subsequent distribution of assets. The scope of this elective relief is limited, however. For example, a parent corporation's sale of subsidiary stock to an individual or partnership has the same triple-tax potential as a comparable sale to a corporate buyer. Yet §338 and its corollary (h)(10) election is available only to *corporate* purchasers. In addition, §338 applies only to 80% acquisitions of control through taxable stock *sales*; it does not extend to taxable *distributions* of a comparable controlling stock interest. Recognizing that other transactions might warrant relief, in 1986, Congress directed the Treasury Department to promulgate regulations providing a §338(h)(10)-like election in appropriate circumstances to a parent corporation upon the sale, exchange, or distribution of subsidiary stock in §336(e).[104]

---

102. If P has purchased the T stock for installment notes, §338 regulations permit old T to report gain from the deemed sale on the installment method. Treas. Reg. §1.338(h)(10)-1(d)(8)(i) ("Old T is treated as receiving in the deemed asset sale new T installment obligations, the terms of which are identical (except as to the obligor) to P installment obligations issued in exchange for recently purchased stock of T."). In addition, on the subsequent deemed liquidation, "[o]ld T is treated as distributing . . . The new T installment obligations that it is treated as receiving in the deemed asset sale." Id. At (d)(8)(ii).
103. I.R.C. §338(h)(9). See earlier discussion in this chapter.
104. I.R.C. §336(e). See H.R. Conf. Rep. No. 841, 99th Cong., 2d Sess. (1986) (authorizing Treasury Department regulations to provide relief from potential multiple taxation through election similar to §338(h)(10)).

Twenty-seven years later, in 2013, the Treasury Department finalized rules for a §336(e) election,[105] the results of which generally "coincide with those of a section 338(h)(10) election."[106] Under these regulations, a §336(e) election permits a domestic corporation to elect to treat a "qualified stock disposition" (QSD) of subsidiary stock as an asset disposition.[107] The §336(e) QSD definition essentially is a reverse image of the §338(d)(3) QSP definition. To be eligible for the §336(e) election, a domestic parent corporation is required to sell, exchange, or distribute subsidiary (old T) stock meeting the 80% control requirements of §1504(a)(2) within a 12-month disposition period.[108] Unlike a §338 election, however, a §336(e) election permits a domestic parent corporation to make a QSD to an *individual or partnership*. The regulations provide that in order to make a §336(e) election, the selling parent corporation and the target corporation must enter into a binding written agreement to make a §336(e) election.[109] Consistent with the §338(a)/(h)(10) model, the §336(e) election triggers a deemed sale of old T's assets at an amount referred to as the aggregate deemed asset disposition price (ADADP)[110] and deemed repurchase by new T using an aggregate grossed-up basis (AGUB).[111] Finally, if this election is made, old T is deemed to transfer its assets in a §332 liquidation.[112]

Consistency Rules

a) Background

When §338 was first enacted in 1982, the old target's deemed sale of assets was eligible for nonrecognition pursuant to the old *General Utilities* doctrine.[113] By making a §338 election, the purchaser could get a stepped-up basis in T's appreciated assets without T recognizing gain on the transfer. Consequently,

---

105. Treas. Reg. §1.336-2. For discussion, see, e.g., Matthew J. Mittman, Final Sec. 336(e) Regulations: Election for Qualified Stock Dispositions, The Tax Advisor, Sept. 1, 2013.

106. 73 Fed. Reg. 49,965, 49,971 (Aug. 28, 2008) (proposed §336(e) regulations). The final regulations include detailed loss limitations rules to prevent abuse, which have already been scrutinized and critiqued by members of the tax bar. See, e.g., N.Y.S. Bar Assoc. Tax Sec., Report on Proposed Regulations Implementing Section 336(e), *reprinted in* Tax Notes Today, 2009 TNT 1-21.

107. Treas. Reg. §1.336-2(b).

108. Treas. Reg. §1.336-1(b)(6)(i).

109. Treas. Reg. §1.336-2(h)(i).

110. Treas. Reg. §1.336-2(b)(1)(i) (similar to the ADSP in Treas. Reg. §1.338-4). See discussion earlier in this chapter.

111. Treas. Reg. §1.336-2(b)(1)(ii) (similar to AGUB in Treas. Reg. §1.338-5). See discussion earlier in this chapter.

112. Treas. Reg. §1.336-2(b)(1)(iii).

113. The doctrine was codified in old §337 and in the original language of §338. See earlier discussion in this chapter and in Chapter 8.

the §338 election was extremely attractive to the purchaser and imposed little tax cost on the target. In designing §338, Congress wanted to prevent corporate purchasers from acquiring a stepped-up basis for *some* target assets by making a §338 election while acquiring a transferred or carryover basis for other assets. In addition, Congress sought to prevent purchasers from preserving certain target tax attributes by making separate stock acquisitions from the target or a target affiliate without making a §338 election. Congress included consistency rules in §338(e) and (f) to prevent this type of selectivity. The "asset consistency" rules in §338(e) created a "deemed §338 election" if the purchasing corporation acquired any assets from the target or a target affiliate[114] within a defined "consistency period."[115] The "stock consistency" rules in §338(f) effectively made the purchaser's decision to elect or not to elect under §338 with respect to a first QSP binding as to subsequent QSPs from one or more target affiliates during the "consistency period."

Since repeal of the *General Utilities* rule in 1986, the §338 election has been less advantageous for most taxpayers and the concern for abuse through selective use of §338 has greatly diminished. The consistency rule regulations under §§338(e) and (f) reflect this diminished concern. Nevertheless, the consistency rules remain in the Code and must be considered by the purchasing corporation, particularly in transactions with a target corporation that is part of a selling group including one or more affiliated corporations. The following sections of this chapter take a closer look at these rules.

b) Asset Consistency Rules: §338(e)

Although the rules have been remarkably relaxed by regulations discussed later in this section, under the *terms* of §338(e), the purchasing corporation is deemed to make a §338 election if it acquires any asset of the target or a target affiliate at any time during the consistency period. Imagine, for example, that P made a QSP of T-1 stock from T, the parent and sole shareholder of T-1, and that P decided *not* to make a §338 election. Imagine further that at some time during the consistency period, P also bought a small piece of property directly from T-1. Under the actual language of §338(e), P is *deemed* to have made a §338 election with respect to the T-1 stock purchase because

---

114. I.R.C. §338(e)(1). See §338(e)(2) for some exceptions to the §338(e)(1) rule.
115. The consistency period includes the 12-month acquisition period up to and including the acquisition date. In addition, the consistency period extends back in time to include the one-year period before the beginning of the 12-month acquisition period and forward to include the one-year period beginning on the day after the acquisition date. I.R.C. §338(h)(4). Thus, the consistency period may be as long as three years.

P bought an asset from T-1 during the consistency period.[116] Pursuant to the statutory language, it appears that the purchase of one small asset from T-1 in this example triggers a "deemed §338 election," requiring T-1 to recognize gain or loss as if it had sold *all* of its assets pursuant to §338(a)(1). The purchased asset triggering the deemed election often was referred to as a "tainted asset."

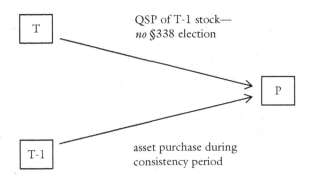

Congress was concerned that without this asset consistency rule, P could pick the T-1 assets for which it wished to receive a cost basis and simply buy those assets directly. At the same time, P could acquire control over the remaining assets through a QSP of T-1 shares *without* making a §338 election. The remaining assets indirectly acquired through this purchase of the T-1 stock would retain the same basis that they had before the transaction. Moreover, since no §338 election was made, T-1 would not lose its identity as "old T-1" and find itself reincarnated as "new T-1," thus enabling P to acquire T-1 with many of its tax attributes still intact.

Strictly applied, §338(e) asset consistency rules created traps for the unwary, and sometimes draconian results. Target selling groups often include several corporations and many assets. Purchasing corporations were at risk that their officers and managers might unwittingly make an asset purchase from some member of the T group, not knowing that even a small asset acquisition could trigger a deemed §338 election with respect to a QSP from T or a T affiliate. Since the deemed election triggered recognition of gain or loss on *all* of the target's assets, this could prove to be a costly mistake. The Treasury Department's initial response to this trap for the unwary was a set of extremely complex temporary regulations.[117]

---

116. The deemed election rule of §338(e)(1) does not apply, however, to the acquisition of target (or affiliate) assets in the ordinary course of the target (or affiliate) trade or business, I.R.C. §338(e)(2)(A), or to the acquisition of a target (or affiliate) asset taking a transferred basis from the selling target or affiliate, I.R.C. §338(e)(2)(B). The statute granted the Treasury Department regulatory authority to promulgate additional exceptions. I.R.C. §338(e)(2)(D).

117. Temp. Treas. Reg. §1.338(b)-4T, removed and replaced with Treas. Reg. §1.338-8(b)-(d).

The final consistency regulations under §338(e) offer an important lesson on the need to examine regulations and not to rely on statutory language alone. In language directly contradicting the terms of §338(e) and (f), the final regulations state that "no election under section 338 is deemed made or required with respect to target or any target affiliate. Instead, the person acquiring an asset may have a carryover basis in the asset."[118] Under the "carryover basis rule" provided in Treas. Reg. §1.338-8(d)(1), when a purchasing corporation makes a QSP without a §338 election and also acquires a "tainted asset" during the consistency period, it simply takes the tainted asset with "its adjusted basis immediately before its disposition." The final §338 regulations further limit the scope of the consistency rules. Although the language of §338(e) itself applies the asset consistency rules to tainted asset acquisitions from any target or target affiliate, the regulations generally apply the consistency rules only when the target is a subsidiary in a consolidated group.[119]

The dramatic relaxation of rules reflected in the final §338 regulations reflects a diminished concern for taxpayer abuse through selective asset acquisition given repeal of the *General Utilities* rule. The remaining concern is more narrowly focused on the combined use of consolidated return reporting provisions with a selective acquisition of assets. This concern is best illustrated in an example offered by the Treasury Department in its preamble to the proposed final §338 regulations. In this example, S and T file consolidated returns. In S's hands, the T stock has a basis of $100 and a fair market value of $200. Assume that T recognizes a $100 taxable gain upon sale of an asset to P and that P shortly thereafter makes a QSP of the T stock from S for $200. Under the consolidated return regulation "investment adjustment rules," S was entitled to increase the basis in its T stock by the $100 gain recognized by T upon the sale of its asset.[120] As a result, the subsequent sale of the T stock to P resulted in no taxable gain to S. The Treasury Department noted that "[i]f the consistency rules did not apply in such a case, P could acquire assets from T with a stepped-up basis in the assets, and then acquire T stock at no additional tax cost to the S group."[121]

---

118. Treas. Reg. §1.338-8(a)(1). Indeed, the regulations no longer permit the government even to impose a deemed §338 election. CO-111-90, 1992-1 C.B. 1000, 1001 (preamble to proposed consistency regulations).

119. Treas. Reg. §1.338-8(a)(2). In addition, the regulations will apply when the target is not a member of a consolidated group, but uses a 100% dividends-received deduction "to achieve an effect similar to that available under the investment adjustment provisions of the consolidated return regulations." Treas. Reg. §1.338-8(a)(4).

120. Treas. Reg. §1.1502-32.

121. CO-111-90, 1992-1 C.B. 1000, 1001. Similar concerns arise when S and T do not file a consolidated return, but T pays a $100 dividend eligible for a 100% dividends-received deduction immediately after T's sale of the asset to P. *Id. At* 1002.

c) Stock Consistency Rules: §338(f)

Under the terms of §338(f), the choice P makes on the first QSP of a selling group of corporations is binding as to subsequent QSPs from the group during the consistency period. Imagine, for example, that T-1 and T-2 are wholly owned T subsidiaries. Assume that P first made a §338 election with respect to the QSP of T-1 stock and later makes a QSP of T-2 stock without a §338 election. Under the actual language of §338(f), P is deemed to have made a §338 election with respect to a QSP of T-2 stock during the consistency period.[122] Similarly, if P had not made a §338 election with respect to the T-1 stock purchase, it would not be permitted to make a §338 election on the subsequent T-2 purchase.[123]

Little is left of the §338(f) stock consistency rules as interpreted by the final §338 regulations, however. First, the regulations eliminate deemed elections altogether for purposes of both the §338(e) asset consistency rules and the §338(f) stock consistency rules.[124] Thus, if P makes a §338 election with respect to one stock purchase, it can no longer be deemed to make a §338 election with respect to a subsequent stock purchase within the consistency period. Second, the scope of both sets of consistency rules is limited by the regulations to targets that are subsidiaries in a consolidated selling group and certain other transactions involving an affiliated selling group using the 100% dividends-received deduction.[125] Third, the regulations specifically limit the stock consistency rules to "cases in which the rules are necessary to prevent avoidance of the asset consistency rules."[126] The only such case described in the regulations is the sale of stock following a QSP for which a §338(h)(10) election was made.[127]

---

122. I.R.C. §338(f)(1).
123. I.R.C. §338(f)(2).
124. Treas. Reg. §1.338-8(a)(2).
125. See discussion in preceding section of this chapter concerning the scope of the asset consistency rules.
126. Treas. Reg. §1.338-8(a)(6).
127. Id. See also Treas. Reg. §1.338-8(b)(2).

An example from the regulations illustrates the remaining selectivity concern in certain cases involving §338(h)(10) elections. Imagine a selling group including S and its wholly owned subsidiary, T. S has a basis of $100 in its T stock. T, in turn, owns all of the stock of second-tier subsidiary T-1, and T-1 owns all of the stock of third-tier subsidiary T-2. T-2's assets have a basis of $100 and a fair market value of $200. Assume that P first purchases all of T-2's stock from T-1 for $200 and makes both a §338 and a §338(h)(10) election with respect to the T-2 stock purchase.

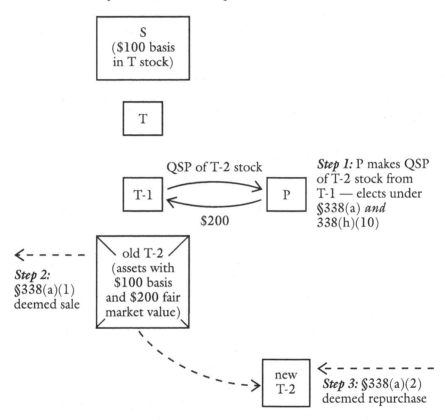

As a result of the basic §338 election, T-2 is deemed to have sold and repurchased all of its assets, thus recognizing a $100 gain, and P effectively receives a $200 cost basis in the T-2 assets. In addition, pursuant to the §338(h)(10) election, T-1 will report no gain or loss on the sale of the T-2 stock and the selling group will be entitled to include any gain or loss from T-2's deemed sale of assets on its consolidated return. Under the investment adjustment provisions in the consolidated return regulations,[128] the $100 gain recognized upon the deemed sale of T-2 assets will increase S's basis in

---

128. Treas. Reg. §1.1502-32.

its T stock to $200. Absent special consistency rules, P might now purchase T stock from S without making a §338 election. If successful, the end result of this selective stock acquisition is a stepped-up basis to P in the T-2 assets and a carryover basis to P in the T-1 assets. Moreover, this result would have been achieved without any taxable gain to either T-1 on the sale of its T-2 stock or to S upon the sale of its T stock.[129] In this limited type of selective §338(h)(10) case, the regulations treat the (h)(10) acquisition as an asset acquisition subject to the carryover basis rule incorporated into the asset consistency provisions of the regulations. Thus, P is denied a stepped-up basis in the T-2 assets and these assets will retain the same basis that T-2 had immediately before P's QSP of T-2.[130]

CREATIVE ACQUISITION STRATEGIES

Eliminating One Layer of the Corporate Tax

At least historically, one important component of taxable acquisitions tax planning was to devise a way to transfer control of corporate assets without imposing a *double* tax on the target corporation and its shareholders. Before congressional repeal of the *General Utilities* doctrine, corporations could distribute assets to their shareholders without recognizing corporate level gain or loss with respect to the distributed assets.[131] Thus, a corporation could arrange first to distribute assets to the shareholders and then to have the shareholders sell the recently distributed assets to the purchaser. If successful, this technique permitted an asset acquisition with a cost basis in the assets to the buyer without a corporate level tax to the selling corporation; in other words, an asset acquisition without the full weight of the corporate "double tax." Congress even extended this opportunity for a "single tax" acquisition of assets by permitting corporations themselves to sell their assets to a purchaser without recognizing corporate level tax under old §337 as long as the sale was pursuant to a "plan of liquidation" and certain other conditions were met.[132] For a time, the "single tax" asset acquisition technique was successful in some cases and unsuccessful in others.

---

129. As an additional bonus, under §338(h)(10), T-2's gain from the deemed asset sale would be included on the S group consolidated return.

130. See Treas. Reg. §1.338-8(e)(2), ex. 2.

131. Discussions of the old *General Utilities* nonrecognition rules appear earlier in this chapter and in Chapter 5 (in the context of nonliquidating distributions) and Chapter 8 (in the context of liquidating distributions).

132. See Chapter 8 for discussion of old §337 and its extension of *General Utilities* nonrecognition to corporate sales of assets in complete liquidation.

Cases that were unsuccessful usually involved a court finding under the step-transaction doctrine that the distribution and the subsequent asset sale by the shareholders should be viewed as a single, integrated transaction in which the corporation really sold assets directly to the purchaser, using the shareholders as a "conduit" for the sale.

Since repeal of the *General Utilities* rule, corporate distributions of assets to shareholders generally trigger recognition of gain or loss to the distributing corporation. Consequently, it has become quite difficult to structure a taxable asset acquisition without a "double tax."[133] On the other hand, creative tax planners continue to seek out new routes to the "single-tax promised land." The playing field in this regard seems to be taking advantage of the one distribution transaction for which the *General Utilities* rule was *not* repealed—distributions in liquidation of a subsidiary under §337. Using the subsidiary liquidation rules along with provisions found in the complex consolidated return regulations, creative tax acquisitions planners have been able to structure unusual acquisition transactions in which the corporate level tax is avoided. As each of these transactions has come to the government's attention, the Treasury Department or Congress has responded with changes to the Code or its regulations. Several of these "mirror" and related transactions were described earlier and will not be revisited here.[134]

Another technique for eliminating or substantially reducing the corporate level tax to the purchasing corporation in corporate acquisitions is the heavy use of debt or leveraging by the purchasing corporation. In a leveraged buy-out (LBO), the purchasing corporation incurs substantial corporate interest expense for the acquisition and hopes to use interest deductions to shelter income. Here again, Congress has responded with statutory provisions that reduce opportunities for using interest deductions to eliminate or substantially reduce the corporate level tax.[135]

The brief description just provided should be sufficient to illustrate the limits on opportunities to eliminate the *corporate* level tax in connection with corporate acquisitions of control. Creative techniques for eliminating the *shareholder* level tax in connection with corporate acquisitions of control also are available, but subject to legal and practical limitations as well. One technique has been for the selling corporation to transfer assets to the purchasing corporation in an asset sale taxable to the corporation. Instead of liquidating, the selling corporation may remain alive as a "shell" and its shareholders will

---

133. Corporate level gain on target assets can be deferred, but not eliminated entirely, through a stock acquisition. See earlier discussion in this chapter on the choice between stock and asset purchases.

134. See discussion of "mirror" and "son of mirror" transactions in Chapter 9 on Liquidation of Subsidiaries.

135. See, e.g., I.R.C. §§ 163(j), 279. For a discussion of these rules see Chapter 3.

receive a stepped-up basis upon death under §1014. If successful, this transaction results in a transfer of assets to the purchasing corporation without the imposition of a shareholder level tax. This technique is limited under the Internal Revenue Code by the personal holding company and accumulated earnings tax rules. Moreover, as a practical matter, it is limited to circumstances involving individual shareholders, who are both eligible for the §1014 step-up in basis and old enough to make this technique viable.

Examples

Each of the following questions will use the same terminology. The purchasing corporation will be P. The target corporation will be T. If a §338 election is made, the target will be old T for purposes of the deemed sale of assets and new T for purposes of the deemed repurchase of assets under §338(a). Affiliated corporations of P or T will be referred to as P-1 or T-1 and so on.

Basic Asset Acquisition

1. a. Lorax, Inc. (T) is a publisher of children's books and is solely owned by Dr. Weiss. Dr. Weiss's basis in the Lorax shares is $2,500. Immediately before the asset acquisition described below, T had the following assets:

	basis	fair market value
portfolio of securities	100	500
inventory (books)	400	500
printing equipment	0	1,000
building	4,000	3,000
land	2,000	5,000
goodwill	0	

For the purposes of this problem, assume that the securities were readily marketable. Arthur Books, Inc. (P) acquired all of T's assets, except the old and obsolete printing equipment, for a total cash purchase price of $9,500. Shortly thereafter, T liquidates, distributing the cash and the unwanted equipment to Dr. Weiss in complete liquidation. What are the tax consequences of this acquisition to Lorax, Dr. Weiss, and Arthur Books?

Adding a Liability Twist

b. How would your answer to Example 1a change if the building had been subject to a $500 mortgage, assumed by P as part of the acquisition transaction?

Bargain Sale

c. How would your answer to Example 1a change if the total purchase price for the desired assets was only $8,000?

Basic §338 Stock Acquisition

2. a. P is a small-town newspaper publisher looking for a new printing plant. P discovers that T has just the plant it's looking for. T recently closed its newspaper operation and the business no longer has any goodwill or going concern value. T's basis in the plant is $20,000. On January 1, P acquired 50% of the T stock for $300,000 in cash. The fair market value of the plant on January 1 was $400,000. T's other assets at that time had a basis of $50,000 and a fair market value of $200,000. On July 1, P acquired the remaining 50% of the T stock for $300,000 in cash. The value of T's assets had not changed between January 1 and July 1. What are the tax consequences to P, T and the T shareholders if P makes no §338 election? How would these tax consequences be different if P makes a §338 election?

b. How would your answer to Example 2a change if P had acquired the remaining 50% in February of the following year?

Adding Minority Shareholders

c. How would your answer to Example 2a change if P had acquired the first 50% of T stock on January 1 for $300,000, but only 30% of the T stock on July 1 for $180,000 cash? Assume that P is unable to acquire any more T shares.

Old and Cold Complications

d. How would your answer to Example 2a change if P purchased 20% of T on January 1 for $100,000 cash and the remaining 80% on February 1 of the following year for $480,000 cash?

Affiliated Corporations: §338(h)(10) Elections

3. a. Bigco owns all of the stock in subsidiary, T. Its basis in the T shares is $400,000 (outside basis). Bigco and T file consolidated returns. T's assets have a basis of $400,000 (inside basis) and a fair market value of $1 million. Bigco has an unused $700,000 net operating loss from last year. P acquires all of the T stock from Bigco for $1 million cash in a QSP and makes a general §338 election. What are the tax consequences to Bigco, T, and P?

b. What would the tax consequences be if P and the selling group also made a joint §338(h)(10) election?

Trouble with Consistency

4. a. T is a parent corporation with subsidiaries, T-1, T-2, and T-3. T-1 owns depreciable equipment with a basis of $10,000 and a fair market value of $60,000. T-2 owns only one piece of highly appreciated property with a basis of $50,000 and a fair market value of $450,000. T-3 owns a large inventory of paper supplies that it sells to newspaper publishers, with a basis of $15,000. P acquires the depreciable equipment for $60,000 cash directly from T-1 on January 1. On July 1, P acquires 100% of the T-2 stock from T for $450,000 and chooses not to make a §338 election. What are the tax consequences to P and the T group?

   b. Assume instead that P acquires 100% of the stock of both T-1 and T-2 on July 1. P chooses not to make a §338 election. On January 1 of the following year, P acquires the paper supplies from T-3. What are the tax consequences to P and the T group?

   c. Assume instead that P acquired 100% of the stock of T-1 on January 1 and filed a timely and proper §338 election. On July 1, P acquired 100% of the T-2 stock and does not wish to make a §338 election. What are the tax consequences to P and the T group?

Explanations

1. a. The seller, Lorax (T) will be required to report gain or loss on each asset sold pursuant to §§61(a)(3) and 1001. To determine the amount of gain or loss on each asset, the $9,500 purchase price must be allocated in accordance with regulations under §1060. The first step in this residual method allocation process is to identify the assets in each Class. No Class I assets such as cash or general deposit bank accounts were included in the sale. The only Class II asset is the portfolio of securities, with a fair market value of $500. No Class III assets were included in the sale. The inventory, with a fair market value of $500, is considered a Class IV asset under the §§338 and 1060 regulations. The building and land are Class V assets, with an overall fair market value of $8,000. T will begin with the $9,500 purchase price, allocating fair market value (but no more) to the Class II asset. Thus, the allocation to the portfolio of securities is $500, resulting in a $400 taxable gain to T (amount realized of $500 less $100 basis). Since this is an investment portfolio, the gain presumably will be capital gain. Next, T will allocate the fair market value of $500 to the inventory, resulting in a $100 gain (amount realized of $500 less $400 basis), presumably ordinary income. Notice that the remaining $8,500 of the purchase price exceeds the total fair market value of the Class V assets. Since no asset can be allocated more than its fair market value,

each of the Class V assets simply receives an allocation equal to its fair market value, resulting in the following gains to T:

building: $3,000 amount realized less $4,000 basis = ($1,000) loss (ordinary loss)

land: $5,000 amount realized less $2,000 basis = $3,000 gain (probably capital gain)

After allocating a total of $8,000 to the Class V assets, a surplus of $500 remains. This surplus is allocated to the goodwill. Assuming a zero basis in the goodwill, T will report a $500 capital gain.

Upon liquidation, Lorax distributed $9,500 cash plus the unwanted printing equipment worth $1,000. Lorax will report a gain of $1,000 upon this liquidating distribution pursuant to §336.[136] Dr. Weiss received $9,500 in cash, plus printing equipment valued at $1,000, for a total liquidating distribution of $10,500. Since his basis in the Lorax shares is $2,500, he will report an $8,000 capital gain ($10,500 less $2,500) from the sale of his shares pursuant to §331.

Arthur Books (P) is entitled to a cost basis in the assets purchased. The same allocations just determined with respect to T also will apply for P. Thus, P's acquired assets have the following §1012 cost basis:

stock portfolio:	$500
inventory:	$500
building:	$3,000
land:	$5,000
goodwill:	$500
TOTAL	$9,500 purchase price

P will use its $3,000 basis for purposes of computing depreciation allowances on the building and will be entitled to amortize the $500 expense for goodwill over 15 years under §197.

b. Under the §1060 regulations, the purchaser's "consideration" to be allocated among the purchased assets is the "cost of purchasing the assets . . . That is properly taken into account in basis," and the seller's "consideration" to be allocated among the assets sold is the seller's "amount realized" under §1001(b).[137] Under general tax principles, the purchaser's "cost" includes liabilities or mortgages assumed and the seller's amount realized also includes liabilities or mortgages from which the seller is relieved. Thus, P's assumption of T's $500 mortgage on the building is considered additional consideration received

---

136. This gain will probably be included as ordinary income under the §1245 recapture provisions.
137. Treas. Reg. §1.1060-1(c)(1).

for the assets, increasing the total purchase price to be allocated to $10,000. Notice that by agreeing to assume the $500 mortgage on the building, P is paying $500 more than it paid in Example 1a for the same assets. Since the mortgage relates to the building, P arguably has paid $500 more than the building's $3,000 alleged fair market value. Why would the buyer do this? Assessing fair market value is not an exact science. Perhaps the buyer is willing to speculate on property it expects to rapidly increase in value, or perhaps the buyer believes that the current fair market value actually is $3,500. On the other hand, the buyer may believe that the overall assets as a package are worth $500 more.

As before, since there are no Class I assets, the purchase price first will be allocated to the Class II stock portfolio in the amount of $500, again resulting in a $400 taxable capital gain to T from the sale of investment stock. Next, $500 will be allocated to the Class IV inventory, again resulting in $100 of ordinary income. The remaining $9,000 will be allocated to Class V assets, but no allocation shall exceed the asset's fair market value. Thus, the land again will receive a fair market value allocation of $5,000, resulting in a $3,000 capital gain from the sale of land.

What about the building? Ordinarily, the amount realized from the sale of an asset subject to a mortgage includes the mortgage amount in the amount realized. Thus, one might expect an allocation of $3,500 to the building, resulting in a loss of $500. Notice, however, that fair market value is defined as "gross fair market value (i.e., fair market value determined without regard to mortgages, liens, pledges, or other liabilities)."[138] Also, §1060 permits an allocation of no more than the fair market value of $3,000. Consequently, despite P's assumption of a $500 mortgage on the building, T's loss from the sale of the building is still $1,000.[139]

After the above allocation of $500 to Class II assets, $500 to Class IV assets, and $8,000 to Class V assets, the $1,000 surplus remaining is allocated to goodwill, resulting in a taxable capital gain to T from the sale of goodwill. In the end, the answers to 1b are the

---

138. Treas. Reg. §1.338-6(a)(2). Notice that the §1060 regulations direct that the allocation of consideration and basis be made under the §338 allocation regulations, substituting the term "consideration" for ADSP and AGUB. Treas. Reg. §1.1060-1(c)(2). The only exception to this use of gross fair market value under the regulations is when a nonrecourse debt exceeds the fair market value of the property. In such cases "the fair market value of any property . . . will be treated as not less than the amount of such indebtedness." Treas. Reg. §1.338-6(a)(2).

139. Since T has a loss on the building, the gross fair market value rule works to its advantage by increasing the permissible loss. Similarly, the gross fair market value rule would have also worked to T's advantage if there had been a gain on the property by reducing T's realized gain.

same as 1a, with the exception of the additional $500 allocation to goodwill.

Notice that the additional "consideration" provided to T through P's assumption of T's mortgage apparently is allocated to the sale of goodwill rather than the building. This may seem an odd result, allocating too much to goodwill and too little to the building. Given that goodwill now is amortizable under §197 over a shorter period than the ACRS recovery period for the building under §167, P may prefer this outcome. If P paid the additional $500 because it believed the overall package of assets was worth $500 more, an allocation of the excess purchase price to goodwill makes sense. On the other hand, the excess $500 should be allocated to the building if the building is undervalued and its *true* fair market value is $3,500. Absent some evidence that the building, in fact, was undervalued, the better default rule would seem to be to allocate any excess purchase price to goodwill.

The tax consequences to Lorax and shareholder Weiss upon liquidation will be the same as in Example 1a.

c. Since the overall value of the desired assets is $9,000, P's acquisition for $8,000 is a below-market or "bargain purchase." Under the §1060 regulations, $500 still will be allocated to the Class II stock portfolio and $500 to the Class IV inventory. The remaining $7,000 of the purchase price will be allocated to Class V assets in proportion to their fair market value. Since only $7,000 in purchase price remains to be allocated, and the overall fair market value of the Class V assets transferred is $8,000, the allocation to each Class V asset will be less than its full fair market value. To allocate the remainder, T must determine the proportionate fair market value of each Class V asset:

                                                    allocated basis

building: $3,000/$8,000 = 0.38 × $7,000 = $2,660

land: $5,000/$8,000 = 0.62 × $7,000 = $4,340

TOTAL ALLOCATED TO CLASS V $7,000

Nothing remains to be allocated to goodwill. This allocation may not reflect the economics of the transaction. Perhaps T was anxious to sell quickly and agreed to sell the entire package, including goodwill, at a discounted price rather than wait for a better offer. If so, it would seem that some portion of the purchase price should be allocable to goodwill.

2. a. Whether or not P makes a §338 election, P will have an overall cost basis in the T shares of $600,000. Also, whether or not P makes an election, the T shareholders will report gain or loss on the sale of their T shares.

If P chooses not to make the §338 election, T simply will be a wholly owned subsidiary of P and will retain its historic basis of $20,000 in the plant and $50,000 in the other assets. P may continue T as a subsidiary, or it may choose to liquidate T and take direct control over the assets. If T is liquidated, T will report no gain from the distribution pursuant to §337 and P similarly will report no gain under §332. P will take T's assets with the same basis they had in T's hands. In other words, P will not be entitled to a step-up in basis to fair market value.

On the other hand, if P makes a §338 election, this will trigger a deemed sale by T of all of its assets at the close of the acquisition date. The acquisition date in this case is July 1, the first day on which P had acquired the 80% interest necessary to make this a QSP. Under the §338 regulations, the price at which T is deemed to sell its assets is the aggregate deemed sales price (ADSP) of the acquisition. This is the grossed-up amount realized on the sale to P of P's recently purchased T stock. The overall ADSP must be allocated to the assets deemed to be sold according to allocation regulations in Treas. Reg. §1.338-6. Assuming that all of T's assets are Class V assets and included no goodwill or going concern value, the purchase price of $600,000 simply is allocated to each asset in proportion to its fair market value as of the acquisition date. Since the fair market value of the plant on July 1 still was $400,000 and T's basis was $20,000, T will report a gain of $380,000 from the deemed sale of the plant. Since the fair market value of the other assets on July 1 was $200,000 and the basis $50,000, T will report a $150,000 gain from the sale of its other assets. T will report this deemed sale gain on "the final return of old target filed for old target's taxable year that ends at the close of the acquisition date." Treas. Reg. §1.338-10(a)(1).

On July 2, the day after the acquisition date, new T will be deemed to repurchase all of the assets that it sold in the deemed sale on July 1. The purchase price for these assets will be the grossed-up basis of P's recently purchased stock. Since recently purchased stock under §338(b)(6)(A) includes any T stock held by P on the acquisition date that was acquired within the 12-month acquisition period, all of P's stock is recently purchased. The grossed-up basis in this case simply is the cost basis of P's stock in T, $600,000, multiplied by 100/100 or $600,000. Thus, as a result of the deemed repurchase, new T will have a basis of $600,000 in its assets. According to the §338 regulations, this overall basis will be allocated among T's assets under the same residual method used for purposes of measuring T's gain on the deemed asset sale. Thus, the plant will receive a $400,000 basis and the other assets will receive a $200,000 basis. The effect of the deemed sale and repurchase is to give P a step-up in the basis of T's assets. To get this step-up, however, T is required to report gain on the deemed sale. P may or may not choose to liquidate T at this point.

a. If P acquired the first 50% of its T stock on January 1 and the remaining 50% in February of the following year, P would not be eligible to make a §338 election since P would not have made a QSP. A QSP is limited under §338(d)(3) to a transaction or series of transactions in which stock meeting the 80% ownership tests is acquired during a 12-month acquisition period. The second purchase was more than 12 months after the first purchase and, therefore, fails this definition. As a result, T simply will be a subsidiary of P and retain T's assets with their historic bases. T will not be required to report any gain or loss. As before, the selling T shareholders will report gain or loss on the sale of stock.

b. Even though P was unable to acquire 100% of T, P has still made a QSP since it has acquired the necessary 80% during a 12-month acquisition period. The remaining 20% of the shares are held by minority shareholders. If P makes a §338 election, T still will be deemed to have sold all of its assets on the close of the acquisition date, which is still July 1. Thus, T will still report a gain of $380,000 on the plant and a gain of $150,000 on its other assets. On July 2, new T will be deemed to repurchase all of its assets. The computation of the purchase price will change a bit here, however. The purchase price again will start with P's basis for the recently purchased stock. Since all of P's stock in T was recently purchased, all of it will be considered here. P's overall basis in its T stock is now $480,000. This cost basis will be multiplied by 100/80 (1.25) as provided in §338(b)(4). Recall that the numerator is 100% minus the nonrecently purchased stock, in this case zero. The denominator is the percentage of recently purchased stock, in this case the full 80% purchased. The result is an overall basis of $600,000 for all of T's assets. Again, this basis must be allocated among T's assets. Notice that P gets the same basis in the assets whether it acquires 100% of the stock, as in example 1a, or only 80% of the stock, as in this variation. In other words, the effect of the "grossed-up basis" computation is to provide a full step-up in basis with regard to *all* of T's assets. Why? Even though P acquired only an 80% interest in T, T still was treated as if it sold *all* of its assets in the §338(a)(1) deemed sale. Since T was taxed as if it had sold all of its assets, P should get a cost basis as if it had acquired all of T's assets. The §338(b) basis formula effectively achieves this result by "grossing-up" the basis to take the additional 20% into account. As before, the selling T shareholders will report gain or loss on the sale of stock.

c. Although the second purchase was more than 12 months after the first, it was a purchase of 80%. This second purchase alone is a QSP.

The first 20% will be considered nonrecently purchased or old and cold stock. If P makes a §338 election, T again will be deemed to sell all of its assets as of the acquisition date, which is now February 1 of year 2. The gain reported by old T will be the ADSP as of that date less T's basis in the assets. On the day following the acquisition date, new T will be deemed to repurchase the assets. The purchase price now will include the grossed-up basis of the 80% recently purchased stock plus the basis of the 20% nonrecently purchased stock. For the first computation, P will start with its cost basis of $480,000 and multiply it by 80/80 leaving a grossed-up basis of $480,000. To this amount, P will add the basis for the nonrecently purchased shares of $100,000. Thus, the overall basis in new T's assets will be $580,000. Again, this amount will need to be allocated among T's assets in accordance with Treas. Reg. §1.338-6.

Notice here that each asset is *not* entitled to a full step-up in basis. Consequently, the "cost" basis for each asset will be less than the fair market value of each asset. This is because the "old and cold" stock that P holds was not acquired as part of the QSP and no gain was taxed with respect to the portion of appreciation reflected in these "old and cold" shares. If P wishes to get a full stepped-up basis, P must make a secondary election under §338(b)(3) and recognize gain as if it had sold the "old and cold" stock. As before, the selling T shareholders will report gain or loss on the sale of stock.

3. a. Bigco will report a taxable gain of $600,000 on its sale of T stock under §§61(a)(3) and 1001. Bigco can use $600,000 of its NOL to offset its taxable gain on the stock sale. P's §338 election will trigger a deemed sale by old T of all of old T's assets, resulting in another $600,000 taxable gain to T under §338(a)(1). Bigco's remaining $100,000 NOL *cannot* be used to offset T's gain on the deemed sale, since §338(h)(9) provides that T is not considered a member of the selling affiliated group for purposes of the deemed sale. The deemed repurchase of assets by new T under §338(a)(2) will result in a $1 million basis in new T's assets. As the new parent of T, P effectively receives a step-up in the basis in T's assets.

   b. If P and the selling group also make a joint (h)(10) election, Bigco will *not* report any taxable gain on the sale of T stock. P's §338 election still will trigger a deemed sale by old T, resulting in a $600,000 gain. However, T will be able to use affiliate Bigco's NOL to fully offset this gain, since §338(h)(10) provides that T *shall* be considered a member of the selling consolidated group with respect to the deemed sale. Old T is deemed to be liquidated under §338 while it was a member of the selling affiliated group. Treas. Reg. §1.338(h)(10)-1(d)(4). As a result, Bigco may be entitled to retain certain T tax attributes that otherwise would have been lost. P still will get the new T assets with a $1 million basis under §338(a)(2). Comparing the two answers to this question should make it clear that the §338(h)(10) election will be rather attractive in many cases involving sales of stock in an affiliated group.

4. a. The purchase of T-2 stock by P is a QSP. Under the *statutory* asset consistency rules in §338(e), P was deemed to have made a §338 election on the T-2 stock purchase since P purchased assets from a target affiliate during the 12-month acquisition period. The congressional concern was that P may have deliberately designed these two purchases in order to acquire depreciable assets from the target group with a cost basis of $60,000 for depreciation purposes while acquiring T-2's asset from the target group without T-2 having to recognize gain on appreciation. The §338(e) statutory consistency rules prevented this result by permitting P to have the $60,000 cost basis in the depreciable assets, but deeming a §338 purchase of T-2 stock, resulting in a substantial taxable gain to T-2. Given the complexity of the §338 rules, P may not in fact have deliberately designed this transaction, but instead may have unwittingly fallen into a trap with rather harsh results.

Under the consistency rules provided in Treas. Reg. §1.338-8(d), no deemed §338 election with respect to T-2 will occur. In fact, the consistency rules will not apply at all unless T-2 is part of a consolidated group filing a consolidated return, and T-1's gain from the sale of the depreciable assets is reflected in T's basis in its T-2 stock under the investment adjustment provisions of the consolidated return rules. Moreover, even if the consistency rules *do* apply, P simply will be denied the cost basis in the depreciable asset acquired from T-1, instead acquiring a carryover basis of $10,000. T-2 would not be required to report any taxable gain.

   b. P has made QSPs of both T-1 and T-2 stock. The issue is whether the asset purchase from T-3, an affiliated corporation, triggers a deemed §338 election. If the sale of paper supplies by T-3 was a sale in the ordinary course of its trade or business, this particular purchase should not trigger a deemed §338 election. I.R.C. §338(e)(2)(A). In any event, under the regulatory consistency rules, there would be no deemed election and the "tainted" assets (paper supplies) will retain their historic basis of $15,000.

   c. Since P made an election with respect to one affiliated corporation during the consistency period, the statute deems P to have made a similar election with respect to the second qualified purchase during the consistency period under the express statutory provisions in §338(f). Under the consistency regulations, however, there is *no* deemed election. The statute and regulations here are in direct conflict.

369

Tax-Free
Reorganizations

SUBPART B

Introduction to Basic Corporate Reorganization Principles

INTRODUCTION

One who has not studied corporate taxation may be surprised to discover that the term "reorganization" for purposes of Subchapter C does not have the same meaning that it might have in the ordinary business setting. A corporation might restructure departments, reassign or redefine personnel responsibilities, or modify or change business operations. Tax consequences do not ordinarily flow from this kind of business change. Corporations also "reorganize" in bankruptcy to restructure debt and to satisfy creditors. Although there are certainly tax consequences to restructuring in bankruptcy, a "reorganization in bankruptcy" is different from a corporate "reorganization" for purposes of Subchapter C of the Internal Revenue Code.

In the corporate tax context of Subchapter C, the term "reorganization" is a statutory term of art. Rather than provide a general definition, Congress attempted to provide precise definitions for the term "reorganization" in §368(a)(1) with an exclusive list of seven specific types of transactions that will be considered "reorganizations." Subparagraphs (A) through (G) of §368(a)(1) each provide a description of a particular reorganization transaction. Unless a transaction fits within one of the seven categories listed in subparagraphs (A) through (G), it simply is not a corporate reorganization. As a shorthand, most tax lawyers, corporate taxpayers, and academics studying Subchapter C identify reorganizations by referring to the appropriate subparagraph. Thus, a Type A reorganization simply is a reorganization that fits within the §368(a)(1)(A) definition, a Type B reorganization is a reorganization that fits within the §368(a)(1)(B) definition, and so on.

At the outset, it is important to notice that §368(a) merely provides a definition of "reorganization." The definitional section says nothing of the tax consequences that flow from classification of a transaction as a corporate reorganization. In general, reorganization exchanges are eligible for nonrecognition treatment and the basis of assets or stock received in the nonrecognition exchange will be a substituted, rather than a cost, basis.[1] The reorganization definition covers several very different types of transactions, the details of which will be considered in the chapters that follow. After a brief description of the different types of transactions that fall within the "reorganization" umbrella, this introduction to general reorganization principles offers an overview and history of tax-free reorganizations and a discussion of the rules and policy considerations that the different types of reorganizations share in common.

CATEGORIES OF REORGANIZATION

Acquisitive Reorganizations

Although the §368(a)(1) reorganization definition contains seven distinct transactions, these distinct transactions fit loosely into three general categories. The first general category is the acquisitive reorganization. In an acquisitive reorganization, the purchasing or acquiring corporation acquires control over or combines with another corporation, usually referred to as the target corporation.[2] This is not to suggest that every corporate acquisition of control over another corporation will be a tax-free reorganization. The critical distinction between a tax-free acquisition of control and a taxable acquisition of control is the consideration used by the purchasing corporation. In a tax-free acquisition, the seller typically receives compensation in the form of stock of the acquiring corporation — also sometimes referred to as the "issuing corporation" — or an acquiring corporation affiliate, thus retaining a proprietary interest in the reorganized or restructured corporate

---

1. The specific tax consequences of reorganization exchanges are outlined at the end of this introductory chapter and are considered in more detail in subsequent chapters.
2. For purposes of §368(a), control generally is defined to mean "the ownership of stock possessing at least 80 percent of the total combined voting power of all classes of stock entitled to vote and at least 80 percent of the total number of shares of all classes of stock of the corporation." I.R.C. §368(c). Notice that this is the same definition of control used for purposes of §351. See Chapter 4.

enterprise.[3] In contrast, sellers in a taxable acquisition typically receive cash or other fairly liquid assets in exchange for stock, thus ending their investment relationship with the corporation.[4] Subparagraphs (A) through (C) of §368(a)(1) generally cover this type of acquisitive reorganization.[5] A Type A reorganization is a "statutory merger or consolidation."[6] In a Type B reorganization, the acquiring or purchasing corporation uses solely voting stock to acquire a controlling interest in the *stock* of another corporation.[7] This is referred to as a "stock for stock" acquisition. In contrast, a Type C reorganization is a "stock for assets" acquisition in which one corporation uses voting stock to acquire substantially all of the *assets* of another corporation.[8]

Divisive Reorganizations

In contrast to the acquisitive reorganization in which two or more corporations are combined, the second major category of reorganizations defined by §368(a)(1) is the divisive reorganization in which one corporation is divided into two or more corporate enterprises in a spin-off, split-off or some other form of division. Most of these transactions are accomplished using §368(a)(1)(D). In a Type D reorganization, one corporation transfers all *or part* of its assets to another corporation. Immediately after the asset transfer, the new corporation must be controlled by the transferring corporation itself, shareholders of the transferring corporation, or some combination of the two.[9] Notice that the new corporation essentially must be controlled by the shareholders of the transferring corporation. Where there once was only one corporation, now there will be two or more corporations controlled by shareholders of the original corporation.

---

3. A more detailed discussion of the continuity of proprietary interest requirement follows in this introductory chapter and in subsequent chapters regarding specific types of reorganization transactions.

4. Taxable acquisitions are covered in Chapter 10.

5. Although §368(a)(1)(D) reorganizations generally are thought of as "divisive," some acquisitive reorganization transactions use the Type D reorganization definition. Chapter 12 discusses each of the acquisitive reorganization types in further detail.

6. I.R.C. §368(a)(1)(A). A "statutory merger or consolidation" is a "transaction effected pursuant to the statute or statutes necessary to effect the merger or consolidation"—in other words, a transaction pursuant to the applicable corporate laws of the relevant jurisdictions. Treas. Reg. §1.368-2(b)(ii). As a result of the merger or consolidation, the assets and liabilities of the merged entity or entities become the assets and liabilities of the surviving entity and the merged entity or entities cease to have a separate legal existence.

7. I.R.C. §368(a)(1)(B).

8. I.R.C. §368(a)(1)(C).

9. I.R.C. §368(a)(1)(D). An additional requirement for a Type D reorganization is that stock or securities of the new corporation must be distributed pursuant to §354, 355, or 356. Further discussion of the details of divisive reorganizations appears in Chapter 13. A divisive reorganization also can be accomplished under §355 through a simple distribution of stock in a subsidiary without using the Type D reorganization definition.

Internal Restructuring

The third general category of reorganizations is internal restructuring. This last category of reorganizations generally is the simplest in the sense that it involves only one corporation that is engaged in restructuring itself. Included here are Type E and F reorganizations. A Type E reorganization is a "recapitalization" in which the bondholders or shareholders of one corporation exchange their bond or stock interests for a different kind of equity interest in the same corporate enterprise.[10] A Type F reorganization involves a "mere change in identity, form, or place of organization of one corporation, however effected."[11] Finally, a Type G reorganization, the last of the §368(a)(1) reorganization definitions, covers certain internal reorganization of one corporation in the bankruptcy setting.[12]

OVERVIEW AND HISTORY: DOCTRINE UNDERLYING TAX-FREE REORGANIZATIONS

The most frequently cited policy reason for the tax-free reorganization rules is that the exchange represents a "mere change in form" of the shareholders' interest in the business enterprise. The participants in a reorganization arguably have not "cashed out" on their investment but instead have substituted one investment in the business enterprise for a similar investment in the same or related business enterprise. Since the immediate transaction affects only the "readjustment of continuing interest in property under modified corporate forms,"[13] recognition of gain or loss is deferred. When shareholders sell their stock in a target corporation for cash or notes from the purchasing corporation, immediate recognition of the shareholders' gain or loss is appropriate. On the other hand, when shareholders exchange their stock in a target corporation entirely for stock of the purchasing corporation, the transaction arguably can be viewed as a mere change in form.

Another explanation for tax-free treatment is to avoid the potential hardship from imposing a tax on parties who receive stock in a reorganization and may not have the cash with which to pay the tax. This reasoning should sound familiar — it is quite similar to the policy behind the tax-free

---

10. I.R.C. §368(a)(1)(E); Treas. Reg. §1.368-2(e).
11. I.R.C. §368(a)(1)(F).
12. I.R.C. §368(a)(1)(G).
13. Southwest Natural Gas Co. v. Comm'r, 189 F.2d 332, 334 (5th Cir. 1951). This language is now incorporated into the Treasury Department regulations. See Treas. Reg. §1.368-1(b).

incorporation rules of §351.[14] The hardship argument is even stronger in the context of a reorganization involving minority shareholders who are effectively forced to exchange their shares in the target corporation involuntarily. The substituted basis rules in §§358 and 362 that apply to corporate reorganizations are the same basis rules that apply to §351 transactions.

As discussed in Chapter 4 on §351 transactions and illustrated further in this chapter and those that follow, the "mere change in form" or "continuity of investment" rationale appears sensible in theory. In practice, however, the nonrecognition rules in some cases sweep so broadly as to include transactions that most would not regard as "mere changes in form" and in other cases to exclude transactions that most would regard as "mere changes in form."

OVERVIEW OF CORPORATE REORGANIZATION TAX CONSEQUENCES

Tax Consequences to Shareholders

a) General Nonrecognition Rule: §354

A shareholder who transfers stock in connection with a reorganization and receives stock or other assets in return has realized a gain to the extent that the value of the stock or other assets received exceeds the basis in the stock transferred. Similarly, the shareholder has realized a loss to the extent that the shareholder's basis in the stock transferred exceeds the value of the stock or assets received in the exchange. Absent a special nonrecognition rule, gains and losses realized from these exchanges would be recognized for tax purposes pursuant to §§61(a)(3) and 1001. Losses also generally would be recognized pursuant to §1001, and subject to the loss rules provided in §165. In §354, Congress provides just such a nonrecognition rule for shareholders who, "in pursuance of a plan of reorganization" exchange stock or securities in a corporation that is a "party to a reorganization" for stock or securities in the same corporation or another corporation that is a "party to the reorganization."[15] Thus, a properly structured reorganization will be tax-free to the participating shareholders.

---

14. In fact, both the §351 incorporation rules and the reorganization rules appear in Part III of Subchapter C, entitled "Corporate Organizations and Reorganizations." For a detailed discussion of incorporation transactions, see Chapter 4.

15. I.R.C. §354(a). Some limitations to this nonrecognition rule apply in the case of transfers of securities. I.R.C. §354(b). In addition, certain "nonqualified preferred stock" will not be considered "stock or securities" for purposes of §354. I.R.C. §354(a)(2)(C). For a more detailed discussion of the tax consequences to shareholders and the definitions of "plan of reorganization" and "party to a reorganization," see Chapters 12 and 13.

The §354 nonrecognition rule contains several parallels to the §351 nonrecognition rule applicable to incorporation transactions.[16] The initial motivating policy behind each of the provisions is similar; that is, providing nonrecognition to exchanges (whether as part of the organization or reorganization) that reflect "merely a change in form." In addition, a shareholder who receives nonrecognition treatment under either §351 or §354 takes a substituted basis in the stock or securities received pursuant to §358. One significant distinction between §§351 and 354, however, is that §354 provides nonrecognition upon receipt of "stock or securities" while §351 only permits nonrecognition upon receipt of stock.[17] Moreover, a second significant distinction between §§351 and 354 is that the shareholders in the §351 context must receive a quantum of stock representing "control" whereas the shareholders of a target may receive only a minuscule ownership in the acquiring corporation and yet be entitled to nonrecognition treatment.

While §354(a)(1) establishes a general nonrecognition rule, limitations are set forth in §354(a)(2). Nonrecognition is not available to the extent that the principal amount of any securities received exceeds the principal amount of securities surrendered.[18] In other words, an exchange of securities for the same principal amount of securities in a reorganization will be a tax-free exchange. Any *excess* securities that the target corporation shareholder receives will be considered boot and will be taxable.[19] Similarly, if any securities are received and no securities are surrendered, the securities received also will be considered boot.[20] In addition, certain "nonqualified preferred stock" will not be treated as stock or securities for purposes of §354.[21] As a result, "nonqualified preferred stock" also will be considered boot, subjecting those who receive such preferred stock in an otherwise

---

16. For an in-depth discussion of §351 and its underlying policy, see Chapter 4.

17. In addition, regulations generally provide that, for purposes of §354, "the term *securities* includes rights issued by a party to a reorganization to acquire its stock." Treas. Reg. §1.354-1(e). These regulations are discussed further in Chapter 12. For many years, §351 did provide nonrecognition upon receipt of "stock or securities." The words "or securities" were deleted from §351 as part of the Omnibus Budget Reconciliation Act of 1989. See Chapter 4.

18. I.R.C. §354(a)(2)(A)(i).

19. Id. See also I.R.C. §356(d)(2)(B). Stock rights are now considered to be "securities" for purposes of §354. See note 17. However, "a right to acquire stock has no principal amount." Treas. Reg. §1.354-1(e). Thus, receipt of a stock option or warrant should not generate any additional principal amount in securities received for purposes of §§354 and 356. Treas. Reg. §1.356-3(b).

20. I.R.C. §354(a)(2)(A)(ii). In addition, under limitations provided in §354(a)(2), shareholders will not be eligible for nonrecognition to the extent that receipt of stock, securities, or other property is attributable to accrued interest on securities. I.R.C. §354(a)(2)(B).

21. I.R.C. §354(a)(2)(C), added by the Taxpayer Relief Act of 1997, Pub. L. No. 105-34, 111 Stat. 788, §1014(b).

tax-free exchange to potentially taxable "boot gain."[22] For purposes of the §354(a)(2)(C) boot rule, "nonqualified preferred stock" carries the same definition that it has under the parallel boot rule applicable to §351 exchanges.[23]

b) Shareholder Receipt of "Boot": §356

i) Basic "Boot" Rule

The nonrecognition language in §354 itself appears quite rigid. It requires that the exchange of stock or securities in one corporation a party to a reorganization be *solely* for stock or securities in the same corporation or another corporation a party to a reorganization. This apparently strict requirement is loosened by §356, which provides that if §354 would apply, but for the fact that something other than stock or securities is received, "then gain, if any, to the recipient shall be recognized, but in an amount not in excess of the sum of. . . money and the fair market value of . . . other property."[24] Thus, to the extent that shareholders receive any "boot" or property other than property permitted to be received tax-free under §354, the "boot" will be taxable under §356 to the extent of realized gain.[25] Any excess securities or "nonqualified preferred stock" received as described in §354(a)(2) will be considered "boot" for purposes of §356.[26]

ii) "Dividend Boot" Versus "Capital Gain Boot"

The §356 "boot" rules are rather unusual. The shareholder who receives §356 boot will either have boot in the form of capital gain under §356(a)(1) or "boot" in the form of a dividend under §356(a)(2). The latter provision simply states that if the boot distribution "has the effect of the distribution of a dividend . . . Then there shall be treated as a dividend to each

---

22. One exception to this boot rule is the receipt of "nonqualified preferred stock" in the case of a §368(a)(1)(E) recapitalization of a family-owned corporation. I.R.C. §354(a)(2)(C)(ii). Regulations add that the term "stock or securities" does not include nonqualified preferred stock (NQPS) received in exchange for stock or rights to acquire stock other than NQPS. Treas. Reg. §1.356-6(a)(2). In other words, receipt of NQPS generally will be considered taxable boot. However, an exchange of NQPS for other NQPS or for rights to acquire such stock should be tax-free.

23. I.R.C. §351(g) treats "nonqualified preferred stock" received in a §351 exchange as boot. For a detailed discussion of this provision and the definition of "nonqualified preferred stock," see Chapter 4 (section entitled "Nonqualified Preferred Stock" Treated as Boot).

24. I.R.C. §356(a)(1). For purposes of §356, the term "other property" includes "nonqualified preferred stock" unless the preferred stock was permitted to be received tax-free in a §368(a)(1)(E) recapitalization of a family-owned corporation. I.R.C. §356(e).

25. The "boot" rules in §356 are similar, but not identical, to the "boot" rules provided in the incorporation context in §351(b).

26. I.R.C. §356(d).

distributee such an amount of the gain . . . As is not in excess of [the share-holder's] ratable share of the undistributed earnings and profits of the corporation. . . ."[27] Although the statute uses the term "dividend," the term as used here is different from an ordinary dividend under §§301 and 316. Two aspects of the §356(a)(2) dividend provision are rather unique. First, under §356, the *amount* of the dividend is limited to the amount of *gain* recognized on the exchange. In contrast, assuming that a distribution meets the §316 dividend definition, the §301 dividend rules impose a tax on the entire amount received without any basis offset. As a result of this difference in treatment, §356(a)(2) sometimes is described as a special "dividend within a gain" rule. The second distinction between the §356(a)(2) dividend and an ordinary dividend is that, unlike §316, the §356(a)(2) dividend is limited to the shareholder's "ratable share of earnings and profits." Moreover, §356(a)(2) looks only to accumulated earnings and profits, unlike §316, under which dividends can arise from either current or accumulated earnings and profits.

A brief look at the history behind §356(a)(2) is useful to get a feel for the underlying purpose or policy behind the "dividend boot" provisions in §356(a)(2). Prior to the addition of the special "dividend boot" provision, boot received in a tax-free reorganization was taxed simply as capital gain. The example used in the legislative history provides a good illustration of congressional concerns leading to adoption of the "dividend boot" provision now found in §356(a)(2). In the example, Corporation A had accumulated earnings of $50,000. A direct distribution of these earnings would result in ordinary dividend income to the shareholders. On the other hand, Corporation A could create, and then merge with, a new Corporation (B), transferring all of its assets and liabilities to the new corporation. As part of the merger transaction, the old Corporation A shareholders would receive B stock and $50,000 cash in exchange for their old A shares. Since this exchange qualified as a tax-free reorganization, the shareholders were entitled to nonrecognition on the receipt of Corporation B stock. And, under the old boot rules, the cash was taxed at capital gains rates. As the example illustrates, §356(a)(2) was designed to prevent an "evasive" bailout of corporate earnings at capital gains rather than ordinary income rates.[28] The rate conversion concern originally animating the §356 "dividend boot" rule is significantly diminished, if not eliminated, by changes to the individual shareholder dividend rules. After the Jobs and Growth Tax Reconciliation Act of 2003,[29] "qualified dividend income" received by individual shareholders is now taxed at the same preferential rates as net capital gains.

---

27. I.R.C. §356(a)(2).
28. H.R. Rep. No. 179, 68th Cong. 1st Sess. 15 (1923).
29. Pub. L. No. 108-27, 117 Stat. 752, §302 (codified at I.R.C. §1(h)(11)). For a detailed discussion of the "qualified dividend income" rules, see Chapter 5.

Thus, for most individual shareholders, the tax rate applicable to §356 boot distributions will be the same under either subsection (a)(1) or (a)(2). Moreover, the shareholder effectively receives a basis offset under either subsection since the (a)(2) "dividend boot" rule is limited to *gain*. Under the 2003 statutory amendments, the only remaining apparent distinction between ordinary "qualified" dividends under §301 and "boot dividends" under §356 is that the latter is limited to the shareholder's ratable share of earnings and profits.

From the time of its enactment, the most difficult and controversial §356 issue has been determining when the shareholder has received a distribution that "has the effect of the distribution of a dividend," thus bringing it within the §356(a)(2) dividend rule as opposed to the §356(a)(1) capital gain rule.[30] After a period during which boot received in tax-free reorganizations was virtually always treated as an "automatic dividend" to the extent of earnings and profits,[31] the Treasury Department and the courts finally agreed that they should look to the §302 redemption rules in designing a "dividend equivalence" test for purposes of §356(a)(2). After all, the point of the §302 redemption rules was to distinguish sale or exchange type redemption distributions eligible for capital gains treatment from dividend-like redemption distributions to be treated as ordinary income dividends. The idea behind §302 is that shareholders receiving distributions in redemption without significantly reducing their proportionate interest in the corporation should not be entitled to capital gain treatment.[32] Similarly, it was thought that shareholders receiving boot in a reorganization transaction should experience a significant reduction in their proportionate interest before being entitled to capital gain treatment under §356(a)(1). Despite agreement that §302 was the appropriate analogy, disagreement quickly emerged regarding how the redemption rules should be applied in the reorganization context. In an acquisitive reorganization, should the redemption tests be applied to stock of the target corporation or to stock of the purchasing corporation? Should the redemption tests be applied just

---

30. Until 2003, individual taxpayers generally preferred to have the boot classified under §356(a)(1) to take advantage of the preferential capital gains rates. Corporate shareholders, on the other hand, would generally prefer to have boot classified under §356(a)(2) to take advantage of the §243 dividends-received deduction.

31. Comm'r v. Estate of Bedford, 325 U.S. 283 (1945). The Service at first adopted this "automatic dividend" approach, Rev. Rul. 56-220, 1956-1 C.B. 191, but later abandoned it. Rev. Rul. 74-515, 1974-2 C.B. 118.

32. Again, however, most "sale or exchange" redemptions and "dividend redemptions" under §302 are subject to the same capital gains rates by virtue of changes to the treatment of dividends under the 2003 Jobs and Growth Tax Reconciliation Act. Just as these changes diminished the underlying driving force behind the §356 distinctions, they similarly diminished concerns animating §302. For a discussion of the §302 redemption provisions, the logic behind them, and the impact of the 2003 changes on these rules and logic, see Chapter 6.

before or just after the reorganization exchange? And finally, whose earnings and profits should count?

The major disagreement between the pre-reorganization and post-reorganization views was finally resolved by the Supreme Court's decision in Commissioner v. Clark.[33] The taxpayer, Clark, was the sole shareholder of a small corporation. He agreed to a transaction in which his wholly owned corporation was merged into a subsidiary of a large publicly held corporation. Clark turned down an offer of 425,000 purchasing corporation common shares in exchange for his stock in the target corporation. Instead, Clark ultimately received only 300,000 shares of the purchasing corporation's stock and over $3 million in cash "to boot." Clark's ownership interest in the publicly held corporation after the reorganization was 0.92%.

Under the pre-reorganization view advocated by the government,[34] the cash boot payment should be regarded as a hypothetical redemption by the target corporation immediately *before* the reorganization. Since Clark was the *sole* shareholder of the target, treating the boot as a hypothetical redemption of target stock would have resulted in dividend treatment under the United States v. Davis principle that a redemption from a *sole* shareholder does not result in a meaningful reduction in the shareholder's interest.[35]

The Supreme Court rejected this approach, instead adopting a post-reorganization view. To reach this result, the Court held that the transaction should be viewed "as a whole" in determining whether it has the effect of the distribution of a dividend.[36] Under the post-reorganization approach, the Court treated the distribution of boot to Mr. Clark as a redemption by the *purchasing* corporation immediately after the acquisitive reorganization transaction. The Court viewed the transaction as if Mr. Clark had received the full 425,000 purchasing corporation shares originally offered and then had 125,000 shares redeemed for cash, thus leaving him with the 300,000 shares he actually received in the transaction. So viewed, his interest in the purchasing corporation was hypothetically reduced from 1.3% to 0.92%. Since this reduction would have been sufficient to qualify as a §302(b)(2) redemption, the Court found that Mr. Clark was entitled to capital gain, as opposed to dividend, treatment under §356(a).

---

33. 489 U.S. 726 (1989).
34. This was the approach adopted in Shimberg v. United States, 577 F.2d 283 (5th Cir. 1978). The Fifth Circuit in *Shimberg* applied a pre-reorganization test under §356, asking "whether the distribution would have been taxed as a dividend if made *prior to* the reorganization or if no reorganization had occurred." *Id. At* 288 (emphasis added).
35. The *Davis* "meaningful reduction" test under §302 is discussed in Chapter 6.
36. 489 U.S. At 737. In adopting this post-reorganization view, the Supreme Court sided with the Eighth Circuit, which applied a post-reorganization test in Wright v. United States, 482 F.2d 600 (8th Cir. 1973). The Eighth Circuit there compared the boot received from the purchasing corporation with what the shareholder hypothetically *would* have received if he had taken stock only from the purchasing corporation without any boot.

In its reasoning, the Court adopted the rule of statutory construction that exceptions to the general rule are to be narrowly construed. Since §356(a)(2) is an exception to the general capital gain rule in §356(a)(1), its scope should be limited. Moreover, it was important to the Court that this was an arm's-length transaction with a purchasing corporation in which Mr. Clark had no prior interest. The Court concluded that "unlike traditional single corporation redemptions and unlike reorganizations involving commonly owned corporations, there is little risk that the reorganization at issue was used as a ruse to distribute a dividend."[37]

Since the Court in *Clark* applied §356(a)(1), it did not reach the issue of which corporation's earnings and profits are relevant in the case of boot which "has the effect of the distribution of a dividend" under §356(a)(2). The traditional view is that one must look to the earnings and profits of the acquired or target corporation for purposes of §356(a)(2). On the other hand, the Supreme Court's view of the *Clark* transaction "as a whole" may suggest that one should look to the earnings and profits of the purchasing corporation, or perhaps, both corporations.[38]

iii) Allocation of Boot

Although §356 clearly requires taxation of target (T) shareholder gains to the extent of boot received in an otherwise tax-free reorganization, it does not specify a method for allocation. Such allocation may be necessary in the event that T shareholders receive boot in an exchange involving multiple classes of T stock or blocks of T shares with different bases. Suppose, for example, that shareholder A transfers T common stock (basis: $10; fair market value: $100) and T preferred stock (basis: $60; fair market value: $100) in exchange for purchasing corporation (P) stock (fair market value: $100) and $100 cash in a qualified Type A tax-free reorganization. Shareholder A has $90 *realized* gain with respect to the T common stock and $40 with respect to the T preferred. The amount of shareholder A's *recognized* gain will depend on allocation of the boot.

On a pro rata basis, the shareholder could be viewed as receiving $50 cash and $50 in P stock in exchange for the T common and $50 cash and $50 worth of P stock for the T preferred. If so, A would recognize only $50 of the realized gain on the common stock and all of the $40 realized gain on the preferred, resulting in $90 total taxable "boot gain." On the other hand, if shareholder A could treat all of the cash as received in exchange for the T preferred, and all of the P stock as received in exchange for the T

---

37. 489 U.S. At 744.
38. In at least one early case, the Fifth Circuit looked at the earnings and profits of both corporations for §356(a)(2) purposes. Davant v. Comm'r, 366 F.2d 874 (5th Cir. 1966), cert. denied, 386 U.S. 1022 (1967).

common, she would recognize the full $40 gain on the exchange of pre-
ferred stock for cash but no gain on the exchange of T common for P stock.
Under this "earmarked" approach, the shareholder would recognize a total
of only $40 "boot gain." While the proper method for allocating §356 boot
in tax-free reorganizations had been uncertain prior to 2006, the regulations explicitly adopt a "tracing approach," clarifying that

> to the extent the terms of the exchange specify the other property or money
> that is received in exchange for a particular share of stock or security surren-
> dered or a particular class of stock or securities surrendered, such terms shall
> control provided that such terms are economically reasonable.[39]

In other words, the reorganization agreement can—and in most cases probably should—designate the particular consideration received in exchange
for each particular share or class of stock or securities surrendered. In
the event that the plan of reorganization fails to identify particular shares
received in exchange for boot, the regulation requires that a *pro rata* portion
of the boot "be treated as received in exchange for each share of stock and
security surrendered, based on the fair market value of such surrendered
share of stock or security."[40]

Tax Consequences to the Corporation in a Reorganization

Absent special rules, a corporation that transfers property in return for stock
or securities of another corporation *realizes* gain or loss from the exchange
under §§61(a)(3) and 1001. In addition, corporations that distribute property to shareholders realize, and ordinarily must recognize, gains and losses.[41]
A special nonrecognition rule is provided in §361 for a corporate "party to
a reorganization" that "in pursuance of a plan of reorganization" exchanges
property in return for stock or securities of another corporate "party to the
reorganization."[42] Even if the corporation receives property other than stock
or securities in the exchange, the receiving corporation will not be required
to recognize gain if the other property is distributed pursuant to the plan
of reorganization.[43] Finally, the corporation is entitled to nonrecognition

---

39. Treas. Reg. §1.356-1(b), 71 Fed. Reg. 4264, 4269 (Jan. 26, 2006) (T.D. 9244 announcing final §356 regulations); Treas. Reg. §356-1(d), ex. 4 (tracing method applied pursuant
to plan of reorganization terms).
40. Treas. Reg. §1.356-1(b), (d), ex. 3.
41. Gains and losses generally are recognized upon liquidating distributions under §336.
In the case of nonliquidating distributions, §311 requires recognition of gain, but does not
permit losses. For a detailed discussion of §§311 and 336, see Chapters 5 and 8, respectively.
42. I.R.C. §361(a).
43. I.R.C. §361(b).

treatment on distributions to shareholders of certain qualified property in connection with the reorganization.[44] Thus, a properly structured corporate reorganization will be tax-free to the participating corporations.

In addition, under §1032, no gain or loss is recognized when a corporation receives money or property in exchange for its own stock.[45] Thus, a corporation that acquires stock or assets in a tax-free reorganization generally will not recognize gain or loss. Finally, in addition to concerns about gain or loss recognition, the acquiring corporation will be concerned about the survival of net operating losses and other tax characteristics of the acquired corporation. These issues will be discussed in the next chapter on acquisitive reorganizations.[46]

Reorganization Basis Rules

Given the nonrecognition provisions of §§354, 361, and 1032, most accountants, lawyers, and academics working with Subchapter C refer to corporate reorganizations as "tax-free reorganizations." As is the case with most nonrecognition provisions in the Internal Revenue Code, however, nonrecognition comes at a price. Specifically, the property permitted to be received tax-free generally receives a substituted, as opposed to a cost, basis.

The shareholders who receive stock or securities tax-free under §354 will take as their basis in the shares received the same basis that they previously had in the shares transferred.[47] Similarly, a corporation receiving property tax-free under §361 or 1032 will take the same basis that the

---

44. I.R.C. §361(c).

45. This provision also was discussed earlier in connection with incorporation transactions. See Chapter 4. Notice that the scope of §1032 is not limited to organizations or reorganizations. A corporation that receives money or other property in return for its own stock recognizes no gain or loss, even if the transaction does not qualify as a tax-free §351 exchange or as a reorganization under §368(a).

46. See Chapter 12 for discussion of the survival of net operating loss and other tax characteristics following a reorganization.

47. I.R.C. §358. Notice that the same §358 rules determine the shareholders' basis in stock received in a §351 exchange. See Chapter 4. Based on its view that "a reorganization is not an event that justifies averaging the bases of exchanged stock or securities," the Treasury Department adopts a "tracing method" for allocating basis for distributions governed by §354, 355, or 356. T.D. 9244, 71 Fed. Reg. 4264, 4265 (Jan. 26, 2006) (preamble to §358 regulations). If only one P share is received for more than one share of T stock, the basis must be allocated "in a manner that reflects, to the greatest extent possible, that a share of stock or security received is received in respect of shares of stock or securities that were acquired on the same date and at the same price." Treas. Reg. §1.358-2(a)(2)(i). As a result, a share of P stock may have a "split basis" and a "split holding period." In a transaction involving boot or multiple classes of stock, terms of the reorganization identifying the particular shares exchanged for boot or particular classes of stock will control for both §356 and §358 allocation purposes. Treas. Reg. §1.358-2(a)(2)(ii). See discussion earlier in this chapter on §356 boot allocation.

transferor had.[48] These substituted basis rules preserve the realized gain or loss for potential later recognition upon subsequent transfer of the property. Thus, the tax-free reorganization provisions do not permanently exclude, but simply defer, realized gains and losses.[49] These basis rules will be taken up in the context of particular reorganization transactions in the chapters that follow.

JUDICIAL GLOSSES ON THE STATUTE

In General

Congress added the distinct reorganization definitions in §368(a)(1) and its predecessors in order to provide clarity for taxpayers. Rather than leave taxpayers to the uncertainty that had evolved under early case law on tax-free reorganizations, the idea was to provide rigid definitions regarding which transactions would be eligible for reorganization treatment. In this statutory environment, one might have thought that literal compliance with the statutory terms of one of the reorganization definitions would suffice to classify a transaction as a tax-free reorganization. Taxpayers soon discovered, however, that simply fitting within one of the apparently precise definitions in §368(a)(1) would not be enough. Perhaps more than in any other area of Subchapter C, the courts have added, and Treasury Department regulations confirm, additional requirements necessary to achieve "reorganization" status. The regulations now summarize law created over the years by court decisions that focused on the purpose and scope of the reorganization provisions:

> The purpose of the reorganization provisions of the Code is to except from the general rule certain specifically described exchanges incident to such readjustments of corporate structures made in one of the particular ways specified in the Code, *as are required by business exigencies and which effect only a readjustment of continuing interest in property under modified corporate forms.* Requisite to a reorganization under the Internal Revenue Code are a continuity of the business enterprise under the modified corporate form as described in paragraph (d) of this section, and . . . A continuity of interest as described in paragraph (e) of this section.[50]

---

48. I.R.C. §362(b).
49. It should be noted, however, that a shareholder who receives stock in a tax-free reorganization effectively can transfer the stock with a fair market value basis upon death under §1014. Thus, in some cases, the realized gain or loss may never be recognized.
50. Treas. Reg. §1.368-1(b) (emphasis added); Treas. Reg. §1.368-1(e)(2). These regulatory provisions are discussed later in this chapter.

This regulatory provision incorporates three requirements governing the §368(a)(1) corporate reorganization definitions that are not otherwise explicitly included in the statutory language: (1) continuity of proprietary or investment interest, (2) continuity of the business enterprise and, (3) business purpose.[51] These three judicial doctrines generally developed in response to the government's litigation position that literal compliance with the reorganization definition, in itself, was insufficient. The two continuity of interest tests and the business purpose doctrine impose *additional* requirements on taxpayers seeking tax-free reorganization status. Thus, historically, the government has insisted on technical compliance with the statutory reorganization definitions *plus* the added judicial requirements. More recently, however, the government has been leaning in a different direction. Through rulings and regulatory changes, the Treasury Department has authorized reorganization treatment for transactions that do *not* meet the literal requirements of §368(a)(1) but otherwise appear to be consistent with the underlying purpose of the tax-free reorganization provisions. The government seems now to focus more on this underlying purpose and to be forgiving in some circumstances when the statutory requirements are not literally met.[52]

Step-Transaction Approaches to Reorganization Transactions

One significant consideration in structuring tax-free reorganizations is the regulatory admonishment that "the transaction must be evaluated under relevant provisions of law, including the step-transaction doctrine."[53] Based on this doctrine, the tax consequences of complex, multistep corporate acquisitions may differ dramatically depending on whether the steps are viewed as part of an integrated plan or, instead, the individual steps are viewed as independent transactions.

---

51. Some of these rules will not be applicable to all §368(a)(1) reorganization categories. No further judicial or regulatory gloss is necessary, for example, if the statutory language *itself* establishes a clear continuity of proprietary interest requirement. See, e.g., §§368(a)(1)(A) and (B), discussed later in this chapter and in Chapter 12. Regulations also explicitly provide that that "a continuity of the business enterprise and a continuity of interest are not required for a transaction to qualify as a reorganization under section 368(a)(1)(E) or (F)." Treas. Reg. §1.368-1(b). See 69 Fed. Reg. 49,836 (Aug. 12, 2004) (explaining that a Type E recapitalization is a mere reshuffling within a single corporation, and that a Type F reorganization, while it may technically involve another corporation, is much like the Type E).

52. See, e.g., Rev. Rul. 2001-24, 2001-1 C.B. 1290; Rev. Rul. 2002-85, 2002-1 C.B. 986. These and other recent rulings reflecting similar trends are discussed later in this chapter and in Chapter 12.

53. Treas. Reg. §1.368-1(a).

Some transactions may fit within one of the reorganization definitions regardless of whether multiple steps are integrated. Even so, step-transaction principles are used in these "overlap" cases to determine which of several subparagraphs of §368(a)(1) should apply. For example, if the end result of a series of corporate transactions is the acquisition of assets by the purchasing corporation, an intermediate acquisition of stock might be ignored.[54]

In the alternative, step-transaction analysis might be used to convert an initial acquisition, which viewed alone would not qualify for tax-free reorganization treatment, into an integrated transaction that does. As a result, the transaction may be recast so as to place it within an entirely different definition of reorganization under §368(a)(1). In Rev. Rul. 67-274, for example, such recasting converted an initially "failed" Type B stock reorganization into a transaction that did qualify as a Type C asset acquisition.[55] The Treasury Department has also used the step-transaction doctrine to convert an initial merger that did not qualify for tax-free treatment as a Type A reverse triangular merger into a qualified direct Type A statutory merger.[56] Similarly, an initial exchange that, by itself, would have qualified for tax-free treatment might not be classified as a tax-free reorganization when viewed as part of a multistep, integrated acquisition transaction.[57]

Step-transaction principles also can be used to effectively aggregate the overall consideration paid to target shareholders in multiple steps, thus potentially converting an initial acquisition that did not qualify for tax-free treatment into an overall transaction that did qualify. For example, in Rev. Rul. 2001-26,[58] the participating target shareholders in an initial tender offer did not receive sufficient target stock to qualify the tender offer as a Type A reverse triangular merger. Viewed together with a subsequent merger, however, the necessary control requirements were met. The integrated transaction ultimately did qualify as a reverse Type A merger.[59]

One real challenge to tax-free reorganizations planning for multistep acquisitions has been predicting whether the courts or the IRS would view the multiple steps independently or as part of a larger whole. Though most of the policy changes have been "taxpayer-friendly," significant shifts in recent decades in the Treasury Department's position on when step-transaction analysis does or does not apply have added to the challenge. These developments are discussed throughout the rest of this chapter and in chapters that follow. A final section in this chapter examines step-transaction issues that

---

54. See, e.g., Rev. Rul. 76-123, 1976-1 C.B. 94. But see Rev. Rul. 88-44, 1984-1 C.B. 105.
55. 1967-2 C.B. 141.
56. Rev. Rul. 2001-46, 2001-2 C.B. 321. This ruling is discussed in detail in the following subsection.
57. See, e.g., Rev. Rul. 2008-25, 2008-1 C.B. 986 (qualified reverse triangular Type A reorganization treated as a failed Type C reorganization when viewed as an integrated transaction).
58. 2001-1 C.B. 1297.
59. See Chapter 12 for further discussion of this ruling.

may arise in distinguishing taxable qualified stock purchases (QSPs) from tax-free reorganizations.

Continuity of Proprietary Interest

a) Introduction

Continuity of the target shareholder's proprietary interest historically has been central to the tax-free reorganization provisions. Taxpayers are entitled to nonrecognition treatment on a reorganization exchange since they are viewed as continuing their investment in the old, albeit now modified, corporate enterprise. If investors remain invested in the modified corporate enterprise, the logic is that the transaction should not trigger immediate recognition of gain or loss. The continuity of shareholder proprietary interest test evolved from court opinions interpreting an early version of the statutory reorganization provisions. Several of the modern reorganization definitions in §368(a)(1) now include a statutorily built-in continuity of investment requirement, making the application of a judicially developed "continuity of proprietary interest" test unnecessary. In these cases, the type and amount of proprietary interest that the transferor must receive to be eligible for tax-free nonrecognition treatment is defined by the statute itself. Under §368(a)(1)(B), for example, the exchange must be *solely* for all or part of the purchasing corporation's voting stock or *solely* for all or part of the voting stock of the purchasing company's parent. In other words *all* of the consideration paid to the sellers must be in the form of voting stock; no cash consideration is permitted. The language of §368(a)(1)(C) is similar, but subsequent paragraphs provide more flexibility with regard to the required proprietary interest in the case of Type C reorganizations.[60]

Today, the statutory definitions in §§368(a)(1)(B) and (C) render the old judicially developed continuity of interest doctrine moot with respect to Type B and C reorganizations. Still, familiarity with the continuity of interest history is important to understanding the logic—or critiquing the *absence* of a consistent logic—behind the various reorganization definitions.[61] More importantly, since §368(a)(1)(A) has no statutorily built-in continuity test, judicially developed tests, as interpreted over time by the Treasury Department, remain directly relevant for Type A reorganizations.

---

60. These issues are considered more fully in Chapter 12.
61. Commentators have been critiquing inconsistencies and incoherence in application of continuity of interest rules for decades. See, e.g., Joshua D. Blank, Confronting Continuity: A Tradition of Fiction in Corporate Reorganizations, 2006 Colum. Bus. L. Rev. 1 (2006); David S. Miller, The Devolution and Inevitable Extinction of the Continuity of Interest Doctrine, 3 Fla. Tax Rev. 187 (1996); Daniel Q. Posin, Taxing Corporate Reorganizations: Purging Penelope's Web, 133 U. Pa. L. Rev. 1335 (1985).

b) Early Case Law

Much of present-day continuity of interest doctrine applicable to Type A reorganizations actually dates back to cases decided in the 1930s under earlier versions of the Internal Revenue Code. Under the Revenue Act of 1921, for example, the term "reorganization" included a "merger or consolidation (including the acquisition by one corporation of at least a majority of the voting stock and at least a majority of the total number of shares of all other classes of stock of another corporation, *or substantially all the properties of another corporation*)."[62] A corporate sale of assets for cash and promissory notes technically fit within the early reorganization definition since it was, after all, an "acquisition by one corporation of substantially all of the properties of another." Nevertheless, the courts were reluctant to grant nonrecognition treatment to transactions that were essentially cash sales. The Second Circuit in Cortland Specialty Co. v. Commissioner[63] rejected tax-free reorganization treatment in the case of a transfer of substantially all of the target corporation's assets in exchange for cash and promissory notes. Even though the transaction technically fit the then applicable reorganization definition, the court found lacking the "requisite that there must be some continuity of interest on the part of the transferor corporation or its stockholders in order to secure exemption. Reorganization presupposes continuance of business under modified corporate forms."[64] The transaction did not satisfy the continuity of proprietary interest test since the target corporation received only cash and notes, rather than an interest in the purchasing corporation.

The Supreme Court considered a similar cash transaction in *Pinellas Ice & Cold Storage* and also refused to interpret the reorganization definition literally. The *Pinellas* Court found that

> the mere purchase for money of the assets of one company by another is beyond the evident purpose of the [reorganization] provision, and has no real semblance to a merger or consolidation. Certainly, we think that to be within the exemption the seller must *acquire an interest in the affairs of the purchasing company more definite than that incident to ownership of its short-term purchase-money notes.*[65]

In other words, the Supreme Court required some continuity of proprietary interest—receipt by the sellers of only cash and short-term notes was not sufficient.

---

62. Revenue Act of 1921, ch. 135, §202(c)(2), 42 Stat. 227, 230 (1921) (emphasis added). This language was reenacted in Revenue Acts through 1932.
63. 60 F.2d 937 (2d Cir. 1932), cert. denied, 288 U.S. 599 (1933).
64. Id. At 940.
65. Pinellas Ice & Cold Storage Co. v. Comm'r, 287 U.S. 462, 470 (1933) (emphasis added).

Two years later, in Helvering v. Minnesota Tea Co.,[66] the Court interpreted the same language[67] in the case of an asset acquisition for cash and voting trust certificates. To the earlier *Pinellas* requirement that the seller receive "an interest in the affairs of the purchasing company more definite than that incident to ownership of its short-term purchase-money notes," the Supreme Court added that "this interest must be definite and material; it must represent a substantial part of the value of the thing transferred."[68]

An unpacking of the *Minnesota Tea* test reveals two components. First, the sellers must receive a "definite and material" interest in the purchasing corporation. The focus here is on the *quality* or type of consideration sufficient to represent a "definite and material" interest in the acquiring corporation. Voting stock of the acquiring corporation, whether common or preferred, represents a definite and material interest in the acquiring corporation. The Court in *Minnesota Tea* found that voting trust certificates representing the purchasing corporation's voting stock also were sufficient.[69] In John A. Nelson Corp. v. Commissioner,[70] a companion case decided on the same day as *Minnesota Tea*, the Supreme Court held that a transfer of assets in exchange for cash and the entire issue of the purchasing corporation's nonvoting preferred stock provided the selling corporation with a "definite and substantial interest in the affairs of the purchasing corporation"[71] sufficient to qualify the transaction as a tax-free reorganization. The *Nelson* case established that the continuity of proprietary interest test did not necessarily require retention of a *voting* or management interest in the modified corporate enterprise; nonvoting preferred stock was sufficient. The Supreme Court later held in LeTulle v. Scofield[72] that the continuity of interest test is not met when the transferor receives only cash and long-term bonds of the purchasing corporation. In such a case, the Court remarked, "we think it cannot be said that the transferor retains any proprietary interest in the enterprise. On the contrary, he becomes a creditor."[73]

---

66. 296 U.S. 378 (1935).

67. The language from §203 of the Revenue Act of 1926 had been carried over to §112(a)(1)(A) of the Revenue Act of 1928.

68. 296 U.S. 378, 385 (1935).

69. A related issue was whether this "definite and material" interest had to be a *direct* interest in the acquiring corporation itself or whether the interest could be an *indirect* interest reflected by stock of a parent of the acquiror or some other affiliated corporate entity. Early case law demanded a *direct* interest. See, e.g., Groman v. Comm'r, 302 U.S. 82 (1937); Helvering v. Bashford, 302 U.S. 454 (1938). This requirement, sometimes referred to as the "remote continuity of interest" doctrine, has been virtually eliminated by subsequent statutory and regulatory developments. See further discussion of triangular mergers in Chapter 12.

70. John A. Nelson Corp. v. Helvering, 296 U.S. 374 (1935).

71. *Id. At* 377.

72. 308 U.S. 415 (1940).

73. *Id. At* 421.

The second component of the *Minnesota Tea* test focuses on the *proportion* of total consideration that must come from these "definite and material" types of consideration. Some portion of the consideration may be paid in the form of cash, notes, securities, or other property without disqualifying the reorganization. As to this second component, the *Minnesota Tea* Court was not bothered by the fact that a large part of the consideration paid to the sellers was cash.[74] "This, we think, is permissible so long as the taxpayer received an interest in the affairs of the transferee which represented a *material part of the value* of the transferred assets."[75] In other words, this second component looks at the *quantity* of consideration received by the target corporation or its shareholders that represents a proprietary stake in the acquiring corporation.

The courts apply the continuity of interest test in the aggregate. Thus, even if some shareholders receive only cash and other shareholders receive only stock, a transaction generally will qualify for tax-free treatment as long as the overall consideration package paid to all of the participating target shareholders meets the continuity of interest requirements and otherwise fits one of the reorganization definitions in §368(a)(1).[76]

c) Evolving Continuity of Shareholder Interest (COSI) Rules[77]

Although the requirement itself had been codified in regulations for many years,[78] the Treasury Department did not provide a detailed regulatory definition of continuity of interest until 1998. Portions of the 1998 regulations since have been revised and replaced by the Treasury Department.[79] Nevertheless, the general rule reflected in Treas. Reg. §1.368-1(e)(1) has not changed. In fact, the regulation's opening sentence could have been taken straight from any number of early reorganization cases from the 1930s: "The purpose of the continuity of interest requirement is to prevent transactions that resemble sales from qualifying for nonrecognition of gain or loss available to corporate reorganizations."[80] The regulation's general

---

74. Approximately 37% of the purchase price was paid in cash, with the remaining 63% paid in the form of voting trust certificates.

75. 296 U.S. At 386 (emphasis added).

76. See also Rev. Rul. 66-224, 1966-2 C.B. 114.

77. Although many refer to these as COI rules, we use the shorthand COSI to refer to these requirements in Treas. Reg. §1.368-1(e), which essentially focus on the extent to which the *target or target shareholders* receive consideration in the form of an equity interest in the acquiring corporation. We use the term COSI to emphasize *shareholder* continuity and distinguish these rules from other continuity-related regulatory provisions that focus on the *acquiring corporation's* continuing connection with the target corporation's assets or stock. See Treas. Reg. §1.368-1(d); §1.368-2(k). These provisions are discussed later in this chapter and again in Chapter 12.

78. Treas. Reg. §1.368-1(b).

79. See Treas. Reg. §1.368-1(e)(2), T.D. 9565, 76 Fed. Reg. 78,540 (Dec. 19, 2011). These changes are discussed later in this chapter and in Chapter 13.

80. Treas. Reg. §1.368-1(e)(1)(i) (added by T.D. 8760, 63 Fed. Reg. 4174 (Jan. 28, 1998).

rule also has unmistakably retained the two-part quality and quantity analysis from earlier cases such as *Minnesota Tea*:

> Continuity of interest requires that in substance a substantial part of the value of the proprietary interests in the target corporation be preserved in the reorganization. A proprietary interest in the target corporation is preserved if, in a potential reorganization, it is exchanged for a proprietary interest in the issuing corporation . . . ,[81] it is exchanged by the acquiring corporation for a direct interest in the target corporation enterprise, or it otherwise continues as a proprietary interest in the target corporation. However, a proprietary interest in the target corporation is not preserved if, in connection with the potential reorganization, it is acquired by the issuing corporation for consideration other than stock of the issuing corporation, or stock of the issuing corporation furnished in exchange for a proprietary interest in the target corporation in the potential reorganization is redeemed. All facts and circumstances must be considered in determining whether, in substance, a proprietary interest in the target corporation is preserved.[82]

Notice that the regulation's general rule does not reflect *fundamental* conceptual differences from the quality and quantity components of the judicially developed continuity of interest requirements. Nevertheless, the regulations *do* change the concept underlying continuity of interest requirements in subtle ways. The regulations are designed to refocus the continuity requirement "on its initial purpose of ensuring that the acquiring corporation furnishes the proper type of consideration."[83] Put differently, the emphasis of the Treasury Department's earlier continuity analysis had been on what the target shareholders *retained* after the reorganization. The emphasis now is on what the acquiring corporation *furnishes* as consideration in the reorganization.[84] The most dramatic changes resulting from this shift in focus involve the effect of pre- and post-reorganization transfers of stock by target shareholders.[85]

In addition to providing detailed interpretation of requirements necessary to satisfy the COSI test, the regulations specifically suggest two situations

---

81. The "issuing corporation" is the acquiring corporation, as the term is used in §368(a), and in the case of triangular reorganizations, the corporation in control of the acquiring corporation. Treas. Reg. §1.368-1(b).

82. Treas. Reg. §1.368-1(e)(1)(i). The proposed COI regulations, 61 Fed. Reg. 67,512 (Dec. 23, 1996), were revised in response to comments and issued as final regulations generally applicable to transactions occurring after January 28, 1998. T.D. 8760, 63 Fed. Reg. 4174 (Jan. 28, 1998).

83. 61 Fed. Reg. 67,512, 67,513 (Dec. 23, 1996) (preamble to proposed COSI regulations).

84. For an interesting discussion, see David F. Shores, Reexamining Continuity of Shareholder Interest in Corporate Reorganizations, 17 Va. Tax Rev. 419 (1998).

85. Most of these changes have broadened availability of tax-free reorganization treatment and, thus, have been viewed as very "taxpayer friendly." The changes and their impact are discussed later in this chapter.

in which the COSI requirement is not met. First, a transaction fails the COSI test if the target corporation is acquired with consideration other than the issuing corporation's stock.[86] This is essentially a restatement of the quality component of traditional continuity analysis. Second, a transaction fails the COSI requirement if stock furnished by the acquiring corporation in the reorganization is redeemed. This seems a sensible result. If the purchasing corporation immediately redeems for cash the stock recently issued in connection with a reorganization, it has effectively made a cash purchase.[87]

One initial concern under the COSI regulations was the effect of a sale by the former target shareholders of recently received purchasing corporation (P) stock back to P under a corporate stock repurchase program. In a ruling on stock repurchase programs issued shortly after the original 1998 COSI regulations revisions, the Service sanctioned reorganization treatment even where the purchasing corporation modified its stock repurchase program in order to prevent dilution that might result from the issuance of its stock in a merger transaction.[88] The ruling disregards any former target corporation (T) shareholders' sales of stock to P under the repurchase program as "mere dispositions" to unrelated persons.[89] The ruling was careful, however, to stress that the repurchase program was not a matter negotiated by the T shareholders as part of the reorganization and that the "mechanics of an open market repurchase" did not favor participation by the former T shareholders. Even if it could be established that some of the former T shareholders participated in the repurchase, the ruling concludes that such purchases would be coincidental.

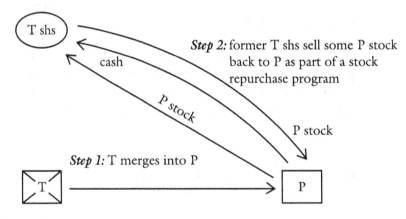

T shs

cash

Step 2: former T shs sell some P stock back to P as part of a stock repurchase program

P stock

P stock

Step 1: T merges into P

T

P

---

86. The issuing corporation will generally be the acquiring corporation, except in certain triangular mergers in which the issuing corporation, will be the corporation in control of the acquiring corporation. A definition of "issuing corporation" is provided in Treas. Reg. §1.368-1(b).

87. See Treas. Reg. §1.368-1(e)(8), ex. 4.

88. Rev. Rul. 99-58, 1999-2 C.B. 701.

89. A more detailed discussion of the COSI regulations' treatment of post-reorganization sales follows in section (e)(ii) of this chapter.

Just as the COSI regulation's required *proprietary interest* in the issuing corporation has its roots in the judicially developed continuity of interest doctrine's *quality* component, the requirement that *a substantial part of the value* of the proprietary interest in the target corporation be preserved has its roots in the doctrine's *quantity* component. Yet, the regulations provide no definition of "proprietary interest" or "substantial part of the value." For the meaning of these terms, taxpayers still must look to case law, IRS rulings, and the occasional regulatory example. As discussed earlier in this chapter, the precedent regarding *quality* has been rather generous. Virtually any equity interest, even if it differs substantially from the equity interests exchanged by the target shareholders, seems to suffice. Apparently, even issuing corporation nonqualified preferred stock (NQPS) received by the target shareholders will be considered a "proprietary interest" for purposes of measuring continuity even though it will be treated as taxable boot to the target shareholders.[90]

d) Measuring Continuity of Shareholder Interest

Not surprisingly, parties interested in a tax-free transaction often demand assurance that the proposed exchange will receive tax-free reorganization classification under §368(a). Assessing continuity for these purposes requires certainty not only about the proprietary quality of the expected consideration, but also its proportion or quantity. For many years, the tax bar had relied for a "quantity" benchmark on the Service's position, for purposes of issuing §368(a)(1)(A) advance rulings, that the continuity of interest test was satisfied if the former target shareholders received a stock interest "equal in value . . . To at least 50 percent of the value of all the formerly outstanding stock of the acquired or transferred corporation . . . ."[91]

Although the Service no longer issues advance letter rulings (sometimes referred to "protective rulings") on Type A reorganization continuity of interest absent significant issues that must be resolved,[92] examples in revised regulations indicate that a transaction in which target shareholders receive as little as 40% of the consideration in the form of an equity interest in the acquiring corporation will satisfy COSI requirements.[93]

One significant issue regarding continuity assessments that had not received focused regulatory attention until relatively recently is the proper

---

90. I.R.C. §354(a)(2)(c) (target shareholder boot rule); §351(g) (NQPS definition). See also discussion of NQPS in Chapter 4.
91. Rev. Proc. 77-37, ¶3.02, 1977-2 C.B. 568.
92. See Rev. Proc. 2017-52, 2017-41 I.R.B. 283 (Sept. 21, 2017).
93. Treas. Reg. §1.368-1(e)(2)(v), ex. 1 (target shareholder receipt of $60 cash and $40 worth of purchasing corporation stock sufficient for continuity of interest). The case law is even more forgiving. For example, in John A. Nelson Corp. v. Helvering, 296 U.S. 374 (1935), a transaction with only 38% equity qualified as a tax-free reorganization.

timing for COSI valuations. If COSI valuation is determined on the acquisition closing date, target shareholders face the risk that a merger that *appeared* to meet proprietary interest requirements at the time of contract would no longer qualify for tax-free treatment if the acquiring (issuing) corporation's stock value declined between the time of contract and closing. Nevertheless, the Treasury Department's past position had been to measure continuity on the effective date of the reorganization.[94]

In a change of position, the Treasury Department has issued regulations that provide that proprietary interest "shall be valued on the last business day before the first date [the potential reorganization contract] is a binding contract (the pre-signing date), if such contract provides for fixed consideration."[95] The preamble explains that this "signing date" rule is "based on the principle that, where a binding contract provides for fixed consideration, the target corporation shareholders generally can be viewed as being subject to the economic fortunes of the issuing corporation as of the signing date."[96] A contract has "fixed consideration" if it states the amount of money, other property, and the *number of shares* of each class of stock of the issuing corporation to be exchanged for *all* the proprietary interests in the target corporation or to be exchanged for *each* proprietary interest in the target corporation.[97] The regulations also explain that a contract still has "fixed consideration" even if it allows a target shareholder to make an election to receive a number of shares of stock, money, or other property (or some combination of these items) in exchange for all of the target shareholder's proprietary interests in the target corporation.[98] The signing date valuation rule makes sense. If the binding contract entitles target shareholders to a fixed number of acquiring corporation shares, regardless of the acquiring corporation's stock value at closing, the target shareholders' proprietary stake really is tied to the economic success or failure of the purchaser. For practical economic purposes under these circumstances, target shareholders

---

94. See, e.g., Rev. Proc. 77-37, 1977-2 C.B. 568, ¶3.02 (assessing value for continuity of interest purposes "as of the effective date of the reorganization").
95. Treas. Reg. §1.368-1(e)(2)(i).
96. T.D. 9565, 76 Fed. Reg. 78,540 (Dec. 19, 2011). On the same day that the Treasury Department issued final regulations regarding the signing date rule, it also issued proposed regulations that identified situations, other than those covered by the signing date rule, in which the value of issuing corporation stock could be determined based on a value other than its actual trading price on the closing date (such as an average of trading prices of issuing corporation stock over a number of days). T.D. 9565, 76 Fed. Reg. 78,540 (Dec. 19, 2011). In 2019, the Treasury Department withdrew those proposed regulations. Prop. Treas. Reg. §1.368-1(e), 84 Fed. Reg. 12,169 (Apr. 1, 2019). For guidance on situations in which the Service will consider alternative stock valuation methods to value issuing corporation stock for purposes of COSI, see Rev. Proc. 2018-12, 2018-6 I.R.B. 1 (Jan. 23, 2018).
97. Treas. Reg. §1.368-1(e)(2)(iii)(A). The regulations also provide detailed rules and useful examples on the related issues of interim contract modifications, contingency adjustments, escrows, and antidilution clauses. This chapter does not include discussion of those details.
98. Treas. Reg. §1.368-1(e)(2)(iii)(A).

become members of the new corporate family from the time of a binding contract.

e) Post-Reorganization Shareholder Continuity

i) Background and History

One concern regarding continuity of interest is the length of time that investors of the old corporate enterprise must *retain* a continuing proprietary interest in the modified corporate form *after* the reorganization exchange. Imagine, for example, a transaction in which shareholders exchange their target corporation stock solely for purchasing corporation stock. Shortly thereafter, a substantial proportion of the old target shareholders sell their recently acquired purchasing corporation stock for cash. In the end, these target shareholders will have cashed out on their investment. Surely, the old target shareholders who sell their new stock for cash will be taxed upon this stock sale. The more difficult question was whether the post-reorganization sale by a substantial percentage of the old target shareholders would jeopardize the tax-free nature of the reorganization to the other shareholders or to the corporations involved. Subchapter C itself contains no specific requirements on the length of time that participating investors must *retain* their continuity of proprietary interest, suggesting that simply satisfying the continuity requirements immediately after the exchange should be sufficient. Until 1998, however, the IRS rather vigorously applied step-transaction analysis, taking the position that "[s]ales, redemptions, and other dispositions of stock occurring . . . subsequent to the exchange which are part of the plan of reorganization will be considered in determining whether there is a 50 percent continuing interest through stock ownership."[99]

This position came back to haunt the Treasury Department in the case of McDonald's Restaurants of Illinois, Inc. v. Commissioner,[100] a case in which McDonald's acquired several target franchisees. The merger agreement provided that the McDonald's stock transferred to the target franchisee shareholders would later be included in a registered public sale of stock for cash arranged by the purchasing corporation.

Taking the view that the transaction was a cash purchase rather than a tax-free reorganization, McDonald's used a cost (or stepped-up) basis in the assets acquired. Viewing the transaction under step-transaction analysis, the Seventh Circuit agreed with McDonald's, concluding that the transaction failed to satisfy the continuity of interest requirement. Viewed as a whole, the transaction, the court concluded, essentially was a cash sale. Although

---

99. Rev. Proc. 77-37, 1977-2 C.B. 568, 569, sec. 3.02. The regulations reflect a dramatically different view, under which the post-reorganization continuity requirement is all but eliminated. These regulations are discussed in detail later in this section.
100. 688 F.2d 520 (7th Cir. 1982).

the franchisees had no formally binding commitment to sell the shares for cash, the court found that the merger would not have taken place without guarantees of saleability to the franchisees who insisted on cash.

Commentators were quick to criticize the Seventh Circuit opinion, arguing that post-reorganization target shareholder sales should be troublesome only when the target shareholders sold the stock back to the acquiring corporation or a party related to the acquiring corporation. If, shortly after the exchange, the target shareholders' recently acquired stock in the purchasing corporation is redeemed or otherwise repurchased by the purchasing corporation, it would appear that such target shareholders have "sold" their interest to the acquiror rather than participated in a reorganization exchange. The post-reorganization sale by the target shareholders in *McDonald's* was to third parties unrelated to the purchasing corporation and was merely *arranged* by the purchasing corporation. This type of post-reorganization sale to an unrelated third party arguably should not defeat continuity of shareholder proprietary interest. The Treasury Department has now adopted this approach.

ii) The Treasury Department's Revised Approach to Post-Reorganization Target Shareholder Transfers

One of the most dramatic Treasury Department changes in 1998 to the COSI regulation was effective elimination of any post-reorganization continuity requirement as long as target shareholders' sales of stock after the reorganization are made to unrelated parties:

> For purposes of the continuity of interest requirement, ... A mere disposition of stock of the issuing corporation received in a potential reorganization to persons not related . . . To the issuing corporation is disregarded.[101]

Put slightly differently, the revised regulations effectively "turn off" the step-transaction rule as applied to post-reorganization target shareholder transfers to unrelated parties. Lest there be any doubt that the Treasury Department has changed its position in the *McDonald's*-type case, the regulations include an example based on the *McDonald's* facts. In this example, the T shareholders receive only P stock in a merger transaction. At the same time, P agrees to register the stock issued in the merger, thus enabling the T shareholders to quickly sell their P shares for cash. The example confirms that T shareholders' sales of P stock immediately after the merger will be disregarded, since the sales are to unrelated parties.[102] Despite the cash sale, the transaction still meets continuity of interest requirements and is treated

---

101. Treas. Reg. §1.368-1(e)(1)(i).
102. Treas. Reg. §1.368-1(e)(8), ex. 3.

as tax-free reorganization. Even a binding contract on the part of target shareholders to sell acquiring corporation stock received in a reorganization will not defeat continuity of interest as long as the target shareholders are selling to unrelated parties.[103] Thus, with the exception of sales to related parties, the regulations now disregard T shareholder post-reorganization sales altogether, even if they were part of an integrated transaction.[104] This is not to suggest, however, that Treasury has otherwise reduced its reliance on step-transaction principles. To the contrary, several rulings suggest a reinvigoration of step-transaction principles as applied to some reorganization issues.

iii) Target Shareholder Transfers to Related Parties

Despite the relaxation of COSI rules regarding post-reorganization transfers to unrelated parties that are considered part of an integrated transaction, such transfers to *related parties* will cause the reorganization to fail the COSI test. The regulations provide:

> A proprietary interest in the target corporation is not preserved if, in connection with a potential reorganization, a person related (as defined in paragraph (e)(4) of this section) to the issuing corporation acquires, with consideration other than a proprietary interest in the issuing corporation, stock of the target corporation or stock of the issuing corporation furnished in exchange for a proprietary interest in the target corporation in the potential reorganization, except to the extent those persons who were direct or indirect owners of the target corporation prior to the potential reorganization maintain a direct or indirect proprietary interest in the issuing corporation.[105]

Two corporations[106] are considered "related" for purposes of the regulations if they are members of the same affiliated group, as defined in §1504, or if purchase by one corporation of stock of the other would be considered a redemption under §304(a)(2).[107] As a basic illustration of such a post-reorganization sale to a related party, imagine that T merges into a subsidiary (S) of the purchasing corporation (P), with the T shareholders

---

103. *Id. At* ex. 1.

104. The Treasury Department takes a similar view with respect to post-incorporation sales pursuant to a binding commitment. See Rev. Rul. 2003-51, 2003-1 C.B. 938, discussed in Chapter 4.

105. Treas. Reg. §1.368-1(e)(3).

106. Individuals or other noncorporate shareholders are not included in the definition of "related persons" for purposes of these regulations. Statements accompanying the announcement of the final regulations explained: "[B]ecause the final regulations focus generally on the consideration P exchanges, related persons do not include individuals or other noncorporate shareholders." T.D. 8760, 63 Fed. Reg. 4174, 4176 (Jan. 28, 1998).

107. Treas. Reg. §1.368-1(e)(4)(i). Section 304's treatment of certain stock sales between related corporations as redemptions is discussed in Chapter 6.

receiving only P stock in the exchange.[108] Immediately after the merger, S purchases the P stock received by the T shareholders for cash. Such a transaction would violate the COSI test, since the former T shareholders made an immediate post-reorganization sale of P stock received in the exchange to a party related to P.[109]

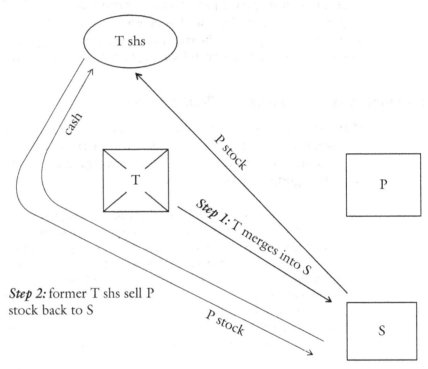

Step 2: former T shs sell P stock back to S

Special rules clarify that corporations are considered related if they meet either of these definitions immediately before or after the stock sale involved.[110] For example, imagine that T shareholders receive stock representing 35% of the outstanding stock of P in connection with a merger of T into P. Immediately after the merger, X Corporation, which already owns 50% of P, purchases for cash all of the P stock received by the T shareholders in the merger. Since X owns 85% of the P stock immediately after the purchase, X is considered a related person. The transaction will fail the COSI test, since a related person acquired T stock with consideration other than a proprietary interest in the issuing corporation.

---

108. Such Type A triangular mergers are considered in detail in Chapter 12.
109. Treas. Reg. §1.368-1(e)(8), ex. 4(iii).
110. Treas. Reg. §1.368-1(e)(4)(ii)(A).

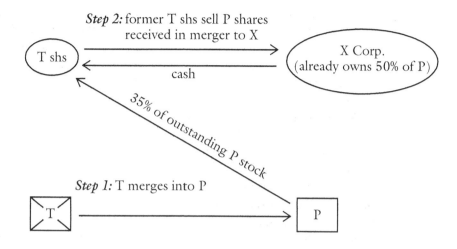

f) Historic Shareholder Continuity

i) Background and History

The issue of pre-reorganization sales arises in cases where the historic shareholders of a target corporation transfer their interest in the target shortly before a reorganization transaction. The new owners of the target stock then participate in a reorganization in which they receive a proprietary interest in the acquiring corporation. The transaction may meet the continuity of interest test with respect to the recent target shareholders. Should it matter that continuity does not exist as to the historic target shareholders, who have recently been cashed-out?

One major early case is Yoc Heating Corp. v. Commissioner,[111] in which the purchasing corporation acquired approximately 85% of the target corporation's stock from the target shareholders for cash and notes. As new owner of an 85% interest in the target, the purchasing corporation then arranged for transfer of all of the target's assets to a newly formed subsidiary in exchange for the new subsidiary's stock, which was distributed to participating target shareholders. Not surprisingly, the only target shareholder to participate was the purchasing corporation itself, which received the subsidiary stock in exchange for its 85% interest in the target. The minority shareholders who disapproved of the asset transfer were paid cash.

Under §362, the purchasing corporation's basis in the target assets in a reorganization transaction should be the same as the basis of the assets in the target corporation's hands. The government in Yoc Heating took the position that the transaction was a reorganization under §368(a)(1)(D),[112]

---

111. 61 T.C. 168 (1973).
112. A §368(a)(1)(D) reorganization is "a transfer by a corporation of all or part of its assets to another corporation if immediately after the transfer the transferor, or one or more of its

which requires that the transferor, or one or more of its shareholders, have control of the new corporation immediately after the exchange. Since the purchasing corporation was the primary shareholder of the target transferor immediately before the exchange, and since the purchasing corporation controlled the new corporation immediately after the exchange, the government argued that the control requirements of §368(a)(1)(D) were met.

The purchasing corporation in *Yoc Heating* used an integrated transaction argument to claim that the target transferors did not have sufficient "control" immediately after the exchange to be considered a reorganization.[113] Instead, it argued that the transaction should be viewed as a cash purchase, resulting in a stepped-up basis in the target's assets.[114] The Tax Court agreed that the transaction should be viewed as an integrated transaction, beginning with the cash sales by the original target shareholders and ending with the later exchange for the new subsidiary's stock. Since approximately 85% of the original target shareholder had been bought out for cash, the target or its shareholders were not in "control" immediately after the exchange as required by §368(a)(1)(D). The court also found that there was no reorganization "[b]y a parity of reasoning rooted in the judicial 'continuity of interest' principle applicable to reorganizations."[115] In other words, the Tax Court in *Yoc Heating* held that continuity of interest requires that the historic shareholders retain a proprietary interest in the newly reorganized enterprise. Since the original or historic shareholders in *Yoc Heating* had sold their stock for cash and were no longer invested in the reorganized corporation, the Tax Court held that the transaction was not a reorganization and that the purchasing corporation was entitled to a stepped-up basis in the acquired target assets.

The historic shareholder continuity of interest doctrine continued to develop with the Tax Court's decision in J.E. Seagram Corp. v. Commissioner,[116] which involved a battle in which DuPont and Seagrams, along with several other corporations, were competing to take over control of the target corporation, Conoco. Each of the competitors successfully

---

shareholders . . . or any combination thereof, is in control of the corporation to which the assets are transferred; but only if, in pursuance of the plan, stock or securities of the corporation to which the assets are transferred are distributed in a transaction which qualifies under section 354, 355, or 356."

113. Since tax-free reorganizations are generally favorable to the taxpayer, one might expect the taxpayer to argue for such treatment and the government to argue *against* it. When the taxpayer is a purchasing corporation, however, as in *Yoc Heating*, the positions often reverse. The purchasing corporation generally will prefer cost basis to the substituted basis that results from reorganization treatment.

114. The *Yoc Heating* case was decided before Congress added §338, which provides an election for such a stepped-up basis following a "qualified stock purchase." This provision, and its relationship to *Yoc Heating*, is discussed in Chapter 10.

115. 61 T.C. 168, 177.

116. 104 T.C. 75 (1995).

acquired substantial amounts of Conoco stock for cash. DuPont, however, was the ultimate winner, having acquired approximately 46% of Conoco's stock. DuPont then arranged for a merger of Conoco into one of its subsidiaries. Conoco shareholders received DuPont stock in connection with the merger. The Conoco shareholders included in this exchange included DuPont itself (approximately 46%), Seagrams (approximately 32%) and the public (approximately 22%).

Seagrams hoped to recognize its realized loss on the exchange of its Conoco stock for DuPont stock. Loss recognition was unavailable to Seagrams, however, if the transaction was classified as a tax-free reorganization and if Seagrams had received its DuPont stock as part of a "plan of reorganization." Although the merger appeared to be a legitimate §368(a)(1)(A) reorganization, Seagrams argued that the transaction failed to meet the shareholder continuity of interest requirements, since only 22% of the participating shareholders to the merger were the original or historic shareholders who owned Conoco stock before the integrated series of events relating to the take-over. Seagrams argued that

> because it acquired approximately 32 percent of [the] shares for cash pursuant to its own tender offer, and DuPont acquired approximately 46 percent of [the] shares for cash pursuant to its tender offer, the combined 78 percent of Conoco shares acquired for cash after the date of the agreement destroyed the continuity of interest requisite for a valid reorganization.[117]

The Tax Court in *Seagrams* took a limited view of the historic shareholder test, distinguishing *Yoc Heating* by observing that in *Yoc Heating* it was the *acquiring* corporation *itself* whose recently acquired shares were not counted toward meeting the continuity of interest requirements. Under this view of the historic shareholder continuity of interest doctrine, the shares recently purchased by the *acquiring* corporation should not count toward continuity of interest. Thus, DuPont's recently acquired 46% of the target Conoco's stock would not count toward continuity. On the other hand, the Tax Court in *Seagrams* held that the 32% of Conoco shares held by Seagrams immediately before the merger *should* be counted toward meeting the continuity of interest requirement even though Seagrams had recently acquired these shares. The Tax Court in *Seagrams* limited the historic shareholder continuity requirement, concluding that

> we must look not to the identity of the target's shareholders, but rather to what the shares represented when the reorganization was completed. In this case, a majority of the old shares of Conoco were converted to shares of DuPont in the

---

117. *Id. At* 99.

reorganization, so that in the sense, at least, that a majority of the consideration was the acquiring corporation's stock, the test of continuity was met.[118]

The court continued:

> [S]ales of target stock for cash after the date of the announcement of an acquisition can be neither predicted not controlled by publicly held parties to a reorganization. A requirement that the identity of the acquired corporation's shareholders be tracked to assume a sufficient number of "historic" shareholders to satisfy some arbitrary minimal percentage receiving the acquiring corporation's stock would be completely unrealistic.[119]

In the end, the Tax Court in *Seagrams* held that the transaction was a reorganization despite the fact that in the transaction transferring shareholders holding a total 78% of the target stock had recently purchased their stock and, therefore, were not the historic shareholders.

ii) The Treasury Department's Revised Approach to Pre-Reorganization Sales by Target Shareholders

As originally proposed, the 1998 COSI regulations focused only on the effect of target shareholder *post*-reorganization sales on continuity of shareholder interest.[120] The preamble to regulations finalized in 1998, however, stated that "the IRS and Treasury Department believe that issues concerning the COSI requirement raised by dispositions of T stock *before* a potential reorganization correspond to those raised by subsequent dispositions of P stock furnished in exchange for T stock in the potential reorganization."[121] Thus, "the final regulations apply the rationale of the proposed COSI regulations to transactions occurring both prior to and after a potential reorganization."[122] These final regulations virtually eliminated the historic shareholder continuity of interest requirement, providing that

> [f]or purposes of the continuity of interest requirements, a mere disposition of stock of the target corporation prior to a potential reorganization to persons not related . . . To the target corporation or to persons not related to the issuing corporation is disregarded . . . .[123]

---

118. Id at 103.
119. Id.
120. See discussion in the section entitled "Post-Reorganization Continuity" earlier in this chapter.
121. T.D. 8760, 63 Fed. Reg. 4174, 4175 (Jan. 28, 1998) (emphasis added).
122. Id.
123. Treas. Reg. §1.368-1(e)(1). In this regard, note that the potential reorganization transaction *itself* can create a relationship meeting the definition of "related persons" under the regulations. For example, the regulations describe a transaction in which X Corporation already held a 60% interest in the purchasing corporation (P) and a 30% interest in the

This regulatory language in §1.368-1(e)(1) gives its blessing to the result in the *Seagrams* case. Under the revised regulations, Seagrams' cash purchases of Conoco stock immediately prior to the reorganization would be disregarded as "mere dispositions," since Seagrams in that case was unrelated to the issuer (acquirer), DuPont, or to the target, Conoco. In other words, shares held by Seagrams immediately before the reorganization would be counted toward the COSI test, even though Seagrams was not a historic shareholder. On the other hand, target corporation stock recently purchased for cash by DuPont would not count toward the COSI test, since DuPont itself was the issuing (acquiring) corporation.

iii) Pre-Reorganization Redemptions and Dividends

The focus of the preceding section was generally on pre-reorganization *sales* by target shareholders. A related set of issues involves pre-reorganization *redemptions from* or *dividends to* target shareholders. At the same time that it finalized its revised COSI regulation in 1998, the Treasury Department issued temporary regulations more specifically addressing such pre-reorganization redemptions and dividends.[124] The temporary regulations swept quite broadly, finding that a proprietary interest in T was not preserved if *any* pre-reorganization redemptions or extraordinary dividends were made with respect to T in connection with a potential reorganization.[125] Commentators pointed out that this approach was inconsistent with authorities addressing Type B and Type C reorganizations. Responding to this concern, the Treasury Department removed the temporary regulations and amended its final regulations, substituting a narrower and more liberal rule. The revised rule provides that

> [a] proprietary interest in the target corporation . . . is not preserved to the extent that consideration received prior to a potential reorganization, either in a redemption of the target corporation stock or in a distribution with respect to the target corporation stock, is treated as other property or money received in the exchange for purposes of section 356, or would be so treated if the target

---

target (T). X bought the remaining 70% of T for cash immediately before a merger of T into P. When the new P shares that X received in connection with the merger are combined with the 60% in P that X already owned, X has an 80% interest. The example concludes that X is a related person whose purchases cannot be disregarded. Since X, now considered a related person, acquired a proprietary interest in T for something other than P stock, the transaction fails the COSI test. Treas. Reg. §1.368-1(e)(8), ex. 2.

124. T.D. 8761, 63 Fed. Reg. 4183 (Jan. 28, 1998).

125. For a discussion of "extraordinary dividends," see Chapter 6 (section entitled "Special Issues for Corporate Shareholders") and Chapter 5 (section entitled "Congressional Response to Dividends-Received Deduction Abuses").

shareholder also had received stock of the issuing corporation in exchange for stock owned by the shareholder in the target corporation.[126]

To understand the link between §356 and continuity of interest, one should recall that §356 is an exception to the general nonrecognition rule for target shareholders who receive stock or securities in a reorganization. Although the transaction may otherwise qualify for tax-free treatment under §354, target shareholders *are* taxed under §356 on the *portion* of consideration received that constitutes "*boot*."[127] Such boot essentially is consideration that does *not* reflect a proprietary interest in the acquiror and arguably should not count toward satisfying COSI requirements. The regulation thus provides that to the extent that any redemption or distribution was treated as boot to the target shareholder under §356 (or *would have been* treated as boot if the shareholder had received any P stock), the portion of target shares attributable to the redemption or distribution will *not* count toward continuity.

Before any consideration could be considered "boot" at all, it would have to be considered part of the reorganization transaction. In deciding whether pre-reorganization redemptions or distributions should be considered part of a reorganization transaction, Treasury rulings and case law regarding Type B and Type C reorganizations historically have focused upon the *source* of funds used for the distribution. These rulings have held that a pre-reorganization redemption would not violate the "solely for voting stock" requirement for Type B and C reorganization, for example, as long as funds for the redemption did not come directly, or indirectly, from P.[128] Consistent with these earlier rulings, the COSI regulations now essentially provide that a pre-reorganization redemption or distribution will cause the transaction to fail COSI requirements if it was directly or indirectly funded by P. A pre-reorganization redemption or distribution funded entirely by T should not affect continuity of interest.[129]

Ownership and Continuity of the Target's Business

a) Introduction

Notice that the continuity principles considered so far in this chapter have focused on *target corporation shareholders*. The primary concern of the COSI rules

---

126. Treas. Reg. §1.368-1(e)(1)(ii), as amended, T.D. 8898, 65 Fed. Reg. 52,909 (Aug. 31, 2000).
127. See discussion of §§354 and 356 earlier in this chapter.
128. Rev. Rul. 68-285, 1968-1 C.B. 147; Rev. Rul. 75-360, 1975-2 C.B. 110; Rev. Rul. 74-565, 1974-1 C.B. 125. See discussion of Type B and C reorganizations in Chapter 12.
129. Treas. Reg. §1.368-1(e)(8), ex. 9.

has been to distinguish cash sales from tax-free reorganizations, and the focus has been on whether the consideration ultimately *received by target shareholders* provided a sufficient proprietary interest in the reorganized enterprise to warrant tax-free treatment. Since its dramatic 1998 policy reversal, the Treasury Department has taken the view that pre- or post-reorganization *target shareholder* transfers will not jeopardize an otherwise tax-free reorganization unless the transfers are made to related parties. In effect, these rules "turn off" the step-transaction rule for COSI purposes.

A related, but somewhat different, dimension to the continuity question is the *purchasing corporation's* connection with the acquired target assets or stock after the exchange. For decades, case law and regulations have incorporated a distinct continuity of the business enterprise (COBE) requirement, separate from the continuity of proprietary interest and business purpose requirements.[130]

Although often thought of as a discrete test, the COBE requirement is more conceptually related to COSI requirements than one might think. As the target's business becomes further removed from the original purchasing corporation, it also becomes further removed from the selling target shareholders. Since eligibility for tax-free treatment in the first place hinged on the target shareholders' receipt of a proprietary stake in the reorganized business entity, it seems logical that what the purchasing corporation does with the target assets or stock is relevant to the target shareholder's continuing connection to the reorganized business. The section that follows discusses the COBE regulations alone. A subsequent section in this chapter introduces another dimension of continuity of interest—remote continuity—and its relationship to COBE requirements.

b) Continuity of the Business Enterprise

In theory, even if the target shareholders retain a substantial proprietary interest in the reorganized corporate enterprise, a reorganization represents more than a "mere change in form" if the type of business conducted or the use of business assets is dramatically transformed. In early cases, the government took the position that to qualify for tax-free reorganization treatment, the new corporation had to engage in a business identical to or similar to the transferor corporation's business.[131] After losing several cases in the courts,[132] the Service revoked its earlier position, concluding

---

130. See Treas. Reg. §1.368-1(b), which cross-references to paragraph (d) for a description of the COBE requirement and to paragraph (e) for a description of the continuity of proprietary interest requirement.
131. See, e.g., Rev. Rul. 56-330, 1956-2 C.B. 204, *revoked*, Rev. Rul. 63-29, 1963-1 C.B. 77, *superseded*, Rev. Rul. 81-25, 1981-1 C.B. 132.
132. See, e.g., Bentsen v. Phinney, 199 F. Supp. 363 (S.D. Tex. 1961).

that "the surviving corporation need not continue the activities conducted by its predecessors."[133] Regulations now provide that the continuity of the business enterprise requirement is satisfied if the issuing corporation either (1) continues the target corporation's historic business or (2) "use[s] a significant portion of [the target's] historic business assets in a business."[134] The regulations confirm that the purpose of this test is to "ensure that reorganizations are limited to readjustments of continuing interests in property under modified corporate form."[135]

As it has evolved, the continuity of the business enterprise requirement is rather loose and reasonably easy to satisfy. If the target corporation has more than one line of business, all that is required to continue the target's historic business is for the purchasing corporation to continue one significant line of business. In the alternative, the continuity of the business enterprise requirement is satisfied if the purchasing corporation simply uses a significant portion of the target's historic business assets in any business. For purposes of this provision, "significance" is a facts and circumstances analysis based upon the relative importance of the assets to the operation of the business.[136] As one example of a transaction that fails the continuity of the business enterprise requirement, the regulations describe a merger of a farm machinery corporation into a lumber mill corporation. Immediately after the transaction, the purchasing lumber corporation disposes of all of the target's farm machinery manufacturing business and continues to engage in milling operations. The purchasing corporation does not continue the farm machinery manufacturing business nor does it continue to use the historic farm machinery business assets. Thus, continuity of the business enterprise is lacking.[137]

One example of a situation in which the continuity of the business enterprise requirement has some remaining bite is when the target corporation sells all or most of its assets for stocks and bonds and shortly thereafter transfers these new assets in exchange for stock in a mutual fund or regulated investment company. For example, suppose that a clothing manufacturer sells all of its assets for cash and a highly diversified portfolio of stocks and bonds. Although this is a taxable asset sale, assume that the asset basis is high enough that the asset sale does not generate significant taxable income for the selling corporation. Shortly thereafter the corporation transfers the recently acquired stocks and bonds to a mutual fund

---

133. Rev. Rul. 63-29, 1963-1 C.B. 77, *suspended*, Rev. Rul. 79-433, 1979-2 C.B. 155 *superseded*, Rev. Rul. 81-25, 1981-1 C.B. 132.

134. Treas. Reg. §1.368-1(d)(1). Note that the continuity of the business enterprise requirement applies only to the business assets of the *target* corporation, and not to the business assets of the purchasing corporation. See Rev. Rul. 81-25, 1981-1 C.B. 132.

135. Treas. Reg. §1.368-1(d)(1).

136. Treas. Reg. §1.368-1(d)(2).

137. Treas. Reg. §1.368-1(d)(5), ex. 5.

or regulated investment company in return for mutual fund or regulated investment company stock, which it then distributes to its shareholders. This transaction meets the technical statutory requirements for a Type C reorganization. It fails the continuity of business enterprise requirement, however, because investment activity is not the target's historic business and stocks and bonds are not the target company's historic assets.[138] The target shareholders are thus prevented from converting their equity interest in a clothing manufacturer tax-free into an equity interest in a mutual fund or regulated investment company.

c) Post-Reorganization Restructuring and Remote Continuity

i) Introduction to the "Remote Continuity" Doctrine: Multiparty Reorganization

Although it sometimes shares the general "continuity of interest" label, the related "remote continuity" doctrine really should be viewed as something apart from the COSI requirements discussed earlier in this chapter. Unlike COSI, which focuses on the quality and quantity of target shareholder consideration received, remote continuity of interest focuses on the location of the target business after the initial exchange, and on the potential impact of any post-exchange transfer of target assets or stock by the acquiring corporation on tax-free reorganization classification.[139] Early iterations of the doctrine were based on strict textual interpretation of predecessors to current statutory reorganization definitions. Several of these early statutory definitions, for example, required that target shareholders receive solely stock in the *acquiring corporation*. Receipt of stock in the *parent* of the acquiring corporation would not suffice.[140] Even if the target shareholders received solely acquiring corporation stock, the transaction also risked reclassification under step-transaction analysis if the acquiring corporation subsequently transferred the target assets or stock to a subsidiary or other related entity after the initial exchange.[141] These early restrictions made it difficult or impossible to structure so-called "triangular" reorganizations. Over time, statutory and regulatory changes expanded the scope of eligible tax-free reorganizations to incorporate a wide variety of multiparty reorganization structures.[142] Still, taxpayers have been concerned that step-transaction

---

138. See Treas. Reg. §1.368-1(d)(5), ex. 3; see also Rev. Rul. 87-76, 1987-2 C.B. 84.

139. It might help to conceptualize this "remoteness" aspect of continuity doctrine as measuring the distance the target business has traveled from its "roots," referring to its "place" immediately before the acquisition. To the extent that the target shareholders received a proprietary interest in the purchasing corporation, this simultaneously measures the distance travelled from them as well.

140. See, e.g., Groman v. Comm'r, 302 U.S. 82 (1937).

141. See, e.g., Helvering v. Bashford, 302 U.S. 454 (1938).

142. For example, all of the acquisitive reorganization definitions today permit the acquiring corporation to transfer stock of a controlling or "parent" corporation in exchange for

analysis of certain post-acquisition transfers of target assets or stock by the acquiring corporation might jeopardize the acquisition's tax-free reorganization classification. Amendments to the COBE regulations, together with final regulations on post-reorganization transfers, have expanded the scope of permissible transfers and provided reassurance to many taxpayers.[143]

ii) COBE Regulations and Remote Continuity

Several rulings have turned to the COBE rules to test whether certain post-reorganization transfers of target stock or assets by the purchasing corporation caused the overall transaction to fail continuity of interest requirements.[144] The regulations now explicitly incorporate the COBE requirements into special rules on post-reorganization transfer of target assets or stock by the issuing corporation.[145]

Amendments to the COBE regulations over time have clarified that the acquiring corporation need not *directly* continue the target's business or use the target's assets. The regulations offer flexibility by effectively deeming the issuing (acquiring) corporation to hold "all of the businesses and assets of all the members of the "qualified group."[146] In other words, an otherwise qualified tax-free reorganization will not be viewed as violating COBE requirements if the acquiring corporation transfers the acquired target assets or stock to members of a "qualified group." As originally conceived, the "qualified group" was limited to a parent corporation and its direct and indirect subsidiaries, as long as each subsidiary in the chain was directly controlled by its immediate parent. In other words, the regulation permitted a series of successive "drop-downs." Regulations have gradually expanded the "qualified group" definition.

In its preamble to regulations amending the "qualified group" definition, the Treasury Department acknowledged that it was loosening the COBE requirements consistent with the trend toward loosening regulatory restrictions on post-reorganization transfers generally.[147] Under the expanded definition, "qualified group" now includes "one or more chains of corporations connected through stock ownership with the issuing corporation, but only

---

target stock or assets, I.R.C. §368(a)(1)(B), (C), (a)(2)(D). Statutory rules also permit a "drop down" of target corporation assets or stock to a controlled subsidiary after the initial exchange, I.R.C. §368(a)(2)(C) Community Renewal Tax Relief Act (2)(C). Triangular mergers and the remote continuity doctrine are discussed in more detail in Chapter 12.

143. Treas. Reg. §1.368-2(k) (as amended by T.D. 9396, 73 Fed. Reg. 26,322 (May 9, 2008).
144. See, e.g., Rev. Rul. 2001-24, 2001-1 C.B. 1290: Rev. Rul. 2002-85, 2002-2 C.B. 986.
145. Treas. Reg. §1.368-2(k)(1) (as amended by T.D. 9396, 73 Fed. Reg. 26,322 (May 9, 2008). A more detailed discussion of remote continuity and triangular reorganizations follows in Chapter 12.
146. Treas. Reg. §1.368-1(d)(4)(i).
147. T.D. 9361, 72 Fed. Reg. 50,552 (Oct. 25, 2007).

if the issuing corporation owns directly stock meeting the requirements of section 368(c) in at least one other corporation, and stock meeting the requirements of section 368(c) in each of the corporations (except the issuing corporation) is owned directly (or indirectly . . .) by one or more of the other corporations."[148] This revised definition includes several significant changes. First, "qualified group" is no longer limited to a chain of direct subsidiaries, but extends to "brother and sister" corporations and other "corporate relatives." The new rules, for example, permit "cross-chain" transfers. One of the most significant expansions here was permitting corporations to aggregate stock ownership for purposes of measuring §368(c) control. Even stock directly owned by a partnership can be aggregated in measuring control as long as members of the qualified group own interests in the "partnership meeting requirements equivalent to section 368(c)."[149] In addition, the definition treats the acquiring corporation as owning target stock or assets transferred to a partnership if members of the qualified group either own a significant interest in the partnership or one or more group members have "active and substantial management functions as a partner."[150] Thus, related partnerships can hold target assets or stock after the initial exchange without violating continuity requirements.

The COBE "qualified group" rules on post-reorganization transfers by the acquirer really speak more to remote continuity concerns than to basic questions regarding continuity of the target's historic business or continued use of its historic assets. In fact, the Treasury Department explained that the "current regulations do not contain separate rules addressing remote continuity because the IRS and Treasury Department believe that these issues are adequately addressed by the rules adopted to implement the continuity of business interest requirement."[151] It seems that the COBE requirement's role has morphed over time. Because current regulations permit target shareholders freely to transfer their purchasing corporation shares immediately after the reorganization without jeopardizing the reorganization's tax-free status, the COBE requirement is no longer used to ensure a link between the historic target shareholders and the target business in its revised form. As one commentator observed:

> It seems the COBE requirement has gone beyond ensuring the linkage to the former T stockholders to become a separate business continuity requirement at the corporate level that — unlike COSI — must survive the transaction . . . .

---

148. Treas. Reg. §1.368-1(d)(4)(ii) (as amended by T.D. 9631, 72 Fed. Reg. 60,552 (Oct. 25, 2007)).
149. Treas. Reg. §1.368-1(d)(4)(iii)(D).
150. Treas. Reg. §1.368-1(d)(4)(iii)(B).
151. T.D. 9361, 72 Fed. Reg. 60,552, 60,553 (Oct. 25, 2007) (preamble to post-reorganization transfer regulations).

Indeed, given the lack of any continuing COSI requirement, administration of the remote continuity doctrine on the transaction itself could be seen as the main function of the COBE qualified group rules.[152]

iii) Post-Reorganization Transfer "Safe Harbor"

Determining whether or not the Service will apply step-transaction analysis to post-reorganization transfers has been a confusing exercise for taxpayers and their advisors. Regulations, referred to by some as the "remote continuity" or "2(k)" provisions, provide a "safe harbor":

> A transaction otherwise qualifying as a reorganization . . . *shall not be disqualified or recharacterized as a result of one or more subsequent transfers* (or successive transfers) of assets or stock provided that the requirements of §1.368-1(d) [COBE] are satisfied and the transfer(s) are described in either (k)(1)(i) or (k)(1)(ii) of this section.[153]

With this provision, the Treasury effectively declared that it is "turning off" step-transaction rules as applied to the purchasing corporation's post-reorganization restructuring as long as the transaction complies with the Treas. Reg. §1.368-2(k)'s requirements.[154] In the first instance, the regulation requires that the post-reorganization transfers satisfy the COBE requirements. In addition, the transfers must be either "distributions" or "transfers other than distributions," as those terms are explicitly defined in subparagraphs (k)(1)(i) and (ii). As a practical matter the COBE "qualified group" definition, mentioned indirectly only by general cross-reference to Treas. Reg. §1.368-1(d), really is the core of these post-reorganization transfer rules; the COBE "qualified group" rules identify the range of entities to which target assets or stock can safely be transferred without jeopardizing tax-free reorganization treatment.[155]

Consistent with the Service's more relaxed interpretations of continuity requirements over the past decade, the definitions of "distribution" and "transfers other than distributions" for purposes of the 2(k) regulations are rather broad. Both definitions cover transfer of assets or stock of "the acquired corporation, the acquiring corporation, or the surviving

---

152. George R. Goodman, Postacquisition Restructuring and Beyond, 170 Tax Notes 577, 581 (2008).

153. Treas. Reg. §1.368-2(k)(1) (emphasis added).

154. Notice also the caveat added to Treas. Reg. §1.368-1(a) immediately after the sentence stating that qualification as a reorganization "must be evaluated under relevant provisions of law, including the step transaction doctrine: *But see* §§1.368-2(f) *and* (k)" (emphasis added).

155. The regulation prohibits any transfer of acquired corporation stock that would cause the acquired corporation to leave the "qualified group." Treas. Reg. §1.368-2(k)(1)(i)(A)(2). This seems redundant, though, given that such a transfer would also cause the corporation to violate the COBE requirements themselves.

corporation, as the case may be."[156] This language simply recognizes that the target stock or assets may be held by any one of the three entities depending on the structure of the acquisition transaction. As a label for purposes of discussion, any one of these different entities might be called the post-acquisition "T business," meaning the entity in which target assets or stock reside after the initial reorganization exchange.

The major limitation built into the post-reorganization transfer definitions appears designed to require that at least *some* connection to the target remain within in the qualified group. Thus, for example, the distribution definition excludes aggregate distributions of "an amount of assets that would result in liquidation . . ." of the T business for tax purposes.[157] Similarly, the "transfer" definition excludes transfers that would "terminate corporate existence"[158] of the T business. Since these issues tend to arise in the context of triangular reorganizations, a closer look follows in Chapter 12. For the moment, though, imagine a straightforward acquisition, in which purchasing corporation (P) first causes a wholly owned subsidiary (S) to acquire target corporation (T) assets in exchange for P stock in an exchange that qualifies as a tax-free reorganization. In a second step, S distributes 80% of the T assets to P. Since P and S are members of a qualified group, the distribution satisfies COBE requirements. The transfer also should qualify under the 2(k) safe harbor since the distribution was not of an amount that would result in a liquidation of S. On the other hand, if S had transferred all of its assets, including the T assets, to P in a liquidation or upstream merger, the acquisition transaction would not have qualified for the 2(k) safe harbor. Keep in mind that the absence of this safe harbor does not necessarily convert this reorganization into a taxable acquisition. The benefit of the regulatory safe harbor simply is assurance that the Service will not apply step-transaction analysis to the transaction.

The Business Purpose Test

A nonrecognition rule permitting taxpayers to defer taxation upon the exchange of appreciated property is obviously appealing to taxpayers. In an early landmark case, the taxpayer structured a transaction to fit literally within the definition of a reorganization, but nevertheless failed to convince the Court that she was entitled to reorganization treatment since the reorganization plan had no "business purpose."[159] Mrs. Gregory's solely owned

---

156. Treas. Reg. §1.368-2(k)(1)(i)(A), (1)(ii)(B).
157. Treas. Reg. §1.368-2(k)(1)(i)(B).
158. Id. At (1)(ii)(C).
159. Gregory v. Helvering, 293 U.S. 465 (1935). The statute involved was the Revenue Act of 1928.

corporation held appreciated stock in another corporation. If her corporation had distributed this appreciated property directly to Mrs. Gregory, she would have received a dividend, taxable as ordinary income. Instead, Mrs. Gregory arranged for transfer of the appreciated stock to a newly formed corporation in which she would hold all of the stock.[160] Shortly thereafter, the new corporation distributed the appreciated stock to Mrs. Gregory in a complete liquidation of the recently formed corporation. The corporation was in existence for only three days and never conducted any business. Mrs. Gregory hoped to treat the liquidating distribution as §331 sale or exchange gain, taxable at lower capital gains rates, thus attempting to convert what otherwise would have been ordinary income into capital gains.[161]

In a famous opinion for the Second Circuit, Judge Learned Hand said first that

> a transaction, otherwise within an exception of the tax law, does not lose its immunity because it is actuated by a desire to avoid, or, if one choose, to evade, taxation. Any one may so arrange his affairs that his taxes shall be as low as possible; he is not bound to choose that pattern which will best pay the Treasury; there is not even a patriotic duty to increase one's taxes.[162]

Reading this far, Mrs. Gregory surely would have thought that she had won the case. However, Judge Hand went on to say that

> the meaning of a sentence may be more than that of the separate words, as a melody is more than the notes. . . . The purpose of the [nonrecognition] section is plain enough; . . . The underlying presupposition is plain that the readjustment shall be undertaken for reasons germane to the conduct of the venture in hand, not as an ephemeral incident, egregious to its prosecution. To dodge the shareholder's taxes is not one of the transactions contemplated as corporate "reorganizations."[163]

In less colorful language, the Supreme Court affirmed the Second Circuit's opinion, firmly establishing the "business purpose" test. In Mrs. Gregory's case, the Court concluded that the operation had no "business or corporate purpose," but was rather "a mere device which put on the form of a corporate reorganization as a disguise for concealing its real character, and the sole object and accomplishment of which was the consummation of a

---

160. Under the modern definitions of reorganization, this transaction would be regarded as a "divisive reorganization" under §368(a)(1)(D).

161. For a complete discussion of §331 sale or exchange treatment to the shareholder upon a liquidating distribution, see Chapter 8.

162. Helvering v. Gregory, 69 F.2d 809, 810 (2d Cir. 1934), aff'd, 293 U.S. 465 (1935).

163. Id. At 810-811. Ironically, Judge Hand's opinion is most often cited for the first quotation without mentioning the second.

preconceived plan, not to reorganize a business or any part of a business, but to transfer a parcel of corporate shares to the petitioner."[164]

Although the "business purpose" test has never been formally incorporated into the statutory reorganization provisions, it is built into the regulations in several places. First, the general regulation regarding the purpose and scope of the tax-free reorganization provisions states that the nonrecognition rules apply to "such readjustments of corporate structures . . . *As are required by business exigencies*."[165] In addition, in order for the shareholders or the corporation to qualify for tax-free treatment under §354 or 361, the transfers must be "in pursuance of a plan of reorganization." The regulations defining "plan of reorganization" require that

> the readjustments involved in the exchanges or distributions . . . must be undertaken for reasons germane to the continuance of the business of a corporation a party to the reorganization. Section 368(a) contemplates genuine corporate reorganizations which are designed to effect a readjustment of continuing interests under modified corporate forms.[166]

Finally, the Treasury Department states that "[i]n order to exclude transactions not intended to be included, the specifications of the reorganization provisions of the law are precise. Both the terms of the specifications *and their underlying assumptions and purposes* must be satisfied in order to entitle the taxpayer to the benefit of the [nonrecognition] exception from the general rule."[167]

MEANING OF "PARTY TO A REORGANIZATION" AND "PLAN OF REORGANIZATION"

The various statutory shareholder and corporate tax-free reorganization provisions require transaction participants to be a "party to a reorganization" and further require that the exchange take place pursuant to a "plan of reorganization." For example, the shareholder nonrecognition rule in §354 requires the exchange of stock or securities in a corporation that is a "party to a reorganization" in return for stock or securities of the same corporation or another corporation that also is a "party to a reorganization." Similar language shows up in the §361 nonrecognition rule applicable to the distributing corporation. Under §361, a corporation that is a "party to the reorganization" is eligible for nonrecognition only upon the exchange

---

164. 293 U.S. At 469.
165. Treas. Reg. §1.368-1(b) (emphasis added).
166. Treas. Reg. §1.368-2(g).
167. Treas. Reg. §1.368-1(b) (emphasis added).

of its property in return for stock or securities in another corporation that is a "party to a reorganization."

The definition of "party to a reorganization" in §368(b) "includes (1) a corporation resulting from a reorganization, and (2) both corporations, in the case of a reorganization resulting from the acquisition by one corporation of stock or properties of another." As opportunities for triangular reorganizations have expanded over the years, Congress has expanded the §368(b) "party to a reorganization" definition to include the multiple corporate participants in the transaction. For example, when a purchasing corporation uses a subsidiary to acquire stock or property of a target, the target corporation, the purchasing corporation and its subsidiary all will be considered parties to the reorganization.[168] Consistent with its trend away from insisting on literal compliance with statutory requirements, the Service has permitted tax-free reorganization treatment even though the corporation ultimately acquiring the assets was not explicitly listed in the expanded §368(b) "party to a reorganization" definition.[169] In so doing, the Service commented that "the use of the word 'includes' in §368(b) indicates that the definition of 'party to a reorganization' is not exclusive."[170]

For the participants to be eligible for nonrecognition treatment, the tax-free reorganization provisions of Subchapter C also generally require that the transaction be pursuant to a "plan of reorganization."[171] The Code itself provides no definition, but the regulations refer to

> a *consummated transaction* specifically defined as a reorganization under section 368(a). The term is not to be construed as broadening the definition of "reorganization" . . . but is to be taken as limiting the nonrecognition of gain or loss to such exchanges or distributions *as are directly a part of the transaction specifically described as a reorganization in section 368(a).*[172]

The regulatory definition of "plan of reorganization" reflects the government's concern that the boundaries of the transaction for which nonrecognition is available not be loosely defined. Nonrecognition should be limited to a discrete reorganization transaction with a beginning and an end and should not extend to peripheral or related transactions.

---

168. See Chapter 12 for a more detailed discussion of this expansion of the "party to a reorganization" definition in the case of triangular reorganizations.

169. Rev. Rul. 2002-85, 2002-2 C.B. 986.

170. Id. At 988. The "party to a reorganization" definition continues to grow through regulation. For example, when the Treasury Department expanded the Treas. Reg. §1.368-2(k) post-reorganization transfer rules discussed earlier in this chapter, it made corollary amendments to the "party to a reorganization" definition. Thus, for example, the regulations provide that "a corporation remains a party to the reorganization even though stock or assets acquired in the reorganization are transferred in a transaction described in paragraph (k) of this section." Treas. Reg. §1.368-2(f).

171. See, e.g., I.R.C. §§354(a), 361(a).

172. Treas. Reg. §1.368-2(g) (emphasis added).

OVERLAPS BETWEEN TAX-FREE REORGANIZATIONS AND TAXABLE QUALIFIED STOCK PURCHASES (QSPS)

An initial taxable acquisition of target (old T) stock by a purchasing corporation (P) that otherwise would be treated as a qualified stock purchase (QSP) under §338 may be immediately followed by a liquidation of the newly acquired subsidiary (new T)[173] or by a merger transaction. Stepped together, the transaction might qualify as a tax-free reorganization. Such transactions raise issues concerning the overlap between tax-free reorganization rules and rules for taxable acquisitions eligible for a §338 election.[174] The most significant overlap question is whether, and if so, when, the step-transaction doctrine should apply. Regulations under §338 address these issues.

The relevant §338 regulatory example, based on the fact pattern in *Yoc Heating*,[175] involves a QSP by P of 85% of T from shareholder A for cash. Shortly after the QSP, and as part of an integrated plan, T merges into X Corporation, a subsidiary of P. Both P Corporation and T's 15% minority shareholder, K, receive X stock in connection with the merger.[176]

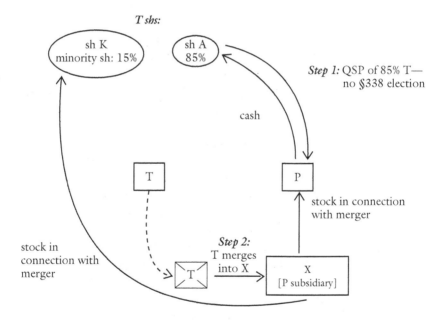

---

173. The liquidation transaction would be treated as tax free to T pursuant to §337 and to P pursuant to §332. T's assets would retain their historic basis under §334(b). See Chapter 9.
174. Further discussion of this overlap appears in Chapter 10 on taxable acquisitions.
175. Further discussion of *Yoc Heating* and the §338 regulations discussed here appears earlier in this chapter and in Chapter 10.
176. Treas. Reg. §1.338-3(d)(5).

Under ordinary reorganization principles, this transaction would not meet continuity of interest requirements. When the dust settles after this integrated transaction, it is simply a cash acquisition by P. A similar example included in the §368 regulations indeed concludes that where P acquires 90% of T's stock for cash and then promptly merges T into a P subsidiary (S), the transaction does not meet COSI requirements and will not be treated as a tax-free reorganization since "P acquired a proprietary interest in T for consideration other than P stock, and a substantial part of the value of the proprietary interest in T is not preserved."[177] The regulation goes on to say, however, that the §338 regulations "*may change the result in this case* by providing that, by virtue of section 338, continuity of interest is satisfied *for certain parties* after a qualified stock purchase."[178] This is precisely how the §338 regulations handle the above 85% QSP example based upon *Yoc Heating*. In contrast to the §368 regulations, the §338 regulations here conclude that "the purchasing corporation's target stock acquired in the qualified stock purchase represents an interest on the part of a person who was an owner of the target's business enterprise prior to the transfer that can be continued in a reorganization."[179] In other words, it is possible for the *purchasing corporation*, or one of its affiliates, to participate in a tax-free reorganization immediately following a QSP.[180]

At the same time, the regulations adopt a bifurcated approach and conclude that the transfer will not be treated as a tax-free reorganization with respect to the minority shareholder "because P's stock purchase and the merger of T into X are pursuant to an *integrated transaction* in which A, the owner of 85 percent of the stock of T, received solely cash in exchange for A's stock."[181] Thus, the transaction is treated as integrated with respect to tax treatment of minority shareholders, but the first-step QSP is viewed as an independent transaction for purposes of §338. The bottom line is that a purchasing corporation that does not make a §338 election following a QSP will be held to a substituted basis under §362. Without this special §338 regulation, P might claim a cost basis in the assets its subsidiary receives in the merger, arguing that the merger is part of an integrated transaction that effectively is a cash acquisition of assets and not a tax-free reorganization. If so, it would be too easy for P to get a cost basis in the T assets acquired by its subsidiary without meeting the requirements of §338.

The bifurcated approach of Treas. Reg. §1.338-3(d) makes sense when the first step alone qualifies as a QSP and the second step, if integrated,

---

177. See Treas. Reg. §1.368-1(e)(8), ex. 4(ii).
178. Id. (emphasis added).
179. Treas. Reg. §1.338-3(d)(2).
180. This is consistent with the Treasury Department's position in Rev. Rul. 90-95, which concluded that a QSP "of target stock is accorded independent significance from a subsequent liquidation of target." 1990-2 C.B. 67, 68-69.
181. Treas. Reg. §1.338-3(d)(5), ex. (v). (emphasis added).

would convert the overall transaction into a taxable acquisition of T assets and not into a tax-free reorganization. This approach preserves §338 as the sole route to a stepped-up basis in T assets. In fact, the Treasury Department in Rev. Rul. 90-95 had even more definitively pronounced that a "qualified stock purchase of target stock is accorded independent significance from a subsequent liquidation[182] of the target regardless of whether a section 338 election is made or deemed to be made."[183] This independent significance rule suggested that the Treasury Department simply would not apply the step-transaction doctrine when a merger-type transaction followed a QSP.

A new wrinkle arises, however, when the first step alone is a QSP but the second step, if integrated, would make the overall transaction a tax-free reorganization. The Treasury Department addressed this issue in Rev. Rul. 2001-46,[184] which involved a first-step QSP followed by an upstream merger of the newly acquired subsidiary.[185] Perhaps surprisingly, the government here rejected the "independent significance of the first step QSP" approach adopted in Rev. Rul. 90-95 and the §338 regulations. In contrast to these earlier positions, Rev. Rul. 2001-46 refused to grant the first step independent significance as a QSP, instead concluding that step-transaction principles must apply. In the end, Treasury treats the overall transaction as a tax-free reorganization and disallows any §338 election with respect to the first-step QSP. Viewed collectively, these regulations and rulings announced the Treasury Department's position that when the first-step in a multistep acquisition is a QSP, the step-transaction doctrine sometimes applies and sometimes does not.[186]

At first blush, it is difficult to reconcile the refusal to integrate transactional steps in Treas. Reg. §1.338-3(d) and Rev. Rul. 90-95 with the insistence on such integration in Rev. Rul. 2001-46. To help understand the difference, keep in mind that the driving concern behind the no-step-transaction approach in the regulations and the 1990 ruling is preventing taxpayers from reverting to old Kimbell-Diamond step-transaction arguments under

---

182. Such liquidation is sometimes referred to as a "upstream merger." See also Chapter 9 on the liquidation of subsidiaries.

183. 1990-2 C.B. 67, 68-69. This approach is confirmed in Treas. Reg. §1.338-3(d).

184. 2001-2 C.B. 321 (situation 1). The first-step transaction effectively was a "busted" reverse triangular Type A merger since the consideration used by the purchasing corporation to acquire T stock was 70% stock and 30% cash. For such reverse mergers the reorganization rules require 80% continuity. I.R.C. §368(a)(2)(E). A detailed discussion of reverse Type A mergers follows in Chapter 12.

185. For purposes of §338, the stock here is acquired by "purchase" since it does not have a transferred or substituted basis in the purchasing corporation's hands. I.R.C. §338(h)(3). See Chapter 10 for further discussion of the §338 "purchase" definition.

186. Some commentators viewed Rev. Rul. 2001-46 as reviving the old Kimbell-Diamond rule thought to have been statutorily overruled by §338. See, e.g., Jerred G. Blanchard, Jr., Reflections on Rev. Rul. 2001-46 and the Continued Viability of Kimbell-Diamond, 93 Tax Notes 1875 (2001). Discussion of the apparent demise of Kimbell-Diamond appears in Chapter 10.

which a target stock purchase followed by liquidation of target was treated as an asset purchase, resulting in a cost or stepped-up basis in the target assets. To bypass §338 in this way would give the purchasing corporation a cost basis in target assets without reporting taxable gain from the deemed target asset sale otherwise triggered by a §338 election.[187] Rev. Rul. 2001-46 explains: "Rev. Rul. 90-95 and section 1.338-3(d) treat the acquisition of the stock of the target corporation as a qualified stock purchase followed by a separate carryover basis transaction in order to preclude any nonstatutory treatment of the steps as an integrated asset purchase."[188] In contrast, the ruling states that the situation presented in Rev. Rul. 2001-46 did not raise similar policy concerns:

> The policy underlying section 338 is not violated by treating [the steps] as a single statutory merger . . . because such treatment results in a transaction that qualifies as a reorganization . . . in which [the purchasing corporation] acquires the assets of T with a carryover basis under section 362, and does not result in a cost basis for those assets under section 1012.[189]

In other words, since integrating the steps will not result in a stepped-up cost basis for T assets, one no longer needs to worry about a possible §338 loophole.

The approach taken in Rev. Rul. 2001-46 is consistent with other rulings suggesting a reinvigoration of step-transaction principles in the reorganization setting. As a practical matter, the step-transaction or integrated approach now seems to be the "default rule" absent some significant policy justification for rejecting it under the particular circumstances presented.

Although a purchasing corporation may want the stepped-up basis in target assets that comes with a §338 election, the price extracted for such an election is a heavy one—taxation of gain upon the deemed sale of target assets.[190] This "toll charge" often makes the election unattractive. Thus, the parties may prefer tax-free reorganization treatment of the integrated steps in any event. In such cases, disallowance of any §338 election, as provided in Rev. Rul. 2001-46, should not be bothersome. On the other hand, the §338 election continues to be attractive when the target is a subsidiary corporation and the transaction qualifies for a special §338(h)(10) election.[191]

---

187. The tax consequences of the deemed sale of target assets following a §338 election are considered in Chapter 10.
188. 2001-2 C.B. 321, 323.
189. Id.
190. See Chapter 10, section entitled "Mechanics of the §338(a)(1) Deemed Sale."
191. The §338(h)(10) election offers numerous advantages, the most significant of which is the corporate seller's relief from taxation upon an otherwise taxable sale of subsidiary stock. I.R.C. §338(h)(10)(A). See Chapter 10, section entitled "The Special §338(h)(10) Election."

One concern or potential trap for the unwary based upon the differential use of step-transaction analysis following a first-step QSP is that the parties may have negotiated the transaction on the assumption that a §338(h)(10) election would be made. If the integrated transaction is viewed as a tax-free reorganization, the opportunity for an (h)(10) election is lost under the rule announced in Rev. Rul. 2001-46. Responding to such concerns, the Treasury Department issued regulations that make step-transaction treatment elective when a first-step QSP is followed by a upstream merger or liquidation of target that, if integrated, would otherwise be treated as a tax-free reorganization.[192] If a §338(h)(10) election is made, the regulations provide that "*for all Federal tax purposes*, P's acquisition of T stock is treated as a qualified stock purchase and is not treated as part of a reorganization described in section 368(a)."[193] On the other hand, if no §338(h)(10) election is made, the overall transaction will be treated as a tax-free reorganization.[194]

A final variation of the tax-free reorganization/QSP overlap theme was considered in Rev. Rul. 2008-25, which involved a first-step exchange that *would* qualify for tax-free reorganization treatment followed by a liquidation that, by itself, would also qualify. Citing Rev. Rul. 67-274 and the step-transaction doctrine,[195] the Service concluded that the steps should be integrated, and the overall transaction viewed as a direct acquisition by the purchasing corporation of the target corporation's assets. As an integrated asset acquisition, however, the transaction did not qualify as a tax-free Type A or C asset acquisition.[196] In the end, step-transaction principles converted what initially appeared to be a tax-free reorganization into a taxable acquisition for the perhaps unsuspecting selling shareholders. Ordinarily, a taxable acquisition would result in a cost-basis for the purchasing corporation. Not so fast, says the Service, arguing that "*further application . . .* [of step transaction rules] would violate the policy underlying §338 that a cost basis in acquired assets should not be obtained through the purchase of stock where no §338 election is made."[197] To determine P's tax consequences, the Service viewed the transaction in two parts: first, a QSP, presumably *without* a §338 election;

---

192. Treas. Reg. §1.338(h)(10)-1(c)(2), as amended by T.D. 9271, 71 Fed. Reg. 38,074 (July 5, 2006). The regulations also apply when target is subsequently merged into "another member of the affiliated group that includes P," id., thus making a subsequent brother-sister merger of target eligible for similar treatment. Treas. Reg. §1.338(h)(10)-1(e), ex. 13.
193. Treas. Reg. §1.338(h)(10)-1(c)(2). The "for all Federal tax purposes" language suggests that if the §338(h)(10) election is made, minority shareholders cannot claim tax-free treatment by arguing that the transaction overall was a reorganization.
194. Treas. Reg. §1.338(h)(10)-1(e), ex. 11.
195. 1967-2 C.B. 141 (stock-for-stock acquisition, which alone failed to qualify as Type B reorganization, became valid Type C reorganization when stepped together with subsequent liquidation of target).
196. The second-step distribution was not covered by the Treas. Reg. §1.368-2(k) "safe harbor" because it was a complete liquidation. See discussion of the 2(k) safe harbor earlier in this chapter.
197. 2008-1 C.B. 986, 988 (emphasis added).

and second, a tax-free complete liquidation of a subsidiary.[198] This approach appears rather contorted. After all, the first step alone was a qualified tax-free reorganization. In the end, the result for the purchasing corporation is the same either way — it will hold target assets with a substituted basis. From the shareholder's perspective, the difference in outcome was more dramatic — a taxable sale as opposed to a tax-free reorganization.

At least in the context of potential QSP overlaps, the Service position appears to be that step-transaction analysis sometimes is applicable in determining tax consequences for all parties, sometimes not applicable for all parties, and sometimes applicable for some parties and not others. The primary concern driving the decision on how to treat the acquisition transaction seems to be protecting the §338 election as the *sole* route to a cost-basis acquisition, thus preventing purchasers from taking a cost basis unless the "toll charge" triggered by a §338 election has been collected in the form of taxable gain or loss from a deemed sale of the target's assets. If so, it seems that the concern should be addressed more directly.

Examples

Hip-Hop ABCs

1. a. Hip Tone Records, Inc. (HTR) is a major music publisher interested in acquiring smaller publishers. It has discovered that Dogg, Inc. (DI) may be amenable to an acquisition. Sloop Dogg owns 75% and Lil Jo owns 25% of DI's outstanding voting common stock. The parties agree on a transaction in which Sloop Dogg and Lil Jo will transfer all of their DI stock to HTR in exchange for HTR voting common stock. In the meantime, Lil Jo has entered into a binding contract to sell his HTR stock to his friend, Beastlie, for cash shortly after the initial exchange. Does this transaction qualify as a tax-free reorganization?

   b. Would your answer to Example 1a differ if HTR, aware of Lil Jo's interest in receiving cash, arranged for one of its wholly owned subsidiaries to purchase Lil Jo's share of the HTR stock received in the exchange for cash shortly after the initial acquisition?

   c. Imagine instead that HTR had approached Sloop Dogg and Lil Jo about the possibility of an acquisition in exchange for HTR stock. Since the two shareholders preferred cash, they sold their DI shares to Snarface, who then exchanged the DI stock for HTR stock. Would the exchange between Snarface and HTR still qualify as a tax-free reorganization?

2. Penelope Cleaners, a corporate dry-cleaning business, acquires all of the assets of Dogg Daze Records, a hip-hop music publisher, in exchange

---

198. Complete liquidations are discussed in Chapter 9.

for Penelope voting stock. Shortly thereafter, Penelope sells off the Dogg Daze assets, except for its plant, which Penelope converts to dry-cleaning use. Does this merger qualify as a tax-free reorganization?

Mixing It Up

3. a. Hipster's four shareholders own the voting common stock as follows: T-Bo: 35%; QT: 30%; Jay: 20%; Zeek: 15%. Hipster has agreed to a merger with Public Friends, Inc. (PFI) under Delaware state law. Under the terms of the merger agreement, T-Bo and QT will receive cash, Jay will receive PFI voting stock, and Zeek will receive PFI nonvoting preferred stock. Will this transaction qualify as a tax-free reorganization?

   b. Would your answer to Example 3a differ if T-Bo and Jay received cash, QT received PFI voting common stock, and Zeek received nonvoting preferred stock?

   c. Would your answer to Example 3b differ if QT received shares of a separate newly created class of nonvoting preferred? What if QT received long-term PFI bonds?

Moving It Around

4. a. Twisto and Ice Cube are both corporate distributors of musical recordings and sheet music. Twisto is the parent to three subsidiaries: S1, S2, and S3. Twisto acquires all of the assets of Ice Cube in exchange for Twisto voting stock. Immediately after the exchange, Twisto transfers portions of the assets to its three subsidiaries. Shortly thereafter, S1 transfers the assets received from Twisto to S2. Would these exchanges qualify for tax-free reorganization treatment?

   b. Imagine that Twisto acquires all of Ice Cube's stock in exchange for Twisto voting common stock and a small amount of cash. Twisto then causes Ice Cube to liquidate and receives all of Ice Cube's assets in complete liquidation. How would this transaction be tested for purposes of meeting the tax-free reorganization definitions in §368(a)(1)?

Explanations

1. a. This initial exchange of DI stock for HTR voting common stock should qualify as a stock-for-stock §368(a)(1)(B) tax-free reorganization. The potential concern here is continuity of shareholder interest. As part of a binding contract, Lil Jo has sold his 25% HTR share for cash. If this is viewed as an integrated transaction, HTR has acquired only 75% of DI in exchange for a proprietary interest. In any event, the transaction would not qualify as a Type B reorganization if the purchasing corporation uses anything other than its own voting stock. Although the cash in this case is not coming from HTR, Lil Jo's

binding contract to sell for cash would have presented a problem under early case law step-transaction doctrine. Current regulations, however, indicate that "a mere disposition of stock of the issuing corporation received in a potential reorganization to persons not related . . . To the issuing corporation is disregarded." Treas. Reg. §1.368-1(e)(1). The transaction will qualify as a Type B reorganization.

b. A cash purchase of Lil Jo's HTR stock just received in the exchange by one of HTR's wholly owned subsidiaries would be considered an acquisition by a "related person." Treas. Reg. §1.368-1(e)(3), (4). The cash received by Lil Jo would now be counted as part of the consideration received in the exchange and the transaction would no longer qualify as a tax-free Type B reorganization. The continuity of shareholder interest test built into §368(a)(1)(B) requires that the purchasing corporation use *only voting* stock. Cash received from a party related to the acquiring corporation effectively is viewed as cash received from the purchasing corporation itself, which would not be permitted in a Type B reorganization.

c. A pre-reorganization sale in anticipation of the acquisition also raises potential continuity of interest concerns. In this case, the historic shareholders have received cash and are not participating in the exchange for a proprietary interest in the acquiring corporation. Although historic shareholder continuity was once a concern, current regulations have relaxed these restrictions as well, providing that a "mere disposition of stock of the target corporation prior to a potential reorganization to persons not related . . . To the target corporation or to persons not related . . . To the issuing corporation is disregarded." Treas. Reg. §1.368-1(e)(1). The transaction should qualify as a Type B reorganization.

2. Continuity of business enterprise (COBE) is the potential concern with this exchange. In addition to a continuity of shareholder interest, the regulations require that the purchaser either continue the target corporation's business or use a significant portion of the target's historic business assets in a business. Treas. Reg. §1.368-1(d)(1). Penelope is not continuing the music publishing business and has sold off the historic business assets except for the plant building here. If the plant building alone represents "a significant portion" of Dogg Daze's assets, the acquisition would meet COBE requirements. This would be determined under a facts-and-circumstances analysis.

3. a. This is a state law merger, which will qualify for tax-free treatment as a Type A "statutory merger" as long as it meets the quality and quantity components of the COSI requirements. PFI voting stock surely is a sufficient "material" or proprietary interest in the purchasing corporation. Nonvoting preferred stock also counts as a proprietary

interest. The cash, of course, would not count as a proprietary interest. In the end, shareholders owning 65% of the Hipster stock (T-Bo and QT) were "cashed out," and 35% received an equity interest in PFI. Although there is no precise quantity test, one regulatory example indicates the government's position that 40% equity is sufficient for continuity of interest purposes. Treas. Reg. §1.368-1(e)(v), ex. 1. Since the equity received in this transaction falls short of 40%, the parties certainly cannot count on tax-free reorganization treatment. Risk-adverse taxpayers would not feel comfortable with this transaction. On the other hand, the courts sometimes have upheld tax-free treatment for transactions with less than 40% equity.

b. Mixing the consideration up this way means that 55% of the target shareholders received cash (T-Bo and Jay) and 45% received equity. This mix of consideration is within the "comfort zone" offered by the regulations. The fact that some shareholders got all cash and others all equity should not be a problem. Continuity of shareholder interest is measured in the aggregate. The transaction should qualify as a Type A reorganization.

c. If QT and Zeek both receive nonvoting preferred stock and the others receive cash, 55% of the target shareholders have been "cashed out" and *none* of the shareholders has received any voting interest in the reorganized enterprise in exchange for their voting interests in the target. Although this arguably is more than a "mere change in form," continuity of interest doctrine historically has treated nonvoting stock as a sufficient proprietary interest. Long-term bonds, on the other hand, are debt instruments that generally do not provide sufficient continuity. Adding QT's bonds to the cash received by T-Bo and Jay would leave only 15% continuity in the stock received by Zeek. This bond variation is not likely to qualify for tax-free treatment.

4. a. The potential problem here is "remote continuity." The target shareholders have a continuing interest through their Twisto stock, but Twisto no longer holds the target assets. Special rules in §368(a)(2)(C), discussed further in Chapter 12, explicitly authorize a "drop-down" of acquired assets to an acquiring corporation subsidiary, but not transfers to multiple subsidiaries or subsequent transfers by those subsidiaries to others. Nevertheless, regulations have substantially relaxed the post-reorganization transfer rules providing opportunities for significant restructuring after the initial exchange. As long as the transfers of assets are made to members of the purchasing corporation's "qualified group" as defined in Treas. Reg. §1.368-1(d) and are transfers or distributions as broadly defined in Treas. Reg. §1.368-2(k), these successive subsequent transfers should not disqualify the transaction from tax-free reorganization treatment. The transaction should qualify as a Type C reorganization.

b. This transaction involves an initial stock-for-stock exchange followed by a liquidation of the target corporation. In the end, the purchasing corporation has acquired the target corporation's assets. The issue is whether step-transaction analysis should apply and the transaction tested under the §368(a)(1)(C) asset reorganization definition, or whether the first step should be regarded as a separate stock acquisition tested under §368(a)(1)(B). The difference in this case is significant because, as will be discussed further in Chapter 12, the small amount of cash transferred would disqualify the transaction as a Type B reorganization. On the other hand, if the transaction is regarded under step-transaction analysis as a Type C asset acquisition, the small amount of cash should not be a disqualifying factor. Treas. Reg. §1.368-2(k) on post-reorganization transfers provides that an otherwise qualifying reorganization "shall not be disqualified or recharacterized" by one or more subsequent transfers. Does this suggest that the first step governs so that this transaction will be tested as a Type B reorganization? Probably not. First of all, the first step here did not "otherwise qualify" as a reorganization. Second, a distribution is not governed by the post-reorganization transfer rules in the 2(k) regulations if it results in liquidation of the target corporation. In the end, if the facts and circumstances indicate that these two steps should be regarded as an integrated transaction, this acquisition should be tested under §368(a)(1)(C). These multistep transaction issues are considered further in Chapter 12.

CHAPTER 12

Acquisitive Reorganizations

INTRODUCTION

Just as taxable acquisitions can be arranged as either transfers of stock or of assets,[1] tax-free acquisitive reorganizations also can be arranged as either stock or asset deals. A tax-free stock acquisition can be structured under §368(a)(1)(B), while a tax-free asset acquisition is possible under either §368(a)(1)(A) or (C).[2] Before moving on to the detailed requirements for each of these transactions, stop for a moment to reconsider the policy for affording nonrecognition treatment to acquisitive reorganizations—the now familiar notion of "mere change in form." In a taxable transaction, the selling target corporation or its shareholders are ending their corporate investment—"cashing out." In the tax-free acquisition, the target corporation and its shareholders have not "cashed out" their investment, but instead have traded an investment in target assets or stock for an investment in the newly reorganized corporate entity. Under these circumstances, Congress felt that recognition of gain or loss could wait until a subsequent sale or disposition by the target shareholders of the purchasing corporation stock or a sale by the purchasing corporation of the target assets received in the acquisition. The parties to the reorganization transaction remain substantially invested in

---

1. Taxable acquisitions are covered in detail in Chapter 10.
2. Although Type D reorganizations are usually divisive, §368(a)(1)(D) can also be used to structure a tax-free asset acquisition. Acquisitive Type D reorganizations are discussed later in this chapter.

the restructured corporate enterprise, and gain or loss left unrecognized can be deferred through the use of substituted basis rules.[3] Since the transaction theoretically represents a "mere change in form," it is not an appropriate moment to impose tax recognition.

Unfortunately, the policy works better in theory than in practice. The Supreme Court itself noted in an acquisitive reorganization case that "[b]ecause of the arbitrary and technical character, and the somewhat 'hodgepodge' form, of the statutes involved, the interpretation problem presented is highly complicated."[4] Our best advice in mastering the mechanics is to take a deep breath and to proceed slowly and carefully. More important, try to keep your eye on the big picture. Keep the underlying nonrecognition policy in mind as you work through the following materials on tax-free reorganizations. Finally, read critically. You will find that many specific aspects of the tax-free reorganization provisions are difficult to justify based upon coherent tax policy objectives. In fact, Treasury Department rulings reflect a tendency toward relaxing rigid textual interpretations in favor of those more reflective of the underlying purposes of the reorganization provisions.[5]

Recall that there are two key differences between taxable acquisitions and tax-free acquisitive reorganizations. First, and most important, the seller will recognize gain or loss in a taxable acquisition, but is eligible for nonrecognition treatment in the case of a tax-free reorganization.[6] In a taxable asset acquisition, the target corporation will report gain or loss on the sale of the assets under §§61(a)(3) and 1001. The target shareholders will also report gain or loss when the target distributes the consideration it received for the asset sale. In a taxable stock acquisition, the selling shareholders report gain or loss upon sale of the target stock. In contrast, the target corporation and its shareholders in a tax-free asset acquisition are eligible for nonrecognition treatment under §§361 and 354. Similarly, the selling shareholders in a tax-free stock acquisition are eligible for nonrecognition under §354.

The second key tax distinction between taxable acquisitions and tax-free reorganizations involves basis rules. Taxable acquisitions often are referred to as "cost basis" transactions. In a taxable asset acquisition, the purchasing corporation simply acquires a cost basis in the target corporation's assets under §1012.[7] In a taxable stock acquisition, the purchasing corporation

---

3. For a complete discussion of this underlying policy and other basic principles applicable to reorganizations generally, you may wish to review Chapters 4 and 11.

4. Turnbow v. Comm'r, 368 U.S. 337, 339 (1961).

5. Many of these rulings also are discussed in Chapter 11.

6. This is not to say that target shareholders will *never* recognize gain or loss in a tax-free reorganization. Shareholders will be taxable immediately on boot received as part of the transaction as well as payments received for accrued interest. The tax treatment of §356 boot is discussed in Chapter 11. These matters will be considered in further detail later in this chapter.

7. Assuming an arm's-length purchase, this cost basis should be equal to the fair market value of the assets.

acquires a cost basis in the target corporation's stock and may effectively receive a cost basis in the target assets with an appropriate election to step-up the basis under §338.[8] Tax-free reorganizations, on the other hand, often are referred to as "substituted basis" transactions. In a tax-free asset acquisition, the acquiring corporation takes the target corporation's assets with the same basis that the target corporation had under §362. In a tax-free stock acquisition, the target corporation's assets simply retain their historic bases.[9]

The combined effect of the nonrecognition and basis rules for reorganizations is effective *deferral* of gain or loss. Although the target and its shareholders in a tax-free reorganization do not recognize *immediate* gain or loss, they will not necessarily escape taxation in the long run. The gain or loss not recognized at the time of the reorganization is preserved through special substituted basis rules. Thus, for example, if the old target shareholders later dispose of the purchasing corporation shares acquired as part of the reorganization, they will measure their gain or loss using the basis from their old target shares. Gain or loss in the old target shares is thus preserved.[10] If the purchasing corporation later disposes of the old target's assets, it will measure its gain or loss using the target's old basis, thus preserving the gain or loss in the assets.

ACQUISITIVE STOCK REORGANIZATIONS: THE BASIC TYPE B REORGANIZATION

Description of the Basic Type B Transaction

In a simple Type B reorganization, the purchasing corporation (P) acquires a controlling interest in the target corporation (T) stock from the T shareholders solely in exchange for all or part of P's voting stock.[11] Two significant elements of the Type B reorganization should be noted at the outset. First, and most important, the purchasing corporation must have *control* over the target corporation immediately after the stock acquisition from the target shareholders. "Control," for purposes of §368, generally requires ownership by the acquiring corporation of "at least 80 percent of the total

---

8. The stepped-up basis election under §338 is covered in detail in Chapter 10.

9. A subsequent upstream merger or liquidation of the subsidiary into the parent also will preserve the target corporation's historic basis in the assets. I.R.C. §334(b). See Chapter 9 for a full discussion of subsidiary liquidations.

10. One way for the shareholders to escape this preserved gain or loss is to leave the purchasing corporation shares to beneficiaries upon death. The beneficiaries will receive a stepped-up (or possibly stepped-down) basis under §1014, and the otherwise preserved gain or loss from the target shares will not be recognized.

11. I.R.C. §368(a)(1)(B).

combined voting power of all classes of stock entitled to vote" *and* "at least 80 percent of the total number of shares of all other classes of stock."[12]

Second, the Type B reorganization definition provides explicit rules regarding the type of consideration that may be used to compensate target shareholders for their stock. The target shareholders must exchange T stock *solely* for all or part of the acquiring corporation's voting stock or *solely* for all or part of the voting stock of the acquiring corporation's parent. Thus, the *only* consideration that may be used in a Type B reorganization is *voting* stock of the acquiring corporation or its parent.[13] One minor exception to this rule is that the "'solely for voting stock' requirement. . . will not be violated where the cash paid by the acquiring corporation is in lieu of fractional share interests to which the shareholders are entitled, representing merely a mechanical rounding-off of the fractions in the exchange, and is not separately bargained for consideration."[14]

As a result of the rigid rules in §368(a)(1)(B), no "boot" is permitted in a Type B reorganization. By specifying that *only* voting stock may be used in a Type B reorganization, Congress has built the continuity of proprietary interest requirement directly into the statute itself, assuring a continued connection between the target shareholders and the assets of the old target corporation. Such continuity of proprietary interest surely exists when the target shareholders receive consideration entirely in the form of the purchasing corporation's voting stock, as required by §368(a)(1)(B). Remember, however, that the transaction must also meet the continuity of business enterprise and business purpose tests discussed in Chapter 11 to qualify for nonrecognition.

Tax Consequences of the Basic Type B Reorganization

The simplest Type B reorganization is one where the purchasing corporation (P) acquires 100% of the stock of the target corporation (T) from T's shareholders entirely in exchange for P voting stock in a single transaction. Since the T shareholders exchanged stock in one corporation a party to a reorganization (T) solely for stock in another corporation a party to a reorganization (P), they will not report gain or loss on the exchange.[15] Under

---

12. I.R.C. §368(c). Notice that the "control" test used for purposes of the tax-free reorganization provisions is the same control test used for purposes of §351 incorporation transactions. For a discussion of the control requirement in connection with incorporation transactions, see Chapter 4.

13. The stock used in the Type B reorganization may be either common or preferred, as long as the stock is voting stock.

14. Rev. Rul. 66-365, 1966-2 C.B. 116, 117.

15. I.R.C. §354(a)(1). The term "party to a reorganization" includes "both corporations, in the case of a reorganization resulting from the acquisition by one corporation of stock or properties of another." I.R.C. §368(b)(2).

§358(a)(1), the T shareholders' basis in P stock received in the exchange will be the same basis that they previously had in their T shares—a substituted basis.[16] As a result of its acquisition of all of the T stock, P is the new owner of T, now a wholly owned P subsidiary. Under §1032, P has no gain or loss upon the receipt of T stock in exchange for its own stock.[17] P's basis in its new T shares will be the same basis the old T shareholders previously had in their T shares pursuant to §362(b).[18] T will retain its historic basis in its assets. Put another way, T's assets will not receive a stepped-up basis as a result of the acquisition.

Type B Reorganization

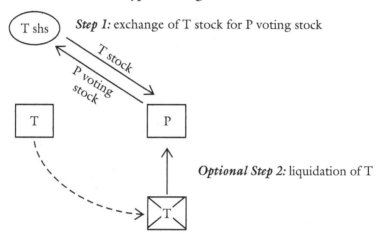

Step 1: exchange of T stock for P voting stock

T stock

P voting stock

Optional Step 2: liquidation of T

P may choose to continue to operate T as a subsidiary, or instead may choose to liquidate or merge T into P in an upstream merger. If the initial Type B reorganization and the subsequent liquidation are respected as separate transactions, T's liquidation will be governed by the subsidiary liquidation rules provided in §332.[19] On the other hand, if the merger of T into P was part of an overall integrated plan, the initial transaction may not be regarded as a Type B reorganization at all, but instead, recast for tax purposes under the step-transaction doctrine as a Type C asset acquisition.[20]

---

16. The holding period for the P stock received will include the period during which the shareholder held the T stock under "tacking" rules provided in §1223(1).

17. I.R.C. §1032(a).

18. Where the target is a publicly held corporation, it may be difficult for P to know each T shareholder's basis in the T shares. P is entitled to use a statistical sampling. See Rev. Proc. 81-70, 1981-2 C.B. 729. Acknowledging that market changes have added burden and complexity to determining target shareholder basis, in 2011, the Service issued procedures that establish safe harbor methodologies that P may use to establish its basis in stock of T when it acquires the T stock in a transferred basis transaction. Rev. Proc. 2011-35, 2011-25 I.R.B. 890.

19. For a detailed discussion of the tax consequences upon liquidation of a subsidiary, see Chapter 9.

20. See, e.g., Rev. Rul. 67-274, 1967-2 C.B. 141. Discussion of the Type C asset acquisition appears later in this chapter.

P may acquire less than 100% of the T stock solely in exchange for P voting stock and the transaction still will qualify as a Type B reorganization as long as P has control immediately after the exchange, as defined in §368(c).[21] If P acquires only 80% of the T stock in the reorganization, the tax consequences to T, to P, and to the participating T shareholders essentially are the same as above.

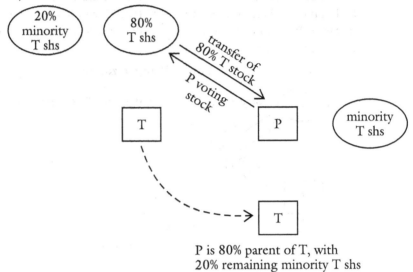

P is 80% parent of T, with
20% remaining minority T shs

The participating T shareholders will not recognize gain or loss, and the T assets will retain their historic basis. P also will recognize no gain or loss, and its basis in its T stock will be the same as the participating old T shareholders' bases in their old shares. Here, however, P is not the *sole* owner of T, but instead a part owner of its new subsidiary, T. The nonparticipating T shareholders are left as co-owners or minority shareholders of the new subsidiary.[22] Their basis in the T shares they continue to hold will remain the same.

Rigidity of the "Solely for Voting Stock" Requirement

The statutory language of §368(a)(1)(B) explicitly requires that the exchange in a Type B reorganization be solely for all or part of the acquiring corporation's voting stock or solely for all or part of the voting stock

---

21. A Type B reorganization also can occur over time in what is referred to as a "creeping acquisition." Such acquisitions are discussed later in this section.
22. The minority shareholders may wish to be "bought out" at some point rather than remain as minority shareholders. Efforts to "buy out" minority shareholders in a Type B reorganization may result in tax difficulties that will be discussed later in this chapter.

of a corporation in control of the acquiror (a parent). This requirement is quite strictly enforced. In the early landmark case of Helvering v. Southwest Consolidated Corporation,[23] the consideration used by the acquiring corporation was voting stock and stock purchase warrants. In addition, some security holders of the old corporation who wished not to participate in the reorganization were bought out for cash. This transaction was held to be an invalid reorganization for several reasons, among them that part of the acquisition was for stock purchase warrants and part for cash. The transaction thus failed the "solely for voting stock" requirement. The Supreme Court noted that

> Congress has provided that the assets of the transferor corporation must be acquired in exchange "solely" for "voting stock" of the transferee. *"Solely" leaves no leeway. Voting stock plus some other consideration does not meet the statutory requirement.*[24]

Strict application of the "solely for voting stock" requirement leaves little room for flexibility in structuring a Type B reorganization.[25] As some put it, there can be "no boot in a B" or "boot busts the B." Since the acquiring corporation cannot use any consideration other than its own voting stock or voting stock of a parent corporation, it will be difficult to compensate target shareholders who wish not to participate in the reorganization. There is no direct way to "buy out" dissenting shareholders. As a policy matter, it makes little sense for Congress to be so rigid with regard to Type B reorganizations when similar economic results can be achieved through a Type A or Type C acquisitive reorganization with much greater flexibility. Nevertheless, the distinctions between the different types of acquisitive reorganizations remain.[26]

Given the strict "solely for voting stock" restriction applied in the Type B reorganization context, acquiring corporations must be creative in dealing with minority or nonparticipating target corporation shareholders. Any cash or notes paid to any target shareholders may cause the transaction to violate the requirements of §368(a)(1)(B).

One technique sometimes used to buy out target shareholders who do not wish to participate in the acquisition transaction is a pre-reorganization redemption of the nonparticipating shareholder's interests by the target corporation using target funds or funds borrowed on the target's own credit.

---

23. 315 U.S. 194 (1942).
24. Id. At 198 (emphasis added).
25. Congress has relaxed the "solely for voting stock" requirement for asset acquisitions under §368(a)(1)(C), however. These more relaxed rules will be considered in subsequent sections of this chapter.
26. Proposals to eliminate traps for the unwary created by the technical and rigid distinctions between the different types of tax-free acquisitions are discussed at the end of this chapter.

A §368 regulatory example now clarifies that such a redemption will not threaten an otherwise valid Type B reorganization.[27]

Target Corporation Liabilities in a Type B Transaction

Ordinarily, if a taxpayer's liability is assumed by another, or if the taxpayer's property is transferred subject to a liability, the taxpayer will have cancellation of indebtedness income or the amount of the liability will be included in the amount realized on the sale. Technically, a Type B reorganization is not a transfer of assets, but a transfer of stock ownership. After the exchange, the target corporation has a new owner, but remains liable to creditors for its debts. Since T simply remains liable for its debts, technically there is no assumption of liability by P and thus no violation of the "solely for voting stock" requirement.

On the other hand, the target's security holders sometimes do exchange T debt for cash or P debt in connection with a Type B reorganization. Historically, the government took the position that such ancillary exchanges were separate transactions not governed by the tax-free reorganization rules. Surely, debt holders should be taxed to the extent that they receive cash in exchange for debt. Under the government's old position, ancillary debt-for-debt exchanges were considered taxable as well. In a significant change, the Service now takes the position that a debt-for-debt exchange that accompanies a Type B reorganization "is not a part of the stock-for-stock exchange which qualifies as a reorganization. It is, however, an exchange of securities in parties to a reorganization which occurs in pursuance of the plan of reorganization and, therefore, meets all the conditions of §354(a)(1)."[28] In other words, the debt-for-debt exchange should now be eligible for tax-free reorganization treatment except to the extent of boot received under §356. Revenue Rule 98-10 is most notable for extending tax-free treatment to these debt-for-debt exchanges. It is also notable, however, because some of the target debentures exchanged for acquiring company debentures were held by target shareholders. Nevertheless, the ruling concludes that the "solely for voting stock" requirement is met

---

27. Treas. Reg. §1.368-1(e)(8), ex. 9. This regulation incorporates positions taken by the Treasury Department in earlier rulings. See, e.g., Rev. Rul. 68-285, 1968-1 C.B. 147. In using this technique, however, the parties must be careful to assure that no funds used in the target shareholder redemption come from the acquiring corporation or an affiliate of the acquiring corporation. See, e.g., Rev. Rul. 75-360, 1975-2 C.B. 110 ("solely for voting stock" requirement not met where cash from acquiring corporation was used to pay off target company bank loan). See also the discussion in Chapter 11 on pre-reorganization redemptions and dividends.

28. Rev. Rul. 98-10, 1998-1 C.B. 643 (emphasis added).

because the target shareholders received only voting stock "in their capacity as shareholders."[29]

Another question arises if the target corporation's shareholders guaranteed the target debts and the debts are later paid off by the acquiring corporation. In such a case, the relief from a guarantor obligation paid by the acquiring corporation may be considered additional consideration other than voting stock. As long as the acquiring corporation's payment of the debt was not a condition for the exchange of stock, the Service regards the payment of debt as a transaction separate from the reorganization and the stock-for-stock exchange should still qualify as a Type B reorganization.[30]

Type B Acquisitions over Time

a) Old and Cold Target Stock Acquired for Consideration Other than Stock

An acquiring corporation does not necessarily purchase all of its stock in the target corporation at one time. The acquiring corporation might own a small amount of the target corporation's stock that it acquired years before, perhaps with no intention of making any additional purchases. Subsequently, the purchasing corporation might acquire additional interests in the target corporation sufficient to acquire control over the target. An issue that arises here is whether the "old and cold stock" held by the purchasing corporation acquired with consideration other than voting stock will prevent the subsequent acquisition from qualifying as a Type B reorganization. The regulations provide an example of a corporation that purchased 30% of the target corporation's stock for cash. Sixteen years later, the purchasing corporation acquired an additional 60% of the target corporation's stock in exchange solely for its own voting stock. Immediately after the acquisition, the purchasing corporation owned 90% of the target. The regulation concludes that this transaction was a Type B reorganization.[31] This regulatory example clarifies that it is not necessary that the purchasing corporation actually acquire an 80% controlling interest in the reorganization exchange itself and that ownership of some "old and cold stock" in the target corporation will not prevent the acquiring corporation from arranging

---

29. Id. One should be cautious in relying upon this ruling for transactions in which there is a substantial overlap of ownership between the target shareholders and security holders. The Service was careful to note that "[t]he fact that a substantial proportion of the Y debentures is held by bondholders who own no stock in Y has the effect of ensuring that the value of the debentures of Y realistically reflects the value of the Y debentures alone and does not constitute indirect nonqualifying consideration for the Y stock." Id.

30. Rev. Rul. 79-4, 1979-1 C.B. 150; Rev. Rul. 79-89, 1979-1 C.B. 152.

31. Treas. Reg. §1.368-2(c).

a subsequent Type B acquisitive reorganization. The statute simply requires that the acquiring corporation have control immediately after the exchange.

Dangers may be lurking, however, for the acquiring corporation with previously acquired stock. If the earlier cash purchase and the subsequent stock-for-stock acquisition are regarded as part of an integrated transaction under the step-transaction doctrine, the transaction will violate the solely for voting stock requirement of §368(a)(1)(B). In Chapman v. Commissioner, the taxpayer argued that it satisfied §368(a)(1)(B) when it acquired 80% control over the target corporation solely in exchange for its own stock even though it had acquired target shares for cash in an earlier acquisition that was conceded to be part of an integrated plan. The First Circuit disagreed, stating: "We believe the presence of nonstock consideration in [a Type B reorganization], . . . is inconsistent with treatment of the acquisition as a nontaxable reorganization."[32] One way to avoid these dangers is for the acquiring corporation to unconditionally sell all of the earlier acquired shares to a third party prior to any offer to acquire the target shareholders' stock in a subsequent Type B reorganization.[33]

b) Creeping Acquisitions

Despite the rigidity regarding the *type* of consideration used in a Type B reorganization, there is some flexibility regarding *timing*. An acquiring corporation need not necessarily take control of the target corporation in one fell swoop. The acquiring corporation may make a "creeping acquisition" in which a controlling interest in the target corporation's stock is acquired over a period of time. The fact that the acquisition takes place over a period of time will not necessarily disqualify it from Type B reorganization treatment as long as each acquisition was part of an integrated plan and as long as the overall transaction meets the "solely for voting stock" requirement. If the acquiring corporation uses any consideration other than its own voting stock for any piece of a transaction viewed as part of an integrated plan, the acquisition will not be a proper Type B reorganization. After the lessons learned from the *Chapman* case, the acquiring corporation must be careful to assure that *each purchase* that is part of the overall acquisition plan meets the "solely for voting stock" requirement, even though 80% or more of the T stock was acquired for P stock.

---

32. 618 F.2d 856, 862 (1st Cir. 1980) (emphasis added).

33. See, e.g., Rev. Rul. 72-354, 1972-2 C.B. 216, in which the Treasury Department permitted Type B reorganization treatment in a case in which the acquiring corporation sold stock previously acquired for cash in an unconditional sale with no agreement or arrangement to reacquire the stock and subsequently entered into a Type B stock-for-stock exchange.

ACQUISITIVE ASSET REORGANIZATIONS: BASIC STATUTORY MERGERS AND CONSOLIDATIONS

Description of the Basic Type A Reorganization

Section 368(a)(1)(A) simply provides that a "statutory merger or consolidation" is a reorganization. Prior to 2006, Type A reorganizations were limited to transactions effected under the domestic laws of a state, U.S. Territory, or the District of Columbia. Recognizing that "many foreign jurisdictions have merger or consolidation statutes that operate in material respects like those of the states,"[34] the Treasury Department amended the regulations to permit mergers involving foreign corporations.[35] As currently defined, a "statutory merger or consolidation" is "a transaction effected pursuant to the statute or statutes necessary to effect the merger or consolidation," in which two events occur simultaneously.[36] Although the description of these two required events introduces some new technical terms designed to accommodate the merger of a target corporation into a limited liability company that is disregarded as a separate entity, the basic requirements are that the operation of the merger or consolidation statute (1) cause the assets and liabilities of each "transferor unit" (target) to become the assets and liabilities of the "transferee unit" (acquirer) and (2) cause the target to cease its separate legal existence.[37]

In the typical merger transaction, one corporation is absorbed into another corporation, with only one of the two corporations surviving. In a typical consolidation, two corporations are combined into a new entity, and both of the old corporate entities disappear.

---

34. T.D. 9242, 71 Fed. Reg. 4259 (Jan. 26, 2006) (preamble to §368 regulatory changes).
35. Id.
36. Treas. Reg. §1.368-2(b)(1)(ii). The Treasury Department promulgated additional regulatory changes addressing the collateral tax consequences of cross-border reorganizations. See T.D. 9243, 71 Fed. Reg. 4276 (Jan. 26, 2009) (amending Treas. Reg. §§1.367(a)-3, 884-2 and adding Treas. Reg. §1.367(b)-13). These foreign collateral issues are beyond the scope of this book.
37. Treas. Reg. §1.368-2(b)(ii). See also Treas. Reg. §1.368-2(b)(iii), ex. 2 (merger of target corporation into a disregarded entity). Limited liability companies and disregarded entities are discussed in Chapter 2.

Type A Merger

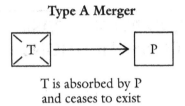

T is absorbed by P
and ceases to exist

T shs must retain a substantial
proprietary interest in P

Type A Consolidation

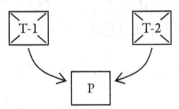

T-1 and T-2 are absorbed by P
and cease to exist

T-1 and T-2 shareholders
must retain a substantial
proprietary interest in P

Historically, corporation laws that permitted mergers or consolidations included strict standards. These included requirements that the target and purchasing corporation engage in similar businesses, that the target shareholders receive a substantial equity interest in the purchasing corporation, and that the target corporation cease to exist. Thus, when Congress first restricted tax-free reorganization treatment to mergers or consolidations meeting statutory requirements, the idea was to limit tax-free treatment to reorganization transactions that met such stringent continuity of interest requirements.[38] Over time, however, it became clear that corporation laws were hardly uniform. A transaction might technically meet the state-law definition of a merger and yet look very much like a sale. Thus, the courts soon began to require that, in addition to qualifying as a state law merger or consolidation, the transaction must meet the continuity of proprietary interest, continuity of business enterprise, and business purpose tests.[39] Some modern corporate law statutes now even include within the definition of a merger transactions in which both the target and the purchasing corporations survive.[40] Such transactions more closely resemble divisive reorganizations than acquisitive reorganizations. In such a case, the Service ruled not only that a Type A reorganization must meet business purpose, continuity of business enterprise, and continuity of interest tests, but also that "a transaction effectuated under a corporate law merger statute must have the result that one corporation acquires the assets of the target corporation by

---

38. For an interesting and useful discussion of this history, see Steven A. Bank, Federalizing the Tax-Free Merger: Toward an End to the Anachronistic Reliance on State Corporation Laws, 77 N.C. L. Rev. 1307 (1999).

39. These rules have since been incorporated into the §368 regulations. Treas. Reg. §1.368-1(b). For a detailed discussion of the judicial development of these requirements, see Chapter 11.

40. See, e.g., Tex. Bus. Corp. Act Ann. Arts. 1.02A(18), 5.01 (West Supp. 1999).

operation of the corporate law merger statute and that the target corporation ceases to exist."[41] These requirements have since been incorporated into the regulations themselves.[42]

Unlike the Type B and C reorganizations, Congress failed to specify precise statutory requirements for the continuity of proprietary interest requirement in the case of Type A reorganizations. Consequently, the early case law on continuity of proprietary interest continues to apply. Recall that the *Minnesota Tea* continuity test requires that the target shareholders receive a "definite and substantial interest" in the acquiring corporation and that this interest must represent a "material part of the value of the transferred assets."[43] As discussed in Chapter 11, this test addresses both the *type* of consideration necessary for a proprietary interest and the *proportion* of total consideration in the reorganization exchange that must consist of such a proprietary interest. Under the Treasury Department's interpretation, as little as 40% of the consideration paid in a Type A reorganization may be something other than stock.[44] The opportunity to use a substantial proportion of assets other than stock as consideration in a Type A reorganization makes this type of acquisitive structure far more flexible than the Type B reorganization. Thus, one advantage of the Type A reorganization is its greater flexibility regarding the buy out of dissenting or otherwise nonparticipating shareholders.[45] On the other hand, the absence of precise statutory rules regarding the continuity of proprietary interest test in the Type A reorganization context may create uncertainty for taxpayers.

Tax Consequences of the Basic Type A Reorganization

Assume that the target corporation (T) is merged into the purchasing corporation (P) in a merger that qualifies as a Type A reorganization. T shareholders who receive only P stock will have no gain or loss pursuant to §354 and their basis in the P shares will be the same basis they previously had in their T shares under §358.[46] Shareholders who receive P stock *and*

---

41. Rev. Rul. 2000-5, 2000-1 C.B. 436.
42. Treas. Reg. §1.368-2(b)(ii).
43. 296 U.S. 378, 386 (1935).
44. Treas. Reg. §1.368-1(e)(2)(v), ex. 1 (target shareholder receipt of $60 in cash and $40 in purchasing corporation stock sufficient for continuity of interest). The case law is even more forgiving. For example, in John A. Nelson Corp. v. Helvering, 296 U.S. 374 (1935), a transaction with only 38% equity qualified as a tax-free reorganization. For a more detailed discussion, see Chapter 11.
45. Similarly, a Type C reorganization provides somewhat greater flexibility in this regard than a Type B reorganization, but still less flexibility than the Type A reorganization. Details regarding Type C reorganizations are considered later in this chapter.
46. Again, the holding period for the P stock received will include the period during which the shareholder held the T stock under "tacking" rules in §1223(1).

boot will get tax-free treatment with respect to the stock, but will be taxable on the boot to the extent of realized gain under §356. The boot will either be considered capital gain under §356(a)(1) or "dividend boot" under §356(a)(2).[47]

P will not report any gain or loss upon the receipt of assets from T as part of the merger transaction pursuant to §1032. P's basis in the assets acquired from T will be the same basis as in T's hands under §362(b).[48] In effect, the transaction is viewed as if T first transferred its assets and liabilities to P in exchange for P stock and then immediately distributed the P stock to its shareholders. T has no gain or loss upon the receipt of any P stock or securities under §361(a). Further, T is entitled to nonrecognition even for any boot under §361(b), since the boot is viewed as immediately distributed to the shareholders as well.[49]

Assumption of Liabilities in Type A Transactions

In a basic two-party merger of a target into a purchasing corporation the target's liabilities simply become liabilities of the purchaser by operation of law with no immediate tax consequence.[50] T remains eligible for nonrecognition under §361(a). And, under §357(a), if another party assumes a liability as part of the consideration in a §361 exchange, the assumption of liability will not prevent the exchange from qualifying for nonrecognition. In other words, the liability assumption will not be considered boot.

A related issue in the Type A reorganization is the treatment of creditors who exchange target securities or debentures for parent securities or debentures. Such creditors are entitled to nonrecognition under §354, subject to taxation on the excess principal amount of securities received over the securities surrendered under §§354(b) and 356.

---

47. Individual shareholders will treat "qualified dividends" as part of net capital gain, thus eliminating much of the distinction between the different types of boot under §356. For a more complete discussion of these issues and the §356 boot rules more generally, see Chapter 11.

48. Notice that §362(b) provides for an increase in the amount of gain recognized to the transferor. Since T is regarded as the transferor and T has no gain or loss in a Type A reorganization, there will be no step-up in the basis of T's assets now held by P. There is no step-up permitted to P for the *shareholders'* gain on any boot because they are not the transferors of the assets within the meaning of §362(b).

49. Any assumption of T liabilities will not be considered boot pursuant to §357(a).

50. On the other hand, if P had any liabilities to T that were discharged as a result of the transaction, P might have cancellation of indebtedness income.

Type A Acquisitions over Time

In a statutory merger, one corporation merges into another at a particular moment in time. At first blush, the concept of a "creeping acquisition" would not appear to be applicable. However, an acquiring corporation may make stock purchases over time with a plan to eventually merge the target. Moreover, unlike the Type B reorganization, under the Service's interpretation, up to 60% of the consideration in a Type A reorganization may take the form of nonequity consideration. Consequently, P may comfortably acquire up to 60% of T's stock for cash and 40% of T's stock for P stock over a period of time culminating in the ultimate merger of T into P. The issue here is whether the ultimate merger of T into P should be treated as a Type A reorganization or instead treated simply as a liquidation of a subsidiary. If all of the purchases of stock are considered part of an integrated acquisition the upstream merger of the subsidiary into the parent will be governed by §332.[51]

ACQUISITIVE ASSET REORGANIZATIONS: THE BASIC TYPE C REORGANIZATION

Description of the Basic Type C Reorganization

a) The "Substantially All of the Properties" Requirement

In a basic Type C reorganization, the purchasing corporation acquires "substantially all of the properties" of another corporation.[52] Consequently, the Type C transaction is referred to as an "asset acquisition." In this respect, the Type C reorganization is much like a Type A statutory merger in which the target assets are similarly transferred to the acquiring corporation. In fact, the Type C merger provision was added to the Code to accommodate transactions that effectively were mergers but that failed to meet the technical corporate law definition as required by §368(a)(1)(A) and accompanying regulations.[53]

---

51. The upstream merger of a subsidiary into a parent is considered in further detail in Chapter 9.
52. I.R.C. §368(a)(1)(C).
53. S. Rep. No. 558, 73d Cong., 2d Sess. 16, 17 (1939).

Type C Reorganization

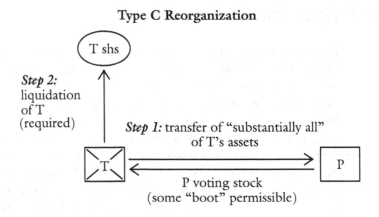

Step 2: liquidation of T (required)

Step 1: transfer of "substantially all" of T's assets

P voting stock (some "boot" permissible)

If the target transfers *less* than substantially all of its assets, the transaction is not "acquisitive" in nature. A transfer of only *part* of a corporation's assets may still qualify for tax-free reorganization treatment, but authority for such nonrecognition will be found in §368(a)(1)(D), which generally applies to *divisive* reorganizations.[54]

Given the tremendous importance of the "substantially all of the properties" requirement in distinguishing acquisitive from divisive reorganizations, it is surprising that neither the statute itself nor the regulations specify what constitutes "substantially all" of a corporation's properties for purposes of §368(a)(1)(C). There is no precise percentage of assets rule. One should take care to look not only to the percentage of assets transferred, but to compare the nature of the property transferred with the nature of the property retained. If the assets transferred are the major operating assets of the business and the assets retained are largely liquid assets retained to pay off debts, the "substantially all" requirement should be satisfied even though the percentage of liquid assets retained is rather high.[55] The Internal Revenue Service takes the position that "substantially all" means 90% of the fair market value of T's net assets and 70% of the fair market value of T's gross assets.[56]

Despite the "substantially all" requirement, one may be surprised that the transferor or target corporation may sell a significant portion of its historic assets immediately before or after the reorganization as part of an

---

54. For a full treatment of §368(a)(1)(D) and divisive reorganizations, see Chapter 13. It also is possible to use §368(a)(1)(D) in connection with an acquisitive reorganization where substantially all of the target's assets are transferred. See the subsequent section in this chapter entitled "Nondivisive Type D Reorganizations."

55. See, e.g., Rev. Rul. 57-518, 1957-2 C.B. 253 (emphasizing the nature of properties retained). See also Robert A. Rizzi, Corporate Organizations and Reorganizations: Quantity and Quality in the Substantially All Requirement, 20 J. Corp. Taxation 171 (1993).

56. Rev. Proc. 77-37, §3.01, 1977-2 C.B. 568. The fair market value of "net assets" is the value of those assets net of liabilities.

overall plan without threatening the tax-free status of the reorganization. For example, in Rev. Rul. 88-48,[57] the transferor sold off one line of business, which accounted for fully half the value of its historic assets, to an unrelated third party for cash and immediately thereafter transferred the remaining assets and cash proceeds in a Type C exchange for the acquiring corporation's voting stock. Even though this was not an acquisition of substantially all of the transferor's *historic* assets, the ruling concluded that the transaction was a valid Type C reorganization.[58] The ruling stressed that the cash sale was to an unrelated party and that the sale proceeds were not retained by the transferor or its shareholders. Thus, the transaction was not divisive in nature. Under these circumstances, it was sufficient that all of the transferor's assets held immediately before the exchange, including the remaining historic assets *and* the cash proceeds received from the prior sale, were acquired in the exchange.

b) Disregarding the Assumption of Liabilities

With regard to permissible consideration paid to target shareholders, the language in §368(a)(1)(C) is virtually identical to the language in §368(a)(1)(B). In each case, the statutory definition requires that the acquisition be in exchange "solely for all or part of its [the acquiring corporation's] voting stock (or in exchange solely for all or a part of the voting stock of a corporation which is in control of the acquiring corporation)."[59] Despite the virtually identical language, Type C reorganizations are different in several respects. One unique feature of the Type C reorganization is treatment of the assumption of target liabilities. In a Type B stock acquisition, the purchasing corporation simply becomes the new owner of the target. There is no formal assumption of the target's liabilities; the liabilities simply remain with the target. On the other hand, in a Type C reorganization, the purchasing corporation becomes the new owner of substantially all of the target's assets. The target corporation's liabilities do not transfer to the purchasing corporation along with these assets unless an express agreement to assume liabilities is made part of the transaction. As a practical matter, however, it is common for asset acquisitions to include an assumption of liabilities. Consequently, Congress added a clause to the Type C reorganization definition to ensure that the mere assumption of liabilities would not threaten eligibility for tax-free treatment of an asset acquisition. This clause provides that "in determining whether the exchange is solely for stock the

---

57. 1988-1 C.B. 117.

58. One ruling suggests the same result when the cash sale of unwanted assets to an unrelated third party takes place immediately *after* a Type A or Type C merger. See Rev. Rul. 2001-25, 2001-1 C.B. 1291.

59. Compare I.R.C. §368(a)(1)(B) with (a)(1)(C).

assumption by the acquiring corporation of a liability of the other shall be disregarded."[60] Thus, the "solely for voting stock" requirement is met if the only other consideration is an assumption of liabilities.[61] Notice that the assumption of liabilities is disregarded *only* in determining whether the transaction meets the "solely for voting stock" requirement. The regulations are careful to stress that disregarding the assumption of liabilities for this limited purpose "does not prevent consideration of the effect of an assumption of liabilities on the general character of the transaction."[62] In some cases, the assumption of liabilities may "so alter the character of the transaction as to place the transaction outside the purposes and assumptions of the reorganization provisions."[63] So, for example, if the bulk of the transaction consists of an assumption of liabilities with only a small asset component, the transaction may not be eligible for reorganization treatment.

c) The Relaxed Solely for Voting Stock Requirement

Perhaps the most significant statutory distinction between Type B and C reorganizations is the boot relaxation rule for Type C asset acquisitions found in §368(a)(2)(B). Under this subsection, a transaction that would otherwise qualify as a Type C reorganization will not be disqualified by the addition of money or other property (boot) so long as the purchasing corporation *does* acquire, solely for voting stock, target property with a fair market value of at least 80% of the fair market value of all of the target corporation's property.[64] In other words, despite the "solely for voting stock" requirement explicitly stated in §368(a)(1)(C), the use of consideration other than voting stock for up to 20% of the acquisition will *not* disqualify the Type C reorganization. Thus, in a case where P is acquiring 100% of T's assets, as long as 80% of the acquisition was "solely for voting stock," the remaining 20% of the assets may be acquired for other consideration or "boot." Notice that the boot relaxation rule in §368(a)(2)(B) requires that at least 80% of *all* of the property of the target corporation be acquired in exchange solely for voting stock. Thus, where the purchasing corporation acquires less than *all* of the assets, the amount of boot that will be permitted

---

60. I.R.C. §368(a)(1)(C) Note, however, that liabilities that were *created* as part of the reorganization transaction itself are not protected by this clause. So, for example, P's assumption of T's liability to pay cash to its dissenting shareholders is not considered a liability for purposes of this clause. See Rev. Rul. 73-102, 1973-1 C.B. 186.

61. If the consideration includes both assumption of liabilities and other boot, additional issues arise. These will be considered shortly.

62. Treas. Reg. §1.368-2(d)(1). For example, some §361 nonrecognition for T might be threatened if P's assumption of T liabilities had a tax avoidance motive under §357(b). See Chapter 4 for further discussion of liabilities and §357.

63. Id.

64. I.R.C. §368(a)(2)(B)(iii).

is reduced accordingly. For example, if P is acquiring only 90% of T's assets, only 10% of the T assets may be acquired for boot.

One caution should be noted, however. In computing the allowable 20% "boot" in a Type C reorganization, the statute requires that liabilities assumed shall be considered as money (boot) paid for the property.[65] Remember that this provision considers the assumption of liability as boot *solely* for purposes of the §368(a)(2)(B) boot relaxation rule. Consequently, if the assumption of liabilities is the *only* consideration other than voting stock, the limitation generally should not present problems. On the other hand, if P is to assume liabilities *and* also pay cash or other boot, the 20% permissible boot must be reduced by the liabilities assumed. In many cases, the practical effect will be that no other boot will be permitted.

Imagine, for example, that P is acquiring 100% of T's assets, valued at $1 million, solely in exchange for P voting stock, plus the assumption of T's liabilities in the amount of $300,000. Even though the liabilities represent 30% of the total fair market value of T's assets, the transaction still qualifies as a Type C reorganization, since the terms of §368(a)(1)(C) itself disregard liabilities in determining whether the exchange is "solely for voting stock." Changing the transaction slightly, imagine that, in addition to the P voting stock and the assumption of T's liabilities, P includes $5 of cash boot in exchange for the T assets. The transaction no longer qualifies as a Type C reorganization since the liabilities *are* considered boot *solely* for purposes of the §368(a)(2)(B) boot relaxation rule. In this transaction, the 20% boot that would otherwise be permissible cannot be used since the liabilities already represent more than 20% of the fair market value.

It is worth taking a moment here to compare the different rules regarding permissible consideration in acquisitive reorganizations. The rules for Type B reorganizations are the most strict, permitting cash only to pay target shareholders for fractional shares. The Type C rules permitting up to 20% boot are more relaxed, but still rather restrictive as a practical matter. Finally, the Type A rules are the loosest, permitting as much as 60%, or perhaps more, boot in a statutory merger or consolidation. Given that the different reorganization definitions in §368(a)(1)(A), (B), and (C) simply represent different routes to achieve similar acquisition results, the differences in these rules are difficult to justify. They create traps for the unwary in some cases, and needlessly increase the cost of transactions in many cases, as taxpayers look for ways around the various restrictions and decide which of the alternative types of acquisition transactions is best for them. Perhaps for this reason, Treasury Department rulings and regulations in recent decades

---

65. This is an exception to the provision in §368(a)(1)(C) discussed above that such liabilities should be disregarded.

reflect a more permissive approach and a movement away from literal inter-pretation of tax-free reorganization requirements.[66]

d) The Liquidation Requirement

Immediately after the target's transfer of substantially all of its property to the purchasing corporation, the target holds its remaining assets along with the voting stock and other boot consideration received from the purchasing corporation. The target is no longer a going concern. Until 1984, however, the target could continue as a holding company. P's failure to distribute money or other boot received to its shareholders allowed the T share-holders to avoid reporting §356 gain on the boot. Responding to this and other related types of perceived manipulation, Congress added the special requirement in §368(a)(2)(G) that, unless the target receives a waiver from the Treasury Secretary, the target corporation in a Type C reorganization must distribute stock, securities, and other properties received in pursuance of the plan of reorganization. Distributions to creditors in connection with the plan of liquidation will be treated as pursuant to the reorganization for purposes of this rule.

Tax Consequences of the Basic Type C Reorganization

Let's begin by considering a simple Type C reorganization in which the target corporation (T) transfers all of its assets to purchasing corporation (P) solely in exchange for P voting stock.

Notice, first of all, that the T shareholders are not exchanging anything directly with the purchasing corporation. T itself is transferring its assets to P in return for P voting stock. This exchange will not be taxable to T pursuant to §361(a).[67] T's basis in the P voting stock will be the same basis it had in the

---

66. These rulings are considered in Chapter 11 and later in this chapter.
67. T might have taxable gain, however, if the principal purpose of P's assumption of T lia-bilities was tax avoidance under §357(b). See Chapter 4 for further discussion of §357(b).

transferred assets. Unless the requirement is waived by the Treasury Secretary, the target corporation will be required to distribute the stock received from P pursuant to a plan of reorganization.[68] T will not be taxed on this distribution pursuant to §361(c). Since the T shareholders are exchanging their T stock for P stock upon this liquidation, they also will be entitled to nonrecognition treatment under §354.[69] Under §358 the T shareholder's basis in the P stock received will be the same as the T shares surrendered in the liquidation.

If the purchasing corporation takes advantage of the opportunity to pay up to 20% of the consideration in the form of boot, T will not be required to report any gain pursuant to §361(b) so long as the boot is distributed to the T shareholders in pursuance of the plan of reorganization[70] or to creditors in connection with the reorganization.[71] Since such distribution is *required* as part of a Type C reorganization, there will be no taxable gain to T upon the receipt of boot. Nor will T be entitled to deduct any losses.[72] P's assumption of T's liabilities will not be considered boot under §357(a), except in cases involving tax-avoidance motives.[73] The rationale for permitting nonrecognition to T even upon receipt of boot is that T is simply acting as an agent or conduit exchanging assets on behalf of the shareholders. The T shareholders will be taxable on the boot received pursuant to §§354(a)(2) and 356. P will report no gain upon receipt of T's assets under §1032 and the assets acquired from T will retain their historic basis in P's hands.[74]

Notice that the example described above envisions a transaction in which T transferred *all* of its assets to P. In such cases, there should be no taxable gain to T either upon the transfer of assets to P, pursuant to §361(a), or upon the subsequent distribution of assets to the T shareholders, pursuant to §361(c). Recall, however, that the Type C reorganization requires only the transfer of *substantially all* of T's assets. When T has transferred substantially all, but retained some, of its assets, T's subsequent liquidation will involve a distribution of both "qualified property" eligible for §361(c) nonrecognition[75] and also the retained assets. T will recognize gain, but is not permitted to recognize loss, upon the distribution of the retained assets.[76]

---

68. I.R.C. §368(a)(2)(G).

69. The §354 nonrecognition rule here operates as an exception to §331, under which the shareholders would ordinarily report gain or loss upon the complete liquidation of a corporation. See Chapter 8 and 9.

70. I.R.C. §361(b)(1)(A).

71. I.R.C. §361(b)(3).

72. I.R.C. §361(b)(2).

73. I.R.C. §357(b).

74. I.R.C. §362(b).

75. "Qualified property" for purposes of §361(c) generally includes stock or obligations of the distributing corporation (T) itself or stock or obligations of the purchasing corporation (P) acquired by T in the reorganization exchange.

76. In this case, upon T's distribution of the retained assets, §362(c)(1) would provide for nonrecognition of losses while §362(c)(2) would provide for recognition of gain.

Type C Acquisitions over Time

Under prior law, a purchasing corporation that already held some target stock and later wished to acquire control through a Type C acquisition of substantially all of T's assets had to be careful to avoid the pitfalls encountered by the taxpayer in Bausch & Lomb Optical Co. v. Commissioner.[77] In that case, Bausch & Lomb already owned 79% of the stock in Riggs corporation and wished to acquire complete control over Riggs' assets.[78] Bausch & Lomb (B&L) acquired control in a two-step transaction, the first part of which was an acquisition of all of Riggs' assets in return for B&L voting stock, followed by a liquidation whereby Riggs distributed its recently acquired B&L voting stock. This surely looks like a Type C acquisition of substantially all of the target's assets followed by the required liquidation of the target under §368(a)(2)(G). The rub is that as a Riggs shareholder itself, B&L surrendered its previously owned Riggs shares as part of the liquidation transaction. The Commissioner took the position that the two steps were part of an integrated plan and that the Riggs stock surrendered by B&L was additional consideration paid by B&L in the acquisition in violation of the "solely for voting stock" requirement. The Tax Court and the Second Circuit agreed. Thus, the liquidation was not considered part of a Type C reorganization, but instead a liquidation taxable to B&L as a shareholder under §331.

The Treasury Department subsequently amended its §368 regulations, effectively overturning the longstanding *Bausch & Lomb* doctrine. For purposes of Type C reorganizations, the regulations now provide that "prior ownership of stock of the target corporation by an acquiring corporation will not by itself prevent the solely for voting stock requirement . . . from being satisfied."[79] Example 1 of the revised regulations involves P, which acquired 60% of T's stock for cash years ago in an unrelated transaction. The remaining 40% of T's stock is owned by X, an unrelated corporation. T transfers all of its assets, with a fair market value of $110, to P in exchange for P stock, $10 in cash, and P's assumption of T's $10 in liabilities. T then liquidates, distributing the P stock and cash to X. The example concludes that the Type C "solely for voting stock" requirement is met, since the $10 in cash and the $10 assumption of liabilities do not exceed 20% of the value of T's assets.[80]

---

77. 267 F.2d 75 (2d Cir.), *cert. denied*, 361 U.S. 835 (1959).
78. Notice that this was just short of the 80% necessary to make Riggs a subsidiary for purposes of §332.
79. Treas. Reg. §1.368-2(d)(4)(i). The preamble to these provisions explicitly addresses Rev. Rul. 69-294, 1969-1 C.B. 110, in which the *Bausch & Lomb* doctrine was applied to a Type B reorganization. Although application to Type B reorganizations was outside the scope of the new regulation, the Treasury announced that it may reconsider this old ruling and the application of *Bausch & Lomb* principles as applied to Type B reorganizations. T.D. 8885, 65 Fed. Reg. 31,805 (May 19, 2000).
80. Treas. Reg. §1.368-2(d)(4)(ii), ex. 1. The results would be different, however, if the prior cash purchase of 60% had been part of an integrated plan. In such a case, the amount of cash involved in the transaction would far exceed even the relaxed boot rules applicable to Type C reorganizations. *Id. At* ex. 2.

TRIANGULAR REORGANIZATIONS

Introduction

Each of the basic acquisitive reorganization transactions discussed earlier in this chapter included only two corporate parties—a target corporation (T) and a purchasing corporation (P). Such basic reorganization exchanges sometimes prove inadequate to meet the needs of the parties. For various nontax reasons, the purchasing corporation might not wish to own T assets or stock directly, but might prefer to have the T stock or assets owned by a subsidiary. Similarly, T or its shareholders might not wish to sell to P directly. A triangular reorganization typically involves *three* corporations—a target (T) on the seller side and a parent (P) and subsidiary (S) on the purchaser side of the transaction. Extension of tax-free reorganization treatment to triangular reorganizations has evolved in piecemeal fashion—one now can structure a triangular reorganization as a Type A, B, or C reorganization.

The "Drop-Down" Transaction

Under case law interpreting early versions of the statutory reorganization provisions, P's acquisition of T stock or assets followed by an immediate contribution of the T stock or assets to a P subsidiary was not eligible for tax-free treatment.[81] Under the step-transaction doctrine, the *true* stock purchaser was the subsidiary. Consequently, P was not a "party to the reorganization," and the T shareholders receiving P stock did not receive stock of another party to the reorganization as required by §354. Also, under the "remote continuity of interest" doctrine, this transaction failed the continuity of proprietary interest test because the target's stock or assets were not held by the corporation that issued the stock in the reorganization. Congress subsequently added a special rule in §368(a)(2)(C), however, providing that a transaction otherwise qualifying as a Type A, B, C, or G reorganization will not be disqualified if the stock or assets acquired are transferred or "dropped-down" to a subsidiary.[82]

Notice that by its terms, §368(a)(2)(C) explicitly is limited to a transfer of the assets or stock *acquired in the acquisition* to a *controlled corporation*—one transfer down the chain to a lower-tier subsidiary. Given the literal interpretation historically applied to §368 reorganization definitions, one would think that transfers of anything *other than* acquired assets or stock, or any

---

81. See, e.g., Helvering v. Bashford, 302 U.S. 454 (1938).
82. In addition, the definition of "party to a reorganization" was amended to ensure that P would be considered a "party" in this drop-down transaction. I.R.C. §368(b).

further transfers that were viewed as part of an integrated acquisition transaction would violate continuity requirements under the remote continuity
doctrine. Not so, according to the Treasury Department's evolving interpretation. Through rulings and regulations in recent decades, the Service has
extended the scope of its position that §368(a)(2)(C) is "permissive and not
exclusive or restrictive."[83] For example, the Treasury Department permitted
a drop-down transfer following a Type D reorganization, even though such
reorganizations are not mentioned in §368(a)(2)(C).[84] Also despite the
statutory text, which explicitly permits only transfers of the *acquired* assets
or stock, the Service permitted a transfer of the surviving *acquiring* subsidiary stock to a second-tier subsidiary after a triangular Type A merger.[85] The
regulations have extended post-reorganization restructuring opportunities
even further by broadly sanctioning successive post-reorganization transfers
or *distributions* to members of the purchasing corporation's "qualified group,"
thus allowing not only "drop-downs," but also "push-ups."[86]

One example of a drop-down transaction is a Type B stock-for-stock
reorganization in which P acquires T shares in exchange for P shares and
subsequently drops the T shares down into a subsidiary (S).

Drop-Down Following a Type B Reorganization

Step 1: transfer of T shares
in exchange
for P voting stock

Step 2: transfer of T stock
by P to Subsidiary S

T becomes a subsidiary of S

---

83. Rev. Rul. 2002-85, 2002-2 C.B. 986.

84. *Id.* Despite the absence of explicit statutory language in the §368 "party to a reorganization" definition, the ruling also concluded that P would continue to be considered such a
party following the drop-down.

85. Rev. Rul. 2001-24, 2001-1 C.B. 1290. This ruling similarly concluded that P would continue to be regarded a "party to the reorganization."

86. See Treas. Reg. §§1.368-2(k) and 1.368-1(d) and discussion in Chapter 11. Drop-downs,
push-ups, triangular reorganizations, and "remote continuity" are discussed further later in
this chapter.

The initial tax consequences will be the same as those described above for the basic Type B transaction—the T shareholders are entitled to non-recognition under §354. The T shareholders' basis in the P shares is determined under §358. P has no gain or loss upon exchange of its P stock for T stock under §1032 and P briefly takes a substituted basis in the T shares from the T shareholders under §362(b).

In transactions involving a "drop-down" of stock after a Type B reorganization, the statute explicitly provides only that "the term `party to the reorganization,' includes the corporation controlling the corporation to which the acquired . . . stock [is] transferred."[87] Thus, P is considered a party, but S is not considered a party to the reorganization. The result here is that P's receipt of S stock in the drop-down portion of the transaction is ineligible for §354 nonrecognition. This should not be a matter of great concern since P should be eligible for nonrecognition under §351.[88] Under the §362 basis rules, S's basis in the T shares will be the same basis that P had immediately before the transfer—the T shareholders' basis in the shares before the exchange.[89]

A similar drop-down technique can be used following a transfer of T's assets. Under this drop-down technique, T is merged into P in a Type A reorganization or transfers assets to P in a Type C reorganization. Shortly thereafter, P transfers the T assets to an existing or a newly created P subsidiary.[90]

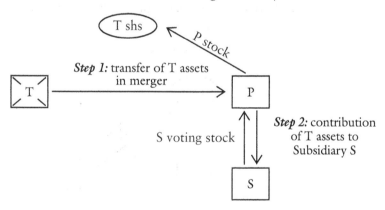

In a drop-down of the T assets received by P following a basic Type A merger or Type C asset acquisition, the tax treatment of the initial Type A or Type C transaction is the same as that described above—no gain or loss to the T shareholders, except to the extent of boot received, and no gain or loss to P or to T. T's asset basis carries over to the assets now in P's hands. Again notice that while T and P are both considered "parties to the

---

87. I.R.C. §368(b)(2).
88. For a full discussion of §351, see Chapter 4.
89. I.R.C. §362.
90. I.R.C. §368(a)(2)(C).

reorganization," the subsidiary (S), to which the assets are dropped, is not a "party to the reorganization" under §368(b). The subsequent drop-down of assets will be treated as an incorporation transaction under §351. There will be no gain or loss to P upon the exchange. Under §362, S's basis in the assets will be the same basis that P had in the assets—T's historic basis in the assets.[91]

Direct Triangular Reorganizations

In a more direct triangular reorganization, the purchasing corporation may compensate the target corporation or its shareholders with a parent corporation's voting stock instead of using its own voting stock to make an acquisition. In this triangular acquisition, the subsidiary corporation (S) technically is the acquiror, but the target corporation or its shareholders receive stock of the acquiring subsidiary's parent corporation (P) in the exchange. Since the rules for direct triangular Type A, B, and C reorganizations vary slightly, each of them is considered separately in the following materials.

a) The Type B Triangular Reorganization

In the Type B triangular reorganization, T shareholders transfer T stock to P's subsidiary (S) solely in exchange for P voting stock.

Type B Triangular Merger

This transaction, too, was not always effective as a tax-free reorganization. Under early case law, the parent was not a "party to the reorganization" and the transaction violated the continuity of proprietary interest requirement

---

91. But see §362(e)(2), which may apply in §351 cases involving "built-in" loss. See Chapter 4.

under the "remote continuity of interest" doctrine—the T stock was not ultimately held by the corporation issuing the stock (P). Consequently, T shareholders who received the parent corporation's stock were ineligible for §354 nonrecognition.[92] The statutory language of §368(a)(1)(B) has since been revised so that the acquiring subsidiary (S) may use solely voting stock of a corporation "in control of the acquiring corporation"—i.e., a parent—in a direct triangular Type B reorganization. The rationale for permitting this direct triangular merger was that if the same results could be achieved through a simple two-party reorganization followed by a dropdown, it made little sense to prohibit corporations from achieving those results more directly through a triangular reorganization.

Notice, though, that the consideration must be *entirely* voting stock of the acquiring corporation (S) itself or *entirely* voting stock of a parent of the acquiring corporation (P). It is not possible to mix parent and subsidiary stock in a compensation package to the target shareholders.[93] The reason for this restriction is not entirely clear. Perhaps Congress was concerned that with a mix of consideration, target shareholders could sell the more readily marketable parent shares without giving up the equity interest reflected in the subsidiary shares.

In the direct triangular Type B reorganization in which the T shareholders transfer their stock to S in exchange for P stock, all three of the corporations are considered "parties to the reorganization."[94] T shareholders who receive P stock clearly are entitled to §354 nonrecognition.

Resolving the proper treatment for P and S in the Type B triangular reorganization is a bit more difficult. S should be entitled to nonrecognition upon its exchange of P shares for T shares. Although this is uniformly accepted as the right answer, the precise statutory authority is less clear. Technically, §1032 nonrecognition applies upon the corporation's exchange of its *own* stock. In the triangular Type B reorganization, S is exchanging its *parent's* stock rather than its own. Regulations under §1032 provide that S will not recognize gain as long as the P stock was provided by P to S or directly to the T shareholders on behalf of S pursuant to the plan of reorganization. On the

---

92. Groman v. Comm'r, 302 U.S. 82 (1937).

93. The regulations provide that the transaction will not be a Type B reorganization "if stock is acquired in exchange for voting stock both of the acquiring corporation and of a corporation which is in control of the acquiring corporation." Treas. Reg. §1.368-2(c) (emphasis added).

94. In this example, S is acquiring T stock. T and S, then, are considered parties by virtue of the general language of I.R.C. §368(b)(2) including "both corporations, in the case of a reorganization resulting from the acquisition by one corporation of stock . . . of another." S's parent, P, also is a party by virtue of language providing that "[in] the case of a reorganization qualifying [as a Type B reorganization] . . . if the stock exchanged for the stock . . . is stock of a corporation which is in control of the acquiring corporation, the term a 'party to a reorganization' includes the corporation so controlling the acquiring corporation." I.R.C. §368(b)(2) (flush language).

other hand, S will recognize gain or loss to the extent that it uses P stock that it did not receive from P pursuant to the reorganization plan.[95] With regard to basis, since S is entitled to nonrecognition treatment upon receipt of the T shares, it follows that S's basis in the T stock should be a substituted basis from the T shareholders. This result is provided under §362(b).

What about the tax consequences to P? P was not directly involved in the exchange, which technically took place between T and S. Nevertheless, P's stock was used in the exchange and the parent corporation now indirectly controls T through its subsidiary. Regulations under §1032 treat the transfer of P shares by S "as a disposition by P of shares of its own stock for T's . . . stock."[96] Thus, P is entitled to §1032 nonrecognition upon the exchange.

A more difficult issue is determining P's basis in its S stock after the triangular reorganization. Treasury Department regulations provide that P's basis in its subsidiary stock should be adjusted after the triangular reorganization as if P had first acquired the T stock *directly* from the T shareholders and then transferred the T stock to S in a transaction in which P's basis in its S stock was determined under §358.[97] In other words, imagine first that P had done a simple two-party Type B reorganization rather than a triangular type. As such, P would take the T shares with a substituted basis from the T shareholders under §362(b). Second, imagine that in a subsequent transfer under §351, P contributed the T shares to its subsidiary. The effect of this regulation is to permit P to increase its prior basis in its S stock by the T shareholders' bases.[98] The end result of this "over-the-top" method of adjusting P's basis in its S stock is the same as if the transaction had been structured as a simple two-party Type B reorganization followed by a drop-down of the T stock to S.

b) The Type A Triangular Reorganization

i) Type A Forward Triangular Merger

Special rules in §368(a)(2)(D) provide authority for a forward Type A triangular merger in which P's subsidiary (S) acquires target assets pursuant to a merger or consolidation in exchange for stock of a controlling corporation—i.e., P stock. In this transaction, the target corporation

---

95. Treas. Reg. §1.1032-2(c). For example, if S used P stock that it previously acquired in a transaction unrelated to the reorganization, S would be required to report gain or loss upon disposition of those previously acquired shares.

96. Treas. Reg. §1.1032-2(b).

97. Treas. Reg. §1.358-6(c)(3). This method is known as the "over-the-top" method for adjusting basis.

98. This adjustment will not apply, however, to the extent that the P shares used by S in the exchange were not provided by P pursuant to the plan of reorganization.

(T) merges directly into S. The parent corporation (P) may establish a new subsidiary for this purpose or may use an already existing subsidiary.

Type A Forward Triangular Merger

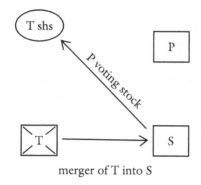

merger of T into S

Several conditions apply to the forward triangular merger under §368(a)(2)(D), however. First, the acquiring subsidiary corporation must receive "substantially all" of the target's properties.[99] In the context of a Type A merger, the requirement that S acquire "substantially all" of T's assets appears a bit odd. After all, by its very nature, a merger involves the acquisition of all of T's assets. The concern that led Congress to include this requirement is the same concern that drove it to include a "substantially all" requirement in the Type C asset acquisition. Specifically, Congress wanted to prevent corporations from using the acquisitive reorganization provisions in a transaction that was truly divisive in nature. Imagine, for example, that the purchasing corporation is interested in only one part of the target's business. The parties might arrange for the target to first spin-off or otherwise rid itself of the unwanted assets followed by an acquisition of T, now holding only the desired assets. In determining whether the "substantially all" requirement is met, one should look at the entire integrated transaction. Under the step-transaction doctrine, a spin-off of a substantial portion of unwanted T's assets followed by an acquisition that was part of an integrated plan would violate the "substantially all" of the assets requirement if former T shareholders retain an interest in the spin-off entity. Such a transaction is essentially divisive in nature. On the other hand, if unwanted assets are directly or indirectly transferred to an unrelated party immediately before or after the merger, the Treasury Department may take a more relaxed approach to the "substantially all" requirement.[100]

---

99. I.R.C. §368(a)(2)(D). The regulations specify that "the term 'substantially all' has the same meaning as it has in section 368(a)(1)(C)." Treas. Reg. §1.368-2(b)(2). The Type C triangular asset acquisition is considered in detail in the following section of this chapter.
100. See, e.g., Rev. Rul. 88-48, 1988-1 C.B. 117; Rev. Rul. 2001-25, 2001-1 C.B. 1291.

The second requirement for a Type A forward subsidiary merger is that no stock of the acquiring corporation (S) be used in the transaction.[101] Thus, the stock consideration that may be used is limited to P stock; it will not be possible to use a mixture of P and S stock as consideration in a forward subsidiary merger. One finds very little in searching for a sensible policy explanation for this restriction. Perhaps Congress was thinking about its 1964 changes to the definition of the Type B reorganization. With those changes, Congress permitted a direct triangular Type B reorganization using solely the voting stock of the acquiror's parent (P), but not a combination of both P and S. Yet, the Type A reorganization much more closely resembles a Type C asset acquisition, which includes boot relaxation provisions. Why not permit the use of 20% S stock, but treat the receipt of S stock as taxable boot? Looking at the problem differently, if T had merged into S in a simple two-party merger, S presumably could have paid 40% of the consideration in the form of P stock and 60% in the form of S stock without running into continuity of proprietary interest problems. Why not permit some similar mix of consideration for forward triangular Type A reorganizations? Whatever the reason, the limit on the use of S stock in a Type A forward triangular merger remains. If the purchasing group wishes to use some S stock in the transaction, alternatives to the Type A forward triangular transaction must be explored.

Notice that the restriction added by §368(a)(2)(D)(i) only prohibits the use of S stock. Since the Type A reorganization is rather generous with regard to permissible boot, a Type A forward triangular merger may include as consideration cash, debentures, and other types of boot, including S debt. Thus, although it is impermissible to use S stock in the transaction, it is permissible to use S debt.[102]

The final requirement for a Type A forward triangular merger is that the transaction would have qualified as a Type A reorganization if it had been a merger of T directly into P.[103] Thus, a merger of T into a P subsidiary will be permissible under §368(a)(2)(D) as long as it meets the business purpose, continuity of proprietary interest, and other tests that would apply in the context of a simple two-party Type A merger. The regulations further clarify that "it is not relevant whether the merger into the controlling corporation could have been effected pursuant to State or Federal corporation law."[104] In fact, one common nontax reason for a triangular, as opposed to a simple

---

101. I.R.C. §368(a)(2)(D)(i).

102. Treas. Reg. §1.368-2(b)(2).

103. I.R.C. §368(a)(2)(D)(ii).

104. Treas. Reg. §1.368-2(b)(2). Given the revised definition of "statutory merger or consolidation" to permit mergers with foreign corporations, this language presumably should be read as referring more generally to "statutes," as the term is used in Treas. Reg. §1.368-1(b)(1)(ii), rather than to state or federal corporate law.

two-party, merger is that a direct merger might not be possible because of some technicality of applicable corporate law.[105]

After an initial Type A triangular reorganization, the assets acquired in the merger may be transferred to another corporation controlled by the acquiring corporation without disqualifying the reorganization transaction pursuant to §368(a)(2)(C). Earlier versions of Treas. Reg. §1.368-2(k)(1) extended this authority to successive transfers to lower-tier subsidiaries. In other words, the statute and regulations permit a "drop-down" or transfer of the acquired *assets* to a second-tier subsidiary of the acquiring corporation's parent. Hinting of expanded interpretations that would follow, the Treasury Department went even one step further in Rev. Rul. 2001-24, in which T was merged into acquiring corporation S, a wholly owned P subsidiary.[106] Standing alone, the forward triangular merger clearly qualified as a Type A reorganization. Shortly after the merger, and as part of an integrated plan, however, P transferred its S *stock* to S1, a preexisting, wholly owned "sister" subsidiary. When the dust settled, the transaction was an asset acquisition by S1, a direct subsidiary of S, but only a second-tier subsidiary of P. Since §368(a)(2)(D) requires the acquiring corporation to use stock of a *controlling*, or parent corporation, the transaction would appear to qualify for nonrecognition only if the T shareholders had received S stock. Since they received only P voting stock in the exchange, the transaction did not meet the literal requirements of §368(a)(2)(D). Moreover, even if the transaction was viewed as an asset acquisition by S followed by a drop-down, the transaction fails the literal requirements of §368(a)(2)(C), which authorizes a transfer of acquired assets, but not a transfer of the acquiring corporation's stock.

Despite the absence of explicit statutory or regulatory authority, the Treasury Department approved the tax-free transaction in Rev. Rul. 2001-24. The ruling notes that "[b]y its terms, §368(a)(2)(C) is a permissive rather than exclusive or restrictive section." In addition, the ruling points out that the *reverse* triangular merger rules permit a prearranged subsequent transfer of either stock or assets of the surviving corporation to a controlled subsidiary without jeopardizing tax-free reorganization status.[107] Given suggestions in the legislative history that forward and reverse mergers should be similarly treated, the ruling concludes that the subsequent transfer of stock pursuant to a similar prearranged plan in a forward merger should not disqualify the transaction.

---

105. Various federal and state banking and insurance laws and regulations, for example, prevent the merging of certain entities.
106. Rev. Rul. 2001-24, 2001-1 C.B. 1290.
107. Reverse triangular mergers are discussed in the next section of this chapter.

Rev. Rul. 2001-24 provided a first glimpse of the government's reliance on the continuity of business enterprise (COBE) regulations, whose requirements are met as long as the issuing corporation (P) continues the target's historic business or uses a significant portion of the target's historic assets in a business, in applying remote continuity principles. For purposes of the COBE regulations, the issuing corporation is treated as holding the assets of *all* members of its qualified group.[108] Since P is thus treated as holding the assets of S and S1 for purposes of the COBE regulations, the ruling concludes that P should be similarly viewed for purposes of interpreting §368(a)(2)(D). The Treasury Department subsequently formally and more broadly adopted this approach by explicitly incorporating the COBE "qualified group" rules for purposes of testing post-reorganization transfers of target assets or stock for remote continuity.[109]

In a forward triangular merger in which T merges directly into S, the T shareholders will receive the same nonrecognition treatment under §354 upon receipt of P stock and the same boot treatment under §356 as described for the basic Type A merger. What about the tax consequences to P and S? Here again, the "right answer" appears to be nonrecognition for both corporations on the acquiring side of the transaction, yet the Code is not clear with respect to the proper tax treatment for P and S. Nonrecognition under §1032 technically applies only upon the corporation's use of its own stock. Again, regulations under §1032 provide that no gain or loss is recognized to P or S in a forward triangular merger, except to the extent that S uses P stock in the transaction that it did not receive from P under the reorganization plan.[110] T's assets will retain their historic bases as in the basic Type A merger.

One further issue in the forward triangular Type A merger is P's basis in its S stock after the merger. Under Treas. Reg. §1.358-6, P's basis in its S stock is adjusted as if P first received the T assets and liabilities through a direct merger of T into P and subsequently P transferred the T assets and liabilities to S in a §351 transaction.[111] In other words, imagine that P had first done a simple two-party Type A merger in which P would take T's assets and liabilities with a substituted basis under §362(b). Next imagine that P contributed those assets and liabilities in a subsequent §351 nonrecognition transaction in which P's basis in the S stock is equal to the basis of the assets transferred under §358. Thus, P's basis in its S stock will include the

---

108. The COBE regulations in general and the definition of a "qualified group" for purposes of these regulations are considered in detail in Chapter 11.

109. Treas. Reg. §1.368-2(k) (as amended by T.D. 9396, 73 Fed. Reg. 26,322 (May 9, 2008). Discussion of these regulations and remote continuity also is included in Chapter 11.

110. Treas. Reg. §1.1032-2. For an earlier discussion of this regulation applied in the Type B context, see the Type B reorganization discussion earlier in this chapter.

111. Treas. Reg. §1.358-6(c)(1).

basis of T's assets plus any basis that P previously had in the S stock. This is the same "over-the-top" method used in connection with triangular Type B transactions. As was the case in the triangular Type B reorganization, the end result is the same as if the parties arranged a simple two-party reorganization followed by a drop-down of the assets into a subsidiary.[112]

ii) Type A Reverse Triangular Merger

Special rules in §368(a)(2)(E) also permit a "reverse triangular merger" to qualify as a Type A reorganization. Congress saw no reason "why a merger in one direction should be taxable when the merger in the other direction [under §368(a)(2)(D)], in identical circumstances is tax-free."[113] In the reverse subsidiary merger, the purchasing corporation's (P's) subsidiary (S) is merged directly into the target corporation (T) so that the *target* survives the merger and the acquiring subsidiary (S) disappears. The target shareholders exchange their T stock for P stock.[114]

Type A Reverse Triangular Merger

merger of S into T
under state law

Here again, Congress imposes conditions, some of which parallel the conditions for the forward subsidiary merger. As in the forward triangular merger, the basic merger of S into T must otherwise qualify as a Type A merger. The reverse subsidiary merger provision also contains a "substantially all" of the assets requirement, which now appears in two parts. First, the corporation surviving the merger (T) must hold substantially all of *its own* properties after the merger.[115] It seems sensible to require that

---

112. Given the application of §351, §362(c)(2) restrictions may apply.
113. H.R. Rep. No. 91-1778, 91st Cong., 2d Sess. (1970).
114. This "reverse triangular merger" is explicitly authorized assuming that the merger of the acquiring subsidiary into the target would otherwise qualify as a Type A reorganization. I.R.C. §368(a)(2)(E).
115. I.R.C. §368(a)(2)(E)(i).

substantially all of the target assets remain in corporate solution. Otherwise, the transaction appears divisive in nature. The first "substantially all of the assets" test thus parallels the Type C reorganization "substantially all" requirement, with one exception. The Type C rule refers to an *acquisition* of substantially all of the target's assets whereas the parallel reverse Type A rule demands that the corporation surviving the merger *hold* substantially all of its *own* assets. Although the term "hold" might appear to connote more permanency and thus perhaps to impose greater restrictions on post-merger transfers, the Treasury Department notes in Rev. Rul. 2001-25 that the term "hold" is used simply because it would not make sense to require a corporation to "acquire" its own assets.[116] The ruling confirms that this reverse Type A "substantially all" language imposes the same requirements as the "substantially all" test in §368(a)(1)(C).

The second part of the "substantially all" test requires that after the transaction T also hold substantially all of the *merged* corporation's (S's) properties (other than P stock distributed in the transaction).[117] Cash or other property contributed by P to S for use as boot consideration to T shareholders or to pay off dissenting T shareholders does not count toward the "substantially all" test and it should not be a problem that T no longer holds these assets. The regulations clarify that "[i]n applying the 'substantially all' test to the merged corporation, assets transferred from the controlling corporation to the merged corporation in pursuance of the plan of reorganization are not taken into account."[118]

One unique quality of the reverse subsidiary merger is the possibility that some of the old T shareholders will dissent and continue to hold T shares as minority shareholders. In the forward subsidiary merger, in contrast, T disappears. The old T shareholders either receive P stock and boot or dissenters are "bought out," usually with cash. This unique characteristic of the reverse subsidiary merger necessitated a final condition for a successful tax-free reverse triangular merger—the "control-for-voting stock" requirement, which provides that former surviving corporation shareholders must exchange "in the transaction" an amount of stock constituting control of the surviving corporation for stock of the corporation (parent) controlling the merged corporation.[119] Given that the reverse subsidiary merger is an acquisitive reorganization, the requirement that the T shareholders transfer control makes sense. The §368(a)(2)(E)(ii) requirement that control be transferred "in the transaction" suggests the impossibility of a qualified

---

116. 2001-1 C.B. 1291.
117. I.R.C §368(a)(2)(E)(i).
118. Treas. Reg. §1.368-2(j)(3)(iii).
119. I.R.C. §368(a)(2)(E)(ii). For this purpose, "control" means 80% control as defined in §368(c).

creeping reverse triangular merger where the acquiring corporation already owns more than 20% "old and cold" stock in the target. One ruling indicates, however, that the "in the transaction" language is not so strict as to demand the transfer of control in the merger itself. In Rev. Rul. 2001-26,[120] the Treasury considered a reverse triangular merger in which the shareholders transferred only approximately 33% of the surviving corporation's (T's) stock in exchange for parent (P) stock of the acquiring corporation. Although control was thus not transferred as part of the merger transaction itself, the ruling held that the reverse merger qualified as a Type A reorganization because it was immediately preceded by a tender offer in which 51% of the T shareholders had exchanged T stock for P voting stock. Viewing the two transactions as integrated under the step-transaction doctrine, the end result was a transfer of control by the T shareholders.

Although forward and reverse triangular Type A reorganizations share several characteristics in common, there are several differences, most of them inexplicable. Perhaps the most significant difference between the forward and reverse subsidiary merger is the requirement in the case of reverse subsidiary mergers that P stock must be used to acquire 80% *control*. This 80% continuity of interest requirement differs from the continuity required in basic and forward triangular Type A mergers, where the Treasury Department has expressed that it will be content with as little as 40% continuity.[121] In addition, the P stock used in a reverse Type A merger must be *voting* stock. This may initially appear a bit odd, given that in the simple Type A merger or the forward subsidiary merger, P nonvoting stock is permissible. Another difference is that the use of S stock as consideration to the T shareholders is expressly prohibited in Type A forward triangular mergers, while it is permitted for reverse mergers. If Congress wished to create reasonable parity between the two types of triangular transactions, these differences are hard to justify. The differences between these transactions reflect deeper and more fundamental problems permeating the whole subject of tax-free reorganizations. It simply makes no sense to have the tax consequences to functionally and economically equivalent transactions turn on the kinds of details now built into the acquisitive reorganization rules. A final section of this chapter briefly considers proposals to provide more simplicity and coherence to the area of acquisitive reorganizations.

As for tax consequences, the T shareholders exchanging T stock for P stock in the reverse subsidiary merger are entitled to nonrecognition pursuant to §354, subject to the §356 boot rules. Treatment of the other

---

120. 2001-1 C.B. 1297.
121. Treas. Reg. §1.368-1(e)(2)(v), ex. 1. See also discussion of basic Type A reorganizations earlier in this chapter and of continuity of interest in Chapter 11.

parties to the transaction is a bit more complex. By analogy to the simple Type B reorganization, nothing of much tax consequence has happened to T; it has simply been acquired. Its assets and liabilities remain with historic basis intact. On the other hand, T, as the surviving corporation, is receiving S assets upon the merger of S into T. There should be no gain or loss on the receipt of these assets, although the statutory authority is not entirely clear. One might argue that nonrecognition should be provided by analogy to §1032. Interestingly, the §1032 regulations directly address the forward triangular merger, but not the reverse subsidiary merger. The regulations simply refer to §361 for "rules governing the use of P stock in a reverse triangular merger."[122] Even though the T stock technically is coming from the T shareholders, T arguably is receiving the S assets in return for T stock. In any event, as a practical matter, T is unlikely to be receiving significant assets from S. S often is merely a transitory shell corporation set up solely for purposes of the merger. Perhaps the best authority for nonrecognition to T, however, is the §118 contribution to capital provision, which covers contributions to capital both from shareholders and nonshareholders.

When P contributes its stock and other assets to S to be used as consideration to the T shareholders, there will be no gain or loss to P pursuant to §351 and no gain or loss to S under either §§1032 or 118. When S is merged into T, again there are no tax consequences to S. Its assets simply transfer to T along with their historic bases. P should receive nonrecognition treatment upon the receipt of T stock pursuant to §1032. In general, the regulations treat P's basis in the T stock in the same manner as a forward triangular merger under the "over-the-top" method—P is viewed first as acquiring the assets directly by a merger of T into P and then P is viewed as transferring the assets to T in a §351 transaction.[123]

c) The Type C Triangular Reorganization

The statutory language of §368(a)(1)(C) itself permits the acquiring corporation to use stock of a parent corporation as consideration in the acquisitive Type C reorganization. In this transaction, the target corporation (T) transfers its assets directly to a P subsidiary (S) in exchange for P stock.

---

122. Treas. Reg. §1.1032-2(b).
123. Treas. Reg. §1.358-6(c). In the forward triangular merger, the latter §351 transfer would be to the surviving corporation, S. Here, since T is the survivor, the transfer is regarded as made to T.

Type C Triangular Reorganization

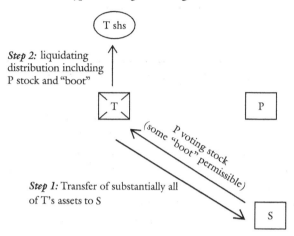

Step 2: liquidating
distribution including
P stock and "boot"

T shs

T

P

(some "boot" permissible) P voting stock

Step 1: Transfer of substantially all
of T's assets to S

S

As with the Type B reorganization, however, the acquiring corporation (S) must use entirely its own voting stock or entirely its parent's (P) voting stock, but not a mixture of the two.[124] It is possible, though, for S to use a mix of S voting stock (or P voting stock) and P *nonvoting* stock (or S *nonvoting stock*) and still participate in a Type C reorganization, as long as the amount of nonvoting stock (of P or S) does not violate the relaxed solely for voting stock rule of §368(a)(2)(B).[125]

In the Type C triangular asset acquisition, the target corporation will have no taxable gain from the receipt of P stock or S stock pursuant to §361. The target shareholders who receive P stock upon liquidation of T will be eligible for §354 treatment and will take as their basis the same basis they previously had in the T shares under §358. Any boot received by T will not be taxable to T under §361(b). Distributions of the boot also will not be taxable to T under §361(c), but will be taxable to the T shareholders pursuant to §356. S now is considered a "party to the reorganization" and S will not report any gain upon receipt of the assets under §1032.[126] Under the "over-the-top" method adopted by the regulations, P would adjust its basis in its S stock as if it first received the assets in a direct Type C asset acquisition and then transferred the assets to its subsidiary in a §351 transaction.[127]

---

124. See I.R.C. §368(a)(1)(C) (note the use of the word "or" in the parenthetical); Treas. Reg. §1.368-2(d)(1).

125. See Treas. Reg. §1.368-2(d)(2).

126. Under Treas. Reg. §1.1032-2(b), S is entitled to nonrecognition except to the extent that the P stock it used as consideration in the exchange was stock that it did not receive from P pursuant to the plan of reorganization.

127. Treas. Reg. §1.358-6(c)(1).

In other words, P would increase its previous basis in its S shares by the basis in the T assets acquired in the transaction.[128]

NONDIVISIVE TYPE D REORGANIZATIONS

Although most reorganizations that rely on §368(a)(1)(D) are divisive reorganizations, the section's statutory terms cover both acquisitive and divisive transactions. In a Type D reorganization one corporation transfers "all or part of its assets to another corporation" and the transferring corporation or one or more of its shareholders (or a combination of the two) must be in control of the corporation to which the assets are transferred immediately after the transfer.[129] One additional §368(a)(1)(D) requirement is that the "stock or securities of the corporation to which assets are transferred [must be] distributed in a transaction which qualifies under section 354, 355, or 356." This required distribution is the feature that distinguishes acquisitive from divisive reorganizations. In order to qualify for tax-free treatment, divisive reorganizations must meet additional stringent requirements codified in §355.[130] In the case of a nondivisive (acquisitive) Type D reorganization qualifying under §354, §354(b) provides that the transferee corporation must acquire "substantially all" of the assets of the transferring corporation.

Notice that the Type D reorganization definition does not require the purchasing corporation to use its own stock or securities or stock or securities of a subsidiary. Instead, continuity of proprietary interest is assured by requiring that the target (T), or one or more of T's shareholders, be in control of the purchasing corporation (P) immediately after the transfer of assets.[131] In other words, the transferor corporation and/or its shareholders must retain control over the purchasing corporation. This is quite unlike the typical acquisitive reorganization, in which the target shareholders typically lose control over the target and its assets.

Since the Type D reorganization involves transfer of "all or part" of the target's assets, there can be overlaps with the Type A and Type C acquisitive

---

128. This basis in the T assets would, of course, be a substituted basis under §362(b). But see I.R.C. §362(e)(2).

129. I.R.C. §368(a)(1)(D).

130. See Chapter 13.

131. In the case of nondivisive Type D reorganizations, the applicable "control" test is the 50% test provided in §304(c), rather than the 80% control test in §368(c) that would otherwise apply. See I.R.C. §368(a)(2)(H). This reduced 50% threshold for control in nondivisive Type D transactions more readily enables the government to recast certain liquidation-reincorporation transactions, in which the liquidating corporation attempts to recognize loss upon a liquidating distribution, as Type D reorganizations in which recognition of loss is not permissible.

asset reorganization definitions. Imagine, for example, that shareholder A controls two corporations, T and P. T transfers all of its assets to P in exchange for P voting stock. T subsequently distributes the P stock to shareholder A in complete liquidation. This transaction fits within the Type C acquisitive reorganization definition. At the same time, it fits within the Type D reorganization definition—T has transferred substantially all of its assets to another corporation (P) and T's shareholder (A) is in control of the acquiring corporation (P) immediately after the exchange. To resolve the potential overlap issue, §368(a)(2)(A) provides that a transaction meeting both the Type C and Type D definitions will be treated as a Type D reorganization. The Treasury Department takes the same position with respect to transactions meeting both the Type A and Type D definitions.[132] These priority rules are designed to prevent transactions that are essentially divisive from bypassing the strictures of §355, but should not pose serious obstacles to tax-free treatment for most acquisitive Type D reorganizations.[133]

Type D Acquisitive Reorganization

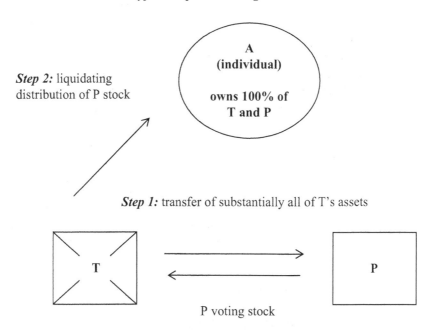

Step 2: liquidating distribution of P stock

A (individual)

owns 100% of T and P

Step 1: transfer of substantially all of T's assets

T

P

P voting stock

One might initially wonder whether these overlaps are any more than technicalities, since the transactions will be within the tax-free reorganization definition in §368(a) in any event. As long as P acquires *substantially all* of T's assets in the Type D reorganization, the target shareholder still should

---

132. Rev. Rul. 75-161, 1975-1 C.B. 114.
133. For detailed coverage of the Type D reorganization provisions, see Chapter 13.

be eligible for §354 nonrecognition.[134] Whether the transaction is classified under the Type A, Type C, or Type D definition can make a significant difference, however. First, the §368(a)(2)(B) "boot relaxation" rules available for Type C reorganizations permit only 20% boot, and the Type A continuity rules permit about 60% boot.[135] Since the Type D reorganization definition is not tied to receipt of a proprietary interest in the purchasing corporation, one might even arguably structure an "all boot" Type D transaction. Short of deciding the extreme "boot only" case, one can at least agree that the Type D reorganization offers greater flexibility with respect to boot.

Second, although assumption of target liabilities is disregarded under the basic Type C definition, assumed liabilities *are* considered boot for purposes of the "boot relaxation" rules. In other words, a Type C transaction with 20% in liabilities has already "used up" its permissible boot under the "boot relaxation" rule. Thus, Type D reorganizations offer greater flexibility with regard to assumption of liabilities. Prior to 2004, however, one concern with Type D reorganizations was the potential for §357(c) gain to the extent that assumed liabilities exceeded the transferor's basis.[136] By its terms, §357(c)(1) previously applied only to §351 nonrecognition exchanges, and to §361 tax-free reorganization exchanges in connection with any Type D reorganization. Notice that, as a general rule, §357(c) does not apply to acquisitive reorganizations. The American Jobs Creation Act of 2004 amended §357(c) to extend this exemption to *acquisitive* Type D reorganizations.[137] The legislative history explains that

> [t]his is because in an acquisitive reorganization under section 368(a)(1)(D), the transferor must generally transfer substantially all of its assets to the acquiring corporation and then go out of existence. Assumption of its liabilities by the acquiring corporation thus does not enrich the transferor corporation, which ceases to exist, and whose liability was limited to its assets in any event, by corporate form. The Committee believes that it was appropriate to conform the treatment of acquisitive reorganizations under section 368(a)(1)(D) to that of other acquisitive reorganizations.[138]

Using similar logic, the Service has ruled that §357(c) does not apply to *any* of the different types of acquisitive reorganizations, even if the acquisition is one to which §351 would also apply.[139]

---

134. I.R.C. §354(a), (b)(1).

135. See discussion of Type C reorganizations and the boot relaxation rules earlier in this chapter.

136. See discussion of §357(c) in Chapter 4.

137. American Jobs Creation Act of 2004, Pub. L. No. 108-357, 188 Stat. 1418 (amending §357(c)(1) to apply only to Type D reorganizations with respect to which stock or securities of the acquiring corporation are distributed in a transaction qualifying under §355 — i.e., divisive reorganizations).

138. S. Rep. No. 192, 108th Cong., 1st Sess. 185 (2003).

139. Rev. Rul. 2007-8, 2007-1 C.B. 469.

ACQUISITIVE REORGANIZATIONS IN INSOLVENCY: THE TYPE G REORGANIZATION

In 1980 Congress added a special category to the §368 reorganization definition dealing with reorganizations of corporations in bankruptcy. The Type G reorganization involves a "transfer by a corporation of all or part of its assets to another corporation in a title 11 or similar case; but only if, in pursuance of the plan, stock or securities of the corporation to which the assets are transferred are distributed in a transaction which qualifies under section 354, 355 or 356."[140] The Type G reorganization definition is similar to the Type D definition, permitting a transfer of all *or a part* of T's assets. Some Type G reorganizations will involve a transfer of substantially all of the bankrupt corporation's assets to another corporation and, thus, will resemble a Type C acquisitive reorganization. In such cases, a new corporation acquires effective control over the bankrupt corporation's assets as a result of a reorganization in bankruptcy. Even though a Type G transaction falls within the §368(a)(1) reorganization definition, the shareholders and security holders will not be eligible for §354 nonrecognition unless the transaction also meets special requirements in §354(b). First, the corporation to which the assets are transferred must acquire substantially all of the assets of the transferor.[141] Thus, §354 nonrecognition applies only in the case of acquisitive Type G transactions and not in the case of divisive Type G transactions. Second, the stock, securities and other properties received by the transferor, as well as all other properties of the transferor, must be distributed as part of the plan of reorganization.[142]

OVERLAPS IN THE ACQUISITIVE REORGANIZATION DEFINITIONS

One aspect of tax-free acquisitive reorganizations that generates tremendous confusion is the many overlaps between various reorganization definitions and other provisions in the Internal Revenue Code. Some reorganization transactions fit one or more of the specific reorganization definitions described above. Since the requirements for each are different one must be clear about which of the definitions applies. Another overlap problem

---

140. I.R.C. §368(a)(1)(G). Regulatory amendments added explicit authority for triangular Type G reorganizations. Treas. Reg. §1.358-6(b)(2)(v) (added by T.D. 9424, 2008-44 I.R.B. 1012 (Nov. 3, 2008)).
141. I.R.C. §354(b)(1)(A).
142. I.R.C. §354(b)(1)(B).

arises because many complex corporate transactions involve multiple steps. Viewed separately, the steps may appear to be one specific type of reorganization. If the step-transaction doctrine is applied, the transaction may take on the characteristics of another specific type of reorganization.[143] This section will address some of the more common overlap problems in the acquisitive reorganization context.

An upstream merger of a subsidiary corporation into its parent technically may be both a Type A statutory merger or consolidation and, at the same time, a liquidation of a subsidiary under §332. In such circumstances, regulations provide that the §332 liquidation rules generally prevail over the reorganization provisions.[144]

Another overlap issue arises when a Type B reorganization is followed shortly thereafter by a liquidation of the newly acquired subsidiary. In Rev. Rul. 67-274, the Treasury Department integrated the two steps to convert an initial Type B to an integrated Type C reorganization.

Type B Stock Acquisition Followed by Seperate §332 Liquidation
OR
Integrated Type C Asset Acquisition?

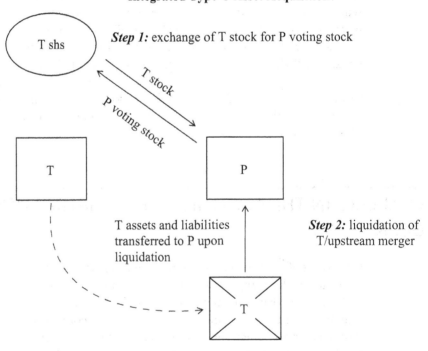

Step 1: exchange of T stock for P voting stock

T stock

P voting stock

T assets and liabilities transferred to P upon liquidation

Step 2: liquidation of T/upstream merger

---

143. Treasury Department rulings reflect a reinvigorated use of step-transaction analysis as applied to reorganizations. See discussion in Chapter 11.

144. Treas. Reg. §1.332-2(d). This is certainly the case when the parent has held stock in the subsidiary for a substantial period of time. If the parent's stock in the subsidiary was recently acquired, however, the upstream merger of the subsidiary into the parent might be recast as an asset acquisition.

When the dust settles from this multi-step transaction, T has ceased to exist, and P holds all of T's assets and liabilities. The end result is exactly the same as it would have been with a direct Type C asset acquisition. If these events were part of an overall plan to acquire assets and occurred within a reasonably short time period, the two steps would be integrated and the overall transaction recharacterized as a Type C asset acquisition. Consequently, eligibility for tax-free reorganization treatment would be governed by the more forgiving boot rules in §368(a)(2)(C).[145]

As noted earlier, revised remote continuity regulations promise that a "transaction otherwise qualifying as a reorganization under section 368(a) shall not be *disqualified or recharacterized* as a result of one or more subsequent transfers . . ." meeting the regulation's requirements.[146] Put differently, the regulation creates a so-called safe harbor, "turning off" the step-transaction doctrine for certain post-reorganization transfers, including distributions, of target assets or stock to members of the purchasing corporation's "qualified group," as defined in the COBE regulations.[147] Although P in the above example surely is a member of the qualified group, the "safe harbor" does not apply to transfers that result in the target's liquidation.[148] Consequently, the transaction *could* be recharacterized as a Type C asset acquisition. On the other hand, if T had transferred only 80% of its assets and liabilities to P, the transaction arguably would be governed by the 2(k) transfer regulations. If so, the initial Type B stock acquisition would not be recharacterized as an asset acquisition.

Step-transaction analysis also has been applied to recharacterize a target stock acquisition followed by a liquidation of the target as an acquisitive Type D reorganization. In Rev. Rul. 2004-83, P was the parent to "brother-sister" subsidiaries, S and T. Pursuant to an integrated plan, S purchased all of T's stock, making T a direct subsidiary of S. Shortly thereafter, S received all of T's assets upon T's complete liquidation. The Service viewed these events as an integrated Type D asset acquisition.[149] Responding to yet another overlap issue, the Service concluded that the Type D tax-free reorganization treatment rules overrode the §304 deemed redemption provisions that otherwise would have applied to the initial sale between related companies.[150]

In addition to these overlap areas, there are also substantial overlaps between the incorporation provisions in §351 and the reorganization

---

145. 1967-2 C.B. 141. A Type B reorganization where the target corporation is a holding company whose only asset is stock in a subsidiary corporation may also be recast as a Type C reorganization. Rev. Rul. 70-65, 1970-1 C.B. 77.

146. Treas. Reg. §1.368-2(k)(1). See discussion in Chapter 11.

147. Treas. Reg. §1.368-2(k)(1) (cross-referencing to Treas. Reg. §1.368-1(d)).

148. Treas. Reg. §1.368-2(k)(1)(i)(B).

149. Rev. Rul. 2004-83, 2004-2 C.B. 157.

150. Id. At 158. See also Rev. Rul. 2015-10, 2015-21 I.R.B. 972 (§351 transfer, followed by Type D reorganization). If the three companies had been members of a consolidated group, the purchase would have been treated as an intercompany transaction to which §304 would not apply. Id. (citing Treas. Reg. §1.1502-80(b)). For a discussion of §304, see Chapter 6.

provisions. This should not be surprising in that all of these provisions are located in Part III of Subchapter C, entitled "Corporate Organizations and Reorganizations." Remember that §351 provides for nonrecognition to persons who transfer property solely in exchange for stock if those persons are in control of the corporation immediately after the exchange. In many respects, the §351 nonrecognition rules parallel those in §354.[151] Since both of these provisions permit nonrecognition, one might wonder if it makes much difference whether the taxpayer is entitled to §351 or §354 nonrecognition. The key difference is that the assumption of liabilities is treated differently in §351 transactions. In the case of incorporation transactions, §357(c) requires the recognition of gain to the extent that liabilities assumed or property taken subject to liability exceeds the basis of property transferred in the nonrecognition exchange. In contrast, in the reorganization context, it is often possible to disregard liabilities and to avoid taxable gain from the assumption of liabilities under §357.[152] In addition, securities received by the transferors in a §351 exchange are *always* considered boot, whereas securities received are not necessarily boot under §354.

An additional twist to the tax-free reorganization overlap problem arises from §362(e), added by Congress in 2004. The §362(e)(2) built-in loss limitation rules require a reduction in the corporation's basis upon a tax-free exchange of property for stock when the aggregate basis exceeds the aggregate fair market value of property transferred.[153] These limitations expressly are applicable only to property described in §362(a); that is, property received in a §351 exchange or as a contribution to capital. Thus, §362(e)(2) does not apply to tax-free reorganizations in which the transferee corporation's basis is determined under §362(b). If the same transaction is governed by both §351 and another tax-free reorganization provision, however, the §362(e) rules presumably will apply. In 2013, the Treasury Department addressed some of the significant issues involving this overlap with §351 in final regulations.[154]

---

151. Control, for purposes of §351, is the same 80% test in §368(c) that is used for reorganizations. Also, the basis rules in §§358 and 362 are applicable both to §351 incorporation transactions and reorganizations. For a detailed discussion of §351, see Chapter 4.

152. Acquisitive Type D reorganizations now are also exempt from §357. I.R.C. §357(c)(1)(B). See also the discussion earlier in this chapter. See I.R.C. §357(c)(1)(B). Another exception is an assumption of liability for tax avoidance purposes. See §357(b).

153. I.R.C. §362(e)(2)(A). See Chapter 4. The restrictions on importation of net built-in loss in §362(e)(1) operate somewhat differently, limiting the basis of individual assets. Since the (e)(1) rules apply primarily to transactions involving foreign corporations, they are not covered in detail in this book.

154. For example, the final regulations include "not only examples from the proposed regulations illustrating the application of section 362(e)(2) to transactions qualifying as both section 351 transactions and reorganizations, they also include an example illustrating the nonapplicability of section 362(e)(2) to triangular reorganizations that do not include a transfer to which section 362(a) applies." T.D. 9633, 78 Fed. Reg. 54,168 (Sept. 3, 2019). See, e.g., Treas. Reg. §1.362-4(h), ex. 3 (§362(e)(2) applies to a transaction that is covered by §§351 and one of the reorganization provisions, §368(a)(1)(A)).

CARRYOVER OF TAX ATTRIBUTES FOLLOWING TAX-FREE ACQUISITIVE REORGANIZATIONS

Every corporation has its own distinct tax characteristics, including its methods of accounting, earnings and profits accounts, various available tax credits, capital loss carryovers, and net operating losses. After a *stock* acquisition, the target corporation remains a distinct legal entity and its tax attributes generally remain intact. After an *asset* acquisition, one would suspect the distinct tax attributes of the target to remain with the target and *not* to transfer to the purchasing corporation. This is certainly true for taxable acquisitions. In the case of tax-free asset acquisitions, however, tax attributes of the target *should* generally survive in the hands of the acquiring corporation. After all, tax-free status was afforded these transactions on the theory that the transaction represented a "mere change in form," and that the original business enterprise continued, albeit in modified form.

As a *general* rule, tax attributes of the target corporation will continue after the target's stock or assets have been acquired in a tax-free acquisitive reorganization. This general rule is subject to numerous judicial and statutory restrictions and limitations, however, designed to prevent "trafficking" in tax characteristics. As one corporate tax treatise has observed, "[i]t seems safe to conclude . . . That the judicial climate is hostile to taxpayer efforts to secure corporate tax benefits by merger or other forms of acquisition; some judges and commentators apparently feel that traffic in corporate tax benefits (most notably, net operating loss carryovers) is akin to original sin . . . ."[155] As suggested by this quote, the tax attribute most frequently subject to perceived "trafficking" abuse is the net operating loss. Consequently, many of the judicial and statutory restrictions and limitations address this attribute in particular. The material that follows presents a brief overview of the rules regarding the carryover of tax attributes following a tax-free acquisition.

To begin, notice that no special rule is required to provide that the tax attributes of the target corporation generally remain intact following a stock acquisition. Such attributes survive simply because the target survives as a distinct entity. On the other hand, absent a special rule, the tax characteristics of the target might well disappear if the purchasing corporation were to liquidate the target immediately after a stock acquisition, or if the purchasing corporation acquired assets directly in the case of a Type A merger or a Type C asset acquisition. Congress provided in §381 for the general carryover of tax attributes for §332 liquidations (upstream mergers) and other

---

155. Boris I. Bittker and James S. Eustice, Federal Income Taxation of Corporations and Shareholders ¶14.01[2] (7th ed. 2015). One might safely add that the statutory climate is similarly hostile.

tax-free acquisitive reorganizations.[156] Although §381 generally permits the target's tax attributes to survive, this general rule is subject to numerous restrictions and limitations included in §381 itself, as well as further restrictions in §§382, 384, and elsewhere. These restrictions and limitations generally apply mechanically, and do not require a finding of tax avoidance motivation or deliberate tax attribute "trafficking." At the same time, the Treasury Secretary is authorized to completely disallow any deduction, credit, or other allowance following an acquisition of control if "the principal purpose for which such acquisition was made is evasion or avoidance of federal income tax by securing the benefit of a deduction, credit, or other allowance which [the acquiror] would not otherwise enjoy."[157]

Section 382 imposes limitations on net operating loss carryforwards (NOLs) following certain ownership changes resulting from either taxable or tax-free acquisitions.[158] In general, §382 addresses the extent to which the acquiring corporation (P) may continue to use the target corporation's pre-acquisition NOLs. The §382 limitations will not apply to all acquisition transactions, but must be triggered by an "ownership change."[159] Generally, a tax-free acquisitive reorganization will constitute such an ownership change if the target shareholders own less than 50% of the acquiring corporation's stock immediately after an acquisitive reorganization. Under §382, T's NOLs are eliminated entirely unless the target meets the continuity of business enterprise test during the two-year period following the ownership change.[160] Even if the target meets the continuity of business enterprise test, the use of T's pre-acquisition NOLs is subject to an annual limitation. This limitation is computed by multiplying T's fair market value immediately before the reorganization by a rate equal to the long-term tax-exempt rate.[161] The idea here is to imagine that the target's value will continue to grow after the acquisition. Rather than look at the *actual* rate of growth, §382(b) presumes a rate of growth equal to the long-term tax-exempt rate. The logic behind the §382(b) annual limitation is to try to allow P to use

---

156. I.R.C. §381(a). The particular tax items that carry over include net operating loss carryovers, earnings and profits accounts, capital loss carryovers, and other items listed in §381(c). Regulations provide that tax attributes are inherited by the "acquiring corporation." If no one corporation acquires all of the assets, the corporation that directly acquired the assets is viewed as the "acquiring corporation" for tax-attribute purposes, even if it does not retain those assets. Treas. Reg. §1.368(a)-1(b)(2).

157. I.R.C. §269(a).

158. The §382 limitations, as applied to taxable acquisitions, are considered briefly in Chapter 10.

159. Details regarding the definition of "ownership change" are extremely complex and beyond the scope of most introductory courses in corporate taxation. The statutory definition appears in §382(g).

160. I.R.C. §382(c).

161. I.R.C. §382(b).

T's pre-acquisition NOLs to the same extent that T alone would have been entitled to use them if T had continued on its own and had experienced a reasonable rate of growth.

In addition to providing limitations on P's ability to use T's pre-acquisition NOLs, the Code imposes limitations on either party's ability to use its pre-acquisition NOLs to offset the other party's built-in gains — unrealized gains with respect to assets for which the pre-acquisition fair market value was higher than the asset's basis. Special rules in §§382(h) and 384 prevent the fusing of such NOLs with such built-in gains for a period of five years following the acquisition.

PROPOSALS TO ELIMINATE THE REORGANIZATION DEFINITIONS

Given the complexities of the acquisitive reorganization definitions and the overlaps between the various definitions, commentators have suggested eliminating the tax-free reorganization framework altogether and substituting a more workable and less complex set of rules.[162] Under such proposals, the parties to a corporate acquisition would simply elect to treat the transaction as a taxable acquisition in which the shareholders who sell their stock report gain, the corporation acquiring the stock receives a cost, often a stepped-up, basis in the assets acquired, and the target corporation reports any gain or loss on its transfer of assets.[163] On the other hand, the parties could elect to treat the acquisition as a tax-free acquisition in which the shareholders who transfer stock are not required to report gain and the acquiring corporation receives a carryover basis in the target corporation's assets. Under these proposals, whether the transaction was taxable or tax-free would be explicitly elective rather than being left to the technical details of the §368(a)(1) reorganization definitions.

---

162. Perhaps the most well-known is the Staff of the Committee on Finance, U.S. Senate, The Subchapter C Revision Act of 1985, A Final Report, S. Rep. 99-47, 99th Cong., 1st Sess. (1985); see also A.L.I., Federal Income Tax Project: Proposals on Corporate Acquisitions and Dispositions and Reporter's Study on Corporate Distributions (1982) (William D. Andrews, rep.). For discussion of explicit tax elections, see Heather M. Field, Choosing Tax: Explicit Elections as an Element of Design in the Federal Income Tax System, 47 Harv. J. on Leg. 21 (2010).

163. This transaction would be quite similar to the current taxable acquisition with a §338 election. See Chapter 10.

Examples

The Basic ABCs

1. Brady Construction, Inc. (BC) is a design/construction corporation, incorporated in the State of Delaware, that is considering an expansion of its operations into a service industry. BC has its eyes on Alice's Housekeeping Services, Inc. (AHS), also incorporated in Delaware. AHS provides housekeeping services on a contract basis to commercial buildings. At the time of the acquisition discussions, AHS had the following assets:

	Basis	fair market value
Cash	$200,000	$200,000
equipment/trucks	250,000	350,000
cleaning supplies	0	50,000
Investments	250,000	800,000
customer lists	0	600,000
Total	$700,000	$2,000,000

Alice was the founder and primary shareholder of AHS. At the time of the proposed acquisition, she held 75% and her original business partner, Sam, held 15% of the authorized and outstanding common stock. Alice's basis in her AHS shares was $825,000. Sam's basis in his shares was $165,000. The remaining 10% was owned by numerous minority shareholders, no one of which held more than 1% of the stock. Alice and Sam are amenable to the acquisition, but the minority shareholders are not.

Assume that the parties agree to a stock-for-stock deal under which Alice and Sam will exchange all of their AHS shares in return for five shares of newly authorized BC voting stock for each AHS share exchanged. Assume further that the BC voting stock Alice received in the exchange is valued at $1.5 million and the BC voting stock received by Sam in the exchange is valued at $300,000. For the moment, BC plans to retain AHS as a subsidiary.

a. What are the tax consequences of the stock-for-stock exchange to BC, AHS, Alice, Sam? What happens to the minority shareholders? What happens to AHS's liabilities to its creditors?

b. What if the parties agreed to a stock-for-stock deal in which Alice and Sam exchanged all of their AHS shares in return for five shares of newly authorized BC voting stock and one share of newly authorized BC nonvoting stock for each AHS share surrendered? For four shares of newly authorized voting stock and ten-year 8% BC debentures for each share surrendered? Assume that the consideration package to

Alice still is valued at $1.5 million and the consideration package to Sam still is valued at $300,000.

   c. How would your answer to Example 1a change if BC paid $200,000 in cash to buy out the dissenting minority shareholders? How would your answer to Example 1a change if, instead, AHS redeemed its minority shareholders with the $200,000 cash on hand immediately before the acquisition?

   d. Based upon the facts in Example 1a, what would be the tax consequence of a subsequent liquidation of AHS in which the $200,000 cash is distributed to the minority shareholders and the remaining assets are distributed to BC?

2. How would your answers to Examples 1a through 1c change, if at all, if the transaction was structured to meet all of the requirements for a statutory merger of AHS into BC under the laws of the State of Delaware?

3. Suppose now that BC arranged to directly acquire all of the AHS assets (described in Example 1), except for the cash. According to the agreement, AHS transfers these assets in exchange for BC voting stock valued at $1.8 million. Assume for the moment that AHS has no outstanding mortgages or liabilities. The BC voting stock received by AHS is subsequently distributed in liquidation to Alice, who receives $1.5 million worth of BC stock, and Sam, who receives $300,000 worth of BC stock. The $200,000 cash is distributed to the minority shareholders in complete liquidation of AHS.

   a. What are the tax consequences of the transaction to BC, AHS, Alice, and Sam? What happens to the minority shareholders?

   b. How would your answer to Example 3a change, if at all, if AHS decided to retain the BC stock and cash as a holding company?

   c. How would your answer to Example 3a change, if at all, if the exchange of AHS assets was for BC voting stock (valued at $1.7 million) and BC nonvoting stock (valued at $100,000)?

   d. How would your answer to Example 3a change, if at all, if BC transferred $1.5 million worth of BC voting stock to AHS and explicitly assumed all of AHS's liabilities to creditors, amounting to $300,000?

   e. How would your answer to Example 3d change, if at all, if instead of $1.5 million voting stock, BC transferred $1.4 million worth of BC voting stock and $100,000 worth of BC nonvoting stock?

   f. How would your answer to Example 3a change, if at all, if the exchange of AHS assets was for BC voting stock (valued at $1.7 million) and ten-year 8% BC debentures (valued at $100,000)?

   g. How would your answer to Example 3a change, if at all, if the asset acquisition called for transfer of all AHS assets other than cash and investments?

Acquisition Geometry

4. Greg, Bobby, and Peter were the founders and shareholders of Interior Decorators, Inc, (IDI) incorporated in the State of Delaware. Greg held 50%, Bobby held 25% and Peter held 25% of the common voting stock. Father Michael lent $50,000 to the corporation in return for a five-year installment note at 8% interest. Carol, Jan, Marsha, and Cindy were the founders and shareholders of a competing firm, Design Studios, Inc. (DSI), also incorporated in Delaware. Each of them holds 25% of DSI's common voting stock. After negotiations, the corporate boards of the two corporations agreed that DSI would acquire IDI. Compare the tax results and the advantages and disadvantages of structuring the transaction in the following different ways:

   a. DSI creates a new subsidiary, S. DSI then acquires all of the IDI stock from Greg, Bobby, and Peter in return for DSI voting stock. Immediately thereafter, DSI contributes the recently acquired IDI stock to S.

   b. DSI creates a new subsidiary, S, by transferring DSI voting stock in return for S stock. S acquires all of the IDI stock from Greg, Bobby, and Peter in return for the DSI voting stock. What difference if S acquired all of the IDI stock in return for DSI voting stock and S voting stock? For DSI voting stock and S debentures?

   c. DSI acquires all of IDI's assets in return for DSI voting stock. Immediately thereafter, DSI contributes the assets to S, a newly created subsidiary. IDI then distributes the DSI voting stock to its shareholders in liquidation.

   d. DSI creates a new subsidiary, S, by transferring DSI voting stock in return for S stock. S acquires all of the assets of IDI in return for the DSI voting stock. IDI then liquidates distributing the DSI stock to its shareholders. What difference if S acquired all of the IDI assets in return for DSI voting stock and S nonvoting stock? For DSI voting stock and debentures?

   e. DSI creates a new subsidiary, S, by transferring DSI stock in return for S stock. IDI then merges into S in a statutory merger under the laws of the State of Delaware. What difference if S merged into IDI?

   f. For each of the above transactions, would it make any difference if, as part of the transaction, DSI pays off the debt to Michael in cash? If DSI contributes cash to S, which S then uses to pay off Michael's debt?

   g. For each of the above transactions, would it make any difference if DSI used an already existing as opposed to a newly created subsidiary?

Taxable Acquisition Overlaps[164]

5. Bobby owned all of the stock of Bobby's Racers, Inc. (BRI), a small business with several valuable racing cars. BRI's assets, including the cars, had a basis of $200,000 and a fair market value of $500,000. Bobby's basis in his BRI stock was $100,000. Dejected after losing several races, Bobby decided to sell his BRI stock to Gibbs Enterprises, Inc. (GEI) for $500,000 cash. GEI did not make a §338 election with regard to this initial acquisition of BRI. Shortly after the cash acquisition, BRI was merged into Gibbs Red Racers, Inc. (GRRI), a preexisting GEI subsidiary. As result of the merger, GEI received additional GRRI voting shares. BRI transferred its assets and liabilities to GRRI and ceased to exist. Standing alone, assume that the merger would qualify as a Type A reorganization.
   a. What are the tax consequences of the initial acquisition to Bobby, BRI, GEI, and GRRI? What are the tax consequences of the subsequent merger to GEI and GRRI?
   b. Imagine that Bobby owned only 90% of BRI, with the remaining 10% owned by his sister, Jan. For purposes of this variation, assume that Bobby's basis in his BRI shares was $90,000 and that Jan's basis in her shares was $10,000. Bobby sold his BRI shares to GEI for $450,000, but Jan refused to sell. In the subsequent merger, both GEI and Jan received GRRI voting stock. Jan's GRRI shares were valued at $50,000. What are the tax consequences of the initial acquisition to Bobby, Jan, BRI, GEI, and GRRI? What are the tax consequences of the subsequent merger to Jan, GEI, and GRRI?

6. a. Imagine that BRI from Example 5 was a wholly owned subsidiary of its parent, Race America, Inc. (RAI), which had a $100,000 basis in its BRI shares. Bobby owned 100% of RAI. In a single first-step acquisition, RAI transferred 80% of its BRI stock to GEI in exchange for GEI voting stock and the remaining 20% in exchange for cash. Shortly thereafter, BRI distributed all of its assets to GEI in a liquidating distribution that would otherwise qualify for tax-free treatment. Can GEI and RAI make a §338 and §338(h)(10) election with respect to the initial acquisition? What are the tax consequences to BRI, GEI, and RAI if no §338 election is made?
   b. How would your answers to Example 6a change if GEI and RAI are entitled to, and do, make a valid §338 and §338(h)(10) election with regard to the initial acquisition?

---

164. You may need to review material from Chapters 10 and 11 to answer these questions.

Explanations

1. a. Since the AHS shareholders are exchanging their AHS stock solely for BC voting stock, the transaction qualifies as a Type B stock-for-stock reorganization. I.R.C. §368(a)(1)(B). Purchaser BC now owns 90% of the target AHS stock, more than sufficient to meet the 80% control tests of §368(c). BC will not recognize any gain upon receipt of the AHS stock in exchange for its own voting stock. I.R.C. §1032. BC's basis in the AHS shares acquired from Alice and Sam will be the same as it was in Alice and Sam's hands (totaling $990,000) pursuant to §362(b).

   Alice and Sam each have a *realized* gain from the exchange of AHS stock for BC stock. Alice's realized gain amounts to $675,000 ($1.5 million amount realized less $825,000 adjusted stock basis) and Sam's realized gain amounts to $135,000 ($300,000 amount realized less $165,000 adjusted stock basis). Neither Alice nor Sam will *recognize* gain, however, since both AHS and BC are parties to the reorganization and the shareholders are each exchanging stock of one corporation that is a party to the reorganization for stock of another corporation that is a party to the reorganization pursuant to §354(a). Alice's basis in her BC shares will be the same basis she had in the AHS shares transferred ($825,000). Sam similarly will receive a substituted basis ($165,000) in his BC shares pursuant to §358(a).

   AHS is now a controlled subsidiary, owned 90% by its new parent (BC) and 10% by the dissenting minority shareholders. If the dissenting shareholders have dissenters' rights under state law requiring that they be bought out, they may jeopardize the Type B status of the reorganization if they insist on being bought out with BC assets and if the buy-out is considered an integrated part of the acquisition transaction. The payment of any BC assets (other than BC voting stock) to minority shareholders will cause the entire transaction to violate the "solely for voting stock" requirement. AHS's assets will retain the same basis that they had prior to the acquisition and AHS will remain liable to its creditors.

   b. If Alice and Sam receive *any* BC nonvoting stock or *any* BC debentures in the exchange, the transaction no longer qualifies as a Type B reorganization since it violates the "solely for voting stock" requirement. Even if it could be shown that BC acquired 80% control over AHS for BC voting stock and the remaining 10% of AHS for BC nonvoting stock or debentures, the transaction still would be disqualified if the two purchases are part of an integrated transaction.[165] Assuming

---

165. See Chapman v. Comm'r, 618 F.2d 856 (1st Cir. 1980); Rev. Rul. 75-123, 1975-1 C.B. 115.

the transaction does not qualify under any of the other reorganization definitions, this failed reorganization would be taxable to Alice and Sam. Alice would realize and recognize a $675,000 capital gain and Sam would realize and recognize a $135,000 capital gain. (See figures in Explanation 1a above.) Since the transaction is taxable to them, Alice and Sam would now take a cost basis in the BC stock and debentures received in the exchange rather than a §358 substituted basis. This cost basis would be the fair market value of the AHS stock transferred, which in an arm's-length transaction is presumed to be the same value as the consideration received.[166] Thus, Alice will take a $1.5 million cost basis and Sam will take a $300,000 cost basis and each of them will apportion the basis between the voting stock and nonvoting stock or between the voting stock and the debentures in accordance with the relative fair market values.

BC would hold its 90% of the AHS stock with a cost basis of $1.8 million (the value transferred to Alice and Sam.) Since the transaction is already disqualified from tax-free treatment under the reorganization rules, BC would be free to pay off the minority shareholders without risk. Unless BC made a §338 election in connection with the acquisition, AHS assets would retain the same basis that they had before the transaction. AHS remains liable to its creditors as before the transaction.

c. As noted in the answer to Example 1a, any cash paid by BC to buy out minority shareholders would cause the entire transaction to fail as a Type B reorganization since it would now violate the "solely for voting stock" requirement. A failed Type B reorganization would be treated as described in Explanation 1b above. On the other hand, if AHS redeemed the minority shareholders with its cash on hand before the acquisition, the transaction could be saved as a tax-free reorganization.[167]

d. As long as the subsequent liquidation is not viewed as integrated with the initial acquisition, a subsequent liquidation of AHS will be treated by the parent, BC, as a liquidation of a subsidiary under rules in §332.[168] BC will report no gain or loss upon the receipt of AHS's assets in liquidation under §332(a), and BC's basis in the assets will be the same basis that the assets had in AHS's hands before the liquidation pursuant §334(b)(1). The minority shareholders will treat the cash as amounts received in exchange for stock pursuant to §331.

---

166. Philadelphia Park Amusement Co. v. United States, 126 F. Supp. 184 (Ct. Cl. 1954).
167. Treas. Reg. §1.368-1(e)(6), ex. 1.
168. If the subsequent liquidation is integrated with the initial stock purchase, the entire reorganization might be recast as a Type C reorganization.

Gain or loss to the minority shareholders will be computed by subtracting the basis in their AHS shares from the amount of the cash received. The cash distribution to the minority shareholders results in no taxable gain to AHS since cash is presumed to have a basis equal to its value. AHS also will not report any gain or loss upon its distribution of assets to its parent, BC, pursuant to §337(a). See Chapters 8 and 9 for discussion of liquidation rules.

Even if the multiple steps are integrated, the overall transaction might be recharacterized as a Type C reorganization under step-transaction analysis. The $200,000 in cash distributed to the minority is within acceptable limits under the Type C "boot relaxation" rule. Even tested under the Type B reorganization rules, one might argue that the $200,000 in cash is being paid out of the target corporation's assets and is not consideration from the purchasing corporation in the exchange.

2. If the transactions described in Example 1a were structured to meet all of the requirements for a statutory merger of AHS into BC, they would now comfortably fit the reorganization definition in §368(a)(1)(A)—statutory merger or consolidation. Once the transaction fits any of the reorganization definitions, the same operating Code sections providing nonrecognition and substituted basis will apply as in Explanation 1a above. The tax consequences described in Example 1a would apply here as well.

Restructuring the transaction in Example 1b as a Type A reorganization makes a significant difference. When the transaction was structured as a Type B reorganization, the presence of any nonvoting BC stock or any BC debentures tainted the entire transaction, causing it to fail to meet the reorganization definition. While the Type A reorganization definition requires a continuity of proprietary interest, it does not require that this proprietary interest be solely voting stock. Nonvoting stock is considered a sufficient proprietary interest for purposes of §368(a)(1)(A). Thus, if Alice and Sam received four shares of BC voting stock and one share of BC nonvoting stock for each share of AHS stock, the transaction still would qualify as a Type A reorganization. BC still would not recognize any gain upon receipt of the AHS assets in exchange for its own voting and nonvoting stock. I.R.C. §1032. BC would hold the AHS assets with the same basis that AHS had in the assets immediately before the exchange. I.R.C. §362(b). As before, Alice and Sam would be entitled to full nonrecognition under §354(a). Their basis in the BC voting and nonvoting stock would be the same basis that they previously had in the AHS stock. They would allocate this basis over the voting and nonvoting shares in accordance with §358(b). BC now also would have more freedom with respect to the dissenting minority shareholders, who could be bought out for cash without jeopardizing tax-free reorganization status for the others. Under most states' merger statutes, BC would become liable after the merger for AHS liabilities.[169]

If Alice and Sam received four shares of BC voting stock and one BC debenture for each AHS share transferred, the tax consequences would differ slightly. The debentures would not be considered a proprietary interest for purposes of the continuity of proprietary interest test. Nevertheless, if the BC voting stock represents at least 40% of the value of the consideration paid for the AHS assets, the transaction should still safely qualify as a Type A reorganization.[170] BC will not report any gain upon receipt of the AHS assets in exchange for BC stock pursuant to §1032. In addition, BC should not have any gain upon the receipt of AHS shares in exchange for BC debentures. The issuance of a security in exchange for property is effectively a purchase of the property by BC, resulting in no gain or loss to the buyer, BC.

Alice and Sam still will be entitled to nonrecognition on the exchange of AHS stock for BC stock. However, §354 nonrecognition will not apply to the extent that the principal amount of the securities received exceeds the principal amount of the securities surrendered. Since Alice and Sam surrendered no securities, the securities received will be treated as taxable boot under §356. Whether the boot gain is treated as sale or exchange gain or "dividend gain" will depend upon the outcome of the §356 boot analysis described in Chapter 11.

Since the Type A reorganization does not contain the "solely for voting stock" limitations of the Type B reorganization, BC should be able to buy out the minority shareholders for cash without jeopardizing the tax-free reorganization status of the transaction as long as the total "boot" consideration paid out to shareholders stays within the 60% range acceptable to the Treasury Department. Thus, the acquisition described in Example 1a (as modified) would result in nonrecognition of gain to Alice and Sam under §354. The minority shareholders receiving cash will be taxable on their stock sales. BC will not report any gain upon the receipt of the AHS stock. Similarly, there should be no problem with tax-free reorganization treatment if, instead, AHS were to redeem the minority shareholders immediately before the acquisition.

---

169. P's continued responsibility for T's liabilities following a Type A merger is a serious concern for many purchasers. Despite the more rigorous requirements of the Type B reorganization, some purchasers may attempt a Type B stock-for-stock reorganization to avoid problems with such liabilities.

170. The Treasury Department's position is that continuity of proprietary interest in a Type A reorganization requires that 40% of the consideration take the form of stock. A Type A transaction could also conceivably qualify with a smaller percentage.

3. a. This acquisition will qualify as a tax-free asset-for-stock reorganization under §368(a)(1)(C). AHS is transferring all of its assets, except for cash. Since the cash represents only 10% of the $2 million value of AHS's assets, AHS has transferred "substantially all of its assets," as required in a Type C reorganization. Since only BC voting stock is used as consideration in exchange for the AHS shares, the transaction meets the Type C "solely for voting stock" requirement. The cash distributed to the minority shareholders in the subsequent liquidation of AHS will not cause the transaction to fail the reorganization definition even though the liquidation is part of an integrated transaction. Notice that the cash in this case comes directly from the target, AHS, and not from BC. Even if the cash had come from BC, under the boot relaxation rules in §368(a)(2)(B), as long as the acquiring corporation acquires 80% of the fair market value of the target's property for voting stock, the transaction would still have qualified.[171] BC will have no gain upon receipt of the AHS assets in return for voting stock under §1032. BC's basis in the assets will be the same basis that the assets had in AHS's hands under §362(b).

   The subsequent liquidation of AHS is required by §368(a)(2)(G) and is considered part of the reorganization transaction. AHS will report no gain or loss upon receipt of the BC voting shares under §361(a), nor will it report any gain or loss upon the distribution of the BC voting stock in liquidation pursuant to §361(c). Alice and Sam will be entitled to nonrecognition under §354 upon receipt of the BC voting shares in liquidation of AHS. Their basis in the BC voting shares will be the same basis they previously had in the AHS shares pursuant to §358(a). The minority shareholders will report the cash received as an amount realized in exchange for their stock under §331. The AHS assets now in BC's hands will retain their historic basis under §362(b).

   b. Unless granted a waiver by the Secretary pursuant to §368(a)(2)(G)(ii), AHS must liquidate in order for this transaction to qualify as a Type C reorganization. Absent such a waiver, if AHS survives as a holding company, the transaction no longer qualifies for nonrecognition.

   c. Under the "boot relaxation" rule, the transaction in Example 3a would still qualify as a Type C reorganization as long as BC acquires 80% of the fair market value of AHS's property for BC voting stock. Here, BC is acquiring 90% of AHS's assets. Since 80% must be acquired for BC voting stock, this leaves room for 10% of AHS's assets to be acquired for something other than voting stock. BC is acquiring 85% of AHS's

---

171. See, e.g., Rev. Rul. 73-102, 1973-1 C.B. 186 (cash paid by acquiring corporation to dissenting shareholders did not violate Type C "solely for voting stock" requirement, since acquiror acquired 80% of the value of the target's assets for voting stock).

assets for BC voting stock ($1.7 million) and only 5% for nonvoting stock ($100,000). Thus, the transaction still qualifies as a Type C reorganization. Since BC is acquiring assets in exchange for its own voting and nonvoting stock, it will have no gain under §1032. The tax consequences will be the same as described in the answer to Example 3a. Alice and Sam will apportion their substituted basis between the voting and nonvoting stock in accordance with §358(b).

d. As long as BC otherwise uses solely its own voting stock as consideration for the AHS assets, its explicit assumption of AHS's liabilities to creditors should cause no problem. The §368(a)(1)(C) reorganization definition itself instructs that assumptions of liabilities should be disregarded. In other words, the assumption of liabilities is not considered boot paid in this transaction. The tax consequences would remain as described in the answer to Example 3a.

e. The answer to Example 3d changes dramatically by the change in facts described here. Although §368(a)(1)(C) instructs us to disregard liabilities, the "boot relaxation" rule *does* consider liabilities as money paid for property solely for purposes of deciding whether the acquired corporation is acquiring 80% of the fair market value of the property solely for voting stock. Thus, the acquiror has paid $400,000 in "boot" for purposes of the boot relaxation rule ($300,000 liabilities assumed plus $100,000 in BC nonvoting stock). Since BC is acquiring only 90% of AHS's assets, it has room to pay for 10% with something other than voting stock.[172] Including liabilities here causes BC to violate the "solely for voting stock" requirement even as relaxed by §368(a)(2)(B). The transaction no longer qualifies as a Type C reorganization. The sale of assets by AHS now becomes a taxable sale requiring it to report gain or loss on the sale of each of its assets. Its basis in the BC stock received will be a cost basis. AHS would no longer be required to liquidate. If it did liquidate, however, the distribution in liquidation would be taxable to Alice and Sam under §331. BC would now acquire the assets with a cost basis.

f. The issue again is whether the transaction fails the Type C reorganization definition for violating the "solely for voting stock" requirement. The exchange would still qualify as a Type C reorganization since the debentures (liabilities) are within the 10% permissible "boot" for this transaction. In other words, as long as BC acquires 80% of the fair market value of AHS's property for BC voting stock, the use of debentures will not disqualify the transaction. Note, however, that Alice and Sam will report gain pursuant to §356 to the extent that the

---

172. Note that if BC had acquired *all* of AHS's assets, the $400,000 boot would constitute 20% of the $2 million of assets, leaving the transaction within the permitted boot relaxation range.

principal amount of securities received exceeds the principal amount of securities surrendered.

g. The issue now raised is whether BC is acquiring "substantially all of the properties" from AHS. The $800,000 fair market value of the investments and the $200,000 cash retained represents fully one-half of the value of AHS's properties. At first glance, one might conclude that the transfer of the other half does not meet the "substantially all" test. On the other hand, the assets that *are* transferred are AHS's operating assets: equipment and trucks, cleaning supplies, and customer lists, while the assets retained are liquid assets that are not integral to the business. Moreover, it does not appear that the investments and cash are being retained to achieve a disguised divisive reorganization. Under these circumstances, the parties have a strong argument that, for purposes of the Type C reorganization definition, BC has acquired "substantially all" of AHS's properties.

4. a. This transaction is a Type B reorganization followed by a drop-down of IDI stock into a subsidiary. The initial Type B reorganization will not be disqualified by virtue of the drop-down. I.R.C. §368(a)(2)(C). Even though Michael will continue to be paid on his installment note, this should not be a problem if the payments to creditors are considered a transaction separate from the acquisition transaction.

The initial incorporation of S is governed by §§351 and 1032 and will not be taxable to either DSI or S. The subsequent stock-for-stock exchange between DSI and the IDI shareholders is treated as a simple Type B reorganization. The IDI shareholders' receipt of DSI stock is entitled to nonrecognition under §354(a). The shareholders' basis in the DSI stock is the same basis they previously had in the IDI shares transferred. DSI has no gain upon receipt of the IDI shares from the IDI shareholders under §1032. DSI's basis in the IDI shares is the same basis that the IDI shareholders had pursuant to §362(b). The subsequent drop-down of the IDI stock to S is not part of the Type B exchange, but instead will be governed again by §§351 and 1032. Under these sections, neither DSI nor S will report any gain or loss from the drop-down transaction.[173] S's basis in the IDI shares will be the same basis that DSI had, which in turn was the same basis that the IDI shareholders had. Put more simply, the IDI stock retains its substituted basis. The basis in the IDI assets will remain as it was. Since this transaction involves an overlap with §351, DSI should be aware of possible limitations to the corporation's basis pursuant to §362(e)(2)

---

173. For a more detailed analysis of §351 incorporation, see Chapter 4.

in the event that the aggregate basis of properties transferred to S exceeds the aggregate fair market value.

b. This transaction is a direct triangular Type B reorganization. The definition of the Type B reorganization itself permits the use of solely voting stock of a corporation which is in control of the acquiring corporation. Since the acquiring corporation, S, is using solely the stock of its parent, DSI, this transaction will qualify. Notice that the transaction would not qualify as a Type B reorganization if S used a combination of DSI and S voting stock to acquire the AHS shares. For purposes of the Type B reorganization, the acquiror must use solely its own voting stock or solely the voting stock of a corporation that controls the acquiror, but not a combination. This rigid rule is a disadvantage to the triangular Type B reorganization. Similarly, a combination of DSI voting stock and S debentures will cause the transaction to violate the Type B definition.

Again, the initial formation of the new subsidiary is governed by §§351 and 1032. Unlike the drop-down transaction, however, the remainder of the transaction is covered by the reorganization rules. S is now treated as the acquiring corporation and S, DSI, and IDI are considered parties to the reorganization. S is entitled to nonrecognition upon the exchange of DSI stock for IDI stock. Under Treas. Reg. §1.1032-2, S would report gain only to the extent that it used DSI stock that it did not receive as part of the reorganization. Since S was newly incorporated for purposes of this transaction, it should be fair to assume that all of the DSI stock used by S was received by S as part of the reorganization plan. S's basis in the IDI shares received will be the same basis that the IDI shareholders had. I.R.C. §362(b). The IDI shareholders receive nonrecognition under §354 and take as their basis in the DSI shares the same basis that they previously had in their IDI shares under §358. Again, DSI and S should be alert to any possible §362(e)(2) issues.

c. This is now a simple Type C asset acquisition followed by a drop-down of the assets to a subsidiary. This type of drop-down will not disqualify an otherwise qualifying Type C acquisition. I.R.C. §368(a)(2)(C). Since DSI has acquired all of IDI's assets solely in exchange for DSI voting stock, this transaction will qualify as a Type C reorganization. DSI will report no gain or loss upon the receipt of IDI assets in exchange for voting stock. I.R.C. §1032. DSI will hold the assets with the same basis that IDI had. I.R.C. §362(b). IDI will report no gain or loss upon receipt of the DSI voting stock in exchange for all of its assets. I.R.C. §361. The subsequent drop-down of assets is governed by §§351 and 1032 with no gain or loss to DSI or S. S will now hold the assets with the same basis that DSI had under §358, which, in turn, is the same basis that IDI had in the assets. In other words, the assets retain the substituted basis from IDI. Upon IDI's required distribution of DSI voting stock received to its shareholders in liquidation, the shareholders will report no gain or loss under §354 and will use the same basis that they previously had in the IDI shares as the basis in their new DSI shares. To the extent that any loss properties are involved, S may face some §362(e)(2) basis limitations.

d. This is now a direct forward triangular Type C reorganization permitted by the Type C definition itself. The Type C definition, like the Type B definition, permits the use of solely voting stock of the acquiring corporation or solely the voting stock of a corporation in control of the acquiring corporation. As a result, S may use DSI stock to acquire IDI's assets. The liquidation of IDI is a required component of the transaction. I.R.C. §368(a)(2)(G). The initial incorporation of S is again governed by §§351 and 1032, with the same potential §362(e)(2) concerns. In the subsequent Type C reorganization, S is treated as the acquiror, but S, DSI, and IDI are all considered parties to the reorganization. I.R.C §368(b). S's receipt of IDI assets in exchange for DSI voting stock is treated as a nonrecognition event under Treas. Reg. §1.1032-2. Its basis in the assets will be the same basis IDI had. I.R.C. §362(b). IDI's receipt of DSI voting stock in return for its assets will not be taxable under §361(a) and its subsequent distribution of the stock to its shareholders will also not be taxable. I.R.C. §361(c). The IDI shareholders who receive the DSI voting stock in liquidation will not report any gain or loss under §354 and will receive a substituted basis under §358.

As in the answer to Example 4b, the use of a combination of DSI voting stock and S voting stock generally is not permitted under the regulations. Using both DSI and S voting stock may threaten Type C reorganization status (to be clear, these are not the facts of this example). On the other hand, if the S nonvoting stock used as a consideration in this example constitutes 20% or less of the total consideration, the S nonvoting stock may be considered legitimate boot under the Type C reorganization "boot relaxation" rules. If the transaction is disqualified as a Type C reorganization, the sale of assets for DSI voting stock and S voting stock would be taxable to IDI. S would be viewed as purchasing the assets in a taxable acquisition and would be entitled to a §1012 cost basis in the assets. Since the transaction did not qualify, the liquidation would be treated as a taxable exchange to the IDI shareholders under §331.

The use of DSI voting stock and debentures will work as a triangular Type C acquisition so long as the debentures fall within the 20% boot relaxation provision. In other words, as long as S acquires 80%

of IDI's assets for DSI voting stock, the transaction will still qualify as a Type C reorganization. The tax consequences will be the same as those just described with the exception that the IDI shareholders will report boot gain or loss to the extent that the principal amount of the debentures (securities) received exceeds the principal amount of the securities surrendered pursuant to §356.

e. A merger of IDI into S would be a forward triangular Type A acquisition. Under §368(a)(2)(D), use of the parent DSI's stock will not disqualify an otherwise qualified Type A reorganization if no S stock is used in the transaction and if the transaction would have qualified if the merger had been a merger of IDI directly into DSI. Since both of these requirements are met, the transaction remains a tax-free reorganization. S's exchange of its parent DSI stock for IDI assets "is treated as a disposition by P [here DSI] of shares of its own stock for T's [here IDI's] assets." Treas. Reg. §1.1032-2(b). In other words, DSI will report no gain or loss under §1032. Similarly, S will report no gain or loss unless S uses P stock that it did not receive pursuant to the plan of reorganization. Treas. Reg. §1.1032-2(c). The IDI assets will retain the same basis in S's hands that they previously had in IDI's hands under §362(b). Under the so-called "over-the-top" method, DSI's basis in its subsidiary stock will be adjusted as if DSI first acquired the assets directly from IDI, thus determining its basis in the assets under §362(b), and subsequently transferred the assets to S in a §351 exchange, again potentially subject to §362(e)(2). In other words, DSI's previous basis in its S stock will be increased by the amount of §362(b) substituted basis in the IDI assets. Treas. Reg. §1.358-6(c)(1). The IDI shareholders are entitled to nonrecognition under §354 upon the exchange with S of their IDI shares for DSI voting shares. Their basis in the DSI shares will be the same basis that they had in the IDI shares pursuant to §358(a).

In the alternative, a merger of S into IDI would be a reverse triangular Type A acquisition. Pursuant to §368(a)(2)(E) an otherwise qualified Type A reorganization is not disqualified by the use of stock of a controlling corporation if the surviving corporation, here IDI, holds substantially all of its properties and the merged corporation's properties [here S's properties] after the exchange. In addition, former shareholders of IDI must have exchanged a sufficient amount of IDI stock for DSI voting stock to constitute control. The first requirement is easily met since S had no assets other than the DSI voting stock used as part of the reorganization. This stock used in the reorganization is not counted for purposes of determining whether the surviving corporation holds substantially all of its own properties after the reorganization. The second requirement is also met since all of IDI's assets were transferred for DSI voting stock.[174]

In the reverse triangular merger, the parent corporation, DSI is entitled to nonrecognition pursuant to §361. See also Treas. Reg. §1.1032-2(b) (last sentence). To the extent that the surviving corporation receives any properties from S, it too receives nonrecognition treatment under §361. Since the IDI assets simply are remaining with IDI, the assets will retain the same basis that they had before the reorganization transaction. IDI now is a controlled subsidiary of DSI. DSI's basis in the IDI stock acquired in the reverse triangular merger "equals its basis in its S stock immediately before the transaction adjusted as if T [here IDI] had merged into S in a forward triangular merger to which paragraph (c)(1) of this section applies." Treas. Reg. §1.358-6(c)(2). In other words, DSI's basis will be computed as described for the forward triangular merger above. The IDI shareholders remain entitled to nonrecognition under §354 upon the receipt of DSI voting stock and will use their IDI stock basis as the basis in their new DSI shares under §358.

f. The key factual question here is whether the payment to Michael is part of, or integrated with, the reorganization plan. To the extent that the payment to Michael is separated from the reorganization plan, it should not affect the answers above. On the other hand, if the payment to Michael is an integral part of the plan, some significant issues arise. In the Type B reorganization followed by a drop-down and the direct Type B triangular reorganization described in Examples 4a and 4b, the use of DSI cash to pay off the debt to Michael (whether directly by DSI, or through a contribution of cash to S, which in turn is used to pay Michael) will disqualify the entire transaction from tax-free reorganization since the transaction no longer meets the "solely for voting stock requirements." In the Type C reorganization followed by a drop-down and the direct triangular C reorganization, the payment of the liability to Michael can be disregarded. Thus, the payment should not disqualify the transaction. If any consideration other than DSI voting stock was used in the transaction, however, the debt to Michael, other liabilities, and other consideration together could not exceed the 20% "boot relaxation" provision. The forward triangular reorganization provides the greatest flexibility here. Under the Service's interpretation, as long as no more than 40% of the consideration takes a

---

174. Notice that the second requirement in the reverse subsidiary merger provides more flexibility than that provided by the forward triangular merger. As long as the IDI shareholders transferred 80% control in return for DSI voting stock, the remaining 20% of the consideration could take the form of S stock. This combination of parent and subsidiary stock consideration is not permissible in the forward triangular Type A acquisition.

nonequity form, the Type A transaction still will qualify. In the reverse triangular merger, however, §368(a)(2)(E) requires that IDI shareholders transfer 80% control in return for DSI voting stock.

g. In each case, it is permissible for the parent to use an already existing subsidiary, as opposed to a newly created subsidiary, for purposes of a triangular reorganization. One concern under the §§358 and 1032 regulations is that the subsidiary will report gain or loss to the extent that it uses parent stock that it did not receive as part of the reorganization transaction. Thus, the reorganization may trigger taxable gain with respect to previously owned parent stock. In addition, in the case of an existing subsidiary, the parent's old basis will be adjusted in accordance with the regulations. In a reverse triangular merger, the parent must also consider the tax consequences of any old stock in the target corporation that it held before the reorganization transaction.

5. a. As a result of the initial cash transaction, Bobby will have a $400,000 gain ($500,000 amount realized less $100,000 stock basis) from the sale of his BRI stock, taxable under §1001, and GEI will have a §1012 cost basis of $500,000 in the BRI stock. BRI has simply become a newly owned subsidiary of GEI, now BRI's parent. The first-step cash acquisition is a QSP for purposes of §338, with no change to BRI's asset basis since GEI has not made a §338 election.[175] The subsequent merger of BRI into GRRI should be respected as a Type A reorganization, resulting in no tax to BRI under §361 and no tax to GRRI under §1032. BRI's assets will retain their historic basis of $200,000 pursuant to §362(b). Under §354, GEI will have no gain or loss on its receipt of additional GRRI shares. Under §358, GEI's basis in the new GRRI shares received will be the $500,000 basis it previously had in its BRI stock.

The key observation here is that BRI will not receive a stepped-up basis in its assets. GEI will be tempted to use a step-transaction approach, arguing that the initial acquisition and the subsequent merger were part of an overall plan. Viewed as an integrated transaction, the two steps appear to be a cash acquisition without sufficient continuity of interest to qualify for tax-free reorganization treatment. Thus, GEI will want to take a cost basis in the BRI assets. Based upon Treas. Reg. §1.338-3(d)(2), however, GEI's integrated transaction argument will fail. Addressing the potential overlap between §338 and the reorganization continuity of interest rules, the regulation provides that "*the purchasing corporation's target stock* acquired in the qualified

---

175. See Chapter 10 regarding §338 elections and their impact upon the target corporation's asset basis.

stock purchase represents an interest on the part of the person who was an owner of the target's business enterprise prior to the transfer that can be continued in a reorganization." GEI will be considered such an owner in this case. Recall that GEI did *not* make a §338 election. An integrated transaction approach to this transaction would permit GEI to take a stepped-up basis in BRI assets without reporting taxable gain pursuant to §338(a)(1) on the deemed sale of target assets.[176] The regulations here preserve the §338 election as the sole route to a stepped-up basis in a target's assets.

b. On the initial cash sale, Bobby will now have a $360,000 gain ($450,000 amount realized less $90,000 stock basis), taxable under §1001, and GEI will have a $450,000 basis in the BRI shares acquired from Bobby. Since Jan did not sell her shares, there are no immediate tax consequences to her. She simply remains a 10% minority BRI shareholder. As in Example 5a, BRI has become a newly owned subsidiary of GEI. Since GEI acquired 90% of BRI by purchase, the first-step cash acquisition is still regarded as a QSP, again with no change to BRI's asset basis given the absence of a §338 election. The subsequent merger should be respected as a Type A reorganization as to all parties *except* Jan. Since Jan is a minority shareholder and not a purchasing corporation, the language of Treas. Reg. §1.338-3(d)(3) does not apply to her. As to Jan, the cash acquisition and subsequent merger *are* viewed together as an integrated transaction in which Jan is *not* eligible for §354 nonrecognition. Regulatory examples describe this bifurcated approach, which applies step-transaction analysis with respect to minority shareholders, but not for the purchasing corporation. Treas. Reg. §1.338-3(d)(5), ex. (v).[177] Thus, Jan will have a $40,000 taxable gain ($50,000 amount realized less $10,000 stock basis) upon exchanging her BRI shares for GRRI shares.

6. a. Standing alone, the initial stock-for-stock acquisition by GEI would not qualify for tax-free treatment. Since it was not *solely* for GEI voting stock, it would be a "failed" Type B reorganization. By itself, then, the initial stock purchase is a taxable QSP. Viewed as an integrated transaction, however, the overall acquisition would qualify as a Type C asset acquisition under the more relaxed boot rules of §368(a)(2)(B). Given its rejection of step-transaction analysis for the purchasing corporation as described in Treas. Reg. §1.338-3(d) and in Explanation 5a, one might think that the Treasury Department would reject such analysis here as well. Moreover, Treas. Reg. §1.338-3(c)(1) explicitly

---

176. See discussion of the deemed sale of target assets in Chapter 10 and the overlaps between tax-free reorganizations and QSPs in Chapter 11.
177. See Chapter 11 for discussion of this bifurcated approach.

permits a §338 election for a first-step QSP even if the target is subsequently liquidated or merged into another corporation. Despite these earlier pronouncements, Rev. Rul. 2001-46 *disallowed* a §338 election for a multistep acquisition, insisting that the overall integrated transaction was a tax-free reorganization.[178] This ruling had particularly harsh implications for transactions involving a target subsidiary where a §338(h)(10) election might be advantageous. Treasury Department regulations have since retreated from the rigid position in Rev. Rul. 2001-46. Treas. Reg. §1.338(h)(10)-1(c)(2). These regulations explicitly *permit* a §338(h)(10) election for a first-step QSP, whether or not the transaction would be regarded as a reorganization under the step-transaction doctrine.

In the end, GEI and RAI *may* jointly make §338 and §338(h)(10) elections for the BRI acquisition. Since GEI and RAI did *not* make such elections in Example 6a, the transaction will be integrated according to the analysis in Rev. Rul. 2001-46 and treated as a Type C reorganization. Under the Treasury Department's reasoning, step-transaction analysis of this acquisition does not violate the underlying logic of §338. After all, GEI would get the §338 stepped-up basis in BRI assets *only* if it made and suffered the tax burdens imposed by the §338 election.

When the dust settles, GEI has received BRI assets in an acquisition that will be tax-free to BRI under §361 and to GEI under §1032. BRI's assets will retain their historic basis under §362(b). RAI will be entitled to nonrecognition under §354, except to the extent of the cash boot received, which will be taxed under §§354(a)(2) and 356. Under §358, RAI's basis in the GEI stock received in the exchange will be substituted from its basis in the BRI shares transferred.

b. If a §338(h)(10) election is made, Treas. Reg. §1.338(h)(10)-1(c)(2) provides that the target stock acquisition is treated as a QSP and *not* as part of a reorganization. Consequently, the election will trigger recognition of a $300,000 gain (amount realized of $500,000 less $200,000 asset basis) on the deemed sale of BRI assets under §338(a). Since the subsequent liquidating distribution from subsidiary BRI to parent GEI will be tax-free to BRI pursuant to §332, there should be no further taxable gain to BRI. GEI's receipt of BRI assets upon liquidation will be tax-free under §337. Immediately after the first-step QSP, the BRI assets in GEI's hands will receive a stepped-up basis pursuant to §338(b). Upon the subsequent liquidation, this same basis serves as the substituted basis of the assets in GEI's hands under §334(b). Under §338(h)(10)(A), RAI will not report gain on its sale of BRI stock.

---

178. This ruling is discussed in detail in Chapter 11.

13

Corporate Divisions

INTRODUCTION

Corporate Divisions in General

The corporate acquisition transactions considered in earlier chapters involved amalgamating or joining the shareholder investments reflected in two or more corporations.[1] Corporate *divisions* involve the reverse— breaking the investment reflected in one corporation into investments in multiple corporations. The reasons for a corporate division or separation can be quite varied. A corporate division might be mandated by an antitrust decree or might otherwise be necessary to comply with statutory or regulatory restrictions imposed by federal, state, or local governments. For example, banking regulations might require a bank holding company to separate its banking operations from other business operations. Corporate divisions can also be used to resolve conflicts between opposing groups of shareholders. Separating the business into two corporations may be more sensible than forcing warring shareholder factions to coexist under one corporate roof. Corporate division also can be useful when two or more separate corporations will have better access to credit or other sources of funding than the single corporate enterprise. Finally, corporate division sometimes is used in connection with an otherwise acquisitive transaction. Such a division

---

1. See Chapters 10 (Taxable Acquisitions) and 12 (Acquisitive Reorganizations).

might be used defensively to make an unfriendly or unwanted takeover less attractive to the acquiror or offensively to facilitate a desired merger or acquisition.

Like the acquisitive transaction, the divisive transaction can be either taxable or tax-free. To illustrate a "taxable division," imagine a corporation with two individual shareholders that has been operating a hotel business and a restaurant business as separate divisions. The corporation might arrange a corporate division simply by distributing the hotel business assets to one shareholder and the restaurant business assets to the other in a complete liquidation.[2] Or, the corporation might distribute the hotel assets to its shareholders in a nonliquidating distribution, remaining alive as a corporation operating only a restaurant business.[3] Finally, the corporation might arrange to distribute all of the hotel business assets in redemption of all of one shareholder's stock, leaving the other shareholder as sole owner of a corporation with only restaurant assets.[4] Although the proper character of gain or loss may be at issue for some of these transactions, each of the above variations reflects a taxable division of the shareholders' investment in one corporation.

In contrast to a "taxable division," the corporation in the above illustration could arrange a tax-free division by using special rules in the "Corporate Organizations and Reorganizations" provisions in Part III of Subchapter C.[5] A tax-free division usually refers to the separation of one corporation into two or more corporations, along with an accompanying distribution of stock or securities to the shareholders or security holders of the original corporation in a distribution that qualifies for nonrecognition under §355.[6] This division or separation may or may not be a "reorganization." Recall that "reorganization" is a term of art, referring only to those transactions defined in §368(a). The term "divisive reorganization" generally refers to a transaction meeting both the requirements of §355 and the reorganization definition in §368(a).[7] The remainder of this chapter discusses tax-free

---

2. Such a liquidating distribution would be taxable to the shareholders under §331 and to the distributing corporation under §336 unless the distribution is in liquidation of a subsidiary governed by §§332 and 337. See Chapters 8 and 9.

3. Such a nonliquidating distribution would be taxable to the shareholders under §301 and to the corporation under §311. See Chapter 5.

4. Such a redemption distribution would be taxable to the shareholders under §302 and taxable to the corporation under §311. See Chapter 6.

5. I.R.C. §§351-368.

6. If a corporation simply transfers some of its assets to a new subsidiary without distributing the subsidiary's stock to its shareholders, the transaction is covered by §351. While this type of transaction technically constitutes a tax-free corporate division, the focus of this chapter is on divisive transactions that include a distribution of stock or securities to shareholders (other than a distribution of taxable boot in a §351 exchange). For detailed discussion of §351 and incorporating a subsidiary, see Chapter 4.

7. The "reorganization" definition typically invoked for divisive reorganizations is §368(a)(1)(D).

divisions, including the subclass of tax-free divisions generally referred to as "divisive reorganizations."

Rationale for Nonrecognition Treatment Balanced Against Potential for Taxpayer Abuse

As discussed in earlier chapters, corporate formation and certain acquisitive reorganizations are entitled to nonrecognition treatment on the theory that these transactions represent "mere changes in form."[8] A corporate division also can be viewed as a mere change in form. Imagine, for example, that the corporation operating a hotel and restaurant business as two divisions of a single entity decides to transfer all the hotel division assets to a newly formed subsidiary. Shortly thereafter, the corporation distributes the new subsidiary stock pro rata to its two equal individual shareholders. Immediately after the transaction, the same two shareholders own the same two business operations in the same proportions as before, but now the businesses are contained in two separate corporate entities. Rather than holding stock in one corporate entity, the shareholders now simply own stock in each of two "brother-sister" corporations. This breaking of corporate divisions into separate corporate entities owned in the same proportions by the same shareholders arguably represents a mere change in form. Consistent with the "mere change in form" rationale, §355 provides nonrecognition treatment for both the distributing corporation and the shareholder or security holder distributees upon certain corporate distributions of stock and securities in a controlled corporation. Unlike many other provisions of Subchapter C that deal with tax consequences to the corporation and its shareholders in separate sections, §355 addresses both the tax consequences to shareholder distributees *and* to the distributing corporation.

Even though many corporate divisions can be appropriately described as "mere changes in form," Congress feared that an overly broad nonrecognition provision would lead to abuses. When §355 was first enacted, the primary concern was potential shareholder bailout of corporate earnings at capital gains rates that otherwise would have been taxable as ordinary income dividends. To illustrate, imagine a corporation holding a highly appreciated asset not needed for current business operations. The corporation might transfer such an asset to a new subsidiary and distribute the subsidiary stock to its shareholders. A subsequent sale of the new subsidiary stock at a gain by the shareholders was eligible for preferential capital gains rather than the ordinary income rates that always applied to dividends prior

---

8. See Chapters 4 (Incorporation and Other Contributions to Capital), 11 (Introduction to Basic Reorganization Principles), and 12 (Acquisitive Reorganizations).

to 2003. Assuming that the distribution of stock to the shareholders was pro rata and that all shareholders subsequently sold the subsidiary stock, the shareholders effectively bailed out corporate earnings and profits at capital gains rates without otherwise altering their proportionate interest in the corporate enterprise. In the end, this corporate separation transaction resembled a direct distribution of the appreciated asset to the shareholders, followed by a shareholder sale of the asset. In either case, the value of the assets was transferred out of corporate solution to the shareholders. In contrast to a tax-free divisive distribution, direct distribution of the asset surely would result in dividend income to the shareholders[9] and—post-*General Utilities* repeal—taxable gain to the distributing corporation.[10] Congress responded to this bailout potential by including in §355 a requirement that both the distributing corporation and the controlled subsidiary be engaged in the active conduct of a trade or business immediately after the distribution[11] and a separate requirement that the distribution not be used principally as a device for the distribution of the distributing corporation's earnings and profits.[12]

Since §355 was enacted, Congress has made several significant tax changes. First, it has tinkered with the differential between ordinary income and capital gains rates, eliminating the difference between rates applicable to sales of stock and "qualified dividends." The shareholder-level bailout concern animating much of §355 is significantly reduced since "qualified dividend income" is eligible for preferential capital gains rates.[13] The second major change since §355's enactment is repeal of the *General Utilities* nonrecognition rule—corporations now generally are taxable on distributions of appreciated property.[14] Many of the §355 requirements that will be discussed throughout this chapter are addressed to the shareholder bailout concern and could be modified in a world in which gains from stock sales and dividends are taxed at the same rates. At the same time, complete repeal of §355 is unlikely. To understand why, it is important to recall that §355 addresses both shareholder *and* corporate-level tax consequences. Even in a

---

9. The dividend result to the shareholders assumes that the distributing corporation has sufficient earnings and profits to cover the distribution. I.R.C. §§301, 316. See Chapter 5. Since the shareholders' basis in the asset received upon distribution would be the asset's fair market value at the time of distribution under §301(d), there would be little or no further taxable gain upon the shareholders' immediate resale of the asset.

10. I.R.C. §311. See Chapter 5.

11. I.R.C. §355(a)(1)(C). A more detailed discussion follows later in this chapter.

12. I.R.C. §355(a)(1)(B). A more detailed discussion follows later in this chapter.

13. Notice that the shareholder bailout concern reflected in §355 is similar to that underlying §306. The "qualified dividend income" rules have similarly diminished much of the driving force behind §306. For detailed discussions of the qualified dividend rules, see Chapters 1 and 5. Chapter 7 considers the impact of the dividend rules on §306.

14. I.R.C. §§311, 336. For detailed discussion of these provisions and repeal of the *General Utilities* principle, see Chapters 5 and 8.

world in which stock sales and dividends are taxed at the same tax rates, however, the *corporate-level* concern underlying current §355 rules remains.[15] Given repeal of the *General Utilities* rule, corporations now generally are taxable upon distributions to shareholders. Yet the distributing corporation recognizes *no* gain or loss upon a qualifying §355 property distribution.[16] The §355 corporate nonrecognition provision is among the primary remaining statutory exceptions to *General Utilities* repeal, thus inviting another potential taxpayer abuse — using §355 as a loophole to avoid corporate level tax on distributions of appreciated property. While the primary concern originally driving §355 was preventing bailout of corporate earnings to the shareholders at capital gain rates, the primary concern now has shifted to preventing tax avoidance at the corporate level.

In the end, §355 is designed to serve multiple functions. First, as a parallel to the corporate organization and reorganization provisions, it attempts to provide tax-free treatment to "mere changes in corporate form" and to distinguish such "readjustments" from transactions that resemble taxable sales. Second, it attempts to prevent a shareholder-level bailout of corporate earnings and profits. Finally, §355 is designed to prevent improper tax avoidance at the corporate level upon distributions of appreciated property. As such, several of the §355 requirements attempt to distinguish appropriate tax-free divisive distributions from those that are inconsistent with the repeal of *General Utilities*. Many complexities and interpretive problems in connection with §355 can be attributed to this congressional attempt to serve too many masters. These problems may be exacerbated under the "qualified dividend income" rules, which arguably alter the second of these considerations but not the others.[17]

Some Introductory Terminology: Spin-Offs, Split-Offs, and Split-Ups

Corporate divisions tend to come in three basic flavors: spin-off, split-off, or split-up. Each variation involves a slightly different type of distribution of stock or securities. In general, if the transaction successfully runs the

---

15. In addition, some shareholder-level concern, albeit reduced, remains given the basis offset available upon a shareholder sale of the distributed shares that would not be available had the distribution been treated as a dividend.

16. I.R.C. §355(c). A similar nonrecognition rule applies to distributions in connection with a "divisive reorganization." I.R.C. §361(c). These rules are discussed later in this chapter.

17. Although they were written shortly before the 2003 "qualified dividend" changes, two articles offer valuable insights into the general tax policies behind §355 and its specific statutory and nonstatutory requirements. Michael L. Schler, Simplifying and Rationalizing the Spinoff Rules, 56 SMU L. Rev. 239 (2003); George K. Yin, Taxing Corporate Divisions, 56 SMU L. Rev. 289 (2003).

gauntlet of §355, the tax treatment to the shareholders and the corporation will be the same regardless of whether the transaction is a spin-off, split-off, or split-up.

In a *spin-off*, the distributing corporation distributes stock of a controlled corporation (a subsidiary) to its shareholders. This subsidiary may be either a recently created or an existing subsidiary. The shareholders in a spin-off generally receive a pro rata share of the controlled corporation's stock and do not transfer anything to the distributing corporation in exchange. If the transaction fails to qualify for nonrecognition under §355, the distribution is treated as a dividend to the shareholder distributees to the extent of the corporation's earnings and profits,[18] and any gain on the distribution of the appreciated assets is taxable to the distributing corporation.[19]

A *split-off* is very much like a spin-off except that the parent's shareholders receive stock in the subsidiary in *exchange* for some of their stock in the parent corporation. In other words, the transaction is structured more like a redemption than a dividend. Although they can be pro rata, split-ups often involve non-pro rata distributions of stock in the controlled corporation to the distributing corporation's shareholders. If the transaction fails to qualify for §355 nonrecognition treatment, the distribution will be treated as a redemption under §302. Consequently, the redemption distribution might be treated by the shareholders either as a dividend under §302(d) or as a sale or exchange redemption under §302(a).[20]

---

18. I.R.C. §301. For detailed discussion of the §301 distribution rules, see Chapter 5.
19. I.R.C. §311. See Chapter 5.
20. The corporation would be taxable on any gain pursuant to §311. For a detailed discussion of redemptions, see Chapter 6.

Split-Off Transaction | **Resulting Corporate Structure**

In a *split-up*, the original corporation effectively disappears. The corporation first transfers all of its assets to two or more new corporations (controlled corporations) in return for stock, which is then distributed to the shareholders of the parent corporation in return for all of the parent stock. The split-up effectively liquidates the original parent corporation. If the transaction fails to qualify for §355 nonrecognition, the distribution will be treated as a complete liquidation to the shareholders, who will report gain or loss based upon the difference between the fair market value of the stock received and their basis in the original corporation's stock.[21] In addition, the corporation would be taxable on any gain upon a distribution of assets in complete liquidation.[22]

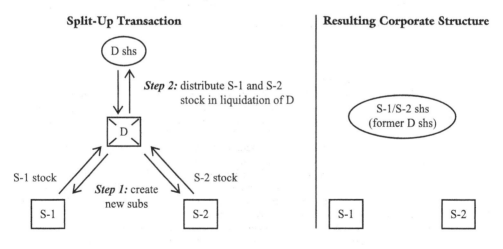

Split-Up Transaction | **Resulting Corporate Structure**

---

21. I.R.C. §331. For a detailed discussion of §331, see Chapter 8. But see §332 (liquidation of subsidiary), discussed in Chapter 9.
22. I.R.C. §336. But see §337 (liquidation of subsidiary).

OVERVIEW OF §355 REQUIREMENTS

A distribution of stock or securities in a controlled corporation will be eligible for §355 nonrecognition treatment only if it meets numerous statutory and nonstatutory requirements. The statute itself requires:

1. *Control immediately before the distribution* — the distributing corporation must distribute solely stock or securities of a corporation that it controls immediately before the distribution;[23]
2. *Distribution requirement* — the distributing corporation must distribute *all* of the stock and securities in the controlled corporation held immediately before the distribution;[24]
3. *Trade or business requirement* — both the distributing corporation and the controlled corporation must be engaged immediately after the distribution in the active conduct of a trade or business;[25]
4. *Non-device requirement* — the transaction must not be used principally as a device to distribute earnings and profits of the distributing corporation, the controlled corporation, or both.[26]

In addition to these statutory requirements, §355 has been interpreted to include several judicially developed requirements paralleling those required for the reorganization provisions generally.[27] These include business purpose,[28] continuity of the business enterprise,[29] and continuity of proprietary interest requirements.[30]

The following sections of this chapter consider each of these statutory and nonstatutory requirements.

---

23. I.R.C. §355(a)(1)(A).

24. I.R.C. §355(a)(1)(D)(i). As an alternative, the distributing corporation may distribute an amount sufficient to constitute control. In such a case, however, the distributing corporation must also establish to the satisfaction of the Secretary that any retention of stock was not in pursuance of a tax avoidance plan. I.R.C. §355(a)(1)(D)(ii).

25. I.R.C. §355(a)(1)(C), (b). The "trade or business" requirement actually incorporates both a post-distribution and a pre-distribution rule, since the statutory definition of an "active trade or business" requires that the corporation's trade or business have been "actively conducted throughout the 5-year period ending on the date of the distribution." I.R.C. §355(b)(2)(B).

26. I.R.C. §355(a)(1)(B). The importance of this particular requirement should be substantially diminished in the "qualified dividend income" world. The impact of these dividend rules on the §355 "device" requirement is discussed later in this chapter.

27. For a discussion of the judicially developed requirements in the reorganization context, see Chapter 11.

28. Treas. Reg. §1.355-2(b).

29. Treas. Reg. §1.355-1(b).

30. Treas. Reg. §1.355-2(c).

A CLOSER LOOK AT THE §355 REQUIREMENTS

Control "Immediately Before the Distribution"

Nonrecognition under §355 is limited to corporate distributions of stock or securities of a *controlled* corporation.[31] Such distribution of stock or securities in a controlled subsidiary to shareholders of the parent arguably reflects a "mere change in form." One might visualize the §355 tax-free stock distribution as a rough complement to the §351 tax-free transfer to a corporation which the transferring shareholders control immediately after the exchange.[32] Reversing directions, a parent corporation under §355 distributes stock or securities in a corporation which it controls "immediately *before* the distribution."[33] The distributing parent may distribute stock or securities in either a preexisting or a newly created subsidiary.[34] As a practical matter, corporations planning for a division frequently create new subsidiaries for the purpose of effecting a spin-off or split-off. So, for example, the distributing corporation may create a new subsidiary under §351 or as part of a Type D reorganization or other tax-free reorganization provision. On the other hand, if the distributing corporation recently acquired control through a *taxable* purchase, §355 will not apply to the subsequent distribution of the stock. The idea here is to restrict nonrecognition to divisions of corporations with a reasonable history of operating a business or at least a business recently created or acquired in a "mere change in form" nonrecognition-type transaction.[35]

---

31. I.R.C. §355(a)(1). Section 355 uses the same 80% control tests from §368(c) that are used for purposes of §351 transactions, discussed in Chapter 4, and for certain acquisitive reorganizations, discussed in Chapters 11-12. In the context of a *nondivisive* Type D reorganization, however, the control test is reduced to a 50% threshold. See I.R.C. §368(a)(2)(H).
32. See Chapter 4.
33. I.R.C. §355(a)(1)(A) (emphasis added).
34. Treas. Reg. §1.355-1(b).
35. The restriction with regard to recent taxable acquisitions is built into §355 via the "active conduct of a trade or business requirement." The "active trade or business requirement" is not met when the distributing corporation acquired control of the controlled corporation within the past five years in a taxable transaction. I.R.C. §355(b)(2)(D). These restrictions are discussed in greater detail later in this chapter. Additional exceptions to §355 nonrecognition may also apply in the case of recent acquisitions of at least a 50% interest in the distributing or the controlled corporation. I.R.C. §355(d), (e). These provisions will also be discussed later in this chapter.

Distribution of Control

A further requirement for §355 nonrecognition involves the amount of stock or securities distributed.[36] The distributing corporation must either distribute *all* of the stock or securities of the controlled corporation held immediately before the distribution or enough stock to constitute control. If the distributing corporation exercises the latter option, it must also establish to the satisfaction of the Secretary that retention of stock (or stock and securities) was not principally for tax avoidance purposes.[37]

The distribution requirements of §355(a)(1)(D) probably stem from concerns that the corporation might otherwise take advantage of the tax-free distribution rules of §355 as a substitute for taxable dividends. If the corporation could periodically distribute small amounts of the controlled corporation's stock, the distribution begins to look more like a distribution of earnings and profits.[38]

Although §355 requires distribution of all, or a controlling amount, of the controlled subsidiary stock, the distributing corporation has substantial flexibility regarding the structure of the distribution. For purposes of §355, the stock need not be distributed pro rata among the shareholders.[39] This flexibility can be especially useful in structuring corporate separations to resolve conflicts among shareholders. In addition, it does not matter whether the shareholders surrender any distributing corporation stock.[40] Finally, the distribution often is, but need not be, part of a Type D reorganization.[41]

---

36. Also note that the distribution must be to a shareholder "with respect to its stock." I.R.C. §355(a)(1)(A). This language parallels language in the §301 distribution rules. As in the case of §301 distributions, this language is designed to limit application of the rules to distributions to the shareholders qua shareholders. For example, a corporation may make a distribution to a shareholder as compensation for services, as payment for goods, or as repayment of debt. Such distributions will not be covered by §355. For more detailed discussion of the "with respect to stock" restriction in the context of §301 distributions, see Chapter 5.
37. I.R.C. §355(a)(1)(D). Section 355(a)(1)(D)(ii) itself requires only a distribution of an amount of *stock* constituting control and says nothing about securities. The regulations clarify that all, or any part, of the securities of the controlled corporation may be distributed. Treas. Reg. §1.355-2(e)(1).
38. This concern is already addressed by the requirement in §355(a)(1)(B) that the transaction not be used "principally as a device for the distribution of the earnings and profits of the distributing corporation or the controlled corporation or both," leading some commentators to question whether the additional restrictions in §355(a)(1)(D) are really necessary. See, e.g., Boris I. Bittker and James S. Eustice, Federal Income Taxation of Corporations and Shareholders ¶11.07 (7th ed. 2015). This "device" restriction is addressed in further detail later in this chapter.
39. I.R.C. §355(a)(2)(A).
40. I.R.C. §355(a)(2)(B). This is the provision that permits the flexibility to structure the corporate division as a spin-off (involving no surrender of stock), a split-off (involving a surrender of *some* of the distributing corporation's stock), or a split-up (involving a surrender of *all* of the distributing corporation's stock).
41. I.R.C. §355(a)(2)(C).

Active Trade or Business Requirement

a) Post-Distribution Active Trade or Business Requirement

Much of §355's complexity enters through the §355(b) requirement that both the distributing corporation and the controlled corporation or corporations be "engaged immediately after the distribution in the active conduct of a trade or business."[42] In the case of a split-up, the distribution effectively is a liquidating distribution of stock in multiple controlled corporations after which the distributing corporation will cease to exist. In such cases, each of the controlled corporations must be "engaged immediately after the distribution in the active conduct of a trade or business."[43] The post-distribution active trade or business requirement is designed to ensure that the distributing corporation is actually breaking off part, or parts, of the business that will continue to operate after the distribution rather than simply distributing assets to shareholders.[44]

The "definition" section in §355(b)(2) offers virtually no guidance on the meaning of the words "active conduct of a trade or business." According to the regulations, a corporation is engaged in a "trade or business" if

> a specific group of activities are being carried on by the corporation for the purpose of earning income or profit, and the activities included in such group include every operation that forms a part of, or step in, the process of earning income or profit. Such group of activities ordinarily must include the collection of income and the payment of expenses.[45]

Whether or not the corporation is *actively,* as opposed to passively, engaged in a trade or business will depend upon the facts and circumstances. Ownership and operation of real estate tends to be largely an investment activity and typically is not a business involving significant management and operational activity. Thus, the regulations eliminate such activity from the definition of an active trade or business unless the owner performs

---

42. I.R.C. §355(b)(1)(A). The provisions of §355(a) explicitly cross-reference to the active business rule, indicating that the requirements of subparagraph (b) must be met if the shareholder distributees are to be entitled to nonrecognition treatment. I.R.C. §355(a)(1)(C).
43. I.R.C. §355(b)(1)(B).
44. This is another requirement that appears to be largely related to shareholder-level bailout concerns.
45. Treas. Reg. §1.355-3(b)(2)(ii). Proposed revisions to the §1.355-3 "active conduct of a trade or business" regulations would make several substantial changes. Nevertheless, the proposed regulations retain this language defining "trade or business." 72 Fed. Reg. 26,012, 26,027 (May 8, 2007) (proposed regulations on the §355(b) active trade or business requirement).

significant services with respect to the operation and management of the property.[46]

Historically, a corporation generally was viewed as engaged in active conduct of a trade or business for §355(b) purposes only if it was directly engaged in the trade or business. Based upon concerns that corporate groups conducting businesses in separate entities were being forced to undertake elaborate restructurings for no reason other than to satisfy §355(b) active trade or business requirements, Congress in 2005 enacted §355(b)(3), which added "special rules for determining active conduct in the case of affiliated groups."[47]

Under §355(b)(3), all members of a corporation's "separate affiliated group" (SAG) are treated as one corporation for purposes of determining whether the corporation is "engaged in the active conduct of a trade or business."[48] A corporation's SAG is the affiliated group determined under the §1504(a) affiliated group definition as if the corporation were the common parent.[49] In other words, the SAG of the distributing corporation (D) includes D as the common parent and all corporations affiliated with D through the §1504(a) control definition.[50] Thus, for example, an active trade or business operated entirely by one of the D's subsidiaries would be treated as if it were operated directly as a division of D.

The affiliated group rules offer structural flexibility by broadening the scope of permissible related entities that may be engaged in the active trade or business yet still satisfy §355(b) requirements.[51] In this sense, they bear

---

46. Treas. Reg. §1.355-3(b)(2)(iv)(B). The issues regarding real estate as a passive activity are similar to issues in connection with the passive activity loss rules of §469. The regulations also specifically eliminate from the active conduct of a trade or business definition the holding of stock, securities, land, or other property for investment purposes. Id. At (b)(2)(iv)(A).

47. Originally enacted as a temporary measure in the Tax Increase Prevention and Reconciliation Act of 2005, Pub. L. No. 109-222, §202, 120 Stat. 345 (2005), the provision was made permanent by the Tax Relief and Health Care Act of 2006, Pub. L. No. 109-432, §410, 120 Stat. 2922 (2006).

48. I.R.C. §355(b)(3)(A). Prior law also had considered a corporation actively engaged if "substantially all of its assets consisted of stock or securities of a controlled corporation directly engaged in a trade or business." I.R.C. §355(b)(2)(A) (prior to amendment). Since the corporation's SAG now is treated as one corporation for §355(b)(2)(A) purposes, the "substantially all of the assets" clause was deleted from §355(b)(2)(A) by the Technical Corrections Act of 2007, Pub. L. No. 110-172, §4(b), 121 Stat. 2473 (2007).

49. I.R.C. §355(b)(3)(B). The statute adds that the §1504(b) limitations on "includible corporations" do not apply for purposes of defining the SAG.

50. Prop. Treas. Reg. §1.355-3(b)(1)(iii) distinguishes the distributing corporation's SAG (DSAG) from the controlled corporation's SAG (CSAG) and indicates that there can be overlap if applicable ownership requirements are met. 72 Fed. Reg. 26,012 (May 8, 2007).

51. At the same time, however, the §355(b)(3) rules have introduced potential confusion and complexity with regard to definitions of "control." Although §355(b)(3) uses the §1504(a) control definition (at least 80% of total combined voting power and at least 80% of the total value of stock), for purposes of assessing whether the corporation meets the (b)(2)(A) active trade or business requirement, other §355 references to "control" or "controlled corporation" use the §368(c) definition (at least 80% of total combined voting power and 80% of the total number of shares).

similarity to the continuity of business enterprise (COBE) regulations, under which the acquiring corporation is deemed to hold businesses and assets of all members of its "qualified group," thus widening opportunities for post-reorganization transfers of target assets or stock without disqualifying an otherwise tax-free reorganization.[52] In fact, the Service explicitly turned to the COBE "qualified group" regulations as authority for a ruling involving a corporation (D) with a one-third membership interest in a limited liability company (LLC) classified as a partnership for tax purposes. Even though D itself performed no services with respect to the LLC's business, the ruling viewed D as actively conducting a business for §355(b) purposes because it "own[ed] a *significant interest* in LLC, and LLC perform[ed] the required activities that constitute an active trade or business under the regulations."[53]

b) Pre-Distribution Active Trade or Business Requirement

The §355(b)(1) pre-distribution active trade or business requirement appears rather inelegantly in the statutory text. It begins by including only a post-distribution trade or business requirement. Yet, the definition section that follows in §355(b)(2) treats a corporation as engaged in the active conduct of a trade or business for purposes of paragraph (b)(1) only if the trade or business "has been actively conducted throughout the five-year period *ending* on the date of the distribution."[54] Thus, the particular trade or business relied upon to meet this requirement cannot be a new trade or business, but must have a five-year history. This required history should not be a straight-jacket preventing any trade or business modifications during the five-year pre-distribution period, however. Changes—including expansion through acquisition of another trade or business in the same line of business—are disregarded under the regulations as long as they "are not of such a character as to constitute the acquisition of a new or different business."[55]

One significant additional statutory limitation is that the distributing corporation must not have acquired the trade or business, or control over the corporation conducting the trade or business, in a taxable transaction within five years prior to the distribution.[56] Absent such statutory restrictions, a distributing corporation without the necessary history simply could

---

52. For discussion of these COBE rules, see Chapters 11 and 12.
53. Rev. Rul. 2007-42, 2007-2 C.B. 44, 47 (emphasis added) (ruling on situation 1, involving D's one-third LLC membership interest). On the other hand, the ruling uses the COBE regulation's one-third "significant interest" test to conclude that D would *not* be viewed as actively conducting the LLC business if it had only a 20% LLC membership interest. *Id.* (ruling on situation 2). The preamble to proposed regulations also explicitly refers to COBE regulation parallels. 72 Fed. Reg. 26,012, 26,024 (May 8, 2007).
54. I.R.C. §355(b)(2)(B) (emphasis added).
55. Treas. Reg. §1.355-3(b)(3)(ii) (sometimes referred to as the "expansion doctrine").
56. I.R.C. §355(b)(2)(C), (D).

finesse the five-year rule by purchasing trade or business assets or acquiring a controlling interest in another corporation with a trade or business that met the five-year requirements. A subsequent distribution of the recently acquired trade or business to shareholders would not be in keeping with §355 as a corporate separation or divisive provision. Congress responded to this concern with statutory limitations to the "active conduct of a trade or business" definition. Pursuant to §355(b)(2)(C), for example, a trade or business acquired in a taxable transaction within the five-year period ending on the distribution date will not qualify for §355(b) purposes.[57] Similarly, control of a corporation conducting an active trade or business received within the pre-distribution five-year period will satisfy §355(b) requirements only if "acquired in transactions in which gain or loss was not recognized in whole or in part."[58]

The logic behind these restrictions applicable only to recent taxable acquisitions is that, unlike taxable acquisitions, tax-free acquisitions typically involve the acquiring corporation's use of equity consideration. If the distributing corporation recently transferred its own equity in exchange for a new trade or business, the historic owners of the recently acquired trade or business will be participants in the divisive transaction. Thus, the distributing corporation and its shareholders, old and new, will have a historic connection to both trades or businesses. On the other hand, a taxable transfer more likely reflects a sale-like acquisition without such continuity of interest. Congress here was trying to limit nonrecognition to "mere change in form" divisions and to prevent corporations from simply siphoning off assets to shareholders that otherwise would have been distributed to them in the form of taxable dividends. The suspicion raised when a corporation spins off a recently acquired business is that the particular business was acquired as part of a plan for sale of the business.[59]

In a lengthy preamble to proposed regulations, the Treasury Department noted that Congress did not make conforming amendments to the statutory limitations on pre-distribution trade or business acquisitions when it added §355(b)(3), which now treats all members of a corporation's separate affiliated group as one corporation for purposes of the active trade or business

---

57. I.R.C. §355(b)(2)(C) (trade or business acquisition "in a transaction in which gain or loss was recognized in whole or in part").

58. I.R.C. §355(b)(2)(D). Under the regulatory "expansion doctrine," acquisition of another trade or business in the same line of business should not be disqualifying under (b)(2)(C). See Treas. Reg. §1.355-3(b)(3)(ii). Proposed regulations would clarify that acquisition of stock of a current subsidiary SAG member also would be considered an expansion, and would not be disqualifying under (b)(2)(D). Prop. Treas. Reg. §1.355-3(b)(1)(ii).

59. Under §355(b)(2)(D), the distributing corporation will not meet the pre-distribution trade or business requirement if it acquired control within the five-year period ending on the date of the distribution. If the distributing corporation acquired not 80% control, but only a 50% interest within this five-year period, restrictions in §355(d) and (e) may apply. These special provisions are considered later in this chapter.

requirement. As a result, "the IRS and Treasury Department . . . believe that a purpose-based interpretation of section 355(b)(2) is essential to harmonize these provisions."[60] The Treasury Department's proposed regulations would permit some taxable trade or business acquisitions with the five-year pre-distribution period that violate the literal requirements of §355(b)(2)(C) and (D). At the same time, certain *tax-free* trade or business acquisitions would nevertheless be treated as prohibited acquisitions of a trade or business for §355(b) purposes. According to the Treasury Department, even though

> the statute prohibits acquisitions of a trade or business in which gain or loss is recognized . . . The recognition of gain or loss, in and of itself, does not violate the purposes of section 355. Rather, recognition of gain or loss is generally *indicative of the type of consideration used in the transaction*. Typically, a transaction in which gain or loss is recognized consists of an acquisition in exchange for assets. On the other hand, a transaction in which no gain or loss is recognized typically consists of an acquisition in exchange for the corporation's equity.
>
> Accordingly, the IRS and Treasury Department believe that the common purpose of section 355(b)(2)(C) and (D) is to prevent distributing from using assets — instead of its stock . . . — to acquire a new trade or business in anticipation of distributing [it] to its shareholders in a tax-free distribution."[61]

Although consistent with the Treasury Department's trend toward more policy-based interpretation over the past decade, adoption of these regulations — traveling so far outside the boundaries of literal statutory text — would represent a rather extraordinary exercise of administrative power.

In 2016, the Treasury Department issued proposed regulations that address situations where a distributing corporation contributes a small active trade or business and a large passive business to a subsidiary corporation and then distributes the stock of the subsidiary corporation to its shareholders.[62] One of the most significant transactions that attempted to utilize this strategy involved Yahoo Inc.'s attempted distribution of its stock in Alibaba Group Holding Ltd. in a tax-free spin-off.[63] In January 2015, Yahoo Inc. Announced that it would distribute its stock in Alibaba Group Holding Ltd. in a tax-free spin-off transaction, enabling Yahoo to avoid over $16 billion in tax liability and that it would seek a private letter ruling.[64] When the IRS announced that it would refrain from issuing

---

60. 72 Fed. Reg. 26,012, 26,015 (May 8, 2007).
61. *Id.* (emphasis added).
62. Prop. Treas. Reg. §1.355-9, 81 Fed. Reg. 46,004 (July 15, 2016).
63. See Press Release, Yahoo, Yahoo Announces Plan for Tax-Free Spin-Off of Remaining Stake in Alibaba Group (Jan. 27, 2015).
64. See *id.* See Vindu Goel & Michael J. de la Merced, I.R.S. Look at Spinoffs May Affect Yahoo Plan, N.Y. Times (May 19, 2015).

private letter rulings on transactions like this, where the active business of the distributing corporation or the controlled corporation was small compared to other assets, the Yahoo-Alibaba spin-off transaction came to an abrupt halt.

Shortly after the attempted Yahoo-Alibaba spin-off transaction, the Treasury Department issued proposed regulations.[65] Under the proposed regulations, the §355(b) active trade or business requirement will only be satisfied if the fair market value of the five-year active business assets constitute at least 5% of the fair market value of total assets of the distributing corporation and at least 5% of the fair market value of the assets of the controlled corporation.[66] Put differently, the distributing corporation and the controlled corporation must each divide the fair market value of its five-year active business assets by the fair market value of each corporation's respective assets in order to determine whether the 5% threshold is satisfied. If this threshold is not satisfied, then, under the proposed regulations, the transaction would fail the active trade or business requirement of §355(b).[67]

c) Particular Applications of the "Active Trade or Business" Requirements

i) Vertical Divisions of a Single Business

Although unresolved for a time, it is now well settled that §355 treatment is possible upon the corporate division of a single trade or business, sometimes referred to as a vertical division. In its early regulations, the Treasury Department had taken the position that the division of a single business was not eligible for §355 nonrecognition, arguing that the active trade or business requirement was met only if there were two or more separate and distinct businesses operating immediately after the distribution. In two landmark §355 cases, however, the Fifth and Sixth Circuits declared these regulations invalid. In the Sixth Circuit case of Coady v. Commissioner,[68] a single corporation engaged in the business of constructing sewage disposal plants transferred half of its assets to a new subsidiary and then distributed the stock in the subsidiary to one of its shareholders in exchange for all of his stock. The corporate division effectively transferred one major construction contract to the new corporation and left the remaining major construction contract with the original corporation. The Fifth Circuit case of United

---

65. Prop. Treas. Reg. §1.355-9.
66. Prop. Treas. Reg. §1.355-9(b).
67. The proposed regulations provide that the five-year active business assets can include a reasonable amount of working capital and assets that are required for business exigencies and regulatory purposes. Prop. Treas. Reg. §1.355-9(a)(3).
68. 289 F.2d 490 (6th Cir. 1961), affirming 33 T.C. 771 (1960).

States v. Marett[69] involved a single business manufacturing edible pork skins. The corporation had a contract with one major customer and others with several smaller customers. The corporation built a new factory to handle orders from its smaller customers and transferred the factory and related assets to a new subsidiary. The stock in this new subsidiary was then distributed to the parent corporation's shareholders. In each case, the courts found that the distributions were valid §355 distributions. Since losing these cases, the government has conceded that the division of a single business into two separate businesses can qualify under §355. In fact, the particular facts of the Coady and Marett cases have received the Treasury Department's explicit blessing in two regulatory examples.[70]

Remember that to meet the "active trade or business" requirement, the distributing and controlled corporations must not only be engaged in an active trade or business immediately after the distribution, but must have actively conducted such trade or business during the five-year period preceding the distribution. The expansion of a business into new geographical areas should not be regarded necessarily as the creation of a new trade or business. If a corporation has been actively engaged in a trade or business in one state and recently expanded into a new state, it should be possible to arrange a corporate division into separate corporations, each conducting business in the separate state. The Treasury Department did not always agree. In one early case, for example, a corporation whose primary operations were in Nebraska had recently opened a branch in Maine. The corporation transferred assets connected with the Maine office to a new subsidiary and then distributed the subsidiary's stock to its shareholders. The government took the position that this was not a valid §355 distribution since the Maine "trade or business" had not been conducted for the necessary five years prior to the distribution. The Eighth Circuit disagreed, holding that the active trade or business requirement was met. The court said that "[n]othing in the language of §355 suggests that prior business activity is only to be measured by looking at the business performed in a geographical area where the controlled corporation is eventually formed."[71] Again, the Treasury Department conceded the point in subsequent regulations.[72]

---

69. 325 F.2d 28 (5th Cir. 1963).
70. Treas. Reg. §1.355-3(c), exs. 4 (Coady case), 5 (Marett case). Beware, however, that there must also be a business purpose for the division and distribution. For example, the separation of the corporation into two corporations in example 5 was designed to eliminate errors in packaging. See also id., examples 6 and 7 involving separation of downtown and suburban retail or department stores into separate corporations.
71. Estate of Lockwood v. Comm'r, 350 F.2d 712, 715 (8th Cir. 1965).
72. Treas. Reg. §1.355-3, ex. 8. See also Prop. Treas. Reg. §1.355-3(d)(2), exs. 14-15.

ii) Horizontal or Functional Divisions of a Single Business

Corporations may wish to separate particular functions, such as research or sales, into separate corporate entities. The potential problem here is that a corporate entity created to engage in a single function of a larger business enterprise may not independently produce income. The §355 regulations envision a corporation as engaged in a "trade or business" "if a specific group of activities are being carried on by the corporation for the purpose of earning income or profit, and the activities included in such group include every operation that forms a part of, or a step in, the process of earning income or profit."[73] To satisfy the "active trade or business" requirement, the activities separated into the new corporation must represent a separate and independent trade or business. Nevertheless, regulations provide several examples of functional divisions that will satisfy the active trade or business requirement. One involves the spin-off of a research division, another a sales function, and another a supply function for a manufacturing business.[74] In each case, however, the regulation cautions that the division must also satisfy the separate requirement that the transaction not be used principally as a device for the distribution of earnings and profits.

Anti-Avoidance Rules for Essentially Nondivisive Distributions

a) Device for the Distribution of Earnings and Profits

In addition to all of the restrictions and requirements discussed above, §355 explicitly demands that the transaction not be used "principally as a device for the distribution of the earnings and profits of the distributing corporation or the controlled corporation or both."[75] Frequently described as the "device requirement," this condition is a nutshell statement of the general shareholder-level concern originally motivating §355. In fact, the "device" requirement regulations perhaps provide the best statement of this original underlying concern. The regulation states that "section 355 recognizes that a tax-free distribution of the stock of a controlled corporation presents a potential for tax avoidance by facilitating the avoidance of the dividend provisions of the Code through the subsequent sale or exchange of stock of one corporation and the retention of the stock of another corporation."[76] In some measure, most §355 requirements are directed at this goal

---

73. Treas. Reg. §1.355-3(b)(2)(ii).
74. Treas. Reg. §1.355-3(c), exs. 9-11.
75. I.R.C. §355(a)(1)(B).
76. Treas. Reg. §1.355-2(d)(1).

of preventing bailout of corporate earnings and profits without paying the "dividend" toll. In fact, some §355 requirements arguably are redundant. The independent "device requirement" may serve as a general safeguard to catch bailouts that the more specific and technical §355 restrictions or requirements fail to cover. Given this redundancy and the diminished shareholder bailout concern under the post-2003 "qualified dividend" rules, the "device" test may well be among the first of the §355 requirements that Congress revisits with an eye toward repeal or substantial modification.

Regulations list a number of factors to be considered in making the facts and circumstances analysis required to determine whether the transaction was used as a "device" to distribute earnings and profits. Not surprisingly, the regulations indicate that "the fact that a distribution is pro rata or substantially pro rata is evidence of device."[77] Subsequent sale of the distributed stock also can be evidence of a device.[78] The greater the percentage of the stock sold and the shorter the period of time between the distribution and the subsequent sale, the stronger the evidence of device.[79] A prearranged or negotiated sale is considered "*substantial* evidence of device," whereas a subsequent sale that was not arranged or negotiated prior to the distribution merely is "evidence of device."[80] Another "device factor" examines the nature and use of the distributing and controlled corporations' assets. The presence of "cash and other liquid assets that are not related to the reasonable needs" of a §355(b) trade or business also is "evidence of a device."[81]

Any device factors present should be balanced against, and may be outweighed by, "nondevice factors." Regulations permit the taxpayer to use corporate business purpose as evidence that the transaction was not used as a device for the distribution of earnings and profits.[82] However, the same regulations caution that "[t]he stronger the evidence of device . . ., the stronger the corporate business purpose required to prevent the determination that the transaction was used principally as a device."[83]

In 2016, the Treasury Department issued proposed regulations that would make the following significant changes to the device test:[84]

Nature and Use of Assets. The proposed regulations create a new term, "business assets."[85] Under the definition provided in the proposed regulations,

---

77. Treas. Reg. §1.355-2(d)(2)(ii).
78. However, the mere fact of a subsequent sale will not be construed as a "device" unless it was pursuant to an arrangement negotiated or agreed upon prior to the distribution. I.R.C. §355(a)(1)(B).
79. Treas. Reg. §1.355-2(d)(2)(iii).
80. Treas. Reg. §1.355-2(d)(2)(iii)(B), (C) (emphasis added).
81. Treas. Reg. §1.355-2(d)(2)(iv)(B).
82. Treas. Reg. §1.355-2(d)(3).
83. Id. Also under these regulations, the fact that the distributing corporation is publicly traded is evidence of nondevice. Id.
84. Prop. Treas. Reg. §1.355-2(d).
85. Prop. Treas. Reg. §1.355-2(d)(2)(iv)(B)(2).

business assets are assets used in an active trade or business, including a reasonable amount of working capital, but that do not need to meet the five-year requirement for the active trade or business requirement of §355(b). Assets that are not business assets are "nonbusiness assets." The proposed regulations state that the ownership of nonbusiness assets by the distributing corporation or controlled corporation is considered to be evidence of a device, unless one of the safe harbors provided in these proposed regulations is satisfied. First, if neither the distributing corporation nor the controlled corporation has nonbusiness assets that comprise 20% or more of its total assets, then the ownership of these nonbusiness assets ordinarily would not be a device.[86] Second, if the percentage of nonbusiness assets of the distributing corporation differs from the percentage of nonbusiness assets of the controlled corporation, then the distribution is not ordinarily a device if (a) the difference is less than 10% or (b) the difference is the result of a need to equalize consideration paid to shareholders in a non-pro rata distribution.[87]

Corporate Business Purpose and Device. The proposed regulations reject an asserted business purpose for a §355 distribution where nonbusiness assets are separated from business assets, unless the business purpose involves "exigency that requires an investment or other use" of the nonbusiness assets.[88]

Per se Device. Finally, under the proposed regulations, some distributions are automatically treated as a "per se device."[89] The proposed regulations provide that a distribution is a per se device if: at least 66.66% of the assets of the distributing corporation or the controlled corporation are nonbusiness assets *and* the percentages of the distributing corporation's and the controlled corporation's nonbusiness assets are significantly different and fall into one of the following three bands: (a) 66.67% to 79.99% of one corporation consists of nonbusiness assets and less than 30% of the other corporation consists of nonbusiness assets; (b) 80% to 89.99% of one corporation consists of nonbusiness assets and less than 40% of the other corporation consists of nonbusiness assets; or (c) 90% or more of one corporation consists of nonbusiness assets and less than 50% of the other corporation consists of nonbusiness assets.[90]

b) Disqualified Investment Corporations: §355(g)

Despite its active trade or business and device for distributing earnings and profits limitations, §355 still has provided opportunities for creative tax

---

86. Prop. Treas. Reg. §1.355-2(d)(4)(C)(1).
87. Prop. Treas. Reg. §1.355-2(d)(4)(C)(2).
88. Prop. Treas. Reg. §1.355-2(d)(3)(ii).
89. Prop. Treas. Reg. §1.355-2(d)(5)(iii)(A).
90. Id.

planners to structure tax-free transactions that more closely resemble sales than divisions. Under one technique, referred to as the "cash-rich split-off," a controlled corporation with a small active five-year trade or business would be loaded up with cash and other liquid assets. Even though the controlled subsidiary's assets consisted almost entirely of cash, the presence of a small five-year active trade or business was sufficient to qualify for §355 tax-free treatment upon a distribution of the controlled subsidiary's stock. This device became especially popular as a way for corporations with a significant investment in another corporation to arrange a largely cash redemption or stock "buyback" with tax benefits for all participants.

In one such well-known transaction, Liberty Media (LM) responded to Time Warner's (TW) announced intention to sell the Atlanta Braves with interest in acquiring the team if the transaction could be coordinated with a tax-free buyback of approximately $1.8 billion in TW stock that LM wished to sell for cash. If the redemption of LM's stock and TW's sale of the team had been structured as sale transactions, both corporations would have incurred substantial taxable gain. Instead, TW created its own new subsidiary, to which it contributed the Atlanta Braves, valued at approximately $450 million, along with $1.35 billion in cash. In other words, only 25% of the new controlled subsidiary's assets consisted of an active trade or business (the team); the remaining 75% of its assets were cash. In the meantime, Liberty Media isolated the portion of its TW stock holdings that it wanted redeemed in a separate LM subsidiary. TW then transferred all the stock in its recently created cash-rich subsidiary to LM in exchange for stock in the LM subsidiary — essentially a redemption of LM's $1.8 million stock interest in TW for 75% cash and 25% in trade or business assets. The transaction qualified as a tax-free split-off.

Congress in 2005 responded to these "liquid-asset" or "cash-rich" transactions by adding §355(g), which disallows §355 tax-free treatment if either the distributing or controlled corporation is a "disqualified investment corporation" immediately after the exchange, and if any person/entity at that time holds a 50-percent or greater interest in such corporation that they did not hold immediately before the transaction."[91] A "disqualified investment corporation" includes "any distributing or controlled corporation if the fair market value of the investment assets of the corporation is . . . ⅔ or more of the fair market value of all assets of the corporation . . . ."[92]

---

91. I.R.C. §355(g)(1) (added by the Tax Increase Prevention and Reconciliation Act of 2005, Pub. L. No. 109-222, §507, 120 Stat. 345 (2005)).

92. I.R.C. §355(g)(2)(A). For the first year following the statute's effective date, the "disqualified investment corporation" designation applied only to corporations whose investment assets were ¾ or more of the fair market value of all assets. Id. At (g)(2)(A)(ii). The Time Warner deal, which included 75% investment assets, apparently closed just before midnight on the last day before the change in order to take advantage of the higher permissible proportion of investment assets.

Thus, the focus of §355(g) is on transactions in which a new owner takes a controlling interest in a corporation whose active trade or business is small relative to its liquid assets.[93] Such transactions appear more "sale-like" than divisive. The relatively small proportion of trade or business assets strongly suggests that the primary motive for the transaction was something other than splitting multiple operating businesses of one corporation into two or more separate corporations to continue those operations.

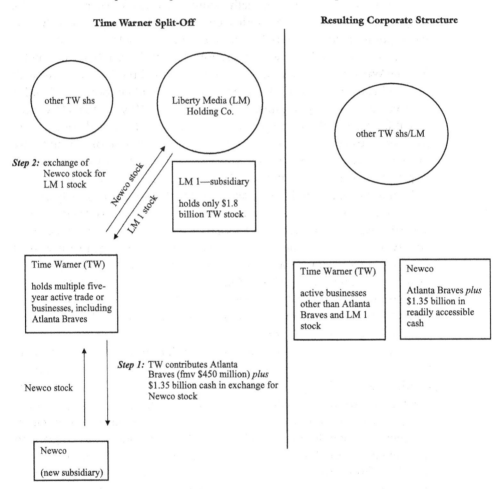

Notice that §355(g) does not prohibit these "investment-rich" transactions, but instead extends its blessing, subject to conditions. In its focus

93. "Investment assets" include cash, corporate stock, partnership interests, debt instruments, options, foreign currencies, and similar assets. I.R.C. §355(g)(2)(B). The statute provides exceptions to the definition for assets used in the active and regular business of certain lending, finance, banking, and insurance businesses, id. At (g)(2)(B)(ii), and for stock or securities in a "20-percent controlled entity with respect to the distributing or controlled corporation." Id at (g)(2)(B)(iv).

on the ratio of trade or business to other assets, §355(g) is similar to the "device regulations," which more generally view assets that are not used in a trade or business as "evidence of device" to distribute earnings and profits.[94] Unlike §355(g), however, the "device regulations" do not offer clear rules as to when the investment asset proportion will be considered too high.

Nonstatutory Requirements

Even if a §355 tax-free separation is not a §368(a) reorganization, the transaction nevertheless must meet business purpose and continuity of interest requirements reminiscent of the rules applied to reorganizations generally under §368.[95] This should not be surprising given the substantial overlap and similarity of underlying concerns behind tax-free reorganizations and tax-free divisions. Although both corporate acquisitions and divisions must meet business purpose and continuity of interest requirements to achieve tax-free status, the requirements are only nominally the same. Actual application of these nonstatutory requirements in the divisive setting can differ significantly from application of the same requirements to an acquisitive reorganization.[96]

a) Business Purpose[97]

Regulations under §355 explicitly incorporate an "independent business purpose" test under which the overall transaction must be motivated, "in whole or substantial part, by one or more corporate business purposes."[98] The §355 regulations insist that both the overall transaction *and* the §355 distribution itself be carried out for one or more business purposes.[99] Making matters more difficult, a separation will not meet the corporate business

---

94. See Treas. Reg. §1.355-2(d)(2)(iv)(B). See discussion in preceding section in this chapter.
95. Divisive reorganizations and §355 distributions may also be subject to nonstatutory step-transaction analysis.
96. Application of these requirements to tax-free acquisitive reorganizations is considered in Chapters 11 and 12.
97. The "business purpose" test that now applies to both the §368 reorganization and the §355 distribution provisions actually grew out of an early landmark case involving a divisive reorganization. Gregory v. Helvering, 293 U.S. 465 (1935). The shareholder in *Gregory* caused her solely owned corporation to transfer highly appreciated stock to a newly formed subsidiary that never conducted any business and was in existence for only three days. Although the transaction met the literal terms of the reorganization statute, the court denied tax-free reorganization treatment, since the transaction lacked a business purpose. For further discussion of the *Gregory* case, see Chapter 11.
98. Treas. Reg. §1.355-2(b)(1).
99. Treas. Reg. §1.355-2(b)(3). At the same time, the *presence* of a business purpose can serve as a "nondevice factor." Id. At (b)(4).

purpose requirement if the business purpose can be achieved in a nontaxable transaction *without* the distribution of stock of a controlled corporation as long as the alternative is "neither impractical nor unduly expensive."[100] In other words, the §355 distribution must be the transaction structure of last resort to achieve the business purpose. To illustrate the point, the regulations include an example of a corporation engaged in the manufacture of candy and toys. In order to protect the candy business from the "risks and vicissitudes" of the toy business, the corporation transferred its toy manufacturing operations to a new controlled subsidiary and then distributed the stock in the new subsidiary to its shareholders. The example concludes that the legitimate business purpose of protecting the candy business is achieved simply by creating the new corporate entity. Since the subsequent distribution to the shareholders is unnecessary to achieve the business purpose, the shareholders are not eligible for §355 nonrecognition.[101]

It is worth noting that the business purpose test under §355 is far more demanding than the parallel test applied to acquisitive reorganizations. Compare, for example, the extensive "business purpose" rules in Treas. Reg. §1.355-2 to the rather minimalist rules applicable to acquisitive reorganizations in Treas. Reg. §1.368-1(c).[102] The difference in emphasis might be explained by observing that although the "mere change in form" notion lies behind both the acquisitive and divisive tax-free treatment provisions, the §355 rules serve the additional important function of ensuring that the distributing corporation not bypass the repeal of *General Utilities* through a tax-free distribution of appreciated assets that would otherwise have been taxable to the corporation under §311 or §336.

The regulatory "corporate business purpose" definition requires "a real and substantial non-Federal tax purpose germane to the business."[103] Examples of acceptable business purpose provided in the regulations include corporate separations designed to comply with federal antitrust or other regulatory restrictions, to settle shareholder conflicts, or to permit employees to share in corporate profits.[104] Despite these examples, the vague "facts-and-circumstances" definition has left taxpayers uncertain and searching for guidance as to permissible purposes. In the past, the Treasury Department was willing to issue advance letter rulings with regard to proper business purposes under §355, even providing a checklist of presumably

---

100. Id.
101. Treas. Reg. §1.355-2(b)(5), ex. 3.
102. Buried in the latter regulation are simply the observations that the reorganization transaction "must be an ordinary and necessary incident of the conduct of the enterprise" and must not be part of "a preconceived plan having no business or corporate purpose. . . ." Treas. Reg. §1.368-1(c).
103. Treas. Reg. §1.355-2(b)(2).
104. See examples in Treas. Reg. §1.355-2(b)(5).

valid business purposes.[105] In 2016, the Treasury Department announced that, after years of not issuing private letter rulings on the business purpose requirement of §355, it would again rule on significant legal issues regarding the business purpose requirement, as long as the issue is not inherently factual.[106]

The Treasury Department has issued several important rulings regarding the business purpose requirement. One of these rulings addresses the rather common "fit and focus" business purpose assertion. In these cases, the taxpayer asserts that a corporate division will enhance business success by resolving management or other systemic problems arising from the operation of two different businesses under one corporate roof. A problem arises in such cases if the original corporation and the "spin-off" entity have a continuing relationship after the separation. After all, such a continuing relationship is inconsistent with the assertion that the businesses needed to be independent. One Treasury Department ruling involved a transaction in which the separated entities had two common directors following the spin-off distribution. The ruling held that this post-separation relationship did not conflict with an otherwise valid business purpose since the common directorships were designed merely to ease transition and reassure financial markets, the directors' terms were short-term, and the two common directors constituted only a minority of each board.[107]

Another common §355 issue arises if the corporate division is designed to serve both shareholder and corporate purposes. Although shareholder purposes do not meet the §355 business purpose requirement, the regulations concede that "a shareholder purpose for a transaction may be so nearly coextensive with a corporate business purpose as to preclude any distinction between them."[108] As an example, the Service offered a ruling in which one corporation conducted two different types of business in separate subsidiaries. Since the two businesses appealed to different investors, the corporation decided to spin off one business as an independent corporation to increase the aggregate stock trading prices for the two corporations as separate entities. By itself, increasing stock price benefits shareholders and is unlikely to satisfy the *corporate* business purpose test. In the ruling's situation one, however, the corporation's directors claimed that they hoped to use the increased stock value to provide stronger equity-based incentives to

---

105. Rev. Proc. 96-30, 1996-1 C.B. 696, app. A, *superseded by* Rev. Proc. 2017-52, 2017-41 I.R.B. 283.
106. Rev. Proc. 2016-45, 2016-37 I.R.B. 1.
107. Rev. Rul. 2003-74, 2003-29 I.R.B. 78. See also Rev. Rul. 2003-75, 2003-29 I.R.B. 79. The latter ruling involved taxpayer assertions that separation of two businesses was necessary to avoid competition for capital. The Treasury Department ruled that a post-separation continuing relationship involving short-term administrative and borrowing agreements between the separated entities would not jeopardize a valid §355 business purpose determination.
108. Treas. Reg. §1.355-2(b)(2), (b)(5), ex. 2.

its employees without diluting existing shareholder interests. In situation two, the directors claimed that stock value increases would make it easier to structure planned acquisitions in a manner that preserved capital with significantly less dilution of existing shareholder interests. In both cases, the ruling concluded that the regulatory business purpose requirement is met "when the increased value is expected to serve a corporate business purpose of either the distributing or the controlled corporation (or both), *even if it benefits the shareholders* of the distributing corporation."[109] In another ruling involving a small family business, the Treasury Department agreed that the separation of two different businesses in order to resolve family disagreements over the appropriate future direction of each business was a valid corporate business purpose despite personal estate planning benefits to the shareholders.[110]

Two additional Treasury Department rulings should provide comfort to taxpayers as well. When one of several different businesses operating under one corporate roof needs additional capital, investment bankers frequently advise that a public stock offering will be more successful if the business planning the expansion is split off. The Treasury Department ruled that this is a valid business purpose even if the public offering is subsequently called off or postponed due to an unexpected deterioration in market conditions.[111] Finally, despite the regulatory provision announcing that potential tax avoidance by the distributing or controlled corporation "is relevant in determining the extent to which an existing corporate business purpose motivated the distribution,"[112] the Treasury Department has reassured taxpayers that "the distributing corporation is entitled to reject a taxable disposition in favor of a tax-free distribution."[113] In other words, as long as there is a business reason for a corporate division, the taxpayer is free to choose a tax-free structure over a taxable one to reduce its overall tax burden.

b) Continuity of Proprietary Interest

The judicially developed "continuity of proprietary interest" or "continuity of shareholder interest (COSI)" doctrine goes to the heart of the "mere change in form" rationale behind the nonrecognition rules. The idea is to provide nonrecognition treatment in transactions where the investors holding an interest before the transaction remain substantially invested in the restructured corporate enterprise after the transaction. Continuity of interest is built in to the §368(a)(1)(D) divisive reorganization definition

---

109. Rev. Rul. 2004-23, 2001-1 C.B. 585 (emphasis added).
110. Rev. Rul. 2003-52, 2003-1 C.B. 960. See also Rev. Rul. 2004-23, 2004-11 I.R.B. 585.
111. Rev. Rul. 2003-55, 2003-1 C.B. 961.
112. Treas. Reg. §1.355-2(b)(1).
113. Rev. Rul. 2003-110, 2003-46 I.R.B. 1083.

since the transferor corporation, or one or more of its shareholders, must be in control of the corporation acquiring the transferor's assets immediately after the transfer. In addition, continuity of interest principles apply even to §355 tax-free distributions that do not meet the §368(a) reorganization definition. Tracking some of the language in Treas. Reg. §1.368-1(b), the §355 regulations require that the separation effect "only a readjustment of continuing interests in the property of the distributing and controlled corporations."[114] As applied in the tax-free separation context, continuity requires that one or more prior owners own, in the aggregate, "an amount of stock establishing a continuity of interest in *each of the modified corporate forms in which the enterprise is conducted after the separation.*"[115]

Although the §368 regulations applicable to acquisitive reorganizations and the §355 regulations applicable to corporate divisions both incorporate nonstatutory continuity of proprietary interest requirements, the application of these requirements in each setting is different. This should not be surprising given the multiple and slightly different roles played by §355. For acquisitive reorganizations, the COSI requirement focuses upon the quality and quantity of *consideration received* by the target (T) shareholders from the purchasing corporation (P).[116] In contrast, the §355 rules focus on the proprietary interest in the original and the "spun off" entity *retained* by the historic shareholders. Recall here that the revised COSI regulations have largely eliminated the historic shareholder continuity requirement in the acquisition setting.[117] Different considerations should apply in determining the significance of pre- and post-division stock transfers in the divisive setting. Not surprisingly, upon issuing its revised and relaxed COSI regulations, the Treasury Department stated explicitly that the revised rules do not apply to §355 distributions and Type D divisive reorganizations, and that it would "continue to study the role of the COSI requirement in section 368(a)(1)(D) reorganizations and section 355 transactions."[118]

OVERLAP OF §368(A)(1)(D) AND §355: DIVISIVE REORGANIZATIONS

Many, but not all, distributions of stock in a controlled corporation will simultaneously be "reorganizations" under §368(a)(1)(D) and also

---

114. Treas. Reg. §1.355-2(c)(1).
115. Id. (emphasis added).
116. For a detailed discussion of the COSI requirement in the acquisitive reorganization setting, see Chapter 11.
117. See section in Chapter 11 entitled "Historic Shareholder Continuity."
118. T.D. 8760, 63 Fed. Reg. 4174, 4176 (Jan. 28, 1998).

distributions under §355. A Type D reorganization involves transfer of "all or a part of [a corporation's] assets to another corporation if immediately after the transfer, the transferor, or one or more of its shareholders . . . , or any combination thereof, is in control of the corporation to which the assets are transferred."[119] In addition, stock or securities of the corporation to which the assets were transferred must be distributed pursuant to the requirements of §§354, 355, or 356.[120] Remember that the Type D reorganization includes both acquisitive and divisive reorganizations. In general, acquisitive Type D reorganizations involve a transfer of *all* of the assets and a subsequent distribution of stock or securities pursuant to the requirements for nonrecognition under §354. On the other hand, a divisive reorganization involves a transfer of *part* of the assets and a subsequent distribution of stock or securities pursuant to the requirements for nonrecognition under §355. Since Congress was more concerned with abuse possibilities in connection with divisive reorganizations, §355 imposes more rigorous requirements for nonrecognition than many of the other tax-free reorganization provisions.

TAX CONSEQUENCES TO SHAREHOLDERS AND OTHER DISTRIBUTEES

Basic Nonrecognition Rule: §355(a)

If all of the requirements for a tax-free division or tax-free reorganization are met, the shareholders and security holders will not report gain or loss or otherwise include any income upon receipt of stock or securities in the controlled subsidiary from the distributing parent corporation.[121]

Receipt of Boot

A transaction that otherwise satisfies the requirements of §355 will not be disqualified simply because the shareholders or security holders receive property other than stock or securities permitted to be received tax-free under §355.[122] Consistent with the other reorganization provisions in

---

119. I.R.C. §368(a)(1)(D) (emphasis added). Contrast the "acquisitive reorganization" provisions of §368(a)(1)(C), which require transfer of "substantially all" of the transferring corporation's assets. See discussion of acquisitive Type D reorganizations in Chapter 12.
120. I.R.C. §368(a)(1)(D).
121. I.R.C. §355(a)(1).
122. Regulations indicate that, with certain exceptions provided in Treas. Reg. §1.356-6, the term "securities" for purposes of §355 "includes rights issued by the distributing

Subchapter C, however, any such additional property received will be treated as boot and taxable according to the reorganization boot rules in §356.[123] "Nonqualified preferred stock" is *not* considered "stock or securities" for purposes of §355.[124] Thus, any such "nonqualified preferred stock" will be treated as boot. Unlike the §351 nonrecognition rules, securities received will not automatically be treated as boot. However, the excess principal of securities in the controlled corporation received over the principal amount of securities surrendered will be considered boot.[125] If securities are received and no securities were surrendered, then all of the securities received will be considered boot.[126]

In the case of a straight §355 spin-off distribution in which the shareholders do not exchange or surrender any shares, §356 provides that the boot distribution shall be treated as a distribution of property to which §301 applies.[127] Thus, if the distributing corporation has sufficient earnings and profits to cover the boot distribution, the shareholders will report the boot as dividend income. In the case of a split-off or split-up in which the shareholders exchange some or all of their shares in return for the stock or securities received, the boot received in the exchange will be governed by §356(a). Unless the exchange is determined to have the effect of the distribution of a dividend, the boot under §356(a) will be treated as gain from the sale of a capital asset.[128]

In addition to the above boot rules, §355 includes a unique rule — sometimes called the "hot stock" boot rule — that applies to recently acquired stock in the controlled corporation. If the distributing corporation acquired stock of the controlled corporation within five years prior to the distribution in a taxable transaction, the distribution of such stock will be treated as the distribution of boot.[129] Keep in mind first of all that §355 nonrecognition treatment applies only to distributions of stock in a *"controlled corporation"*

---

corporation or the controlled corporation to acquire stock of that corporation." Treas. Reg. §1.355-1(c).

123. See I.R.C. §355(a)(4)(A), which explicitly cross-references to the §356 boot rules.

124. I.R.C. §355(a)(3)(D). "Nonqualified preferred stock" is defined in §351(g) and is discussed in detail in Chapter 4. See also Treas. Reg. §1.356-6 (rights to acquire nonqualified preferred stock).

125. I.R.C. §§355(a)(3)(A), 356(d)(2)(B). This security boot rule parallels the §354(a)(2) boot rule that applies to reorganizations generally. For a detailed discussion of these boot rules as applied to other reorganizations, see Chapter 11. A right to acquire stock, which is considered a "security" for purposes of §355, is considered to have no principal amount. Treas. Reg. §1.355-1(c). See also Treas. Reg. §1.356-3(b).

126. I.R.C. §355(a)(3)(A). Even though a stock option or warrant is considered a security for purposes of §355, it is *not* considered "other property" for purposes of the §356 boot rules, since it has no principal amount. Treas. Reg. §1.356-3(b). See also id. At exs. 7-9.

127. I.R.C. §356(b).

128. For a more detailed discussion of the §356 boot rules and the distinction between "dividend" boot and "capital gain" boot under these rules, see Chapter 11.

129. I.R.C. §355(a)(3)(B).

as defined in §368(c). Moreover, the distribution will not qualify at all as a tax-free §355 distribution if the necessary control was acquired in a taxable transaction during the five years leading up to the distribution.[130] Thus, the "hot stock" boot rule apparently serves a narrow function. If the distributing corporation already owns sufficient stock for §368(c) control, but acquires *additional* stock in the controlled corporation in a taxable transaction during the five-year period before the distribution, §355(a)(3)(B) will classify the additional shares as boot taxable to the shareholders.

Potential new twists have resulted from the separate affiliated group (SAG) active trade or business requirement regime. To address these issues, Congress granted the Treasury Department explicit authority to modify the "hot stock" boot rules in a manner consistent with new §335(b)(3). To illustrate potential conflicts between the two sets of rules, the Treasury Department's preamble to regulations describes a distributing corporation that acquired control over another corporation in a taxable transaction and then distributed the stock to its shareholders within five years. Since the acquired and distributing corporations were in the same line of business, the acquisition satisfied the 355(b) trade or business requirements under the Treasury Department's regulatory expansion doctrine.[131] Yet, absent a special rule, *all* of the stock distributed would be taxable boot pursuant to §355(a)(3)(B). Finding this result inconsistent with congressional intent,[132] and despite the literal statutory text, regulations effectively provide that recently acquired stock will not be treated as "hot stock" or boot "if the controlled corporation is a [member of the distributing corporation's SAG] at any time after the acquisition (but prior to the distribution)."[133] Under this interpretation, additional controlled corporation shares acquired by the distributing corporation in a taxable transaction within the five-year period will not be treated as boot if the distributing corporation already has both §368(c) control and the controlled corporation is a member of the parent's SAG for §355(b)(3) purposes, or if the distributing corporation has §368(c) control and the additional acquired shares cause the controlled corporation to become a member of the parent's SAG.[134] Thus, under these regulations §355(a)(3)(B) should play an even more limited role. Recently acquired controlled corporation stock will be treated as boot only in cases where the distributing corporation's control—even after purchasing the recent shares—meets the §368(c) control definition, but does not satisfy the control test as defined in §1504(a) for purposes of identifying the SAG.

---

130. I.R.C. §355(b)(2)(D).
131. Treas. Reg. §1.355-3(b)(2)(iv); Prop. Treas. Reg. §1.355-3(b)(3)(ii).
132. 73 Fed. Reg. 75,946, 75,946 (Dec. 15, 2008) (preamble to final and temporary §1.355-2T regulations).
133. Treas. Reg. §1.355-2(g)(2).
134. See, e.g., Treas. Reg. §1.355-2(g)(5), ex. 2.

The application of these two different definitions of control within the same statute adds unnecessary complexity to an already complex provision. Congress should rethink its control definitions for §355 purposes, and perhaps use this as an opportunity to reassess more generally the value added to Subchapter C by the different sets of control definitions in §§368(c) and 1504(a).

Basis in the Stock or Securities Received

In the case of split-offs and split-ups, each of which involves an *exchange* of stock or securities by the shareholder or security holder, §358(a) provides that the basis of the stock or securities received shall be the same as the stock or securities surrendered, decreased in the amount of any boot received and increased by the amount of gain or amount treated as a dividend. With regard to spin-offs, §358(c) deems the transaction to be an exchange in which the stock or securities of the distributing corporation retained is viewed first as surrendered and then received back in the exchange. The effect of both of the §358 basis rules is to allocate the old basis over all of the stock or securities owned after the distribution in accordance with fair market values on the date of distribution.

TAX CONSEQUENCES TO THE CORPORATION

A corporation distributing stock or securities of a controlled subsidiary in a transaction meeting the requirements of §355 generally will recognize no gain or loss upon the distribution. Lest there be any doubt, §355(c)(3) explicitly states that the general recognition rules in §§311 and 336 that otherwise would apply to corporate distributions will not apply to §355 distributions. Section 355(c) provides such nonrecognition for §355 distributions that are "not in pursuance of a plan of reorganization."[135] Notice that §355(c) nonrecognition technically applies only to tax-free divisions that are not also "divisive reorganizations" under §368(a)(1)(D). Similar nonrecognition is provided to the distributing corporation in a Type D divisive reorganization via §361(c), and §361(c)(4) explicitly states that §311 shall not apply. If any appreciated property, other than stock or securities in the controlled corporation, is distributed as boot in connection with the §355 separation distribution, the corporation will be required to recognize

---

135. I.R.C. §355(c)(1).

gain upon the distribution of the boot.[136] Similar treatment is provided in §361 for boot distributed in a divisive Type D reorganization.[137]

Generally speaking, the tax consequences to the distributing corporation will be the same regardless of whether the transaction is a Type D divisive reorganization or a tax-free division not classified as a reorganization. One notable exception, however, is the treatment of certain liabilities. In a Type D divisive reorganization, the distributing corporation may be required to report capital gain to the extent that the liabilities transferred exceed the adjusted basis of the property pursuant to §357(c).[138]

Corporations planning a divisive transaction often will contribute assets to a new subsidiary immediately before distributing the subsidiary's stock to its shareholders. If the transaction qualifies as a Type D reorganization, the corporation is entitled to nonrecognition on its transfer of assets in exchange for subsidiary stock under §361. Even if the transaction technically is not a Type D reorganization, the corporation transferring assets to a new subsidiary in exchange for stock should be eligible for nonrecognition treatment under §351. Recall, however, that the transferors must have control immediately after the exchange in order to qualify for §351 nonrecognition.[139] Special provisions in §351(c) ensure the corporate transferor that the control test is not violated if the stock received in the initial §351 exchange is distributed to its shareholders.[140] Moreover, in the case of such a §355 distribution following a §351 exchange, the control required by the shareholders is reduced to 50% control, rather than the 80% control that would otherwise be required under §368(c).[141] The reduced control requirement offers greater flexibility to corporations planning spin-off transactions.

---

136. I.R.C. §355(c)(2).

137. I.R.C. §361(c)(2).

138. These are the same §357 rules that apply in the case of §351 exchanges. A detailed discussion of §357 appears in Chapter 4. Rev. Rul. 78-442, 1978-2 C.B. 143 clarifies that §357(c) gain required to be recognized will not prevent the transaction from satisfying the trade or business requirements under §355(b)(2)(C). Rev. Rul. 2007-8, 2007-1 C.B. 469 clarifies that §357(c) does not apply to *acquisitive* Type D reorganizations. See discussion of acquisitive Type D reorganizations in Chapter 12.

139. For discussion of the §351 control test, see Chapter 4. To the extent that §351 applies, the §362(e) loss limitation provisions added by Congress in 2004 may also apply. See discussion of §362(e) overlaps with tax-free reorganization rules in Chapter 12, and general discussion of the §362(e) rules in Chapter 4.

140. Special rules also provide that if the corporation forms a new subsidiary under §351 and distributes the subsidiary stock to its shareholders pursuant to §355, the fact that the shareholders dispose of all or part of the new subsidiary stock, or that the new subsidiary issues additional shares, is disregarded in determining control for purposes of the §351 exchange. I.R.C. §351(c)(2).

141. I.R.C. §368(a)(2)(H).

Special Corporate Gain Recognition Rules: Preventing Corporate Escape from *General Utilities* Repeal

Since the repeal of *General Utilities*, corporations have focused upon using §355 as the primary remaining exception to the general rule requiring corporate recognition of gain or loss upon the distribution of appreciated property. Responding to this potential loophole, Congress added two special provisions requiring the recognition of gain upon certain distributions of stock or securities in a controlled corporation. Both of these special provisions, found in §355(d) and (e), deny tax-free treatment to the distributing corporation and yet retain tax-free treatment for the shareholder distributees as long as the distribution otherwise meets the requirements of §355. This bifurcated approach confirms that the primary focus of these special provisions is not to acknowledge the "mere change in form" reflected in divisive transactions but rather to prevent corporate abuse of §355 as a way of bypassing the repeal of *General Utilities*.

a) Disguised Sales: §355(d)

Absent special restrictions to §355 nonrecognition, a corporation might convert an otherwise taxable sale of a controlling interest in a corporation into a tax-free sale through use of §355 nonrecognition distributions. Imagine, for example, a holding company (T) with two subsidiaries, T-1 and T-2. Unrelated corporations X and Y each acquire 50% of T's stock from the T shareholders for cash. Immediately thereafter, T liquidates, distributing the T-1 stock to X and the T-2 stock to Y.

In this transaction, the holding company (T) effectively is selling its subsidiaries, T-1 and T-2, in a transaction that otherwise would trigger a corporate level gain to T.[142] T's liquidation ordinarily would trigger a corporate level gain under §336.[143] Notice, however, that the transaction is designed to meet the requirements of §355. The distributing corporation (T) is distributing solely stock of two controlled corporations (T-1 and T-2) to its shareholders, X and Y. Prior to the enactment of §355(d), this hypothetical transaction was eligible for §355 nonrecognition to both the shareholders receiving the distribution, X and Y, and the distributing corporation (T).

---

142. Since X and Y corporations are unrelated, their purchases will not be combined, and the transaction cannot be a §338 QSP eligible for a §338(h)(10) election that would eliminate the corporate level taxable gain. For a discussion of §338, see Chapter 10.

143. For a discussion of liquidations, see Chapter 8.

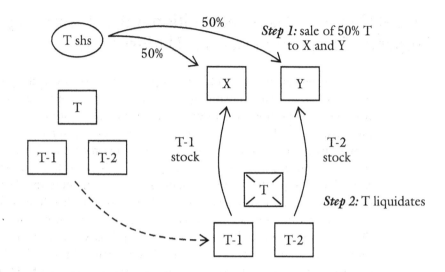

Congress responded to this type of "disguised sale" transaction by adding §355(d).[144] Legislative history accompanying §355(d) notes a congressional intent "to prevent taxpayers from using section 355 to dispose of subsidiaries in sale-like transactions, or to obtain a fair market value stepped-up basis for future dispositions without incurring a corporate-level tax."[145]

Under §355(d), distributions of certain "disqualified stock" will trigger recognition of gain to the distributing corporation, contrary to the general corporate level nonrecognition rule in §355(c)(1). Briefly summarized, stock in the distributing corporation itself, or stock in a corporation controlled by the distributing corporation (its subsidiaries), is considered "disqualified stock" under §355(d) if it was acquired by purchase within the five-year period ending on the date of the distribution.[146] Distribution of such disqualified stock is not a qualified distribution for purposes of §355(c)(2). As such, the distribution will trigger gain to the distributing corporation as if the stock were sold to the distributee shareholders at fair market value.[147] The §355(d) rules do not alter the nonrecognition available to the shareholder distributees, but T now will be taxable upon the distribution of its T-1 and T-2 stock to X and Y.

The conference report accompanying §355(d) explicitly invited the Treasury Department to promulgate regulations "to exclude from the provision transactions that do not violate the purposes of the provision"; in

---

144. Revenue Reconciliation Act of 1990, Pub. L. No. 101-508, §1132(a) (codified at I.R.C. §355(d)).

145. H.R. Rep. No. 101-881, 341 (1990).

146. I.R.C. §355(d)(3). As defined in §355(d)(5), "purchase" generally includes any acquisition other than property received in certain nonrecognition exchanges or with a transferred basis. Put differently, the "disqualified stock" definition focuses on stock acquired in a taxable transaction.

147. I.R.C. §355(d)(1), (c)(2).

other words, it authorized the Treasury Department to depart from the literal statutory text.[148] The report further announced that "[t]he purposes of [§355(d)] are not violated if . . . The effect of the distribution is neither (1) to increase ownership in the distributing corporation or any controlled corporation by persons who have directly or indirectly acquired stock within the prior five years, nor (2) to provide a basis step-up with respect to the stock of any controlled corporation."[149] Pursuant to this authority, Treasury Department regulations offer examples of transactions that will not be considered "disqualified distributions" for purposes of §355(d), even though the transactions otherwise fit within the language of the statute.[150]

b) The Anti-"*Morris Trust*" Rules: §355(e)

In another reaction to transactions designed to prevent recognition of corporate level gain, Congress added §355(e), which has come to be known as the "*Morris Trust*" rule, in reference to the early case that ultimately stimulated this statutory response. Commissioner v. W. Morris Trust[151] involved the merger of a state bank into a national bank. One barrier to the proposed merger was an insurance division operated for many years by the state bank—federal banking law prohibited national banks from engaging in insurance operations. To facilitate the merger, the state bank spun off its insurance operations by transferring them to a new subsidiary and immediately distributing stock in this new subsidiary to its shareholders in a transaction otherwise qualifying as a Type D divisive reorganization. The stock distribution included as part of the Type D reorganization also otherwise qualified for nonrecognition under §355. As planned, the state bank was then merged into the national bank in a Type A reorganization. The Fourth Circuit in Morris Trust gave its blessing to the tax-free divisive reorganization preceding the merger. The Morris Trust transaction offered a blueprint for transaction planners who wish to spin off unwanted assets in a Type D reorganization just prior to a tax-free acquisitive reorganization. If effective, target corporations could transfer *less than* substantially all of their assets and still be eligible for tax-free nonrecognition in the acquisition of the desired assets that followed.

The structure of §355(e) is similar to that of §355(d). If the §355(e) rules are triggered, the distribution of stock or securities will not be a distribution of qualified property eligible for §355(c)(1) nonrecognition to the distributing corporation. The shareholder distributees, on the other hand, still will be eligible for tax-free treatment as long as the distribution

---

148. H.R. Conf. Rep. No. 101-964, 1092 (1990).
149. Id. At 1093.
150. Treas. Reg. §1.355-6(b)(3)(vi).
151. 367 F.2d 794 (4th Cir. 1966).

otherwise meets the requirements of §355. Briefly summarized, the corporate level gain recognition rules are triggered by a distribution that is "part of a plan (or series of related transactions) pursuant to which 1 or more persons acquire" a 50% or greater interest in the distributing corporation or any controlled corporation.[152] Acquisition of a 50% or greater interest during the four-year period beginning two years before the date of the distribution is *presumed* to be part of such a plan unless the contrary can be established.[153]

A related provision included along with §355(e) was §355(f), which provides that §355 will not apply to a distribution from one member to another member of an affiliated group if the distribution was part of a plan for one or more persons *outside* the group to acquire a 50% or greater interest as described in §355(e).

Subparts (d), (e), and (f) of §355 are controversial and complex. In large part, these complexities stem from §355's multiple purposes. The §355 rules simultaneously attempt to provide tax-free treatment to "mere changes in form" but not to "disguised sales," to prevent the shareholders from bailing out corporate earnings and profits as capital gains, *and* to prevent the distributing corporation from escaping corporate level recognition, thus effectively escaping the repeal of *General Utilities.* Congress is packing a lot into one statutory provision.

For many years prior to the enactment of §355(e), *Morris Trust*-type transactions had been blessed by the Service, and used regularly by taxpayers, as a technique to spin off a target corporation's unwanted assets prior to a tax-free reorganization. From the beginning, practitioners argued that the new provision swept too broadly, extending far beyond the "abusive" transactions that provided the impetus for §355(e).[154] These "abusive" transactions involved highly leveraged transactions, in which the purchasing corporation became responsible for substantial target corporation debts.[155] Nevertheless, §355(e) extends more generally to 50% or greater changes in interest in the distributing or the controlled corporation. Of greatest concern to taxpayers was the meaning of the vague "plan (or series of related transactions)"

---

152. I.R.C. §355(e)(2)(A).

153. I.R.C. §355(e)(2)(B).

154. *See, e.g.,* Mark J. Silverman and Lisa M. Zarlenga, Proposed Section 355(e) Regulations: Broadening the Definition of a Plan, 87 Tax Notes 117, 118 n.10 (2000) ("Section 355(e) is a poorly drafted statute based on flawed principles.... Section 355(e) was aimed at certain abusive transactions ... one feature [of which is] that the corporation to be acquired borrows money (or assumes a large amount of debt) and distributes ... The proceeds of such debt to its parent before a spin-off.").

155. The most frequently mentioned among these "abusive" transactions was the Viacom/TCI merger. Viacom contributed its "unwanted" assets along with $1.7 billion in borrowed funds to a spun-off subsidiary. The subsidiary stock was distributed to shareholders pursuant to §355. In the subsequent merger, TCI was left with the wanted assets and liability for the $1.7 billion debt.

language in §355(e)(2)(A) and the requirements that would be necessary to rebut the §355(e)(2)(B) *presumption* that the distribution was part of such a plan in the case of acquisitions within two years prior to the distribution. Beginning in 1999, the Treasury Department proposed and reproposed several sets of regulations, stimulating voluminous and largely critical comments from the tax bar. Ultimately, Treas. Reg. §1.335-7 was promulgated in 2005 in what many describe as "the final chapter in the saga."[156] Although the regulations adopt a general "facts-and-circumstances" approach, they include nine specific safe harbors.[157] Of greatest relief to taxpayers, the regulations create what might be referred to as a "super-safe harbor," providing that a post-distribution acquisition (other than involving a public offering) will be considered part of a plan only if "there was *an agreement, understanding, arrangement, or substantial negotiations* regarding the acquisition . . . At some time during the 2-year period ending on the date of the distribution."[158] Although existence of some type of agreement or substantial negotiations tends to show a plan, the parties may offer rebuttal evidence indicating that the "transaction was motivated in whole or substantial part by a corporate business purpose . . . other than a business purpose to facilitate the acquisition . . . ."[159] In response to comments on the proposed regulations, the final §355(e) regulations also include a safe harbor specifically addressed to distributions and acquisitions involving public offerings.[160]

Examples

Basic Separations

1. a. Shareholders A and B each own 50% of the outstanding common stock of Corporation C, which has been operating a flower delivery and a singing telegram business for ten years. The flower delivery business assets have an aggregate basis of $100,000 and a fair market value of $500,000 and the singing telegram business assets have an aggregate basis of $75,000 and a fair market value of $300,000. Shareholders A and B each have a basis in the C shares of $25,000.

---

156. T.D. 9198, 70 Fed. Reg. 20,279 (Apr. 19, 2005) (final regulations under §355(e)). Commentators who had been critical of both the statute and early regulatory efforts praised the final regulations. See, e.g., Mark J. Silverman and Lisa M. Zarlenga, Anti-Morris Trust Plan Regulations: The Final Chapter in the Saga, 110 Tax Notes 967 (2006) ("plan regulations have evolved from an extremely rigid set of rules that defined the term 'plan' broadly to include the intent of either party without regard to whether there had been any bilateral discussions or negotiations to a very administrable set of rules that reflect both the purpose of section 355(e) and business realities").

157. Treas. Reg. §1.355-7(b)(1) (general facts-and-circumstances rule); Treas. Reg. §1.355-7(d)(1)-(9) (safe harbors).

158. Treas. Reg. §1.355-7(b)(2) (emphasis added).

159. *Id.*

160. Treas. Reg. §1.355-7(d)(6).

Because each of its operations requires different types of management skills and has different inventory requirements, Corporation C's Board of Directors has decided to separate the two businesses. To achieve this result, C first transfers its flower delivery business assets to Newco, a newly formed subsidiary, in exchange for all of Newco's stock. Newco will continue operating the flower delivery business. Immediately thereafter, C makes a pro rata distribution of the Newco stock to shareholders A and B. What are the tax consequences of this transaction to shareholders A and B and to Corporation C?

b. Assume instead that Corporation C itself had been operating only the singing telegram business, but had long been operating its flower delivery business through Oldco, a wholly owned subsidiary. C now makes a pro rata distribution of its Oldco stock to shareholders A and B. What are the tax consequences to Corporation C and shareholders A and B?

c. What if shareholders A and B were each required to surrender one-half of their C shares in exchange for the Newco shares in Example 1a?

d. Would your answer to Example 1a differ if Corporation C instead transferred its flower delivery business assets to Newco 1 and its singing telegram business to Newco 2 in exchange for all of the stock of Newco 1 and 2, respectively, and thereafter distributed all of the Newco 1 and Newco 2 stock to shareholders A and B in exchange for all of their Corporation C shares?

e. Would your answer to Example 1a differ if Corporation C had transferred only the real estate associated with the flower delivery operation to Newco in exchange for all of the Newco stock and subsequently distributed the Newco stock pro rata to shareholders A and B?

Shareholder Conflicts, Boot, and Other Matters

2. Corporation N is a magazine publisher, publishing largely sports magazines. It recently acquired a highly controversial, politically incorrect magazine in a tax-free reorganization. Shareholder group A, which holds 20% of N's stock, is quite upset and threatening to sell its N shares. Shareholder group B, which holds the remaining 80%, does not object to the recent acquisition. In response to this conflict, Corporation N transfers the new magazine business assets to Newco in exchange for all of the Newco stock and subsequently distributes the Newco stock to shareholder group B and cash to shareholder group A. What are the tax consequences to Corporation N and the two shareholder groups?

3. Corporation D is a toy manufacturing company, with two distinct business operations. One division manufactures children's toys and the other manufactures games and puzzles designed for adults. D has owned and operated each of these businesses for at least ten years. D transfers its adult

division to Newco, a newly formed subsidiary, and immediately thereafter transfers the Newco stock to its shareholders. Within two weeks of the distribution, 90% of the Newco shareholders sell their Newco stock to a purchasing corporation interested in getting into the adult game and puzzle business. The sale transaction was not prearranged at the time of the initial spin-off. What are the tax consequences of the spin-off transaction and the subsequent sale to D and its shareholders?

4. Shareholder A is the sole owner of Corporation X, which operates funeral homes in small communities a, b, and c. Corporation X's key, and only full-time, employee at the community c location threatened to quit and start a competing business. Loss of this key employee and subsequent competition from another funeral home in this small community would have a significant adverse impact on Corporation X's profits. Corporation X contributes all assets related to the community c location to Newco, a newly formed subsidiary, in exchange for Newco stock. Immediately thereafter, Corporation X distributes all of the Newco stock to shareholder A, who immediately sells 49% of the Newco stock to the key employee, pursuant to a prearranged plan, for cash and notes. What are the tax consequences of these transactions to Corporation X and shareholder A?

5. Corporation F has owned and operated several diners in city Z for over five years. F's wholly owned subsidiary (S), in turn, wholly owns three separate subsidiaries (S1, S2, and S3), which have been engaged in the manufacture of soft drinks for over five years. Each of the subsidiaries performs an essential part of the soft drink manufacturing business. Although none of the subsidiaries alone would be viewed as engaged in the active conduct of a trade or business for purposes of §355(b), the three subsidiaries together would be considered as conducting such a trade or business. F distributes all of its S stock to the F shareholders. Would this transaction meet the §355(b) active trade or business requirements?

Explanations

1. a. The transaction described in this Example is a basic spin-off. The initial exchange creating Newco will be tax-free to Corporation C and Newco under §§351 and 1032. Thus, under §358 the Newco stock in Corporation C's hands will have the same aggregate basis that the flower delivery business assets had before the exchange — $100,000. The flower delivery business assets will have a substituted basis of $100,000 in Newco's hands under §362. In other words, these assets retain their historic basis.[161]

---

161. See Chapter 4 for a discussion of §§351, 362, and 1032.

The value of the Newco shares presumably is the same as the $500,000 value of the assets contributed by Corporation C. Thus, shareholders A and B have each received a distribution worth $250,000. Ordinarily, a distribution of stock other than the corporation's own stock would be taxable to the recipient shareholders pursuant to §301.[162] If this distribution qualifies under §355, however, shareholders A and B will report no gain or loss upon receipt of the Newco shares pursuant to §355(a). Their basis in the Newco shares received would be a substituted basis determined under §358. Under §358(a), the basis in property received in a tax-free exchange shall be the same as the property exchanged. In this spin-off, however, shareholders A and B have not "exchanged" anything in return for their Newco shares. Nevertheless, under §358(c), shareholders A and B will be regarded as if their shares in the distributing corporation were surrendered and then received back. In other words, they are viewed as having exchanged their C shares with a basis of $25,000 for a return of the same C shares along with the Newco shares. Thus, shareholder A and B's aggregate basis in the Corporation C and Newco shares is the same $25,000 basis they had before. This $25,000 now will have to be allocated between the C shares and the Newco shares. This allocation will be based upon the relative fair market values immediately after the distribution. Thus, five-eighths ($500,000 fair market value of Newco shares/$800,000 total value of Newco and Corporation C shares) will be allocated to the Newco stock and three-eighths ($300,000 value of Corporation C remaining after distribution/$800,000 total value of Newco and Corporation C shares) will be allocated to the Corporation C stock.

Ordinarily, the distribution of appreciated property is taxable to the distributing corporation under §311.[163] If the distribution qualifies, §355(c) provides that Corporation C will not be taxed upon the $400,000 gain realized upon the distribution of Newco stock with a basis of $100,000 and a fair market value of $500,000. The flower delivery business assets would still retain their historic basis in Newco's hands.

This transaction appears to meet the statutory requirements of §355. Corporation C was in control of Newco immediately before the exchange, both corporations are engaged in the active conduct of a trade or business immediately after the exchange, both the flower delivery and singing telegram business have at least a five-year history, Corporation C has distributed all of its Newco stock, and the

---

162. See Chapter 5 for a discussion of the §301 nonliquidating distribution rules.
163. See Chapter 5 for a discussion of the nonliquidating distribution rules.

transaction does not appear to be principally a device for the distribution of C's earnings and profits.

There may be a problem, however, in meeting the nonstatutory business purpose test. The need to separate the two businesses due to different management requirements may be a perfectly appropriate business purpose. The regulations require, however, that the distribution of stock also have a business purpose. Since the initial creation of Newco without the subsequent distribution arguably fulfills the stated business purpose, this distribution may not be eligible for §355 treatment unless the corporation provides an additional business purpose for distributing the Newco shares to A and B.

b. Although §355 transactions frequently include a new subsidiary, a newly created subsidiary is not necessary. Thus, assuming the business purpose issue is resolved in the taxpayers' favor, the distribution of Oldco stock also would be eligible for §355 treatment as provided in the answer to Example 1a.

c. This variation is an illustration of a basic split-off, with similar tax consequences. The key difference in the transactions is that shareholders A and B now have each received $250,000 worth of Newco shares in exchange for one-half of their C shares. Ordinarily, such a distribution would be treated as a redemption and would be taxable to the shareholders pursuant to the rules in §302 and to the corporation under §311.[164] Assuming the transaction meets the business purpose hurdle discussed in the answer to Example 1a, however, A and B should be entitled to nonrecognition upon receipt of the Newco shares under §355(a) and the corporation should be entitled to nonrecognition under §355(c). The shareholders' basis in the Newco shares will again be determined under §358. Unlike the spin-off in Example 1a, however, the shareholders now have actually exchanged shares. At first blush, it might appear that the substituted basis would be only $12,500 (one-half of the $25,000 basis of each shareholder in the C shares exchanged). However, §358(b)(2) provides a special rule for §355 cases under which the allocation of basis shall take into account not only the property permitted to be received without gain recognition, but also stock of the distributing corporation which is retained. In other words, the substituted basis for allocation purposes will include the full $25,000 basis that shareholders A and B had in the Corporation C shares and the basis will be allocated between the Newco and C shares as described in the answer to Example 1a.

d. This variation now illustrates a basic split-up. Since shareholders A and B are exchanging *all* of their C shares in exchange for the Newco

---

164. See Chapter 6 for a discussion of redemptions.

stock, this transaction is effectively a liquidation distribution, which ordinarily would be taxed to the shareholders under §331 and to the corporation under §336.[165] If the transaction overcomes the business purpose hurdle described in the answer to Example 1a, however, the shareholders again should be entitled to nonrecognition under §355(a) and the corporation should be entitled to nonrecognition under §355(c). The shareholders' basis in the Newco shares again would be determined under §358. The substituted basis rule works more simply in this case to reach the same $25,000 substituted basis result. Since all of the shares were exchanged in this variation, one need not resort to the metaphysical "deeming" rules of §358(b)(2) or §358(c).

e. A transaction in which Corporation C transfers only the real estate associated with the flower business should appear quite suspicious. This transaction is unlikely to qualify for §355 nonrecognition for several reasons. First of all, the real estate held by Newco immediately after the distribution probably is not sufficient to constitute the active conduct of a trade or business. Second, the transaction does now appear to be a device for the distribution of earnings and profits.

2. This transaction represents a spin-off of the new magazine business. Surely the cash received by shareholder group A will be taxable pursuant to the §301 distribution rules. The distribution of Newco shares to shareholder group B raises several issues under §355. Corporation N had control of Newco immediately before the distribution, as required by §355(a)(1)(A). Moreover, it appears that both Corporations N and Newco will be engaged in the active conduct of a trade or business immediately after the distribution. Recall, however, that §355(b)(2)(B) also requires a trade or business "actively conducted throughout the five-year period ending on the date of the distribution." The statute goes on to require in §355(b)(2)(C) that this trade or business not have been acquired *in a taxable transaction* within the same five-year period. The facts in this question indicate that the new magazine business was acquired by Corporation N in a *tax-free reorganization*. Thus, even though Corporation N itself has not been operating the new business for five years, the business should be considered a business with the necessary five-year history. The fact that some shareholders are receiving cash and others are receiving Newco stock makes this a non-pro rata distribution. This too should not prevent the transaction from qualifying for §355 nonrecognition since the statute explicitly states in §355(a)(2)(A) that the distribution need not be pro rata. Resolving conflicts among shareholders is among the acceptable business purposes for a §355 distribution. Thus,

---

165. See Chapter 8 for a discussion of liquidations.

the distribution of Newco stock to the group B shareholders should be eligible for nonrecognition to the shareholders under §355(a) and to the distributing corporation under §355(c).

3. This transaction appears to be a rather staightforward spin-off, which should be eligible for §355 nonrecognition treatment. If so, the initial receipt of the Newco stock would be tax-free to the D shareholders. Pursuant to §358, they would allocate a portion of their basis in the D shares to the Newco shares received in the distribution. Those shareholders participating in the subsequent sale of Newco stock would be taxable, however, upon the subsequent sale of the Newco shares. To compute gain or loss, these shareholders would subtract the portion of their original D stock basis that was allocated to the Newco shares.

   On the other hand, the sale of 90% of the Newco stock within such a short time after the distribution raises questions as to whether or not the transaction was a "device for the distribution of earnings and profits." The statute itself provides, in §355(a)(1)(B), that the mere fact of a subsequent sale "shall not be construed to mean that the transaction was used principally as such a device." On the other hand, the regulations do consider such a sale to be "evidence of a device." The regulations further suggest that the greater the percentage of stock sold and the shorter the time period between the distribution and the subsequent sale, the stronger the evidence of a device for the distribution of earnings and profits.[166] These factors point toward a finding that the transaction was used as a device. At the same time, the corporation and its shareholders will point out that the transaction was not prearranged. Such a prearranged sale would have been considered *substantial* evidence of a device under the same regulation. In the end, whether the transaction was used as a device will be determined based upon *all* the facts and circumstances. If the transaction is viewed as a "device," the initial shareholder distribution would be governed by §301. Assuming sufficient earnings and profits, the full fair market value of the Newco shares received would be a taxable dividend and the shareholders would take a fair market value basis in the shares under §301(d). Although the subsequent sale of shares by 90% of the shareholders would technically be a taxable event, there should be no further gain if the shareholders sell the stock for fair market value. Under the "qualified dividend income" rules, the stakes from the shareholder's perspective are lower than they were prior to 2003. Regardless of whether the shareholders are treated as receiving dividend income under §301 or gain from the sale of a capital asset, the applicable tax rates are likely to be the same. On the other hand, §355 treatment would provide them a tax-free recovery of capital for a portion of their

---

166. Treas. Reg. §1.355-2(d)(2)(iii).

original basis in the D shares that would not be available if the initial distribution was treated as a dividend.

Corporation D should be eligible for nonrecognition on the contribution of assets in exchange for Newco stock under either §361 or 351. Its basis in the Newco stock will be the same basis that it previously had in the assets contributed under §358. If the transaction qualifies under §355, both D and its shareholders will be eligible for nonrecognition upon the distribution of Newco stock. If the transaction does *not* qualify under §355, D will be required to report gain on the distribution of the Newco stock under §311.[167]

4. If this transaction qualifies as a tax-free spin-off, shareholder A will not recognize any gain on the receipt of Newco stock from Corporation X pursuant to §355(a), nor will Corporation X recognize any gain on the distribution of the Newco stock pursuant to §355(c). Basis in the Newco shares will be determined under §358, and shareholder A will report capital gain or loss from the sale of Newco shares to the employee. If the transaction does not qualify under §355, and presuming sufficient earnings and profits to cover the distribution, shareholder A will report the fair market value of the Newco stock received as §301(c) dividend and take a fair market value basis in the Newco shares under §301(d). Although the subsequent sale technically is a taxable event, there should be no further taxable gain if shareholder A receives a fair market value price for the Newco shares. Corporation X's distribution of the Newco stock would be governed by §311.

This transaction should raise serious questions about whether the transaction was "used principally as a device for the distribution" of earnings and profits under §355(a)(1)(B). Although the mere fact of a subsequent sale to the employee should not be construed to mean that the transaction was used principally as a device for distributing earnings and profits, numerous other "device factors" are present. First, the distribution is pro rata to a sole shareholder. According to the regulations, such a distribution "presents the *greatest potential for the avoidance of the dividend provisions*" and should be regarded as evidence of a device. Treas. Reg. §1.355-2(d)(2)(ii). Second, the immediate sale of a substantial amount of stock is evidence of a device. The regulations further provide that the "greater the percentage of the stock sold" and the "shorter the period of time between the distribution and the sale or exchange, the stronger the evidence of device." Treas. Reg. §1.355-2(d)(2)(iii). Moreover, since it was pursuant to a prearranged plan, the subsequent sale is *substantial* evidence of a device. Id.

---

167. For an interesting case analyzing a similar transaction that did involve a pre-arranged plan, see South Tulsa Pathology Laboratory v. Comm'r, 118 T.C. 84 (2002).

These device factors must be balanced against nondevice factors under a facts and circumstances balancing test. On the "nondevice factor" side, shareholder A will point to the corporate business purposes of the transaction: avoiding loss of a key employee and the threat of competition. Treas. Reg. §1.355-2(d)(3)(ii). Note, however, the regulatory caution that "the stronger the evidence of device . . . , the stronger the corporate business purpose required to prevent the determination that the transaction was used principally as a device." Id. In addition, the alleged business purposes may not be sufficient for purposes of §355 if the "corporate business purpose can be achieved through a nontaxable transaction that does not involve the distribution of stock of a controlled corporation and which is neither impractical nor unduly expensive." Treas. Reg. §1.355-2(b)(3). In an example similar to the transaction here, the regulations found that the transaction should be considered to have been used as a device, noting that the corporation *could* have achieved its business purpose by directly issuing shares to the employee. Treas. Reg. §1.355-2(b)(4), ex. 8. Surprisingly, in a case presenting facts remarkably similar to those here and in Example 1, the Tax Court ruled that the transactions *did* qualify for §355 tax-free treatment. Pulliam v. Comm'r, T.C. Memo 1997-274, 73 T.C.M. 3052 (1997), *nonacq.* 1999-1 I.R.B. 5. In a rather weak effort to distinguish its case from the regulatory example, the Tax Court noted that the taxpayers before the court *thought* that they were required by state law to have the stock distributed to the sole shareholder, since only individual licensed funeral directors and embalmers could hold stock in an incorporated funeral business. Given the reduced tax consequences at stake in the "qualified dividend income" world, the IRS might be less inclined to vigorously litigate cases such as this one, however.

5. Prior to the enactment of §355(b)(3), this transaction would not have satisfied the §355(b) trade or business requirement because S itself did not operate the soft drink business, and it did not control a single corporation that was engaged in the active conduct of a trade or business. For purposes of determining whether a corporation meets the §355(b)(2)(A) active conduct of a trade or business requirement, however, §355(b)(3)(A) now treats all members of the corporation's separate affiliated group (SAG)—which includes any corporation that would be a member of the corporation's §1504(a) affiliated group if the corporation were the common parent—as one corporation. Under this new provision, the activities of S and all of its subsidiaries are viewed as one corporation. Thus, the active trade or business requirement should be considered satisfied. See, e.g., Prop. Treas. Reg. §1.355-3(d)(2), ex. 5.

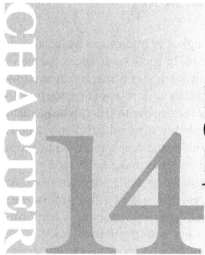

Recapitalization and Other Corporate Restructuring

INTRODUCTION

The reorganization definition in §368(a)(1) includes two types of transactions involving the restructuring of only *one* corporation, as opposed to an acquisition joining two or more corporations or a division resulting in two or more corporations. In each of these restructuring transactions, the shareholders exchange stock or securities for stock or securities in the same corporation.[1] As with any corporate reorganization, the participating shareholders will not report gain or loss upon the receipt of stock and certain securities in the reorganization transaction pursuant to §354, except to the extent that they receive taxable boot under §356. The shareholders' basis in the shares received will be governed by the substituted basis rules of §358. Similarly, there will be no gain or loss to the corporation.[2]

Various factors might encourage a corporation to implement a recapitalization plan. The corporation might recapitalize in order to simplify its capital structure.[3] Or the corporation might recapitalize to create stock that

---

1. In the case of a Type F reorganization, the old corporate enterprise (the predecessor) technically may be transformed into a new corporate entity (the successor).
2. The corporation simply receives its own stock or securities. This receipt should be nontaxable under either §§361 or 1032.
3. See, e.g., Rev. Rul. 77-238, 1977-2 C.B. 115 (recapitalization to encourage the conversion of preferred stock into common stock to simplify capital structure); Rev. Rul. 72-57, 1972-1 C.B. 103 (subsidiary corporation simplifies capital structure by eliminating minority shareholders).

will be more attractive in a public offering[4] or to improve its financial condition by restructuring its debt obligations. In some cases, the corporation recapitalizes in order to increase the equity interest of management employees who have made a significant contribution to the corporate enterprise.

In other cases, the corporation might recapitalize to reflect management changes upon the retirement of one of its key shareholders. For example, upon retirement of the corporation's founder, the corporation might adopt a plan of recapitalization in which the founder exchanges her voting common stock interest in return for newly issued nonvoting preferred stock. As a result of the recapitalization, the shareholder retains a financial interest in the corporation through her preferred stock, but eliminates her management interest previously reflected in her voting common stock.[5] One might initially think that the §302 redemption rules should apply to this retirement of the shareholder's voting common stock. Despite appearances, however, this is not a redemption. In a redemption, the corporation must acquire its stock from the shareholder in return for *property*,[6] which is defined to exclude the corporation's own stock.[7] When a corporation acquires old stock and issues new stock in return, the exchange will be treated as a recapitalization under §368(a)(1)(E), and not as a redemption under §302.

The simplest of the two internal restructuring reorganizations is a Type F reorganization involving a "mere change in identity, form, or place of organization of one corporation, however effected."[8] For example, the corporation might choose to change its incorporation from New Jersey to Delaware.[9] The Type E reorganization is slightly more complex. A Type E reorganization is defined, without further elaboration, as a "recapitalization." Each of these reorganizations will be considered in this chapter.

A third related type of corporate reorganization, a Type G reorganization, involves the restructuring of a corporation in bankruptcy. The Type G reorganization permits more flexibility than the E and F types and, unlike the E and F internal restructuring reorganizations, may involve more than one corporation. The insolvent corporation may be acquired by another

---

4. See, e.g., Rev. Rul. 77-479, 1977-2 C.B. 311. A "parent" corporation with less than 80% voting control might also engage in a preliminary recapitalization, converting the shareholders' voting common stock into a new class of "high vote" common stock, thus providing the parent with the 80% voting control necessary for a successful §355 spin-off. See Rev. Rul. 69-407, 1969-2 C.B. 50.

5. See, e.g., Rev. Rul. 74-269, 1974-1 C.B. 87.

6. I.R.C. §317(b).

7. I.R.C. §317(a). For a more detailed discussion of corporate redemptions, see Chapter 5. Notice, however, that the definition of "property" in §317(a) applies only for purposes of Part I of Subchapter C (§§301 through 318). Thus, the definition of property applies for redemption and distribution but not for reorganization purposes.

8. I.R.C. §368(a)(1)(F).

9. This was the situation in the early case of Marr v. United States, 268 U.S. 536 (1925), in which the Supreme Court held that the transaction was not a tax-free reorganization. The transaction surely would qualify today as a Type F reorganization.

corporation as part of the bankruptcy reorganization, or the insolvent corporation may be divided into several separate corporate entities in the bankruptcy reorganization. Thus, Type G reorganizations may take an acquisitive or a divisive form.

RECAPITALIZATIONS: THE TYPE E REORGANIZATION

A Stab at a Definition

Neither the Code nor the regulations provide a definition of the term "recapitalization" as used in §368(a)(1)(E). In an early reorganization case, the Supreme Court, in dicta, described recapitalization as a "reshuffling of a capital structure, within the framework of an existing corporation."[10] Although the regulations do not provide a definition, they do provide five examples of transactions that will be considered recapitalizations.[11] Deciding whether a particular transaction constitutes a recapitalization often simply involves a comparison with the illustrations provided in the regulations. The closer a transaction is to fitting the five described transactions, the more likely it is to be treated as a recapitalization.[12] Most of the examples in the Treasury regulation involve stock-for-stock transfers. Thus, shareholder exchanges of preferred stock for common stock or exchanges of common stock for preferred stock generally will be considered recapitalizations.[13] A transaction in which the corporation pays off bonds with preferred stock, as opposed to cash, is also considered a recapitalization.[14] Under appropriate circumstances, the conversion of common stock into preferred stock or preferred stock into common may constitute a recapitalization.[15]

One might imagine that a recapitalization requires an actual exchange or transfer of stock, securities, or other financial instruments. However, a simple amendment to the articles of incorporation may be a "deemed recapitalization" even if no shares actually are exchanged if "the change

---

10. Helvering v. Southwest Consolidated Corp., 315 U.S. 194, 202 (1942). This particular case involved what would now be considered a Type G reorganization. Although the Court's definition of "recapitalization" was dicta, the case continues to be frequently cited as a starting point for the definition of recapitalization.

11. Treas. Reg. §1.368-2(e).

12. Certainly, one making a case to the IRS also should be prepared to argue that the exchange results only in a change in form.

13. Treas. Reg. §1.368-2(e)(2)-(5).

14. Treas. Reg. §1.368-2(e)(1).

15. See, e.g., Rev. Rul. 77-238, 1977-2 C.B. 115.

in the outstanding stock is so substantial as to constitute, in substance, an exchange . . . in a recapitalization of the corporation."[16]

The following sections of this chapter consider numerous different exchanges that fall within the "recapitalization" definition. Some of these exchanges are non-pro rata, some change proportionate shareholder interests and otherwise may appear on the surface to be more than a "mere change in form." Again, the "change in form" rationale sounds nice in theory, but fails to account, in practice, for several nonrecognition transactions.[17] Keep in mind that none of the exchanges described here will be eligible for tax-free reorganization treatment unless it also meets the general business purpose requirement applicable to all reorganizations.[18]

Equity Exchanges

a) Common for Common or Preferred for Preferred

One of the simplest recapitalizations is an exchange by the shareholders of old common for new common shares or of old preferred for new preferred shares. Several changes may occur as the result of such exchanges. The new shares may have different voting rights and thus alter the proportionate voting interest of the shareholders.[19] Or, the new shares may have different preemptive rights. The corporation may have had only one class of stock before the recapitalization and have several different classes of stock after the recapitalization. In the alternative, the number of classes of common shares might be reduced. Despite these relative changes in shareholder rights, the transaction still is considered a "mere change in form" and still qualifies for nonrecognition treatment as a reorganization.

In fact, a simple exchange of common stock for common stock in the same corporation or of preferred stock for preferred stock in the same corporation is entitled to nonrecognition treatment under §1036. This provision simply states that "no gain or loss shall be recognized if common stock in a corporation is exchanged solely for common stock in the same corporation, or if preferred stock in a corporation is exchanged solely for preferred stock in the same corporation."[20] Notice that §§1036 and

---

16. Rev. Rul. 56-654, 1956-2 C.B. 216 (amendment to articles increasing the per share redemption price and liquidation value of preferred stock deemed to be a recapitalization).
17. In some cases, though, a recapitalization resulting in changes in proportionate interest will result in a deemed stock dividend taxable under §305(c). See Chapter 6 for a discussion of §305(c) deemed stock dividends.
18. See Chapter 11 for a full discussion of the business purpose requirement. The continuity of proprietary interest and continuity of business enterprise tests will not be applicable in the case of recapitalizations. See section later in this chapter entitled "Application of General Reorganization Principles."
19. See, e.g., Rev. Rul. 69-407, 1969-2 C.B. 50.
20. I.R.C. §1036(a).

368(a)(1)(E) overlap in their coverage of recapitalizations involving an exchange of common for common stock or of preferred for preferred stock.[21] A simple recapitalization involving an exchange of common for common stock or preferred for preferred stock generally can be handled under §1036. If "boot" is transferred as part of a such a recapitalization, however, the reorganization provisions will "trump" §1036.[22]

At this point, one may wonder why Congress has overlapping provisions providing nonrecognition treatment to the same transaction. Notice that the overlap is not perfect. Section 1036 nonrecognition is not limited to exchanges between the corporation and its shareholders, but also applies to an exchange between two shareholders.[23] Moreover, as noted, the more complex reorganization provisions will be necessary for transactions involving boot.

b) Common Stock for Preferred Stock

When shareholders exchange old common shares for new preferred shares, they are exchanging what often is referred to as a "junior" equity interest for a "senior" equity interest in the corporation. The preferred shares are "senior" in that they typically receive priority in dividend and liquidation rights.[24] A transfer of old common shares for new preferred is an "upstream equity exchange." Although the shareholders have received a more secure equity interest in the corporation, this transfer still is considered a recapitalization representing a "mere change in form." The exchange fits within the §368(a)(1)(E) reorganization definition.[25]

A shareholder who receives preferred stock in a recapitalization must also be concerned about the possibility that certain preferred shares received will be classified as "§306 stock," which could result in dividend income upon later sale or redemption of the shares.[26] The preferred shares will be §306 stock if they were received by the shareholder in a plan of reorganization and if gain or loss was not recognized, "but only to the extent that either the effect of the transaction was substantially the same as the receipt of a stock dividend, or the stock was received in exchange for section 306

---

21. The regulations are explicit that "a transaction between a stockholder and the corporation may qualify not only under section 1036(a), but also under section 368(a)(1)(E) (recapitalization)." Treas. Reg. §1.1036-1(a).

22. See, e.g., Rev. Rul. 72-57, 1972-1 C.B. 103, modified by Rev. Rul. 78-351, 1978-2 C.B. 148.

23. See Treas. Reg. §1.1036-1(a); Rev. Rul. 72-199, 1972-1 C.B. 228.

24. Although it is common for preferred shares to be senior to common shares in dividend rights or rights to assets upon liquidation, this will not always be the case. There may be common and preferred shares with equal dividend and liquidation rights.

25. See Treas. Reg. §1.368-2(e)(3).

26. This classification is less likely to be of great concern to the shareholder under the "qualified dividend income" rules. For a complete discussion of §306 stock and the impact of these rules, see Chapter 7.

stock."[27] Under this definition, the shareholder will have §306 shares where the shareholder in a recapitalization receives preferred shares in excess of the preferred shares surrendered. In the common for preferred exchange, the receipt of preferred shares in the exchange is much like the receipt of a preferred stock dividend. Unless the receipt falls within one of the §306(b) exceptions, the stock will be §306 stock.

c) Old Preferred for New Common

When shareholders exchange old preferred stock for new common, they generally are exchanging a "senior" interest for a more "junior" interest.[28] Even though the shareholders have received an interest somewhat different from the interest they previously held, this "downstream equity exchange" still is considered a "mere change in form."[29]

d) Convertible Shares

When the articles of incorporation provide stock conversion rights, shareholders who convert their common shares into preferred shares or those who convert preferred shares into common should be eligible for tax-free reorganization treatment under §354 if the transaction qualifies as a recapitalization. The transaction will qualify as long as the exchanges are pursuant to a plan of reorganization and there is a business purpose for the conversion privilege.[30]

e) Dividend Arrearages and Other Potential §305 Issues[31]

Although a recapitalization technically is not a stock dividend, §305(c) authorized the Treasury Secretary to prescribe regulations under which any transactions, including recapitalizations, resulting in a change in the proportionate interests of shareholders will be treated as deemed stock dividends taxable under §301. Since stock distributions with respect to preferred stock generally are thought to increase the preferred stockholders' proportionate interest, §305(b)(4) provides that such stock distributions

---

27. I.R.C. §306(c)(1)(B).
28. Here, there will be no issue with respect to §306, since the definition of "§306 stock" includes only "[s]tock which is not common stock." I.R.C. §306(c)(1)(B).
29. Treas. Reg. §1.368-2(e)(2), (4). In the latter paragraph, the regulations make it clear that the transaction will be treated as a recapitalization if the preferred stock carried certain priorities regarding dividends and assets upon liquidation that the common shares do not carry.
30. For further discussion of the "plan of reorganization" and "business purpose" requirements, see Chapter 11.
31. This section will consider limited applications of §305 in the context of recapitalizations. For a more detailed discussion of §305 stock dividends, see Chapter 7.

are taxable. Recapitalizations may achieve comparable results. For example, if a corporation finds itself in arrears on dividend obligations to preferred shareholders, it may arrange a recapitalization in which the shareholders transfer their preferred stock, including the right to dividend arrearages, to the corporation in return for other stock of the corporation. Such a transfer is considered a recapitalization under §368(a)(1)(E).[32] However, if the stock received in the exchange increases the preferred shareholders' proportionate interest in the assets or earnings and profits of the corporation, the shareholders may have taxable income from a deemed stock dividend under §305(c). The regulations provide that an exchange of preferred stock with dividends in arrears for other stock increases the shareholders' proportionate interest whenever the fair market value or the liquidation preference of the new stock exceeds the issue price of the preferred stock surrendered in the exchange.[33] The amount of the deemed §305(c) distribution generally will be the lesser of (1) the amount in arrearage or (2) the excess of the fair market value of the new stock or the liquidation preference (whichever is greater) over the issue price of the stock surrendered.[34]

Assume, for example, that the corporation has preferred shares outstanding that are four years in arrears on dividends. The arrearages exceeded $20 per share and the issue price of the preferred shares was $100 per share. In a recapitalization, the shareholders exchange each old preferred share, including the right to dividend arrearages, in return for 1.2 newly authorized preferred shares. Immediately after the exchange, the new preferred shares are valued at $100 per share. Notice that the shareholders have increased their proportionate interest in the corporation since they have received $120 worth of new shares in return for the $100 issue price on each of the old shares. Each shareholder will have a $20 taxable stock dividend on each share of old preferred exchanged for new preferred.[35]

In addition to the preferred stock with dividend arrearages transaction described above, other recapitalizations may have deemed stock dividend consequences under §305(c) where the recapitalization results in a change in proportionate interests among the shareholders. Under the regulations, a recapitalization will be deemed a taxable stock distribution if "[it] is pursuant to a plan to periodically increase a shareholder's proportionate interest in the assets or earnings and profits of the corporation."[36] Notice that an *isolated* recapitalization that is not part of a periodic plan to alter the shareholders' proportionate interests in the corporation's assets or earnings and

---

32. Treas. Reg. §§1.368-2(e)(5), 1.305-7(c)(1)(ii).
33. Treas. Reg. §1.305-7(c)(1)(ii).
34. See Treas. Reg. §§1.368-2(e)(5), 1.305-7(c)(2).
35. This $20 amount is the difference between the fair market value of the stock received over the issue price of the stock surrendered pursuant to Treas. Reg. §1.305-7(c)(2).
36. Treas. Reg. §1.305-7(c)(1)(i).

profits should not result in any deemed stock dividend consequences for the shareholders.[37] Corporations frequently take advantage of this exception in the regulations for recapitalizations in which a retiring shareholder exchanges old stock for new.

Debt and Equity Exchanges

a) Debt for Equity Exchanges

i) Tax Consequences to the Debt Holders

A debt holder may receive stock in exchange for outstanding debt in a tax-free recapitalization. This type of transaction may be arranged as part of a "workout" to improve the financial condition of a troubled corporation by substituting equity interests for debt interests on the balance sheet. In fact, the first example in the regulations illustrating the definition of "recapitalization" describes a corporation with bonds outstanding that discharges the bond obligations by issuing preferred shares to the bondholders rather than paying the bonds off with cash.[38] As a result of this "downstream" exchange, the bondholders have exchanged a "senior" debt interest for a more "junior" equity interest in the form of preferred stock. The bondholders will be entitled to nonrecognition upon the exchange of their securities in return for stock under §354. Notice that §354 allows nonrecognition only where "stock or *securities*" are exchanged solely for stock or securities.[39] Thus, in order for the debt holder to qualify for nonrecognition under §354, the debt interest surrendered must be considered a "security." Short-term notes and other forms of indebtedness surrendered in the exchange that do not constitute "securities" will not be eligible for nonrecognition treatment. Although the debt holder generally is entitled to nonrecognition upon the exchange of debt for equity, §354 provides an exception to account for accrued interest on the surrendered debt. Neither §354 nor 356 will apply to the extent that "any stock, . . . securities, or other property received is attributable to interest which has accrued on securities on or after the beginning of the holder's holding period."[40] Note that §354(a)(2)(B) simply provides that the general nonrecognition rules of §354(a)(1) and the related §356 boot rules do *not* apply to that portion of the stock received in return for *interest accrued* on the debt surrendered in the exchange. This makes sense. Interest income is treated as ordinary income and typically

---

37. See, e.g., Treas. Reg. §1.305-5(d), ex. 2.

38. Treas. Reg. §1.368-2(e)(1). See also Lorch v. Comm'r, 605 F.2d 657 (2d Cir. 1979), cert. denied, 444 U.S. 1076 (1980).

39. Note the contrast to §351, which provides nonrecognition only for exchanges of property in return for stock. For a complete discussion, see Chapter 4.

40. I.R.C. §354(a)(2)(B).

is recognized for tax purposes as it is received or as it accrues under special provisions of the Code.[41] The shareholder involved in a debt-for-stock exchange should not be entitled to avoid tax on the interest income. All we know so far, then, is how *not* to treat the portion attributable to interest. Section 354 simply sends the taxpayer to the general definition of income in §61. The portion of the stock value that is received in return for accrued interest simply should be treated as ordinary income upon receipt of the stock.[42]

ii) Tax Consequences to the Corporation

Under basic cancellation of indebtedness principles, when a corporation discharges its debt obligations with stock or other assets worth less than the principal amount of the debt, the corporation will be required to report cancellation of indebtedness income.[43] Under §108, a solvent debtor corporation that "transfers . . . stock to a creditor in satisfaction of its . . . indebtedness . . . shall be treated as having satisfied the indebtedness with an amount of money equal to the fair market value of the stock."[44] In other words, if the fair market value of the stock transferred is less than the principal amount of the debt, the corporation must report cancellation of indebtedness income. If the corporate discharge of indebtedness occurs in a Title 11 bankruptcy proceeding or occurs when the corporation is insolvent, however, the corporation may exclude the cancellation of indebtedness income.[45] This exclusion will provide the corporation with only a temporary break since the corporation will be required to reduce its tax attributes, potentially resulting in increased income in later years.[46]

b) Equity for Debt Exchanges

In contrast to the "downstream" exchange described above, a shareholder might transfer his stock to the corporation in return for a debt interest in an "upstream" exchange. By exchanging stock for debt, the shareholder has converted a "junior" stock interest for a more "senior" debt interest. He now typically has a priority interest assuring his payment of interest before dividends are paid to shareholders. Moreover, he now typically stands in line ahead of the shareholders when creditors are paid off upon liquidation.

---

41. See, e.g., the original issue discount rules in §§1271-1275.
42. Amounts reflecting market discount are not immediately recognized. I.R.C. §1276(c)(2).
43. I.R.C. §61(a)(12); United States v. Kirby Lumber, 284 U.S. 1 (1931).
44. I.R.C. §108(e)(8).
45. I.R.C. §108(a)(1)(A), (B). Section 108(a) also provides more narrow exceptions for "qualified farm indebtedness," I.R.C. §108(a)(1)(C), and "qualified real property business indebtedness," I.R.C. §108(a)(1)(D).
46. See I.R.C. §108(b).

Although the exchange might technically qualify as a "recapitalization" under §368(a)(1)(E), limitations to the general shareholder nonrecognition provisions in §354 provide that the nonrecognition rules shall not apply if the principal amount of securities received exceeds the principal amount of securities surrendered, or if any securities are received and no securities are surrendered.[47] Any excess securities will be treated as taxable "boot" under §356.[48]

There is also the possibility in an "upstream" exchange of stock for debt, that the transaction may not qualify as a "recapitalization" at all. In the case of Bazley v. Commissioner,[49] a closely held family corporation arranged a plan of reorganization under which each shareholder would exchange one share of $100 par value stock in return for five shares of no par stock and new debenture bonds callable at any time. The corporation had substantial earnings and profits. The Supreme Court appears to conclude in this case that the transaction was not a tax-free reorganization *at all* since "nothing can be a recapitalization . . . unless it partakes of those characteristics of a reorganization which underlie the purpose of Congress in postponing the tax liability."[50] The Court apparently found that the distribution of debentures was a "disguised dividend," concluding that

> if the Bazley corporation had issued the debentures to Bazley and his wife without any recapitalization, it would have made a taxable distribution. Instead, these debentures were issued as part of a family arrangement, the only additional ingredient being an unrelated modification of the capital account. The debentures were found to be worth at least their principal amount, and they were virtually cash because they were callable at the will of the corporation which in this case was the will of the taxpayer.
>
> A "reorganization" which is merely a vehicle, however elaborate or elegant, for conveying earnings from accumulations to the stockholders is not a reorganization. . . .[51]

At the end of its opinion the Court further concludes that "*even if this transaction were deemed a reorganization, the facts would equally sustain the imposition of the tax on the debentures under [§356]*."[52] Whether the transaction was classified as a recapitalization or not, the debentures would still be considered taxable boot under the reorganization boot provisions. The Supreme Court's opinion in *Bazley* leaves the legal uncertainty that, in some cases,

---

47. I.R.C. §354(a)(2)(A).
48. For a further discussion of the §356 boot rules, see Chapter 11.
49. 331 U.S. 737, reh'g denied, 332 U.S. 752 (1947).
50. Id. At 741.
51. Id. At 742-743.
52. Id. At 473 (emphasis added). This result is formally incorporated into Treas. Reg. §1.301-1(l). This provision was included and redesignated in proposed regulations issued in 2019. Prop. Treas. Reg. §1.301-1(j), 84 Fed. Reg. 11,263 (May 26, 2019).

an exchange of stock for debt might fail to qualify as a reorganization at all. As a result, the exchange of stock for stock may be a taxable event and the receipt of debt will be fully taxable as a dividend governed by §301 as opposed to §356. As such, the dividend would be taxable regardless of whether or not there was any realized gain on the exchange.

c) Debt for Debt Exchanges

i) Tax Consequences to Debt Holders

Corporations sometimes restructure debt through an exchange of old debt for new debt. The new debt may provide for a reduced interest rate, a reduction in the principal amount, a delayed payment date, or other modification of terms. These debt exchanges have been especially useful to financially stressed corporations seeking a "workout" of their difficulties short of a formal declaration of bankruptcy.

In a debt-for-debt exchange, the debt holder realizes gain or loss from "the exchange of property for other property differing materially either in kind or in extent."[53] The difficulty here is determining when one debt differs "materially either in kind or extent" from another, resulting in realization under the §1001 regulations. In Cottage Savings Association v. Commissioner,[54] the Supreme Court reviewed mortgage swap transactions among various financial institutions. Cottage Savings Association exchanged mortgage participation interests for substantially identical mortgage participation interests from another lending institution. The loan interests exchanged were all similar-type, single-family residence loans with the same term to maturity, identical interest rates, and virtually identical terms and conditions. Cottage Savings deducted a loss on these exchanges. The Internal Revenue Service argued that there was no realization event since the mortgages exchanged were economic equivalents. According to the Service, the properties exchanged were not "materially different." Rejecting the government's argument, the Supreme Court adopted "a much less demanding and less complex test,"[55] concluding that the exchanged mortgage interests were materially different since they embodied "legally distinct entitlements." Since the mortgage participation interests were made to different obligors and secured by different homes, the Supreme Court concluded that the taxpayer "received entitlements different from those it gave up,"[56] treating the exchange as a realization event. The Court thus upheld Cottage Savings' recognition of losses on the mortgage swaps.

---

53. Treas. Reg. §1.1001-1(a).
54. 499 U.S. 554 (1991).
55. Id. At 562.
56. Id. At 567.

The significance of *Cottage Savings* in the recapitalization context is that under the Supreme Court's "less demanding and less complex" test, most actual exchanges of one debt obligation for another will be considered realization events under the §1001 regulations. Even without a formal exchange of debt instruments, a "significant modification of the debt instrument" may be considered a realization event.[57] Assuming that there is a significant modification of the debt instrument, the debt holders will recognize gain or loss *unless* the exchange or modification is a §368(a)(1)(E) recapitalization.[58]

For many years, the Internal Revenue Service regarded the exchange by debt holders of old debt for new debt in the same corporation, or the modification of debt terms without a formal modification of the corporation's capital structure, as a "mere refinancing" rather than a "recapitalization." In an early case, however, the Second Circuit noted that

> in common financial parlance the long term funded debt of a corporation is usually regarded as forming part of its capital structure. . . . By changing the interest rate and date of maturity of its old bonds and adding a conversion option to the holders of the new, the corporation could strengthen its financial condition, while the bondholders would not substantially change their original investments by making the exchange. "Recapitalization" seems a most appropriate word to describe that type of reorganization.[59]

As long as the exchange or significant modification of debt is part of a plan of reorganization with a business purpose, it should be treated as a recapitalization under §368(a)(1)(E).

Assuming that a debt-for-debt exchange is a recapitalization, the debt holders who exchange old securities for new securities should be eligible for nonrecognition under §354. Since §354 nonrecognition is limited to exchanges of "stock or securities," exchanges of short-term and other debt instruments that are not "securities" will not be eligible for §354 nonrecognition. Moreover, to the extent that the principal amount of

---

57. In regulations written and finalized after the *Cottage Savings* decision, the Treasury Department provides that a "significant modification of a debt instrument . . . results in an exchange of the original debt instrument for a modified instrument that differs materially either in kind or in extent." Treas. Reg. §1.1001-3(b). The regulations provide a detailed description of what constitutes a "significant modification," Treas. Reg. §1.1001-3(e), and a number of detailed examples, Treas. Reg. §1.1001-3(g). In 2019, the Treasury Department issued proposed regulations that provide guidance on the tax consequences of the transition to the use of reference rates other than interbank offered rates (IBORs) in debt instruments and non-debt contracts. Prop. Treas. Reg. §1.1001-6, 84 Fed. Reg. 54,068 (Oct. 9, 2019).

58. Of course, if the exchange is of properties that are *not* materially different, or if the modification is *not* a "significant" modification, there is no realization event in the first instance. Consequently, there will be no gain or loss and there should be no need to consider the tax-free reorganization provisions.

59. Comm'r v. Neustadt's Trust, 131 F.2d 528, 529-530 (2d Cir. 1942), acq. 1951-1 C.B. 2.

securities received exceeds the principal amount of securities surrendered, the exchanging debt holders will recognize gain under §356.

ii) Tax Consequences to the Corporation

A corporation issuing new debt in exchange for old debt has potential discharge of indebtedness income. Unless the discharge fits within one of the exclusions provided in §108(a),[60] gain from the cancellation of indebtedness must be recognized. In computing this gain, the "debtor shall be treated as having satisfied the indebtedness with an amount of money equal to the issue price of such debt instrument."[61]

MERE CHANGE IN IDENTITY, FORM, OR PLACE: TYPE F REORGANIZATION

A Type F reorganization involves "a mere change in identity, form, or place of organization of *one corporation*, however effected."[62] The highlighted language, added in 1982, was intended to simplify the Type F reorganization provision. The revised language makes it clear that the Type F reorganization applies to the change in identity, form, or place of a single corporation, rather than an acquisitive or divisive reorganization. In its Conference Report accompanying the 1982 changes, however, the Committee clarified that "[this] limitation does not preclude the use of more than one entity to consummate the transaction provided only one operating company is involved. The reincorporation of an operating company in a different State, for example, is an F Reorganization that requires that more than one corporation be involved."[63]

The major tax advantage to classification as a Type F reorganization is the preferential set of rules that will apply after the transaction regarding the carryover of tax attributes. For example, following any other reorganization, the new corporation's opportunity to use net operating losses against the income of the old corporation will be restricted.[64] Since Type F reorganizations presumably involve continuation of the same corporation with the same shareholders, the rules regarding carryover of tax attributes are far

---

60. Section 108(a) excludes cancellation of indebtedness income if the discharge occurs in title 11 bankruptcy, if the taxpayer is insolvent, or if the debt is qualified farm indebtedness or qualified real property business indebtedness. I.R.C. §108(a)(1).

61. I.R.C. §108(e)(10)(A).

62. I.R.C. §368(a)(1)(F) (emphasis added).

63. H.R. Rep. No. 760, 97th Cong., 2d Sess. (1982).

64. I.R.C. §§381, 382. For a more detailed discussion of the carryover of tax attributes following corporate acquisitions, see Chapter 12.

less restrictive.[65] Thus, net operating losses can be more freely used to offset income from the old corporation prior to the reorganization.[66]

Prior to the 1982 changes, the scope of §368(a)(1)(F) had expanded to cover and overlap with many of the other reorganization definitions, creating much confusion for taxpayers. Since 1982, the Type F reorganization largely has returned to the more simple role that it once had.[67] The classic Type F reorganization is a reincorporation in another state. A California corporation may decide that it is more advantageous to incorporate in Delaware. Upon reincorporation in Delaware, the shareholders of the old California corporation will be issued shares in the new Delaware corporation.[68] Or the corporation might simply change its name. Another simple Type F reorganization is a change in the corporation's charter or articles of incorporation.[69] These "mere changes in form" will be treated as tax-free reorganizations to the shareholders.[70]

Although the 1982 changes simplified the Type F reorganization provisions, a Type F reorganization still may be used in connection with a more complex transaction. For example, one corporation may change its state of incorporation in a Type F reorganization in anticipation of an impending acquisitive reorganization transaction. Whether the transaction should be respected as a Type F reorganization followed by another type of reorganization in an independent transaction or should be integrated into one transaction may be determined under the step-transaction doctrine.

---

65. See, e.g., I.R.C. §§381(b), 382.

66. A similar provision for recapitalizations (Type E reorganizations) is unnecessary, since the same corporation remains after the internal restructuring.

67. The Type F reorganization was so little used that the House of Representatives proposed its repeal in 1954. The provision was retained, however, and rulings and cases in the 1950s through the 1970s expanded the scope of §368(a)(1)(F) until Congress amended the language in 1982.

68. If the shareholders receive virtually identical interests in the new corporation that they previously held in the old corporation, the transaction will be a Type F reorganization. On the other hand, if the corporation also uses the transaction as an opportunity to do some capital restructuring, the transaction will be regarded as a recapitalization under §368(a)(1)(E).

69. Ahles Realty Corp. v. Comm'r, 71 F.2d 150 (2d Cir.), cert. denied, 293 U.S. 611 (1934).

70. In 2015, the Treasury Department issued final regulations that provide guidance on qualifications for Type F reorganizations. Treas. Reg. §1.368-2(m). The final regulations refer to the corporations involved in this transaction—the original corporation and the corporation to which its assets are transferred—as the "transferor corporation" and the "resulting corporation." Treas. Reg. §1.368-2(m). These regulations include requirements regarding the distribution of stock of the resulting corporation stock to shareholders, the identity of shareholders of the resulting corporation, the prior assets or attributes of the resulting corporation, and the liquidation of the transferor corporation. They also provide that the resulting corporation must be the only acquiring corporation and the transferor corporation must be the only acquired corporation involved in the reorganization. Treas. Reg. §§1.368-2(m)(i)-(vi).

APPLICATION OF GENERAL REORGANIZATION PRINCIPLES

Business Purpose Test

As with any other reorganization, a recapitalization will not qualify as a tax-free reorganization unless it has a business purpose.[71] For example, the Treasury Department ruled that the conversion of stock pursuant to a conversion privilege may constitute a recapitalization if there is a sufficient business purpose for the conversion privilege. Rev. Rul. 77-238 involved a manufacturing business whose corporate employees owned substantial amounts of common stock. Upon retirement, employees were entitled either to have their stock bought out for cash or to convert the common stock into preferred shares according to the terms of the articles of incorporation. The Treasury Department concluded that the retiring shareholder employees' conversion of common stock into preferred was a recapitalization, emphasizing that the purpose of the conversion privilege was to "eliminate common stock ownership by retiring employees and to reduce the cash expenditures . . . That would otherwise result if the common stock of retiring employees were redeemed for cash."[72] The articles of incorporation of a second manufacturing corporation in the same revenue ruling provided preferred shareholders the privilege of converting their shares into common stock. Shareholder conversions in accordance with this privilege were also considered recapitalizations since the business purpose of the privilege was to "encourage the conversion of preferred stock into common stock in order to simplify the capital structure of the corporation by eliminating the preferred stock."[73]

---

71. The regulations provide that the tax-free reorganization provisions are available to "such readjustments of corporate structures . . . As are required by business exigencies." Treas. Reg. §1.368-1(b). For more detailed discussion of the general business purpose rule as applied to reorganizations, see Chapter 11.

72. Rev. Rul. 77-238, 1977-2 C.B. 115.

73. Id. One should not assume that all stock conversions pursuant to a conversion privilege in the articles of incorporation will necessarily be viewed as recapitalizations. The facts and circumstances in these cases are sufficiently complex that even the Service is unwilling to rule in advance regarding whether or not there is a sufficient business purpose for the conversion such that the conversion should be regarded as a recapitalization. See Rev. Proc. 2003-3, sec. 3.01(26), 2003-1 C.B. 113, 115.

Continuity of Interest Tests

In general, the continuity of proprietary interest and the continuity of the business enterprise test must be met before a transaction will be eligible for tax-free reorganization treatment.[74] The continuity of proprietary interest test first emerged in early acquisitive reorganization cases. In these cases, a purchasing corporation acquired stock from target corporation shareholders in exchange for cash or notes or debentures of various types. Because the transferors in these early cases had not retained a significant proprietary interest in the corporate enterprise, the court denied tax-free reorganization treatment. In numerous cases involving an exchange of common or preferred stock by the shareholders of one corporation in return for debentures in the same corporation, the Commissioner initially argued that the exchanges were not entitled to reorganization treatment because ownership of debentures did not represent a sufficient continuity of proprietary interest.[75] The courts rejected these arguments, holding that the "continuity of proprietary interest" test simply did not apply in the recapitalization setting. Since, by definition, a recapitalization involves only an internal reshuffling of the capital structure of a single corporation, continuity of proprietary interest is not at issue. The following passage from the Hickok case is representative:

> [T]he "continuity of interest" doctrine, which was developed by the courts to serve a necessary purpose in the merger and consolidation types of reorganizations, need not be a necessary ingredient in the cases where a recapitalization occurs. It is quite apparent that the considerations which make such a doctrine necessary in the merger and consolidation cases are simply not present in a recapitalization. . . . We think that the "continuity of interest" doctrine has no application to a recapitalization such as took place in the instant case.[76]

The Treasury Department decades ago conceded that the continuity of proprietary interest test does not apply to Type E recapitalizations.[77]

Under the continuity of the business enterprise (COBE) requirement, reorganized corporations must either continue the target corporation's historic business or use a significant portion of the target corporation's

---

74. For a detailed discussion of these requirements, see Chapter 11.
75. See, e.g., Penfield v. Davis, 105 F. Supp. 292 (N.D. Ala. 1952), aff'd, 205 F.2d 798 (5th Cir. 1953); Berner v. United States, 282 F.2d 720 (Ct. Cl. 1960).
76. Hickok v. Comm'r, 32 T.C. 80, 89–90 (1959). See also Erwin Griswold, Securities — Continuity of Interest, 58 Harv. L. Rev. 705, 716-717 (1945).
77. See Rev. Rul. 77-415, 1977-2 C.B. 311. Moreover, since the continuity of proprietary interest test does not apply to recapitalizations, the Treasury Department has ruled that a prearranged plan to sell stock received in a recapitalization will not disqualify the transaction from tax-free reorganization treatment. Rev. Rul. 77-479, 1977-2 C.B. 119.

historic business assets in a business.[78] The Treasury Department years ago also conceded that the COBE requirement does not apply to Type E recapitalizations.[79] This makes sense. Since only one corporation is involved in a recapitalization, the corporation in its newly reorganized form presumably will continue either to use its historic assets or continue its historic business. In any event, a single corporation could change its business or fail to use its historic assets without tax penalty. An internal restructuring of one corporation should have no different result.

Treasury Department concessions that the continuity of proprietary interest and COBE requirements did not apply to Type F reorganizations were slower in coming, however. Ultimately acknowledging that "F reorganizations involve only the slightest change in the corporation and do not resemble sales" and that applying continuity of interest and COBE requirements to such reorganizations "is not necessary to protect the policies underlying the reorganization provisions,"[80] the Treasury Department issued regulations providing that satisfaction of the continuity of interest and COBE requirements is not required to in order to qualify for tax-free Type F reorganization treatment.[81]

Examples

A Simple Starter

1. a. Several years ago, Jerry received a large inheritance and decided to incorporate a business shirt distribution business to be named Steinfeld's Shirts, Inc. He persuaded several friends to provide capital. Jerry himself put in $170,000 for 85% of the common stock (850 shares). Elaine, George, and Kramer contributed $10,000 each in return for 5% of the common stock (50 shares each). Although the first few years were rough, the corporation began to see substantial profits after five years. The Board of Directors decided to issue five new shares of common stock in exchange for each old share. As a result of this stock exchange, Jerry received 4,250 shares valued at $425,000 and Elaine, George, and Kramer each received 250 shares valued at $25,000. What are the tax consequences to each shareholder upon this exchange of stock? Are there any tax consequences to the corporation?

   b. Assume that Jerry and George were much more actively involved with the company than Elaine and Kramer. As a result, the Board decided to

---

78. Treas. Reg. §1.368-1(d)(2). For a more detailed discussion of the COBE requirement, see Chapter 11.
79. Rev. Rul. 82-34, 1982-1 C.B. 59.
80. 69 Fed. Reg. 49,836, 49,837 (Aug. 12, 2004) (proposed regulations).
81. Treas. Reg. §1.368-1(b) (as amended by T.D. 9182, 70 Fed. Reg. 9219 (Feb. 25, 2005)).

create two different classes of stock: voting common and nonvoting 10% preferred. Jerry exchanged his 4,250 old shares for 4,250 shares of voting common (valued at $450,000) and George exchanged his 250 old shares for 250 shares of voting common (valued at $26,470). Elaine and Kramer each exchanged their 250 old shares for 250 shares of nonvoting 10% preferred (valued at $26,500). What are the tax consequences to each shareholder upon the stock-for-stock exchange? Are there any tax consequences to the corporation?

c. Now assume that George is annoyed with the whole enterprise. He can't agree with Jerry on anything and no longer wants to actively participate in the business. The Board of Directors agrees to accept his 250 voting common shares in return for 500 nonvoting 10% preferred (valued at $50,000). What are the tax consequences to George and the other shareholders? Any tax consequences to the corporation?

Financial Difficulties

2. a. Kramer's Hair Studio, Inc. is owned 50% by Kramer (200 common shares with a basis of $5,000) and 50% by his sister (200 common shares also with a basis of $5,000). Kramer's father loaned the corporation $10,000 in return for a ten-year bond at 8% interest. The corporation encounters financial difficulties and is unable to make timely payments of principal and interest on the bond. The corporation is two years in arrears on interest payments. The corporation reaches an agreement with Kramer's father under which he exchanges his bond for 400 shares of newly authorized preferred stock. What are the tax consequences to father and the other shareholders upon this exchange? What are the tax consequences to the corporation?

b. Would your answer to Example 2a change if, instead of exchanging the bond for stock, father exchanged the bond for an identical bond except that the new bond's interest rate was reduced to 7.5% interest?

Throwing in a Little Boot

3. a. Elaine owned 75 shares (basis $75,000) and her sister, Judy, owned 25 shares (basis $25,000) of the stock in Elaine's Advertising, Inc. They wanted to bring down the per share price to facilitate a possible future sale of shares to other stockholders. They agreed on a plan under which Elaine exchanged her 75 common shares for 225 new common shares (fair market value $80,000) plus a ten-year bond at 8% interest (fair market value $30,000). Judy exchanged her 25 common shares for 75 new common shares (fair market value $23,000) plus a ten-year bond at 8% interest (fair market value $14,000). To keep things simple, assume that the principal amount of the bonds in this question is equal to the fair market value of the bonds. What are

the tax consequences to Elaine, Judy, and the corporation from the exchanges?

   b. How would your answer change if the value of the stock Elaine and Judy received had been $50,000 and $17,000 respectively, and the value of the bonds they received had been $25,000 and $8,000 respectively?

Explanations

1. a. Each of the shareholders in this Example has *realized* a gain. For Jerry, this realized gain is $255,000 ($425,000 fair market value of the shares received less $170,000 basis in the shares exchanged). For Elaine, George, and Kramer, this realized gain is $15,000 ($25,000 fair market value of the shares received less $10,000 basis in the shares exchanged).[82] Absent a special nonrecognition provision, these gains would be taxable as capital gains. Taxpayers may find it somewhat unusual to have two overlapping provisions permitting nonrecognition treatment for the same transaction. Yet, one can arrive at the answer to Example 1a under *either* §1036 or the tax-free reorganization provisions.

   The simpler provision is §1036(a), providing nonrecognition where common stock is exchanged solely for common stock in the same corporation. Jerry now owns 4,250 shares in lieu of his old 850 shares and Elaine, George, and Kramer each own 250 shares in lieu of their old 50 shares. With regard to the basis of these new shares, §1036(c)(2) simply cross-references to §1031(d)—the basis rules attached to the like-kind exchange provisions. This cross-reference suggests that, although the like-kind exchange rules in §1031 generally do not apply to stock, one can conceptually think of the common stock received for common stock in the *same* corporation as a like-kind exchange. Under §1031(d), the basis in the new shares will be the same as the old shares exchanged. Thus, Jerry will have a basis of $170,000 in his new shares and Elaine, George, and Kramer will each have a basis of $10,000 in their new shares. Prior to the exchange, Jerry's basis *per share* was $200 ($170,000 basis/850 shares). After the exchange, the basis is allocated among the new shares under §1031(d). Thus, his basis *per share* will now be $40 ($170,000

---

82. In several respects, the transaction is similar to the type of stock dividend involved in Eisner v. Macomber. The only difference is that the shareholders here actually exchanged shares for the shares received. Recall that in the *Macomber* case, the Supreme Court found that no income had been realized from a similar common stock dividend issued with respect to common stock. The modern and widely accepted view, however, is that *Macomber* was wrong with regard to its definition of income. Most would view the stock dividend there, and the stock exchange here, as a realization event.

basis/4,250 shares). Similarly, Elaine, George, and Kramer's *per share* basis was $200 ($10,000 basis/50 shares) and now will be $40 ($10,000 basis/250 shares).

One reaches the same tax results under the tax-free reorganization provisions. The exchange of common for common stock in the same corporation is a "recapitalization" under §368(a)(1)(E), and thus a "reorganization." Under §354(a), the shareholders shall not recognize the gain realized from the exchange. Under §358(a), the basis of the new shares will be the same as the basis in the old shares. The basis will be allocated among the new shares pursuant to §358(b)(1).

Notice that whether the shareholders use §1031(d) or §358(b) to determine basis, the basis in each case is a substituted basis. Gain not recognized at the time of the exchange is preserved through this substituted basis for potential taxation later on.

The corporation does not recognize any gain upon the receipt of property in exchange for stock pursuant to §1032. See Treas. Reg. §1.1032-1(b), (c). Notice that the corporation's own stock can constitute property for purposes of §1032. The §317(a) definition of property, which excludes the corporation's own stock, is limited to Part I of Subchapter C.

a. Again, each of the shareholders has realized a gain from the exchange. Jerry's realized gain is $280,000 ($450,000 fair market value of shares received less $170,000 basis of the shares exchanged). George's realized gain is $16,470 ($26,470 fair market value of the shares received less $10,000 basis of the shares exchanged). Elaine and Kramer have a realized gain of $16,500 ($26,500 fair market value of the shares received less $10,000 basis in the shares exchanged).[83] Jerry and George again have the choice of relying upon either §1036 or the reorganization provisions, since they have exchanged common stock for common stock in the same corporation. Under either provision, it initially appears that they will not be required to recognize any gain and their basis in the new shares will be the same basis as the basis in the shares exchanged. Since they received the same number of shares that they previously held, no allocation of basis will be necessary. Jerry and George may have problems, however, under §305(c). Stay tuned for more on this issue in a moment.

Since the §1036 provision is only available upon exchanges of common for common in the same corporation or preferred for preferred in the same corporation, Elaine and Kramer must treat this exchange under the reorganization provisions. An exchange of

---

83. Notice that at the time of the exchange, each nonvoting preferred share is valued just slightly higher than the voting common shares.

common for preferred in the same corporation will be considered a "recapitalization" covered under the tax-free reorganization rules. In other words, Elaine and Kramer will not report any gain pursuant to §354, and will have a substituted basis in the new shares under §358.

Notice that after this exchange, Jerry retains 85% of the overall stock and the others each retain 5% of the overall stock. Although the overall exchange does not change the proportionate stock holdings, it does change the proportionate *voting* rights. Elaine and Kramer's voting interest has been reduced from 5% to zero. Jerry's voting interest has increased from 85% to 94%.[84] George's voting interest has increased from 5% to 6%.[85] In addition, the exchange changes the shareholders' status vis-á-vis one another. Elaine and Kramer now have a "senior" interest relative to Jerry and George. One must consider here whether either Jerry and George's increase in proportionate voting rights or the change in shareholder status triggers a §305(c) deemed taxable stock dividend.

Recapitalizations in which shareholders receive new shares resemble stock dividends. The simple difference between a stock dividend and a recapitalization is that in the latter case, the shareholder actually exchanges old shares for new. Had this transaction been a simple stock dividend, it would have been taxable under §305(b)(3) as a distribution resulting in the receipt of preferred stock by some common shareholders and the receipt of common stock by other common shareholders. In other words, such a transaction is considered disproportionate.[86] This should give all of the shareholders in this problem cause for concern. On the other hand, several examples in the §305 regulations indicate that an *isolated* transaction that is not part of a periodic plan will not trigger deemed §305(c) stock dividend treatment. Treas. Reg. §1.305-3(e), exs (10)-(13). If the shareholders here can satisfy the Secretary that this is an isolated transaction and not part of a periodic plan to alter proportionate interests, they can avoid the §305 pitfall, and the transaction will retain its nonrecognition treatment.

One additional issue for Elaine and Kramer is whether or not the nonvoting preferred shares received will be classified as tainted §306 stock. Recall that the §306 stock definition includes stock, other than common, received in a tax-free reorganization to the extent that "the effect of the transaction was substantially the same as the receipt of a stock dividend." I.R.C. §306(c)(1)(B). Since Elaine and Kramer exchanged *all* of the old common shares (none of which were §306

---

84. Of the total 4,500 voting shares, he owns 4,250.
85. Of the total 4,500 voting shares, George owns 250.
86. See Chapter 7 for a discussion of stock dividends.

stock), this exchange does not appear substantially the same as a stock dividend of preferred stock to common shareholders. Moreover, since the underlying common shares have been relinquished, the anti-bailout purpose of §306 would not be served by classifying these shares as tainted. See I.R.C. §306(b)(4).

b. Again, George has *realized* a $40,000 gain (the $50,000 fair market value of the shares received less his $10,000 substituted basis in the shares surrendered). He will not be required to *recognize* this gain, however. His basis in the new shares will remain $10,000 under §358. The potential §§305 and 306 issues should be analyzed as above in the answer to 1b. One might be tempted to treat this transaction as a redemption subject to §302. Note that this is not a redemption as defined in §317(b) since George is receiving the corporation's own stock. This will be treated as a recapitalization, the business purpose of which is to "retire" a major shareholder from active participation.

2. a. One often sees application of the tax-free reorganization provisions as part of a workout for a financially troubled corporation such as this. The exchange of Dad's outstanding bonds for preferred stock is a recapitalization. See Treas. Reg. §1.368-2(e)(1). Assuming that the ten-year bond is considered a "security," Dad will not report any gain or loss pursuant to §354, providing nonrecognition upon exchange of "stock or securities" for "stock or securities" in a reorganization. Note, however, that §354 nonrecognition will not extend to the portion of the stock received that is attributable to the two years' accrued interest. I.R.C. §354(a)(2)(B). The amount realized (fair market value of the stock received) must be apportioned between accrued interest and the bond. The portion of amount realized attributable to interest will be taxable as ordinary income. The corporation has effectively cancelled a debt and will have cancellation of indebtedness income.

b. Dad will *realize* a gain or loss upon this debt-for-debt exchange. Under Treasury regulations, "an exchange of property for other property differing materially either in kind or extent" is a realization event. Treas. Reg. §1.1001-1(a). Given the change in interest rates, the properties should be considered materially different. See Treas. Reg. §1.1001-3(e)(2).[87] Assuming a sufficient business purpose, however, this transaction should be treated as a recapitalization, with no gain or loss recognized to Dad under §354, except to the extent of amounts attributable to accrued interest as described above in the answer to 2a. As for the corporation, notice that the principal amount of its

---

87. Under this regulation, a change in interest rate is considered a significant modification if the modified rate varies from the original rate by more than 1/4 of 1%.

obligation remains the same. Since the only change is a prospective alteration of the rate of interest, there should be no cancellation of indebtedness to the corporation.

3. a. Elaine has realized a $35,000 gain from the exchange of her old stock for new stock and a bond (fair market value received of $110,000 less basis in old shares of $75,000). Judy has realized a $12,000 gain from the exchange (fair market value received of $37,000 less basis in old shares of $25,000). The first issue here is whether the transaction should be classified as a tax-free Type E recapitalization. As in the *Bazley* case, the concern here might be that the distribution of bonds simply is a disguised dividend. A few distinguishing factors might make ours a stronger case than *Bazley*. First, the restructuring here arguably had a business purpose — reducing the price of shares for a potential future sale of stock. On the other hand, this alleged business purpose does not explain the need for including bonds in the exchange. Second, the bonds in the *Bazley* case were callable at will, and thus virtually the equivalent of cash. The bonds in our case are not callable and thus not cash equivalents.

   Assume, then, that Elaine and Judy are successful in their claim that the exchange is a recapitalization. If so, they are eligible for §354 non-recognition. In any event, §354 nonrecognition does *not* apply to the extent that the principal amount of any securities received exceeds the principal amount of any securities surrendered. I.R.C. §354(a)(2)(A). Moreover, Treasury Department regulations take the position that the bond distribution should be considered as a separate transaction from the stock exchange. Consequently, the regulations would treat the bond distribution as taxable under §301 to the extent of earnings and profits. Treas. Reg. §1.301-1(l) (redesignated as Prop. Treas. Reg. §1.301-1(j)).

   b. The analysis of the Example is the same except that neither Elaine nor Judy has *realized* a gain from the exchange since each has received a value equal to her basis. Note that the §356 boot rules provide for taxation of boot income to the extent of gain. Since there was no gain here, neither shareholder will report taxable income even though boot has been paid to each of them.

Table of Cases

Table of Cases

Table of Internal Revenue Code Sections

Table of Internal Revenue Code Sections

Table of Treasury Regulations and Revenue Rulings

Index

Index

Index